CRIMINAL JUSTICE
94/95

Editor

John J. Sullivan
Mercy College, Dobbs Ferry, New York

John J. Sullivan, professor and chairman of the Department
of Law, Criminal Justice, and Safety Administration at
Mercy College, received his B.S. in 1949 from Manhattan
College and his J.D. in 1956 from St. John's Law School.
He was formerly captain and director of the Legal Division
of the New York City Police Department.

Editor

Joseph L. Victor
Mercy College, Dobbs Ferry, New York

Joseph L. Victor is professor and assistant chairman of the
Department of Law, Criminal Justice, and Safety
Administration at Mercy College, and coordinator of
Criminal Justice Graduate Study at the Westchester Campus
of Long Island University. Professor Victor has extensive
field experience in criminal justice agencies, counseling, and
administering human service programs. He earned his B.A.
and M.A. at Seton Hall University, and his Doctorate of
Education at Fairleigh Dickinson University.

A Library of Information from the Public Press

Cover illustration by Mike Eagle

The Dushkin Publishing Group, Inc.
Sluice Dock, Guilford, Connecticut 06437

The Annual Editions Series

Annual Editions is a series of over 60 volumes designed to provide the reader with convenient, low-cost access to a wide range of current, carefully selected articles from some of the most important magazines, newspapers, and journals published today. Annual Editions are updated on an annual basis through a continuous monitoring of over 300 periodical sources. All Annual Editions have a number of features designed to make them particularly useful, including topic guides, annotated tables of contents, unit overviews, and indexes. For the teacher using Annual Editions in the classroom, an Instructor's Resource Guide with test questions is available for each volume.

VOLUMES AVAILABLE

Africa
Aging
American Foreign Policy
American Government
American History, Pre-Civil War
American History, Post-Civil War
Anthropology
Biology
Business Ethics
Canadian Politics
Child Growth and Development
China
Comparative Politics
Computers in Education
Computers in Business
Computers in Society
Criminal Justice
Drugs, Society, and Behavior
Dying, Death, and Bereavement
Early Childhood Education
Economics
Educating Exceptional Children
Education
Educational Psychology
Environment
Geography
Global Issues
Health
Human Development
Human Resources
Human Sexuality
India and South Asia
International Business
Japan and the Pacific Rim

Latin America
Life Management
Macroeconomics
Management
Marketing
Marriage and Family
Mass Media
Microeconomics
Middle East and the Islamic World
Money and Banking
Multicultural Education
Nutrition
Personal Growth and Behavior
Physical Anthropology
Psychology
Public Administration
Race and Ethnic Relations
Russia, Eurasia, and Central/Eastern Europe
Social Problems
Sociology
State and Local Government
Third World
Urban Society
Violence and Terrorism
Western Civilization, Pre-Reformation
Western Civilization, Post-Reformation
Western Europe
World History, Pre-Modern
World History, Modern
World Politics

Library of Congress Cataloging in Publication Data
Main entry under title: Annual editions: Criminal justice. 1994/95.
     1. Criminal Justice, Administration of—United States—Periodicals.
I. Sullivan, John J., *comp.* II. Victor, Joseph L., *comp.* III. Title: Criminal justice.
HV 8138.A67   364.973.05   LC 77–640116
ISBN: 1–56134–268–8

Eighteenth Edition

Printed in the United States of America

160065

Printed on Recycled Paper

To the Reader

In publishing ANNUAL EDITIONS we recognize the enormous role played by the magazines, newspapers, and journals of the *public press* in providing current, first-rate educational information in a broad spectrum of interest areas. Within the articles, the best scientists, practitioners, researchers, and commentators draw issues into new perspective as accepted theories and viewpoints are called into account by new events, recent discoveries change old facts, and fresh debate breaks out over important controversies.

Many of the articles resulting from this enormous editorial effort are appropriate for students, researchers, and professionals seeking accurate, current material to help bridge the gap between principles and theories and the real world. These articles, however, become more useful for study when those of lasting value are carefully *collected, organized, indexed,* and *reproduced* in a *low-cost format,* which provides easy and permanent access when the material is needed. That is the role played by *Annual Editions.* Under the direction of each volume's *Editor,* who is an expert in the subject area, and with the guidance of an *Advisory Board,* we seek each year to provide in each *ANNUAL EDITION* a current, well-balanced, carefully selected collection of the best of the public press for your study and enjoyment. We think you'll find this volume useful, and we hope you'll take a moment to let us know what you think.

During the 1970s, criminal justice emerged as an appealing, vital, and unique academic discipline. It emphasizes the professional development of students who plan careers in the field and attracts those who want to know more about a complex social problem and how this country deals with it. Criminal justice incorporates a vast range of knowledge from a number of specialties, including law, history, and the behavioral and social sciences. Each specialty contributes to our fuller understanding of criminal behavior and of society's attitudes toward deviance.

In view of the fact that the criminal justice system is in a constant state of flux, and because the study of criminal justice covers such a broad spectrum, today's students must be aware of a variety of subjects and topics. Standard textbooks and traditional anthologies cannot keep pace with the changes as quickly as they occur. In fact, many such sources are already out of date the day they are published. *Annual Editions: Criminal Justice 94/95* strives to maintain currency in matters of concern by providing up-to-date commentaries, articles, reports, and statistics from the most recent literature in the criminal justice field.

This volume contains units concerning crime and justice in America, victimology, the police, the judicial system, juvenile justice, and punishment and corrections. The articles in these units were selected because they are informative as well as provocative. The selections are timely and useful in their treatment of ethics, punishment, juveniles, courts, and other related topics.

Included in this volume are a number of features designed to be useful to students, researchers, and professionals in the criminal justice field. These include a *topic guide* for locating articles on specific subjects; the *table of contents abstracts,* which summarize each article and feature key concepts in bold italics; and a comprehensive *bibliography, glossary,* and *index.* In addition, each unit is preceded by an *overview* that provides a background for informed reading of the articles, emphasizes critical issues, and presents challenge questions.

We would like to know what you think of the selections contained in this edition. Please fill out the article rating form on the last page and let us know your opinions. We change or retain many of the articles based on the comments we receive from you, the user. Help us to improve this anthology—annually.

John J. Sullivan

John J. Sullivan

Joseph L. Victor

Joseph L. Victor
Editors

Contents

Unit 1

Crime and Justice in America

Seven selections focus on the overall structure of the criminal justice system in the United States. The current scope of crime in America is reviewed; topics such as criminal behavior, drugs, and organized crime are discussed.

Unit 2

Victimology

Eight articles discuss the impact of crime on the victim. Topics include the rights of crime victims, the consequences of family violence, rape, and incest.

The concepts in bold italics are developed in the article. For further expansion please refer to the Topic Guide, the Index, and the Glossary.

Unit 3

Police

Seven selections examine the role of the police officer. Some of the topics discussed include police response to crime, utilization of policewomen, and ethical policing.

The concepts in bold italics are developed in the article. For further expansion please refer to the Topic Guide, the Index, and the Glossary.

Unit 4

The Judicial System

Five selections discuss the process by which the accused are moved through the judicial system. Prosecutors, courts, the jury process, and judicial ethics are reviewed.

Unit 5

Juvenile Justice

Eight selections review the juvenile justice system. The topics include effective ways to respond to violent juvenile crime, juvenile detention, female delinquency, and children in gangs.

The concepts in bold italics are developed in the article. For further expansion please refer to the Topic Guide, the Index, and the Glossary.

Unit 6

Punishment and Corrections

Seven selections focus on the current state of America's penal system and the effects of sentencing, probation, overcrowding, and capital punishment on criminals.

The concepts in bold italics are developed in the article. For further expansion please refer to the Topic Guide, the Index, and the Glossary.

Charts and Graphs

The concepts in bold italics are developed in the article. For further expansion please refer to the Topic Guide, the Index, and the Glossary.

Topic Guide

This topic guide suggests how the selections in this book relate to topics of traditional concern to students and professionals involved with the study of criminal justice. It is useful for locating articles that relate to each other for reading and research. The guide is arranged alphabetically according to topic. Articles may, of course, treat topics that do not appear in the topic guide. In turn, entries in the topic guide do not necessarily constitute a comprehensive listing of all the contents of each selection.

TOPIC AREA	TREATED IN:	TOPIC AREA	TREATED IN:
Alcohol	2. Campus Crime Wave 7. Untold Story of the L.A. Riot	**Crime (cont'd)**	3. Breeding Hate 4. Seeking the Roots of Violence 5. Tunnel Vision 6. Street Guns 7. Untold Story of the L.A. Riot
Attorneys	24. Abuse of Power in the Prosecutor's Office 25. Trials of the Public Defender	**Crime Victims**	*See* Victimology
Battered Families	9. Hunted 10. 'Til Death Do Us Part 11. When Men Hit Women 13. Incest: A Chilling Report 14. Repeating a Study 15. Where to Now on Domestic Violence?	**Criminal Behavior**	2. Campus Crime War 3. Breeding Hate 4. Seeking the Roots of Violence 7. Untold Story of the L.A. Riots
Biology	4. Seeking the Roots of Violence	**Criminal Justice**	1. Overview of the Criminal Justice System 24. Abuse of Power in the Prosecutor's Office 25. Trials of the Public Defender 26. Twelve Good Reasons
Children	*See* Juveniles		
Civilian Review Boards	17. Public Solidly Favors Mixed Police/Civilian Review Boards	**Cultural Awareness**	20. Future of Diversity in America
Community Policing	18. Beyond 'Just the Facts, Ma'am' 20. Future of Diversity in America	**Death Penalty**	42. 'This Man Has Expired'
Constitutional Rights	25. Trials of the Public Defender 27. Double Exposure	**Defense Counsel**	25. Trials of the Public Defender
		Delinquency	*See* Juveniles
Corrections	36. Sentencing and Corrections 37. Women in Jail: Unequal Justice 38. Pennsylvanians Prefer Alternatives to Prison 39. Detoxing of Prisoner 88A0802 40. Do We Need More Prisons? 41. Evaluating Intensive Supervision Probation/Parole	**Discrimination**	3. Breeding Hate 7. Untold Story of the L.A. Riot 19. Is Police Brutality the Problem? 20. Future of Diversity in America
		Double Jeopardy	27. Double Exposure
Courts	23. Judicial Process 24. Abuse of Power in the Prosecutor's Office 25. Trials of the Public Defender 26. Twelve Good Reasons 27. Double Exposure 28. Handling of Juvenile Cases 30. Girls' Crime and Woman's Place 31. Juvenile Court	**Drugs**	5. Tunnel Vision 39. Detoxing of Prisoner 88A0802
		Environment	4. Seeking the Roots of Violence
		Ethics	17. Public Solidly Favors Mixed Police/Civilian Review Boards 19. Is Police Brutality the Problem? 24. Abuse of Power in the Prosecutor's Office 26. Twelve Good Reasons
Crime	1. Overview of the Criminal Justice System 2. Campus Crime Wave		

Crime and Justice in America

The past few years have been explosive ones in so far as crime and justice have been concerned. We have witnessed unpopular jury verdicts, crime on our campuses, a rise of "hate crimes," an increase in racial tensions, and drugs remain a scourge on society.

The articles found in this section are intended to serve as a foundation for the materials presented in subsequent sections. "An Overview of the Criminal Justice System" charts the flow of events in the administration of the criminal justice system.

Rising crime on American university campuses is explored in "The Campus Crime Wave." A disquieting factor is the involvement of alcohol use by young students who commit crimes. "Breeding Hate" notes that hate crimes are on the rise and the number of white racist groups is increasing. The issue of violence is explored further in "Seeking the Roots of Violence," which discusses the ongoing research into biological causes of violence.

According to "Tunnel Vision: The War on Drugs," the punitive approach to controlling drugs is not working and new approaches are needed. Along with the scourge of drugs, America is facing a major problem with the influx of guns on the streets. "Street Guns: A Consumer Guide" presents a detailed essay on some of the new weapons in current use.

The Rodney King story does not seem to want to go away, and its impact on the American justice system will be felt for a long time. "The Untold Story of the L.A. Riot" reviews some of the reasons for the riot. The article's perceptions are interesting and controversial.

Looking Ahead: Challenge Questions

What can be done to control violence?

What new approaches in the war on drugs should be tried?

Can illegal guns be controlled?

An Overview of the Criminal Justice System

The response to crime is a complex process that involves citizens as well as many agencies, levels, and branches of government

The private sector initiates the response to crime

This first response may come from any part of the private sector: individuals, families, neighborhood associations, business, industry, agriculture, educational institutions, the news media, or any other private service to the public.

It involves crime prevention as well as participation in the criminal justice process once a crime has been committed. Private crime prevention is more than providing private security or burglar alarms or participating in neighborhood watch. It also includes a commitment to stop criminal behavior by not engaging in it or condoning it when it is committed by others.

Citizens take part directly in the criminal justice process by reporting crime to the police, by being a reliable participant (for example, witness, juror) in a criminal proceeding, and by accepting the disposition of the system as just or reasonable. As voters and taxpayers, citizens also participate in criminal justice through the policymaking process that affects how the criminal justice process operates, the resources available to it, and its goals and objectives. At every stage of the process, from the original formulation of objectives to the decision about where to locate jails and prisons and to the reintegration of inmates into society, the private sector has a role to play. Without such involvement, the criminal justice process cannot serve the citizens it is intended to protect.

The government responds to crime through the criminal justice system

We apprehend, try, and punish offenders by means of a loose confederation of agencies at all levels of government. Our American system of justice has evolved from the English

What is the sequence of events in the criminal justice system?

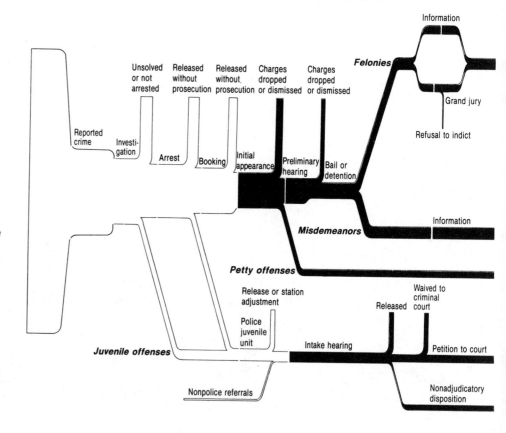

Note: This chart gives a simplified view of caseflow through the criminal justice system. Procedures vary among jurisdictions. The weights of the lines are not intended to show the actual size of caseloads.

common law into a complex series of procedures and decisions. There is no single criminal justice system in this country. We have many systems that are similar, but individually unique.

Criminal cases may be handled differently in different jurisdictions, but court

decisions based on the due process guarantees of the U.S. Constitution require that specific steps be taken in the administration of criminal justice.

The description of the criminal and juvenile justice systems that follows portrays the most common sequence of events

From *Report to the Nation on Crime and Justice,* Bureau of Justice Statistics, U.S. Department of Justice, March 1988, pp. 56-60.

in the response to serious criminal behavior.

Entry into the system

The justice system does not respond to most crime because so much crime is not discovered or reported to the police. Law enforcement agencies learn about crime from the reports of citizens, from discovery by a police officer in the field, or from investigative and intelligence work.

Once a law enforcement agency has established that a crime has been com-

Prosecution and pretrial services

After an arrest, law enforcement agencies present information about the case and about the accused to the prosecutor, who will decide if formal charges will be filed with the court. If no charges are filed, the accused must be released. The prosecutor can also drop charges after making efforts to prosecute (nolle prosequi).

A suspect charged with a crime must be taken before a judge or magistrate

nation of guilt and assessment of a penalty may also occur at this stage.

In some jurisdictions, a pretrial-release decision is made at the initial appearance, but this decision may occur at other hearings or may be changed at another time during the process. Pretrial release and bail were traditionally intended to ensure appearance at trial. However, many jurisdictions permit pretrial detention of defendants accused of serious offenses and deemed to be dangerous to prevent them from committing crimes in the pretrial period. The court may decide to release the accused on his/her own recognizance, into the custody of a third party, on the promise of satisfying certain conditions, or after the posting of a financial bond.

In many jurisdictions, the initial appearance may be followed by a preliminary hearing. The main function of this hearing is to discover if there is probable cause to believe that the accused committed a known crime within the jurisdiction of the court. If the judge does not find probable cause, the case is dismissed; however, if the judge or magistrate finds probable cause for such a belief, or the accused waives his or her right to a preliminary hearing, the case may be bound over to a grand jury.

A *grand jury* hears evidence against the accused presented by the prosecutor and decides if there is sufficient evidence to cause the accused to be brought to trial. If the grand jury finds sufficient evidence, it submits to the court an indictment (a written statement of the essential facts of the offense charged against the accused). Where the grand jury system is used, the grand jury may also investigate criminal activity generally and issue indictments called grand jury originals that initiate criminal cases.

Misdemeanor cases and some felony cases proceed by the issuance of an *information* (a formal, written accusation submitted to the court by a prosecutor). *In some jurisdictions*, indictments *may* be required in felony cases. However, the accused may choose to waive a grand jury indictment and, instead, accept service of an information for the crime.

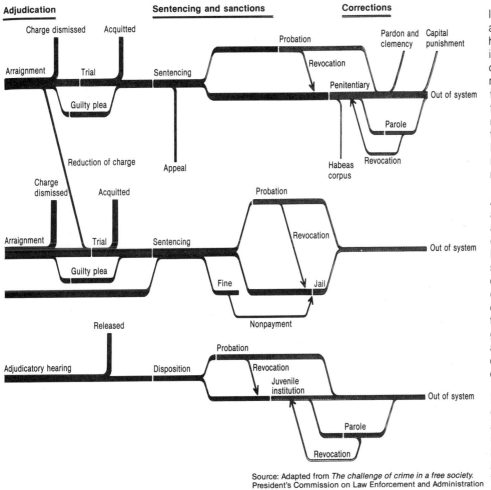

Source: Adapted from *The challenge of crime in a free society.*
President's Commission on Law Enforcement and Administration of Justice, 1967.

mitted, a suspect must be identified and apprehended for the case to proceed through the system. Sometimes, a suspect is apprehended at the scene; however, identification of a suspect sometimes requires an extensive investigation. Often, no one is identified or apprehended.

without unnecessary delay. At the initial appearance, the judge or magistrate informs the accused of the charges and decides whether there is probable cause to detain the accused person. Often, the defense counsel is also assigned at the initial appearance. If the offense is not very serious, the determi-

Adjudication

Once an indictment or information has been filed with the trial court, the accused is scheduled for arraignment. At the arraignment, the accused is informed of the charges, advised of the

1. CRIME AND JUSTICE IN AMERICA

rights of criminal defendants, and asked to enter a plea to the charges. Sometimes, a plea of guilty is the result of negotiations between the prosecutor and the defendant, with the defendant entering a guilty plea in expectation of reduced charges or a lenient sentence.

If the accused pleads guilty or pleads *nolo contendere* (accepts penalty without admitting guilt), the judge may accept or reject the plea. If the plea is accepted, no trial is held and the offender is sentenced at this proceeding or at a later date. The plea may be rejected if, for example, the judge believes that the accused may have been coerced. If this occurs, the case may proceed to trial.

If the accused pleads not guilty or not guilty by reason of insanity, a date is set for the trial. A person accused of a serious crime is guaranteed a trial by jury. However, the accused may ask for a bench trial where the judge, rather than a jury, serves as the finder of fact. In both instances the prosecution and defense present evidence by questioning witnesses while the judge decides on issues of law. The trial results in acquittal or conviction on the original charges or on lesser included offenses.

After the trial a defendant may request appellate review of the conviction or sentence. In many criminal cases, appeals of a conviction are a matter of right; all States with the death penalty provide for automatic appeal of cases involving a death sentence. However, under some circumstances and in some jurisdictions, appeals may be subject to the discretion of the appellate court and may be granted only on acceptance of a defendant's petition for a *writ of certiorari*. Prisoners may also appeal their sentences through civil rights petitions and writs of habeas corpus where they claim unlawful detention.

Sentencing and sanctions

After a guilty verdict or guilty plea, sentence is imposed. In most cases the judge decides on the sentence, but in some States, the sentence is decided by the jury, particularly for capital offenses such as murder.

In arriving at an appropriate sentence, a sentencing hearing may be held at which evidence of aggravating or mitigating circumstances will be considered. In assessing the circumstances surrounding a convicted person's criminal behavior, courts often rely on presentence investigations by probation agencies or other designated authorities. Courts may also consider victim impact statements.

The sentencing choices that may be available to judges and juries include one or more of the following:
• the death penalty
• incarceration in a prison, jail, or other confinement facility
• probation—allowing the convicted person to remain at liberty but subject to certain conditions and restrictions
• fines—primarily applied as penalties in minor offenses
• restitution—which requires the offender to provide financial compensation to the victim.

In many States, State law mandates that persons convicted of certain types of offenses serve a prison term.

Most States permit the judge to set the sentence length within certain limits, but some States have determinate sentencing laws that stipulate a specific sentence length, which must be served and cannot be altered by a parole board.

Corrections

Offenders sentenced to incarceration usually serve time in a local jail or a State prison. Offenders sentenced to less than 1 year generally go to jail; those sentenced to more than 1 year go to prison. Persons admitted to a State prison system may be held in prisons with varying levels of custody or in a community correctional facility.

A prisoner may become eligible for parole after serving a specific part of his or her sentence. Parole is the conditional release of a prisoner before the prisoner's full sentence has been served. The decision to grant parole is made by an authority such as a parole board, which has power to grant or revoke parole or to discharge a parolee altogether. The way parole decisions are made varies widely among jurisdictions.

Offenders may also be required to serve out their full sentences prior to release (expiration of term). Those sentenced under determinate sentencing laws can be released only after they have served their full sentence (mandatory release) less any "goodtime" received while in prison. Inmates get such credits against their sentences automatically or by earning it through participation in programs.

If an offender has an outstanding charge or sentence in another State, a detainer is used to ensure that when released from prison he or she will be transferred to the other State.

If released by a parole board decision or by mandatory release, the releasee will be under the supervision of a parole officer in the community for the balance of his or her unexpired sentence. This supervision is governed by specific conditions of release, and the releasee may be returned to prison for violations of such conditions.

The juvenile justice system

The processing of juvenile offenders is not entirely dissimilar to adult criminal processing, but there are crucial differences in the procedures. Many juveniles are referred to juvenile courts by law enforcement officers, but many others are referred by school officials, social services agencies, neighbors, and even parents, for behavior or conditions that are determined to require intervention by the formal system for social control.

When juveniles are referred to the juvenile courts, their *intake* departments, or prosecuting attorneys, determine whether sufficient grounds exist to warrant filing a petition that requests an *adjudicatory hearing* or a request to transfer jurisdiction to criminal court. In some States and at the Federal level prosecutors under certain circumstances may file criminal charges against juveniles directly in criminal courts.

The court with jurisdiction over juvenile matters may reject the petition or the juveniles may be diverted to other agencies or programs in lieu of further court processing. Examples of diversion programs include individual or group counseling or referral to educational and recreational programs.

If a petition for an adjudicatory hearing is accepted, the juvenile may be brought before a court quite unlike the court with jurisdiction over adult offenders. In disposing of cases juvenile courts usually have far more discretion than adult courts. In addition to such options as probation, commitment to correctional institutions, restitution, or fines, State laws grant juvenile courts the power to order removal of children from their homes to foster homes or treatment facilities. Juvenile courts also may order participation in special programs aimed at shoplifting prevention, drug counseling, or driver education. They also may order referral to criminal court for trial as adults.

Despite the considerable discretion associated with juvenile court proceedings, juveniles are afforded many of the due-process safeguards associated with adult criminal trials. Sixteen States permit the use of juries in juvenile courts; however, in light of the U.S. Supreme Court's holding that juries are not essential to juvenile hearings, most States do not make provisions for juries in juvenile courts.

The response to crime is founded in the intergovernmental structure of the United States

Under our form of government, each State and the Federal Government has its own criminal justice system. All systems must respect the rights of individuals set forth in court interpretation of the U.S. Constitution and defined in case law.

State constitutions and laws define the criminal justice system within each State and delegate the authority and responsibility for criminal justice to various jurisdictions, officials, and institutions. State laws also define criminal behavior and groups of children or acts under jurisdiction of the juvenile courts.

Municipalities and counties further define their criminal justice systems through local ordinances that proscribe additional illegal behavior and establish the local agencies responsible for criminal justice processing that were not established by the State.

Congress also has established a criminal justice system at the Federal level to respond to Federal crimes such as bank robbery, kidnaping, and transporting stolen goods across State lines.

The response to crime is mainly a State and local function

Very few crimes are under exclusive Federal jurisdiction. The responsibility to respond to most crime rests with the State and local governments. Police protection is primarily a function of cities and towns. Corrections is primarily a function of State governments. More than three-fifths of all justice personnel are employed at the local level.

	Percent of criminal justice employment by level of government		
	Local	State	Federal
Police	77%	15%	8%
Judicial (courts only)	60	32	8
Prosecution and legal services	58	26	17
Public defense	47	50	3
Corrections	35	61	4
Total	62%	31%	8%

Source: *Justice expenditure and employment, 1985,* BJS Bulletin, March 1987.

Discretion is exercised throughout the criminal justice system

Discretion is "an authority conferred by law to act in certain conditions or situations in accordance with an official's or an official agency's own considered judgment and conscience."[1] Discretion is exercised throughout the government. It is a part of decisionmaking in all government systems from mental health to education, as well as criminal justice.

Concerning crime and justice, legislative bodies have recognized that they cannot anticipate the range of circumstances surrounding each crime, anticipate local mores, and enact laws that clearly encompass all conduct that is criminal and all that is not.[2] Therefore, persons charged with the day-to-day response to crime are expected to exercise their own judgment within *limits* set by law. Basically, they must decide—
• whether to take action

• where the situation fits in the scheme of law, rules, and precedent
• which official response is appropriate.

To ensure that discretion is exercised responsibly, government authority is often delegated to professionals. Professionalism requires a minimum level of training and orientation, which guides officials in making decisions. The professionalism of policing discussed later in this chapter is due largely to the desire to ensure the proper exercise of police discretion.

The limits of discretion vary from State to State and locality to locality. For example, some State judges have wide discretion in the type of sentence they may impose. In recent years other States have sought to limit the judges' discretion in sentencing by passing mandatory sentencing laws that require prison sentences for certain offenses.

Who exercises discretion?

These criminal justice officials. . .	. . .must often decide whether or not or how to—
Police	Enforce specific laws Investigate specific crimes Search people, vicinities, buildings Arrest or detain people
Prosecutors	File charges or petitions for adjudication Seek indictments Drop cases Reduce charges
Judges or magistrates	Set bail or conditions for release Accept pleas Determine delinquency Dismiss charges Impose sentence Revoke probation
Correctional officials	Assign to type of correctional facility Award privileges Punish for disciplinary infractions
Paroling authority	Determine date and conditions of parole Revoke parole

1. CRIME AND JUSTICE IN AMERICA

More than one agency has jurisdiction over some criminal events

The response to most criminal actions is usually begun by local police who react to violation of State law. If a suspect is apprehended, he or she is prosecuted locally and may be confined in a local jail or State prison. In such cases, only one agency has jurisdiction at each stage in the process.

However, some criminal events because of their characteristics and location may come under the jurisdiction of more than one agency. For example, such overlapping occurs within States when local police, county sheriffs, and State police are all empowered to enforce State laws on State highways.

Congress has provided for Federal jurisdiction over crimes that—
• materially affect interstate commerce
• occur on Federal land
• involve large and probably interstate criminal organizations or conspiracies
• are offenses of national importance, such as the assassination of the President.[3]

Bank robbery and many drug offenses are examples of crimes for which the States and the Federal Government both have jurisdiction. In cases of dual jurisdiction, an investigation and a prosecution may be undertaken by all authorized agencies, but only one level of government usually pursues a case. For example, a study of FBI bank robbery investigations during 1978 and 1979 found that of those cases cleared—

• 36% were solved by the FBI alone
• 25% were solved by a joint effort of the FBI and State and local police
• 40% were solved by the State and local police acting alone.

In response to dual jurisdiction and to promote more effective coordination, Law Enforcement Coordinating Committees have been established throughout the country and include all relevant Federal and local agencies.

Within States the response to crime also varies from one locality to another

The response differs because of statutory and structural differences and differences in how discretion is exercised. Local criminal justice policies and programs change in response to local attitudes and needs. For example, the prosecutor in one locality may concentrate on particular types of offenses that plague the local community while the prosecutor in another locality may concentrate on career criminals.

The response to crime also varies on a case-by-case basis

No two cases are exactly alike. At each stage of the criminal justice process officials must make decisions that take into account the varying factors of each case. Two similar cases may have very different results because of various factors, including differences in witness cooperation and physical evidence, the availability of resources to investigate

and prosecute the case, the quality of the lawyers involved, and the age and prior criminal history of the suspects.

Differences in local laws, agencies, resources, standards, and procedures result in varying responses in each jurisdiction

The outcomes of arrests for serious cases vary among the States as shown by Offender-based Transaction Statistics from nine States:

	% of arrests for serious crimes that result in...		
	Prosecution	Conviction	Incarceration
Virginia	100%	61%	55%
Nebraska	99	68	39
New York	97	67	31
Utah	97	79	9
Virgin Islands	95	55	35
Minnesota	89	69	48
Pennsylvania	85	56	24
California	78	61	45
Ohio	77	50	21

Source: Disaggregated data used in *Tracking offenders: White-collar crime,* BJS Special Report, November 1986.

Some of this variation can be explained by differences among States. For example, the degree of discretion in deciding whether to prosecute differs from State to State; some States do not allow any police or prosecutor discretion; others allow police discretion but not prosecutor discretion and vice versa.

THE CAMPUS CRIME WAVE

THE IVORY TOWER BECOMES AN ARMED CAMP.

Anne Matthews

Anne Matthews teaches nonfiction writing at Princeton University.

International House is a sturdy Victorian mansion at the edge of the Brown University campus in Providence, R.I. On a late morning, just before the start of fall classes, Brown undergraduates in backpacks and Birkenstocks flow past its steps, heading for the cappuccino bars and bookstores of Thayer Street, the main campus shopping avenue. But inside the international center, incoming students from more than 80 nations, some just hours off the plane, are being given the drill on basic survival tactics, learning what alumni and parents are rarely told, what many students discover too late: no American campus in the 1990's is as idyllic as it looks.

"If threatened, do not—how do you spell 'struggle' in English?" mutters a doctoral candidate from South Korea. In the back row, an agitated hand. "With 34 assaults near this campus last year, do you recommend that we equip ourselves with stun guns or Mace?" ("He's from Beirut," whispers a Danish student.)

Brown's police chief, Dennis Boucher, his New England voice as crisp as his khaki uniform, replies: "I've been attacked on the street in broad daylight, so it's impossible to be too careful. Lock your room when you go to shower. Call the shuttle or the escort service rather than walk alone after dark. Call me when you feel in danger, on campus or off. And memorize the university emergency number: 3322."

When Wayne Lo, 18, roamed Simon's Rock College in Massachusetts last December, shooting four people and

killing a professor and a fellow student, his armed violence was not unprecedented. In 1991 alone, five University of Iowa employees—three professors, one staff member and an associate vice president—were shot to death by a former physics graduate student irate at losing a research prize. At Temple Junior College in Texas, the chairman of the sociology department was held hostage by an armed student displeased by her sociology grade. At Yale, a sophomore died only yards from the university president's house, fatally shot in a street holdup.

Campus murders or threat of murder invariably make it to page 1 of local and national newspapers, but they are still rare. Other crimes, however, usually less publicized, are not. An American college or university (enrollment ranges from under 100 students to 45,000 and more) averages three reported violent assaults a year, eight incidents of hate crime or hazing violence, 430 property crimes and countless alcohol violations. Like much off-campus crime, many more incidents go unreported. One in three students will be the victim of some kind of campus crime. Estimates on the number of women raped or sexually assaulted during their college years range from 1 in 7 to 1 in 25.

From 13th-century riots at Oxford to today's armed clashes at college campuses in Bangladesh (where rival student organizations rely on rocket-propelled grenade launchers, rifles and submachine guns to get the most desirable dorm rooms), collegiate violence is not new. Yet only a generation ago, American campuses were tranquil enclaves in both image and fact. Most still feel like privileged and peaceful islands, the nearest thing in secular society to sacred ground, but since the early 1980's, image has less and less to do with reality.

From *New York Times Magazine*, March 7, 1993, pp. 38-42, 47. © 1993 by The New York Times Company. Reprinted by permission.

1. CRIME AND JUSTICE IN AMERICA

From ax attacks in libraries to shootings at dances, violence on urban, suburban and rural campuses has transformed many schools into discreetly armed camps: electronic passkeys for dormitories, cold-steel mesh on classroom windows, computer-controlled cameras in stairwells, alarm strips in toilet stalls. Messy realities, however, rarely surface in the glossy catalogues and upbeat recruiting brochures by which many schools now live or die. With an anemic recovery going on, the earning power of a bachelor's degree declining and the pool of 18-to-22-year-olds shrinking, many of the 3,600 or so institutions of higher education are promoting, as never before, the campus as intellectual resort—Club Med with books.

"Campuses today are Athenian city-states," observes Vartan Gregorian, president of Brown, gazing with urbane weariness at the ceiling of his 18th-century office. "Laundry, concerts, parking, catering—some days I feel like Job: 'Hit me again!' But as Harvard's president said recently, 'Where else in America can you get hotel, health club, career advice and 1,800 courses for $90 a day?'"

Keeping the tuition-paying customers happy is far easier than keeping them safe, however. Administrators, faculty and students, when aware of campus crime at all, frequently attribute it to faceless hit-and-retreat raiders from the world beyond the ivy curtain: professional criminals, the homeless, local gangs. Dorothy G. Siegel, a vice president and associate professor of psychology at Towson State University in suburban Baltimore, is not so sure.

"Our only campus crime used to be plagiarism, but so much odd stuff appeared in the 80's—rapes, robberies, even the kid who used his prosthetic arm to beat up a dormmate—that I decided we needed to know: Is it us or is it society?" She opens a thick printout: a 1989 survey of 1,100 colleges and universities by Towson State's Center for the Study and Prevention of Campus Violence.

"By guarding against strangers," Siegel says, "we were locking in the aggressors already with us. Almost 80 percent of campus crime appears to be student-on-student."

Although the number of crimes on campus is rising but not soaring, she emphasizes, the intensity of violence has radically increased. The Towson State study reveals a distinct subculture, common to campuses nationwide, of victims and victimizers. Student crime victims drink and use drugs significantly more often than nonvictims, have lower-than-average grades and tend disproportionately to be fraternity or sorority members. Perpetrators, who often commit multiple crimes, also usually have low grade-point averages, drink heavily and tend disproportionately to be athletes.

"Though over 90 percent of campus crime is alcohol-related," Siegel adds, "chances of becoming a victim of crimes other than theft are remote if you avoid drugs and drink infrequently and sensibly. That's a big if." A Harvard study released last year of 1,669 college freshmen found a radical increase in students' drinking to get drunk since 1977. Many women now binge-drink as well. One college student in three today, in fact, drinks primarily to get drunk—which is why so little campus crime is premeditated. Strong-arm robbery or auto theft becomes an impulsive event after a big bash.

Siegel sighs. "These aren't juvenile offenders, nor do they continue to behave badly as adults. But many just want career credentialing, not true learning, and the myth of college as a time of absolute freedom is extremely strong. Too often, the result is a four-year madness, morality suspended."

At Arizona State University in the tidy city of Tempe, serious weekend partying begins on Thursday, as it does at most American campuses. Asked at 1 in the morning, "Why do you drink so much?" undergraduates are succinct.

"Stress!" says a blond business major in tennis shorts outside a cafe-bar on Mill Avenue, Tempe's main thoroughfare. Watched by a bored bouncer, he turns away to vomit deftly into a crimson bougainvillea bush.

"Stress," whispers an elementary-education major in purple spandex and gold ear cuffs as she clings to a palm tree by an apartment patio near campus. Two bull-necked boys (wearing T-shirts with the slogans "Take Me Drunk, I'm Home," and "From Zero to Horny in 2.5 Beers") hoist the disoriented and giggling girl by the ankles over a nearby keg. She seizes its plastic hose and, hanging upside down, begins to gulp.

"Outrageous, awesome, major stress," a leisure-studies major says apologetically outside a Tempe club, aiming her too-drunk-to-walk roommate at the front seat of a silver BMW coupe. The roommate, long hair soaked with beer, promptly hangs out the car window, hiccuping and crying. Two girls in the back seat haul her in, whip moist towelettes from their purses and, crooning gently, wipe her face. But her howls draw jeers from a nearby huddle of boys in Malcolm X caps. As they advance on the car, the girls roar away into the desert night, crossing four lanes of traffic in a $31,000 blur.

Dr. Ellen C. Yoshimura is the only substance-abuse counselor for 43,000 Arizona State students. "This is a huge commuter school, where it's easy to be lonely and alienated," she explains. "They join fraternities and sororities to make friends, or hang out in bars for 1-cent drink nights and wet T-shirt contests. I see a lot of crash-and-burn semesters. Some experiment with hallucinogens, including Ecstasy and LSD, or IV cocaine, or heroin. Yet the typical student I treat looks astonishingly clean-cut—a hearty, sunny, polished, perfect child."

Under President Lattie Coor, the school is attempting, despite legislative budget cuts, to attract and keep a higher-powered faculty and upgrade its academic programs. Thousands attend Arizona State, the nation's sixth-largest university, then proceed respectably into adulthood. Many do not. They enroll for the resort-brochure weather (flawless, 80-degree days in November, for instance) and for the all-pro partying, which, as at many campuses, is often sponsored or encouraged by beer companies. Typical ads in student papers: "Lake Tahoe All-Greek Blowout... Booze Cruise." "Miller Genuine Draft Ski Utah! Round Trip Video Bus... Of Course All the Beer You Can Drink All Weekend Long!!"

Arizona State has seen a rash of off-campus sexual assaults and other crimes by often-intoxicated student athletes (the football team's starting quarterback was found guilty of several burglaries), as well as an increase in the number of underage drinkers among its freshmen. The school and Tempe police are now stricter about enforcing the conduct code, especially the ban on under-21 drinking. Of course, under recent laws requiring that work places and schools be drug-free, any school tolerating illegal drinking risks forfeiture of Federal funds. But most schools fear they may antagonize parents by arresting their intoxicated offspring or, by enforcing drinking laws, alienate alumni in their 30's and 40's who still party at campus fraternities or clubs.

Often forgotten in the current turmoil, though, are other tuition-paying individuals. Many students have no time to party: they work two jobs and carry full course loads, knowing their parents have remortgaged the house to finance a six-figure college bill. Degree candidates over the age of 25—the fastest-growing campus population—worry more about day care than dating rituals. Students from abroad consider American attitudes on alcohol primitive. To undergraduates with Asian, black, Jewish or Hispanic backgrounds, in which serious drinking is rarely central to socializing, six tequilas with brandy or six vodkas with Triple Sec (a sweet orange liqueur) "just to relax" before a night on the town seem ridiculous, if not pathetic.

Schools have neither a single solution to campus crime, especially drunken crime, nor a consistent policy of discipline for offenses to person and property. Though intoxicated students routinely smash toilets, yank out sinks, punch through ceilings, head-butt street lamps, uproot ornamental trees and body-slam vending machines, few are reprimanded or caught. Repairs become a hidden cost underwritten by the taxpayer, or squeezed from the library or faculty-salary budget. (There are exceptions. At Princeton, willful vandals must pay up and go on mandatory 5 A.M. cleaning-crew duty.)

Some schools, especially those in small towns, have tried late-night alternatives to drinking: keeping weight rooms and coffeehouses open till 2 A.M., sponsoring midnight basketball leagues or late-night concerts. But even at schools in culture-rich cities, drinking and crime stay high. "Remember, much campus violence is basically domestic violence," notes Dorothy Siegel of Towson State, "fueled by alcohol and drugs, committed by people who know each other. And if anecdotal reports of college students bringing guns to school continue to rise, 90's America will have come to campus indeed."

Until recently, you could walk onto the grounds of any college or university and be, legally speaking, on another planet. Employees have attempted computerized embezzlement of university funds and students have printed counterfeit money in their dorm rooms. But following seven centuries of jealously guarded tradition, instances of lawlessness have almost always been handled internally, with local police or F.B.I. involvement a last resort, even for felonies.

Recent legislation, however, has sharply challenged such convenient informality. Three important new rulings insist that schools have a duty to protect students from, and to warn them of, crime and danger, both on campus property and in off-campus housing recommended by the school.

First, in July 1992, the Campus Sexual Assault Victims' Bill of Rights, introduced by Representative Jim Ramstad, a Republican from Minnesota, became law. It stems from lawsuits like the landmark case in which four women—current and former students—charged Carleton College in Northfield, Minn., with negligence in allowing two male students accused of prior sexual assaults to remain on campus. (The case was settled out of court in 1991.) Under the Ramstad law, sexual-assault victims have the right to call on off-campus authorities to investigate campus sexual crimes. Universities also have to set up educational programs and notify students of available counseling.

Second, under a clarification of the Buckley Privacy Amendment, victims of campus violence can now have easier access to the previous criminal records of student perpetrators.

Third, last fall marked the first reporting period of the first national law to require disclosure of crime rates on campuses. Sponsored by two Pennsylvania Republicans, Representative William Goodling and Senator Arlen Specter, the Student Right-to-Know and Campus Security Act has its origins in the 1986 death of a 19-year-old Lehigh University student who was raped, sodomized, tortured and murdered in her dorm room by a drunken fellow student. This act requires all colleges and universities receiving Federal funds to publish annually their security and crime-reporting policies, and to make public the number of on-campus incidences of murder, sexual assault, robbery, assault, burglary and motor-vehicle theft, as well as arrests for weapons possession and drug and alcohol offenses. (Larceny, arson, vandalism or disorderly conduct need not be reported.)

The Campus Security Act is a consumer-information law, treating higher education not as privilege but as product. But ease of public access to Security Act data varies. Columbia University and the University of Alaska mailed all requested information within hours. The University of Florida, four of whose students were murdered by unknown assailants in off-campus housing in 1990, dawdled two months, then sent nearly a pound of perky but largely unrelated brochures. The security office of the City University of New York said, testily, that they had never heard of the Campus Security Act. Adelphi University, on Long Island, went into a frenzy: "Why do you want to know? We can't release that. Can you prove authorization from the legal department?"

According to The Chronicle of Higher Education, in the first annual crime statements submitted by more than 2,400 schools, there was a total of 30 murders, nearly 1,000 rapes, more than 1,800 robberies, 32,127 burglaries and 8,981 motor-vehicle thefts. The low figures furnished by many colleges especially on rapes make some security experts and victims' rights advocates openly skeptical. And since the Department of Education is not required to analyze campus-crime data, only collect it, a list of America's 10 Most Dangerous Campuses is not in the offing.

These days, colleges and universities have to struggle with a thorny question: to escape liability, how much must students, faculty and staff be protected? A major issue is foreseeable crime: a student raped or robbed, say, in a dark parking lot where previous assaults had occurred. Increasingly, colleges must invest in crime-proofing measures like shrubbery trimming, improved lighting and emergency phones campuswide.

All this resembles a revival of the in loco parentis doctrine—the assumption that a university stands in for a student's parents, safeguarding life and morals. In loco parentis flourished between 1913 and 1945, as did its daily rituals, from grace before family-style meals to supervised socializing. (Should a girl sit on a boy's lap, some dorms and sororities insisted, she must first put down a magazine across his lap, the larger the better.) In loco parentis weakened after World War II with the arrival of older G.I. Bill students, and it vanished altogether in the 60's and 70's following demands that students be treated as adults. Lowering the voting age and in many states the drinking age to 18 in the early 70's cemented the national shift from student ward to student citizen.

Today's students, trained as consumers from the cradle, frequently prefer service to empowerment. In spirit if not in statute, in loco parentis is back. The widespread attitude "I get to do whatever I want but you have to protect me" is forcing overwhelmed, under-financed student-life staffs and campus security forces to improvise a new care-giving role: part concierge, part social worker, part bodyguard.

At Brown University's student union on a recent afternoon, a dozen women—most young, one silver-haired, one heavily pregnant—lie on a carpeted floor looking up at Lesley Pan, then director of special services for the campus police and safety department. Pan is a 1989 Brown graduate, slender and straightforward.

"Let's review an oral-sex scenario," she tells her self-defense class, a mix of undergraduates and research staff members from Brown's medical school. From a nearby sofa, the sole man present, a visiting literature major from the University of California at Santa Barbara, offers a dutiful nod.

"If you wake up in your apartment or dorm room and find a 240-pound assailant on your chest, or if what began as consensual activity turns to date rape," says Pan, her voice level and professorial, "chomp down on his offending anatomy, brace your feet against the mattress, bring your locked hands up like a volleyball serve—scraping the scrotum as hard as possible—then heave him off with a strong fast hip thrust and come around with your leg cocked, ready to kick. Try it."

Flailing feet fill the room, as the women grunt and lunge. The literature major is pressed back against the sofa cushions now, his eyes averted, face pale. "Rats, I have physics lab," says a petite senior, sending a last invisible rapist reeling. Lesley Pan bounds to her feet, looking proudly at her panting pupils. Some are somber, some grinning. "Next week," she tells them, "knockout blows."

Asked if women's self-defense classes could be made mandatory, Pan shakes her head. "This is Brown. We don't do mandatory." Argument is an intramural sport at Brown. As on many campuses, the quest for perfect freedom, equality and safety involves a great deal of talk. (Should Brown security officers be permitted to carry weapons? Should female undergraduates write the names of male students believed to be sexually aggressive on the walls of public bathrooms? Impassioned committees deadlock for months, even years.) Meanwhile, Brown's net of student services grows increasingly fine-meshed: grief-therapy groups, support sessions for students with mentally ill families, an on-campus drug and alcohol rehabilitation program, a bouquet of 24-hour hot lines: dean on call, women on call, chaplains on call, psychologist on call.

By trying outreach and prevention programs, by offering safety education for women and men, schools like Brown and Arizona State are facing up to campus crime. But it's a constant uphill battle.

Quite simply, college students are walking security risks.

Bored, healthy, smart and underworked (one recent study found that American undergraduates transact all school-related business in a mere 30 hours a week), their idea of a good time often involves breaking into steam tunnels or climbing onto steep roofs. The mechanically inclined play with elevators in high-rise residence halls, practicing "surfing" (riding on top of the cars), "action" (jumping from car to car) and "helicopter" (hanging from cables under the car).

Academic culture—anarchic, self-centered, trusting, impractical—is itself a contributing factor in campus crime. Forgetful faculty leave the keys in unlocked cars. Some alumni return to campus to steal computers or office equipment. Naïve undergraduates keep homeless people in their dorm lounges, like pets; buy Girl Scout cookies from adorable tots with a sideline in wallet-lifting; offer mendicants rides to distant parts of town only to discover a knife against the ribs. At 18, you think you're immortal.

Even before they begin their first day of college, say many experts on student life, a large number of undergraduates are messed-up, increasingly adept (often since high school) at reckless drinking and reckless sex, increasingly burdened by messy family histories, increasingly unprepared for college course work. Winning such hearts and minds, or at least opening them to current campus concerns—from safe sex to racial harmony to homosexual rights—is hard work.

After 10 P.M., the campus, with its wild drinking and reckless sex, is almost entirely adultless.

Some schools turn to theater: student-produced improvisations with titles like "Sex on a Saturday Night" and "Coming Out 101," followed by audience discussion. Or they offer peer-to-peer counseling—useful for a generation strikingly short on adult heroes or role models. Although such efforts lead some students to seek help or alter their behavior, many experts say that for the vast majority of collegians, knowing and doing are rarely the same. Only two forces can bring about change, some contend. One is a moral campus administration. ("Possibly an oxymoron, like jumbo shrimp," murmurs one Big 10 professor.) The other, asserts a recent study of administrative responses to campus sexual assault, is an informed student conduct code.

This code, or contract between school and student, often fails those who need it most, says Andrea Parrot, an assistant professor of human service studies at Cornell University. "Some schools, like Stockton State in New Jersey, or St. Norbert's in De Pere, Wis., make it very clear they won't tolerate people who rape. After enough suspensions, word gets around. Other campuses are ostriches. 'Our kids are nice, kind, moral,' they claim. 'We've never had trouble.' In between are mildly concerned schools—look-the-other-way, don't-rock-the-boat schools, schools that whisper, 'There but for the grace of God go we.'"

Meanwhile, according to the National Clearinghouse for Alcohol and Drug Information in Maryland, college students continue to spend $5.5 billion on alcohol each year. Carl Wartenburg, for 20 years a college dean, now executive director of Alcohol Congress on Responsible Decisions, or Acord, a New Jersey-based effort to organize strategy conferences on student drinking, summarizes the views of many campus professionals.

"Raising the drinking age drove abuse behind closed doors and made social drinking impossible," he says. "So often, in alcohol-linked campus crime, actions and consequences are separated: 'Oh, I didn't know what I was doing; I was drunk.'"

When Jonathan Greenberg, 34, a Manhattan financial writer, spent a fellowship year at Yale a decade after he went to college (at the State University of New York at Binghamton, from 1976–80), the change in student attitude toward drug use astonished him, as it does many of his peers.

"Their social drug of choice is alcohol," says Greenberg. "My generation's was marijuana. The behavioral consequences of legal versus illegal drug couldn't be more striking. Stoned kids withdraw or ramble inanely about the meaning of life. Drunk kids turn hostile and abusive. It seems to me a depressing shift from the nonconformist dress codes and anarchistic leanings of the Question Authority generation to some 'fondle the babes, bash the queers' reversion to an unthinking, pre-60's, 'Father Knows Best' mentality."

The newfound paternalism notwithstanding, an unnerving disconnection distinguishes, and impoverishes, much of contemporary college life. Increasingly, faculty and administrators live far from campus. Some commute from other cities, even other states. Others hold down second jobs or teach at several schools. After sundown, certainly after 10 P.M., the campus, with its night world of wild drinking and unprotected sex, is almost entirely adultless. One price of such institutionalized inattention: at least 1 undergraduate in 12 suffers from a sexually transmitted disease; 1 in 10 becomes a chronic substance abuser. An increasing number—how many, no one is sure—are H.I.V.-positive.

At the Sixth National Conference on Campus Violence, 200 deans, student-services managers, counselors and security officials converge on downtown Baltimore, crowding into presentations on ethnoviolence in cafeteria lines, nodding at a panel's findings regarding "The Psychopathology of Machismo and Beer Dependency as Precursors to Campus Violence," trading data after a spirited session on "Fatal Misogyny: Femicide on College Campuses."

During coffee break, college officials browse among the new-product booths lining the hallways of the Baltimore Marriott. Many, looking thoughtful, tuck away brochures for dormitory-room doors guaranteed to resist both a sledgehammer and a .44 Magnum slug. Clients for such doors already include Harvard University and the Los Angeles Public Housing Authority.

Throughout the first two days of the conference, delegates from the University of California at Berkeley are treated with nervous respect. In the campus-crime world, as in many aspects of American life, California functions as an early-warning system, a canary in the academic mine. From 1990 to 1992, 11 Berkeley students were killed or wounded, including three dead in a fraternity-house fire and one slain (six injured) when an Iranian immigrant and gun collector held 33 people hostage at a popular campus-area bar. Even the chancellor spent a morning last August barricaded in his bedroom, stalked by a female nonstudent carrying a machete and a hunting knife; an Oakland police officer shot her dead. Conference attendees are eager for wisdom from the Bay Area trenches. "I want to ask them about student snipers," a security officer from Pennsylvania confides.

But on the third morning of the conference, the Berkeley chairs are empty. A Berkeley janitor discovered a body in the offices of the university's Filipino-American Student League. While working late, Grace Rualo Asuncion, 20, a junior, had been stabbed to death. No suspects, no clues. The Berkeley administrators caught the first plane west.

BREEDING HATE

*White racist organizations are growing in the U.S.,
though to what extent no one knows.*

**Michael Connely and
David Freed**

Los Angeles Times

LOS ANGELES—Hitler was a saint.
The Holocaust never happened.
Jews are the children of Satan and are
destroying the United States along
with other "mud people"—African-
Americans, Asians, Latinos—anyone
not descended from Anglo-Saxon
stock.

Such are the bizarre fomentations of
the shadowy, often violent world
known as white supremacy.

Federal agents in Los Angeles provided a rare window on that world
earlier this month in breaking up what
they described as a plot by heavily
armed white supremacist skinheads to
assassinate Rodney G. King, the motorist whose beating by Los Angeles
Police gained international attention,
bomb a prominent black church and
incite a race war. Three suspects said
to be Fourth Reich skinheads, were arrested, two of them juveniles.

How much of a presence do these
groups have? How much of a threat do
they pose?

Membership in hard-core, white
racist organizations is growing in the
United States, many authorities
believe, though to what extent no one
knows.

Statistics suggest that racially motivated hate crimes also are on the rise,

though it is uncertain how many are
committed by white racist groups.

Various organizations that closely
monitor white racist activities estimate
there are between 250 and 300 skinhead and other Aryan-type groups
nationwide. Among the largest are the
Nebraska-based New Order, which
wants to bring back Nazism; the
Church of the Creator, which is head-
quartered in Niceville, Fla., and
advocates a racial holy war; and the
Aryan Nations in northern Idaho,
whose members believe that computer
bar codes on food packages are part of
a Jewish plot to kill Christians.

Membership in these groups is estimated by private watchdog
organizations to range anywhere from
10,000 to 30,000 and growing.

A notable exception has been the Ku
Klux Klan, whose tactics have been
branded as outdated by some racist
leaders and whose hard-core ranks are
believed to have thinned in recent
years to no more than a few hundred.

"It's very difficult to get an accurate
gauge on how many people are involved because for every hard-core
member of an organization, there are
probably four to five sympathizers,"
said Lawrence Jeffries, spokesman for
the Atlanta-based Center For Democratic Renewal.

"Acts of violence (by) skinheads . . .
have given a wakeup call to local law
enforcement," said Barry Kowalski,
deputy chief of the criminal section of

the civil rights division of the U.S. Justice Department. "Prior to this, many
in law enforcement thought that this
(white supremacist) phenomenon was
something confined to kooks and people who were not really that
dangerous."

A report released this month by the
Anti-Defamation League of the B'nai
B'rith entitled "Young Nazi Killers,
the Rising Skinhead Danger" estimated
that the number of skinheads had
grown since 1985 from about 1,500
in 12 states to about 3,500 in 40
states.

Between 1987 and mid-1990, according to the ADL, skinheads were
responsible for six murders across the
country. In the three years since, there
have been at least 22 killings.

Experts across the country offer
varying theories of why white youths
shave their hair and don steel-toed
Doc Marten boots to embrace a typical
skinhead lifestyle of beer, hard rock
music and "boot parties"—where
roaming packs of skinheads beat and
stomp minorities. Most come from
dysfunctional or blue-collar families
who resent their lot in life and blame
minorities, experts say.

"In general, these are young people
whose lives are a mess," said Jack
McDevitt, a hate crime expert at
Northeastern University in Boston.
"We are more likely to get struck by a
comet than they are likely to join together in a big national movement.

From *Gannett Suburban Newspapers,* August 1, 1993, pp. 1E, 4E. Reprinted by permission of Los Angeles Times Syndicate.

These are people who find it hard to get to work in the morning."

Joe Roy, chief investigator for the Southern Poverty Law Center's Klan-watch project in Montgomery, Ala., said feuds and competition have prevented white racist organizations from forming nationwide coalitions. "There are a lot of groups out there," he said, "and they can't get their act together."

"Nothing was going my way. It is very easy to start scapegoating. It's the Jews' fault that I don't have a job. Or the blacks."

—Tom Martinex,
former Klan member.

The eroding economy, experts believe, is helping fuel an increase in the numbers of young people joining white racist groups, including the skinheads.

"These (hate) groups say, 'You aren't getting your piece of the American pie because the Jews and minorities are taking over,' " said Roy of Klanwatch.

Tom Martinez, 37, a white supremacist turned FBI informant, said he decided to join the Ku Klux Klan at the age of 19 while working at a Dunkin' Donuts shop.

"Nothing was going my way," Martinez recalled. "It is very easy to start scapegoating. It's the Jews' fault that I don't have a job. Or the blacks."

Martinez became a Ku Klux Klan recruiter. He ultimately belonged to other racist groups during the 1980s, including the American Nazi Party and an ultraviolent organization known as the Order, whose members murdered Denver radio talk show host Alan Berg in 1984 and committed a series of high-profile bank robberies.

"The groups made me feel important," Martinez said. "It was the first time in my life I felt like it was part of something, part of a family."

Martinez now goes to schools speaking out against racism, telling his personal story.

"The movement," he warns, "has become more violent."

Statistics indicate that hate crimes are increasing. But it remains unclear how much of the trend can be attributed to organized groups. Few local law enforcement agencies keep such data—and most hate crimes are never solved.

"There are definitely more recorded acts of racially motivated crime than 10 years ago," said Kowalski of the Justice Department. "But I'm not sure if that's because there are more such incidents, or better reporting mechanisms."

There is no authoritative nationwide picture of hate crime trends.

The FBI since 1990 has been required by federal law to publish annual reports on hate crime but many local and state agencies do not submit data, resulting in undercounting.

The FBI counted 4,558 hate crimes throughout the United States in 1991.

Instead of armed confrontation to effect change, former Ku Klux Klan leader Tom Metzger said he has begun encouraging the racists he meets to "worm your way into the system itself." Metzger, a toupeed television repairman who heads the White Aryan Resistance, thought to be the largest white racist group in California and among the best organized in the nation, maintains that gaining political and economic power while helping promote other whites, he explained, is the surest way to achieve the goal of an all-Aryan state.

Other prominent racists have gone even deeper into the mainstream. Consider, for example, former Klan leader-turned Louisiana state legislator David Duke who lost a gubernatorial bid in 1991—while capturing 39 percent of the vote.

But even as Duke and others attempt to work within the system, Metzger speculated, random acts of violence increasingly will be carried out by whites frustrated by what they see as reverse discrimination and dwindling opportunities in the workplace.

"These are acts of desperation that will become more and more common," Metzger said. "The government will try to stop it, but there's no way they can."

SEEKING THE ROOTS OF VIOLENCE

The search for biological clues to crime is igniting a brutal political controversy

Anastasia Toufexis

It's tempting to make excuses for violence. The mugger came from a broken home and was trying to lift himself out of poverty. The wife beater was himself abused as a child. The juvenile murderer was exposed to Mötley Crüe records and *Terminator* movies. But do environmental factors wholly account for the seven-year-old who tortures frogs? The teen-ager who knifes a teacher? The employee who slaughters workmates with an AK-47? Can society's ills really be responsible for all the savagery that is sweeping America? Or could some people be predisposed to violence by their genes?

Until recently, scientists had no good way to explore such questions—and little incentive: the issue was seen as so politically inflammatory that it was best left alone. But advances in genetics and biochemistry have given researchers new tools to search for biological clues to criminality. Though answers remain a long way off, advocates of the work believe science could help shed light on the roots of violence and offer new solutions for society.

But not if the research is suppressed. Investigators of the link between biology and crime find themselves caught in one of the most bitter controversies to hit the scientific community in years. The subject has become so politically incorrect that even raising it requires more bravery than many scientists can muster. Critics from the social sciences have denounced biological research efforts as intellectually unjustified and politically motivated. African-American scholars and politicians are particularly incensed; they fear that because of the high crime rates in inner cities, blacks will be wrongly branded as a group programmed for violence.

The backlash has taken a toll. In the past year, proposed federal research initiative that would have included biological studies has been assailed, and a scheduled conference on genetics and crime has been canceled. A session on heredity and violence at February's meeting of the American Association for the Advancement of Science turned into a politically correct critique of the research; no defenders of such studies showed up on the panel. "One is basically under attack in this field," observes one federal researcher, who like many is increasingly hesitant to talk about his work publicly.

Some of the distrust is understandable, given the tawdry history of earlier efforts to link biology and crime. A century ago, Italian physician Cesare Lombroso claimed that sloping foreheads, jutting chins and long arms were signs of born criminals. In the 1960s, scientists advanced the new discounted notion that men who carry an XYY chromosome pattern, rather than the normal XY pattern, were predisposed to becoming violent criminals.

Fresh interest in the field reflects a recognition that violence has become one of the country's worst public-health threats. The U.S. is the most violent nation in the industrialized world. Homicide is the second most frequent cause of death among Americans between the ages of 15 and 24 (after accidents) and the most common among young black men and women. More than 2 million people are beaten, knifed, shot or otherwise assaulted each year, 23,000 of them fatally. No other industrialized nation comes close: Scotland, which ranked second in homicides, has less than one-fourth the U.S. rate.

This cultural disparity indicates that there are factors in American society—such as the availability of guns, economic inequity and a violence-saturated culture—that are not rooted in human biology. Nevertheless, a susceptibility to violence might partly be genetic. Errant genes play a role in many behavioral disorders, including schizophrenia and manic depression. "In virtually every behavior we look at, genes have an influence—one person will behave one way, another person will behave another way," observes Gregory Carey, assistant professor at the University of Colorado's Institute for Behavioral Genetics. It stands to reason that genes might contribute to violent activity as well.

Some studies of identical twins who have been reared apart suggest that when one twin has a criminal conviction, the other twin is more likely to have committed a crime than is the case with fraternal twins. Other research with adopted children indicates that those whose biological parents broke the law are more likely to become criminals than are adoptees whose natural parents were law-abiding.

No one believes there is a single "criminal gene" that programs people to maim or murder. Rather, a person's genetic makeup may give a subtle nudge toward violent actions. For one thing, genes help control production of behavior-regulating chemicals. One suspect substance is the neurotransmitter serotonin. Experiments at the Bowman Gray School of Medicine in North Carolina suggest that extremely aggressive monkeys have lower levels of serotonin than do more passive peers. Animals with low serotonin are more likely to bite, slap or chase other monkeys. Such animals also seem less social: they spend more time alone and less in close body contact with peers.

A similar chemical variation appears to exist in humans. Studies at the National Institute on Alcohol Abuse and Alcoholism conclude that men who commit impulsive crimes, such as murdering strangers, have low amounts of serotonin. Men convicted of premeditated violence, however, show normal levels. As for aggressive behavior in women, some researchers speculate that it might be tied to a drop in serotonin level that normally occurs just before the menstrual period. Drugs that increase serotonin, researchers suggest, may make people less violent.

Scientists are also trying to find inborn personality traits that might make people more physically aggressive. The tendency to be a thrill seeker may be one such characteristic. So might "a restless impulsiveness, an inability to defer gratification," says psychologist Richard Herrnstein of Harvard, whose theories about the hereditary nature of intelligence stirred up a political storm in the 1970s. A high threshold for anxiety or fear may be another key trait. According to psychologist Jerome Kagan, also of Harvard, such people tend to have a "special biology," with lower-than-average heart rates and blood pressure.

Findings like these may be essential to understanding—and perhaps eventually controlling—chronic wrongdoers, argue proponents of this research. "Most youth or adults who commit a violent crime will not commit a second," observes Kagan. "The group we are concerned with are the recidivists—those who have been arrested many times. This is the group for whom there might be some biological contribution." Kagan predicts that within 25 years, biological and genetic tests will be able to pick out about 15 children of every thousand who may

have violent tendencies. But only one of those 15 children will actually *become* violent, he notes. "Do we tell the mothers of all 15 that their kids might be violent? How are the mothers then going to react to their children if we do that?"

It is just such dilemmas that have so alarmed critics. How will the information be used? Some opponents believe the research runs the danger of making women seem to be "prisoners of their hormones." Many black scholars are especially concerned. "Seeking the biological and genetic aspects of violence is dangerous to African-American youth," maintains Ronald Walters, a political science professor at Howard University. "When you consider the perception that black people have always been the violent people in this society, it is a short step from this stereotype to using this kind of research for social control."

The controversy began simmering more than a year ago, when Louis Sullivan, then Secretary of Health and Human Services, proposed a $400 million federal research program on violence; 5% of the budget would have been devoted to the study of biochemical anomalies linked to aggressive behavior. The program was shelved before being submitted to Congress, and one reason may have been the reaction to an unfortunate statement by Dr. Frederick Goodwin, then director of the Alcohol, Drug Abuse and Mental Health Administration. Commenting about research on violence in monkeys, Goodwin said, "Maybe it isn't just the careless use of the word when people call certain areas of certain cities 'jungles.' " African Americans were outraged. The ensuing furor forced Goodwin to resign, though Secretary Sullivan then appointed him to head the National Institute of Mental Health, a job he still holds.

Soon after that episode, the federally endowed Human Genome Project agreed to provide the University of Maryland with $78,000 for a conference on violence. When the program's organizers

announced that the session would look at genetic factors in crime, opponents torpedoed the meeting. "A scandalous episode," charges Harvard's Herrnstein. "It is beneath contempt for the National Institutes of Health to be running for cover when scholars are trying to share their views."

Dr. Peter Breggin, director of the Center for the Study of Psychiatry in Bethesda, Maryland, who led the opposition that scuttled the conference, has no apologies. "The primary problems that afflict human beings are not due to their bodies or brains, they are due to the environment," he declares. "Redefining social problems as public health problems is exactly what was done in Nazi Germany."

Some critics see the current interest in heredity as part of an ugly political trend. "In socially conservative times," argues political scientist Diane Paul of the University of Massachusetts at Boston, "we tend to say crime and poverty are not our fault and put the blame not on society but on genes."

Even staunch believers in heredity's influence do not discount environment. In fact, the two are intimately entwined, and separating cause and effect is not easy. Biology may affect behavior, but behavior and experience also influence biology. Serotonin levels, for example, are not only controlled by genes but, according to research in monkeys, they can be lowered by regular exposure to alcohol. By the same token, says Kagan, a child with a fearless personality may turn into a criminal if reared in a chaotic home, but given a stable upbringing, "he could well become a CEO, test pilot, entrepreneur or the next Bill Clinton."

No one thinks that discovering the roots of violence will be simple. There may be as many causes as there are crimes. The issue is whether to explore all possibilities—to search for clues in both society and biology.

—Reported by Hannah Bloch/New York and Dick Thompson/Washington

Tunnel Vision

THE WAR ON DRUGS, 12 YEARS LATER

Dan Baum

Dan Baum is a free-lance writer in Missoula, Mont.

The nation ringing in the Clinton administration is, by several measures, a healthier and more health-conscious nation than it was when Ronald Reagan took office. Americans exercise more, eat less fat, drink less alcohol and smoke less tobacco than they did a dozen years ago. Public awareness campaigns, strong leadership from the surgeon general's office, and laudable efforts at enlightening schoolchildren have, for the nation as a whole, significantly reduced demand for cigarettes, alcohol and butterfat.

Cocaine and marijuana, though, are different. So gravely did the Reagan and Bush administrations view these public health problems that they fought them not with persuasion, but with what they called a "war." George Bush devoted his first televised presidential address entirely to cocaine, calling it the nation's "most serious problem."

To be sure, cocaine, marijuana and other illegal drugs have ruined a lot of lives during the past dozen years, and each story of addiction or death is more heartbreaking than the last. But the dangers of pharmacological substances pale beside other threats accepted more calmly by the public and politicians.

For every person who dies from cocaine poisoning, 15 people die from the direct effects of alcohol and 60 from tobacco-related illnesses, according to the Public Health Service (PHS). No deaths from marijuana have ever been reported.

Dramatic headlines notwithstanding, cocaine touches relatively few lives. According to the General Accounting Office (GAO), six million Americans used cocaine in 1990, but fewer than 350,000 used it daily—a big number, but not compared to that of people plagued by other public-health problems, like the five million children under 12 who go hungry at some point each month (according to the Food Research and Action Council in Washington, D.C.).

"On the grounds of the health costs, it could scarcely be claimed that use of illicit psychoactives constitutes a social problem of the first order," writes Peter Reuter, co-director of the Drug Policy Research Center of the RAND Corp.

Nonetheless, so convinced were the Reagan and Bush administrations that drugs were society's greatest evil that they chose to fight the use of these illegal drugs with a "war."

To fight this war, federal, state and local governments spent about $100 billion during the Bush administration. In the 1980s, a decade supposedly devoted to shrinking the federal government, the federal drug-fighting budget grew ninefold to almost $13 billion a year, or about twice that of the Environmental Protection Agency.

But only about a third of the federal drug budget goes toward trying to get users off drugs and toward educating children and other nonusers not to start. The rest goes to pay for more police, more drug agents, more prosecutors and more prisons.

The nation's strategy in the war on drugs has been to spend twice as much on law enforcement as on treatment and education. By handing responsibility for this public health problem to the attorney general instead of the surgeon general, the United States has become the nation with the largest percentage of its people behind bars.

America has doubled its prison population since 1980. The number of federal prison inmates doing time for drugs is now greater than the entire federal prison population was in 1980.

In California, the portion of state prison inmates doing time for drugs has doubled to one-quarter of all inmates just since 1985; one of every five California state employees now works for the department of corrections.

"Drug czar" William Bennett created a network of high-level drug officials in the Interior, Education, Defense and other departments to give drug policy top priority. The highest-placed single-issue office at the Department of Health and Human Services, for example, is the counsel to the secretary for drug abuse policy. No other health or human-service issue—not AIDS, alcoholism, hunger or poverty—rates a secretary-level special counsel. As of press time, this specialized drug-fighting network remains within the Clinton administration.

Judges and police chiefs are beginning to criticize such worrisome byproducts of the drug war as mandatory life sentences without parole for nonviolent drug offenses, government seizure each year of $1.6 billion worth of citizens' property, and the criminalization of a generation of black men. (Across the country, one of every four black men between the ages of 18 and 30 is under some form of correctional control; in Baltimore and Washington, D.C., the figure approaches 50 percent.)

"I don't feel that you and I could sit down and take two weeks and design a system worse than the one we've got," says James Gray, a self-described conservative Republican superior court judge in Santa Ana, Calif., since 1989 and former federal prosecutor. "The courts are doing a good job, as is the DEA and everybody else. But we're farther away from a resolution than when I started on the bench."

Gray, who is careful to refer to drugs as "garbage" and abhors their use even as he promotes legalization, joins other state and federal judges in lamenting the crippling burden drug cases place on the courts. President Bush let the number of sitting federal judges decline during his administration, while tripling the number of federal prosecutors and spurring them to bring three times more drug cases to federal court in 1990 than in 1980.

The result has been havoc in the federal courts so acute that Chief Justice William Rehnquist told the 1992 midyear meeting of the ABA that the explosive rise in federal drug prosecutions is "making it next to impossible for many judges to give timely and adequate attention to their civil dockets."

Despite the country's unprecedented law-enforcement effort, overall consumption of illegal drugs hasn't declined appreciably, and in the inner cities it appears to have skyrocketed. Rates of violent and property crime likewise don't seem much affected, according to figures from the Federal Bureau of Investigation. Still, "getting tough" on drug users and drug dealers has remained the national strategy. The Bush administration consistently treated drugs as the root of society's ills.

Bush's annual National Drug Control Strategy, the written conscience of the war on drugs, justified the emphasis on enforcement by focusing all blame for drug use on the individual, explicitly rejecting any notion that drug use is a symptom of economic, social and political distress.

"To explain the drug problem by pointing to social conditions is to 'victimize' drug users and deprive them of personal autonomy—the freedom and will not to use drugs," Bush's 1992 National Drug Control Strategy states. "The drug problem reflects bad decisions by individuals with free wills." Adds John Walters, the outgoing deputy director for supply reduction in the Office of National Drug Control Policy (ONDCP): "Poverty doesn't cause drugs; drugs cause poverty."

The strategy based the war on assertions about drug use stated as fact. But these assertions are questioned by independent researchers, who produce an endless stream of studies that challenge the central tenets of the drug war.

To cite a few examples: The strategy's notion that babies exposed to crack in the womb will never recover and constitute a "time bomb" that will "explode 20 to 30 years from now" is challenged by researchers at both Emory University Medical School and the National Association of Perinatal Research and Education.

They find instead that most effects of cocaine exposure pass within several months, and that most of the sad long-term symptoms popularly associated with "crack babies" stem instead from other conditions that commonly accompany cocaine use, such as poverty, violence, malnutrition and poor prenatal care.

The shibboleth that increased drug enforcement can reduce other types of crime is questioned by studies in Florida and Chicago, where diverting extensive police resources to drug enforcement had the unintended consequence of allowing both property crime and alcohol-related traffic deaths to increase.

The common belief that high murder rates are caused by people driven insane by drugs is contradicted by an examination of 218 New York City homicides recorded as "drug-related" in 1988. Five were caused by the psychoactive effects of crack (as opposed to 21 by the effects of alcohol); motives for the rest lay not in the pharmacological substance but in the nature of the illegal drug trade—either turf wars or robberies by addicts desperate to buy another dose.

And the government's assertion that cocaine can be "instantly addictive" is upended by its own numbers; of the more than six million Americans who used cocaine in 1990, only about one-tenth used it weekly and only about half of those, or 5.4 percent of all cocaine users, used it daily, according to the GAO.

While none of the studies challenging "instant addiction," "drug-crazed" crime or a generation of "crack babies" is conclusive, they at least begin to lend academic support to a re-examination of current drug policy.

On the other hand, research supporting the policy—detailing the health dangers of drugs and linking drug abuse to crime, for example—isn't available from ONDCP or the Department of Health and Human Services. Both agencies ignored repeated requests, by phone and fax, for studies that support the assertions about drug abuse made in the 1992 Drug Control Strategy.

"If you want mass studies, there aren't any," said Walters, who charted national drug-enforcement policy for four years. "It's very hard to get to the bottom of some of this."

Instead of "mass studies," ONDCP, the White House and their allies in Congress and the courts generate support for the government's enforcement-heavy policies through moral assertions about drugs and the people who use them.

Speaking at Harvard in 1989, the new ONDCP director, William Bennett, summed up his abhorrence of drug use this way: "It makes a mockery of virtue."

"It's a moral question," Walters said, during an interview in his Washington office two weeks after the November election. "The question of right and wrong is crucial."

Federal judges have written into their opinions

comparisons of drug users and dealers to "the vampire of fable," and an "external enemy," and one judge even suggested that compared with drug trafficking, "violent crimes may well be considered the lesser of two evils."

Building more prisons is "the morally right thing to do," Attorney General William Barr said in a speech last April. Drug czar Bennett even suggested, on "Larry King Live," beheading dealers.

Such medieval reasoning permeates the National Drug Control Strategy, which effectively equates drug users with lepers, comparing them "in epidemiological terms" to a "carrier" whose drug use is "highly contagious." The casual user is singled out for punishment more than the hard-core addict because "he is likely to have a still-intact family, social and work life. He is likely still to 'enjoy' his drug use for the pleasure it offers."

Each year since 1989 the strategy has called for ever-tougher sanctions against nonaddicted, non-dealing consumers of illegal drugs. "Who's responsible?" George Bush asked in his 1989 speech. "Let me tell you straight out: Everyone who uses drugs. Everyone who sells drugs. And everyone who looks the other way." The Bush White House called this principle "user accountability." Critics call it cruel and repressive.

"The mentality here is a concern not with health, but with compliance," says Professor Lynn Zimmer of the City University of New York. "That's why there's no parallel concern with alcohol and tobacco." She points to the circular logic that gives rise to such a position: "Drugs are illegal because they're immoral, and immoral because they're illegal."

Congress has eagerly played along with the White House. "In the war on narcotics, we have met the enemy, and he is the U.S. Code," Rep. Earl Hutto, D-Fla., complained during a 1981 hearing. "I have never seen such a maze of laws and hangups."

Since then, Congress abolished federal parole. It let police share in the confiscated assets of drug dealers, giving them a financial interest in the drug economy they're supposed to eradicate (state and local police collected $218 million in shared assets in fiscal year 1992). Congress let police hold drug defendants without bail. It required states to revoke drug offenders' driver's licenses or lose federal highway funds.

Congress also removed federal judges' authority to decide sentences, writing in 1984 a long list of mandatory minimum sentences that judges must apply without consideration of the circumstances of the particular crime or the defendant's character. (Predictably, defense attorneys hate mandatory minimums. But so do federal judges. The judicial councils of all 12 federal circuits passed resolutions in 1990 and 1991 asking Congress to reconsider mandatory sentencing. Even federal prosecutors are divided on it, according to a survey by the federal Sentencing Commission.)

Anyone defending a client in federal court also now faces the Speedy Trial Act of 1984, which says a federal case must come to trial within 70 days of indictment. "That sounds good," says Louisiana defense attorney Thomas Lorenzi, "but the feds take

five years to prepare a case, then issue an indictment and bam! You're arraigned today, motions are due in 15 days, trial in six weeks."

Also in 1984, Congress passed a law allowing prosecutors to appeal a sentence, a right that used to be enjoyed almost exclusively by the defense. "They don't do it much, but they do have the right and the threat," says Judy Clarke, a Spokane, Wash., federal defender who privately publishes the monthly "Guideline Grapevine," which tracks federal sentences. "Prosecutors use it to intimidate the defense into not appealing a trial issue if they [prosecutors] won't appeal a sentencing issue."

All in all, the passion to fight drugs has reversed the federal government's traditional leadership in holding states to a higher standard of civil rights. "When I started to practice law, the state legislature would have to go into session every year to restrict their laws to comply with federal law," says Lorenzi. "Now they go into session every year to change their laws to take advantage of federal laws' new laxity."

Drug use and drug sale are crimes committed among willing participants—unlike robbery, rape or burglary. So investigating drug crime requires intrusion into peoples' lives. And the courts have shared Congress' willingness to make that intrusion ever easier. Every one of the federal wiretap warrants requested of federal judges in 1990 was approved; in fact, the annual use of federal wiretaps has more than quadrupled since 1980.

In drug case after drug case, the U.S. Supreme Court has loosened the rules surrounding search warrants, too. *Illinois v. Gates*, 462 U.S. 213 (1983), and *McCray v. Illinois*, 386 U.S. 300 (1987), permitted the issuance of search warrants based on anonymous information; *Oliver v. United States*, 466 U.S. 170 (1984), permitted warrantless searches of fields, barns and other private property near a residence; *United States v. Leon*, 468 U.S. 897 (1984), *Massachusetts v. Sheppard*, 468 U.S. 981 (1984), and *Maryland v. Garrison*, 480 U.S. 79 (1987), allowed the use of evidence obtained under a defective search warrant if officers acted "in good faith." *California v. Ciraolo*, 476 U.S. 207 (1986), permitted warrantless aerial surveillance of a home, and *Florida v. Riley*, 488 U.S. 445 (1989), lowered the permissible ceiling for aerial warrantless searches to 400 feet.

The Court justified its decision to permit pretrial preventive detention, in *U.S. v. Salerno*, 481 U.S. 739 (1987), by explicitly comparing the war on drugs to a war against another nation, ruling that in times of "war or insurrection ... the government's regulatory interest in community safety can ... outweigh an individual's liberty interest."

Conversely, the law increasingly fails to protect drug suspects from crimes committed against them. Prosecutors, judges and juries have begun going easy on people—especially parents—accused of killing or abusing drug users, according to Abraham Abramovsky of the International Criminal Law Center at Fordham University Law School in New York.

In one recent New York case, the Bronx district attorney dropped charges against a couple who chained their daughter to a radiator to prevent her from using drugs. In another, a Queens grand jury refused to indict a mother for murder for shooting her crack-addicted daughter; it indicted instead for manslaughter. "There's not a flood of these cases yet," said Abramovsky. "But I do see an emerging pattern."

In such cases, people who use drugs are considered beneath the full protection of the law. Women who are on drugs while pregnant are likewise demonized. Prosecutors around the country are charging women with everything from drug trafficking to homicide for using illegal drugs during pregnancy, even though no state assigns statutory penalties for doing so.

The Center for Reproductive Law & Policy has collected 167 cases of women thus tried, and though many were acquitted or had their cases dismissed, many others lost custody of their children and many went to prison. Perhaps most frightening, defense lawyers rarely challenge the validity of the charge and instead convince their clients to plead guilty. "As a result," says a report by the center, "many women in America are serving jail terms or are on probation for non-existent crimes."

The mainstream press doesn't seem concerned; in one rather strident dispatch, *New York Times* columnist A.M. Rosenthal dismissed women who use drugs as "monsters."

Doctors, however, are becoming increasingly vocal about the intrusion of the punitive drug-war mentality into the field of medicine. Six prominent medical associations, including the American Medical Association, the American Academy of Pediatrics and the American Public Health Association, publicly deplore the prosecution of pregnant women.

"Criminal prosecution of chemically dependent women will have an overall result of deterring such women from seeking both prenatal care and chemical dependency treatment, thereby increasing rather than preventing harm to children and society," the American Society for Addiction Medicine argues.

The government has steadfastly refused to allow doctors to prescribe marijuana to AIDS and terminal cancer patients who are relieved of debilitating nausea by no other drug, even though the DEA's own administrative law judge ruled in 1988 that as no long-term health effects and no marijuana deaths had ever been recorded, the drug should be reclassified as a legal medicine.

The government can't allow marijuana to be given to AIDS patients, Assistant HHS Secretary James O. Mason said in 1991, because that would send a "bad signal" that "this stuff can't be so bad." (This is one policy that might change quickly under the Clinton administration. Surgeon General-designate Jocelyn Elders told a reporter that she supported allowing the medical use of marijuana.)

New York City canceled its only clean-needle exchange program for intravenous drug addicts in 1990 because, the health commissioner said, it would be "sending the wrong message." In New York, some 60 percent of needle-drug addicts are HIV-positive; in Liverpool, England, which has a needle-exchange program, the rate of infection approaches zero.

"We're sending a message, all right," says Dr. John Morgan, professor of pharmacology at City University of New York Medical School. "The message we're sending to IV drug users is: 'We want you to die.'"

Even the use of legal medication is affected by the drug-war mentality. Several recent studies report that complicated paperwork surrounding opiate pain-killers, outright restrictions on the use of opiates and what one doctor calls "opiophobia" are leading to underuse of legitimate pain medication in hospitals.

This not only increases suffering, it also prolongs surgical patients' recovery, says Dr. C. Stratton Hill of the M.D. Anderson Cancer Center in Houston, who helped write pain-medication guidelines for the federal Agency for Health Care Policy and Research. "We confuse the legitimate use of drugs with the illegitimate," he says. "The illegitimate image so dominates our thinking that we believe anybody who uses them is a criminal."

Despite the evident drawbacks to a policy that criminalizes rather than treats behavior, the end of the Bush administration probably doesn't mean an end to the drug war. Judging by signals from the Democrats on the subject so far, the government may become even more punitive toward drug use.

In the first televised presidential debate, Bill Clinton said, "the criminal justice system saved the life" of his half-brother Roger, who was convicted in 1984 on federal conspiracy and cocaine trafficking charges and sentenced to two years in prison, of which he served 16 months. It isn't clear whether Clinton thinks his brother's life would have been saved by 10 years in a federal penitentiary, the minimum mandatory penalty he'd get today on the trafficking charge alone.

Although Clinton told the *ABA Journal* he thinks "a large part of the substance-abuse problem can be best dealt with as a public health and education issue," his only specific proposals are a "National Police Corps" to put 100,000 more police on the streets and an archipelago of "boot camps" to straighten out young drug users through "shock incarceration."

As for the Democratic leadership in Congress, the Senate Judiciary Committee chaired by Sen. Joseph Biden, D-Del., attacks Bush's drug war for being too soft. In a report titled, "The President's Drug Strategy: Has it Worked?" the Biden committee argues, no, but only because President Bush hasn't spent enough money on law enforcement, hasn't been tough enough on drug addicts, hasn't given enough power and money to the military to shift its mission to fighting illegal drugs. In 194 pages, the report never once uses the words "racism," "AIDS," "poverty," "tobacco," or "civil liberties." As much as Republicans, Democrats like their drug war rhetoric served hot.

"There is no drug exception to the Constitution," Justices Thurgood Marshall and William Brennan wrote in 1989. But both, of course, are gone from the Court.

Street Guns

A CONSUMER GUIDE

Waves of crime, fear and drug money relentlessly sweep new generations of guns into the streets. Vast numbers are legally for sale in gun and sporting goods stores across America, but even where sales are restricted by Federal or local laws the guns may be purchased illegally if you know the right people and can pay the right price.

DAVID C. ANDERSON

David C. Anderson is a member of The New York Times editorial board.

THE NINES

THE NINES

LENGTH
7 to 8 inches.

WEIGHT
1.5 to 3 pounds.

AVAILABILITY
Difficult to get only in a few places with strict laws.

PRICE
In stores, $95 to $900, depending on quality; on the street, $700 to $1,000.

PEOPLE SEEKING GUNS FOR PERsonal combat want reliable "stopping power" — the devastation to human tissue when a bullet strikes. That requires a bullet with a diameter of 9 millimeters, similar in size to a caliber of .357 of an inch. Larger bullets have greater stopping power, but must be fired from bigger guns that are hard to conceal, heavy to carry.

Guns using .357- or 9-millimeter cartridges are either revolvers or semiautomatic pistols known as "nines." The revolver, a comparatively simple device dating from the early 19th century, commonly fires six rounds from a cylinder that rotates with each pull of the trigger. The semiautomatic, which dates from the late 19th century, typically fires cartridges from a magazine that fits in the gun's grip. As each cartridge is discharged, the recoil drives a heavy slide surrounding the gun's barrel. Traveling back and forth in a fraction of a second, the slide automatically recocks the firing pin, ejects the spent casing and moves a fresh cartridge from the magazine into the firing chamber.

These differences are easy to feel. Pick up a .357 magnum revolver and your wrist muscles strain to level the weight, centered well forward of the handle. Fire it for the first time and the bullet is likely to fly wild as the recoil jolts your arm and shoulder.

By comparison, the semiautomatic nine seems lighter and more balanced. The popular Glocks, for example, are made partly of plastic, greatly reducing their weight. In addition, the semiautomatic's grip is just beneath the barrel, so that the gun seems to snuggle down in your hand. Firing the nine means less jolt and more control as the slide absorbs some of the recoil. The gun is also more responsive, requiring less force to pull the trigger. Its magazine holds 9 to 16 cartridges.

These no-nonsense advantages have, especially since the mid-1980's, made the nine the weapon of choice for career robbers and foot soldiers in drug gangs. A study conducted by the Federal Bureau of Alcohol, Tobacco and Firearms suggests that since 1987 the number of nines used in crimes has nearly doubled. Another study by the bureau found that of the 966 homicides committed with guns in New York City during the first half of 1992, 283 were committed with nines, placing these firearms at the top of the list. In response, law enforcement agencies in many cities are equipping their officers with nines.

Even so, the nines are not about to make .357 magnum revolvers obsolete. Fans debate the merits of the two weapons the way music buffs compare long-play records with compact disks. Those sticking with revolvers point out that unless the nines are manufactured with precision and maintained carefully, their complicated action may malfunction, most commonly by jamming as cartridges misfire. In fact, New York City police officers are seeing an increasing number of "perp-jams" (when a perpetrator's semiautomatic pistol misfires), deepening the department's misgivings about allowing all of its 30,000 officers to carry nines.

The revolver, meanwhile, can be depended upon

to get off its six shots no matter how dirty or neglected the gun may be. And the virtues of the larger magazine aren't necessarily obvious. Extended firefights are rare events on city streets. Furthermore, the connoisseur may find a .357's familiar weight and feel reassuring: Snap open the dark, gleaming weapon's well-oiled cylinder, feel the silken weight of cartridges sliding into their chambers — the elegance and sensuous simplicity make the cranky semiautomatic's advantages seem marginal.

The nines, however, now lead in sales. In places where local gun regulations impede quick purchases, criminals are likely to buy from traffickers bringing weapons in from states with wide-open laws. On the street, one can expect to pay anywhere from $700 for a clunky Stallard to $1,000 for the top-of-the-line German-made SIG-Sauer. The cheaper the gun, of course, the more profit for the smuggler; he probably purchased the SIG legally for $800 to $900, the Glock for $450 to $500 and the Stallard for only $95 to $120.

An Atlanta company, S.W.D. Inc., developed the Cobray M-11 after the Bureau of Alcohol, Tobacco and Firearms decided that the MAC-10 the company was selling as a semiautomatic was actually a submachine gun. Gun owners had discovered how to make it fire automatically, using nothing more sophisticated than a paper clip. Classified as a submachine gun, the MAC-10 became subject to stringent regulations that sharply restricted sales. The gun bureau approved the Cobray as a semiautomatic after extended negotiations with S.W.D.

Intratec, a Miami company founded by Cuban exiles, introduced the TEC-9 in the 1980's. Intratec claims it has sold the gun to police and military forces abroad; they like the TEC-9's menacing appearance, the company says, because they believe it deters political street violence without bloodshed. But the main market for Cobray M-11's, TEC-9's and their imitators remains domestic, and follows the trend for other nines. Research by the firearms bureau suggests these weapons now account for nearly 10 percent of crime guns it traces for criminal investigations.

THE UGLY GUNS

THE COBRAY M-11 AND THE TEC-9, along with their relatives and clones, are an important subcategory of the nines. When firing semiautomatically, these handguns don't fire any more rapidly or powerfully than the conventional models. Their obvious advantage is that they can take long magazines holding up to 30 cartridges. Because of their fearsome appearance, experts at the firearms bureau call them "ugly guns."

The Cobray looks like a quart-size milk carton turned on its side and fitted with a barrel. The handle is attached at about the midpoint of the box; with its deep magazine in place, the gun takes on a distinctive T-shaped profile. The TEC-9 is about the same size but shaped differently, with a rounder frame, a grip set farther back and a barrel surrounded by a shroud ventilated with holes the size of nickels.

These guns can't be tucked discreetly in a waistband or shoulder holster. But they confer upon their bearers, commonly drug dealers, an aura of big-time criminality, evoking images of terrorists or Colombian cocaine cartels.

In truth, the guns owe part of their reputation to more than appearance. Gunsmiths with access to instructions and parts can alter them so that they fire as fully automatic submachine guns. (Machine guns are defined as firearms that discharge more than one shot with each pull of the trigger. Submachine guns are machine guns that fire handgun, as opposed to rifle, ammunition.)

These are not just any submachine guns. The Cobray is descended from the MAC-10, which fired an astonishing 1,000 rounds per minute as an automatic weapon. The TEC-9 converted for automatic fire shoots at a similar rate. The novice who tries to fire one quickly understands the inherent dangers of automatics. Pull the trigger and the barrel jumps up as repeated recoils throw the gun's weight back. Try to hold it down and it's likely to swing about, spraying its hundreds of rounds per minute across wide arcs.

THE JUNK

GERMAN, ITALIAN AND SPANISH manufacturers used to supply most of the American market with the $20 to $30 weapons called "Saturday night specials." But in the landmark 1968 gun control law, Congress banned their importation — instantly creating a vast market for American entrepreneurs to exploit.

Today, a California family led by George Jennings dominates the domestic market through several companies that manufacture and wholesale more than 400,000 cheap handguns a year. Big sellers are crudely made small-caliber — .22 or .25 — semiautomatics that barely fill the hand. Except for its weight, the popular Raven MP-25 might be mistaken for one of the palm-size water guns that appear on school playgrounds.

Small size and caliber do allow for considerable control. But that's about the only advantage. Cheap junk guns remain very much the despised "rejects" of street weapons, the pathetic choice of unsophisticated criminals. Even so, products of Jennings and related companies appear to be volume leaders in crime guns sold in recent years, accounting for more than 30 percent of such weapons traced by the firearms bureau.

Their ubiquitousness simply confirms that much crime is committed by amateurs, experimenters and adolescents acting out. The cheap pocket guns are found in the hands of small-time drug dealers, teen-agers looking for a way to get started in armed robbery and, increasingly, students in inner-city high schools who believe they have a need for self-defense.

The guns' low price makes them accessible to nearly everyone. Dealers sell them for $45 and up depending on the model. That allows black-market gun runners to make an easy profit, selling them for less than $100 on the street. The Jennings companies also reap an ample legitimate profit, since the guns cost less than $20 to produce.

THE ASSAULT RIFLES

THE ASSAULT RIFLES

LENGTH
About 3 feet (shorter if folding stock is folded).

WEIGHT
7 to 9 pounds.

AVAILABILITY
Rare if foreign made; widely available if American made.

PRICE
In stores, $700 to more than $1,000, depending on model; on the street, more than $2,000.

DURING THE 1980'S, SEMIAUTOMATIC versions of infantry rifles acquired a following in the United States. This generated much debate and prohibitions in many localities because the guns often turned up in the hands of deranged people who vented their rage by shooting randomly at innocent targets.

The gun lobby argues that gun control supporters exaggerate the extent to which assault rifles are used in crime. Studies by the firearms agency show that though they account for less than 2 percent of all guns in the United States, they turn up as 6 to 10 percent of crime guns the agency traces. Law enforcement agents say they are likely to find these weapons in raids on drug distributors, urban street gangs and far-right revolutionaries.

Still, these weapons are hard to conceal and not particularly useful for street crime. They remain more the choice of people seriously involved in criminal organizations who feel a need for military-level weapons with which to war on one another or to pursue paranoid fantasies.

Such guns are descended from the MP-44 developed by the Germans at the end of World War II. The MP-44 was the first to combine features now considered standard by armies all over the world: a pistol grip as well as a rifle stock, a selection lever for shifting from semiautomatic to automatic fire, a detachable magazine and fittings for muzzle attachments like bayonets and flash suppressors.

The assault weapons in circulation today are mostly substantial, well-designed guns. Purists insist that those sold legally in the United States should not be called assault rifles because in order to stay within the law, they are capable only of semiautomatic fire. A true military weapon ought to function as a machine gun as well. As with the Cobray M-11 and the TEC-9, however, instructions and parts for converting semiautomatic assault rifles to automatic fire are available to those who know where to look.

The AK-47 was designed for the Soviet Army after World War II; millions have been distributed in Communist countries around the world. The AK, often fitted with a curved "banana" magazine, commonly appears in news photos of conflict in the Balkans, the Middle East and elsewhere.

Chinese manufacturers produce a semiautomatic version that was exported in huge quantities to the United States in the 1980's. It was sold in gun shops for $250 to $300 until 1989, when President Bush imposed a ban on imports of assault rifles for sale to civilians. Those in inventory now might sell for more than $700 in a store and more than $1,000 illegally on the street, especially with automatic firing restored.

The famous Israeli-designed Uzi submachine gun has a sportier image and great street appeal: Fold its slender wire stock alongside the frame and it looks a bit like one of the ugly guns. But it settles more solidly in your arms — it was made for the battlefield rather than the street. Its importation, too, is now banned by the 1989 order. Semiautomatic models still available in stores would sell for $800 to $1,000; the street price might reach $1,800 for one converted to automatic fire.

THE STREET SWEEPERS

LENGTH
About 3 feet.

WEIGHT
9.25 pounds.

AVAILABILITY
Legal in most places, but may be hard to find.

PRICE
In stores, $300 to $400; on the street, more than $1,000.

Colt's Manufacturing in Connecticut, along with some imitators, produces the AR-15, a civilian semiautomatic version of the M-16 rifle issued to United States armed forces. A few years ago, AR-15's were relatively easy to convert to automatic fire, especially with the help of manuals and parts available from mail-order suppliers. But in 1990, Colt's, in consultation with the gun bureau, made conversion much more difficult on new models.

Where legal, the AR-15 costs $1,500 to $1,800; at that price, the street markup may be comparatively small. But despite the cost, say agents of the firearms bureau, the AR-15 appears frequently in criminal hands.

THE STREET SWEEPERS

THE WILDEST, AND PERHAPS THE deadliest, gun on the street looks like the mutant progeny of a coffee can and a giant grasshopper. Its oversize handgun frame is fitted with a folding stock, a forward grip and a large drum magazine. A big butterfly-shaped key protrudes from its face. The gun, developed in South Africa for "crowd control" of a brutal and bloody sort, is called the Striker 12 or the Street Sweeper. With importation also banned, two American companies now produce the gun.

The Street Sweeper is basically a large revolver whose drum cylinder holds 12 shotgun shells. The key winds a spring that keeps the cylinder under tension. As the trigger releases after the gun is fired, the spring quickly rotates the cylinder for the next shot, greatly increasing the rate of fire. The Street Sweeper can discharge 12 shells in a few seconds, spewing as much lethal fire across a wide area as rapidly as any machine gun.

Because its action depends entirely on trigger pull and spring tension rather than the force of recoil, the Street Sweeper does not qualify as an automatic or even a semiautomatic weapon. Except where local jurisdictions have banned it by name, it remains in legal terms of no greater official concern than a simple revolver.

Some experts say the gun is poorly designed and shabbily made. In most hands, it is nearly impossible to control. If fired from the shoulder with the stock unfolded, its powerful recoils are likely to overcome all but the most massively built shooter. That is why those who use the weapon mostly fire it from the hip.

The Street Sweeper, though not a familiar tool of armed robbery, is commonly found on drug raids. It may qualify as the ultimate perversion of the gunsmith's craft — a cross between deadly firearm and wind-up toy.

EASY PIECES

STREET GUNS ARE EASY TO GET because laws controlling sales are relatively lax. A 1935 Federal law imposed stiff tax and registration requirements on "gangster" weapons (machine guns, sawed-off shotguns and short-barreled rifles), but since then Washington has imposed only light restrictions on other firearms.

27

Federal law prohibits sales of guns to convicted felons, mental patients, drug abusers, illegal aliens. Handguns can be sold only to people over the age of 21; rifles and shotguns, to those over 18. Some states require waiting periods between purchase and delivery of guns so police can check the would-be buyer's background. New Jersey and California ban assault weapons. South Carolina prohibits purchases of more than one handgun per month, as well as sales of any handgun made of metal that melts at a low temperature. Counties and cities may add sales limits and license requirements of their own.

The differences in laws among states create a powerful motive for gun running. Typically, the smuggler drives to Virginia, Ohio or Florida, where guns are easily purchased over the counter. With the help of a straw man who can document local residence, he then purchases several guns and carries them back to New York or another city with strict gun laws. There the weapons sell quickly on the street for a handsome profit.

Federal laws that might inhibit the smuggling include a proposal to limit handgun purchases to one per month and the Brady Bill, which would impose a five-day waiting period for handgun purchases everywhere. Since the Brady Bill was first proposed in 1987, its supporters have contended that the prospect of police scrutiny could deter out-of-state purchases. Named for James Brady, the White House press secretary wounded in the assassination attempt on President Reagan, the bill has won substantial support, though not yet enough to make it law. With President Clinton indicating strong backing, this year could be different.

THE UNTOLD STORY OF THE LA RIOT

The prevailing view about its causes is flawed. The unsettling truth is that incompetence, alcohol, greed and hatred helped make it happen.

Well before he heard the first siren, Rodney King knew he never should have slipped that key into the ignition. They had been having so much fun, he and his buddies Bryant Allen and Freddie Helms, just kicking back, sipping some inexpensive 40-ounce bottles of malt liquor at the local park as they jawed and laughed while the daylight ebbed away. Afterward, they had stood in front of Allen's mom's house trying to croon a few tunes. King wasn't much of a singer but, when he switched to rapping, his buddies felt he was almost in a groove. And then it was after midnight, and suddenly King was driving his car, flying down the highway at 80 miles per hour, the radio blaring, he and Allen singing again, and then there it was—the flashing light atop the highway patrol car bouncing off his rearview mirror, filling his car with a red light that King had learned to dread.

King knew, as he later testified, that he was drunk and that if the police caught him speeding he'd soon be back in prison for violating parole. The fact was that liquor had tempted and cursed him for years. His father, an alcoholic, died at age 42, and King himself had built up quite a tolerance for "eightballs," the street name for Olde English 800, a high-alcohol beer. That evening King had consumed enough eightballs—roughly the equivalent of a case of regular 12-ounce beers—to put his blood alcohol level at twice the legal limit. But he wanted still more: When he spotted the highway patrol car behind him around 12:40 a.m., he had just exited the free-

way on his way to another liquor store. Once the chase began, he ran red lights, pushed the speedometer up to 80 mph in 35 mph speed zones and ignored the hollered pleas of his childhood friend Allen to please "pull over." By the time King finally stopped, nearly 8 miles later, a small army of cop cars had joined the chase and a Los Angeles Police Department chopper was whirring overhead.

A Los Angeles jury decided last month that nothing King did justifies his manhandling by the LAPD. But even those who testified *against* the police described an encounter that was complicated by King's drunkenness. They say he responded slowly or not at all to commands to lie down and place his hands above his head. He smiled and danced a little pitter-patter, waving to the helicopter; he threw a kiss and wiggled his butt at a female officer who had ordered him, at gunpoint, to lie down; finally, he heaved four male officers off his back who tried to handcuff him and seemed to shrug it off when police stunned him with a Taser. King's behavior so alarmed the arresting officers that they mistakenly assumed he was on PCP. A second Taser dart fired by Sgt. Stacey Koon failed to incapacitate the 6-foot, 3-inch, 225-pound King. Then, across the street, an amateur videotaper named George Holliday turned on his camcorder and taped the conclusion of what soon became the most infamous beating in history. George Bush later called the footage "revolting." Afterward, as King lay hogtied on the ground, the bloodied, angry victim alternately laughed and

cursed into the chill night air. " . . . you!" he screamed. " . . . you!"

THE 'REBELLION'

The story of how the worst American riot in this century began is a little like the story of Rodney King's beating: By now it has been twisted into a series of half-truths and misconceptions. Just as King was not simply a speeding motorist who was beaten after a routine traffic stop, so, too, the analyses of the roots of the Los Angeles riot require some revision. The official version runs roughly as follows: Angry blacks, indignant over a suburban jury's decision on April 29, 1992, to acquit four LAPD cops in the King beating, started the riot by pulling white trucker Reginald Denny from the cab of his truck and then beating him brutally to avenge the King beating. The subsequent riot was bred out of decades of racism and police brutality and nourished by the enraging conditions of ghetto life: unemployment, poverty, family breakdown, gangs, drugs, welfare and Reagan-era cutbacks in aid. When it was over, more than 50 people lay dead, 2,300 had been injured and $1 billion in property had been damaged.

No one doubts that deprivation and bitterness fill many neighborhoods in South Central Los Angeles or that outrage at the cops' acquittal set the stage for the riot. But there are two core premises to the official version of the riot that are wrong in some instances and exaggerated in others. The first is that the grim conditions of South Central and the surprise acquittals combined to make

Anatomy of a riot

Violence at ground zero preceded Reginald Denny's beating. Times are approximate —

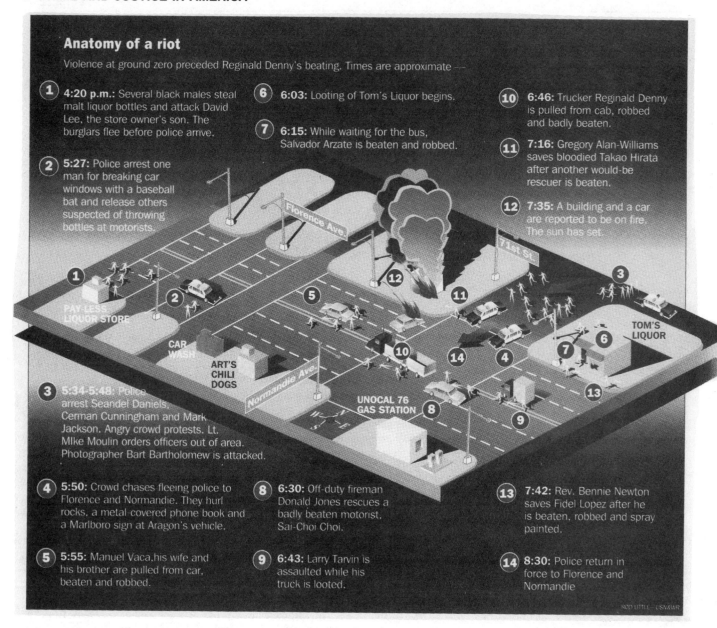

(1) 4:20 p.m.: Several black males steal malt liquor bottles and attack David Lee, the store owner's son. The burglars flee before police arrive.

(2) 5:27: Police arrest one man for breaking car windows with a baseball bat and release others suspected of throwing bottles at motorists.

(3) 5:34-5:48: Police arrest Seandel Daniels, Cerman Cunningham and Mark Jackson. Angry crowd protests. Lt. Mike Moulin orders officers out of area. Photographer Bart Bartholomew is attacked.

(4) 5:50: Crowd chases fleeing police to Florence and Normandie. They hurl rocks, a metal-covered phone book and a Marlboro sign at Aragon's vehicle.

(5) 5:55: Manuel Vaca, his wife and his brother are pulled from car, beaten and robbed.

(6) 6:03: Looting of Tom's Liquor begins.

(7) 6:15: While waiting for the bus, Salvador Arzate is beaten and robbed.

(8) 6:30: Off-duty fireman Donald Jones rescues a badly beaten motorist, Sai-Choi Choi.

(9) 6:43: Larry Tarvin is assaulted while his truck is looted.

(10) 6:46: Trucker Reginald Denny is pulled from cab, robbed and badly beaten.

(11) 7:16: Gregory Alan-Williams saves bloodied Takao Hirata after another would-be rescuer is beaten.

(12) 7:35: A building and a car are reported to be on fire. The sun has set.

(13) 7:42: Rev. Bennie Newton saves Fidel Lopez after he is beaten, robbed and spray painted.

(14) 8:30: Police return in force to Florence and Normandie

ROD LITTLE — USN&WR

a riot *inevitable.* The second is that the Los Angeles riot was fundamentally a massive protest over social injustice. Many liberal commentators, as well as prominent black and Latino Angelenos, now insist that the riot should be referred to as a "rebellion" or an "uprising." The men accused of beating, trampling and robbing Reginald Denny have thus been dubbed the "L.A. Four"—a moniker usually reserved for political martyrs.

The true story of the riot is more disquieting. Contrary to conventional wisdom, it began in one of South Central's better-off neighborhoods. Avenging Rodney King was only superficially present in the minds of those who *started* the riot at the now infamous intersection

of Florence and Normandie avenues. And the young men who nearly killed Reginald Denny were distinguished neither by their notoriety as thugs (as some conservatives would have it) nor by their militancy (as some liberals suggest).

A richer explanation of the riot's genesis must extend beyond the usual suspects. Neighborhood loyalties and simple greed motivated the mob as much as the desire to right a warped system of justice. And a massive riot might not have occurred at all were it not for a Keystone Kops performance by the LAPD. Liquor played a little-noticed role throughout the disaster, from King's arrest to the attacks at Florence and Normandie to the targets of the looters. Last, and most sad, blacks

attacked Anglos and Hispanics because of their skin color. Thankfully, numerous black bystanders dissented from that racial litmus test, coming to the rescue of the victims.

The popular understanding of how the riot began is based on the much replayed television clip of one incident, the beating of Denny. Once seen, the gruesome footage is indelible. Even so, it actually understates the reign of terror that prevailed at Florence and Normandie. *U.S. News* has reconstructed a fuller picture of how this epic riot started by interviewing residents, businessmen, police officers, reporters and photographers who were present at ground zero and by reviewing court records, police radio transmissions and amateur videotapes taken on the ground during the violence.

Collectively, they show how several dozen victims were assaulted and robbed. Sometimes, the perpetrators raged as they attacked passing motorists and pedestrians. Yet just as often they cheered, laughed and even danced. Their unadulterated language is profane and occasionally chilling. But as the opening of the devisive Denny trial looms this summer [1993], a candid reassessment of the outbreak may assist officials in preventing future disturbances and help Americans understand just what it means to grow up in South Central Los Angeles.

THE NEIGHBORHOOD

At first glance, the area around Florence and Normandie seems an unlikely site to start a riot. There are virtually no highrises or housing projects, the streets are wide and uncluttered and the vast majority of blocks consist of single-level, owner-occupied homes with neat lawns and trim hedges. Families—about 3 in 4 are black—hold weekend barbecues, friends pull up chairs to play outdoor games of dominoes and kids race around on 12-speed bikes. In the census tract that was home to Reginald Denny's attackers, 1 in 6 black households made more than $50,000 in 1990, and the majority of black males work. By contrast, in South Central as a whole, more than half of all residents age 16 and over don't hold jobs.

Ironically, the comparative success of the Florence and Normandie neighborhood may have made it a candidate for havoc. After the riots of the 1960s, sociologists found that neighborhoods characterized by "relative deprivation" were more often riot flash points than were the worst slums. Once some residents start seeing neighbors achieve upward mobility, expectations can get both raised and dashed. During the 1980s, the area around Florence and Normandie improved in economic terms: The poverty rate dropped from 33 percent to 21 percent, and even the proportion of households headed by single mothers dipped. Covetousness, more than rage, filled the streets. One example: The 1991 homicide rate in this census tract was not much above that of the average U.S. community; the robbery rate was nearly four times the national average.

Not so exotic. News accounts often portray South Central L.A. as an exotic world filled with Uzi-toting gang members, promiscuous teenage girls looking for crack and innocent children who dive for cover on bullet-riddled playgrounds. To be sure, such characters and events do exist. But day-to-day life at Florence and Normandie was far more ordinary. Young males hoping to meet girls headed to Kakawana's car wash or lingered at Art's Chili Dogs next door. A half-dozen winos hung out in the parking lot at the corner at Tom's Liquor, where they were sometimes joined by a few crack addicts who occasionally hustled tips pumping gas at the Unocal 76 station across the street. And almost anyone who was hungry was welcome on 71st Street, where several moms always seemed to cook enough to feed the entire block.

To outsiders, however, the neighborhood was far more forbidding. In particular, a significant segment of residents—especially young black men—detested cops. That antagonism had grown during the 1980s, as overwork and serious understaffing forced officers to have less contact with law-abiding residents and more encounters with an ever more violent criminal underclass, leaving many officers jaded. Then, in 1988, Chief Daryl Gates launched a controversial series of gang-member roundups. In one night, 1,000 extra-duty patrol officers rounded up 1,453 black and Latino teenagers. By the time "Operation Hammer" was over, LAPD files listed nearly half of all black males in Los Angeles ages 21 to 24 as gang members, and every neighborhood was rife with kids who told tales of dubious arrests and petty harassment.

The residents distrust of outsiders also extended to young black males from outlying areas. Florence and Normandie was near the center of Eight Tray Gangster Crips turf, one of Los Angeles's most violent gangs. Wearing the wrong color, bearing an alien tattoo or flashing the wrong gang sign all could lead to a bullet. The 800 or so Eight Tray members fought not only with their traditional enemies, the Bloods, but with another Crips set, the Rollin' Sixties. Though news reports often painted Crips gangs as major crack distributors, most Eight Trays slept late, hung out with their "homeboys," partied with girlfriends and often imbibed fortified wine or 40-ounce bottles of malt liquor. When violence did erupt it was rarely over drugs; typically, it was the same issues that preoccupied the Jets and Sharks of "West Side Story": "dissing" (showing disrespect), girls and turf.

THE SPARK

When the jury in Simi Valley acquitted four LAPD cops in the King beating, the verdict hit millions, especially African-Americans, like a sucker punch to the stomach. At the prominent First AME Church in Los Angeles, stunned black leaders wept openly after the verdicts were read at 3:10 p.m. At the grungy 77th Street LAPD station several miles away, the officers sat riveted to the TV announcement, too. Everyone felt edgy. When the cops went out on patrol, a few pedestrians screamed obscenities; others watched silently. Bart Bartholomew, a photographer on assignment for the *New York Times,* finally inquired of officers on the station roof: "Where should I go?" They hollered: "The liquor stores. That's where it will start."

Sure enough, at the Pay-less Liquor and Deli, three short blocks from Florence and Normandie, it did start. Right around 4 p.m., five youthful gang associates decided to make a run up to "Mr. Lee's," as the Korean-owned store was known, to get some Olde English 800. Once they arrived, however, the young men decided to steal the malt liquor, each cradling three or four of the large bottles in their arms as they headed for the door. When David Lee, son of the owner, tried to block their path, one of them smashed him in the head with a bottle. Then the others hurled a couple of bottles against the door, shattering the glass. "This is for Rodney King!" one youth yelled.

From behind the bulletproof shield at the counter, Samuel Lee, David's father, pushed the silent alarm. At 4:23, an LAPD dispatcher sent two officers to the scene, but the suspects had run away.

For the next half-hour the Florence and Normandie intersection remained eerily quiet. Jim Galipeau, a member of a gang unit at the county probation department who probably knows the Eight Trays better than any white man in L.A., stopped his car a few minutes after 5 p.m. to banter with 10 to 12 male blacks who were hanging out drinking beer near Tom's Liquor. "They didn't care about Rodney King," he recalled. "Guys like King had been beaten up for decades in these neighborhoods. They were just using the verdict as an excuse to party—

they weren't getting armed and mobilized."

Yet just as Galipeau was readying to leave, Mayor Tom Bradley went on the air stating that "we will not tolerate the savage beating of our citizens by a few renegade cops." Though Bradley also appealed to Angelenos to stay calm, no one will know whether his comments helped incite a riot. But at 5:22, shortly after he finished speaking, an LAPD dispatcher reported that a group of eight black males were using baseball bats to break the car windows of passing motorists at Florence and Halldale avenues about 100 yards from Mr. Lee's store. Shouting "Rodney, Rodney," the group had attacked two whites who had driven an old Cadillac through the area and thrown rocks and beer bottles at other drivers. When officers drove up to interrogate the group of young men and two girls, they were met with a fusillade of insults. " . . . y'all," one of the men screamed. "What you gonna do, beat me?" "You sold out to the white man, Uncle Tom," another one told officer Rick Banks, who is black. After searching and handcuffing several youths, the sergeant on the scene made a fateful decision: They would arrest the kid who still had a baseball bat and let the others go. The small crowd that had gathered seemed to have quieted down and most of the white motorists whose windows had been smashed had left.

Before long, the cops were second-guessing themselves. The four cars that had been on the scene had driven only a few blocks when they heard a help call at 5:34 from another 77th unit that was being pelted with rocks and bottles at Florence and Normandie. Before five minutes had passed, 18 cop cars and some 35 officers had sped there. But the crowd was swelling, too, and eventually, more than 100 residents surrounded the police. The first face-off was about to begin—and it was the LAPD that would blink.

THE RETREAT

As residents ran to the intersection, one question mattered: Were the cops going to brutalize someone again? Two black cops had chased and caught a 16-year-old youth named Seandel Daniels, who they claimed had thrown rocks at them (a charge he later denied). Cornering Dan-

iels in a yard, the cops passed him over a chain-link fence at 71st and Normandie and pressed him to the ground. "I can't breathe," Daniels shouted. "Don't make this another Rodney King beating," one of the black officers warned him.

While the police wrestled with Daniels and hogtied him, the crowd got more incensed. Daniels "was just a kid," people screamed. Soon, onlookers—mothers, teenage girls, older men and gang members—started bellowing curses, and a few teens threw a smattering of rocks and bottles. To the white cops, they hollered " . . . all you white men," "Get the . . . out of here" and "It's Uzi time. Cops gonne die tonight." Black cops came in for even harsher invective as "Uncle Toms" and "kiss-ass niggers."

After subduing Daniels, officers arrested two men in their late 20s, Cerman Cunningham and Mark Jackson. Both had once run with the Eight Trays, but now they were two of the more gainfully employed neighborhood men. Jackson installed car stereos in his back yard and Cunningham worked part time repairing cars over by the car wash. Their arrests, when they seemed only to be doing what everybody else was doing—threatening and taunting the police—ratcheted the fury of the crowd even higher. "Kill me, nigger, kill me. . . . Why don't you just kill me?" Cunningham screamed as three white cops cuffed him. Several men in the crowd grabbed Jackson and tried to pull him back from four policemen, so the officers quickly formed a skirmish line to separate him from the crowd. Complicating matters, the cops could see that two men were standing on the fringe of the crowd, videotaping them for evidence of misconduct. Instead of jabbing with their batons to make the crowd move back, the officers stood stoically, merely asking people to step back and calm down.

Lt. Mike Moulin, the supervisor on the scene, had seen enough. "Anarchy was occurring before our very eyes," he said later. Once the squad cars had pulled away with the three arrestees, Moulin hollered "Let's go!" through a squad car public address system, ordering the officers to pull out to de-escalate the tension and prevent injuries. Embarrassed, the other officers walked briskly back to their cars—a few even trotted—as rocks and bottles fell around them and the crowd roared in approval. As the patrol cars pulled away, Moulin ordered his troops again to stay away from Florence

and Normandie and got a one-word radioed retort from an officer: "Bullsh—."

The only white left behind in the crowd, photographer Barthlomew, realized it was time for him to scram. As he turned to walk back to his car on 71st, someone cold-cocked him with a two-by-four under his chin, shaking his whole body. "Give me the . . . film, give me the . . . film," a man in dreadlocks chanted to the photographer. Bartholomew pulled out a roll of film and handed it to the cheering crowd. Ahead, he saw four black males dancing on the hood and trunk of his car as though in "a joyous rage." By the time he got his car going and pulled away—amid high-fives between two of his attackers—looters had stolen thousands of dollars in equipment and a hurled rock had smashed his window and face, leaving his left cheek the size of a grapefruit.

At last, the crowd turned and started to jog the short distance to Florence and Normandie, yelling at the fleeing cop cars. One of the crowd members was 19-year-old Damian "Football" Williams, who had a special reason for being angry. Mark Jackson, whom police had just arrested, was his older brother, and some girls had called Williams a "pussy" for standing by and watching the arrest. Now, after pulling his shorts and underwear down to flash the girls and the police, the angry Williams strode jauntily with the crowd to Florence and Normandie, yelling " . . . that . . .!"

THE ACCUSED

Three men—Williams, Henry Watson and Antoine Miller—stand accused of attempting to murder Reginald Denny. The former district attorney, Ira Reiner, said the trio were "simply gangsters." yet the Denny attack is chilling in part because it was *not* carried out by especially notorious gang members or violent criminals. In fact, Williams—whom a local magistrate singled out for "braining" Denny—was something of a mama's boy.

Williams's mother, Georgiana, was a devout Christian who had left the cotton fields of Mississippi to work as a nurse caring for the homebound in Los Angeles. She worked full time during the week and often toiled on weekends, somehow managing to raise not only three of her own children but also numerous foster kids. An unmistakable presence on 71st Street, Mrs. Williams kept vast vats of chili, greens or spaghetti on the stove during dinner hours for hungry neighbors and teens. When the rotund matron, broom in hand, hollered from her porch for the kids to "act right," they listened.

Damian, the baby of the family by 10 years, had many advantages over his peers in South Central. From the time he was 2 $1/2$ until he was in 10th grade, he attended a strict Christian academy. After Mrs. Williams's brother Alandress was brutally beaten in a robbery and moved into the Williamses' house, Damian helped tend his uncle, cleaning him up when he was incontinent and lifting him back into bed after his seizures. There was no indication that Damian bore whites a grudge: His best high-school buddy was white, and Williams was so light-skinned as a child that he sometimes wondered whether he, too, was white.

Gang time. Williams started drifting into trouble at age 16, dropping out of school because he disliked wearing a uniform, and soon joined the 71 Hustlers, a feeder gang of young teens affiliated with the Eight Trays. With his mother away at work all day and no regular male discipline in his life (he had never known his father), Williams eventually started hanging out with local Eight Tray members. He was arrested several times for auto theft, robbery and other offenses but never convicted; by Eight Tray standards, his criminal record was of the garden variety. But before long, he started growing bored with gang life, with its endless gambling, rapping and trips to Mr. Lee's for Olde English 800. Williams spoke of going back to school, and the morning of the Florence and Normandie assaults, he had interviewed for a renovation job down the street. He dreamed of bigger things, too. The night manager at Tom's Liquor knew that the 5-foot, 9-inch, 180-pound Williams had been a talented high-school running back, and he had helped Williams get a stint earlier that year with the L.A. Mustangs, a semipro team. Though Williams stopped attending practices at the end of the season, he still bragged that one day he would be in the pros and "have me a big mansion."

Antoine Miller bore even less resemblance to a remorseless hoodlum. A thin, introverted 19-year-old, Miller had lived with the Williamses for seven years because his mother had struggled with a

drug problem and his grandmother, in his presence, had shot and killed his grandfather during a quarrel. As a would-be gang member and "tagger" (i.e., someone who paints graffiti), Miller had spray painted his moniker, "Twan," all over the neighborhood and had been picked up for small-time offenses like joy riding.

The only accused Denny assailant who came close to fitting the thug stereotype was 27-year-old Henry "Kiki" Watson. The 6-foot, 1-inch, 215-pound Watson had served time for holding up an armored car in 1990 and had a menacing glower that accentuated his muscular build. Even so, Watson had never joined a gang. He married after he left prison and was working two jobs to support his family when he was arrested. No one in the neighborhood considered Watson to have a violent or racist disposition; if he argued with someone it was usually over sports trivia or one of the basketball games he liked to round up. Watson, Damian Williams later told a detective, was "a gentleman."

THE FIRST VICTIMS

When the police vanished at 5:45 p.m., the angry crowd turned into an out-of-control mob. Residents started throwing rocks, bottles and bricks at passing cars, periodically pulling motorists out of their vehicles to beat and rob them. All told, at least 30 persons were eventually victimized by the throng.

There was, however, a partial method to the disorganized madness: Blacks could pass safely through the intersection. (Subsequently, a small number of motorists, most of them fair-skinned, did have rocks thrown at their cars.) Kirk McKoy, a black photographer for the *Los Angeles Times,* arrived right as the crowd was running over to Florence and Normandie and soon saw that perhaps a dozen individuals in the 100-person mob were doing most of the hurling of rocks and racial slurs—hollering phrases like " . . . the white man," "Mexican . . .," "Asian . . . " and "Get the . . . out of my neighborhood"—while the rest of the crowd stood by either watching passively or cheering them on. "A guy in the center of the intersection would unload a rock and then folks would follow suit," McKoy says. Later, Damian Williams boasted to the police that he was throwing rocks "like Darryl Strawberry," the

all-star outfielder of the Los Angeles Dodgers.

Ironically, virtually all of the victims were struggling Hispanic and Asian immigrants who spoke little or no English, rather than representatives of the white establishment. The first target was a family of three Hispanics: Marisa Bejar, her husband, Francisco Aragon, and Josh, their 7-month-old baby. As Marisa drove through the intersection, their Volvo was met by rocks, bricks, a piece of wood and a metal-covered phone book, opening up a 13-stitch cut on Marisa. Her husband quickly got clobbered on his forehead, and a man leaned in and told him to give up his cash "or I'm going to kill you" as others screamed "We'll whip your . . ."; the infant, meanwhile, suffered minor scratches after a youth tried to throw a large, stand-up Marlboro sign through the rear window of the car.

"Get 'em." The attacks on the innocents continued minutes later when another Hispanic family, the Vacas, drove into the intersection in a beat-up '73 Buick Regal. In a scene captured on videotape, Antoine Miller and other males threw rocks at the frightened motorists, prompting the panicked driver, Manuel Vaca, to fishtail and crash into a pickup truck. Miller, his arms stretched into the air, leapt for joy and sprinted with Williams up to the car as people screamed "Get 'em." This time a group of six males pulled Vaca, his wife and his brother from the car, beat and robbed them. Eight Tray member Anthony Brown later explained to police that he kicked at Manuel Vaca "because he was Mexican and everybody else was doin' it." After the Vacas managed to struggle away on foot, a carload of five Anglo nuns entered the intersection, driven by a sister in a habit. She, too, was immediately hit in the left arm by a brick that shattered her window.

Perhaps none of the early victims, however, was more stunned than Sylvia Castillo, a fourth-generation Mexican-American and prominent activist from South Central who had worked closely with gang members to reduce liquor stores and crack abuse in the area. As her car crawled into the intersection, bricks, cement chunks and bottles shattered the windows and a startled Castillo looked up in the rearview mirror to see a streak of blood running down her nose. Out of nowhere, a young black man leaned in the window and blurted " . . ., you are going to die." Castillo sped away. "I knew I was outraged by the verdict," she says, "and had always struggled against racism. All I could think was: 'Why are they doing this to me?' "

THE LIQUOR SPREE

Minutes after the mob started pelting motorists, Wes Wade, the night manager of Tom's Liquor—the same man who had helped Damian Williams get his start in semipro football—padlocked the metal gate that fronted the store. But Wade's efforts to save the Korean-owned shop proved futile. Just after 6 p.m., a group of young black males smashed the padlock and gate, one of them hurling a steel light pole through the window. Blissfully unaware of history, the pole thrower sported a black-and-white T-shirt depicting Malcolm X, an ardent advocate of abstinence. Looters gleefully piled in, with the party atmosphere captured on amateur videotape. "Bring all that . . . out," "Y'all can thank Rodney King for this" and "Go back there and get the rest—Yeah!" Above, a local news helicopter was broadcasting the looting live, advertising to residents, as owner Tom Suguki later put it, "Hey, free beer!"

Booze out. During the next hour every bottle of beer, wine and liquor in Tom's was either stolen or smashed, including the roughly 100 cases of 40-ounce malt liquor bottles and an additional 90 cases of 16-ounce malt liquor cans ordinarily stashed in the storage room. The sudden presence of gallons of free liquor plainly inflamed the violence—albeit indirectly—of a crowd that had grown to perhaps 200 persons. There is no evidence that Denny's assailants themselves were drunk, though three of them (Williams, Miller and Anthony Brown) told police they went into Tom's Liquor during the conflagration and a fourth man later picked the pocket of the unconscious Denny while holding a bottle of liquor. But many looters simply carted the wares home while others heaved liquor bottles at passing motorists. Before long, the entire intersection was covered with finely crushed shards of glass, and a significant segment of the crowd had started drinking. Pete Demetriou, a reporter for news radio station KFWB who was standing near Tom's, reports that by 6:15 p.m. "you could smell the liquor on people's breath

from several feet away as they walked by. You already had anger and frustration at the intersection—and when you fueled it with alcohol it turned into insanity."

As motorists alternately sped through or made desperate U-turns, Florence and Normandie started resembling a scene out of the movie "Road Warrior." "I hate to use this term," says Roy Walker, a black state police officer who was watching the violence from his home at the corner of 71st and Normandie, but "young men and women were driving around in trucks, hollering and taking over the streets like it was a Nazi gala." Five minutes after the looters hit Tom's, a man in the mob informed a resident with a video camera that the ringleaders of the violence were " . . . up everything white and Mexican that comes through here. "The race hatred finally peaked when Larry Tarvin—the "other" white trucker—drove his small delivery truck into the intersection.

Tarvin worked for a black-owned company and was carrying medical equipment bound for Chile that doctors use to oxygenate blood during open-heart surgery. Lacking a radio, he knew nothing about the verdict. But the frail 52-year-old driver, all of 5 feet, 7 inches and 130 pounds, was halted by a hail of rocks when he stopped for a red light. The hulking Watson then helped yank and throw Tarvin from his truck like a sack of potatoes, stomped on him and delivered a soccer-style kick to his head. "Enough is enough," Tarvin pleaded. But it wasn't enough for his assailants. Another man threw a fire extinguisher at him, while others kicked him senseless, fracturing his ribs, cracking his pelvis and leaving him with an infected abscess in the nose and permanent facial scars. "Oh, yeah, yeah," one onlooker is recorded saying.

Bleeding profusely, Tarvin lay unconscious in the street for more than a minute. As he haltingly pushed himself up a man nearby declared, "No pity for the white man. Let his white . . . down. Now you know how Rodney King felt, white boy." For a moment, several bystanders looked as if they might come to Tarvin's aid, but one man yelled: "Hey—don't help his white . . .!" Tarvin finally staggered back to his truck. And with the help of an African-American named Rodney (Tarvin never learned his last name), the disfigured trucker slowly pulled away at 6:46, preceded by a chorus of "White boy!" Just then, Reginald

Denny drove into Florence and Normandie.

THE ATTACK ON DENNY

The white male who became the nationally televised symbol of retribution for the King beating was a simple self-effacing man who didn't care for much besides driving a truck and hanging around his buddy's boat shop. That day, Reginald Denny had just followed his usual routine when he exited the 10 Freeway west onto Florence Avenue, hoping to avoid traffic. He was headed to the batch plant across town—where he would dump his two trailers of gravel—when he saw that something was terribly wrong up ahead.

Without power steering, Denny knew that he would never be able to turn his huge load around. Still, no one would want to steal gravel, and since Denny was driving just about the biggest rig on the highway, he figured that he could just "tiptoe across this intersection and get on down the road." When several black males motioned him to stop, he wasn't about to run them over. Immediately, rocks came whistling through his window and Antoine Miller jumped up to open the door of Denny's cab, allowing several men to yank him into the street. At first, a man kicked Denny in the belly as Henry Watson held Denny's head down with his foot. Then the man in the Malcolm X T-shirt (the liberator of Tom's Liquor) threw a 5-pound oxygenator stolen from Tarvin's truck on Denny's head, pushed Denny's head down with his foot and hit him three times in the head with a claw hammer. Somehow, Denny got up on all fours and stated to rise, when Damian Williams, at point-blank range, winged a piece of concrete into Denny's right temple—knocking him unconscious for close to five minutes. The blows were so savage that they crushed pieces of Denny's skull into his brain, fractured his face in 90 to 100 spots and dislocated his left eye so that it would have dropped into his sinus cavity had surgeons not replaced a crushed bone with a piece of plastic.

His assailants, though, still weren't satisfied. Next they proceeded to demean Denny. As the 36-year-old trucker lay bleeding and senseless, Damian Williams thrust his arms upward in celebration and did a victory dance, imitating a receiver who has just beaten his defender

BEYOND THE RIOT EPICENTER

Latinos were prominent as victims and victimizers

On April 26, 1992, three days before the Los Angeles riot erupted, more than half a million Latinos filled city streets to inaugurate the festival of Cinco de Mayo at the "L.A. Fiesta." They danced, ate, drank and shopped, purchasing leather goods and electronic appliances from a multitude of trusting merchants. Not a single crime was reported, not even a picked pocket.

Yet four days later—and just blocks away—mobs of Latinos looted and torched store after store, yelling "Burn, baby, burn." In fact, by the time the riot ended on May 4, the LAPD had arrested *more* Latinos than blacks. Fifty-one percent of the 5,000 arrested within the city limits were Latino; 38 percent were black. And Hispanic merchants suffered more damage at the hands of rioters than any other ethnic group except Koreans.

Equal opportunism. The heavy involvement of Latinos in the riot, as both victims and victimizers, has prompted commentators to call the L.A. unrest a unique multicultural uprising. But it may have been less an equal-opportunity revolt than an equal-opportun*ism* riot. Popular lore and some photos notwithstanding, the looters were neither chiefly indignant citizens protesting the Rodney King verdict and police brutality nor impoverished mothers seeking baby formula. On the whole, they were rootless. Often, they were ill-educated and had criminal records.

The special nature of Latino involvement can best be understood by comparing the quiescence of the vast eastside barrio of Los Angeles during the riot with the explosion in South Central. East Los Angeles, home to some 2 million Latinos, was almost free of violence during the riots, though it contains some of the worst gangs in the nation. Looters there struck only 10 business in a 15 1/2-square-mile area, and in one case parents forced their children to return many of the goods taken from a Sears store.

A recent study by the Latino Coalition for a New Los Angeles suggests that the difference lay in the depth of ties residents had in each community. Eastside residents have often lived in their neighborhoods for generations, and many own their homes. By contrast, only a quarter of the Hispanics in South Central own their residences, and the area is flooded with tens of thousands of recent immigrants from Mexico, El Salvador and Guatemala. They share some of the most overcrowded housing in the country, as well as a distrust of the police imported from their homelands. (One neighborhood, immediately to the east of famed MacArthur Park, contains 147 people per acre, roughly four times the population density of New York City.) The lack of local roots was especially evident in a recent *Los Angeles Times* analysis of the probation reports of 694 individuals convicted of riot-related felonies: Fully 79 percent of the Latino looters turned out to be foreign-born, and a quarter had moved to the United States in the previous two years. The *Times* study indicated that black looters—half the sample—were also rootless. Half of the 694 felons were homeless or had been at their residences for less than a year; 66 percent were unemployed, and 60 percent had criminal records. A stunning 3 out of 5 had dropped out of high school.

In the hundreds of incidents reviewed by the paper, Rodney King's name came up just once—and it wasn't on the lips of an outraged African-American. Two days after the riot started, an Anglo and a Latino went into a San Fernando Valley grocery run by a black storekeeper and started stealing 12-packs of beer. " . . . Rodney King!" one shouted triumphantly.

DAVID WHITMAN

---

for a touchdown and then points back at him in taunting recognition. Williams then flashed the Eight Tray Gangster Crips sign to the crowd across the street and looked up at the news helicopters and pointed out Denny. Another gang member, Anthony Brown, joined him, flashing the Eight Tray sign before spitting on Denny.

As Williams and Brown walked away, Denny lay in the street like a curiosity item. Several men darted up to throw liquor bottles at him. A man whom police identified as Lance Parker—a process server for a law firm—calmly halted his motorcycle, stepped off, pulled a shotgun from a gym bag and shot at Denny's gas tank, narrowly missing. Next, Gary Williams, a crack user who ordinarily hung out at the Unocal 76 station, sauntered over and went through the trucker's pockets, balancing a bottle of liquor in his free hand.

Finally, Denny rose to his knees, blood seeping from his head into a 1-foot pool in the street. He reached out with a trembling left hand, fumbling in the air as though he was trying to feel his way in a dark closet and beseeching the mercy of the crowd. What he got instead was the man in the Malcolm X T-shirt, who jumped across Denny, using the kneeling man's head as a stepping stone.

Somehow, Denny managed to crawl back into the cab and start his truck. Fortunately, a fellow trucker—an African-American named Bobby Green—had seen Denny on TV and came running to the intersection. Green knew how to drive Denny's truck, which requires a special license, and with the help of three other blacks, two of whom led him in a convoy, got him to a local hospital. Had Denny arrived minutes later, he would have been dead.

Only after Denny pulled away from Florence and Normandie did the first belated protest sign appear on videotape. Spray painted on a white placard, it said "Kill Gates" and "LAPD 187" (187 is the number of the California penal code section for murder). A couple of men took up the demonstration, chanting. "All we want is to kill Gates. Kill Gates. Kill Gates," while another chimed in, "Kill that little rednecked. . . ." But Daryl Gates—and the LAPD, for that matter—were nowhere to be found. The officers of the 77th division were sitting at their special command post.

THE POLICE

The plaintive radio plea of a female LAPD officer a half-hour before the

Denny beating—"What the . . . is going on? What are we doing here?"—effectively encapsulates the 77th divisions no-show response to the mob. Senior cops in the division either directed officers to disregard emergency calls about victims at Florence and Normandie or ordered cars out of the area at least nine times during the hour preceding Reginald Denny's arrival—even though two squad cars that did barrel through the intersection managed, one at gunpoint, to rescue beaten-up motorists who were stranded within a couple of blocks of the mayhem. A half-hour *after* the Denny beating, as 911 calls poured in, Lieutenant Moulin and other supervisors were still advising officers to stay put because they "had squads forming" at a bus depot that was serving as the command post.

In fact, the special "command post" was a sham. It had no TV in it, so while hundreds of thousands of Americans watched the looting of Tom's Liquor and the beating of Denny live, none of the officers of the 77th did. Its few telephones were set up only to receive incoming calls. Lacking a working computer, supervisors had to track multiple emergency calls and deployments of police cars with pencil, paper and street maps. Officers stood disgusted beside their squad cars, listening with impatience to ever more urgent calls on the police radio while LAPD supervisors debated whether they had sufficient officers and riot equipment to intervene.

In the hour that followed Moulin's retreat, the LAPD officers failed to implement virtually every time-honored crowd-control tactic. They failed to take the elemental step of sealing off traffic to Florence and Normandie by cordoning off nearby streets. They failed to confront the mob with a squadron of, say, 50 officers marching in riot gear—which ordinarily will make even a rowdy crowd disperse. They had no field-jail units and buses in place—which would have enabled officers to arrest unruly crowd members and then turn them over to detectives without having to leave the scene to bring arrestees to the station. They failed to use tear gas or pepper gas to disperse the mob. They did not send their vice and narcotics cops in undercover to spy on the mob or place police snipers atop tall buildings in the area. They failed to provide police escorts for firefighters, so they could safely combat early outbreaks of arson. And they failed to secure local gun stores (one of which

lost 1,150 firearms during the first night of the riot). Not until 6:43, an hour after the police retreat, did LAPD dispatchers even issue a tactical alert for south Los Angeles, which finally freed supervisors to assign emergency calls to units from other parts of the city.

AWOL brass. The 77th's lack of preparedness was exacerbated by gaps in the chain of command. In the midst of the biggest crisis of his career, Daryl Gates left police headquarters to attend a fundraiser in posh Brentwood about 6:20 p.m., temporarily turning over command to a deputy. Meanwhile, two thirds of the LAPD's 18 patrol captains were out of commission, returning from a training seminar outside the city.

To be sure, a rapid and decisive response by the 77th at Florence and Normandie would not have prevented some kind of disturbance from evolving in Los Angeles that day; isolated incidents of blacks assaulting whites and looting stores started popping up on a small scale at several locations in South Central about 15 minutes before Denny was beaten. Even so, the prolonged, televised absence of police at the riot's epicenter virtually invited thousands of would-be looters to believe they could steal and rampage with impunity. In fact, no riot-related fires started in Los Angeles until after the Denny beating—some four hours after the acquittals were announced—and the number and location of lootings mushroomed immediately following the attack on the trucker.

The fact that the riot could have turned out differently was illustrated at the LAPD Foothill division, the very precinct that had housed the cops who beat Rodney King. By early evening, a crowd numbering 400 people—twice the size of the mob at Florence and Normandie—had started a fire outside the station and were throwing rocks and bottles. But unlike their peers in the 77th, the Foothill cops had completed some serious riot training that taught them crowd-control techniques. They went into the crowd in formation, employed a skirmish line to push the crowd back, sensibly dropped to their knees when someone in the crowd fired a couple of shots in the air (instead of returning fire) and dispelled the crowd after arresting individuals who had started fires or thrown rocks. "It was a critical mistake not to go back in to Florence and Normandie," says Robert Vernon, the former assistant chief of the LAPD, who retired from the force just

days before the riot. "You cannot have a limited riot—any more than you can have a forest fire that burns a handful of trees."

THE HEROES

Ultimately, the same community that produced the mob at Florence and Normandie also nurtured African-American men and women with the courage to face down the crowd. In the hour following the Denny beating, one black man after another stepped forward to save the victims. James Henry left the safety of his porch to pull Raul Aguilar, a diminutive immigrant from Belize, out of harm's way after gang members beat Aguilar into a coma and let a car run over his legs; Donald Jones, an off-duty fireman, comforted Sai-Choi Choi after several men ripped him from his car, beat and robbed him; John Mitchell of the *Los Angeles Times* abandoned his customary spectator role as a reporter to save Tam Tran, a 34-year-old Vietnamese woman who was robbed and bashed in the head with a brick; Gregory Alan-Williams told a group of men who were beating Takao Hirata senseless, "Y'all know this ain't right. Leave him alone," and pulled the badly wounded man to safety.

No one battled the tide of race hatred more tenaciously than an ex-convict and onetime pimp named Bennie Newton. When Newton, who then ran an inner-city ministry, saw the Denny beating on TV, he headed to Florence and Normandie to stop the violence. But when the reverend arrived, around 7:40, a mob of young black males was savaging Fidel Lopez, a self-employed construction worker. After stopping Lopez in his 1980 GMC pickup, they spray painted his face black, pulled him from his truck and robbed him of $2,000 he had saved to buy construction materials. When Lopez tried to run, someone hit him on the head with a stereo speaker, and his attackers punched and kicked him into unconsciousness before dousing his pants with gasoline. Then, one of them indulged in a final act of humiliation. Damian Williams has been charged with spray painting Lopez, who ended up with his chest, penis and testicles painted black after his assailants slid down his pants and underwear. "He's black now," said a man on videotape. "He's black now."

That was too much for Newton. He stopped pleading with Lopez's assailants and threw himself over the stranger's fallen body, yelling, "Kill him and you have to kill me, too." When the attackers withdrew, Newton—clad in the white collar and black garb of a minister—stood over Lopez with a Bible in his hand and stretched his arms and cried, "Someone help this man!" Newton himself ended up taking Lopez to the hospital—and later started a fund-raising drive at his congregation to replace Lopez's money. "The simplest description that I can use to describe what I've done is the word L-O-V-E," Newton explained to a television interviewer, "It's not about being black, white, Korean or Latino.

His message got swallowed up that night. When the sun set around 7:30 p.m., the crowd at Florence and Normandie started lighting fires; before the night was over, two nearby auto repair stores, a gas station, a TV repair shop, the house of a minister and a church dining room were aflame. Around 8:30 p.m., LAPD squad cars finally returned, but the crowd had dissipated. Meanwhile, under cover of darkness, the violence was shifting from people to property, as looting and arson exploded throughout South Central. The party had begun—and greed and hate, rather than L-O-V-E, were the passwords of the night.

By David Whitman

Victimology

Victimology focuses on crime victims. The popularity of this area of study can be attributed to the early work of Hans von Hentig and the later work of Stephen Schafer. These writers were the first to assert that crime victims play an integral role in the criminal event, that their actions may actually precipitate crime, and that unless the victim's role is considered, the study of crime is not complete.

In recent years, a growing number of criminologists have devoted increasing attention to the victim's role in the criminal justice process. Generally, areas of particular interest include calculating costs of crime to victims, victim surveys that measure the nature and extent of criminal behavior, establishing probabilities of victimization risks, studying victim precipitation of crime and culpability, and designing services expressly for victims of crime. As more criminologists focus their attention on the victim's role in the criminal process, victimology will take on even greater importance.

Articles in this unit provide sharp focus on key issues. From the lead essay, "The Fear of Crime," we learn that fear of being victimized is pervasive among people, including some who have never been victims of crime. This article addresses the effects of crime on its victims.

The horror of family violence and limitations of the criminal justice system in dealing with it are clearly evident in "Hunted: The Last Year of April LaSalata."

The intractability of the problem of battering is made evident in "When Men Hit Women." Though widely considered the model for the rest of the country, a Duluth, Minnesota, program for battered women has its limitations.

Should women's unique perspectives be taken into account in areas of legal doctrine? The essays, "The Reasonable Woman" and "'Til Death Do Us Part" explores this controversial issue.

Heidi Vanderbilt's essay, "Incest: A Chilling Report," provides a revealing look at child abuse victims and offenders.

Does arrest work best to deter future incidents of domestic violence? The essay "Repeating a Study, If Not Its Results: Five Projects Rethink Domestic-Violence Response" offers mixed evidence in support of an initial finding on the arrest of domestic violence offenders.

The closing essay in this section, "Where to Now on Domestic Violence?" shows that making effective police policy decisions regarding domestic violence is not an easy matter.

Looking Ahead: Challenge Questions
Is the fear of crime realistic?

What lifestyle changes might you consider to avoid becoming victimized?

Are you familiar with victim service programs in your area?

How does crime affect the victim's psyche?

Unit 2

The Fear of Crime

The fear of crime affects many people, including some who have never been victims of crime

How do crime rates compare with the rates of other life events?

Events	Rate per 1,000 adults per year*
Accidental injury, all circumstances	242
Accidental injury at home	79
Personal theft	72
Accidental injury at work	58
Violent victimization	31
Assault (aggravated and simple)	24
Injury in motor vehicle accident	17
Death, all causes	11
Victimization with injury	10
Serious (aggravated) assault	9
Robbery	6
Heart disease death	4
Cancer death	2
Rape (women only)	2
Accidental death, all circumstances	.5
Pneumonia/influenza death	.3
Motor vehicle accident death	.2
Suicide	.2
Injury from fire	.1
Homicide/legal intervention death	.1
Death from fire	.03

These rates approximate your chances of becoming a victim of these events. More precise estimates can be derived by taking account of such factors as your age, sex, race, place of residence, and lifestyle. Findings are based on 1982–84 data, but there is little variation in rates from year to year.

*These rates exclude children from the calculations (those under age 12–17, depending on the series). Fire injury/death data are based on the total population, because no age-specific data are available in this series.

Sources: *Current estimates from the National Health Interview Survey: United States, 1982,* National Center for Health Statistics. "Advance report of final mortality statistics, 1983," *Monthly Vital Statistics Report,* National Center for Health Statistics. *Estimates of the population of the United States, by age, sex, and race: 1980 to 1984,* U.S. Bureau of the Census. *The 1984 Fire Almanac,* National Fire Protection Association. *Criminal victimization 1984,* BJS Bulletin, October 1985.

The chance of being a violent crime victim, with or without injury, is greater than that of being hurt in a traffic accident

The rates of some violent crimes are higher than those of some other serious life events. For example, the risk of being the victim of a violent crime is higher than the risk of death from cancer or injury or death from a fire. Still, a person is much more likely to die from natural causes than as a result of a criminal victimization.

About a third of the people in the United States feel very safe in their neighborhoods

The fear of crime cannot be measured precisely because the kinds of fears people express vary depending on the specific questions asked. Nevertheless, asking them about the likelihood of crime in their homes and neighborhoods yields a good assessment of how safe they feel in their own immediate environment.

In the Victimization Risk Survey, a 1984 supplement to the National Crime Survey, most people said that they felt at least fairly safe in their homes and neighborhoods. Yet, the people who said that they felt "fairly safe" may have been signaling some concern about crime. Based on a "very safe" response, a little more than 4 in 10 people felt entirely safe in their homes and about 1 in 3 felt totally safe in their neighborhoods—
• homeowners felt safer than renters
• people living in nonmetropolitan areas felt safer than those living in cities
• families with incomes of $50,000 or more were most likely to report their neighborhoods were very safe from crime.

The Victimization Risk Survey found that—
• 9 in 10 persons felt very or fairly safe in their places of work
• few persons—about 1 in 10—felt in danger of being a victim of a crime by a fellow employee, but persons working in places that employ more than 50 people were more likely to express fear of possible victimization.

The groups at the highest risk of becoming victims are not the ones who express the greatest fear of crime

Females and the elderly generally express a greater fear of crime than do people in groups who face a much greater risk. The Reactions to Crime project found that such impressions are related to the content of information about crime. Such information tends to emphasize stories about elderly and female victims. These stories may influence women and the elderly in judging the seriousness of their own condition. Perhaps groups such as females and the elderly reduce their risk of victimization by constricting their activities to reduce their exposure to danger. This behavior would account, at least in part, for their high levels of fear and their low levels of victimization.

Relatives, friends, and neighbors who hear about a crime become as fearful as the victim

When one household in a neighborhood is affected by a crime, the entire neighborhood may feel more vulnerable. This suggests that people who have not been victimized personally may be strongly affected when they hear about how others have been victimized. The Reactions to Crime project found that

From *Report to the Nation on Crime and Justice,* Bureau of Justice Statistics, U.S. Department of Justice, March 1988, pp. 24-25.

How does crime affect its victims?

indirect reaction to crime is often very strong.

$13 billion was lost from personal and household crimes in 1985

The direct cash and property losses from personal robberies, personal and household larcenies, household burglaries, and privately owned motor vehicle theft in 1985 was slightly more than $13 billion. This NCS finding probably underestimates the amount covered by insurance because the claims of many respondents had not been settled at the time of the NCS interview.

UCR data show that in 1985 losses from reported robberies, burglaries, and larceny/theft surpassed $5.9 billion. Among the many economic consequences of crime are lost productivity from victims' absence from work, medical care, and the cost of security measures taken to deter crime.

Other costs of crime include the economic costs of the underground economy, lowered property values, and pain and suffering of victims, their families, friends, and neighbors.

The economic impact of crime differs for different groups

The cost of crime is borne by all segments of society, but to different degrees. A study on the economic cost of crime using NCS data for 1981 shows that the dollar loss from crimes involving money, property loss, or destruction of property rises with income.

• Median losses were higher for households with incomes of $15,000 or more than for households with incomes of

less than $7,500 from burglary ($200 vs. $100) and from motor vehicle theft ($2,000 vs. $700).

• Median losses from personal crimes were higher for blacks ($58) than for whites ($43).
• Median losses from household crimes were higher for blacks ($90) than for whites ($60).
• More than 93% of the total loss from crime was in crimes without victim-offender contact (such as burglary, theft without contact, and motor vehicle theft).

Many victims or members of their families lose time from work

Along with injuries suffered, victims or other members of their household may have lost time from work because of a violent crime. Lost worktime was reported in 15% of rapes and 7% of assaults (11% of aggravated assaults, 6% of simple assaults).

Violent crimes killed 19,000 and injured 1.7 million in 1985

NCS data for 1985 show that of all rape,

robbery, and assault victims—
• 30% were injured
• 15% required some kind of medical attention
• 8% required hospital care.

The likelihood of injury was—
• greater for females than males even when rape was excluded from the analysis
• about the same for whites and blacks
• greater for persons from lower than from higher income households.

Who is injured seriously enough to require medical attention?

An analysis of NCS data for 1973–82 found that—
• Female victims are more likely than male victims to be injured, but they have about the same likelihood of requiring medical attention (13% of female vs. 12% of male victims).
• Blacks are more likely than whites to require medical attention when injured in violent crimes; 16% of black violent crime victims and 16% of the victims of all other racial groups required medical attention, while 11% of white victims required such care.

How seriously a victim is injured varies by type of crime

	Percent of all violent victimizations requiring:			Median stay for those hospitalized overnight
	Medical attention	Treatment in hospital emergency room	Overnight hospital stay	
Rape	24%	14%	3%	4 days
Robbery	15	7	2	5
Assault	11	5	1	5
Aggravated	18	9	3	5
Simple	7	3	—	2

—less than .5%

Source: BJS National Crime Survey, 1973–82.

HUNTED

THE LAST YEAR OF APRIL LaSALATA

She thought the criminal-justice system would protect her from her ex-husband. But the system was no match for his lethal rage.

Richard C. Firstman

Richard C. Firstman is a contributing writer of
The Newsday Magazine.

Her body a pattern of scars, April LaSalata stared up at the young woman standing uneasily at her bedside.

"How old are you?" April asked warily.

Frances Radman, a 27-year-old assistant district attorney with a gentle manner, had heard that one before. "How old are *you*?" she asked gamely.

April laughed; she was feeling better this March day in 1988. But still she worried: It seemed to her that the prosecutor was as vulnerable as she was. For her part, Radman hadn't expected April to be so tiny, just 85 pounds and barely five feet tall. When April displayed the scars that split her upper body in two, Radman was amazed that such a delicate woman had managed to survive so brutal an attack.

"He won't get out of jail, will he?" April asked.

Knowing the events of the past months, now seeing this torn body before her, Radman knew this was not a trivial question.

"No," she said, "he won't."

Four months before, in the fall of 1987, a Suffolk County judge had signed the papers terminating the marriage of April and Anthony LaSalata, high school sweethearts from Brentwood. To the mind of her ex-husband, April had been the winner in this divorce; he had been the loser. She got the kids, the house and freedom from a calamitous marriage. He got a trailer and a court order barring him from menacing his ex-wife. It had been the kind of divorce that had produced almost monthly police reports: domestic dispute, 110 McKinley.

On the ninth call to the Third Precinct, in February, the police had found Anthony LaSalata trying to get into the house with a crowbar. They had arrested him for harassment. Then he had been released.

After work on Friday, Feb. 26, April, as was her custom, drove to her mother's house to pick up her sons, Justin, 10, and Anthony Jr., 4. She decided to leave Anthony overnight and drove the few blocks home with Justin. They scanned the front lawn, then walked into the house. The phone in the kitchen, the red one with "911" written on it, was ringing. Justin answered; it was his grandmother, checking to see that they had gotten home all right. Justin said they were fine.

And then, the closet door flew open.

April screamed. Justin cried out, "Dad, what are you doing here?" His father told him to be quiet and then cut the telephone cord. The receiver fell onto a sweater on the floor.

LaSalata, according to the police, pushed his son into a bedroom and closed the door. He grabbed April, dragged her downstairs and started stabbing her. He twisted the knife inside her abdomen. She screamed to Justin to get out of the house, and Justin bolted and began banging on the doors of neighbors.

When LaSalata heard Justin leave, he looked up reflexively, stabbed April a third time, and stopped. He left her bleeding in the basement and fled the house. April dragged herself to the basement phone. After all her instructions to Justin about how to call for emergency help, it was Gerard, her brother who lived 25 miles away, whom she called first.

"Whatsa matter? Whatsa matter?" Gerard screamed into the phone. In his house, a room full of guests stood horrified. April was describing her wounds to her brother. "Close your arms around them! Hold them tight!" Gerard yelled into the phone. When rescue came, April was bleeding so relentlessly that she kept sliding off the stretcher.

She was in surgery through the night. The doctors did not believe she would live — her wounds suggested to them an autopsy had already been performed. But somehow, she reached the recovery room. She spent the next week on life-support machines.

LaSalata was charged with attempted murder and held in the Riverhead jail.

No, Fran Radman told April in the hospital room, he would not get out. His lawyer was arguing that LaSalata was not competent to stand trial, and so there would be no bail until there was a decision on that issue. Or so Radman thought.

TWO weeks later, in what Radman would later describe as a critical bureaucratic "mix-up," Judge Morton Weissman set cash bail at $25,000 while she was appearing in another court on another case. Kevin Fox, LaSalata's attorney, told Radman not to worry: LaSalata would never raise that kind of money.

But five months later, in midsummer, LaSalata's parents decided to mortgage their house to get him out of jail. And from that day forward, as her life was defined by a collection of motions and briefs, April LaSalata came to know on the deepest level that she would not survive.

On New Year's Eve, 1988, when a radio announcer reported on the second woman in Suffolk County in three days to be killed by her estranged husband, despite orders of protection, April turned to her oldest friend and said, "Sharon, I'm next."

* * *

April LaSalata, 34 at her death, was not an anonymous victim crying in the dark. In her world, she was surrounded by many people who cared a great deal about her, a prosecutor who fought for her, a cop who tried to protect her.

And still, she died.

The questions raised by her death a year ago have less to do with why some men are driven to such desperate acts of domestic terrorism than with why the legal system sometimes fails to protect the women they kill. April LaSalata's case played to the fears of all women who saw her death as a confirmation of a terrible truth: that even at its best, the system is not designed to keep a hunted woman alive.

Her case is closed now, her onetime husband having seen to that with five shots from

'WHAT APRIL SAW WAS THAT HE WAS SO MACHO.'

a rifle last January, three to her, two to himself. But her death touched so many lives — people who knew her intimately, others who were more familiar with her case file — and they struggle still for acceptable explanations, to place blame on someone or something other than Anthony LaSalata alone.

April's family is suing the Suffolk County Police Department for failing to protect her, but others argue that the police did all they could. An examination of the last year of her life shows that many factors contributed to her death, including miscalculations by some members of the criminal justice system, perhaps an insensitivity by others, and some ambiguities born of the bureaucracy itself.

In the end, despite the depth of April's fears and the brutality of the stabbing attack, Anthony LaSalata was just another defendant awaiting trial on a charge of attempted murder. The case dragged on as many cases do. LaSalata was released on bail as many defendants are.

And April LaSalata was left to wonder on what night in the near future her ex-husband would come again to kill her.

* * *

April Principio, a bricklayer's daughter, was in the eleventh grade at Brentwood High when she met Tony LaSalata, a senior. April liked to read and Tony liked to fix cars, but they shared ethnic background and neighborhood ties, and April was not attracted to gentle boys. Among the things she found appealing about Tony was the strength of his wrists: She liked the way he shifted his car. When he was 18, LaSalata acquired a tattoo: *Live and Let Die.*

"Tony was the first person who paid attention to her," recalled Sharon Millard, April's close friend. "What April saw was that he was so macho, in total control, which she felt she needed, someone to guide her."

But Tony's control bordered on compulsion. If April was out with a girlfriend, Tony was likely to turn up agitated, demanding her return to his car. April was ambivalent about Tony's tyrannical tendencies. Of course, she found them annoying — his jealousy became so much a part of her daily life that she was moved to write about it, prophetically if with some bemusement, in her yearbook inscription to Millard, her friend since kindergarten:

I'll never forget the time [we] had to hide on wet grass behind Debbie Mann's car because LaSalata was passing, and many more of those "times" to come.

But in her innocence, April took Tony's attentions as a sign of love. "You get all sorts of attention from someone and it makes you feel good," Millard said. "You go on the assumption that it's true love. Tony was her first one, and that was it."

Her parents were so opposed to the rela-

'SHE SLEPT WITH THE DRESSER IN FRONT OF THE BEDROOM DOOR.'

tionship that they begged her to go away to college. But April was headstrong, a lifelong trait, and at the time reasonably rebellious. Despite her parents' urgings, she cast her lot with Tony. She went to work in a bank, Tony got a job on the pie line at Entenmann's Bakery, and in June, 1975, they were married.

In those early years, April and Tony continued the rancor that often marked their courtship. In an interview with a court-appointed psychiatrist after his arrest in 1988, LaSalata said: "The only complaint she ever had about me and our marriage early on was that I smoked too much pot. Other than that there were no other complaints except me yelling at her."

She had one other complaint, however: Tony's employee file was getting thick with reprimands and warnings for missing work and for not getting along with co-workers. April felt at times that she was doing more than her share of supporting the family.

The turning point in the marriage — the point from which it would deteriorate beyond hope of repair — came in 1982, when April and Tony went to the wedding of a friend from high school. April wasn't feeling well and left early with a friend of theirs, and when Tony came home and found the friend in the house, he believed that April had been unfaithful to him. April insisted that she had not.

Whatever happened that night, the incident became so much a point of contention in the marriage that nearly everyone who knew the LaSalatas — their friends, their relatives and ultimately the corps of lawyers, prosecutors and psychiatrists who would populate their lives — would hear a version of it.

WAS always angry with her," LaSalata told the psychiatrist in 1988. "I wouldn't let that night go. She swore she didn't, then she said if she did or didn't, she would swear that she didn't. That one incident for over five years has been constantly on my thoughts. I keep asking friends and they are all sticking together and telling me I was crazy. It was like a conspiracy. When they all looked at my wife, I know they all wanted her. They all wanted to take turns with my wife. They didn't give a —— if I was their friend, they just wanted her."

April would later tell Radman, "You'd think I was Christie Brinkley, the way he was acting."

In 1983, LaSalata was fired from Entenmann's. He found work at Fairchild Republic, and later at Grumman. Down in the basement, which he had finished himself, he also cooked up get-rich-quick schemes. The marriage grew more acrimonious, and then abusive. April would vilify Tony for not working, Tony would bring up the wedding incident. And Jus-

tin would follow his mother around with a bow and arrow to protect her. April taught him how to dial 911.

Finally, in 1986, April decided to see a lawyer about divorcing Tony. The following April, she called the police for the first time. She said that Tony was threatening her. She went to court and was granted an Order of Protection.

"He would be mean one day, begging her the next," said Millard. "Some days he stuck to her like glue. He would follow her around the house. She hated that. She couldn't wait to go to work."

The couple slept in separate rooms, but a few times April woke up with Tony standing over her. For a while, she slept with the dresser in front of the bedroom door. At one point, she told friends, Tony put a gun to her head and threatened to kill her. During the divorce proceedings April called the police eight times.

April decided to move with her sons to her mother's house, but her lawyer advised her to move back in so she would be on firmer ground when she asked the judge to award her the house.

But when she moved back in, she told friends and Radman, her husband raped her. Her lawyer, William Griffin, says April never told him this.

The divorce was granted in the fall of 1987, with April getting custody of the children and sole occupancy of the house. Family Court Judge John Dunn gave LaSalata 60 days to find another place to live, leaving a bitterly divorced couple living under the same roof.

In December, LaSalata moved into a $90-a-month house trailer in Bay Shore. But the terms of the divorce decree only seemed to intensify his violent tendencies. When April gave her brother Gerard a shotgun for Christmas, he told her, "You're the one that needs this."

It is difficult to learn much about LaSalata's view of what was happening in his life because nearly all of his friends and relatives declined to be interviewed for this article. But one friend said that LaSalata had become fixated on April's refusal to sell the house and split the money.

"The guy was strapped," said the friend, who asked not to be identified. "He was working nights at Grumman, he was living in this dinky trailer, he couldn't even watch TV except for Channel 12 because he couldn't afford an antenna. He wanted some money so he could start his life over."

Wary of LaSalata, Gerard Principio, who taught martial arts, arranged for one of his students, Billy Woods, to live in the basement apartment Tony had finished. Billy was 25, slightly built and wore longish hair and an earring. He worked as a maintenance man for Slomin's fuel oil. April was glad to have someone else in the house. Billy was glad to know April. Soon they became involved, and Woods' mission took on greater importance.

April had iron gates installed over the front door.

One late night in February, 1988, LaSalata went to the house and found Woods' fuel truck parked outside. When he saw Woods in the house, he tried to break through the gates with a crowbar. April called the police and Tony was arrested for harassment. Out on bail, he called her and said he would shoot her.

In a few days, April was scheduled to go to court for a stronger Order of Protection. But Tony had other ideas.

"Tony told me that if the judge didn't modify his decision, it was time for this," an acquaintance of LaSalata's said in a statement to police. "As he said this, he picked up a big Rambo-type knife off the table. Tony said that he was going to 'kill the bitch.' . . . Tony then said that he was at the house a few nights before to kill April, that he had cut the telephone lines and then he changed his mind. . . . I got in touch with April and told her what Tony had said. April told me that she would be careful."

SHE came in dead," recalls Dr. Alexander Melman, the surgeon at Southside Hospital in Bay Shore who sewed April back together on the night of Feb. 26. "She had no blood pressure, she had wounds to the lungs and the diaphragm and part of her liver was sticking out. The son of a bitch turned the blade, an old trick to create more injuries. It reminded me of a wartime injury."

April spent six days on life-support systems as her hosptial room filled with flowers, balloons, cards and visitors. Members of the Long Island Women's Coalition came to offer their help, but April didn't feel a part of them, didn't feel they were living in her world. To April this was not a political issue. This was *her* issue.

"I thought I was going to die," she told Newsday reporter Dan Fagin, who was preparing a story on how local police respond to domestic violence. "It's been getting worse and worse, but I never thought it would come to this. I'm terrified. You can't imagine what it's like to be living with this every day."

Another visitor was Vincent O'Leary. He had known April since high school, and now he was a police detective, working in their home precinct, the Third. He was assigned to her case. Though such a convenience has the ring of a cheap trick by a screenwriter, in this true story O'Leary was the friend on the force. But it did not seem to relieve April's fear. "I just think of what his jail sentence is going to be and him getting out and getting me," she told Fagin.

LaSalata was initially charged by police with first-degree assault and held on $25,000 bail by District Court Judge Francis Caldeira.

From jail, he wrote a letter to his older son:
Dear Justin,

I am writing you this letter to tell you how sorry I am about what happened to your mother. If you hate me now and never want to see me again I can understand why. I just wanted to tell you that I was very very sick that night and that I did not know what I was doing. I hope and pray to God that you and your mother can forgive me. I wish that there was some way that the pain that your mother has in her body now can somehow be transformed into my body . . . I miss you and Anthony so much. Take care and be a good boy. Please send me a letter. I wish there was something that I could send you but right now I have nothing to send you other than my love. I love you Justin!

On the same day that LaSalata wrote the letter, he was served in jail with this County Court decree: "It is ordered that the above named defendant observe the following conditions of behavior: Stay away from the home, school, business, or place of employment of: April LaSalata."

The next day, LaSalata appeared before County Court Justice Morton Weissman, to whose court the case was transferred after a grand jury indicted him on a charge of attempted murder. Kevin Fox, LaSalata's attorney, indicated he would argue that his client was not competent to stand trial, and Weissman, as is customary when a competency issue is raised, held him without bail.

Fran Radman was brand new to the district attorney's family crimes bureau when she was handed a pile of cases from a departing prosecutor. She had been handling drunk-driving and misdemeanor, child sex-abuse cases in the District Court bureau, and People vs. Anthony LaSalata would be her biggest case to date. A couple of years out of Brooklyn Law School, she had joined the district attorney's office because she felt that was where she could do the most good. Her sympathies lay with victims of crime.

Radman's inexperience was disquieting to April and her family. But what she lacked in seasoning she would try to make up for with dedication. Like April, she was the daughter of a working-class family, had grown up in western Suffolk County and had never wandered far. Now, Radman was living with her parents in East Northport. And when she met April for the first time in the hospital, she felt more than the usual compassion.

"She said that even in the hospital she was afraid he would come get her," Radman recalls. "But she was composed. She always was. Usually she would be kidding, smiling, pleasant, but when it was about being afraid, she got very straight-faced. I thought when I walked out, Wow, that is some strong woman."

* * *

Thursday, April 7, 1988, was a very busy day in the Suffolk County criminal courts.

Radman was scheduled to present evidence to a grand jury on a sex abuse case that day, so she asked another member of the bureau, Gaetan Lozito, to stand in for her at a conference with Judge Weissman on the LaSalata case. Radman's primary concern — for April's peace of mind, as well as her own — was that LaSalata remain in jail. And Fox, she says, had assured her in a phone conversation that he wouldn't be making a bail application. So Radman didn't regard the conference as key.

But there was a crack, after all, and April was about to fall through it.

Weeks before, Dr. Allen Reichman, a psychiatrist who judges the competency of defendants in Suffolk's criminal cases, had found that LaSalata did, in fact, understand the charges against him and was capable of aiding his defense. Now, in the conference in the judge's chambers, a kind of dress rehearsal for open court, Fox told Weissman and Lozito that he would seek to have his own psychiatrist contradict that finding, and also advance his defense of mental impairment on the night of the attack. At Radman's instruction, Lozito told Weissman that April was afraid that her ex-husband would be released, and showed photographs of the weapon he had used.

Then Lozito had to leave for another case. She handed the file over to Matthew Parella, an assistant district attorney who had never seen the case but who was covering Weissman's courtroom for the major crimes bureau. "Nothing's going to happen," he says Lozito told him.

In the courtroom, Fox repeated his intentions for the record. Then Weissman surprised everyone.

"Do you have a bail application?" he asked Fox, according to a transcript of the session.

"No," Fox said, "we reserve it."

"You never made a bail application before this?" Weissman persisted. He seemed to be indicating he wanted to set bail.

Fox was unprepared, but he took his shot. He asked that bail be set at $25,000, the same amount as when the charge was assault.

Weissman looked at Parella. "We'll ask that no bail be continued until the results of the defense psychiatric exam," Parella said.

"No, I won't do that," Weissman said. "Give me a monetary recommendation."

Parella asked for $100,000, but he did not present arguments for the higher bail.

"Hundred thousand bond, twenty-five thousand cash," Weissman said.

To this day, Radman sees that moment as the "mix-up" that made the job of protecting April much more difficult. She says that had she been been there, she would have argued strenuously that the bail wasn't high enough. But now she was stuck with it.

Later, she called Fox. "You said you weren't going to make a bail application," she recalls telling him. Fox explained the circumstances, then said, "Don't worry, Fran, he'll never make that kind of bail."

(Asked to comment for this article, Weissman said he could not recall the case and, anyway, did not discuss cases he had handled.)

MEANWHILE, Fox was finding that his client was still obsessed with his divorce. "Obviously [in retrospect] there was something boiling inside, but it didn't show," he said. "He seemed very subdued, polite, sort of defeated. He wasn't a raving lunatic."

In the spring, April went back to work in the credit department at J.C. Penney, but she was still in pain from her wounds and preoccupied by the court case against Tony. She believed in the *victim's* right to a speedy trial.

The case was transferred to Judge Rudolph Mazzei, and on Aug. 5, a conference was scheduled. April told Radman she wanted to be there.

Also in attendance that day were John and Otille LaSalata, Tony's father and mother. They were like a lot of parents of accused criminals — they were sick over it. And in their sadness, they had an inverted view of the situation. To them, Tony was the victim, April the victimizer.

Afterward, as April walked toward her car with Gerard and Radman, John LaSalata drove up beside them. Throughout, April feared him as much as she feared Tony.

"You slut!" LaSalata screamed at April, according to Radman. "You're the reason my son's in jail!"

John LaSalata was charged with harassment, and although it was later dismissed at April's behest, the incident set the tone for his son's defense.

"His parents saw their son as being sick, and they felt she was one of the causes," said Charles Russo, Fox' law partner. "They didn't say [the stabbing] was justified, but they didn't understand why the criminal justice system was involved. They wanted to get help."

Three days after the incident in the parking lot, and 163 days after their son went to jail, the LaSalatas decided to mortgage their home to get him out.

In April's world, alarms went off. Vinnie O'Leary was the first to call: *He's out.* April couldn't believe it, and when Radman called, the prosecutor found a very nervous woman on the other end of the line.

"Do you have any place to go?" Radman asked.

"*Any place to go?*" April repeated angrily. "He did this to me, and now I have to change my whole life? I live here. My kids go to school here."

A siege mentality set in as word of LaSalata's release spread. Radman had a portable panic button delivered to April's house; she could wear it around her neck and summon the police instantly. And a tape recorder was installed on her kitchen phone. When Det.

Frank Fallon came to install the tape machine, April showed him a picture of her wounds after surgery. "Every noise, every sound, a car or somebody starting a lawn mower, made her nervous," Fallon recalls. "She didn't sleep at night. I told her, 'That's a hell of a way to live. Why don't you move?'"

At home, Justin took to following his mother around with a baseball bat. "He follows me everywhere," April told Radman. "It drives me crazy."

At work, April was allowed to park in the fire zone directly outside the store. A security guard escorted her to her car each night after work.

And at the district attorney's office, the case took on the qualities of a cause. The family crimes unit was staffed mainly by young women whose caseloads were dominated by crimes against women and children, usually involving sexual and physical abuse. It was not unusual for the prosecutors to become emotionally involved with their "clients," and this was especially true of the case of April LaSalata. Radman, whose office was decorated with artwork by victims of child abuse, felt that this time she carried the burden of keeping the victim alive. And she would not play it safe.

Among prosecutors, Mazzei had a reputation, justified or not, as a "defendant's judge." In late August, with Mazzei on vacation, Radman went to Judge Charles Cacciabaudo to try to have LaSalata returned to jail, at a higher bail. To do this, she needed some new evidence. She told Cacciabaudo that April had been receiving "unusual phone calls," since her ex-husband's release, related the incident involving his father, and said that LaSalata had been found competent to stand trial.

Kevin Fox told the judge that LaSalata, suffering from depression, would be voluntarily admitted to South Oaks Hospital in Amityville on that day.

Cacciabaudo rejected Radman's bail request. Then he looked at LaSalata and warned him not to go near his ex-wife.

"Yes, sir," LaSalata said.

As LaSalata underwent psychiatric treatment in South Oaks, Radman pushed for a trial date. To impress upon Mazzei the seriousness of the case, she showed him the photographs of April after the attack. This was an off-the-record move not generally regarded as proper. But LaSalata was due to get out of South Oaks in 60 days, and Radman wanted to jar Mazzei into action. The judge said the case ought to come up soon. But he gave no commitments.

On Sunday, Oct. 16, as Tony's stay in South Oaks was drawing to a close, April was outside the house with Justin and Anthony when a gray car slowed as it passed. In the passenger seat, April was sure, was Tony, wearing a red shirt she had bought him years before.

April called the police, who said they couldn't make an arrest because Tony hadn't come close enough. But Radman said it was enough for her, and had two detectives go to South Oaks to pick him up on charges of criminal contempt.

Radman took the case to District Court

Judge William Bennett. But there was one problem: Fox produced a letter from Dr. Nicholas Samios, LaSalata's physician at South Oaks, saying that the record showed LaSalata had not left the hospital on the day in question.

Radman went to see Bennett in his chambers. "Judge, he's going to kill her," Radman says she told Bennett. "He should be nowhere near this house. We're trying to protect her."

But Bennett said his hands were tied — LaSalata had an alibi. He released him on his own recognizance.

Radman was furious. "His defense [in the stabbing] was mental defect," she says now. "He wasn't saying he didn't do it. So why not keep him in jail? Why not be safe? The problem is we don't have preventative detention in New York and we should."

In New York, as in most other states, the purpose of bail is to insure that a defendant will appear for trial. There, a cornerstone of the criminal justice system, the presumption of the accused's innocence, comes in conflict with the victim's presumption of danger.

After Bennett's decision, Radman called and visited April frequently, if only to let her know she wasn't alone. "I was so afraid," she said. "I don't know if she knew that. Now what do we do? I was afraid that this aggravated everything. April was angry, afraid and wiped out."

In her anxiety, knowing Tony was about to be released from South Oaks, did April imagine seeing him that Sunday? Or did Samios assume that because there was no record of his absence LaSalata must have been in the hospital?

Radman decided to take the South Oaks case to a grand jury and let April tell her story. The grand jury indicted LaSalata, but on Nov. 15, Mazzei, clearly angered at Radman, called it "the proverbial ham sandwich indictment" — referring to a legal truism that prosecutors can lead a grand jury to indict anybody for anything. Mazzei refused to impose bail.

A few weeks before, while Radman was planning her strategy on the South Oaks incident, she had asked Mazzei to move the attempted-murder case up on the calendar. When Mazzei refused, Radman suggested April come to court to make a personal pitch. That day, Radman asked Mazzei again to raise or revoke bail. Mazzei again rejected the request. Then April approached the bench. She spoke softly and nervously.

"I just would like to know how long it's going to take to get a court date. I mean, from Aug. 7 since he's been out on bail, I have been living in fear. I have an 11-year-old son walking around with a baseball bat."

"I understand your concern," Mazzei told her. "The problem is at the present time there are more than 35 defendants who are in custody on murder charges and attempted murder charges who have to be given preference and they have been in custody over a year. Constitutionally that's the way I have to do it."

One factor in the waiting time was the temporary transfer of four criminal court judges to the civil part in April, 1988, to relieve a backlog there. They would not return until December. But another factor that might have been working against April was the trial record of the judge assigned to her case.

AMONG some lawyers, Mazzei is a jurist who has a reputation for delaying or avoiding trials. In 1988, the year the LaSalata case was before him, Mazzei presided over just two trials, according to the court clerk's office. The year before, he had three. In terms of numbers of trials, this placed him 14th among the 15 County Court judges working in Suffolk during those two years.

Mazzei declined to be interviewed for this article, saying through a secretary that he was too busy.

At every turn, Radman felt she was coming up against a rigid legal system whose arbiters were insensitive to the peril that was consuming a woman's life and unresponsive to the urgings of a young, female prosecutor.

"It's still the old boys' network," she said. "I'm little, I'm young. You can sense they treat you differently."

Indeed, her adversaries, Fox and Russo, agree that a different prosecutor might have gotten an earlier trial date. But they lay some of the blame on the district attorney's office for assigning the case to a young prosecutor working in a bureau with a relatively low profile in the office.

"Fran became very involved," Fox said. "She did a good job, but somebody with more authority could have pushed things along." Some of April's family felt likewise. But a former member of the family crimes unit, who asked not to be identified, said a more experienced prosecutor might not have fought as hard: "Fran did more than any other prosecutor would have. She saw the injustice and she went in to Mazzei and kept fighting. A lot of people would have been afraid to."

Chief Assistant District Attorney Mark Cohen added that Radman was well supervised and took counsel from others. "The attention and dedication that assistant paid to the case are beyond question," he said. "To suggest that she was 'inexperienced' and somehow that becomes a logical connection to what happened is misplaced."

As Radman struggled with the system, Fox had troubles of his own. In recent months, LaSalata's parents had been insisting that their son's defense be based on his ex-wife's character. In effect, they wanted Fox to blame April for pushing Tony too far. In October after a series of heated arguments with John LaSalata, Fox took the unusual step of asking to be released from the case. Mazzei granted the request. Fox's withdrawal would delay matters further, as a new attorney would have to be appointed by the court.

Mazzei took the opportunity to remind Anthony LaSalata about the Order of Protection. "I don't want you to go anywhere near your wife," Mazzei said, apparently unaware that they were no longer married.

"No sir," LaSalata said.

But despite his courtroom passivity, it is clear now that LaSalata remained a man possessed. "Some people's self-involvement is so unreasonable that they have enormous trouble dealing with rejection," Dr. Reichman, the court-appointed psychiatrist who examined LaSalata, said in an interview.

April knew this better than anyone. All these months, Fran Radman fought for her and Vinnie O'Leary checked on her. Pictures of LaSalata were kept in the Third Precinct's sector cars. But April told friends she was sure she would not survive Tony's rage. She wrote her will and selected an urn to hold her ashes.

"She *knew* he was going to kill her," Billy Woods said. "She told everybody. Her mother, her brother. She told me every day."

Despite her resignation, April's determination was seen in the way she lived her last months. She went to work in the credit department, shepherded her children to soccer practice, cared for her plants, mowed her mother's lawn.

"A lot of people would have given in," said Kevin Mack, a family friend. "But that was not April's way. She was resolute. She loved her boys and worked hard. And she didn't want to hide. People would say, 'Go away for a while,' or 'Carry a weapon.' "

"We all approached her," Radman said. "I knew she had relatives in New Jersey. But all I got was screaming: 'Here I am, raising two kids, why should we have to leave?' Was it worth it more to her to maintain her life here? Hard question. I think she felt that no matter where she went he would find her. I suggested Ridge, where her brother lives. And she said, 'It's all wide open spaces, he can get me from anywhere.' "

APRIL went to court in Riverhead on Dec. 20. She sat on the opposite side of the room from LaSalata. The defense asked for a three-week adjournment, setting a trial date of Jan. 11. April slipped into the next courtroom to watch the proceedings there. It was the murder trial of Matthew Solomon, accused of strangling his wife the previous Christmas.

The next day, Tony LaSalata went to Edelman's Sporting Goods store in Farmingdale and bought a .22-cal. Marlin rifle, the same model he'd carried with him the night he stabbed April. He filled out the requisite form, which asked, "Are you under indictment . . .?" LaSalata wrote, "No."

On Dec. 26, Lydia Grohoski was shot to death by her estranged husband, Joseph, in the basement of their home in Cutchogue. An Order of Protection was in effect at the time. On Dec. 29, Elizabeth Croff was shot by her estranged husband, William, in front of a cookie factory in Islip. An Order of Protection was in effect at the time. Both men then killed themselves.

On New Year's Eve, Sharon Millard brought her children to April's house for dinner. From the radio in the kitchen they heard a newscaster discussing the cases of Grohoski and Croff. April looked squarely at her oldest friend.

"Sharon," she said. "I'm next."

On the evening of Tuesday, Jan. 3, LaSalata left his parents' house in his mother's car. He said he was going to visit a woman friend. He was wearing his red-and-black hunter's jacket.

At the holidays, he had been feeling low, detectives would learn later. He was living with his parents, was about to come to trial, but was still obsessed with his divorce.

LaSalata drove to 110 McKinley St. He began walking back and forth out front. Justin and

Anthony were inside with their grandmother, who was preparing dinner. The television was on, the volume high. The boys were waiting for Woods to come home with two mice for their pet boa constrictor. Woods had a last-minute call from Slomin's, so he couldn't meet April at work and escort her home, as he liked to do.

April arrived on McKinley Street about 6:30. As she reached the concrete steps in front of her door, LaSalata came out from behind some shrubs. He aimed his sawed-off rifle at her chest and fired. Then he stood over her body and shot her twice in the head. Inside, Justin and Anthony watched television and their grandmother cooked dinner. Their mother lay in the bushes until Woods came home and found her.

"Frannie," Mary Werner, the chief of the family crimes bureau, told Radman over the phone an hour after the fatal shots were fired, "they got April." Radman cried; she didn't sleep for three days. "I kept thinking of her children, of the little boy coming to my office saying he'll do anything to help his mother."

In the end, Radman realized she was part of a system that couldn't help enough. "I had tried to be optimistic," she said. "Gerard wanted to get a gun. I said no, don't do that. I should have told him, yeah. Going to law school, you think the system works, but here's someone I knew and liked and she's dead."

People in the office asked Radman if she'd request a transfer out of family crime, but she felt that would be letting April down somehow. Now, she takes some comfort from the belief that judges in her part of the world seem to be setting higher bails in domestic abuse cases. And in the year since the murders of April and the two other women, reports and arrests for family violence increased dramatically in Suffolk County. But still, when battered women descend the stairs to her basement office and sit before her, it is April whom Radman sees in her mind. And she worries for them.

"We all feel part of it," said Charles Russo, Fox' partner. "When you wake up in the morning and hear, 'April LaSalata is killed,' you feel part of the system. . . . You can't help but have this big empty hole in you."

It was, Mazzei said a day after the murder, "a judge's nightmare."

On Jan. 6, the police discovered LaSalata's frozen corpse slumped in the front seat of his mother's car at a rest stop beyond Exit 52 of the Long Island Expressway. There were two gunshot wounds.

Two days later, more than 100 people crowded into two rows at St. Luke's Church in Brentwood for April's funeral mass. "She will never be forgotten," a friend told a reporter. "She will be in our hearts forever." April was cremated, her ashes placed in the urn she had picked out.

In the spring, LaSalata's family petitioned for guardianship of Justin and Anthony, who were living with their grandmother Lillian Principio. April's friends gathered 2,000 names on petitions opposing the idea, and in the fall the petition was withdrawn.

Last month, over the airwaves of radio station WBLI came the voice of Steve Harper, the afternoon disc jockey.

"We've got a special request right now for two little guys, Anthony and Justin, who've had a very tough year. And I understand . . . they're on their way to New York City to see the tree at Rockefeller Center. And we want to wish them all the best. We've got a song for them."

He played "This One's for the Children."

'Til Death Do Us Part

When a woman kills an abusive partner, is it an act of revenge or of self defense? A growing clemency movement argues for a new legal standard.

Nancy Gibbs

The law has always made room for killers. Soldiers kill the nation's enemies, executioners kill its killers, police officers under fire may fire back. Even a murder is measured in degrees, depending on the mind of the criminal and the character of the crime. And sometime this spring, in a triumph of pity over punishment, the law may just find room for Rita Collins.

"They all cried, didn't they? But not me," she starts out, to distinguish herself from her fellow inmates in a Florida prison, who also have stories to tell. "No one will help me. No one will write about me. I don't have a dirty story. I wasn't abused as a child. I was a respectable government employee, employed by the Navy in a high position in Washington."

"To this day, I don't remember pulling the trigger."

Her husband John was a military recruiter, a solid man who had a way with words. "He said I was old, fat, crazy and had no friends that were real friends. He said I needed him and he would take care of me." She says his care included threats with a knife, punches, a kick to the stomach that caused a hemorrhage. Navy doctors treated her for injuries to her neck and arm. "He'd slam me up against doors. He gave me black eyes, bruises. Winter and summer, I'd go to work like a Puritan, with long sleeves.

Afterward he'd soothe me, and I'd think, He's a good man. What did I do wrong?"

The bravado dissolves, and she starts to cry.

"I was envied by other wives. I felt ashamed because I didn't appreciate him." After each beating came apologies and offerings, gifts, a trip. "It's like blackmail. You think it's going to stop, but it doesn't." Collins never told anyone—not her friends in the church choir, not even a son by her first marriage. "I should have, but it was the humiliation of it all. I'm a professional woman. I didn't want people to think I was crazy." But some of them knew anyway; they had seen the bruises, the black eye behind the dark glasses.

She tried to get out. She filed for divorce, got a restraining order, filed an assault-and-battery charge against him, forced him from the house they had bought with a large chunk of her money when they retired to Florida. But still, she says, he came, night after night, banging on windows and doors, trying to break the locks.

It wasn't her idea to buy a weapon. "The police did all they could, but they had no control. They felt sorry for me. They told me to get a gun." She still doesn't remember firing it. She says she remembers her husband's face, the glassy eyes, a knife in his hands. "To this day, I don't remember pulling the trigger."

The jury couldn't figure it out either. At Collins' first trial, for first-degree murder, her friends, a minister, her doctors and several experts testified about her character and the violence she had suffered. The prosecution played tapes of her threatening her husband over the phone and portrayed her as a bitter,

unstable woman who had bought a gun, lured him to the house and murdered him out of jealousy and anger over the divorce. That trial ended with a hung jury.

"They say I'm a violent person, but I'm not. I didn't want revenge. I just wanted out."

At her second, nine men and three women debated just two hours before finding her guilty of the lesser charge, second-degree murder. Collins' appeals were denied, and the parole board last year recommended against clemency. Orlando prosecutor Dorothy Sedgwick is certain that justice was done. "Rita Collins is a classic example of how a woman can decide to kill her husband and use the battered woman's syndrome as a fake defense," she says. "She lured him to his death. He was trying to escape her." Collins says her lawyers got everything: the $125,000 three-bedroom house with a pool, $98,000 in cash. "I've worked since I was 15, and I have nothing," she says. "The Bible says, 'Thou shalt not kill,' and everybody figures if you're in here, you're guilty. But I'm not a criminal. Nobody cares if I die in here, but if I live, I tell you one thing: I'm not going to keep quiet."

If in the next round of clemency hearings on March 10, Governor Lawton Chiles grants Collins or any other battered woman clemency, Florida will join 26 other states in a national movement to take another look at the cases of abuse victims who kill their abusers. Just before Christmas, Missouri's conservative Republican Governor John Ashcroft commuted the life sentences of two women who claimed they had killed their husbands in self-defense. After 20 years of trying, these women have made a Darwinian claim for mercy: Victims of perpetual violence should be forgiven if they turn violent themselves.

More American women—rich and poor alike—are injured by the men in their life than by car accidents, muggings and rape combined. Advocates and experts liken the effect over time to a slow-acting poison. "Most battered women aren't killing to protect themselves from being killed that very moment," observes Charles Ewing, a law professor at SUNY Buffalo. "What they're protecting themselves from is slow but certain destruction, psychologically and physically. There's no place in the law for that."

As the clemency movement grows, it challenges a legal system that does not always distinguish between a crime and a tragedy. What special claims should victims of fate, poverty, violence, addiction be able to make upon the sympathies of juries and the boundaries of the law? In cases of domestic assaults, some women who suffered terrible abuse resorted to terrible means to escape it. Now the juries, and ultimately the society they speak for, have to find some way to express outrage at the brutality that women and children face every day, without accepting murder as a reasonable response to it.

But until America finds a better way to keep people safe in their own homes or offers them some means of surviving if they flee, it will be hard to answer the defendants who ask their judges. "What choice did I really have?"

HOME IS WHERE THE HURT IS

Last year the A.M.A., backed by the Surgeon General, declared that violent men constitute a major threat to women's health. The National League of Cities estimates that as many as half of all women will experience violence at some time in their marriage. Between 22% and 35% of all visits by females to emergency rooms are for injuries from domestic assaults. Though some studies have found that women are just as likely to start a fight as men, others indicate they are six times as likely to be seri-

ously injured in one. Especially grotesque is the brutality reserved for pregnant women: the March of Dimes has concluded that the battering of women during pregnancy causes more birth defects than all the diseases put together for which children are usually immunized. Anywhere from one-third to as many as half of all female murder victims are killed by their spouses or lovers, compared with 4% of male victims.

"Male violence against women is at least as old an institution as marriage," says clinical psychologist Gus Kaufman Jr., co-founder of Men Stopping Violence, an Atlanta clinic established to help men face their battering problems. So long as a woman was considered her husband's legal property, police and the courts were unable to prevent—and unwilling to punish—domestic assaults. Notes N.Y.U. law professor Holly Maguigan. "We talk about the notion of the rule of thumb, forgetting that it had to do with the restriction on a man's right to use a weapon against his wife: he couldn't use a rod that was larger than his thumb." In 1874 North Carolina became one of the first states to limit a man's right to beat his wife, but lawmakers noted that unless he beat her nearly to death "it is better to draw the curtain, shut out the public gaze and leave the parties to forget and forgive."

Out of that old reluctance grew the modern double standard. Until the first wave of legal reform in the 1970s, an aggravated assault against a stranger was a felony, but assaulting a spouse was considered a misdemeanor, which rarely landed the attacker in court, much less in jail. That distinction, which still exists in most states, does not reflect the danger involved: a study by the Boston Bar Association found that the domestic attacks were at least as dangerous as 90% of felony assaults. "Police seldom arrest, even when there are injuries serious enough to require hospitalization of the victim," declared the Florida Supreme Court in a 1990 gender-bias study, which also noted the tendency of prosecutors to drop domestic-violence cases.

Police have always hated answering complaints about domestic disputes. Experts acknowledge that such situations are often particularly dangerous, but suspect that there are other reasons for holding back. "This issue pushes buttons, summons up personal emotions, that almost no other issue does for police and judges," says Linda Osmundson,

who co-chairs a battered wives' task force for the National Coalition Against Domestic Violence. "Domestic violence is not seen as a crime. A man's home is still his castle. There is a system that really believes that women should be passive in every circumstance." And it persists despite a 20-year effort by advocates to transform attitudes toward domestic violence.

While most of the effort has been directed at helping women survive, and escape, abusive homes, much of the publicity has fallen on those rare cases when women resort to violence themselves. Researcher and author Angela Browne points out that a woman is much more likely to be killed by her partner than to kill him. In 1991, when some 4 million women were beaten and 1,320 murdered in domestic attacks, 622 women killed their husbands or boyfriends. Yet the women have become the lightning rods for debate, since their circumstances, and their response, were most extreme.

WHAT CHOICE DID SHE HAVE?

"There is an appropriate means to deal with one's marital problems—legal recourse. Not a .357 Magnum," argues former Florida prosecutor Bill Catto. "If you choose to use a gun to end a problem, then you must suffer the consequences of your act." Defense lawyers call it legitimate self-protection when a victim of abuse fights back—even if she shoots her husband in his sleep. Prosecutors call it an act of vengeance, and in the past, juries have usually agreed and sent the killer to jail. Michael Dowd, director of the Pace University Battered Women's Justice Center, has found that the average sentence for a woman who kills her mate is 15 to 20 years; for a man, 2 to 6.

The punishment is not surprising, since many judges insist that evidence of past abuse, even if it went on for years, is not relevant in court unless it occurred around the time of the killing. It is not the dead husband who is on trial, they note, but the wife who pulled the trigger. "Frankly, I feel changing the law would be authorizing preventive murder," argued Los Angeles Superior Court Judge Lillian Stevens in the Los Angeles Times. "The only thing that really matters is, Was there an immediate danger? There can't be an old grievance." And even if a woman is allowed to testify about past violence, the jury may still condemn her response to it. If he was really so savage, the prosecutor typically asks, why didn't she leave, seek shelter, call the police, file a complaint?

"The question presumes she has good options," says Julie Blackman, a New Jersey-based social psychologist who has testified as an expert witness in abuse and murder cases. "Sometimes, they don't leave because they have young children and no other way to support them, or because they grow up in cultures that are so immersed in violence that they don't figure there's any place better to go, or because they can't get apartments." The shelter facilities around the country are uniformly inadequate: New York has about 1,300 beds for a state with 18 million people. In 1990 the Baltimore zoo spent twice as much money to care for animals as the state of Maryland spent on shelters for victims of domestic violence.

Last July, even as reports of violence continued to multiply, the National Domestic Violence Hotline was disconnected. The 800 number had received as many as 10,000 calls a month from across the country. Now, says Mary Ann Bohrer, founder of the New York City-based Council for Safe Families, "there is no number, no national resource, for people seeking information about domestic violence."

The other reason women don't flee is because, ironically, they are afraid for their life. Law-enforcement experts agree that running away greatly increases the danger a woman faces. Angered at the loss of power and control, violent men often try to track down their wives and threaten them, or their children, if they don't come home. James Cox III, an unemployed dishwasher in Jacksonville, Florida, was determined to find his ex-girlfriend, despite a court order to stay away from her. Two weeks ago, he forced her mother at gunpoint to tell him the location of the battered women's shelter where her daughter had fled, and stormed the building, firing a shotgun. Police shot him dead. "This case illustrates the extent to which men go to pursue their victims," said executive director Rita DeYoung. "It creates a catch-22 for all battered women. Some will choose to return to their abusers, thinking they can control their behavior."

"After the law turns you away, society closes its doors on you, and you find yourself trapped in a life with someone capable of homicide. What choice in the

end was I given?" asks Shalanda Burt, 21, who is serving 17 years for shooting her boyfriend James Fairley two years ago in Bradenton, Florida. She was three months pregnant at the time. A week after she delivered their first baby, James raped her and ripped her stitches. Several times she tried to leave or get help. "I would have a bloody mouth and a swollen face. All the police would do is give me a card with a deputy's name on it and tell me it was a 'lover's quarrel.' The battered women's shelter was full. All they could offer was a counselor on the phone."

"I didn't mean to kill him. He had hit me several times. Something inside me snapped; I grabbed the bottle and swung."

Two weeks before the shooting, the police arrested them both: him for aggravated assault because she was pregnant, her for assault with a deadly missile and violently resisting arrest. She had thrown a bottle at his truck. Her bail was $10,000; his was $3,000. He was back home before she was, so she sent the baby to stay with relatives while she tried to raise bail. The end came on a Christmas weekend. After a particularly vicious beating, he followed her to her aunt's house. When he came at her again, she shot him. "They say I'm a violent person, but I'm not. I didn't want revenge. I just wanted out." Facing 25 years, she was told by a female public defender to take a plea bargain and 17 years. "I wanted to fight. But she said I'd get life or the electric chair. I was in a no-win situation."

It is hard for juries to understand why women like Burt do not turn to the courts for orders of protection. But these are a makeshift shield at best, often violated and hard to enforce. Olympic skier Patricia Kastle had a restraining order when her former husband shot her. Lisa Bianco in Indiana remained terrified of her husband even after he was sent to jail for eight years. When prison officials granted Alan Matheney an eight-hour pass in March 1989, he drove directly to Bianco's home, broke in and beat her to death with the butt of a shotgun. Last March, Shirley Lowery, a grandmother

of 11, was stabbed 19 times with a butcher knife by her former boyfriend in the hallway of the courthouse where she had gone to get an order of protection.

THE MIND OF THE VICTIM

Defense lawyers have a hard time explaining to juries the shame, isolation and emotional dependency that bind victims to their abusers. Many women are too proud to admit to their family or friends that their marriage is not working and blame themselves for its failure even as they cling to the faith that their violent lover will change. "People confuse the woman's love for the man with love of abuse," says Pace's Dowd. "It's not the same thing. Which of us hasn't been involved in a romantic relationship where people say this is no good for you?"

It was Denver psychologist Lenore Walker, writing in 1984, who coined the term battered-woman syndrome to explain the behavior of abuse victims. Her study discussed the cycle of violence in battering households: first a period of growing tension; then a violent explosion, often unleashed by drugs or alcohol; and finally a stage of remorse and kindness. A violent man, she argues, typically acts out of a powerful need for control—physical, emotional, even financial. He may keep his wife under close surveillance, isolating her from family and friends, forbidding her to work or calling constantly to check on her whereabouts. Woven into the scrutiny are insults and threats that in the end can destroy a woman's confidence and leave her feeling trapped between her fear of staying in a violent home—and her fear of fleeing it.

Many lawyers say it is virtually impossible to defend a battered woman without some expert testimony about the effect of that syndrome over time. Such testimony allows attorneys to stretch the rules governing self-defense, which were designed to deal with two men caught in a bar fight, not a woman caught in a violent relationship with a stronger man.

In a traditional case of self-defense, a jury is presented a "snapshot" of a crime: the mugger threatens a subway rider with a knife; the rider pulls a gun and shoots his attacker. It is up to the jurors to decide whether the danger was real and immediate and whether the response was reasonable. A woman who shoots her husband while he lunges at her with a knife should have little trouble claiming that she acted in self-defense. Yet lawyers still find jurors to be very uncomfortable with female violence under any circumstances, especially violence directed at a man she may have lived with for years.

Given that bias, it is even harder for a lawyer to call it self-defense when a woman shoots a sleeping husband. The danger was hardly immediate, prosecutors argue, nor was the lethal response reasonable. Evidence about battered-woman syndrome may be the only way to persuade a jury to identify with a killer. "Battered women are extraordinarily sensitive to cues of danger, and that's how they survive," says Walker. "That is why many battered women kill, not during what looks like the middle of a fight, but when the man is more vulnerable or the violence is just beginning."

"Delia was driven to extremes. The situation was desperate, and she viewed it that way."

A classic self-defense plea also demands a fair fight. A person who is punched can punch back, but if he shoots, he runs the risk of being charged with murder or manslaughter. This leaves women and children, who are almost always smaller and weaker than their attackers, in a bind. They often see no way to escape an assault without using a weapon and the element of surprise—arguing, in essence, that their best hope of self-defense was a pre-emptive strike. "Morally and legally a woman should not be expected to wait until his hands are around her neck," argues Los Angeles defense attorney Leslie Abramson. "Say a husband says, 'When I get up tomorrow morning, I'm going to beat the living daylights out of you,' " says Joshua Dressler, a law professor at Wayne State University who specializes in criminal procedures. "If you use the word imminent, the woman would have to wait until the next morning and, just as he's about to kill her, then use self-defense."

That argument, prosecutors retort, is an invitation to anarchy. If a woman has survived past beatings, what persuaded

her that this time was different, that she had no choice but to kill or be killed? The real catalyst, they suggest, was not her fear but her fury. Prosecutors often turn a woman's history of abuse into a motive for murder. "What some clemency advocates are really saying is that that s.o.b. deserved to die and why should she be punished for what she did," argues Dressler. Unless the killing came in the midst of a violent attack, it amounts to a personal death-penalty sentence. "I find it very hard to say that killing the most rotten human being in the world when he's not currently threatening the individual is the right thing to do."

Those who oppose changes in the laws point out that many domestic disputes are much more complicated than the clemency movement would suggest. "We've got to stop perpetuating the myth that men are all vicious and that women are all Snow White," says Sonny Burmeister, a divorced father of three children who, as president of the Georgia Council for Children's Rights in Marietta, lobbies for equal treatment of men involved in custody battles. He recently sheltered a husband whose wife had pulled a gun on him. When police were called, their response was "So?" Says Burmeister: "We perpetuate this macho, chauvinistic, paternalistic attitude for men. We are taught to be protective of the weaker sex. We encourage women to report domestic violence. We believe men are guilty. But women are just as guilty."

He charges that feminists are trying to write a customized set of laws. "If Mom gets mad and shoots Dad, we call it PMS and point out that he hit her six months ago," he complains. "If Dad gets mad and shoots Mom, we call it domestic violence and charge him with murder. We paint men as violent and we paint women as victims, removing them from the social and legal consequences of their actions. I don't care how oppressed a woman is; should we condone premeditated murder?"

Only nine states have passed laws permitting expert testimony on battered-woman syndrome and spousal violence. In most cases it remains a matter of judicial discretion. One Pennsylvania judge ruled that testimony presented by a prosecutor showed that the defendant had not been beaten badly enough to qualify as a battered woman and therefore could not have that standard applied to her case. President Bush signed legislation in October urging states to accept expert

testimony in criminal cases involving battered women. The law calls for development of training materials to assist defendants and their attorneys in using such testimony in appropriate cases.

Judge Lillian Stevens instructed the jury on the rules governing self-defense at the 1983 trial of Brenda Clubine, who claimed that she killed her police-informant husband because he was going to kill her. Clubine says that during an 11-year relationship, she was kicked, punched, stabbed, had the skin on one side of her face torn off, a lung pierced, ribs broken. She had a judge's order protecting her and had pressed charges to have her husband arrested for felony battery. But six weeks later, she agreed to meet him in a motel, where Clubine alleges that she felt her life was in danger and hit him over the head with a wine bottle, causing a fatal brain hemorrhage. "I didn't mean to kill him," she says. "He had hit me several times. Something inside me snapped; I grabbed the bottle and swung." The jury found Clubine guilty of second-degree manslaughter, and Judge Stevens sentenced her to 15 years to life. She says Clubine drugged her husband into lethargy before fatally hitting him. "It seemed to me [the beatings] were some time ago," Stevens told the Los Angeles *Times*. Furthermore, she added, "there was evidence that a lot of it was mutual."

It is interesting that within the legal community there are eloquent opponents of battered-woman syndrome—on feminist grounds—who dislike the label's implication that all battered women are helpless victims of some shared mental disability that prevents them from acting rationally. Social liberals, says N.Y.U.'s Maguigan, typically explain male violence in terms of social or economic pressures. Female violence, on the other hand, is examined in psychological terms. "They look to what's wrong with her and reinforce a notion that women who use violence are, per se, unreasonable, that something must be wrong with her because she's not acting like a good woman, in the way that women are socialized to behave."

Researcher Charles Ewing compared a group of 100 battered women who had killed their partners with 100 battered women who hadn't taken that fatal step. Women who resorted to violence were usually those who were most isolated, socially and economically; they had been the most badly beaten, their children had been abused, and their husbands were drug or alcohol abusers. That is, the common bond was circumstantial, not psychological. "They're not pathological," says social psychologist Blackman. "They don't have personality disorders. They're just beat up worse."

Women who have endured years of beatings without fighting back may reach the breaking point once the abuse spreads to others they love. Arlene Caris is serving a 25-year sentence in New York for killing her husband. He had tormented her for years, both physically and psychologically. Then she reportedly learned that he was sexually abusing her granddaughter. On the night she finally decided to leave him, he came at her in a rage. She took a rifle, shot him, wrapped him in bedsheets and then hid the body in the attic for five months.

Offering such women clemency, the advocates note, is not precisely the same as amnesty; the punishment is reduced, though the act is not excused. Clemency may be most appropriate in cases where all the circumstances of the crime were not heard in court. The higher courts have certainly sent the message that justice is not uniform in domestic-violence cases. One study found that 40% of women who appeal their murder convictions get the sentence thrown out, compared with an 8.5% reversal rate for homicides as a whole. "I've worked on cases involving battered women who have talked only briefly to their lawyers in the courtroom for 15 or 20 minutes and then they take a plea and do 15 to life," recalls Blackman. "I see women who are Hispanic and don't speak English well, or women who are very quickly moved through the system, who take pleas and do substantial chunks of time, often without getting any real attention paid to the circumstances of their case."

The first mass release in the U.S. came at Christmas in 1990, when Ohio Governor Richard Celeste commuted the sentences of 27 battered women serving time for killing or assaulting male companions. His initiative was born of long-held convictions. As a legislator in the early '70s, he and his wife helped open a women's center in Cleveland and held hearings on domestic violence. When he became lieutenant governor in 1974 and moved to Columbus, he and his wife rented out their home in Cleveland as emergency shelter for battered women. He and the parole board reviewed 107

cases, looking at evidence of past abuse, criminal record, adjustment to prison life and participation in postrelease programs before granting the clemencies. "The system of justice had not really worked in their cases," he says. "They had not had the opportunity for a fair trial because vitally important evidence affecting their circumstances and the terrible things done to them was not presented to the jury."

The impending reviews in other states have caused some prosecutors and judges to sound an alarm. They are worried that Governors' second-guessing the courts undermines the judicial system and invites manipulation by prisoners. "Anybody in the penitentiary, if they see a possible out, will be claiming. 'Oh, I was a battered woman,' " says Dallas assistant district attorney Norman Kinne. "They can't take every female who says she's a battered woman and say, 'Oh, we're sorry, we'll let you out.' If they're going to do it right, it's an exhaustive study."

Clemency critics point to one woman released in Maryland who soon afterward boasted about having committed the crime. Especially controversial are women who have been granted clemency for crimes that were undeniably premeditated. Delia Alaniz hired a contract killer to pretend to rob her home and murder her husband in the process. He had beaten her and their children for years, sexually abusing their 14-year-old daughter. The prosecutor from Skagit County, Washington, was sufficiently impressed by the evidence of abuse that he reduced the charge from first-degree murder and life imprisonment to second-degree manslaughter with a sentence of 10 to 14 years. In October 1989, Governor Booth Gardner granted her clemency. "Delia was driven to extremes. The situation was desperate, and she viewed it that way," says Skagit County public defender Robert Jones. "The harm to those kids having a mom in prison was too much considering the suffering they went through. As a state, we don't condone what she did, but we understand and have compassion."

THE ALTERNATIVES TO MURDER

There is always a risk that the debate over clemency will continue to obscure the missing debate over violence. "I

grew up in a society that really tolerated a lot of injustice when it came to women," says Pace University's Dowd. "It was ingrained as a part of society. This isn't a woman's issue. It's a human-rights issue. Men should have as much to offer fighting sexism as they do racism because the reality is that it's our hands that strike the blows." The best way to keep battered women out of jail is to keep them from being battered in the first place.

In a sense, a society's priorities can be measured by whom it punishes. A survey of the population of a typical prison suggests that violent husbands and fathers are still not viewed as criminals. In New York State about half the inmates are drug offenders, the result of a decade-long War on Drugs that demanded mandatory sentences. A War on Violence would send the same message, that society genuinely abhors parents who beat children and spouses who batter each other, and is willing to punish the behavior rather than dismiss it.

Minnesota serves as a model for other states. In 1981 Duluth was the first U.S. city to institute mandatory arrests in domestic disputes. Since then about half the states have done the same, which means that even if a victim does not wish to press charges, the police are obliged to make an arrest if they see evidence of abuse. Advocates in some Minnesota jurisdictions track cases from the first call to police through prosecution and sentencing, to try to spot where the system is failing. Prosecutors are increasingly reluctant to plea-bargain assault down to disorderly conduct. They have also found it helpful to use the arresting officer as complainant, so that their case does not depend on a frightened victim's testifying.

Better training of police officers, judges, emergency-room personnel and other professionals is having an impact in many cities. "We used to train police to be counselors in domestic-abuse cases," says Osmundson. "No longer. We teach them to go make arrests." In Jacksonville, Florida, new procedures helped raise the arrest rate from 25% to 40%. "Arrests send a message to the woman that help is available and to men that abuse is not accepted," says shelter executive director DeYoung, who also serves as president of the Florida Coalition Against Domestic Violence. "Children too see that it's not accepted and are more likely to grow up not accepting abuse in the home."

Since 1990 at least 28 states have passed "stalking laws" that make it a crime to threaten, follow or harass someone. Congress this month may take up the Violence Against Women bill, which would increase penalties for federal sex crimes; provide $300 million to police, prosecutors and courts to combat violent crimes against women; and reinforce state domestic-violence laws. Most women, of course, are not looking to put their partners in jail; they just want the violence to stop.

A Minneapolis project was founded in 1979 at the prompting of women in shelters who said they wanted to go back to their partners if they would stop battering. Counselors have found that men resort to violence because they want to control their partners, and they know they can get away with it—unlike in other relationships. "A lot of people experience low impulse control, fear of abandonment, alcohol and drug addiction, all the characteristics of a batterer," says Ellen Pence, training coordinator for the Domestic Abuse Intervention Project in Duluth. "However, the same guy is not beating up his boss."

Most men come to the program either by order of the courts or as a condition set by their partners. The counselors start with the assumption that battering is learned behavior. Eighty percent of the participants grew up in a home where they saw or were victims of physical, sexual or other abuse. Once imprinted with that model, they must be taught to recognize warning signs and redirect their anger. "We don't say, 'Never get angry,' " says Carol Arthur, the Minneapolis project's executive director. "Anger is a normal, healthy emotion. What we work with is a way to express it." Men describe to the group their most violent incident. One man told about throwing food in his wife's face at dinner and then beating her to the floor—only to turn and see his two small children huddled terrified under the table. Arthur remembers his self-assessment at that moment: "My God, what must they be thinking about me? I didn't want to be like that."

If the police and the courts crack down on abusers, and programs exist to help change violent behavior, victims will be less likely to take—and less justified in taking—the law into their own hands. And once the cycle of violence winds down in this generation, it is less likely to poison the next. That would be a family value worth fighting for.

—Reported by Cathy Booth/Miami, Jeanne McDowell/Los Angeles and Janice C. Simpson/New York

WHEN
MEN
HIT WOMEN

■

A program for battered women in Duluth, Minn.—though widely considered the model for the rest of the country—has enjoyed only limited success. Nothing speaks more eloquently to the intractability of the problem.

Jan Hoffman

Jan Hoffman, a staff writer for The Village Voice, *recently completed a journalism fellowship at Yale Law School.*

This Saturday night shift has been excruciatingly dull for the police in Duluth, Minn., a brawny working-class city of 90,000 on the shoreline of Lake Superior. The complaints trickle into the precinct, the callers almost embarrassed: black bear up a tree; kids throwing stuffed animals into traffic. But it's 1 A.M. now, and the bars are closing. People are heading home.

1:02 A.M.: Couple arguing loudly. Probably just "verbal assault," the dispatcher tells the car patrols.

1:06 A.M.: Two squad cars pull up to the address. A tall blond man opens the door as a naked woman hurriedly slips on a raincoat. The man looks calm. The woman looks anything but.

"We were just having a squabble," he begins.

"He was kicking the [expletive] out of me," she yells.

"Let's go in separate rooms and talk," says one of the officers, following the Duluth Police Department procedure for domestic disputes.

In the living room, George G. tells his side of the story. "We've been trying to work on things. And so we were talking. And wrestling."

How does he explain the blood oozing from the inside of her mouth? "She drinks, you know. She probably cut herself." From inside the bedroom, Jenny M., whose face is puffing up, screams: "Just get him out of here! And then you guys leave, too!"

The police officers probe for details, telling her that

something must be done now, or there will probably be a next time, and it will hurt much worse. Jenny M. glares, fearful but furious. "He slapped me and kicked my butt. He picked me up by the hair and threw me against the wall."

"She lies, you know," George G. confides to an officer, who remains stone-faced. Jenny M. starts crying again. "I don't want him hurt. This is my fault. I'm the drinker. He's not a bad guy."

Following protocol, the officers determine that the couple live together. And that she is afraid of him. Next, they snap Polaroids of her bruised face, and of his swollen, cut knuckles. Then the police head toward George G. with handcuffs. He looks at her beseechingly. "Jenny, do you want me to go?"

An officer cuts him short. "George, it's not her choice."

George G. thrusts his chin out and his fists deep into the couch. "But this is just a domestic fight!"

One cop replies: "We don't have a choice, either. We have to arrest you." They take him away, handcuffed, leaving Jenny M. with leaflets about the city's Domestic Abuse Intervention Project (D.A.I.P.).

By 1:34 A.M. George G. has been booked at the St. Louis County jail, where he will sit out the weekend until arraignment on Monday morning. Within an hour, a volunteer from the city's shelter will try to contact Jenny M., and in the morning, a man from D.A.I.P. will visit George and explain the consequences in Duluth for getting into "a domestic fight."

It was 10 years ago this summer that Duluth became the first local jurisdiction in America to adopt a mandatory arrest policy for misdemeanor assaults—the criminal charge filed in most domestic-violence cases. But the arrest policy alone is not what makes Duluth's perhaps the most imitated intervention program in the country. Its purpose is to make every agent of the justice system—police, prosecutors, probation officers, judges—deliver the same message: domestic violence is a crime that a community will not tolerate. The program's centerpiece is D.A.I.P., which acts as a constant, heckling monitor of all the organizations. The project, which also runs batterers' groups and supervises custody visits between batterers and their children, chugs along on $162,000 a year. Financing comes from the state's Department of Corrections, foundation grants and fees for D.A.I.P.'s manuals and training seminars.

The Duluth model—pieces of which have been replicated in communities throughout Minnesota, in cities like Los Angeles, Baltimore, San Francisco, Nashville and Seattle, and in countries like Canada, Scotland, New Zealand and Australia—has been admiringly described by Mary Haviland, a New York City domestic-abuse expert, as "an organizing miracle."

Typically, a first-time offender is incarcerated overnight. If he pleads guilty, he'll be sentenced to 30 days

in jail and put on probation, pending completion of a 26-week batterer's program. If he misses three successive classes, he is often sent to jail. Men who are served with civil orders of protection are routinely sent into the same treatment program. Staff members and volunteers from the shelter maintain contact with victims throughout the process.

Many experts regard Duluth as embodying the best of what the almost 20-year-old battered-women's movement has sought to achieve. The movement, inspired by the grass-roots feminist campaign that opened rape-crisis centers in the late 60's, sprang up in the mid-70's as a loose coalition of emergency shelters. Duluth's own shelter, the Women's Coalition, was founded in 1978. Reflecting the national movement's multiple approaches a few years later, Duluth activists then prodded local law-enforcement agencies to take the issue seriously and eventually urged that batterers be offered treatment as well as punishment.

. . . while intervention may be possible, prevention seems all but unimaginable.

Nowadays in Duluth, women who seek help from the legal system do receive some protection, and their batterers are usually held accountable. After a decade of many trials and many errors, Ellen Pence, one of the project's founders and its national proselytizer, estimates that 1 out of every 19 men in Duluth has been through the program. During that same period, not one Duluth woman died from a domestic homicide. Given the rate of Duluth's domestic homicides in the 70's, says Pence, "there are at least five women alive today that would have otherwise been killed."

The results from Duluth are not, however, wholly triumphant. One study shows that five years after going through the Duluth program and judicial system, fully 40 percent of the treated men end up reoffending (or becoming suspects in assaults), either with the same woman or new partners. Pence thinks the real number may be closer to 60 percent. And the number of new cases each year that come before either criminal or family court judges has remained constant—about 450 a year.

"The changes in the country have been enormous," says Elizabeth M. Schneider, a Brooklyn Law School professor and expert on battered women. "But we seriously underestimated how wedded our culture is to domestic violence." Upward of four million American women are beaten annually by current and former male partners, and between 2,000 to 4,000 women are murdered, according to the National Woman Abuse Prevention Center. C. Everett Koop, the former Surgeon General, has identified domestic violence as the No. 1 health problem for American women, causing more injuries than automobile accidents, muggings and rapes combined. The connection with child abuse in a family has been well documented: between 50 and 70 percent of the men who physically harm their partners also hit their children.

At this point, while intervention may be possible, prevention seems all but unimaginable. Despite the community's exceptional efforts, as Pence flatly admits: "We have no evidence to show that it has had any general deterrent effect. The individual guy you catch may do it less. But in Duluth, men don't say, 'Gee, I shouldn't beat her up because I'll get arrested.' After 10 years, we've had a lot of young men in our program whose dads were in it.

"I have no idea where the next step will come from," she adds. "We're too exhausted just trying to stay on top of things as they are."

Ellen Pence's commitment to ending family violence is hard-earned. An aunt was shot to death by her husband, a sister is a former battered wife and, one night about 20 years ago, a neighbor fleeing an abusive partner left her boy with Pence, who subsequently helped raise him. In 1981, D.A.I.P. received a $50,000 state grant for Pence's bold new experiment. Duluth was chosen for a simple but powerful reason: the city's judges and police chief were the only ones in Minnesota willing to take her proposal seriously. A Minnesota native, Pence, now 43, is an exasperating, indefatigable earthshaker, who, by dint of her salty wit and impassioned outbursts, simply will not be denied.

Duluth, she concedes, is not exactly the mayhem capital of the Midwest. In 1990, homicides hit a record high of three. The local scourge is predominantly alcoholism, not drug addiction. The people are mostly Scandinavian and Eastern European, with a modest minority of Ojibwa Indians, blacks and Southeast Asians. With fir-dotted hills that swoop sharply down to the largest fresh-water lake in the world, Duluth appears to be a pretty decent place to live—particularly for those with a fondness for ice fishing and months of subfreezing weather. Its incidence of domestic violence is probably no worse than anywhere else in the country, and, a decade ago, was treated just as casually. In 1980, there were just 22 arrests for domestic assault, and only four convictions.

First, Ellen Pence took on the cops.

Traditional practice: If an officer doesn't witness a misdemeanor assault, the officer won't arrest.

New practice: If an officer has probable cause, including a victim's visible injury, to believe a misde-

meanor domestic assault occurred within four hours of the arrival of the police, the officer must arrest. In 1990, the Duluth police arrested 176 men and 23 women for misdemeanor domestic assaults—of whom almost all were convicted. (Experts agree that violence by women against men is usually in self-defense or retaliation, and is often less severe.)

Over the years, mandatory arrest has become increasingly popular, having been adopted, though inconsistently enforced, in dozens of municipalities and 15 states—although recent studies have called into question whether police arrests are the best way to protect domestic-abuse victims.

Still, mandatory arrest earns favorable reviews from police and prosecutors, and a D.A.I.P. survey found that 71 percent of the victims approved of the Duluth police's handling of their situations. But some battered-women's advocates remain skeptical, particularly because the policy can be disproportionately tough on poor minority families. Most experts point out that while battering occurs across all races and classes, poor people are more likely to be reported to authorities and punished than men from middle-class households. "For people who are more disadvantaged economically, like Native Americans, blacks and Hispanics, there are higher levels of all kinds of victimization, including family violence," says Angela Browne, the author of "When Battered Women Kill."

Another significant problem with mandatory arrest is that it can backfire: on occasion, when faced with two bloodied people accusing each other of attacking first, police have arrested the woman as well as the man. When this happens, children may be sent into foster care. In Connecticut, which has one of the country's toughest domestic-violence policies, the dual-arrest rate is 14 percent.

. . . women just want their abusers out of the house but not sent to jail . . .

Many police are still reluctant to arrest because prosecutors tend to put the cases on the back burner. Prosecutors, in turn, blame their lack of action on the victims, who, they say, often refuse to press charges, fearing a batterer's revenge or believing his promise of reformation. Duluth, however, has what officials call a "flexible no-drop" policy: regardless of the victim's wishes, the prosecutor will almost always pursue the case.

"I assume that victims won't cooperate," says Mary

E. Asmus, the chief prosecutor of Duluth's city attorney's office. Asmus has a working procedure for obtaining evidence independent of the victim's cooperation. At trial, she'll offer police photographs, tapes of calls to 911 and medical records. She also subpoenas all victims. If the victim recants on the stand, Asmus, making unusual use of a state rule of evidence, will offer the woman's original statement to police – not to impeach her witness, but to assert the facts of the incident. In her nine years as a Duluth prosecutor, Asmus has lost only three domestic-violence cases in court.

Nationwide, some of the most aggressive domestic-violence prosecutors are in Philadelphia, San Francisco and San Diego, which files at least 200 new cases each month. To pressure women to testify, some prosecutors have gone so far as charging them with filing false police reports and perjury, issuing contempt-of-court citations, and, in rare instances, even jailing them. The no-drop policy has ignited fiery debate. One prosecutor argued in a recent national District Attorneys Association Bulletin that it "smacks of the worst kind of paternalism." In Westchester County, N.Y., Judge Jeanine Ferris Pirro retorts, "Some jurisdictions allow a victim to drop charges, and that's sending a subtle message that they don't take the crime seriously."

Not surprisingly, a no-drop policy often puts prosecutors at odds with the same activists who are demanding that the justice system go after batterers. Susan Schechter, author of "Women and Male Violence," contends that such a policy can erode a battered woman's sense of self-esteem and control, "particularly when she has a good sense of her own danger and what's best for her and the kids." Pence says that in Duluth, D.A.I.P. has managed to cut the dual-arrest rate way down. "We trust our system," she says, "so we're willing to force a woman into it." But Pence doesn't condone mandatory arrest or no-drop prosecutions unilaterally.

While tougher policies have diverted more cases into criminal court, women just want their abusers out of the house but not sent to jail seek relief through a different route: the civil order of protection, which limits the batterer's contact with the woman and her children. Applying for such an order can be a labyrinthine undertaking – even on a good day. Every jurisdiction has its own criteria for who qualifies, as well as for the duration of the protection order. Women with mixed feelings about getting the order in the first place can quickly become frustrated.

And judges become frustrated with them. Gender-bias studies of various state court systems have sharply criticized judges for penalizing battered women. In Duluth, the D.A.I.P. targeted the judiciary. "We explained why they were seeing what they were seeing," Pence recalls. "They were interpreting a woman's fear as ambivalence and masochism. We showed them what happened in cases when they just gave a guy a lecture or a fine." Now she occasionally trots out one or two

Duluth judges on her judicial-training sessions around the country. One grumbles fondly that "Ellen Pence is turning us into feminist tools."

Judge Robert V. Campbell of Duluth's District Court presides over most of its order-of-protection hearings. If a woman fails to appear in court because her abuser may be present, "I'll continue the order for a month or so, on the theory that she's being intimidated," Campbell says. A Duluth woman named Brenda Erickson, whose request for an order against her husband alleged that he'd raped her, had her first brush with the

---

"If she'd been raped by a stranger, would you expect her to live with him, too?"

---

justice system before Judge Campbell. Her husband's attorney argued that his client could not have raped her. "Your honor," Erickson remembers the lawyer protesting, "she's his wife!"

The judge, she says, all but leaped down from the bench, sputtering, "If she'd been raped by a stranger, would you expect her to live with him, too?" "And I thought, Oh God, he understands how I feel," Erickson says.

Six glum faces, 12 crossed arms – nobody thinks they did anything wrong, so why do they have to be here? Ty Schroyer, a D.A.I.P. group leader, assumes an expression of determined cheeriness as he greets this week's recruits, all ordered by the court to the batterer's program. Some ground rules:

"We don't call women 'the old lady,' 'the wife,' 'that slut,' 'that whore,' 'the bitch,' 'that fat, ugly bitch.'. . . ." The list quickly becomes unprintable.

"So what should we call her – 'it'?" says a man who calls himself Dave, as the others snicker.

"How about her name?" snaps Schroyer, who himself was arrested nearly a decade ago for pounding his wife's head against a sidewalk.

Trying to change a batterer's behavior toward women makes pushing boulders uphill look easy. Nonetheless, at least 250 different programs around the country, filled with volunteer and court-referred clients, are having a go at it. Among them, no consensus has emerged about philosophy or length of treatment: Phoenix courts send their batterers to 12 weeks or more of counseling sessions; San Diego batterers must attend for a year.

Edward W. Gondolf, a Pittsburgh sociologist who has evaluated and developed batterers' programs for 12 years, says, "We're making a dent with garden-variety batterers"–first-time or sporadic offenders–"but there's another cadre, the most lethal, who are still out of our reach." Batterers who go through the legal system should be more carefully screened, he says, and some confined. Men whom he would categorize as antisocial or even sociopathic batterers–about 30 percent–not only resist intervention, but may be further antagonized by it.

He cautions women not to be taken in when their partners enter counseling. "Counseling is the American way to heal a problem," he says. "She'll think, 'If he's trying, I should support him,' while he's thinking, 'I'll go to the program until I get what I want–my wife back.' But his being in counseling may increase the danger for her because she has got her guard down."

In Duluth, when a batterer enters D.A.I.P., officials at the Women's Coalition shelter will stay in close touch with the victim; a woman who is reluctant to report another beating to police can confide in a shelter counselor, who will tell a group leader, who may confront the man in the following week's session.

Nearly half of all batterers have problems with substance abuse, especially alcohol, and D.A.I.P. group leaders often have difficulty persuading men not to blame their violence on their addictions. John J., 35, a Duluth man who once beat a marine senseless with a lug wrench, raped the women he dated and kicked the first of four wives when she was pregnant, thought he'd become violence-free after going through the D.A.I.P. batterers' program and Alcoholics Anonymous. One night several years later, though sober, he shoved his third fiancée so hard that she went flying over a coffee table. "Men have more courage when we're drunk," he says, teary-eyed with shame, during an interview. "But the bottle didn't put the violence there in the first place."

Why do men hit women? "Men batter because it works," says Richard J. Gelles, director of the Family Violence Research Program at the University of Rhode Island. "They can not only hurt a woman but break down her sense of self-worth and belief that she can do anything about it."

Some programs use a therapeutic approach, exploring family history. Others employ a model inspired by the psychologist Lenore Walker's "cycle of violence" theory of battering: the man goes through a slow buildup of tension, explodes at his partner and begs her forgiveness during a honeymoon period.

But Pence criticizes both approaches for failing to confront a batterer's hatred of women, as well as his desire to dominate them. Duluth's 26-week program is divided in two sections. The first, usually run by a mental-health center, emphasizes more traditional counseling that tries to teach men to walk away from their anger. The second, run by D.A.I.P., provokes men to face up to their abuse and to identify the social and cultural forces underlying it. (In 1990, Duluth sent 350

men through its program. By comparison, Victim Services in New York City sent 300.)

Bill, 30, admits that he once believed "you were allowed to hit a woman if you were married–the license was for possession." A sense of entitlement pervades the men's groups: when Schroyer asked one man why he cut telephone cords in his house, the man shouted, "Why should she talk on something I paid for?"

Duluth batterers don't necessarily have to slap, punch, choke, kick with steel-toed boots or crush empty beer cans against a cheekbone to keep their partners terrified. During arguments, abusers will floor the gas pedal, clean hunting rifles or sharpen knives at the kitchen table, smash dishes and television sets, call her office very two minutes and hang up. One man smeared a peanut butter and jelly sandwich in his wife's hair. One woman's ex-husband wrote her phone number in the men's rooms of Duluth's seediest bars, with an invitation to call for a good time.

Then there are the outright threats. If she leaves him, he'll tell child-welfare services that she's a neglectful mother. Or he'll kill her. Or himself.

Schroyer and the other group leaders stress that when the violence does erupt, contrary to a batterer's favorite excuse, he has not lost control. "You chose the time, the place, the reason, how much force you'd use," Schroyer tells them. "She didn't."

But convincing men that they are better off without that control is perhaps the most challenging impediment to treatment. One night a batterer huffily asked, "Why should men want to change when we got it all already?"

Brenda Erickson, one of the Duluth women who appeared before Judge Campbell, had been thinking about leaving her husband, Mike, for a long time. Mike had always told her that she was fat, ugly and stupid, and besides, no man would want a woman with three children, so she'd better stay with him. Brenda never thought she was a battered woman, because Mike had never punched her.

The social psychologist Julie Blackman points out that a byproduct of the attention given to the Lisa Steinberg tragedy several years ago is that the public now mistakenly associates battered women with the smashed, deformed face of Hedda Nussbaum. Susan Schechter finds that many abused women who are not as bloodied as the character portrayed by Farrah Fawcett in "The Burning Bed" do not believe they deserve aid. "Many battered women see themselves as strong, as keeping together a family, in spite of what's going on," Schechter says.

Mike often assured Brenda that if he went to jail, it wouldn't be for wife-beating–it would be for her murder. When he was angry, he would shatter knickknacks or punch a hole in the wall right next to her head. Brenda is 5 foot 1 and Mike is 6 foot 3. "Imagine an 18-

wheeler colliding with a Volkswagen," she says. "So I learned how to say 'yes' to him, to defuse situations."

Over the eight years of their marriage, the family subsisted on welfare and Mike's occasional earnings as a freelance mechanic. In the final years, Brenda cooked in a restaurant, worked as an aide for Head Start and cared for their three sons. According to Brenda, Mike chose not to seek a full-time job in order

---

Women stay in abusive relationships too long for many reasons.

---

to keep an eye on her. She couldn't even go to the grocery store alone.

Frequently, he raped her. "He'd rent pornographic films and force me to imitate them," Brenda says. The sex was often rough and humiliating. "He thought that if we had sex a lot I wouldn't leave him." Mike acknowledges that there was "mental abuse" in their marriage, but not what he'd call rape. "I'm oversexed, but there's nothing wrong with that."

A friend at work, sensing Brenda's distress, gave her the number of the Women's Coalition shelter. Brenda would call anonymously, trying to figure out if she could possibly escape. Finally, she just picked a date: Feb. 9, 1988.

That morning, she told Mike she was taking the kids to school. Once there, a shelter official picked them up. When Brenda walked into the handsome Victorian house filled with women and children, she felt an overwhelming sense of relief.

Women stay in abusive relationships too long for many reasons. Susan Schechter says it can take years before physical abuse starts, even longer for a woman to learn "not to blame herself or his lousy childhood for his violence." Brenda refused for years to believe her marriage wasn't working. Another Duluth woman, who endured a decade of stitches and plaster casts, sobbed, "We did have some wonderful times, and he was my entire world."

Some women stay because they may have reasonable expectations that they will die leaving. As many as three-quarters of the domestic assaults reported to authorities take place after the woman has left.

Some women stay because they can't afford to leave—or because, long since alienated from friends and family, they have no place to go. There are about 1,200 shelters scattered across the country, many reporting that they must turn away three out of every four women who ask for help. Duluth's shelter can house up to 30 women and children; the shelter in Las Vegas, Nev. (population: 850,000), has only 27 beds.

But when Brenda finally made the decision to leave, she had more options than most battered women in the country—the full resources of the shelter and D.A.I.P. were available to her. Shelter staff members screened her phone calls, and Pence spoke with Mike on Brenda's behalf; she joined a women's support group, and a counselor led her through the first of what would be many appearances before Judge Campbell in family court. But things did not go smoothly.

Mike did manage to complete the batterers' group program and made several passes through substance-abuse treatment. Yet, even though Brenda had filed for three separate orders of protection, the net effect was negligible: she claims to have suffered harassing phone calls, slashed tires and broken car windows. D.A.I.P. officials pressed police to investigate, but because the officers never caught Mike on the premises, he was never arrested.

After the divorce was granted, they continued to battle over visiting the children. Brenda had ultimately left Mike because of her children—the eldest, then in kindergarten, was already angry and traumatized. Research indicates that children exposed to family violence are 10 times as likely to be abused or abusive in adult relationships.

Two years ago, D.A.I.P. opened a visitation center at the Y.W.C.A. for noncustodial parents whom the court has granted supervised time with their children. The entrances and exits are such that neither parent has to see the other, and, under the watchful gaze of a D.A.I.P. staff member, parent and children have the run of two large living rooms, a small kitchen and a roomful of toys. This is where Brenda's boys have been seeing their father and his new wife.

Brenda Erickson is now an honor student at the University of Minnesota in Duluth, majoring in family life education. "Mike has some good qualities," she allows, "but this sure as hell beats walking around on eggshells. The boys and I are so much more relaxed and able to love each other. And I found a strength I never knew I had."

On a Friday night last fall, Mike Erickson was finally arrested for domestic assault and violently resisting arrest. The victim was not Brenda, however, but his new wife, Deborah, and her teen-age son. In the ensuing brawl, it took four officers and a can of Mace to get him into the squad car, as he howled: "I wasn't domesticating with her. I was drinking!" He pled guilty to all charges and served 36 days on a work farm. Mike is now enrolled in the D.A.I.P. program. "That night I pushed my stepson and backhanded my wife because she pulled the phone out and I got irritated," he says. "It's hard for me to shut up when I get going."

But Deborah Erickson refused to file charges against Mike or even to speak to a volunteer from the Women's Coalition. She has been in abusive relationships before, but she's certain this marriage is different. "I told the cops, 'Hey, it happened, but it's not happening again.'"

Those who are in a position to help battered women tend to deny the gravity of the problem. "Doctors still believe the falling-down-stairs stories, and clergy still tell women to pray and go to a marriage counselor," says Anne Menard of the Connecticut Coalition Against Domestic Violence.

But Congress has begun to act. In 1990, it passed a resolution, adapted by 30 states, urging that domestic violence by a parent be a presumption against child custody. The most dramatic policy reform, however, may be Senator Joseph R. Biden Jr.'s pending Violence Against Women Act, which proposes, among other things, to stiffen penalties for domestic abusers.

But while the use of the criminal-justice system to quash domestic violence has gained currency around the country, Ellen Pence's advice to women in battering relationships is simply this: leave. Leave because even the best of programs, even Duluth's, cannot insure that a violent man will change his ways.

The Reasonable Woman

Kim Lane Scheppele

In the intense tribalism of our times, empathy seems in short supply, but also in little demand. Newly or partially empowered groups use their small and fragile power to say, "You can't understand me unless you're *like* me, where "like" means of a similar gender or race or other social grouping now acutely aware of its own historical disempowerment. "You can't understand me" sounds like an accusation, and also a warning not to try.

But it is simply not true that people can't understand those whose experiences and values are very different from their own. It isn't easy; it requires work; it takes a certain humility to learn how much of one's own way of seeing the world is dependent on features of oneself that one cannot easily imagine away. But it is possible, with concentrated effort, much willingness to listen to others, and genuine good faith. So perhaps "you can't understand me" shouldn't be understood as a statement about what's possible. Instead it might be heard as a demand that statements about me must be heard in my voice, or at least in the voice of someone who shares my experience and my point of view. "You can't understand me" is a way of saying that you can't flatten my perspective into your perspective on the world. It is a call to stop the effort to find the "view from nowhere" or the apparently point-of-viewless point of view. It is an attack on the conception of objectivity that sees one unitary and coherent point of view as privileged over all the others.

A serious problem for the legitimacy of public institutions occurs when truths become multiple, when stories proliferate in incommensurable versions, when different people with different ways of seeing become empowered to be heard in public debate. The problem is particularly evident in the law. How do courts continue to figure out "what happened" for the purposes of finding a resolution in disputes when the ideal in a multicultural society is no longer a single unassailable truth, but plural and various truths?

We can see the problem of multiple truths most clearly by focusing on consent. Consent is crucial to the legal status of many actions. Consent transforms actions from criminal to legal. For example, a surgical operation is converted from a severe battery to a legitimate procedure by the consent of the patient. Taking someone's car is converted from theft to borrowing by the consent of the owner. Determining whether relevant people have consented is, then, a crucial part of judging actions to be legal. And where disputants diverge over how consent is to be imagined, disputants will also diverge over basic issues of legitimacy.

People with different backgrounds and experiences have different experiences of consent. Consent is often associated with choice, but a great deal of the legitimating force of choice depends on how the choices are seen. Most people would agree that the gunman who approaches and says "Your money or your life" is giving you a choice, but it's hard to say that you consented if you hand over your wallet. That's because it is widely recognized that almost everyone would see the "life" option as an unattractive choice. Handing over money feels, understandably, compelled, not chosen. But assume that the choice is between living with someone who beats you or moving out. Moving out sounds like the clear choice—unless you have no money,

From *LSAmagazine,* Spring 1993, pp. 12-16, College of Literature, Science, and the Arts, University of Michigan. Abridged from *The Responsive Community, Rights and Responsibilities,* Vol. 1, Issue 4, 1991. *The Responsive Community,* 2020 Pennsylvania Avenue, NW, Suite 282, Washington, DC 20006. Reprinted by permission.

little chance of supporting yourself, and no independent support system to help you through the transition—and you believe that if you leave, the person you're living with will track you down and beat you worse than before. Men who are self-supporting and physically strong will tend to see that choice differently from women who are not. And if judges are men who assume their partial views represent the only truth, they may see women as having consented to stay, because, after all, the women chose to do so when they could have done otherwise. A judge who decides this way has no empathic imagination. He fails to see the choice as someone else might. He assumes that there is some single right answer in the choice, a right answer whose very claim to universality disguises the partiality of his own perspective. And with this totalizing point of view, his version of consent wins out over the real experience of feeling that one has no choice.

Rape is an area of law in which consent is crucial. If an accused rapist can demonstrate that the victim consented, sex is no longer rape. Many accused rapists use the consent defense at trial, forcing the focus of the trial onto the actions of the victim, who is almost always (and in some states has to be by statute) a woman. Though consent is defense to other crimes as well—theft, for example, or battery—consent poses a particular problem in rape cases, because consent to sex is often thought to be more problematic than consent to being beaten or having one's possessions taken. Sex, after all, is almost always emotionally complicated, and there may well be reasons for appearing to consent at the time and appearing not to have consented later. At least, that's what those who judge often think. This, of course, already tells us something crucial about consent—whether it will be believed in a particular context depends on its plausibility, judged against a set of implicit background standards. But those background standards may not always be shared by all those concerned, particularly the victims. Women have experiences of the world that are not the same as men's, especially when it comes to sex. And given the different perceptions of what is going on, women's views about consent in sex differ systematically from men's.

Let's look at one example. In *Rusk v. State*, a Maryland case, Eddie Rusk was convicted by a jury of raping a woman, referred to in the opinions only as Pat, whom he had met at a singles bar.

> Being female or a person of color in this society is relevant to one's social point of view, and the law would better serve everyone if it recognized that the melting pot no longer melts all points of view into one, if it ever did.

When she said she was leaving, shortly after meeting him, Rusk asked Pat to drive him home. She agreed, drove him to his apartment in a part of the city that she didn't know, and refused his several invitations to come in. He took the car keys from the ignition and invited her in again. At the trial, Pat said that she was stranded in a strange and dangerous part of Baltimore. She said she believed it was unsafe to try to escape on foot and that she hoped to be able to convince Rusk to give back her car keys and to let her go. She followed him into his room and made no attempt to leave, even when he went down the hall to go to the bathroom. She asked for her car keys back and, when he refused, begged to be able to leave with her car. Rusk repeatedly said she couldn't, but he had no weapon and did not use overwhelming physical force. Rusk pulled her onto the bed and undressed her. Pat started to cry and Rusk put his hands on her throat and "started lightly to choke" her. She then asked, "If I do what you want, will you let me go without killing me?" and he answered yes. She performed oral sex, and then they had sexual intercourse, after which he gave her back the car keys and said she could leave. Charged with rape, Rusk claimed she had consented to sex with him. The appeals courts were called upon to determine whether her actions counted as consent.

This is where the 20 judges who heard the case on appeal (13 in the Court of Special Appeals, the intermediate appeals court in Maryland, and 7 in the Court of Appeals, the state supreme court) split all over the map. In the Court of Special Appeals, in 1979, the vote went 8–5 in favor of reversing the conviction, and in the Court of Appeals, in 1981, the vote was 4–3 in favor of reinstatement. The judges who wanted to overturn the conviction said that Rusk had not used enough force to overcome Pat's resistance if she had really meant not to consent; those who wanted to uphold the conviction said that Pat was afraid enough to make consent implausible.

The judges who found that Pat consented saw her options very differently from the way she reported them. Judge Thompson, for the Court of Special Appeals, noted that she could have sought help or tried to leave without her car. He minimized her reports that she was in a completely strange part of town and was frightened. Justice Cole, dissenting in the Maryland Court of Appeals, stressed that Pat was on an ordinary city street, that she was with a man who did not "grapple with her," and that she *followed* this man (Justice Cole's emphasis) into his apartment knowing what would happen if she did. "She certainly had to realize that they were not going upstairs to play Scrabble," Justice Cole observed.

The judges who found that Pat had *not* consented saw her options at the time more the way Pat said she did. Judge Wilner, dissenting in the Court of Special Appeals, quoted Pat's own words frequently throughout his description of the facts, and emphasized that Rusk's theft of her car keys was equivalent to a threat of force. And Justice Murphy, writing for the Court of Appeals, concluded Pat was "badly frightened . . . unable to think clearly . . . and believ[ed] that she had no other choice in the circumstances."

What these four opinions disagree about is precisely how to see her options and how she might have "reasonably" considered them. But, where the person whose consent is being constructed sees the world very differently from the judges, should judges be using universal (i.e., apparently point-of-viewless) standards that represent how a "reasonable man" would have acted at the time? Or should they consider how Pat herself, or a reasonable person with Pat's background, should have acted?

Good-faith efforts to understand the multiplicity of perspectives and the serious incommensurability of many points of view should make some difference here. Consent matters precisely because the consenter's point of view is crucial to the legitimacy of the actions she takes. To substitute what some hypothetical consenter unlike the particular person whose consent is being sought *would have* done in that circumstance undermines the very idea that makes consent a moral force—respect for the person's self-believed descriptions are checked not against the world that the individual sees but against a world that she does not see because she has a different socially grounded perspective.

In a number of areas of the law, courts already find ways to incorporate the distinctive social knowledge of socially diverse actors. In tort cases, for example, courts adopt some formulation, either explicitly or implicitly, that inquires into what the reasonable man would have done under the circumstances. As tort doctrine has evolved, the unitary reasonable man has multiplied into the reasonably prudent doctor, the reasonable pilot, and the ordinarily careful horse trainer, among other characters recognizable in law. This multiplication of types of persons shows that existing legal doctrine and considerations of fairness do not require that everyone's perceptions be measured against the same social standard of reasonableness. But the law only incompletely recognizes that special knowledge is acquired not only in occupations but also in other sociological categories that give rise to different ways of seeing the world. The few cases that do mention a reasonable woman in tort law do so only for grammatical consistency, because one of the parties happens to be a woman, not because anything different results from noticing the gender of the parties. The reasonable woman is just like the reasonable man, only with a different pronoun.

But the reasonable woman could be a more sociologically powerful construction if we believed that everyone has "expertise" obtained from living a particular life in a particular social environment. Some of that expertise comes from living as a woman or a person of color. The choices each of us makes, and the degree of consent we express in those choices, depend on how our expertise tells us to evaluate the availability and attractiveness of alternatives. Being female or a person of color in this society is relevant to one's social point of view, and the law would better serve everyone if it recognized that the melting pot no longer melts all points of view into one, if indeed it ever did.

Considering a reasonable woman standard with gender-specific content is, in some ways, nothing new, though it is still controversial. In some areas of legal doctrine, women's unique perspectives have already been taken into

> The choices each of us makes, and the degree of consent we express in those choices, depend on how our expertise tells us to evaluate the availability and attractiveness of alternatives.

account in this way, though only quite recently. In sexual harassment cases, a number of courts have said that the point of view of the reasonable woman should be adopted in determining whether men's behavior in the workplace is disruptive enough to qualify as sexual harassment. In *Ellison v. Brady* (1991), for example, the Ninth Circuit Court of Appeals found that any reasonable woman would have found the persistent and threatening "love letters" from her co-worker objectionable, reasoning:

> We adopt the perspective of a reasonable woman primarily because we believe that a sex-blind reasonable person standard tends to be male-biased and tends to systematically ignore the experiences of women. The reasonable woman standard does not establish a higher level of protection for women than men . . . Instead, a gender-conscious examination of sexual harassment enables women to participate in the workplace on an equal footing with men.

The reasonable woman was also decisive in *Robinson v. Jacksonville Shipyards* (Federal District Court, Middle District in Florida, 1991), and in *Yates v. Avco Corp* (6th Circuit, 1987). And it's not only in sexual harassment cases that the reasonable woman makes an appearance. She appears in murder or assault cases where a woman has killed or injured her attacker. In *State v. Wanrow* (1977), the Supreme Court of Washington reversed Yvonne Wanrow's conviction for assault and murder of a man who had allegedly molested her children. The court reversed because the jury had been instructed to consider the woman defendant's actions according to the standard of the reasonable man:

[The jury instruction] not only establishes an objective standard, but through the persistent use of the masculine gender leaves the jury with the impression the objective standard to be applied is that applicable to an altercation between two men. The impression created—that a 5'4" woman with a cast on her leg and using a crutch must, under the law, somehow repel an assault by a 6'2" intoxicated man without employing weapons in her defense, unless the jury finds her determination of the degree of danger to be objectively reasonable—constitutes a separate and distinct misstatement of the law and, in the context of this case, violates the respondent's right to equal protection of the law. The respondent was entitled to have the jury consider her actions in the light of her own perceptions of the situation, including those perceptions which were the product of our nation's 'long and unfortunate history of sex discrimination.'

The "reasonable woman," then, has been accepted by some judges (though rejected by others) when the standard would involve importing a substantive judgment into the law that is different from the judgment of the reasonable man. But the places where the reasonable woman has already won some qualified acceptance in legal doctrine present fewer serious challenges to business-as-usual in the law than the rape cases do. In sexual harassment complaints, the relevant law is Title VII of the Civil Rights Act of 1964, whose primary purpose is to remedy past discrimination by stopping present and future discrimination. Seeing the harm from the point of view of the class explicitly protected by the statute is not a radical move, particularly given that the litigated complaints are civil cases. In the criminal cases with women defendants, the *mens rea* ("guilty mind") requirement for almost all crimes already focuses inquiry on the point of view of *this particular defendant*. If this particular defendant happened to be a woman, it would stand to reason that her perspective should be given due consideration without radically challenging existing law. Neither the civil cases involving sexual harassment nor the criminal cases involving women defendants contest the point of view already built into the doctrine for other reasons. But the rape cases are different.

Using the reasonable woman standard in rape cases like *Rusk* means asking the court to see the criminal nature of the defendant's conduct as dependent upon the *victim's* point of view. This is a radical departure for the criminal law, which customarily considers the victim to be just another witness at the trial and which privileges the perspective of the defendant through the *mens rea* requirement. But most crimes have as part of their definitions the lack of consent of the victim. For example, as we have seen, theft becomes borrowing if the owner consents, and battery becomes legitimate surgery with the consent of the patient. Usually consent isn't at issue in criminal trials for battery or theft. But in rape cases, consent is used frequently as a defense, and consent in rape has been taken as consent from men's point of view. Eleven of the 20 judges who heard the *Rusk* case adopted this perspective and the conviction was upheld only because the highest court had a slim majority in Pat's favor. Given the overwhelming focus in criminal cases on the defendant's perceptions of events (even if the defendant is a woman, as we have seen), introducing the perspective of the reasonable woman as a victim represents a major change.

The reasonable woman victim is not in the usual cast of characters of rape cases. Instead, the consent of the rape victim is usually assumed to be a flat fact that can be determined by an outsider's assessment of the evidence: Did she kick and scream? Did she try every avenue of escape? Was her fear the sort of fear I (the judge) would have had under the circumstances? Under these questions, the power of legitimation that consent is supposed to bring evaporates. The consent that is found does not respect the potential consenter's perspective. And if consent is to have the moral force assigned to it in liberal moral theory, the consent must not be imposed by someone who does not attempt to understand the potential consenter's point of view.

Does this mean that a search for consent should always be a quest for what *this* particular person thought at *that* particular time, no matter what the reasonableness of the perception? It would be easy, using the sort of perspective I've been encouraging here, to have as many standards as there are potential consenters and to make the legitimacy of actions requiring consent rest on detailed inquiries in individual instances. And that would be the best possible result for women who

> The reasonable woman standard does not require men to guess what is in each woman's mind but it does require men to respect that women have the right to claim difference.

are victims of sexual assault. But there are some claims that defendants can make here that need to be considered as well. Criminal law is a vehicle for the expression of the moral standards of the community. The penalties are harsh and the stigma great for criminal conviction. As a result, criminal prosecutions are more serious for the defendants than ordinary civil trials. To base criminal convictions on potentially idiosyncratic perceptions of victims is unfair to those accused. If a woman says yes while meaning no, for example, we cannot expect the accused rapist to figure out what she means. This is why the reasonable woman standard has something to offer here. Adopting the reasonable woman as a social construct in the law allows women's views to have a strong impact on the outcome of rape trials while simultaneously putting men on notice that they must consider how women's perceptions of sexualized situations may be very different from their own. The reasonable woman standard does not require men to guess what is in each woman's mind, but it does require men to respect that women have the right to claim difference. It requires men to see the world through women's eyes.

For women, politically disadvantaged in the construction of sexuality, gender crucially shapes the world. As we saw in the *Rusk* case, Pat, like most women, learned to fear city streets, to count on the men she knew to protect her from lurking dangers. Women don't sexualize situations as quickly as men do, and so they may be slower to recognize danger in the first place. Pat's choice to go into Rusk's room because she was frightened to walk alone at night was an understandable choice, in

the same way that the choice to stay in a dreadful living situation is understandable when the alternative is a reasonably seen threat of homelessness. Pat said "no" to sex. Rusk tried to override that "no" by limiting her means of escape. Pat decided it was less dangerous to go with Rusk and not fight him off physically than to risk the streets alone at night. The fact that she chose this option doesn't mean that she consented to sex with him. Her "no" meant no. The reasonable man, who does not fear city streets the way a reasonable woman does and who can fight physically with the expectation of success, may have tried to leave or fight. He would have had other options to reinforce what he meant by "no."

Women, people of color, and other politically disadvantaged groups are ill-served by a standardized concept of a reasonable man or an average person or a point-of-viewless point of view. So, the multiplication of standards against which perception might be judged is crucial to deciding whether women or people of color might have in fact consented to the conditions that the law holds them responsible for. And for starters, women in rape cases will see the world differently than men who face similar choices.

The intense tribalism of our time is a sign that conditions are improving for those whose voices have been silenced in the past. Women and people of color are calling for the recognition of multiple truths and many versions to replace the false unity of totalizing standards. We all owe each other a good-faith attempt to understand how people differently situated in the social order may reasonably see the same set of choices differently. In a pluralistic community, empathy is one of our most crucial resources. Extending the standard of the reasonable woman would be one good way to bring empathy to the law.

Kim Scheppele is associate professor of political science and public policy in LS&A, associate research scientist in the Institute for Public Policy Studies, and adjunct associate professor of law in the Law School. She is the author of Legal Secrets: Equality and Efficiency in the Common Law, *and she is working on two books,* Nothing But the Truth: Fact, Fiction and Narrative in Law *and* Abortion, Contention and Hypocrisy.

INCEST

A Chilling Report

Do you want to know what incest is? What it really is? No euphemisms, evasions, excuses, or intellections? Are your sure? Then read this. Every word of it is true. The horror is unimaginable. But in the end, at least you will know.

Heidi Vanderbilt

Heidi Vanderbilt is an award-winning writer who lives in New England.

Where there is no last name identifying details have been changed.

The Children

I am five. The July sun shines on my shoulders. I am wearing a dress I have never seen before, one I don't remember putting on. The door opens and a little girl runs to me her face delighted. I have never seen her before. I am completely terrified and try to hide behind my astonished and irritated mother.

CASE STUDIES

Rikki and Nick's parents were members of a satanic cult. The children were sexually abused and tortured. When the parents left the cult, they got their children into therapy. Rikki is three. Nick is four. Both have full-blown multiple personality disorders.

Lauren was five when she told her mother that a family friend who often took care of her had "fooled" with her. Her mother was relieved when the doctors found no physical evidence of sexual abuse. She wondered if her daughter's story was true. Then Lauren told her mother that the friend had taken photos of her. The photos were found; they revealed that Lauren had been raped and sodomized over a period of more than a year.

Sharon's mother masturbated her to sleep from the time she was born. As Sharon grew older, her mother would sometimes stare at her for long periods. "I love you too much," she would repeat, over and over. Now 44, Sharon says, "I still don't know where my mother ends and I begin."

"I take responsibility for what happened," she says. "I bought into it. I know my mother shouldn't have done it, but I'm responsible, too."

"How could you be responsible for something that began when you were only a baby?" a friend asks.

"I just am," she insists.

Sharon has been in Freudian analysis for 15 years.

"But she's your best friend!" my mother says, and tells me that I played at the girl's house just yesterday. I don't remember. When my mother tells me her name, I've never heard it before.

Other children arrive. I remember some of them, but from long ago. They're older now. They've grown. Some have lost their teeth.

I pretend that everything is all right.

At night I lie awake as I have for years, listening. I hear footsteps coming down the hall. I hold my breath. I watch the edge of the door to my bedroom. I watch for the hand that will push it open. If it is my mother's hand or my father's, I am all right. For now. If it is the hand of the woman who lives with us and sticks things into me, I move out of my body. I disappear into a painting on the wall, into my alarm clock with its rocking Gene Autry figure, into imaginary landscapes. Usually I come back when the woman leaves. But not always.

I am eight. I have spoken French from the time I was three. I attended a French kindergarten, and now the Lycée Français. I have just spent the summer in France. My French is fluent when we leave Nice. Four days later, after my return to the woman who hurts me, I can no longer understand or speak a single word of French. Sitting at my gouged wooden desk, my classmates sniggering around me, I feel terrified and ashamed, certain that whatever is wrong is my fault.

She told me she would cut out my tongue. She told me I would forget. I remember how tall she was, how she wore her hair pulled back with wisps breaking loose at the temples. I knew then that I would never forget.

I am 40. There are things I have always remembered, things I have forgotten, things that exist in shadows only, that slip away when I try to think about them. I can't remember all that she did that sent me "away." Nor do I know what I was doing while I was "away." I only know that these episodes began with periods of abuse so frightening, painful, and humiliating that I left my body and parts of my mind.

I rarely talk about what happened to me. I have never discussed the details with my parents, my husband, or anyone else. Whenever I think of telling, she returns in my dreams.

I dream that I am a child and she chases me with a sharp knife, catches me, and gouges out my eyes. I dream that I have to protect little children at night, even though I am alone and a child myself. I tuck in the other children and get into my bed. Her arm reaches for me and pulls me down. I dream that I run for help, enter a phone booth, hear a dial tone. When I reach up I see the phone has been torn from the wall. I dream of animals skinned alive while I scream.

Sometimes when I sleep I stop breathing and can't make myself start until I wake gasping, my fingers blue.

Incest can happen to anyone: to rich and to poor; to whites, blacks, Asians, Native Americans, Jews, Christians, and Buddhists. It happens to girls and to boys, to the gifted and to the disabled. It happens to children whose parents neglect them, and those—like me—whose parents love and care for them.

What exactly is incest? The definition that I use in this article is: any sexual abuse of a child by a relative or other person in a position of trust and authority over the child. It is the violation of the child where he or she lives—literally and metaphorically. A child molested by a stranger can run home for help and comfort. A victim of incest cannot.

Versions of this definition are widely used outside the courtroom by therapists and researchers. In court, incest definitions vary from state to state. In many states, the law requires that for incest to have taken place, vaginal penetration must be proved. So if a father rapes his child anally or orally he may be guilty of child sexual abuse but may not, legally, be guilty of incest.

I believe that if incest is to be understood and fought effectively, it is imperative that the definition commonly held among therapists and researchers—the definition I have given here—be generally accepted by the courts and public. I am not alone in this belief. As therapist E. Sue Bloom, for one, writes in *Secret Survivors: Uncovering Incest and Its Aftereffects in Women:* "If we are to understand incest, we must look not at the blood bond, but at the emotional bond between the victim and the perpetrator. . . . The important criterion is whether there is a real relationship in the experience of the child."

"The crucial psychosocial dynamic is the *familial* relationship between the incest participants," adds Suzanne M. Sgroi, M.D., director of the Saint Joseph College's Institute for Child Sexual Abuse Intervention in West Hartford, Connecticut, writing in the *Handbook of Clinical Intervention in Child Sexual Abuse.* "The presence or absence of a blood relationship between incest participants is of far less significance than the kinship roles they occupy."

Incest happens between father and daughter, father and son, mother and daughter, mother and son. It also happens between stepparents and stepchildren, between grandparents and grandchildren, between aunts and uncles and their nieces and nephews. It can also happen by proxy, when live-in help abuses or a parent's lover is the abuser; though there is no blood or legal relationship, the child is betrayed and violated within the context of family.

No one knows how many incest victims there are. No definitive random studies on incest involving a cross section of respondents have been undertaken. No accurate collection systems for gathering information exist. The statistics change depending on a number of variables: the population surveyed, the bias of the researcher, the sensitivity of the questions, and the definition of incest used. This is an area "where each question becomes a dispute and every answer an insult," writes Roland Summit, M.D., a professor of psychiatry at Harbor-UCLA Medical Center in Torrance, California, in his introduction to *Sexual Abuse of Young Children.* "The expert in child sexual abuse today may be an ignoramus tomorrow."

As recently as the early '70s, experts in the psychiatric community stated that there were only 1 to 5 cases of incest per one million people. When I began work on this article, I thought that maybe one person in a hundred was an incest victim. How wrong I was. Sometimes called "rape by extortion," incest is about betrayal of trust, and it accounts for most child sexual abuse by far. To be specific:

In 1977, Diana E. H. Russell, Ph.D., professor emeritus at Mills College in Oakland, California, and author of *The Secret Trauma: Incest in the Lives of Girls and Women* and *Sexual Exploitation: Rape, Child Sexual Abuse and Workplace Harassment,* questioned 930 San Francisco women and found that 38 percent had been sexually abused by the time they had reached the age of 18. She further found that of those women who were victims, 89 percent were abused by relatives or family acquaintances. Using Russell's figures as my guide—they are widely cited by other authorities in the field and have been duplicated in other studies—the estimate of the incidence of incest that I came up with is one in three; which is to say that incest happens to about one person in three before the age of 18.

Incestuous acts range from voyeurism and exhibitionism to masturbation, to rape and sodomy, to bestiality, to ritualized torture in cults. Incest may or may not include penetration, may or may not be violent. It may happen only once or continue for decades. It usually exists in secret, but not always.

Kim Shaffir was four and a half years old when her divorced mother remarried. Her stepfather, John Hairsine, showed Kim pornographic photographs and read aloud to her from pornographic novels. He took Polaroids of himself and Kim's mother having sex and showed Kim the pictures. He arranged for her to watch him and her mother having intercourse; he told her when they would be doing it and left the door open. Hairsine kept Kim quiet with the threat that if she told anyone, her mother would send her away.

From exhibitionism and voyeurism, Hairsine moved on to fondling. He made Kim perform oral sex on him. Then he forced her to have anal sex. As he had photographed himself with her mother, he now photographed himself with Kim.

When Kim was 13 her mother discovered the blurred backings of the Polaroid pictures of her husband and Kim. She broke the camera as a symbolic statement. "We're going to put it all behind us," she announced. But she was wrong.

Hairsine made peepholes throughout their Maryland house so he could spy on Kim. He drilled through the bathroom door. Kim repeatedly stuffed the hole with soap and toilet paper, which he would remove and she would replace. For three years she tried to avoid showering when her mother was out of the house.

Every morning, under the guise of waking

her for school, Hairsine entered her room and masturbated in her presence. Kim, now 30 and living in Washington, D.C., says, "That's how I'd wake up, to him coming into a dish towel as he stood by my bed."

One reason for the imprecise nature of the incest statistics is that when children try to tell, they aren't believed. Another is that many victims don't recognize certain behaviors as abusive. My parents would never have let anyone abuse me—if they had known. They didn't know because I didn't know to tell them.

Small children understand very little about sex. Even kids who use "dirty" words often don't understand what those words mean. And as little as they know about normal sex, they know less about deviant sex. They simply trust that whatever happens to them at the hands of those who take care of them is supposed to happen. Children know that adults have absolute power over them, and even in the face of the most awful abuse, they will obey.

The victim who does tell is almost always asked: Why didn't you tell sooner? The answers are:

I didn't know anything was wrong.
I didn't know it was illegal.
I didn't know who to tell.
I did tell and no one believed me.
I was ashamed.
I was scared.

The abuser keeps the incest secret through threats:

If you tell, I will kill you.
If you tell, you'll be sent away.
If you tell, I'll kill your little sister.
If you tell, I'll molest your little brother.
If you tell, I'll kill your dog.
If you tell, it will kill your mother.
If you tell, no one will believe you.
If you tell, then you will go to the insane asylum.
If you tell, I'll go to jail and you'll starve.
If you tell, they'll give you to someone who will really hurt you.
If you tell, you'll go to hell.
If you tell, I won't love you anymore.

Many abusers make good on their threats, but most don't need to. "Small creatures deal with overwhelming threat by freezing, pretending to be asleep, and playing possum," says Dr. Roland Summit, the Harbor-UCLA Medical Center psychiatrist who, in a paper titled "The Child Sexual Abuse Accommodation Syndrome," sets forth a widely accepted explanation of how children behave when molested.

The classic paradigm for an incestuous union is between an older male (father or stepfather or grandfather or uncle) and a younger female. The male is pictured as seduced by a conniving and sexually precocious child who wants sex, power, and presents. Or he is seen as a snaggletoothed tree dweller with an IQ below freezing who rapes his daughter because she is female, his, and nearer to hand than a cow. Yet Massachusetts therapist Mike Lew, author of *Victims No Longer: Men Recovering from Incest and Other Sexual Child Abuse*, told me that as many as 50 percent of victims may be boys. As therapist Karin C. Meiselman, Ph.D., writes in *Resolving the Trauma of Incest*, "The fact that many males are abused as children and adolescents is only beginning to receive adequate professional attention."

Difficult as it is for girls to talk about their abuse, it is even harder for boys. Boys are taught that they must be strong and self-reliant. For a boy to report that he was abused, he must admit weakness and victimization. If he was molested by a male, he will fear that this has made him homosexual.

Then, too, many boys simply don't know they have been abused. Deborah Tannen, Ph.D., professor of linguistics at Georgetown University and author most recently of *You Just Don't Understand: Women and Men in Conversation*, suggests that girls and boys are raised in different cultures. The world expects one set of behaviors and attitudes from girls and another, quite different set from boys.

We teach girls to avoid sex, to wait, and to protect themselves. We teach them that men are not allowed to do certain things to them. But we teach boys that any sex—any heterosexual sex—is good, the earlier the better. We tell them they "scored," they "got lucky." But consider the impact when a boy "gets lucky" with his mother.

"My first really clear memory," says Michael Smith, 30, "is of my mother performing oral sex on me. I was seven. My parents would make me watch them have sex before or after my mother had oral sex with me."

Ralph Smith, the family patriarch, is now 65 years old. His wife, Betty, is 58. They are gray-haired, churchgoing, God-fearing people whose eight children range in age from 20 to 40. The Smiths say they tried to give their kids a good childhood.

"What happened to me was bad," says Michael, "but it was nothing compared to what happened to Lisa." Lisa is Michael's sister. Her earliest memory is of being five and her father fondling her and performing oral sex on her. She told her mother. "I was in the bathtub when I told her," Lisa says. "She slapped me around. She said, 'You're dirty. Don't ever say that again.' "

Lisa's parents had sex in front of her, and when she turned 12 her father had intercourse with her—a pattern he continued until she turned 23 and left home. "I didn't like it," she says. "But he said it was right. He said it even said in the Bible that it was okay to have sex with your children and sex with your parents. He quoted Job. I begged my mother not to leave me alone with him anymore. She said, 'I know you love him.' I asked her to help me, but she wouldn't."

Lisa's sister Michelle slept in a room next to Lisa's. She would hear her father go into Lisa's bedroom at night. "I would hear Lisa crying and screaming and telling him no," Michelle recalls.

Ralph and Betty Smith made Michael and Lisa perform oral sex on each other while they watched and gave instructions. "They said they were teaching us about sex," Michael says. "They were teaching us how to be good mates when we grew up, how to keep a mate satisfied. I would know how to please a woman. I could stay married."

Ralph and Betty kept the children silent by beating them and threatening to kill them and their brothers and sisters. Ralph Smith regularly held a gun to Lisa's head while he had intercourse with her.

Lisa believed that she and Michael were the only ones being molested. She believed that her being abused was protecting her younger siblings. "Until Michelle came and told me she was also being molested," Lisa says, "I thought I had protected them. My whole goal was to protect them. When I found out they had all been abused . . . " Her voice trails off. "We were afraid of our parents and the outside world. The very few people we tried to tell didn't believe us or only believed a little, not enough to do anything."

"I even told a priest once," Michael says. "He gave me a bunch of leaflets and told me to go home and work it out with my family."

Abused children assume that they are responsible for the abuse, believing they brought it on themselves. One man said to his 13-year-old victim, "I'm sorry this had to happen to you, but you're just too beautiful." Some victims feel guilty because they accepted presents or felt pleasure. Victims who experience orgasms while being molested suffer excruciating guilt and conflict.

2. VICTIMOLOGY

While there have been articles by pedophiles arguing that incest is good and natural and that its prohibition violates the rights of children, psychiatrist Judith Lewis Herman, M.D., writes in her pioneering book, *Father-Daughter Incest*, that the actual sexual encounter, whether brutal or tender, painful or pleasurable, "is always, inevitably, destructive to the child." And Maryland psychotherapist Christine A. Courtois, Ph.D., author of *Healing the Incest Wound: Adult Survivors in Therapy*, is firm in her belief that incest "poses a serious mental-health risk for a substantial number of victims."

Mariann's father began taking her into his shower when she was five. He washed her and taught her to wash him. He took her into his bed for snuggling, which turned into fondling. He taught her to masturbate him and made her perform oral sex on him. When she was ten he forced her to have vaginal and anal intercourse.

Mariann's father told her he was teaching her about sex. He said he was teaching her to control her sexual feelings so she wouldn't get swept away. He told her that if she was ever with a boy and got sexually aroused, she was to come to him and he would "help" her.

When Mariann's mother caught her husband fondling their daughter, she called Mariann a whore and accused her of trying to seduce her father. Yet when Mariann's father got a job in another state that required him to move early one spring, her mother stayed behind until summer but insisted that Mariann go with him.

As Mariann grew older her father experienced periods of impotence. When he could no longer manage penetration, he masturbated between his daughter's breasts, ejaculated onto her chest, and rubbed his semen over her.

"There was no escaping it, no safety," Mariann remembers. "I started to feel crazy. I wanted to be crazy. I remember thinking, I want to take LSD and go crazy so they'll lock me up and I can stay there for the rest of my life." At 17, Mariann cut her wrists. The wounds were superficial, but she bled into her sheets all night and came down to breakfast with Band-Aids lined up along her arms. No one asked what had happened.

In spite of her objections and efforts to avoid her father, he continued to have sex with her, until he died when she was in her 20s. She has been hospitalized several times for severe depression and suicidal impulses. "I was invisible," she says. "That's all I was—a vagina. Nothing else existed."

If incest can lead to suicide, it can also lead to homicide. Witness Tony Baekeland. Tony's mother, Barbara, seduced him when he was in his early teens. She openly boasted of their affair, and Tony talked of it as well. When he became violent in his late teens and early 20s, neither of his parents got him psychiatric help. At 26, Tony stabbed his mother to death in their apartment. He was incarcerated at a facility for the criminally insane. His grandmother rallied friends and family to have him released. It took six years. Once freed, Tony stabbed his grandmother eight times at her apartment in New York. She survived. He was imprisoned on Rikers Island, where he suffocated himself with a plastic bag.

In young children who are victims of incest, the vast array of physical and psychological symptoms suffered include injuries to the mouth, urethra, vagina, and anus; bedwetting and soiling; fear of everyone of the perpetrator's gender; nightmares and/or sleep loss; compulsive masturbation, precocious sexual knowledge, and sexual acting out; running away, suicide attempts, and sexually transmitted diseases. Judge Jeffry H. Gallet of the New York State Family Court, sitting in Manhattan, perhaps best known as the judge who heard the Lisa Steinberg case, told me he had once seen a baby with pelvic inflammatory disease so severe that as an adult she will never be able to conceive. And as is well known to health workers and court officials, not all AIDS babies contract the virus before they are born.

It is not at all unusual for victims to grow up with sexual problems. Some can't touch or be touched. Others become wildly promiscuous. Or act out in other sexual ways. That was the case with my friend Nina, who told me that she had been her "father's mistress."

Nina then went on to defend her father. "I hate it," she said, "when people say, 'Any man who'd do that is sick.' He wasn't sick. Except for the incest my dad was totally reliable and helpful and loving. He was the only loving parent I had. He was my role model when I was growing up. He taught me about morals and gave me all the important lessons of my life. If I have to give up my love for my father, what will I have left? I hate what he did, but I love him."

In what she now understands was an unconscious need to reenact in adulthood her secret, duplicitous life with her father, Nina became a bigamist. She married two men, maintained two households, and simultaneously raised three children—two of them in one house and a stepchild in the other.

Some victims become prostitutes. Others believe that incest forced them into lifelong sexual behaviors that they would not have chosen for themselves, including homosexuality. Victims experience not only guilt, shame, fear, and a broad range of psychosocial disorders. They are unable to trust. They have severe problems maintaining intimate relationships, including those with their children.

Journalist Betsy Peterson, in *Dancing with Daddy: A Childhood Lost and a Life Regained*, describes how incest with her father affected her relationship with her sons. "To know how much I love them is to know what I didn't give them, what they missed and what I missed," she writes. "I use my hands to stuff the sobs back in, to eat the terrible grief . . . because I spent their childhood as I spent my own, trying to protect myself."

Michigan therapist Kathy Evert, author of the autobiographical *When You're Ready: A Woman Healing from Childhood Physical and Sexual Abuse by Her Mother*, recently completed a study of 93 women and 9 men abused by their mothers. She found that almost a fourth of the men and more than 60 percent of the women had eating disorders. "I can't tell you the number of women I've seen who weigh over five hundred pounds," Evert says. One woman told her she ate to get bigger and more powerful than her mother. Another woman in the group weighed more than 600 pounds. "Food was my weapon against her," she said of her mother.

More than 80 percent of the women and all the men in Evert's study had sexual problems as adults that they attributed to the abuse by their mothers. And almost two thirds of the women said they rarely or never went to the doctor or dentist because to be examined was too terrifying for them. Thus they are unable to avail themselves of the diagnostic benefits of modern medicine, such as pelvic exams, PAP smears, breast examinations, and mammography.

Some victims are unable to feel physical pain. Some self-mutilate—they burn or cut themselves. Mariann told me that the impulse to cut herself is almost constant and almost uncontrollable. "You get to feeling like your body is full of something rotten," she says. "If you can make an opening, somehow the pressure will be relieved and everything will come out."

Dr. Roland Summit says that a victim of incest "will tend to blame his or her own body for causing the abuse." Some victims may go so far as to seek repeated cosmetic surgeries in an attempt to repair physically the damage that was done to them psychologically, according to a 1990 paper written by Elizabeth Morgan, M.D., a plastic surgeon, and Mary L. Froning, who holds a doctorate in psychology. (Dr. Morgan herself had made headlines in the late '80s, when she sent her daughter into hiding to keep her away from the father that Dr. Morgan alleged had sexually abused the child.) Perpetual plastic surgery, in fact, was to become one of the consequences of incest for Cynthia, who was raped by her father and her brother Eugene but had blocked all memory of the assaults.

Even when her brother sexually abused Cynthia's daughter Kit, Cynthia failed to recall her own assaults. Kit was three and a half when Eugene came to visit and, one afternoon, took her upstairs to the bathroom. When Cynthia discovered them, both were naked. Kit was sitting on the sink and Eugene, standing between her legs, was slowly rocking back and forth. Cynthia threw her brother out of the house. Then she said to the confused child, "This never happened. Understand? Forget it ever happened." By the time Kit was 20, she had only vague memories of childhood trips to the doctor for pelvic examinations and ointments.

Cynthia spent years in psychoanalysis, which didn't seem to help her severe depressions—nor restore her memory of having been sexually assaulted as a child. She kept telling Kit—who didn't understand why she was being told—that incest is so rare that it almost never happens. Kit was in her 30s when she remembered that afternoon in the bathroom with her uncle, and she understood then that he had probably given her a sexually transmitted disease.

Cynthia began to have plastic surgery in her middle 40s. She approached each operation as if it were The Solution, and she was briefly delighted with the results. Within months of each lift, tuck, or suction, however, she began to prepare for the next one. Cynthia didn't remember her own abuse until she was in her late 60s and a grandmother. Now in her middle 70s, she is planning on having a breast reduction as soon as she can find the right surgeon.

Also prevalent among incest victims is post-traumatic stress disorder (PTSD), which I discussed at length with Mary W. Armsworth, Ed.D., the author of dozens of articles on incest and its aftermath, as well as a professor of educational psychology at the University of Houston who teaches one of the few courses in this country on trauma. In the early '80s, Armsworth noticed that incest patients, who "live in a bath of anxiety," had the same PTSD symptoms demonstrated by some Vietnam War veterans and most victims of torture. These symptoms include but are not limited to amnesia, nightmares, and flashbacks. People who have PTSD may "leave their bodies" during the abuse, and they may continue to dissociate for decades after the abuse ends.

(In 1990, *The New York Times* reported that Dennis Charney, M.D., a Yale psychiatrist and director of clinical neuroscience at the National Center for Post-Traumatic Stress Disorder, had found that even one experience of overwhelming terror permanently alters the chemistry of the brain. The longer the duration and the more severe the trauma, the more likely it is that a victim will develop PTSD.)

Most of the dreams told to me by victims of incest involve being chased and stabbed, suffocated, made immobile and voiceless. I myself have a recurring dream of a man who gouges out my eyes and of a woman who rips out my tongue. One woman who has been in long-term therapy owing to years of abuse by her aunt, uncle, and mother told me she dreamed she was at a beautiful, crowded picnic in the woods when she vomited feces. The dream so revolted and shamed her that she had never before told it to anyone, not even her therapist.

Children forced to perform fellatio may grow up to be adults with flashbacks triggered by the smell of Clorox, the feel of melted butter, the sight of toothpaste in their mouth. It is difficult for people who don't have flashbacks to know what one is like. Flashbacks are not memories—memories have distance, are muted and selective. A flashback is a memory without distance. It can bring all the terror of an original event, triggered by something utterly innocuous.

A few months ago I was daydreaming in a friend's kitchen. Her husband, on his way to get the mail, came up quietly behind me, speaking softly to himself. The sensation of being approached (sneaked up on) from the rear by a much larger person who was muttering triggered a flashback—terror so acute that I had to get him away from me with the same urgency I would feel if my shirt were on fire.

Flashbacks can be almost continuous and overwhelming. People who experience them without knowing what causes them can feel crazy. An incest survivor's friend, seeing her run to hide for no apparent reason, might agree that she is. When flashbacks come less frequently, they can be handled almost as fast as they happen. The man who accidentally terrified me never knew it, and I was able to check back in with where I really was and what had really happened almost as quickly as I had checked out.

At the extreme edge of post-traumatic stress disorder lies multiple personality disorder (MPD). It was once thought to be rare and is still disbelieved entirely by some (one of the more noted skeptics is Paul McHugh, M.D., head of psychiatry at Johns Hopkins in Baltimore). But while MPD has been called the UFO of psychiatric disorders, a growing number of cases are being treated.

Researchers believe that children develop multiple personalities as a way of coping with abuse so violent and sadistic that the mind fractures. Each assault is then handled by one or more personalities—"selves," or "alters." Some personalities hold pain, others grief, others rage. Even happiness may be segregated into a discrete "self." The personalities often have no knowledge of one another, so a person with MPD "loses time" when one personality gives way to another, and can "come to" hours or years later without any way of knowing what had happened in the interim.

Brad, a victim of incest who suffers MPD, has learned to recognize a particular feeling that warns him he is about to switch into one of his alters. It happens under stress, he says. "My eyes all of a sudden blur and everything goes to gauze."

I met another sufferer of multiple personalities—a young woman—the day after she fled a cult. My husband and I were guests of the people she ran to, and I sat up with her until early morning because she was afraid to be alone. She had been sexually tortured by her father, brothers, and other cult members for all of her 28 years. As we talked, she switched personalities.

One of her alters was suicidal. Another wanted to call her family and tell them where she was. One was very young, five or six. One knew the dates of satanic holidays and the rituals she had performed on them. At one point during the night she closed her eyes, then opened them again and looked at me with such an evil stare that the hair on my neck stood up. Later, she asked me to put my arms around her and hold her, and I did.

"I was my mother's gift to my father," says Sylvia, yet another woman who suffers multiple personalities. "My dad's a pedophile. He had sex with me until I was seven. My mom's a sociopath. She tried to suffocate me many, many times. She slept with my brother until he was fourteen. She made him her husband, even though my father lived with us. The last time I saw her was twenty years ago. I came by the house where she was living with my brother. He opened the door with a gun in his hand. She had told him to shoot me."

Sylvia and her family lived in a cult that practiced blood sacrifices. When she was three, she was ritualistically raped and sodomized by the cult leaders: Her life was so torturous that she split into alternate selves who carried on when she couldn't.

"The one thing a child learns from sexual abuse," Dr. Summit told me, "is how to be abused." Sexually abused children teach themselves to endure assault. Instead of learning to protect themselves, they learn that they *can't* protect themselves. As adults they can be blind to dangers others would find obvious. They may freeze or go limp when threatened. Someone who has never been abused can say no, can walk or run away, can scream and fight. The incest victim often doesn't know what to do except to wait for the danger to be over.

Child incest victims often become adult rape victims. Almost one quarter of the incest victims Mary W. Armsworth studied went on to be sexually abused by their therapists. Many incest victims as adults choose abusive partners.

Judy, who was abused from infancy by her grandmother, grew up with what she describes as free-floating feelings of shame. "I always felt there was something wrong about me," she says, "something loathsome."

She married a violent man. She believed that when he beat her it was her fault and what she deserved. She believed the beatings were a sign of his love. She stayed with him for more than a decade, leaving him only when she became afraid that her suicidal feelings would overwhelm her and that she would die, leaving her child alone and in danger from his father.

Only later did Judy remember the abuse at the hands of her grandmother. "Every night, I lay awake listening for the sound of her feet on the hall carpet," she now recalls. "I taught myself to leave my body when she came into the room, and to forget. I forgot so well that whole years vanished from my life."

When victims do finally remember their abuse, they are often hushed by friends and told to "put it in the past," to "forgive and forget." But that is precisely what they unwittingly had done so very long ago. In *Incest and Sexuality: A Guide to Understanding and Healing,* psychotherapists Wendy Maltz and Beverly Holman point out that "many women (estimates run as high as 50 percent) do not remember their incestuous experiences until something triggers the memory in adulthood."

"Sometimes my body remembered," says therapist Roz Dutton of Philadelphia, "and sometimes my mind remembered." Roz was an infant when her father began coming into her room at night. He placed one hand on her back and inserted a finger in her anus. He continued doing this until she was two and her baby sister was born. As a teenager and young woman Roz had no conscious memory of these events, though her life had been punctuated with "nudging feelings and disturbing thoughts."

Roz became a therapist with a thriving practice. In working with her clients, she noticed that she had "triggers"—things she heard or saw that sent her into a dissociative state. These things tended to have to do with certain settings but included once the unexpected sight at a professional meeting of a man's hairy hands. Though she questioned herself for years in therapy and in clinical supervision, it wasn't until she was in her early 40s that a chance remark to a colleague about brainwashing—and the colleague's reply that maybe Roz was afraid of brainwashing herself—evoked memories of her father.

Says Roz: "As I talked about myself and my symptoms—eating disorders, depression, inability to protect myself from emotional danger, dissociating emotionally—I began to make clear connections between myself and other abuse victims." Roz's memories were of early infancy. She remembered feelings of dread and terror associated with her father coming into her room. Images came to her of his hands reaching over the slats of her crib, and she experienced body memories from infancy of being held facedown and penetrated.

Just how reliable are memories? Can they be manufactured? How reliable, especially, is the memory of a child? Do leading questions by parents, therapists, or investigators—or the use of anatomically detailed dolls in the questioning of children who may have been abused—create false accusations that lead to false convictions? These were the sort of questions addressed by Gail S. Goodman, a psychologist at the State University of New York, Buffalo, and her colleagues in studies designed to test not only the accuracy of children's recall under stress and over time but also how children respond to leading or strongly suggestive questions devised to bring about false accusations. "If children are indeed as suggestible as some have claimed, then we should be able in our studies to create false reports of abuse," Goodman writes in the chronicle of her studies, published in 1990. Child-abuse charges, after all, have often been dismissed by judges on this ground.

The scenes acted out in one of Goodman's studies were based on actual child-abuse cases. Pairs of four- and seven-year-olds were taken into a dilapidated trailer where they encountered a man who talked to them while using hand puppets. Then he put on a mask. While one of the children observed, he played a game of Simon Says with the other child, during which he and the child touched knees. He photographed the children and played a game where one child tickled him while the other child watched. All of this was videotaped through a one-way mirror so that researchers could have a precise record.

Ten to 12 days later the children were asked the kinds of questions that might lead to a charge of sexual abuse: "He took your clothes off, right?" The seven-year-olds remembered more than the four-year-olds, but whatever both groups remembered they remembered accurately and could not be led into sexualized answers. They became embarrassed by the leading questions, looked surprised, covered their eyes, or—according to Goodman—"asked in disbelief if we would repeat the question."

Goodman and her colleagues used anatomically detailed dolls when questioning the children to see if the dolls would encourage false reports. The study's conclusion on this point: "Whether or not the children were interviewed with anatomically detailed dolls, regular dolls, dolls in view, or no dolls did not influence their responses to the specific or misleading abuse questions."

Because some people believe that a child under stress can't remember accurately and may escalate what really happened in order to match the stress felt, Goodman also studied children who had to go for shots at a medical clinic. "We know of no other scientific studies in which the stress levels were as high as they were for our most stressed children," she writes. The children had to sit in the clinic waiting room and listen to other children scream as they got a needle, knowing they would get one, too.

"These children's reports were completely accurate," Goodman writes. "Not a single error in· free recall was made." The most stressed children remembered best and in the greatest detail. One year later Goodman and her colleagues reinterviewed as many participants as they could find. Even after the children had listened repeatedly to leading questions, most persisted in reporting the incident exactly as it had taken place. "Child abuse involves actions directed against a child's body," Goodman writes. "The violation of trivial expectations would probably not be very memorable. The violation of one's body is."

The Offenders

Jerry "Bingo" Stevens was born in 1910 in New Orleans. He was the third of five children and the first and only boy, hence his nickname. Bingo's father, Joe, was tall, handsome, redheaded, and smart. A supremely successful real estate developer, Joe believed that men should be strong and that women should smell good, keep the house clean, and serve dinner on time. He smoked a cigar and drank quietly and steadily from the moment he came home from the office until he went to bed.

Bingo's mother, Trudy, sometimes took the boy to bed with her to relieve her loneliness. She snuggled him in the dark, trying to block the sounds Joe made on his way into the girls' rooms, and any sounds that came later.

Joe died of cirrhosis of the liver when Bingo was 13. "You're the man of the house now," his mother told him.

By the time Bingo was 30, he had molested not only his sisters but most of their children. Trained from infancy to keep sexual abuse a secret, they never talked about it, even among themselves.

Bingo fell in love and married. The marriage was, apparently, a happy one. He had three daughters of his own, a son, and, eventually, an infant granddaughter. When his wife died he mourned. Then, after an interval, he married again and had a happy second marriage. He owned and operated a successful real estate business. In addition, he was a champion polo player and a member of the Explorers Club.

Bingo died of a heart attack in 1988 while sailing on Lake Pontchartrain with the nine-year-old daughter of his best friend.

He was, as anyone who knew Bingo was quick to say, brilliant, funny, charming, gifted, and successful with women. There was nothing about him that would have identified him as an incestuous father, brother, uncle, cousin, and grandfather. I am one of the children he abused.

After Bingo's death I visited his psychiatrist. "Bingo was one of my favorite patients ever," he told me.

"He molested me," I said.

"He molested everyone," his psychiatrist said. "Why not you?"

Everyone reading this article probably knows—whether aware of it or not—more than one incestuous man or woman. "Offenders don't have horns and a tail," says incest survivor Kim Shaffir. "They look like nice guys. They are not strangers. Everyone tells you to say no to strangers. No one tells you to say no to your family."

In *Broken Boys, Mending Men: Recovery from Childhood Sexual Abuse,* incest survivor Stephen D. Grubman-Black points out that "perpetrators who commit sex crimes are rarely the wild-eyed deviants who stalk little boys. They are as familiar and close by as the same room in your home, or next door, or at a family gathering."

Offenders come from the ranks of doctors, construction workers, hairdressers, building contractors, teachers, landscapers, philosophers, nuclear physicists, and women and men in the armed forces. David Finkelhor, Ph.D., director of the Family Research Laboratory at the University of New Hampshire, and his associate, Linda Meyer Williams, Ph.D., had just concluded *Characteristics of Incest Offenders,* their landmark study of incestuous fathers, when they saw nearly half of their subjects sail off to the Persian Gulf to serve their country.

Some offenders prefer girls, others boys. Some abuse both. Some are interested only in adolescents, or preteens, or toddlers, or newborns. Some, though not most, molest only when they are drinking or depressed or sexually deprived. Some don't abuse until they are adults, but more than half start during their teens.

Like Bingo, some victims go on to become abusers. Seventy percent of the incestuous fathers in the Finkelhor study admitted that they were abused during their own childhood. Judith V. Becker, Ph.D., a professor of psychiatry and psychology at the University of Arizona College of Medicine who has supervised or been involved in the assessment and/or treatment of more than 1,000 abusers, reports that some 40 percent said they had been sexually abused as children. Ruth Mathews, a psychologist who practices with Midway Family Services—a branch of Family Services of Greater St. Paul—has seen a similar number of adolescent offenders, male and female, and has arrived at a similar conclusion.

Mathews went on to tell me about a girl whose father abused her with vibrators after her mother's death. He also brought in other men to abuse her and, with his new wife, had sex in front of her. When she was 12, a city agency, acting on a neighbor's complaint, removed her from her father's house and placed her in a foster home. There she inserted knitting needles into her foster sister's vagina. Asked why, she replied, "For fun." In therapy, asked to draw a picture of herself, she chose a black magic marker and wrote, over and over again, the words *hate, disgust,* and *hell.*

In another instance of children acting out their own abuse on other children (animals are also frequent targets), one little boy was referred for therapy because he tried to mount most of the children in his kindergarten. His parents told the therapist that they made him ride on his father's back while they had intercourse. They said that this excited them.

Although we want to believe that we can spot evil when we confront it, the truth is that nothing about a perpetrator would alert us. Offenders are good at hiding what they do. They are master manipulators, accomplished liars. Those few who aren't get caught; the others molest dozens or even hundreds of children over many decades.

On January 15, 1991, 67-year-old Raymond Lewis, Jr., a retired aerospace designer, son of the founder of the Lewis Pharmacies in Los Angeles, wrote to his middle-aged daughter Donna that he "was the father who begat you; the knight on a white horse who protected you. The guy who had no lover other than your mom till well past his teens. A no smoking, no drinking, no drugs man of restraint."

This man of restraint had raped his five daughters (Donna's first memory of abuse is of her father molesting her while he was taking her to her first day of school in the first grade) and each of the female granddaughters he had access to—five out of seven. In the letter, Lewis wrote: "What is going on in Marlon's twisted mind when he tells of me, deathly ill and post-operative from my prostectomy, licking Nicole's vagina making slurping noises? . . . Why would I *lick* a female? Wrong modus operandi. Wrong age. And a relative! A grandchild! Totally insane! Granddaughters have fathers and no father would permit such a thing to happen. Nor would any mother. Had it happened, hell would have been raised."

But for more than 40 years, hell had not been raised. When Lewis's daughters tried to avoid him, when they cried and told him it hurt, when they threatened to tell on him, he showed them photographs of decapitated murder victims. They endured his rapes in silence, convinced from earliest childhood that they were protecting one another and themselves.

Says DeeDee, now 38: "My father said, 'People who betray their father are like people who betray their country. They should be executed.' He carried a gun in his car, in some black socks. He also kept a gun between the mattress and box spring.

"At first he'd molest me in the bathtub. He'd say, 'I'm the baby. Clean me up. Here's the soap.' Every time before he molested me and my sisters, he'd put his foot on the bed and beat on his chest like King Kong. He penetrated me when I was eight. When I was thirteen he bought me a ring. He told me we could cross out of California and get married, because I was illegitimate. He said exactly the same thing to my daughter when *she* was thirteen. I fooled around with the first boy I could. I got pregnant. I thought, Thank goodness, Dad won't touch me now. For a while, he didn't.

"When my little sister was fifteen she was living alone with Dad. I waited one day until he'd gone out, and went in the house. I found her in a corner, naked, crying. She said, 'I'll be okay. Don't tell. Don't tell.' I thought that if I told, Dad would find out and kill me."

One daughter broke away from Lewis when she was in her 30s and went into therapy. Then, recognizing signs of sexual abuse in her five-year-old niece, Nicole, DeeDee's youngest child, she reported her father to the authorities. In his letter to Donna, Lewis wrote about Nicole: "I fooled with the petite perjurer's pudendum! She said it! Crazy story! Totally insane!" He denied that he had done anything. At first his other daughters defended him. Then they began to talk—16 relatives, including his daughters, told the same story.

Most of his crimes were wiped out by the statute of limitations. He was charged with only four counts of child sexual abuse against his five-year-old granddaughter, and one count of incest—a lesser charge in California, as in most states—against her mother, DeeDee, whom he had coerced into sex when she was a grown woman by promising to leave her daughter alone.

During the trial Lewis's daughters—all professional women, one a college professor—were unable to meet his gaze in the courtroom. It fell to his five-year-old granddaughter

to face him. Although Lewis had threatened that he would kill her if she ever talked about what he had done, the judge ordered her to tell the truth. Seated on the witness stand, shaking and crying, she testified for two days. Lewis denied everything.

Three times the judge asked him if there wasn't anything he was sorry for. "How could they say such terrible things about me?" Lewis asked by way of an answer. "I drove a rusted wreck of a car so that I could give them good cars."

"Isn't there something you think you did to make your family say these things about you?" the judge asked.

"Well, maybe," Lewis replied. "A long time ago."

The five-year-old handed the judge a note she had written. "My granddaddy is a bad man," it read. "I want him to go to jail for two hundred years."

Lewis was convicted of one count of incest against his daughter and three counts of lewd acts, including oral copulation, involving his granddaughter. Expressing the opinion that Raymond Lewis, Jr., represented a threat to all females and that the only place where he would have no access to them was in prison, Superior Court Judge Leslie W. Light sentenced him to the maximum: 12 years and 8 months. But with time off for good behavior, he will probably serve only half his sentence, which means that he will be released from Mule Creek Prison in 6 years.

Says DeeDee: "Until I was twenty-three, I thought I was retarded. He told me I was brain damaged. He told me I was neurotic, manic-depressive, a damaged genius. He thought he was a genius. He said we could have a child together and it would be a genius. Six months before going to jail, he offered me one hundred thousand dollars to bear his child.

"I always hoped he would love me. I just wanted to be his daughter. But now I have my own home, my own checking account. I give sit-down dinners. I feel special. I have knowledge. I am a great mom and I'll be a great grandmom. I love myself, finally. And now I can die without that secret."

Lewis never said he was sorry. In the letter to Donna—one of a stream that he continues to send to his daughters—he wrote: "Loneliness was the reason that I had enslaved myself in my youth to raise kids, and now in the illnesses of old age 14 of my loved ones had abruptly dumped me! *Licked!* How bizarre! A puzzle."

Lack of empathy for the victim is typical of offenders. Every therapist I spoke to commented on this characteristic. All said that for offenders to be rehabilitated they must take responsibility for what they did and develop empathy for their victims. With one possible exception, not one of the offenders I interviewed had done this.

I am talking to Joe. His daughter accused him of sexually abusing her. He pleaded nolo contendere. "But I didn't do it," he says. His sentence: four years probation, with therapy. He has been in treatment for two years. "When I first came to therapy," he says, "I had an attitude that I was being punished for what I didn't do. I had no rights, when you got right into it."

I ask how he feels about the therapy he is required to undergo now. "It's a little inconvenient," he says, "but it helps me in dealing with other people to understand them. I think it would be helpful if a lot of people could go through a program to give them understanding and another outlook, instead of being negative or feeling put down."

I ask him again about his daughter. "I never touched her," he says.

Later I talk with Joe's therapist. "Is he in denial?" I ask.

"Denial," the therapist replies, "is when someone says 'She asked for it' or 'She didn't say no.' Joe's not in denial. He's lying."

I am talking to Chris. His sentence: 8 to 23 months in jail plus 5 years probation, with therapy. He has served 8 months and has been in therapy for 2 years.

"My stepdaughter and I had an affair when she was thirteen," he says. "It lasted a year. I got sick and had to go on dialysis. My wife was working. My stepdaughter was taking care of me. She was like the wife. She never refused me or anything. I really believe she fell in love with me. More than like a father. She met a boy and fell in love. He was into selling cocaine. I didn't want him in the house. I slapped her. She ran to her grandmother and told. She didn't want to take it to court, didn't want me to go to jail. But her grandmother and Women Against Rape stepped in. The grandmother never did like me anyway. They blew it out of proportion and it got all stinky. I did what I could to keep it out of the paper. I could have beat it. I have to come here [to therapy] or I'd have to serve all my time. But if I didn't have to come, I wouldn't."

"Is there a message you would like me to pass on to the people who read this?" I ask him. "Can you tell me something that would help them?"

"Yes!" he replies. "I want you to tell them that if their child gets a boyfriend, don't stand in the way. Don't say no. If I hadn't said no to her, this would never have happened."

I am talking to Bob. He, too, is in court-ordered therapy. Two and a half years ago he was convicted of indecent assault on his girlfriend's 15-year-old daughter. "She was curious about drinking," he says. "Her mother and I decided we would all get together and drink. Better at home, you know?"

The first time, all three drank together. But later the drinking took place when Bob's girlfriend was away. "The first time it went okay," he says. "Then two weeks later, we did it again. I talked her into giving me a back rub. Then I gave her one. I felt her breasts. She didn't say no. I was very attracted. She got up and went upstairs. She got on the phone, but she didn't say 'Stop.' Then she pretended to fall asleep facedown. I fondled her buttocks, pulled her pants down, felt her vagina.

"She was crying. I started to get scared. For myself. I really got scared. I'm trying to figure out how to react. I ask her, 'You want me to leave?' She says to me, 'No. Mom loves you.' She went outside and didn't come back. She called her girlfriend whose mom works at the courthouse. The cops showed up. I was thinking, Oh shit, this is real."

Bob was given a two-year probation, with therapy. (The sentence was light because this was his first offense and the molestation hadn't progressed beyond fondling.) "She would have dropped it," Bob says, "but the courts already had it."

I ask Bob about his therapy. "I have a lot more knowledge now than I had," he replies— "about how many lives I can screw up. Every time she goes through something in the future I'm going to have to ask myself, 'Was I responsible for that?' "

Males who molest children have traditionally been lumped into two broad categories, violent and nonviolent. Included in the latter are offenders who are fixated and regressed. Psychologist A. Nicholas Groth, Ph.D., founder of the Sex Offender Program at the Connecticut Correctional Institution at Somers, describes fixated offenders as adult men who "continue to have an exclusive or nearly exclusive sexual attraction toward children." Regressed offenders are attracted to their peers, but under

stress—illness, loss of job or spouse—turn to children as substitutes.

To refine these categories, Robert A. Nass, Ph.D., a Pennsylvania therapist who treats sex offenders, suggests a third group: quasi-adult sex offenders—men who yearn for a loving relationship with another adult but, because of their own immaturity, are unable to have one and turn to children instead.

In researching *Characteristics of Incest Offenders*, the most detailed study of male perpetrators to date, David Finkelhor and Linda Meyer Williams of the University of New Hampshire questioned 118 incestuous fathers in exacting detail. Based on the men's explanations about why and how the incest started and how the men felt about what they had done, the researchers identified five distinct types of incestuous father: the sexually preoccupied—men who are obsessed about sex and tend to sexualize almost every relationship; adolescent regressives—men who have adolescentlike yearnings for young girls generally and direct them toward their daughter; instrumental self-gratifiers—men who molest their daughter while fantasizing about someone else; the emotionally dependent—men who turn to their daughter for emotional support they feel deprived of from others; and angry retaliators—men who assault their daughter out of rage at her or someone else.

And what of the women who sexually abuse children in their care? What patterns, if any, are they cut from? Psychologist Ruth Mathews of St. Paul, in a study of more than 100 female sex offenders—65 adult women and 40 adolescent girls—found that they fall into four major categories.

The first is teacher-lover—usually made up of older women who have sex with a young adolescent. This category often goes unnoticed by society as well as by the offender because the behavior is socially sanctioned. For confirmation, one has only to look to films such as *The Last Picture Show, Summer of '42*, and *Le Souffle au Coeur*.

The second category is experimenter-exploiter, which encompasses girls from rigid families where sex education is proscribed. They take baby-sitting as an opportunity to explore small children. Many of these girls don't even know what they are doing, have never heard of or experienced masturbation, and are terrified of sex. One girl who had seen a movie with an orgasm scene said, "I wondered if *I* could get that 'ah' feeling. I was waiting for the 'ah' to happen, then I got into all this trouble."

The third category is the predisposed,

meaning women who are predisposed to offend by their own history of severe physical and/or sexual abuse. The victims are often their own children or siblings. As one woman in this category said, "I was always treated as an animal when I was growing up. I didn't realize my kids were human beings."

Mathews's final category is male-coerced women—women who abuse children because men force them to. These women were themselves abused as children, though less severely than the predisposed. As teens they were isolated loners but anxious to belong. Many are married to sex offenders who may abuse the kids for a long time without the wife's knowledge. Ultimately, she is brought into it. Witness a typical scenario.

He: "Let's play a game with the kids."
She *(surprised and delighted)*: "Great!"
He: "Let's play spin the bottle."
She: "No!"
(He slaps her face, then beats her head on the floor. The child tries to stop him.)
Kid *(yelling)*: "Mom, do it. *He's* been doing it for years."

Deeply dependent and vulnerable to threats, these women are easily manipulated. As one of them said, "If he would leave me, I would be a nobody." Once such a woman molests a child, however, she may go on to offend on her own. As the mother of a five-year-old put it, "Having sex with my son was more enjoyable than with my husband."

While more than a third of the survivors I interviewed told me that they had been molested by women, true female pedophiles, Mathews says, are relatively rare—about 5 percent of her sample. Those she interviewed had themselves been abused from approximately the age of two onward by many family members. They received virtually no other nurturing—most of the nurturing they received was from the offender—and came to link abuse with caring.

Like male offenders, some females molest many, many children, their own and those in their care. But Mathews feels that women may take more responsibility for their acts than men do. Only one girl she worked with blamed her victim. Seventy percent of the females took all the blame if they acted alone. One half took 100 percent of the responsibility if they molested with a man. Where the men minimized what had happened—"We were only horsing around"—the women were "stuck in shame."

In Atlanta at a poetry reading, the woman sitting next to me asks what I write about. When I tell her, she leans close. "I molested my son," she whispers. I ask if she wants to talk about it. "No," she says. "But I will say that it will take me the rest of my life to even begin to deal with it."

Therapist Kathy Evert of Michigan, extrapolating from her 450-question survey of 93 women and 9 men who were abused by their mothers, sees a more general problem. "I believe that no one, including me," she says, "knows the extent of sexual abuse by females, especially mothers. About eighty percent of the women and men reported that the abuse by their mothers was the most hidden aspect of their lives. Only three percent of the women and none of the men told anyone about the abuse during their childhood." Instead they endured their own suicidal and homicidal feelings.

A. Nicholas Groth, the Connecticut psychologist, suggests "the incidence of sexual offenses against children perpetrated by adult women is much greater than would be suspected from the rare instances reported in crime statistics." He further suggests that women offenders may not be recognized as such because it is relatively easy to get away with abusive behavior under the guise of child care.

Female offenders wash, fondle, lick, and kiss the child's breasts and genitals, penetrate vagina and anus with tongue, fingers, and other objects: dildos, buttonhooks, screwdrivers—one even forced goldfish into her daughter. As one survivor told me, "My mom would play with my breasts and my nipples and insert things into my vagina to see if I was normal. 'I'm your mother,' she'd say. 'I need to know you're growing properly.' She'd give me enemas and make me dance for her naked. It lasted until I was twenty. I know it's hard to believe, but it's true. I was petrified of her. Absolutely."

It has long been believed that any woman who sexually abuses a child is insane and sexually frustrated but that her abuse is less violent than a man's. None of this is true. Only a third of the women and men in Kathy Evert's study, for example, said they thought that their mother was mentally ill. (According to Ruth Mathews, a tiny percentage of abusing mothers are severely psychotic.) Not only were most of the mothers in the study sane, but almost all had an adult sexual partner living with them. Furthermore, the mothers in Evert's study abused their daughters violently, beat and terrorized them, and raped them with objects. But they treated their sons like substitute lovers. Evert postulates that the abusing mothers projected self-hate from their own history of sexual abuse onto their daugh-

A PIONEERING NEW

David Finkelhor, Ph.D., and Linda Meyer Williams, Ph.D., who are sociologists at the Family Research Laboratory of the University of New Hampshire, have recently completed the most thorough study to date of men who have sexually abused their daughters. The sample consisted of 118 incestuous fathers—55 men in the U.S. Navy and 63 civilians from treatment centers around the country— and a carefully matched control group of nonincestuous fathers.

In this landmark study on the characteristics of incest offenders, Finkelhor and Williams set out to determine whether men are socialized to see all intimacy and dominance as sexual, whether fathers separated from their daughter for long periods soon after birth are more likely to molest her than fathers who have not been absent, and whether incestuous men had themselves been abused as children more than had nonoffenders. The researchers also sought to learn each man's feelings about his daughter, his outlook on sex, and his attitudes toward incest.

Many theories have been posited about why fathers molest their daughters. Everything from alcoholism to a frigid wife has been blamed. With this study, Finkelhor and Williams have shed new light on the subject and produced much new insight. They have established, for example, that there are distinct differences in the onset of abuse: Daughters ranged in age from 4 weeks to 15 years old when the incest began. "Fathers were more likely to start abuse when their daughter was four to six years old or ten to twelve years old," the study reveals, "than to initiate abuse when she was seven, eight, or nine years old." Men reported various behaviors leading up to the abuse. Some of the fathers said they had masturbated while thinking of their daughter, had exposed themselves to her, or had made her touch their genitals before they began touching hers. A substantial percentage of the men—63 percent—had been sexually attracted to their daughter for a period of years before the abuse began. Most significantly, the findings reveal that there are many paths to incestuous behavior and that there is not just one type of man who commits such abuse.

Each man was interviewed for at least six hours and was asked hundreds of questions. The results—many presented here for the first time—dispel some common myths and prompt the following typology.

Type 1.

SEXUALLY PREOCCUPIED

Twenty-six percent of the fathers studied fell into this category. These men had "a clear and conscious (often obsessive) sexual interest in their daughters." When they told what attracted them to their daughter, they talked in detail about her physical qualities—the feel of her skin, for example, or the smell of her body.

Type 1 subcategory: *Early sexualizers*

Among the sexually preoccupied fathers, many regarded their daughter as a sex object almost from birth. "One father reported that he had been stimulated by the sight of his daughter nursing and that he could never remember a time when he did not have sexual feelings for her. . . . He began sexually abusing her when she was four weeks old."

Many of the offenders were themselves sexually abused as children.

STUDY OF INCESTUOUS FATHERS

"These men are so sexualized that they may simply project their sexual needs onto everybody and everything. . . . The children may be those who are most easily manipulated to satisfy the preoccupations."

Type 2.
ADOLESCENT REGRESSIVES

About a third of the fathers—33 percent—became sexually interested in their daughter when she entered puberty. They said they were "transfixed" by her body's changes.

For some the attraction began when the daughter started to act more grown up, before her body changed. Some of the fathers in this group became aroused by a daughter after having been away from her for a long time. Her new maturity and developing body caught them by surprise. Sometimes the fathers let the attraction build for years, masturbating to fantasies of the daughter, before they acted.

These men acted and sounded like young adolescents themselves when they talked about their daughter. One said, "I started to wonder what it would be like to touch her breasts and touch between her legs and wondered how she would react if I did."

"The father-adult in me shut down," said another offender, "and I was like a kid again."

Type 3.
INSTRUMENTAL SELF-GRATIFIERS

These fathers accounted for 20 percent of the sample. They described their daughter in terms that were nonerotic. When they abused her, they thought about someone else—their wife, even their daughter as an adult.

In contrast to the sexually preoccupied and adolescent-regressive fathers who focused on their daughter, the instrumental self-gratifiers blocked what they were doing from their mind: "They used their daughter's body as a receptacle." The fact that they were abusing a daughter or that a daughter was so young was actually "a distracting element" that these fathers had to work to ignore. While one man was giving his seven-year-old a bath, she rubbed against his penis. "I realized that I could take advantage of the situation," he said. "She wasn't a person to me." Another man said, "I abused her from behind so I wouldn't see her face."

Instrumental self-gratifiers abused sporadically, worried about the harm they were causing, and felt great guilt. To alleviate the guilt, some convinced themselves that their daughter was aroused.

Type 4.
EMOTIONALLY DEPENDENT

Just over 10 percent of the sample fit this category. These fathers were emotionally needy, lonely, depressed. They thought of themselves as failures and looked to their daughter for "close, exclusive, emotionally dependent relationships," including sexual gratification, which they linked to intimacy and not to their daughter's real or imagined sexual qualities.

One man, separated from his wife, saw his five-year-old daughter only on weekends. "It was companionship," he said. "I had been alone for six months. We slept together and would fondle each other. The closeness was very good and loving. Then oral sex began."

The average age of the daughter when the incest began was six to seven years. But it happened with older daughters as well. The fathers of older daughters described the girls as their "best friends," and the relationships had a more romantic quality: The men described their daughter as they might have described an adult lover.

Type 5.
ANGRY RETALIATORS

About 10 percent of the men were in this category. These fathers were the most likely to have criminal histories of assault and rape. They abused a daughter out of anger at her or, more often, at her mother for neglecting or deserting them. Some denied any sexual feelings for the daughter. One father of a three-year-old said, "My daughter has no sex appeal for me at all. What I did was just an opportunity to get back at my daughter for being the center of my wife's life. There was no room for me."

Sometimes the daughter was abused because she resembled her mother, sometimes because of the father's desire to desecrate her or to possess her out of an angry sense of entitlement. Some angry retaliators tied up, gagged, beat, and raped their daughter and were aroused by the violence.

OTHER FINDINGS Alcohol and drugs: While 33 percent of the men reported being under the influence of alcohol when the abuse occurred, and 10 percent reported that they were using drugs, only 9 percent held alcohol or drugs responsible. "Preliminary analysis indicates that the incestuous fathers are not more likely than the comparison fathers to have drug or alcohol abuse problems, although they may use alcohol or drugs to lower their inhibitions to abuse."

Marital discord: Forty-three percent of the men felt that their relationship with their wife was part of the reason for the incest. "However, the wife was rarely the only factor mentioned. . . . Different men probably come to incestuous acts as a result of different needs, motives, and impairments."

Sexual abuse of the offender as a child: Significantly, 70 percent of the men said they themselves had been sexually abused in childhood. Half were physically abused by their father and almost half—44 percent—had been physically abused by their mother. "Although not all who are abused go on to become perpetrators, it is critical that we learn more about how child sexual victimization affects male sexual development and male sexual socialization."

RECOMMENDATIONS Finkelhor and Williams suggest, considering the "intergenerational transmission of sexual abuse," men be given improved opportunities for positive fathering—including paternity leave and more liberal visitations in cases of divorce or separation. Also that they be encouraged to be intimate in nonsexual ways, beginning in boyhood. The study argues that, based on the evidence, it's very likely that people can become more aware of the precursory signs of incest. "It is conceivable," Finkelhor and Williams conclude, "that the sequence of events that leads to abuse can be interrupted."

CASE STUDIES

When Anne-Marie's 17-year-old daughter, Maureen, left home, she told an aunt that her father had molested her and her brothers and sisters. While the case was being investigated, Maureen's father killed her mother. Out on bail pending trial, he moved back in with his younger children. When a child-welfare worker came to question him, he said, "Get out of my face or I'll do to you what I did to my wife."

Jenny, who had been sexually abused as a child, refused to believe it when a neighbor filed a complaint charging that her ten-year-old had been molested by Jenny's husband, Norman. Then her own child, five-year-old Emma, told Jenny that her father had abused her and her baby brothers while Jenny was at work. Norman went to prison.

Jenny poured gasoline over herself and her children and struck a match. The mother and both sons were enveloped in flames, but Emma was able to escape. Jenny, two-year-old Adam, and three-year-old Gerry burned to death.

Alison was eight when she was raped by her stepfather, Buddy, a drug user. HIV positive, Buddy had infected his wife, who later gave birth to an HIV-positive son and, the following year, a second daughter, who is HIV negative. In 1987, Alison's mother, who was carrying twins at the time, died of AIDS in her seventh month of pregnancy. Convicted of Alison's rape, Buddy is currently serving time. From prison he is seeking visitation rights to his son and daughter, who are now in foster care.

---

ters. "This causes rage and anger that don't go away," she says.

Not all incest is intergenerational, committed by adult against child. "There is more sibling incest than parent-child," David Finkelhor told me. And in *Sibling Abuse: Hidden Physical, Emotional, and Sexual Trauma,* Vernon R. Wiehe, Ph.D., professor of social work at the University of Kentucky, writes: "There is evidence . . . that brother-sister sexual relationships may be five times as common as father-daughter incest."

There are problems with numbers and definitions in this area, as in others. How, for example, does one define consensual versus forced sexual contact between siblings? Finkelhor says that an age gap of five years implies coercion. Others feel that a five-year gap is too wide. What about children who are close in age but different in size? What about children who have much more or much less power in the family? What about children who are more gifted or less gifted physically or intellectually?

Coercion aside, "sibling abuse has been ignored in part," writes Vernon Wiehe, "because the abusive behavior of one sibling toward another is often excused as normal behavior. Sibling rivalry must be distinguished from sibling abuse."

Certainly, sibling sexual abuse is no different from other sexual abuse in that it is self-perpetuating. According to the Fin-

kelhor study: "The role of physical and emotional abuse in childhood should not be overlooked. . . . Arousal to very young children may be the result of early sexual victimization."

The Finkelhor study has profound implications for the possible prevention of father-daughter incest. Over 50 percent of the men in the study reported that their sexual interest in the daughter developed slowly. Is it possible that prevention programs could have helped them clarify and deal with their feelings about her before sexual contact occurred? According to the researchers, "It is conceivable that men can interrupt the sequence of events which led to the abuse."

Currently, the statistics on recidivism are predictably dismal. The rehabilitation of offenders has always been approached as a matter of jail, probation, or court-ordered therapy. Only some few medical institutions in the country—notable among them, Baltimore's Johns Hopkins—offer impressive inpatient treatment involving drugs and therapy, but treatment is expensive, and not all medical-insurance plans will cover it.

While some nonmedical rehab programs claim up to a 95 percent "cure" rate, they are misleading in their optimism. Jim Breiling of the National Institutes of Mental Health says

that the results of many studies are suspect owing to the unreliability of statements by offenders, many of whom lie. According to one study, a 38 percent dropout of participants can be anticipated in any program. Of those who receive the full course of treatment, 13 percent reoffend during the first year. After that, who knows?

The rare offender who voluntarily seeks help can get trapped in a bind. Therapists are legally required to inform the local police if they hear about a specific child-abuse crime. Massachusetts therapist Mike Lew cautions his clients at the outset that if they tell him they have offended, he must report them. Even so, the authorities tend to look more favorably on those who turn themselves in than on those who get caught or accused.

Ruth Mathews believes that women may be easier to rehabilitate than men because, as noted, they may feel more empathy for their victims than male offenders do. But she points out that her opinion is based on the women she sees, who have come voluntarily for treatment. A sample of women in prison for sex crimes would probably yield very different results. Child offenders who receive treatment, on the other hand, do much better than adults. They need less long-term help and are less likely to reoffend.

Mental-health providers are key to spotting and treating offenders and their victims. But, says psychologist Mary W. Armsworth, the Houston trauma specialist, "we don't train mental-health providers properly." Incest victims who need psychiatric care are often misdiagnosed. Victims of child sexual abuse who suffer symptoms of post-traumatic stress disorder have been hospitalized for everything from manic depression to schizophrenia and have been subjected to shock treatments, insulin shock, and other inappropriate therapies.

Misdiagnosis occurs because the therapist, psychiatrist, or doctor doesn't know what to look for, doesn't consider childhood sexual abuse a possibility, or doesn't believe the patient's account of what has occurred. For almost a century, Freud and his followers have led us astray.

Vienna, Austria. April 21, 1896. Sigmund Freud stands before his colleagues at the Society for Psychiatry and Neurology, reading his paper "The Aetiology of Hysteria." He informs his listeners that mental illness is the result of childhood sexual abuse. The words he uses to describe the abuse are *rape, assault, trauma, attack.*

He has based his findings—which he has used to formulate what he terms the seduction theory—on the testimony of his patients. These are both women and men who have told him of their childhood abuse, often by their fathers. He has listened to them, understood them, and believed them. He has reason to. As he has written to his friend and colleague Wilhelm Fliess, "My own father was one of these perverts and is responsible for the hysteria of my brother . . . and those of several younger sisters."

But Freud is soon under attack by his colleagues, many of whom denounce his argument. He retracts the seduction theory. The accounts of incest, he now says, were fabricated by hysterical women who were not assaulted. Like Oedipus, he says, they yearned for intercourse with one parent and wanted to murder the other, and these yearnings produced such a profundity of guilt and conflict that they caused a lifetime of mental illness.

Unlike the seduction theory, for which Freud was ostracized, the Oedipal theory finds favor with the great majority of his colleagues. It becomes the cornerstone, the bible, of all psychoanalysis to come.

Jeffrey Moussaieff Masson, Ph.D., former project director of the Sigmund Freud Archives in Washington, D.C., and a self-described "former psychoanalyst," has written three books detailing first his affection for, then his disaffection from, Freud and his teachings. According to Masson, Freud's reversal of his position represented a monumental loss of moral courage that served to save his professional skin to the detriment of his patients.

In *Banished Knowledge: Facing Childhood Injuries,* Alice Miller, Ph.D., like Masson a former Freudian psychoanalyst, argues that Freud suppressed the truth to spare himself and his friends the personal consequences of self-examination. "Freud has firmly locked the doors to our awareness of child abuse and has hidden the keys so carefully that ensuing generations have been unable to find them."

Miller goes on to make a startling revelation about Freud's great friend Wilhelm Fliess. She writes that many decades after Freud suppressed his data, Wilhelm's son Robert found out that "at the age of two,

[Robert] had been sexually abused by his father and that this incident coincided with Freud's renunciation of the truth."

Some scholars have expressed the wish that the seduction theory and the Oedipal theory could work together. But they can't. The seduction theory states that child sexual abuse is the cause of most—or even all— mental illness. The Oedipal theory, on the other hand, states that child sexual abuse almost never happens, that a person's memories are false, and that mental illness and neuroses come from a child's conflicted desires for sex and murder.

Ever since Freud, the Oedipal theory has been used to refute claims of child sexual abuse. In *Healing the Incest Wound,* Dr. Christine Courtois, the Maryland psychotherapist, writes that "many survivors report that they were medically examined and treated for their various symptoms, but for the most part the symptoms were never attributed to abuse even when the evidence was obvious. Instead, symptoms were most frequently described as psychosomatic or without basis or another diagnosis was given." Some therapists still tell their patients that their memories— no matter how degrading, detailed, or sadistic— are really their wishes. Freud placed the responsibility for the deed and the memory not with the offending adult but with the child victim—and his adherents continue the sham. As Alice Miller writes: "I often hear it said that we owe the discovery of child abuse to psychoanalysis. . . . In fact it is precisely psychoanalysis that has held back and continues to hold back knowledge of child abuse. . . . Given our present knowledge of child abuse, the Freudian theories have become untenable."

But most people don't know this. To accept that Freud lied means that nearly a century of child rearing, analytic training, law enforcement, and judicial and medical attitudes must be reconsidered. As the matter rests now, the men and women who should be able to identify abuse and help prevent and punish it have never even learned the basics. Our doctors, analysts, and judges have been taught to mistake victim for offender. They allow offenders to remain untreated, free to infect the next generation.

Alice Miller writes that Freud "wrote volume after volume whose style was universally admired and whose contents led humanity into utter confusion." His legacy has been in part to blind us to the prevalence of incest, to make the offenders in our midst invisible.

At the Sexual Abuse Center of the Family Support Line in Delaware County, Pennsylvania, therapists who work with perpetrators and survivors showed me paintings done by children aged 7 to 12 who had participated in an incest survivors' support group.

Monica, 10, had drawn the outline of an adult, six feet tall, on butcher paper. With the help of her therapist she titled it *Diagram of a Perpetrator.* She drew in hair, a brain, eyes, ears, nose, mouth, shoulders, big hands, a heart, and a penis. Next to each feature, down each finger, and around the penis, she wrote the things her father had said to her:

TRUST ME.

I'LL PROTECT YOU.

I'M NOT GOING TO HURT YOU.

IT'LL FEEL GOOD.

DON'T FIGHT ME.

DON'T MOVE.

THEY'RE SOFT.

I THINK WITH MY PENIS.

I DON'T CARE WHAT YOU SAY.

I NEED SOME.

BETTER ME THAN SOMEONE ELSE.

IT'LL MAKE YOU A WOMAN.

I'M BIG.

Editor's note: This is a four-part report, of which two parts are included here. Parts two and three addressing the courts and recovery factors may be found in the February 1992 issue of *Lear's.*

Repeating a study, if not its results

Five projects rethink domestic-violence response

Jacob R. Clark

A decade ago, a landmark study of police response to domestic violence suggested that arresting offenders better deterred future violence than such non-arrest tactics as separating the couple for a period of time or having policy mediate the problem.

But replications of that Minneapolis experiment which were undertaken to test its conclusion that "arrest works best" now offer no better than mixed evidence in support of that initial observation. In fact, findings from three of the follow-up studies suggest that arrest may actually backfire in some cases, making suspects more hostile and increasing the likelihood of subsequent violence against the same victim. The finding appears especially valid for offenders with little or no stake in social conformity, such as the unemployed.

Two replication studies, on the other hand, offer evidence that arrest does deter future violence among most couples.

The findings have ominous overtones for the many states that have legislated mandatory arrest in misdemeanor domestic violence cases, and pose complex questions about the kind of policies that should be adopted to deal with what is probably the most common form of violence confronted by police in this country.

The replication studies had been called for by the Minneapolis researchers, who urged further analysis of their results before wide-ranging statutory and policy changes were made. The studies, funded in 1986 by the National Institute of Justice, were conducted in Milwaukee, Charlotte, N.C., Colorado Springs, Colo., Dade County, Fla., and Omaha, Neb.

All of the studies focused on "treatments"—arrest or non-arrest actions taken against offenders at the scene when police arrived. In Omaha, a second experiment was conducted to determine whether issuing an arrest warrant to an absent offender might deter future violence.

NO SIMPLE ANSWERS

The five sites have reported their findings, but unlike the Minneapolis study, which generated major press coverage nationwide, few have actually been publicized. Richard A. Berk, a professor of sociology at the University of California-Los Angeles who served as a consultant to the Colorado Springs Police Department during its replication, said the findings were underpublicized because they "are not simple."

"The reason why you haven't seen much [about the replications] is because there is no simple, straightforward story from these studies," Berk said in a LEN interview. "The findings differed across cities. It's not as if there's a blanket statement about what will work for everybody."

More than the findings differed. The methodologies varied from one city to another, and from the original Minneapolis study. Within individual cities, findings may have varied depending on the data source used—police records or victim interviews.

Only the Colorado Springs and Metro Dade studies tended to support the findings of the Minneapolis experiment. In Colorado Springs, four treatments were randomly assigned: police arrested the suspect at the scene and gave an emergency protection order to the victim; the suspect was not arrested, but taken to the police station for immediate crisis counseling, while the victim was given an

order of protection; police issued an emergency protection order only, or they simply restored order at the scene and advised the suspect he could be arrested for the offense in the future. More than half of the suspects had committed "verbal" crimes such as harassment and menacing, while 38 percent of the cases involved an actual assault.

VICTIMS HAVE THEIR SAY

The official data from the Colorado Springs experiment showed that arrest did not deter recidivism by suspects, but victim interviews seemed to tell another tale. According to the 58 percent of the victims who were questioned by researchers six months after the initial incident, arrest did provide a deterrent effect. "Basically what we found was that [arrest] didn't do any harm for the people who had a lot to lose—a job and so on," said Berk. "Then, as a deterrence, it worked. Otherwise, it was just kind of a wash."

The Metro Dade experiment, which was coordinated by Police Foundation research director Antony Pate, offered perhaps the most concrete evidence of the deterrent value of arrest. Cases were randomly assigned to arrest or non-arrest intervention. In a second stage of the experiment, victims were randomly assigned to receive follow-up intervention, assistance and referrals from a Safe Streets Unit, made up of detectives and supervisors specially trained to handle domestic violence cases. The unit, which was eventually disbanded, "had no effect of any sort," said Pate, because it was left up to victims to actually seek help.

In Dade County, researchers found that only 10.9 percent of the suspects who were arrested went on to repeat violence, while 18.3 percent of the suspects who were not arrested committed further violent acts. Six-month follow-up interviews with victims showed that 14.6 percent of those arrested repeated violence, compared to only 26.9 percent of the unarrested suspects.

Any deterrent value seemed to end there, however, as the three other sites showed a tendency for arrests to increase violence over a six-month period. Omaha researchers found that 11.9 percent of the suspects arrested for a domestic violence offense were rearrested within six months, compared to 11.3 percent of the suspects who were sent from the home and 8.7 percent of the suspects who were advised by police of the possibility of future arrest.

Interviews with victims in Omaha suggested that arrest provided some deterrence, at least initially. Victims reported one physical injury after the police intervention in 14.7 percent of the arrest cases compared with 20.4 percent of the nonarrest cases. But the Omaha researchers also found that arrest can have an "escalation" effect on violence with the passage of time, with a higher level of repeat violence being committed by the group originally assigned to arrest, as measured by new arrest reports.

"IN NO WAY A DETERRENT"

Arrest, or even other formal sanction such as the issuance of citations, was also seen leading to subsequent violence in the long term in the Charlotte study. The study's six-month follow-up period showed that 18 percent of the arrested suspects were rearrested, while 19 percent were arrested after initially being issued a summons. Only 12 percent of the suspects who were advised or separated from the spouse were later arrested. The number of repeat arrests bore out this finding further. The arrest group produced 201 repeat arrests per 1,000 suspects, while the citation group had 259, and the advise/separate group logged 123 arrests.

"There's no reason, based on our results to think that arrest is a deterrent to subsequent abuse," said Ira Hutchison, an associate professor of sociology at the University of North Carolina who assisted in the Charlotte study. "We were really hoping that [arrest] would make a

difference and we looked at our data every which way—incidence, frequency, time to failure. In none of those ways was arrest an effective deterrent."

Hutchison said one reason why arrest did not show a deterrent effect could be because a significant number of the suspects had been arrested before. "These were not virgins. We had guys in our sample who had been in prison for killing people."

In Milwaukee, where the study was led by Dr. Lawrence Sherman, who coordinated the original Minneapolis experiment, researchers examined the effect of a 12-hour arrest and two other treatments—a "short arrest" of three hours and a warning that arrest would take place if police had to return to the scene. At 30 days after an incident, arrest was found to have some deterrent effect, with a 7-percent chance of repeat violence by unarrested suspects compared to 2 percent for arrested suspects.

But any protection against future violence was short-lived, researchers found. Within two months after a domestic violence incident, there was no difference in the rate of repeat assaults between men who had been arrested and those who had received warnings from police. Sherman and his research team found that for suspects taken into custody under a three-hour "short arrest," an escalation of violence occurred after one year against any victim just as it did for the other treatments.

Repeat violence was reported during victim interviews in 30 percent of the short-arrest cases, 35 percent of full-arrest cases and 31 percent of the warning cases.

MARRIAGE, EMPLOYMENT FACTORS

The research also showed that full arrest offered a modest deterrence in the case of married suspects. Among unmarried suspects, on the other hand, full arrest increased the frequency of repeat violence by 30 percent, and short arrest increased the frequency rate even higher.

But perhaps the most important finding of the Milwaukee study is that arrest increased subsequent violence among unemployed suspects. The study found that arrested suspects who were unemployed were 49 percent more likely to assault their partners in the year follow-

ing the arrest, compared to men who held jobs. The researchers discovered a rate of 750 repeat assaults per 1,000 unemployed men and 503 assaults per 1,000 employed suspects.

Sherman, who is the author of a recent book on the replication studies titled "Policing Domestic Violence," said the Milwaukee results show that "unemployment is the most consistent indicator of when arrest backfires, compared to when arrest is going to work."

Unemployment, Sherman stated, "is probably the most symbolic indication of people not having a stake in conventional society." Jobless suspects have a lot less to lose and thus are less fearful of the consequences of arrest, he added.

Data analyses focusing on the employment status of suspects also showed that arrest appears to deter future violence among employed suspects in Metro Dade and Colorado Springs. Six-month interviews with victims in the Metro Dade study revealed that 33.3 percent of the unemployed arrestees committed further violence, compared with 8.6 percent of the arrested suspects with jobs.

"We're not about to say that police ought to make an arrest depending on employment status," said Pate. "But we've got to to be aware of the fact that there is a risk that making an arrest in some cases may not help and might even endanger the victim."

DETERRING THE DETERRABLE

In Colorado Springs, arrest serves as a deterrent "for the people who could be deterred," said Berk. Unlike samples in some of the other replications, most of the suspects in Colorado Springs were employed—20 percent of them by the military—with greater stakes in conformity.

"If you have something to lose, arrest makes a difference," Berk observed. "If you don't have something to lose—you've been arrested about a half-dozen times and you're unemployed and nobody cares about you anyway—then an arrest is no big deal."

An analysis of the Omaha data by the Crime Control Institute also found a deterrent effect of arrest for employed suspects. Arrest increased the frequency of recidivism among unemployed suspects by 52 percent, from 412 to 627 incidents per 1,000 suspects. But among the employed, arrest reduced the rate of subsequent violence by 37 percent, from 280 to 176 incidents per 1,000 annually.

Researchers in Omaha also tested the effects of another alternative approach—issuing on-the-spot arrest warrants for suspects not at the scene when police arrived—which appeared to offer an even more effective deterrent to future violence than immediate arrest, separating the couple, offering counseling or warning suspects about the risk of arrest in future incidents.

To compare the effect of the warrants, police took an offense complaint from victims but did not issue a warrant. Instead, they advised victims on how to obtain an arrest warrant. Suspects were either served with a warrant, received a letter from the prosecutor's office advising them to come in to discuss the matter or were told by victims or others that a warrant was to be issued. Prosecutors issued warrants to about 75 percent of the suspects.

WHAT, BUT NOT WHY

The researchers found that suspects in the no-warrant group were twice as likely to be rearrested for a domestic violence incident against the same victim than those in the warrant group. At six months, 12 percent of the suspects in the no-warrant group were arrested compared to 5 percent in the warrant group, and at one year, 21 percent of the no-warrant suspects were arrested compared to 11 percent of the warrant suspects.

Interviews with victims revealed that 30 percent were injured by suspects in the no-warrant category after six months, compared to 16 percent in the warrant group. At the one-year mark, 35 percent of the victims reported new attacks by no-warrant suspects compared to 19 percent in the warrant cases.

The suspects who received warrants "had a substantive and statistically significant lower recidivism rate across all the variables we looked at compared to those who did not have a warrant issued. And we don't know why," said Franklin Dunford, the principal investigator of the Omaha study.

Dunford, a researcher at the Institute of Behavioral Science at the University of Colorado-Boulder, said the finding begs further study—perhaps through replications in other cities.

"We did a good deal of work to try to see if there was something about the two groups that would give us some clues as to why in one group, warrants might be more effective than another," he said. "I wasn't able to identify anything but that's not to say further research may not identify something. We weren't able to explain it."

But Dunford has theorized that the warrant may have a "sword of Damocles" effect on suspects, representing a hovering threat of arrest that motivates the suspect to avoid any behavior that might put him into contact with police.

Where to now on domestic-violence? Studies offer mixed policy guidance

Jacob R. Clark

Second of two parts.

When it comes to practical application to law enforcement policy-making, the complex and sometimes contradictory findings of five follow-up studies to the widely cited Minneapolis domestic violence experiment may prompt more head-scratching than serious contemplation among police officials. The studies, conducted in the late 1980's and early 1990's in Colorado Springs, Colo.; Dade County, Fla.; Omaha, Neb.; Charlotte, N.C., and Milwaukee, offer no better than conflicting evidence to support the Minneapolis study's original finding that arrest works best to deter future incidents of domestic violence. [See LEN, March 31, 1993.]

Viewed as a whole, the studies' divergent results pose for police what researcher Dr. Lawrence Sherman has termed a series of "dilemmas" because different approaches, such as arrest, separation of the couple, or mediation, appear to work differently for different kinds of suspects, couples and communities. Indeed, the studies suggest that arrest has a much more substantial deterrent effect on employed suspects than on those who are jobless, and may even increase the likelihood of recidivism among unemployed suspects.

In a policy context, Sherman asserts, that conclusion sounds a radical note that strikes at the very heart of criminal justice principles—that some forms of legal sanction, such as arrest, may actually cause more criminal behavior.

"The whole idea that the criminal law backfires has no acknowledgement in American criminal law," he observed, "and it's going to take a long time before jurisprudence catches up with social science. We're showing increasingly, not just in this area, that criminal law can backfire and cause more crime. Of course, that's not its intent. But we have to reconcile justice and crime causation, and when justice causes crime, it ought to be a source of concern."

POLICY MADE IN A VACUUM?

As he has since the Minneapolis data were released in 1984, Sherman argues strongly against instituting mandatory arrest policies—a stance that has earned him harsh criticism from victims' advocacy groups. He has also urged—so far, without success—that such policies already enacted be repealed, particularly in jurisdictions where large numbers of residents live in concentrated areas of high poverty, as in Milwaukee.

"The political forces in support of mandatory arrest have been completely unmoved by the research findings," Sherman told LEN. "They would rather have the research findings go away. What they're revealing is the primary interest in mandatory arrest is punishment for the sake of punishment rather than for reducing violence against victims. They're looking for symbolic justice as opposed to violence prevention."

What states should do, Sherman recommends, is legislate warrantless arrest on probable cause for misdemeanor assaults the officers did not witness. All but a handful of states have enacted such statutes, according to Sherman.

Sherman also advocates a community-specific law enforcement policy based on some of the replication studies' varied findings—one that takes the socioeconomic characteristics of the policy constituency into account. "Communities with low unemployment would have mandatory arrest. In communities with high unemployment rates, I would urge police to try to develop some alternative policies and rely very little on arrest," he said.

PROFILES OF VIOLENCE

Tactical information can be vitally important for responding officers, who should know whether they're dealing with a domestic violence incident involving chronically violent couples, who account for the majority of domestic violence complaints to police, and whether couples reside in so-called "problem buildings" that account for a disproportionate number of calls for police service.

"It's important for them to be told which ones are the chronically violent couples, what their recent history has been and some indication of what's been tried in the past, so they can perhaps tailor their responses to the specific features of that couple," said Sherman.

Ira Hutchison, an associate professor of sociology at the University of North Carolina who assisted in the Charlotte study, said police departments should develop ways to profile chronically violent households, with the profiles being used to formulate effective strategies for dealing with future problems. "I think where the police have gotten the most s—t is when some woman gets killed and the police have been there a dozen times in the last three years. But the fact is that they can't prevent some guy from killing his wife. There is no way to do that. But if they can somehow respond differently to those households . . . I think that it would be an advantage."

Sherman added that since there is no scientific evidence that a one-time arrest in a misdemeanor domestic violence incident will help reduce the likelihood of a

From *Law Enforcement News*, April 30, 1993, pp. 1, 17. Reprinted by permission.

subsequent, more violent attack, police should not be held civilly liable for failing to prevent future domestic assaults that result in severe injury or death.

"SMART POLICING"

In his book "Policing Domestic Violence," Sherman outlines several recommendations for "smart policing" to deal with domestic violence. He calls on individual police departments to replace mandatory arrest policies with mandatory actions chosen from a list of options that could include transporting victims to shelters, taking intoxicated victims or suspects to detoxification treatment centers, giving the victim more of a say in deciding whether an immediate arrest should be made, and using the victim's own social networks to provide short-term protection against repeat attacks.

Police and prosecutors should also cooperate to develop offender-absent warrant procedures, which at least in Omaha, appeared to offer a deterrent against future violence, Sherman advises.

But Franklyn Dunford, the Omaha project director, warned against summarily adopting the offender-absent warrant approach before it can be tested further. Such an action would be "premature," he said, because "we don't know why it works. And we don't know if it would work in any other site."

Despite the research findings that pointed to a flat or negative effect of arrest in the Omaha replication, police officials there adopted a new mandatory arrest policy for offenders present at the scene. "We recommended that police arrest," Dunford said, "even though our data suggested that it didn't do any good, and not because an arrest would deter continued violence, but because it is illegal to assault folks. People who go around assaulting others should be held accountable for that. And what's important in Omaha was that our data suggested that arrest did not have a negative effect on offenders."

SENDING A SYMBOLIC MESSAGE

Other researchers in the replication studies agreed that arrest sends an important symbolic message to domestic violence victims and their communities that society will not condone violent behavior, regardless of the context in which it occurs.

"If we're arresting spouse abusers, what we're saying as a society is this is wrong, this is illegal, and we are not going to tolerate this," said Hutchison. "That in my mind is a step better than not arresting at all . . . I think it's got a symbolic value for the next generation growing up. I think it's important that kids see that somebody gets arrested if they hit their spouse."

"I still think that the presumption of arrest is the sensible thing to do for legal reasons if no others," agreed Richard A. Berk, a professor of sociology at the University of California-Los Angeles who served as a consultant to the Colorado Springs Police Department during its replication study. "There are good moral and legal grounds for arresting people. I mean an assault is an assault is an assault. And it's the thing police know how to do. They aren't social workers, they're not psychiatric counselors. We shouldn't ask them to do things that their training doesn't provide for. So we would get police doing what they know how to do best—and that's to enforce the law."

"If we want arrest to be an effective deterrent, then very clearly, these police departments who went ahead and changed the laws did so prematurely and unnecessarily," added Hutchison. "On the other hand, we don't have arrest be a deterrent in most other forms of crime. We don't say, 'Let's not arrest drug pushers because it doesn't stop them from pushing drugs.' "

STUDIES' UTILITY IN EVIDENCE

While law enforcement policymakers looking to the replications for definitive answers to dealing with domestic violence may come away disappointed, police officials in some of the study sites insist that the research has given law enforcement a body of invaluable information that simply wasn't available before. In some cases, the new studies have given rise to revisions or wholesale changes in the way the agencies deal with the crime.

Colorado Springs police can now issue summons and complaints in misdemeanor domestic violence incidents without the consent or signature of the victim. In addition, they may make custodial arrests based on probable cause "whenever circumstances warrant," according to a domestic violence protocol by the state's Fourth Judicial District, which includes Colorado Springs, that was implemented in March.

The protocol also allows police to phone judges from the scene of a domestic disturbance to obtain an emergency protection order, should the officer feel such a measure is warranted.

"We can simply call the judge right from the scene and get a verbal OK and just write his name in for him," said Sgt. John Anderson, a 21-year veteran and former supervisor at the Colorado Springs Police Academy, where he has trained officers to respond to domestic violence calls. "He doesn't have to see the form. He gets a short statement from the officer in the field and we're able to issue that EPO immediately and serve it while both parties are right there."

The protocol requires violators of EPO's to be arrested and detained until they [are] brought before the judge who issued the order, Anderson added. If necessary, EPO's can be upgraded to a temporary, then to a permanent restraining order, violations of which result in mandatory arrests.

INTEGRATED APPROACHES

Defendants in domestic violence cases who have no prior criminal history and who meet other eligibility criteria can receive a deferred sentence, usually of two years, with mandatory participation in a 36-week domestic violence counseling program. In addition, counselors from the city's Center for the Prevention of Domestic Violence, which receives copies of summonses issued by police in domestic violence cases, offer aid and counseling to the victim, as well as to the offender. "We've really tried to open it up to where it's a community-based problem," said Det. Howard Black, who helped coordinate the Colorado Springs replication.

Probable cause-based arrests and protection orders are being used increasingly in Omaha as well, according to police spokesman Sgt. William Muldoon. And prosecutors are more likely to try offenders—even without the cooperation of victims—which Muldoon says is in marked contrast with past practice of dropping cases if the victim refused to cooperate.

"Now, they are not deterred by a spouse's refusal to cooperate," he said.

"They go ahead anyway. In many cases, these suspects end up striking some kind of plea bargain deal and are ordered into some type of diversion program or probation is arranged where counseling is offered. And we think that's significant progress from what used to take place."

"The vast majority of the population still thinks it's all right to beat your spouse. That's an attitude we're going to have to change, otherwise we're going to be a lot busier in the future."
—**Capt. Howard Lindstedt, Milwaukee PD**

Muldoon and others interviewed by LEN also say the studies have prompted their agencies to strive for an integrated approach to domestic violence, involving the police along with the judiciary, victim's advocates and social services agencies. "The studies raised awareness of the magnitude of the problem and forced us to look into some different strategies for dealing with domestic violence," said Muldoon. "We are talking more with the YWCA, the Women Against Violence group, our victim-witness unit and prosecutors. We're trying to look at this whole thing from a quality-of-life standpoint—is there a drug or alcohol problem or something that, if not treated, will fester and continue?"

A LEGACY OF AWARENESS

Increasing police awareness of domestic violence, as well as the body of knowledge and data available about what is arguably the most common form of crime they confront, may well be the legacy of the Minneapolis experiment and its follow-up studies. "Just because we're not seeing major outcomes, they've still been of great assistance in the area of training and understanding just how complicated this whole area of domestic violence is," said Detective Black of the studies. "This is a very, very difficult area because you're always dealing with two different perceptions—the victim and the offender. And no two calls are ever the same."

"Awareness in any manner, shape or form is more important than anything else," said Capt. Howard Lindstedt of the Milwaukee Police Department, where a statewide mandatory arrest policy in domestic violence cases is still in force despite Sherman's call for a repeal of the law. Lindstedt, who is a member of a Common Council task force on sexual assault and domestic violence, said his belief is based on a perception that a "vast majority of the population still thinks it's all right to beat your spouse. That's an attitude we're going to have to change, otherwise [police] are going to be a lot busier in the future."

Wilmington, N.C., Police Chief Robert Wadman, who headed the Omaha Police Department while the study in that city was being conducted, said that the studies have increased awareness not only of domestic violence but of the importance of research in formulating police policy.

"We have a better body of knowledge [about domestic violence] to make decisions than we've ever had," he said. "Law enforcement has been slow to use research in a positive way to make better decisions. The domestic violence studies were really in the forefront in allowing law enforcement to benefit from quality research."

Police

The police officer of today faces a wide range of problems that were not the concern of the police officer a generation ago. Racial tensions are high, the criminal is more violent and heavily armed, and drug use is on the increase, bringing with it more violent crime. As the police turn to new technologies, new methods of patrolling, and so forth, the human impact of the tensions of the work load are being felt.

The spotlight has been on the police, as never before, since the Rodney King incident in Los Angeles in March 1991. That case highlighted the issues of racial tension, police tactics, and community relations.

The stressful nature of the police job is outlined in "The Most Stressful Job in America: Police Work in the 1990s." Adding to the stresses of the job are influences from outside the department calling for the creation of civilian complaint review boards. The issues of police misconduct and civilian review boards are discussed in two articles, "Public Solidly Favors Mixed Police/Civilian Review Boards" and "Is Police Brutality the Problem?" In the latter article, the author expresses concern that the emphasis on recent cases of police brutality is diverting attention from the problem of violent crime.

"Community policing" is now the practice in many police departments. The final verdict is not yet in on just how successful the programs are and the article "Beyond 'Just the Facts Ma'am' " discusses the problems that have been experienced in some communities.

Diversification in our society and the need for police to develop systems to deal with various groups is the subject of "The Future of Diversity in America: The Law Enforcement Paradigm Shift." Diversification in police ranks with the appointment of more women is discussed in "Dragons and Dinosaurs: The Plight of Patrol Women."

An interesting study conducted by the FBI in which killers of police officers were interviewed is summarized in "Police-Killers Offer Insights Into Victims' Fatal Mistakes."

Looking Ahead: Challenge Questions

Are the police of today being adequately trained to deal with the diverse cultures in modern society?

Are women being accepted by their male peers and supervisors?

Is "community policing" working?

Unit 3

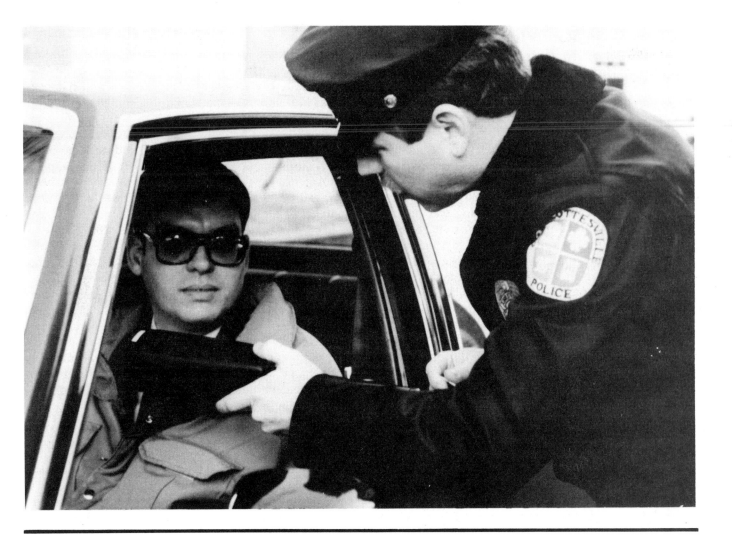

The most stressful job in America: Police work in the 1990s

The news media have so sensationalized recent brutality reports that many segments of the public are now suspicious of all policemen. Yet police today face a gauntlet of stresses and obstacles so formidable that it is a wonder they can do their job at all.

David Kupelian
With reports by Robert Just, Elizabeth Newton, Jeanne A. Harris, and Jacqueline Hewko.

David Kupelian is Managing Editor of New Dimensions.

In 1991, America's police are subject to greater scrutiny, second-guessing, and Monday-morning quarterbacking than at any other time in history. Their misdeeds and mistakes, real or alleged, are given saturation publicity. The videotaped beating of Rodney King was aired so many times that most Americans have its image etched permanently in their minds.

Yet, there are other videos that the public rarely sees. One month before the Rodney King beating, a Texas policeman, having routinely stopped a truck, was shot as he approached the driver. That video was shown on national TV for about one day. A week later a North Carolina state trooper was intentionally run over by a truck—also video taped. It received very little air time. Is there a double standard here?

By sensationalizing and endlessly harping on several isolated incidents, the media, in conjunction with grandstanding politicians, have fostered a new and increasingly widespread perception of America's police as the enemy, rather than the protector, of decent society. Los Angeles is a city "under siege by occupying forces," claims Roland Coleman of the Southern California Civil Rights Coalition. Jesse Jackson practically accused the entire Los Angeles Police Department of being racist.

Rep. John Conyers (D, Mich.) warns that the nation faces "a crisis of confidence in law enforcement." Responding to this intense political pressure, the U.S. Justice Department has mounted a major effort to review its file of 15,000 cases of alleged brutality, some of which are six years old.

Did all this hysteria really result from three L.A. cops beating Rodney King?

Police brutality has always existed, and it *is* a problem today. But is it true, as current media reporting implies that American law enforcement is increasingly populated by racists and bullies? "Any police brutality is a serious matter and deserves attention and correction," says former Attorney General Edwin Meese. "But you also have to maintain a perspective that these events are relatively rare." Meese faults the media for distorting the issue. "More and more of the police-beat reporters just do not understand what the police go through, as the older reporters did. Instead, they are young hot-shots fresh out of journalism school who want to make a name for themselves by castigating the police."

In fact, police brutality may actually be *less* prevalent today than it was twenty years ago. Civil liberties groups and police departments report *fewer* brutality complaints filed in recent years, not more. And while the FBI's Civil Rights Division reports 2,450 complaints involving law enforcement in 1989, during the same period, 62,172 law enforcement officers were victims of assaults.

This month (*August, 1991*) New Dimensions takes a close look at the men and women who make up America's police force—their almost impossible job, their frustrations, and their pain at being judged so harshly by the

Reprinted from *Police Career Digest*, January/February 1992, pp. 2-11.

public. It is a shocking story, so far unreported by the popular media, of life on the front lines of America's increasingly violent crime war.

THE VERY THIN BLUE LINE

"Every time you go out on duty you're going out there with a full deck of cards, and you have absolutely no idea how they are going to be dealt to you," muses Gary Steiner, an eight-year member of the Santa Monica Police Department in Los Angeles County. "Very often officers are put into situations where one minute everything is fine and next second, literally, you are going to be killed unless you act."

During street training as a San Francisco police officer, Peggy Wu discovered what was required of her. "I was called to one of the housing projects in the Mission District. My partner and I, who were the first police officers to arrive, found a child who had just been scalded to death in the tub by her mother. There were heroin and drug paraphernalia all over that squalid apartment. We arrested the mother as a suspect for the murder of her child, who was scalded and basically drowned in the tub. It was absolutely horrifying," she said.

"I spent most of the night there, talking with the woman for hours and hours. It was basically a negligence situation. She was high and the child ended up dead." According to Wu, nothing from her former life as a civilian could possibly have prepared her for being a policewoman.

Every cop has his or her own personal horror stories, nightmarish dramas into which the police willingly thrust themselves to play their valiant roles. Indeed, the only thing standing between average citizens and the hellish world of murder, drugs, and violent crime is a thinning blue line of beleaguered police men and women. Their task is formidable. Crime is up, way up. Police in New

---

Cop-bashing media-style

■ On a recent episode of "L.A. Law," a black motorist is signalled by Los Angeles Police to pull over after failing to make a complete stop at a stop sign. But just the sight of police flashers in his rear view mirror terrifies the motorist—it is one week after the Rodney King incident—so he takes off at high speed. A dangerous 60 mph chase through a residential area ends at the man's house, where he threatens the police, "If you try to get me, I'll shoot."

Arrested and charged with running a red light, speeding, reckless endangerment, and failing to obey a police officer, the man pleads innocent on all charges. At his trial, he argues that he was afraid for his life and feared putting himself at the mercy of a police department with a reputation—recently documented—of brutality, especially against minorities.

The jury's verdict: not guilty.

Just in case any viewers missed the show's point that Los Angeles Police are brutes, "L.A. Law's" scriptwriters arranged to have the black man's attorney, Jonathan Rawlings, also be brutalized by L.A.'s finest while being stopped for a minor traffic violation.

Clearly, the belief that police brutality is rampant in American is becoming integrated into the thought-stuff of current popular mythology, one of the hot new prejudices that Hollywood writers can exploit in the creation of prime time entertainment. And no wonder, Hollywood borrows its subject matter from the news media, who are currently engaged in one of their favorite armchair sports: cop-bashing.

Ever since the brutal beating of Rodney King by three Los Angeles policemen on March 5, a seemingly endless stream of stories in the print and television media have been painting America's law enforcement community as brutal, racist, and trigger-happy.

■ After the network news shows kicked off the cop-bashing season, ABC's "The West" picked up the ball and trounced the San Diego Police Department. "In Los Angeles," reported anchor Joe Oliver, "what begins as a routine traffic stop (*Editor's note: Rodney King actually led police on a high-speech chase.*) ends with a violent beating, while in San Francisco, highway patrol officers use riot batons against passive protesters. In each of those confrontations, the citizen lived to testify. But further south in San Diego, people have not been so lucky."

In an almost embarrassing display of one-sided reporting, Oliver proclaimed: "On a per-capita basis, San Diego police are killing people at a greater rate than anywhere in the West . . . San Diego police killed 12 people in 1990. . . ." Oliver made very little mention of the circumstances surrounding the killings.

■ On ABC's "Prime Time Live," Sam Donaldson's report on the U.S. Border Patrol, which focused on two police shootings, suggested that the Patrol wantonly shoots innocent Mexicans trying to cross the border. Rep. Edward Roybal (D, Calif.), a member of the House Hispanic Caucus, is seen on camera stating: "[The Border Patrol] think that they have a God-given right to abuse people, to violate individuals and human rights." Yet, while there were 53 cases of alleged abuse in 1989, the Patrol arrested 945,000 illegal aliens that year—one charge of abuse for every 17,000 arrests.

York City answered 4 million 911 calls last year alone, up from 2.7 million in 1980. But the numbers tell only half the story.

IN COLD BLOOD

Criminals, many experts agree, are simply worse today than in previous eras. Vaguely reminiscent of the Biblical warning of an age "when love of one for another will grow cold," a new, more violent, more death embracing trance of hatred seems to have captivated armies of social outcasts, especially in the inner cities.

Whereas 20 years ago a fender bender might have resulted in an argument or fist fight, today it is not uncommon to hear reports of one driver shooting the other in cold blood, then coolly getting back into his car and driving off.

David Kalich, a Houston policeman, contemplates this modern phenomenon: "Two brothers were fighting over a pork chop that their mother had left one of them," he says, recalling a recent incident he investigated. "The other one got mad enough that he stuffed it down his brother's throat and choked him to death. When I got there, he said, 'Yeah. I killed him. He took my pork chop.' Then he kicked the body lying there in the living room and said, 'I'd kill him again if he was alive.' "

Fueled by the lust of drug trafficking profits, tens of thousands of gang members have turned many of America's inner cities into Beiruts of gang warfare. "In the 1940s and 1950s, a single police officer could face down a crowd of two or three dozen young people," says Meese. "Just by his presence, he would restore order. If he asked them to move on, they would move. Today that isn't necessarily the case." Indeed, for many youths who have known nothing from the day they were born except violence and abuse, killing a cop is a badge of honor.

There is a new meanness on the streets. The Jamaican drug gangs, for instance, which control much of the U.S. crack trade, "are absolutely the most vicious organized crime group today," says Joe Vince of the Miami office of the bureau of Alcohol, Tobacco, and Firearms. With a combined membership of over 10,000, the Jamaican gangs, or "posses," turn to violence and torture at the slightest provocation. They often dispose of rival gang members, or just someone who gets in their way, by cutting that person into pieces in a bathtub, and then disposing of the pieces in dumpsters all over town. They call it "jointing."

HOLDING BACK THE TIDE

To fight back these incarnated demons of the underworld, police must play the role of combat soldier, referee, psychologist, urban negotiator, social worker, doctor, and older brother. To do all this, they must be supermen. "I will keep my private life unsullied as an example to all,"

Criminals, many experts agree, are simply worse today than in previous eras. . . . 20 years ago a fender bender might have resulted in an argument or fist fight, today it is not uncommon to hear reports of one driver shooting the other in cold blood, then coolly getting back into his car and driving off.

reads the National Law Enforcement Code of Ethics, "maintain courageous calm in the face of danger, scorn, or ridicule, develop self-restraint and be constantly mindful of the welfare of others, honest in thought and deed in both my personal and official life." While there are some rotten apples, most cops try diligently to live up to their profession's call for Herculean strength and nobility. Indeed, as any cop will tell you, sometimes the most difficult recruitment of the job is simply being strong and calm in the midst of chaos and tragedy.

"I responded to a traffic accident where a two-year-old boy had broken away from his bigger sister and run across the street," recalls Philip Hurtt, an El Cajon Police Officer in San Diego County. "The boy made it as far as the middle of the street before a car hit and killed him. My responsibility was to stay with his mother, brothers, and sisters. Just having to be strong in dealing with trauma of his brothers and sisters, who were only eight or nine at most, talking to the mother, trying to keep her and the kids calm while her son was being picked up off the street and taken to the hospital—that was really hard."

OVER THE EDGE

Such are the formidable stresses police must deal with—the need to remain calm, strong, and in control in the face of tragedy, frequent danger, and constant exposure to the worst side of life. But police today are burdened by a whole slew of additional—mostly politically motivated—stresses that too often push them over the edge.

Race relations has emerged as an explosive law enforcement issue. While the Rodney King case virtually *invited* the charge of racism, the shooting of an Hispanic man by a black female officer in Washington, D.C.—after the suspect had pulled a knife on the policewoman—also resulted in racial riots. Why?

In an age when an increasing number of Al Sharptons and Jesse Jacksons purposely stir up racial resentments to galvanize a power base to support their own agendas, the nation's police are fighting a no-win war. It does not matter how tactfully, professionally, and impartially they might perform their jobs. They can, on a political whim, be branded racists.

America's increasing factionalization—one Los Angeles precinct hosts 43 different languages and dialects—has made the policeman's job extremely difficult. He inevitably feels like an outsider, and is viewed as one—far from the ideal of the neighborhood cop who knows and befriends the people on his beat. In such neighborhoods, which generate a disproportionate number of calls for serious problems compared to less divided communities, the value placed on human life is often low. Going into such a neighborhood knowing that their lives are on the line, it is easy for cops to develop a siege mentality—an "Us vs. Them" attitude.

Lewis Alvarez is all too familiar with the dangers of being a cop in a racially explosive powder keg. In 1982, Alvarez, then a Miami police officer, shot and killed a black man in self-defense. "I went to arrest him and he pulled his gun, so I shot and killed him. That's all that happened."

But that wasn't all. In an area already boiling with racial tensions, there was tremendous public pressure to "get" Alvarez, and the state attorney succumbed, indicting the young officer for homicide. Seven months and $200,000 in attorney's fees later, a jury found him not guilty. Alvarez's case is a prime example of politics at war with law enforcement. "The justice system and law enforcement cannot withstand the weight of politics," says Alvarez, who is now in private business. "It's like putting a 300-pound brick on a 40-pound scale. It just cannot hold it."

THE INJUSTICE SYSTEM

Indeed, one of the worst stresses for police today is the criminal justice system, the very system that is supposed to back them up. "A lot of people get into police work because they believe they can do something about criminals and crime," remarks Detective Jack Luther, an 18-year veteran of the Los Angeles Police Department. "They get a rude awakening when they realize that felonies get knocked down so easily it's pathetic."

Police today are constantly frustrated and frequently betrayed by a judicial system that has become skewed in favor of criminals at the expense of victims and police. The universal frustration cops feel when they risk their lives to make an arrest, only to hear that the criminal is back on the street before the paperwork is completed, has led to widespread cynicism, burnout, and sometimes corruption and brutality.

Disillusion with the system "has a serious impact on police," says Meese, "which we have seen in the increased cynicism, and which has led, I think, in some cases to misconduct by police over the last 25 years." Learning from experience how quickly many offenders exit the system's revolving door may tempt some police officers to mete out a distorted version of "curbside justice" a la Rodney King. Frustrated at seeing criminals go free and getting rich off their crimes can lead to the temptation, to which a few cops succumb, to get rich off

"Over the years, the justice system has had more and more technicalities imposed upon it that have nothing to do with the guilt or innocence of the accused, and which frequently turn a trial into an inquisition into the conduct of the police officer rather than the misconduct of the defendant."
—Former Attorney General Edwin Meese

of *their* work, i.e., by taking a payoff for not busting a rich drug lord.

More commonly, however, frustration with the justice system results in burnout. Officers who feel that arresting dangerous suspects just doesn't produce results often stop trying. "I guess you'd call it the 'on-the-job retirement syndrome,'" says Steiner. "A burned out police officer basically gives up and just answers radio calls, and spends hours filling out reports." Wu refers to this syndrome as the "four reports a day formula."

What has happened to America's justice system? In the '60s and the early '70s, Americans virtually enshrined personal freedom. Mass demonstrations involving violence to people and the destruction of property became an everyday occurrence, but were considered expressions of free speech to be contained, rather than crimes to be punished. The free speech movement became a kind of on-going drug party. As the national preoccupation with self-gratification grew it took on increasingly bizarre forms. (Of course, varieties of self-expression considered "normal" today—obscene rap music, sacrilegious art, homosexual marriages—would have been viewed as outrageous even during the '60s and '70s.)

During that period of "personal freedom" mania, the Warren Court, controlled by a liberal majority, rendered a series of opinions which inserted into the laws of criminal procedure restrictions on police behavior that had never even been considered throughout America's history. For instance, the birth of the "exclusionary rule" meant that evidence could not be used in prosecuting a suspect unless it was seized in exactly the right way—and "the right way" seemed to change from case to case. "The rights of the accused," says Meese, "must be protected, but in a way that doesn't defy common sense, and which provides for getting all the truth in front of the jury."

The Supreme Court does not exist in a vacuum. Although the Warren Court's decisions dealt with technical areas of criminal procedure, they reflected, at the highest level of America's judiciary, the prevailing attitude of the times: the elevation of personal liberty over every other consideration.

The result? "Over the years," says Meese, "the justice system has had more and more technicalities imposed upon it that have nothing to do with the guilt or innocence of the accused, and which frequently turn a trial into an inquisition into the conduct of the police officer rather than the misconduct of the defendant. This disturbs police officers, who have an innate sense of fairness and justice, which is often violated."

Don Baldwin, Executive director of the National Law Enforcement Council, agrees: "Today, there is the likelihood that somebody can commit a heinous crime and get off almost scot-free because there is a violation under the exclusionary rule. You go out and risk your life to bring a criminal in, and a shrewd lawyer points out that you overstepped the bounds of proper procedure in some small way."

What would police like to see in the way of system reform? According to Baldwin, whose organization serves as an umbrella for 14 law enforcement organizations with a combined membership of 450,000 officers: "The thing that would help law enforcement the most is to get some laws on the books that have teeth in them, that would mandate that if a person commits a crime, that they have to pay for it. If the sentence says ten years, they get ten years."

Besides mandatory sentencing and modification of the exclusionary rule, says Baldwin, many police would also like to see speedier court action, more jails and prisons, the death penalty, and *habeas corpus* reform—limiting the number of times a convicted felon can appeal his case, since his opportunities currently are virtually unlimited.

REPEATING THE VIETNAM MISTAKE

Struggling against a web of criminal brutality, personal tragedy, racial politics, and a lenient judicial system, America's police force today finds itself in a war zone. But not just any war zone. As in the Vietnam War—a conflict in which America's young soldiers fought as bravely as in any war before or since, but who were not allowed to win—today's police, particularly in the nation's troubled inner cities, increasingly feel as though they, too, are fighting a war that they are not being allowed to win.

Whereas U.S. troops in Vietnam were hamstrung by confused an indecisive administration policies, today's domestic troops find their efforts being sabotaged by a judicial system overly concerned with the rights of the accused at the expense of the victim. In Vietnam, isolated reports of atrocities, such as at My Lai, led to the grossly unjust spectacle of American anti-war demonstrators condemning all U.S. soldiers. Today, isolated reports of police brutality are resulting in much the same thing: mass condemnation of America's police force.

Without the support of the public, a nation's soldiers simply cannot win the war they have been sent off to fight. As General Schwarzkopf said at the stunning conclusion of the gulf ground war: If U.S. troops had to fight using Iraq's inferior weapons, and Iraq had fought

us using our superior weapons, the U.S. still would have won—because our troops had great morale, and theirs didn't. Without the strong support of the public and the backing of the justice system, America's police are in danger of losing the war they have been asked to fight.

THE HIGH COST OF POLICE STRESS

The stress of being a soldier in a no-win war results in many casualties among our troops:

• **23 percent of police officers are alcoholics.** In one study of 2,300 police officers, it was found that 23 percent had serious alcohol problems. One contributing problem is that drinking is very much a part of the police subculture.

• **28 percent are at high risk for heart attacks.** 15 percent of police have cholesterol levels twice the level required to render them coronary heart disease risks.

• **36 percent have serious health problems.** More than thirty-five physiological and many other psychological problems have been attributed to job-related stress.

• **Divorce is a serious problem.** In the United States, police divorce rates have been found to be as high as 75 percent. The critical period for police marriages appears to be the first three years when the anxiety of "reality shock" is at peak for new officers.

• **Cops are prone to suicide.** Compared to workers in other occupations, police officers are particularly prone to killing themselves. Some believe that the police suicide rate is artificially low due to the tendency of departments to report any suicide that can possibly be viewed in another way as accidental. Most often, they list the cause as "heart attack."

WHEN COPS CROSS THE THIN BLUE LINE

Given the nature of the job, it is understandable that police suffer greater physical and family problems than does the average person. While the police officer who turns his stress inward may end up with the kind of problems that add to these statistics, the individual who turns his frustration and rage outward can find himself taking unnecessary risks, isolating himself from friends (particularly friends who are not police), becoming increasingly callous, and even turning to extortion and other criminal behavior, as well as using unnecessary violence in dealing with citizens.

On the other hand, some individuals are attracted to police work in the first place simply because they are bullies looking for the opportunity to push other people around. These are the rotten apples of law enforcement. Stress management programs and system reform will not help them. They just need to be weeded out. But this is not easily done because of the code of silence among police. "There are so many good officers, but they all protect the worst officer. That's just the code," says Wu. "It's a shame."

Most policemen agree that brutality would not go on if the administration didn't approve it, or at least tolerate it. Decent cops who become brutal are overreacting to the stresses of their job—and that overreaction should be caught by supervisors before it becomes a problem. Unfortunately, many departments still do not have adequate stress training programs to help supervising officers find and diffuse overstressed officers. In addition, cops wrestle with their own macho image, says Ed Donovan, a retired 32-year veteran of the Boston Police Department and founder of the first organization to deal with cops under stress.

"What police have in common all over the world is that tough-guy image, the John Wayne syndrome," says Donovan. "That is what they die from."

To Donovan, the problem is simple: A cop who is stressed and has become a problem is ignored by his supervisors because they don't want to acknowledge there is a problem—it's bad PR to advertise that your cops are not well. Second, the cop takes refuge in his own macho image, which he believes he must maintain in order to do his job. These two factors, says Donovan, lead police, who are seldom adequately prepared to deal with stress anyway, to ignore it.

The department sometimes ignores it as well. Supervising officers have been notorious for transferring troubled officers out of one assignment into another precinct, just to get rid of the problem. But problems that are not addressed get worse—sometimes much worse.

THE SERPICO SYNDROME

The most disturbing part of her police job, says Wu, was the occasional brutality on the part of certain cops. "Once, in the Mission Station, one particular officer who had a terrible temper brought in a handcuffed prisoner. I didn't see what started it, but he angered that officer who started beating this cuffed man. He pulled him out of the bookies room and brought him into the common room in front of all the officers, and continued to beat up on him.

"I couldn't take it," Wu remembers. "I just stood up and went over to the training officer and said, 'He can't do that in front of me because I have to do something about it. You make him stop because I'll report to you.' He went to the officer and pointed me out and said, 'Don't do it in front of her, because she's going to do something about it.' So they pushed him into the men's locker room and continued to beat him. The captain never looked up, and that was the end of it for that night—but not the end of it for me.

"The next time I worked, I was out on the street on a call, and called for a 1025, 'officer needs assistance.' My sergeant and someone else came. But as we were leaving, the sergeant said, 'You know, you called for a 1025. Sometimes you never get the backup when you need it.' I knew immediately that was a warning, so I confronted my partner and said, 'Hey, I'm here for you, you're here for me or I assume you are, but if I needed help, and if this sergeant's telling me that I'm not going to get it, you'd better tell me right now, because I'm not going to work under those conditions.' "

Such incidents have always been an ugly part of the police world. The film "Serpico" portrayed the true story of New York City police officer Frank Serpico, who exposed the corruption that was rampant in that department during the 1960s. In retaliation for "ratting," Serpico was denied the crucial backup he needed during a drug raid—and was shot. He lived to testify and subsequently his department was cleaned up.

Unfortunately, the "code of silence" among police—the powerful taboo against "ratting" on a fellow officer who is crooked or brutal—makes it almost impossible to weed out the bad members. Feeling they have no other friends—the criminals, the justice system, the press, the politicians, and frequently the public all arrayed against them—police feel they have no other natural allies except each other. Like soldiers at war, who, during the heat of the battle find themselves fighting not for God, mother, country, or freedom, but for each other, so do cops protect one another fiercely, including the rotten ones. They are all cops, and cops don't rat on other cops.

"Cops stick together right or wrong because they get screwed all the time," says Alvarez. "If the standards were changed and things were done by the book, by the law, cops would not stick together when they are wrong. A good cop is not going to put up with an individual who violates the law or tarnishes everything he stands for when there is no need."

SOLUTIONS

In the war between good and evil, there are casualties on the front lines. Cops are only human, made of the same mortal flesh and blood as the rest of us. The stresses can be overwhelming, and when they are, something has to break.

"Most policemen in this country—and I've been involved in numerous shootings, so I can tell you from personal experience—are crying on the inside," says Bill Arnado, who was a S.W.A.T. instructor for the Los Angeles Police Department until an injury forced him off the force in 1976. "They're torn up on the inside. They have that macho image on the outside, but if you could really look into a policeman, most of them are real emotional. They're very pro-American, but they're crying on the inside and they don't know how to let it out."

Policemen have got to learn to open up and show their emotions, says Arnado. It can be difficult. "If you shot somebody, it's hard to go home and tell your wife 'I just shot a person' or 'My partner was killed in front of me.' You can't take that home. So it builds up and pretty soon you explode. I almost exploded. I've been through it.

"Let's say the police officer responds to a robbery in progress. Maybe he gets into a fight, or a shooting, or an argument. Afterwards, he gets in his car and heads down the road. He pulls over a speeder, but he still hasn't come down from the stress level of the robbery—his heart is still pounding. The speeder just so much as says something wrong, and right away *boom*. Then the cop goes right out on another hot call. You have to walk in his shoes to understand what I'm trying to tell you. The stress is there. It's how he controls that stress, that's what counts."

Arnado, now a Sheriff of Josephine County, Oregon, echoes the voice of many in law enforcement that say there may indeed be a way out, a way to allow America's police to win the no-win war—not only against crime, but against the stress that is killing them.

"The first thing I do when I get a new employee," he says, "is to sit him down and tell him, 'Law enforcement is *not* the most important thing in your life.' The first, most important thing you have is faith in God, your family, and your community. . . . While you're on duty, give 110 percent, but once your tour of duty is up, when you hang up your gun and badge and get away from the job, go home and be with your family and loved ones."

The biggest danger a police officer has, says Arnado, is becoming just a police officer. "A lot of cops—especially young ones, the three-to-five year cops—think everybody's a dirtbag. But after they get a little more time on the job, they realize it's not true."

THE RETURN OF THE PEACE OFFICER

"Police badly need to move into a new era," says Arnado. "They need to go into what is called Community Oriented Policing." Currently being employed in over 300 cities and towns nationwide—including Boston and San Francisco—Community Oriented Policing (COP) is essentially the resurrection of the traditional "beat cop" style of policing. "Since the '60s," says Arnado, who trains departments throughout the Northwest in COP principles, "policemen have mainly responded to radio calls." Whereas cops once knew their neighborhoods intimately, talked to its residents, engaged in social work, rounded up stray animals, and generally befriended the community, for the last three decades police work has been reduced to an endless stream of 911 calls—"You call, we haul," in police lingo. The cop sees only the worst side of the community and constantly reacts to trouble, instead of stopping it before it happens.

The COP approach: Many calls coming from one area may signal a root problem. If police and the community can solve that root problem, then there will be less need for law enforcement. Example: a broken window in a building encourages disrespect, and then more windows are broken by kids. Or a bar in a neighborhood may be a problem. When police focus on eliminating specific problems they tend to plug the leak in the boat, so to speak, rather than constantly bail out the boat without plugging the leak.

"This is an important thing," says former Attorney General Meese, "where police officers get out of their cars, become acquainted with the local population they serve, deal with people as human beings in a one-to-one relationship, obtain information from the public about community conditions, about criminal activity that's going on, about specific suspects—and then use this cooperation to do a better job of protecting the community."

Already, COP has paid handsome dividends in many communities throughout the nation. "Police who have

Balancing the scales

The police and public alike have become cynical over a justice system that sentences Lawrence Singleton—a man who raped a 15-year-old girl, cut off her arms, and left her for dead—to 14 years, only to release him after eight. On the other extreme, evangelist Jim Baker received a 45-year sentence for fraud in a country where convicted murderers are sentenced to an average of 20 years.

As a stem in rectifying this imbalance, the Federal Sentencing Commission set up guidelines that went into effect on November 1, 1987. Before then, sentencing had been totally up to the discretion of individual judges. And whatever sentence *was* handed down wasn't real. The average convicted criminal served only one-third of the time imposed, at which time the parole commission would decide whether or not he was to be released.

Congress scrapped the system due to its obvious inequities. Now the sentences generated under the guidelines are so-called "real time sentences." Parole has been abolished in the Federal Courts; it is no longer available for anyone sentenced under these guidelines.

"I think the system is more fair now, especially to the defendants," says Paul Martin of the Federal Sentencing Commission. "It used to be that if one man robs a bank in South Carolina and another robs a bank in New York City, the first man could get 20 years and the second could get three." That kind of discrepancy "breeds disrespect for the law," says Martin. "Oftentimes it mattered more who the particular judge was than what particular crime a person had committed." Martin believes the new system will also benefit the victims of crime.

tried community policing have found that they can be a catalyst for developing neighborhoods," says Meese. This is important, he says, because "one of the reasons people have given up is there doesn't seem to be anybody in a position of authority who is going to take an interest in them."

In a rural community like Arnado's, Community Oriented Policing comes naturally. Officers live in the community they serve, they know its people and its problems, and COP just extends and enhances an on-going process. It is in the big cities of the nation that community policing offers the greatest challenges.

Looking at the nation's major cities, Ed Donovan is pessimistic. "With the layoffs of police, with the recession, with the lack of housing and the homeless and the drugs and AIDS and the lost youth of America, I only see more and more fear. I see television condoning violence. It's nothing for a kid to go to a movie and see someone kick somebody in the stomach or hit him over the head with a baseball bat and then laugh about it afterwards.

"If it gets any worse, we're going to have to put the National Guard in the streets of major cities. In 1991 we're already ahead of 1990's murder record, which is an all-time high."

Yet, through the gloom, Donovan sees a solution: "The public has to take a hand in this. It's not going to turn around by itself." Indeed, community involvement seems to be the wave of the future. According to the FBI, the 1990s will be the decade of greatly increased citizen participation in helping the police to enforce the laws and make America's communities livable again. But in some communities, such as Macon, Georgia, the future is now.

THE CIVIL RESPONSIBILITY MOVEMENT

"No one could have disliked law enforcement [more] than I did," admits Rev. Charles Jones, a Macon, Georgia, Baptist minister. "I constantly blamed the police for the problems in the community." In Jones's neighborhood of Bellevue, residents were close to despair. The combined effect of gangs and drugs had devastated the area and created a siege mentality.

Macon Police Chief Jim Brooks was just as frustrated. "We used every kind of police technique you can imagine and still we didn't accomplish anything over there."

Rev. Jones confronted Chief Brooks at every opportunity, demanding that he do more to clean up the drug- and crime-infested community. "He wore me out," remembers Brooks, referring to Jones's angry calls for everything from more cops and patrol cars to a whole new police precinct in Bellevue. Jones recalls: "I took busloads of people down there to 'give them hell'—but that wasn't the answer."

Jones laughs about it now. So does Brooks. They discovered a secret weapon: "The answer," says Jones, "was the community standing up, *with* the police, and saying 'we've had enough!' "

Who gave them the answer? A man named Herman Wrice from a tough Philadelphia neighborhood called Mantua. Wrice and his group, *Mantua Against Drugs*, spend their time organizing citizens who are sick of seeing their children die—either suddenly on the streets or slowly in a drugged haze of lost hope and broken dreams. "When a city or a small town can find no resources to meet this epidemic, then they go back to basics," says Glenn McCurdy, an early member of MAD. The "basics" in this case is *citizen action*.

CONFRONTING THE PROBLEM

Wrice's method is simple confrontation on a mass scale. His method is the essence of elegant simplicity: He and concerned citizens in the community walk through crime-infested neighborhoods and order the drug dealers out. Amazingly, it works. "The drug dealer is someone who has never had to deal with real confrontation in his life," says Wrice. But the drug dealers weren't the only ones afraid. After years of living under a siege mentality, the citizens themselves weren't too eager for confrontation. "First time out people are afraid," Wrice admits. "They are under the impression that these dealers are invincible." Wrice corrects that impression as fast as he can. "I always take the worst corner first," he chuckles. His reasoning is simple—after that it can only get easier, and the citizens know it.

Although his intent is to intimidate the criminal through direct action, Wrice has no interest in vigilantism. Involving law enforcement is the key to the whole idea. When he started *Mantua Against Drugs*, Wrice did it with full police involvement as members, and within the first three weeks, the group had closed down 14 crack houses. With patrol cars parked nearby, citizens chanting "Up with hope—Down with dope" would approach the crack houses and surround them using bullhorns to scold the dealers inside.

"The drug dealers get moving for one simple reason," says Wrice. "Someone is putting the light on them." Chief Brooks is more specific: "The single greatest weapon that we have used against them to date is the video camera. I guess you could take an Uzi out there but I don't think you'd move them any faster," he jokes. Of course, the crowd itself makes a big impression, and although the dealers wave guns and make threats, they eventually take off into the night.

Wrice and his movement don't threaten easily. He has obvious contempt for the dealers who he complains are portrayed falsely on TV as tough guys. "They remind me of Saddam Hussein—if you go after them, they'll surrender. You can't go believing that 'Republican Guard' line—remember that?—how deep they were dug in, and how many body bags we were going to need. You can't believe that fear stuff. The enemy came at us through psychology, not through warfare. We gave Iraq the psychological

Building shattered lives

When people have their backs to the wall, who do they call? A cop. When a cop has his back to the wall, who does he call? When Boston patrolman Ed Donovan was in trouble, the answer was a resounding "nobody." A cop at age 26, a full-fledged alcoholic by 29, Donovan found himself outside Boston's Fenway Park one steamy summer day in 1969 pushing the barrel of his .38-caliber service revolver into his mouth, panicked, depressed, ready to end his life.

As a police photographer Donovan had spent 10 years looking through a camera lens at an endless stream of victims of brutal murders, rapes, car accidents, and violent assaults. He coped with the constant images of carnage by attending "choir practice" (police jargon for drinking with their buddies) and popping anti-depressants, never once daring to face the grim reality that his life was falling apart.

To this day Donovan doesn't know what stopped him from pulling the trigger. But the near-suicide marked the turning point in his shattered life. From that moment forward, Donovan—almost without realizing it—began devoting his life to helping stressed-out cops.

With the encouragement of some tough cop friends, Donovan checked himself into a detox center in the summer of 1970, joined Alcoholics Anonymous after sobering up, and started putting his life back together. Fellow cops who had witnessed the dramatic change in Donovan began coming to him for help with their own problems. By 1972 he had teamed up with fellow Boston policeman Joe Ravino to form what would become, in 1974, the Boston Police Stress Program. The success of that program prompted Donovan to establish the International Law Enforcement Stress Association (ILESA), located in Matapan, Massachusetts, in 1978.

Donovan's near 20-year odyssey into the world of police stress management has been the focus of a 1986 book, *The Shattered Badge*, by Canadian Bill Klankewitt, and a soon-to-be-aired TV movie starring David Soul (of "Starsky and Hutch" fame).

Whether he's running weekly meetings of the Boston stress program, lecturing on police stress around the world, or talking to a single, distressed cop, Donovan's message is the same: When you're in trouble, get out from behind your badge.

The job of police officer comes complete with a macho image, he explains, a "tough guys don't cry" syndrome that teaches cops to hold in their feelings—on and off the job—at any cost. "The enemy within, the silent killer, is cops suppressing their feelings and thinking they can handle it. Instead, it handles them," he says.

Treating stressed-out law enforcement officers has its hitches, as Donovan discovered early on. Because police departments had no way of treating overstressed officers, most dealt with the problem simply by ignoring it. For their part, troubled officers were reluctant to admit problems for fear they would lose their jobs. This combination of factors made cops unwilling to open up to anyone outside of the police's tightly knit rank and file. But they listen to the likes of Donovan—a tough, non-nonsense cop like themselves who had been in their shoes—and survived.

While there has been a gradual change in police work during Donovan's 32-year career—there is more violence and less respect for police officers today, he comments—the stress has always been there. That's why Donovan likes to counsel young police academy recruits; it gives him a chance to stop problems before they start. "Prevention is the key," he explains. "We can't just keep patching up cops and putting them back on the streets."

Donovan's persistence in this field is beginning to pay off. Stress management courses are becoming an integral part of police training. "Police academies are letting recruits know beforehand that they are human," he says, "that when they hurt they have a place to go."

One place troubled officers go is Seafield 911, a Davie, Florida treatment center exclusively for chemically dependent and stressed-out cops. Begun in 1989, a brainchild of Donovan and George Benedict, owner of Seafield Treatment Centers, Seafield 911 has helped hundreds of cops overcome their alcohol and drug dependencies. Seafield is different from many treatment centers in that it is staffed mostly by former law enforcement professionals—men and women who can readily relate to the unique stresses that tip cops over the edge.

Despite the stress of police work, Donovan says there is no shortage of young men and women wanting to become cops. Their reasons are still altruistic, he says; they want to make a difference in society. Donovan sees his role as injecting a bit of cool reality into their sometimes rosy expectations, giving recruits a good, hard look at what it really takes. And if the going gets tough, thanks to Donovan's tireless efforts, there's a safety net—a place to fall back and regroup.

Retired for 2 years now, Donovan has not slowed down. His latest endeavor is to revive *Police Stress* magazine, ILESA's house publication. Lack of funds prompted him to suspend publication several years ago, even though the demand for it has remained high. If he can line up the funding, Donovan intends to market the new *Police Stress* magazine to a huge readership of law enforcement personnel around the world.

The need to get the message to cops is still great, says Donovan. "There are still many cops who have the Neanderthal attitude that 'we don't have problems,' that 'we don't air our troubles to anybody,' " he says. "As long as they have that attitude, cops are going to get sicker and sicker."

Donovan won't rest until that attitude is wiped out. "I'm a survivor. "I'm the guy who had the gun in my mouth cocked many times," he says. "When I think about it, I just thank God I didn't die."

attitude that they were going to win. 'It's going to be another Vietnam!' we said. The heck with that!"

UP WITH HOPE

A former coach, Boy Scout leader, and father of 7, Herman Wrice has begun what could fairly be called a *civil responsibility movement.* Although his effort to get citizens to take back the streets began locally, it is growing into an impressive national campaign dedicated to training and inspiring citizens and local law enforcement officials to join together to throw the drug dealers out.

It's easy to see why President Bush has referred to Wrice as "the John Wayne of Philadelphia," but John Wayne walked alone and Wrice is very much a team player. "I've never seen a coming together between a law enforcement agency and a community like this," says Chief Brooks. These days the Chief is a true believer. "I can tell you about cold nights when there were 14 young black children inside a police van to stay warm with a white police officer demonstrating an in-car computer. I can tell you about a 76-year-old woman who came to me and said, 'Chief, I haven't been out of my house after dark in 7 years, and it's a wonderful feeling to be able to do it now.'" Bellevue's crime rate is substantially down since the program started last November.

Brooks's stories aren't just about civilians. He tells of a 17-year police veteran who was so burnt out from the hopeless crime situation that he was ready to quit the department. The Wrice method turned him around. "The second or third night we were out," says Brooks, almost incredulous, "he was off duty, but he and his family were there, marching in the streets. It's that powerful."

Today, police from many towns and cities are asking Herman Wrice to give them training in his methods. As a result, from Akron to Savannah to St. Louis to Chicago, citizens and police are reaching out to each other as friends. "You don't need a national guard. You don't need 50 police officers," says Reverend Jones, "All you need is just a few folks in the streets telling those drug dealers they've got to go." Says Brooks, looking back on the experience of community and cops standing by each other. "It's more grand than anything that I'm capable of telling you about."

EPILOGUE

Why do well-armed criminals leave communities where cops and housewives march around chanting slogans and shouting at them through bullhorns? What is the magic that melts the invincible drug dealer?

They are literally shamed out. Such demonstrations of solidarity between the community and the police breathe conscience back into the nation's communities. Rundown neighborhoods where nobody cares are irresistibly inviting to the criminal element, which regards broken windows and the like as engraved invitations to move in. Dope dealers simply feel comfortable in a community that doesn't care. But when people do care, and care courageously, the dealer feels unbearable discomfort and shame, and runs off into the night.

Why does fixing that broken window prevent crime and delinquency in a neighborhood? It is a clear signal of that community's caring and vigilance. Like the human body, where an open wound can result in infection, neighborhoods must also clean up their wounds to keep out the infection of crime. The cooperation of police and community produces a profound change of chemistry in a community's body politic. It reaffirms the value of the police, who are no longer looked upon as hired guns, but as true representatives of the people.

For what they do, for what we pay them, police are the best employee value there is. And because cops are under such stress, Americans would do well to exercise a little compassion toward them. Cops have a difficult job to do, and that job becomes nearly impossible without the support of both the court system and the public. Lacking such support, there will be no incentive for good people to go into law enforcement, and they will gradually dropout. The only incentive left will be for people to work with unworkable options—the perfect excuse for abusing power, taking bribes, and being brutal.

After all, if it's a no-win game, why play by the rules? If there's no way out and no options, why even try?

We expect our police not only to protect us from the criminal underworld, but increasingly to solve every problem of our own making, from child abuse and domestic fights to drunk driving accidents and drug addiction. We created the problems; they have to deal with the results—and they are the ones that end up with suicide, alcoholism, and divorce rates doubles those of the rest of the population.

It does not have to be so. The individual citizen holds the key: First support your police then get involved in helping them, not blaming them.

Like troops in a foreign land, unless they are supported and loved by those on the home front whom they are defending, police all the more easily become demoralized, and fall to corruption and cynicism. They are soldiers, and just as some of our soldiers in Vietnam found it easier to take dope and break the rules when they heard reports that many Americans did not support their efforts, so are America's police also made more vulnerable to temptation through our abuse of them. Public support provides the stability and faith that these men and women need in order to fight the good fight for the rest of us.

A LEN exclusive:

Public Solidly Favors Mixed Police/Civilian Review Boards

Perhaps no issue in policing currently evokes more heated debate or frayed nerves than civilian review, which in city after city has driven wedges between political officials and the police rank and file. Police labor leaders insist that only a police officer can understand and judge the actions of another officer. Local officials, for their part, worry that justice may not be served if the police judge themselves.

But while the issue simmers on the front burner of many an urban political agenda, where does the public stand?

A new survey shows that an overwhelming majority of people, across a broad spectrum of demographic groupings, believe that police officers accused of misconduct should have their cases reviewed by a committee composed of both civilians and other officers.

According to the nationwide telephone survey of 1,248 adults, conducted in early October by the polling organization of Louis Harris and Associates Inc. and John Jay College of Criminal Justice, 80 percent of all respondents felt that review boards with both police and civilian members could better judge allegations of misconduct than those formed only of police officers or only of civilians. Only 4 percent felt that review committees should be composed solely of police offi-

cers, while support for all-civilian review boards was slightly higher at 15 percent.

All-civilian police review boards garnered the greatest support among Hispanics, people ages 18 to 24, and those with incomes of $7,500 or less, with 23 percent of each group preferring that form of police oversight.

Humphrey Taylor, the president and chief executive officer of Louis Harris and Associates, took note of the "broad public consensus" on the question of how police accused of misconduct should be judged, but added, "On balance, however, many more people trust civilians than the police to be fairer judges of police conduct."

Dr. Gerald W. Lynch, the president of John Jay College, said the poll shows that the public are "wiser than they know" on the subject of police review boards.

"The mix of civilians and police is a dynamic combination of all interests in considering all aspects of police misconduct," Lynch noted. "Mixing police and civilians is not oil and water, it is oil and vinegar. It takes two to tango in the area of police complaints and without a partner, neither side will believe the results."

The survey, the first in an ongoing series of joint ventures between the Harris organization and John Jay Col-

lege, also found strong positive responses to the questions of whether police treat people fairly and refrain from using excessive force.

Solid public support for review boards of mixed composition was consistent in nearly every demographic grouping examined by the survey. Analyzed by age group, that support ranged from a low of 71 percent among those age 18–24 to a high of 84 percent among those age 50–64. In terms of educational level, mixed boards were supported by 73 percent of those with less than a high school education, 78 percent of high school graduates, 83 percent of those with some college education or college degree, and 87 percent of those with a post-graduate education.

Seventy-two percent of the self-described political liberals, 81 percent of conservatives and 82 percent of political moderates said they supported the mixed approach. Across racial lines, mixed police/civilian review boards were favored by 80 percent of whites, 78 percent of blacks, and 75 percent of Hispanics.

Dr. William McCarthy of the Criminal Justice Center at John Jay College said he found it "surprising" there was not a wider diversity of opinion about police review boards between racial groups. "I think people would have expected a much wider distinction between the ethnic groups," he said.

McCarthy went on to speculate that the relatively low support for mixed police/civilian boards among those age 18–24 may stem from the fact that persons in that age group are likely to have more adversarial contact with police.

"Their negativity may not indicate inappropriate behavior, just that they are subject to the authoritarian behavior of police," he opined. "The behavior itself is what the society wants the police to control and the police are doing it professionally, but that doesn't mean the person who is subject to that control is ever going to be pleased with it."

Overall, 60 percent of the respondents felt that police officers would be too lenient in judging officers accused of misconduct, a finding that varied little between males and females, or among age, racial or income groupings. Just under one-third of those questioned—31 percent—felt that police officers would adequately judge other officers accused of misconduct. The rates were lower among males (29 percent), 18- to 24-year-olds (28 percent), 40- to 49-year-olds (26 percent), and blacks (22 percent).

The ability of police to fairly judge another officer got slightly higher marks from those with less than a high school education (37 percent), those with an income of $7,500 or less (38 percent) and those with incomes of $15,000 to $25,000 (36 percent). Only among those age 65 and older did a plurality—44 percent—believe that police officers would be "about right" in their judgment of other police, compared to 43 percent who said police would be too lenient.

By contrast, more than half of those surveyed believe that civilians would do an adequate job of judging police misconduct, with 56 percent saying civilians would be "about right" in their judgment of officers. Only 7 percent thought civilians would be too lenient, while 35 percent thought civilians would be too strict.

When the survey asked whether police treated people fairly, it found that 63 percent of the respondents gave the police favorable grades, while 35 percent responded negatively. Perceptions that police treated people fairly were split along racial lines, with 68 percent of

Judging the Police

Some responses from a Louis Harris/John Jay College public opinion survey

(results in percentages)

When Police Officers Are Charged with Alleged Misconduct, What Kind of a Committee Do You Think Should Judge Them?

	RACE			AGE						RESIDENCY				INCOME					
	White	Black	Hisp.	18-24	25-29	30-39	40-49	50-64	Over 65	City	Rest of Metro Area	Small Town	Rural	Less than $7,500	$7,501 to $15K	$15K to $25K	$25K to $35K	$35K to $50K	$50K and up
All Police	4	6	3	4	5	2	3	4	7	5	4	2	3	4	6	3	3	4	2
All Civilian	15	14	23	23	15	15	13	12	15	16	14	17	13	23	20	11	14	16	11
Mixed	80	78	75	71	80	82	82	84	76	78	80	81	83	70	75	85	81	80	87

How Would You Rate the Police in Your Community on NOT Using Excessive Force — Excellent, Pretty Good, Only Fair, Poor?

	RACE			AGE						RESIDENCY				INCOME					
	White	Black	Hisp.	18-24	25-29	30-39	40-49	50-64	Over 65	City	Rest of Metro Area	Small Town	Rural	Less than $7,500	$7,501 to $15K	$15K to $25K	$25K to $35K	$35K to $50K	$50K and up
Excellent	29	11	22	22	15	24	30	33	31	20	32	20	37	17	21	27	28	31	31
Pretty Good	42	43	39	42	46	44	39	38	38	41	40	45	41	37	38	42	42	41	44
Only Fair	19	30	24	19	21	22	21	19	21	26	16	25	16	29	26	22	18	21	17
Poor	7	16	13	13	17	8	7	6	7	12	9	6	3	15	12	8	10	6	6

How Would You Rate the Police in Your Community on Treating People Fairly — Excellent, Pretty Good, Only Fair, Poor?

	RACE			AGE						RESIDENCY				INCOME					
	White	Black	Hisp.	18-24	25-29	30-39	40-49	50-64	Over 65	City	Rest of Metro Area	Small Town	Rural	Less than $7,500	$7,501 to $15K	$15K to $25K	$25K to $35K	$35K to $50K	$50K and up
Excellent	22	9	17	12	9	18	22	27	30	15	24	20	24	11	16	19	23	23	27
Pretty Good	46	29	37	40	42	50	43	40	40	44	43	40	45	42	36	44	41	49	44
Only Fair	21	36	30	29	30	22	23	20	23	28	21	30	12	27	31	26	24	21	20
Poor	9	26	13	19	19	9	10	8	6	13	9	8	19	19	17	11	10	7	8

whites giving positive responses such as "excellent" or "pretty good," and 62 percent of blacks giving the police negative responses such as "only fair" or "poor."

Police tended to receive positive responses on the fair-treatment question from people age 40 to 65 (up to 70 percent) and those living in rural areas (69 percent). Highly educated respondents were more likely to perceive police favorably (about 70 percent) than those with less than a high school education, 50 percent of whom perceived police negatively.

Asked to rate police in their community on not using excessive force, 68 percent said police made an "excellent" or "pretty good" effort, while 30 percent rated those efforts "only fair" or "poor." Generally, blacks judged the police more harshly in this regard than whites did.

"Following the Rodney King trial, it is not surprising that blacks are more critical of the police for their excessive use of force," said Taylor. "What is more surprising is that, overall, only 46 percent of blacks rate their local police negatively on this."

Overall, 71 percent of whites felt police efforts against the use of excessive force were adequate. Young people, inner-city residents, people with low incomes and those with less than a high school education were more likely to rate police negatively. Those with higher levels of education and income were more likely to rate police positively.

"These poll results show most Americans have favorable opinions about the police in their communities," Taylor observed, "but that the police have much worse relations with blacks, with young people and with the disadvantaged. However, this is a nationwide poll. No doubt some individual police departments have much better relationships with their communities, while others do much worse."

Crime Data

Law Enforcement Officers Slain

During 1992, 59 law enforcement officers were killed feloniously in the line of duty, according to preliminary figures released by the FBI's Uniform Crime Reporting Program. This represents the lowest annual total of officer deaths recorded in the past 20 years.

As in previous years, firearms continued to be the weapon most used in the slayings. During 1992, handguns were used in 40 of the murders, rifles in 9, and shotguns in 2. In addition, one officer was killed with a knife, one was killed by a bomb explosion, two were beaten with blunt objects, and four were intentionally struck by vehicles.

Twenty-five officers were slain during arrest situations, including 9 while preventing robberies or apprehending robbery suspects, 5 while apprehending burglary suspects, 3 while involved in drug-related situations, and 8 while attempting arrests for other crimes. Eleven officers were answering disturbance calls when slain, 9 were enforcing traffic calls, 7 were investigating suspicious persons or circumstances, 4 were ambushed, 2 were handling mentally deranged persons, and 1 was handling a prisoner.

Nineteen officers were wearing body armor at the time of their deaths, and 3 were slain with their own weapons. Law enforcement agencies have cleared 54 of the 59 slayings.

Geographically, the Southern States recorded 27 officer slayings; the Western States, 13; the Northeastern States, 8; the Midwestern States, 6, and Puerto Rico, 5. An additional 63 officers lost their lives due to accidents that occurred while performing their duties.◆

Beyond 'Just the facts, ma'am'

*Community policing is law enforcement's
hottest new idea. But its promise is elusive*

**CRIME &
JUSTICE**

In Philadelphia, a pulsating tavern jukebox that had caused irate neighbors to log 500 police calls in six months was moved away from a common wall with the adjoining building. The calls stopped. Though it seems simple, such a move is at the heart of what is known as community policing, which has become a mantra for police chiefs and mayors in cities big and small across the country. Indeed, community policing is the new orthodoxy of law enforcement: Rather than just reacting after crimes by racing to a ceaseless string of 911 calls, police should try to create partnerships with communities in advance to solve problems that otherwise lead to crime. "Thoughtful administrators are asking themselves, 'Is there a better way?'" says Lee Brown, the nation's new drug czar.

If community policing isn't in your town yet, it's probably coming. "We're determined to put more police officers on the street and to expand community policing," President Bill Clinton has said; he hopes to fund 100,000 more cops for America's crime-ridden cities. In a recent survey by the FBI and the National Center for Community Policing at Michigan State University, 50 percent of police officials serving cities with populations of more than 50,000 people

said they were following this approach to policing, and an additional 20 percent planned to inaugurate it within a year. "It's reached the point that it's like mom and apple pie," says John Eck of the Police Executive Research Forum.

And therein lies a problem. Despite its allure on paper, turning the theory into practice on the unforgiving streets of urban America is proving complicated. If community policing can't deliver quantifiable results quickly, it could end up on the scrap heap of innovation.

In Brooklyn, N.Y.'s Sunset Park neighborhood, where immigrants and tidy row houses uneasily coexist with prostitutes and graffiti-covered small businesses, patrol officer Russ Amato provides an example of how to make community policing work. Strolling along Third Avenue underneath the Brooklyn-Queens Expressway, Amato banters with shop owners, who see him as "their" cop. Sometimes, his contribution has little to do with fighting crime directly, as when Amato prodded local officials to remove abandoned cars from underneath the expressway.

Crimebuster. But Amato is proudest of the role he played in clearing rampant crack dealing from the corner of 45th Street and Third Avenue. Local residents and merchants came to trust him enough to tell him that a man working out of a nearby apartment was behind it all; Amato called in narcotics detectives and worked with the building's landlord to arrange to monitor the situation from

adjacent units. That led to arrests and contacts with informants who helped the police bring down the main pusher in late June. The crack dealing dried up.

"Community policing made that possible," insists Amato. "A patrol car wouldn't have had the time to spend on it." At Sunset Check Cashing, President Vinny Babino sings Amato's praises: "Russ is always around. And the neighborhood has been cleaned up nicely. The old ladies were afraid to come down here, and now they're not."

But in Houston, neither old ladies nor many others were very happy with community policing—called neighborhood-oriented policing in their city. "The words 'neighborhood-oriented policing' are cuss words around here now," says Sam Nuchia, Houston's police chief since 1992. It was drug czar Lee Brown, then Houston's chief (and later New York's commissioner), who instituted NOP as a pilot program in 1983 and citywide in 1987. The idea improved relations between cops and residents in inner-city neighborhoods. But for community policing to work, several goals need to be met, and Houston is a cautionary tale for the idea's boosters across the country.

First, crime rates soared from 1985 through 1991. Meanwhile, Brown and his successor, Elizabeth Watson, had to scale back their plans because Houston lost 655 of its 4,500 officers to budget cutbacks from 1986 to 1991; NOP was ridiculed as "nobody on patrol." And middle managers gave line officers little flexibility in decision making, diminishing enthusiasm for the approach down the line. Management consultants hired by the city said that some officers were so preoccupied with NOP that they lost sight of the need to catch crooks, and the consultants concluded that NOP had "not produced any comprehensive improvement." Nuchia has now shelved most aspects of NOP, preferring old-fashioned get-tough tactics.

Even proponents recognize the pitfalls. False advertising is one recurring problem. Police experts say departments in cities like Richmond, Va.; Portland, Ore., and San Diego have made major commitments to community policing, but many other cities have borrowed the name while making only cosmetic changes. "The variety of programs that are described as 'community policing' is truly bewildering," wrote Jerome Skolnick and David Bayley in a study for the National Institute of Justice, the Justice Department's research arm. In 1992, for example, a panel studying the Boston police department singled out that city's program as "incomplete and superficial, and lacking the problem-solving component."

The difference between the genuine article and the fakes often comes down to whether the police department appreciates the depth of change needed to make an honest go of community policing. In New York, Lee Brown and his brass identified 57 major changes that had to be made within that department in everything from reward and evaluation systems to criminal investigative techniques. The task is so broad, asserts Robert Trojanowicz, director of the National Center for Community Policing, that "in my opinion, there is no one doing it on a departmentwide basis."

Indeed, the changes recommended typically cut to the core of a stubborn, paramilitary police culture. For one thing, departments must recruit differently, attracting people interested in service, not just adventure. Police academy training needs to expand beyond arrest procedures to include building skills like community organizing. Bean-counting performance measures—like counting summonses—have little meaning in such a system.

Call waiting. Departments must also find ways to free officers from what's called the "tyranny of 911": nonstop calls that send cops bouncing around like pinballs. In some departments, dispatchers query callers aggressively to screen out nonemergency calls. But the problem persists. On a recent night in Sunset Park, patrol officers Ricky Lopez and Brian Fusco were tied up on a numbing series of 911 calls for false burglar alarms,

domestic disputes and heat exhaustion. "There really isn't the time to work problems," says Fusco. "People call 911, and they want a cop." Community-policing advocates say solving problems at their core will eventually reduce 911 calls, and argue that residents will accept a different response time for nonemergencies if the payback from community policing is clear; studies in Greensboro, N.C., and Toledo, Ohio, back them up. But in Houston, where community-po-

licing efforts faltered, "the public was enraged" by slower emergency-response times, says patrolman Mike Howard.

Ideally, experts say, all officers should participate in community policing, but the crush of 911 forces some departments to split their troops, with a few officers working full time on community problems while others answer radio calls. In New York, this has caused animosity between the two groups. The reality, contend some experts, is that com-

---

NEW YORK STORY

The power of an insider

When recruiters sought a top cop for New York City last year, Acting Commissioner Ray Kelly was an early favorite. But there were doubts. As the department's former second in command, Kelly was regarded as an insider who might not make the tough changes required. That concern vanished after a riot in which thousands of off-duty cops stormed City Hall, some shouting racial epithets at Mayor David Dinkins. Kelly came down hard with charges against dozens of officers. His performance reinforced just how steady the ex-Marine could be. And it showed the difference between what a committed insider can do compared with some of the new chiefs who come from outside the forces they lead.

The police disturbance brought back images of Kelly during the otherwise dismal police performance in the 1991 Crown Heights riots. As a stinging 600-page report issued last week made clear, Kelly's bosses, notably Dinkins and then Police Commissioner Lee Brown, instructed police to let marauding black youths vent their rage after a car driven by a Hasidic Jewish man killed a 7-year-old boy. But it was Kelly who helped devise a plan to intervene after several nights of rioting. And it was Kelly's insider status that made him the right person for the job—and, his supporters hope, for bringing the reform to New York's police force that outsider Brown could only theorize about.

Community policing isn't new to New York. It was introduced in 1984, and since then, the number of officers on foot has jumped from 750

to 4,000. By early next year, 2,863 officers and thousands of civilians are expected to be added to the city's community-policing project. A 30-year veteran of the force, Kelly is using his savvy to forge consensus about necessary adjustments without getting too far ahead of his some 29,000 troops. "It's going to take years to get officers top to bottom reading from the same sheet of music," he predicts.

Kelly is helped by the fact that he came up through the ranks. And it probably doesn't hurt that he has a bit of a tough, by-the-book image. His jaw looks like it's wired to crush stone, and he can bench press 300 pounds. Indeed, Kelly has shown his mettle in several recent crises, without letting his insider role obscure his vision of the need for change. Last year, five officers were charged with selling cocaine, raising an old question: Can the force police itself? Kelly conducted an investigation of how the internal affairs unit failed to detect the dealers, finding no corruption and refusing to fire anyone. But he ordered the unit overhauled and placed a civilian over the restructuring, an unpopular move within the department.

Even for someone with wide support like Kelly, there are no guarantees about the future. Kelly's boss, Dinkins, is up for re-election this year. And he is facing a hard challenge from former federal prosecutor Rudolph Giuliani, who has some ideas of his own about law enforcement. Even insider Kelly might have to contemplate life on the outside someday soon.

SCOTT MINERBROOK

munity policing requires more cops, a tough sell for budget-strapped cities.

Real work. When practiced well, community policing assumes each neighborhood has unique problems, so precinct commanders and line-level cops are encouraged to customize service, not just follow general edicts from headquarters. Yet many cops feel the philosophy is soft on crime or isn't "real" police work, says Randolph Grinc of New York's Vera Institute of Justice, which is completing an evaluation of eight programs. And many sergeants and lieutenants have resisted allowing street cops to devise their own solutions, fearing a loss of control.

The challenges don't stop with the police. Bringing other government agencies and the community at large into the process as partners is crucial. But overworked city agencies have at times had trouble responding when police have asked for their help. New York's housing agency, for instance, told one Sunset Park cop seeking help in sealing an abandoned building filled with squatters that it would take months of legal hassling before they could do it. And many neighborhoods aren't taking up the new role demanded of them, especially if they're plagued by crime or have a history of bad relations with the police. "People don't care enough, or they're afraid," says a frustrated Sunset Park activist.

Even if all the obstacles can be overcome, there is no clear verdict on whether community policing makes a difference. Research in Newark, N.J.; Madison, Wis.; Baltimore, and Flint, Mich., indicates it can reduce fear and increase citizen satisfaction. But hard evidence of actual reductions in crime is hazy, and the most rigorous evaluations are only now being conducted. As Skolnick and Bayley have written in their National Institute of Justice study, "Community policing is advancing because it seems to make sense, not because it has yet been shown to be demonstrably superior." But for crimeweary cops, citizens and politicians, the clock is ticking.

GORDON WITKIN WITH
DAN MCGRAW IN HOUSTON

Is Police Brutality the Problem?

William Tucker

WILLIAM TUCKER is the author of *Vigilante: The Backlash Against Crime in America* and *Progress and Privilege*. He has also contributed to many periodicals, including *Harper's*, the *Atlantic*, the *New Republic*, and the *New York Times*. The present article, sponsored by the Harry Elson Commentary Fund, marks his first appearance in COMMENTARY.

ITEM: On July 20, 1992, Sergeant Peter Viola, and four other New York City police officers, were summoned to the home of Annie Dodds, a politically prominent black woman in Brooklyn, to settle a domestic dispute. It was one of those routinely dangerous, noncriminal confrontations that the police have learned to abhor.

Mrs. Dodds's two sons, Harold Dodds, 34, and Tyrese Daniels, 28, were engaged in a violent argument. Although the police could not then know it, both brothers had extensive criminal records. Daniels in particular had been charged several times with assaulting police officers.

As the five cops worked patiently to soothe tempers, Daniels suddenly turned on his brother and hit him over the head with a metal pipe he had been brandishing. In the ensuing melee, all five cops were injured, one suffering a fractured shoulder. Mrs. Dodds also suffered a few scratches. Nevertheless, she went to the Brooklyn district attorney, Charles Hynes, and complained of Sergeant Viola's behavior. Viola was subsequently charged with felonious assault and is now awaiting trial.

Item: In January 1992, Scott Baldwin, a 210-pound running back at the University of Nebraska, underwent a "psychotic episode," jumping out of a friend's car and running naked through the streets of Omaha. Coming across a woman walking her dog, Baldwin smashed her head into a parked car, nearly killing her. He was charged with assault, but acquitted by reason of insanity.

The coach of the Nebraska football team, Tom Osborne, then took Baldwin into his home for several months. But on September 5, the evening of Nebraska's first game of the season, Baldwin again turned up in Omaha, this time trying to break through the glass door of a stranger's apartment. Two female police officers were dispatched to the scene. When they tried to handcuff Baldwin, he wrestled one to the ground and attempted to grab her gun. The other officer drew her gun, held it to Baldwin's head, and threatened him. When Baldwin kept fighting, she lowered the gun and shot him in the ribs, paralyzing him for life.

State Senator Ernie Chambers of Omaha, Nebraska's only black legislator, blamed the police for sending two women to the scene and called the shooting "avoidable and therefore unjustified."

Item: On October 7, 1992, Jerry Haaf, a 30-year veteran of the Minneapolis police department assigned to traffic duty, stopped at a pizza shop at 2 A.M. for a cup of coffee. While he was sitting at a table filling out reports, two young black males, in full view of several witnesses, walked up behind him and shot him through the heart. Despite an episode like this, and despite a general rise in crime and gang violence, Minneapolis's liberal city administration continues to insist that police behavior is the city's major problem. Says Mayor Donald Fraser: "I've never met a black family in Minneapolis that hadn't been abused by the police."

Item: On September 16, 1992, three off-duty New York City police officers became embroiled in an argument with 18-year-old Ywanus Mohamed as they were entering a subway station. During the argument, Mohamed pulled a box-cutting razor knife and slashed officer John Coughlin in the face, cutting him so badly he nearly died. The wounds required 500 stitches. Officers Thomas Cea and Patrick O'Neill subdued Mohamed, but after they had him handcuffed they allegedly continued punching him and broke his jaw. Mohamed, and Officers Cea and O'Neill, have all equally been charged with felony assault.

Item: Again in New York City, a riot erupted and the entire city spent the summer of 1992 on edge after an undercover police officer named Michael O'Keefe killed 23-year-old Kiko Garcia, a suspected drug dealer, in a street confrontation in Washington Heights. A grand jury eventually exonerated the officer, but Mayor David Dinkins

Reprinted from *Commentary*, Vol. 95, No. 1, January 1993, pp. 23-28, by permission.

used the occasion to push for the removal of the remaining six police officials from the city's twelve-member police-review board, and to turn it into a completely civilian body.

Item: And again in Brooklyn, on August 19, 1991, in the Crown Heights section, a young Orthodox Jew named Yankel Rosenbaum was set upon by a mob of black teenagers yelling "Get the Jew." One of them stabbed him, and before he died he identified his killer as Lemrick Nelson, Jr. The police also found a knife in Nelson's possession with blood stains on it that matched Rosenbaum's, and two detectives testified that Nelson had confessed. But on October 30, 1991, in a verdict that seemed to many a mirror image of the Rodney King case, the jury (made up of six blacks, four Hispanics, and two whites) acquitted Nelson of all charges. Evidently the reason was that the jurors did not believe the testimony of the police officers on the scene and concluded that they had framed Nelson.* The *New York Times*, which had scarcely been able to contain its outrage over the white and Hispanic jury that had acquitted the police officers in the Rodney King case, now blamed not the jury but the police department—for the crime of having "lost all credibility with the neighborhoods it serves." For good measure, the *Times* also attacked the policemen's union for having "forfeited public faith" through its "callous arrogance." And the moral it drew from the occasion was that the city needed "a more independent board to review complaints of police misconduct."

IN ADVANCING the bizarre suggestion that the police rather than the criminals are the real problem confronting us, and that the solution therefore lies in civilian oversight, Mayor Dinkins, District Attorney Hynes, Senator Chambers, Mayor Fraser, the *New York Times*, and the many other politicians and media pundits who agree with them, have a good deal of support from the academic world. For example, according to David Bayley, professor of criminology at SUNY Albany, and the leading American authority on foreign police forces,

We're way behind the rest of the English-speaking world on this issue. England, Canada, Australia, and New Zealand all have strong systems. The best civilian-review board in North America is in Ontario. Their police department has completely lost sovereignty with respect to internal punishments.

Yet that did not prevent Toronto from erupting in riots last June when a 22-year-old black youth was shot to death by an undercover police officer. Nor is there any evidence that civilian-review boards do any better in this country in defusing the tensions between minority communities and the police.

Sam Walker, professor of criminology at the

University of Nebraska, who specializes in civilian-review boards, has just completed a survey in which he found that 35 of the nation's largest cities now have such boards. Walker argues that they act as an outlet to deflect police-civilian confrontations and prevent violence and frustration from building up within poor and minority communities:

The experience is that when the procedure for filing complaints is made more open to the public, the number of complaints rises. San Francisco has a very open system and has lots of complaints, while Los Angeles has no complaint procedure and is not even talking about one. San Francisco also didn't have any riots. The Mayor of Omaha recently changed the system so that complaints could be filed at city hall rather than at the police stations. The number of complaints immediately doubled. In my judgment, the number of complaints a city has about police brutality is a reflection of public confidence in the police.

Yet public opinion, led by local anti-police activists, is likely to conclude the opposite. First, the number of complaints filed is seen as evidence that police brutality is "widespread." Second, since only a very small number of complaints ever lead to disciplinary action (just as a very small number of criminal complaints ever lead to jail sentences), the vast number that fall apart or are not resolved will usually be taken as proof that "the system isn't working."

The truth, however, is that most complaints are either frivolous or unjustified. This is borne out by the experience of the old New York City Board, which the Vera Institute for Justice, a nonpartisan organization, found to be prejudiced neither for nor against civilians or police officers.

In 1990, the Board's annual report showed a total of 2,376 complaints for "excessive force," 1,140 for "abuse of authority," 1,618 for "discourtesy," and 420 for "ethnic slurs." Among the 2,376 complaints for excessive force (presumably the most serious charge), injuries were documented in 267 cases. These involved 71 bruises, 92 lacerations requiring stitches, 30 fractures, 22 swellings, and 41 "other." In the 2,286 cases that were pursued, 566 were dropped because the complainant became uncooperative, 234 were dropped because the complainant withdrew the charge, and 1,405 were closed with less than full investigation, usually because the complainants became unavailable. Only 81 cases resulted in a finding against the policeman.

To understand why there is such an overload of frivolous cases, it is first necessary to realize that the vast majority of complaints do not involve serious charges. In 80 percent of the New York cases, the complainant did not even seek

---

* For a fuller discussion of what happened in Crown Heights, see the article by Philip Gourevitch [*Commentary*, January 1993]—ED.

punishment or further investigation, but only wanted to confront the officer.

Furthermore, the serious complaints are often the work of criminals who are seeking some leverage in the charges against them. "They file a complaint as soon as they are arrested and hope to use it as a trade-off in bargaining their case," says Robert M. Morgenthau, the district attorney of Manhattan. Drug dealers in particular have become adept at using the complaint system as a bargaining tool. In the 34th precinct (Washington Heights), which led all New York City precincts for homicides in 1991, arresting officers now routinely hand drug suspects the civilian-complaint form as an ironic gesture in "community relations."

When Professor Walker was asked to point to a system that works, he replied:

> That's a question I've been asked a hundred times and I don't know the answer. I was talking to a reporter from the *Detroit News* and he told me that Detroit has a strong civilian-review board and few complaints about police brutality. Maybe the system works there. I'm going to have to go up and see.

Detroit, of course, is a city where, as one columnist wrote recently, "the wheels have fallen off Western civilization."

THERE are people who contend that to downgrade the problem of police brutality is to adopt a white perspective and to manifest insensitivity, or worse, to the black condition. No doubt there is some truth to this charge. After all, as Mayor Fraser points out, law-abiding blacks are more likely to be harassed by cops than are their white counterparts, so that for the former, police misconduct is indeed something to worry about. But a cursory glance at the FBI's Uniform Crime Reports makes it clear why focusing on police misbehavior is so perversely misplaced an emphasis.

Since 1986, the incidence of all crimes per 100,000 population is only up 6 percent, and some property crimes (pocket-pickings, purse-snatchings, and motor-vehicle accessory theft) have actually shown a slight decline. But these small decreases in property crimes have been more than offset by a huge increase in personal and violent crimes.

Thus, the rate of violent crime is up 29 percent overall and 24 percent in per-capita terms. Murder rates are up 23 percent and 18 percent per capita. Robbery rates have risen 33 percent in real terms and 28 percent in per-capita terms. This includes an absolute increase of 50 percent for bank robberies, 38 percent for street robberies, 27 percent for convenience-store robberies, 16 percent for residential robberies, and 11 percent for gas-station robberies. Aggravated assault is also up 28 percent in absolute terms and 23 percent per capita.

Does all this mean that America is becoming a far more violent society? Not entirely. What is unique about this crime wave is that it has been confined almost completely to black juveniles. The lines for "white" and "other" (Hispanic, Oriental, American Indian, etc.) are almost perfectly flat over the same period. But the arrest rates for blacks has gone nearly vertical.

What is more, violent blacks are getting younger and younger. In an analysis of the Uniform Crime Reports, James Alan Fox, dean of the Northeastern University College of Criminal Justice, found that crime rates were up the steepest for the youngest groups. Arrest rates for murder climbed 121 percent for 17-year-olds, 158 percent for 16-year-olds, and 217 percent for 15-year-olds. Even 12-year-olds were up 100 percent.

This unprecedented crime wave among young blacks has hit the cities hardest. Minneapolis, for example, has 40 percent of Minnesota's crime, even though it has only 8 percent of the state's population. In New York, 85 percent of the state's record 2,200 crimes in 1990 were in New York City (less than half the state's population). And within New York City, 70 percent of the murders were concentrated in a few neighborhoods—Washington Heights, Harlem, East Harlem, the South Bronx, East New York, and Bedford Stuyvesant. Brooklyn's 75th precinct (East New York), a drug-infested wasteland with a population of 160,000, had more murders than Buffalo, Rochester, Syracuse, and Albany combined (total population 880,000).

The reasons for the upsurge in inner-city violence are by now familiar. The most obvious is the introduction of crack cocaine, which has transformed drug addiction from a messy, disease-ridden, needle-passing subculture to a cleaner, inhaling-based "mainstream" habit among major portions of the underclass population. Once again, the arrest statistics reflect this change. While juvenile arrests for marijuana and other drugs are down or level since 1985, arrests for cocaine have soared during the same period. And once again, this increase has been concentrated entirely among blacks.

Beyond that, there is the disintegration of normal social life in many black ghettos. What is most striking is the loss of the mediating institutions of society—the churches, stores, schools, voluntary organizations, commercial activities, and ordinary street life that once formed a buffer between criminals and law-abiding citizens. On the streets surrounding the Robert Taylor Homes, a dreaded housing project on the South Side of Chicago, there is little sign of life except for a few graffiti-scarred playgrounds and scattered rows of desolate—though still inhabited—homes. Among the ruined buildings are an abandoned factory and a burned-out YMCA. Over nearly twenty square blocks, the only commercial advertising is a ubiquitous billboard on the back of bus-stop benches, advertising: "Beepers. Call 633-9610." Beepers, of course, are the standard equipment of the drug trade.

Most forbidding of all, however, is the collapse of history's oldest bulwark against crime and violent behavior—the nuclear family.

The majority of black males in ghetto areas no longer have any real adult role to play, either at home or in society. Their role as breadwinner—however poorly it may have been played in the past—has now been usurped by the welfare system. In projects like the Robert Taylor Homes, where more than 90 percent of the households involve only women and children, adult men have all but disappeared.

Over half of all black children born in this country are now born to unwed mothers, and in many poor areas, the figure exceeds 80 percent. Some of these women may supplement their welfare grant with some kind of furtive arrangement with a new man. But family units built around stable marriages are essentially unknown.

Nationwide, 25 percent of black men between the ages of 15 and 35 are entangled in the criminal-justice system—as prison inmates, defendants, parolees, or probationers. In cities like Washington, the number approaches 40 percent. Homicide is now the most common cause of death for black men between the ages of 20 and 35, and one in every 22 black men can expect to be murdered.

From the time they reach physical maturity until the time they disappear into the netherworld of dereliction and homelessness, these young black men lead lives of stupefying violence. In this unrelenting free-for-all, there are no qualms about killing someone for a pair of sneakers or sunglasses or because the other person is wearing the wrong colors or looks the wrong way. Listen to the voices of Sidewinder and Bopete, two fourteen-year-olds, as recorded in a California youth-detention center by Lèon Bing for her chronicle of Los Angeles gang life, *Do or Die*:

[Bopete:] "Sometimes I think about not goin' back to bangin' when I get outta here. I play in sports a lot here, and I. . . ."
Sidewinder's laugh interrupts. "Sound like a regular ol' teenager, don't he? I sound like that, too, after the drive-by. I got shot twice in the leg, 'cause they was shootin' at the car, and when that happen I didn't want to bang no more, either. Makin' promises to God, all like that. But when it heal up. . . ." He is silent for a moment; maybe he's thinking about a freedom he won't taste for a while. Then, "I tell you somethin'—I don't feel connected to any other kids in this city or in this country or in this world. I only feel comfortable in my 'hood. That's the only thing I'm connected to, that's my family. One big family—that's about it."
"In my 'hood, in the Jungle, it ain't like a gang. It's more like a nation, everybody all together as one. Other kids, as long as they ain't my enemies, I can be cool with 'em." Bopete lapses into silence. "I'll tell you, though—if I didn't have no worst enemy to fight with, I'd probably find somebody."
"Ye-eeeeeeh," Sidewinder picks it up. "*I'd* find somebody. 'Cause if they ain't nobody to fight, it ain't no gangs. It ain't no life. I don't know . . . it ain't no. . . ."
"It ain't no fun."
"Yeah! Ain't no fun just sittin' there. Anybody can just sit around, just drink, smoke a little Thai. But that ain't fun like shootin' guns and stabbin' people. *That's* fun."

It might seem that nothing more could be piled atop this disintegrating social scene to make a policeman's life more difficult and dangerous. But something has been: the proliferation of illegal guns, particularly automatic and semi-automatic weapons.

Says Hubert Williams, head of the Police Foundation:

There's a strong feeling among the departments around the country that we're being outgunned in our own neighborhoods. You can see it in the number of high-power, high-tech weapons confiscated off the streets. I mean, add it up. There are only about 70 patrolmen in every precinct and each one has one gun. How many guns are there in the neighborhoods we're patrolling?

The speed and sophistication of the weapons in the hands of today's drug dealers have made the rap singer Ice Cube's description of South Central Los Angeles—"the concrete Vietnam"—no exaggeration. According to Jack Killorin, of the Federal Bureau of Alcohol, Firearms, and Tobacco:

The kind of semi-automatic weapons in the hands of criminals today means even one bad guy can do a devastating amount of damage. It's not necessarily the power of the guns—although certainly that makes a difference. But many criminals are now armed with semi-automatic weapons that can literally fill the air with bullets. Not only are guns faster and more powerful, but there's an almost psychopathic willingness to use them.

In 1981, American gunmakers manufactured 1.7 million revolvers and 837,000 semi-automatic pistols. In 1991, the ratio was completely reversed—1.3 million semi-automatics to 456,000 revolvers. Standard revolvers, carried by most police officers, fire six shots and then require reloading, while semi-automatic pistols usually contain a clip of 16-24 bullets. "It's during that reloading time, when the first round of bullets runs out, that a lot of officers are killed," says Killorin.

Nevertheless, in New York City, Mayor Dinkins—against the urging of the FBI—has personally prevented the police from switching to semi-automatic 9-mm. weapons, even though such weapons are now carried by his own bodyguards.

WHAT can we expect the police to do under these circumstances?

In 1968, James Q. Wilson examined the problem in his classic book, *The Varieties of Police Behavior*. In that long-lost era, when the principal problems of police work involved dealing with drunks and breaking up fights at parties, Wilson discovered three styles of police action, which he termed the "watchman," the "legalistic," and the "service."

The "watchman," or "order-maintenance" style, common in cities with old political machines, tended to concentrate on maintaining order, giving individual patrolmen a lot of latitude to enforce the law as they saw fit. Large concentrations of gambling and prostitution were usually tolerated—often in black neighborhoods—as long as they did not offend the "respectable" people of the town.

The "legalistic" departments had usually been through some kind of reform period. Police stuck by the letter of the law and were impeccable about corruption. They wrote speeding tickets on an equal basis for city councilmen and black ghetto residents alike. The police force had usually been put out of the reach of politics and a strict civil-service or merit system prevailed.

The "service" style was a kind of middle ground, found mostly in the suburbs. The police were not "pro-active," but extremely conscious of the desires of their constituents. The law was upheld in a neutral way, but the police were unobtrusive about it as well. Although this style worked well in homogeneous suburbs, Wilson doubted that it could serve as a model in heterogeneous urban populations.

Regrettably enough, Wilson discovered that both the laissez-faire order-maintenance style *and* the reform-minded legalistic style (which was in many ways its opposite) *both* aroused resentment in black communities:

Order maintenance means managing conflict, and conflict implies disagreeing over what should be done, how, and to whom. Conflict is found in all social strata and thus in all strata there will be resentment, often justified, against particular police interventions (or their absence), but in lower-class areas conflict and disorder will be especially common and thus such resentment will be especially keen. It is hardly surprising that polls show young lower-income Negro males as being deeply distrustful of and bitter about the police; it would be a mistake, however, to assume that race is the decisive factor.

But when minimal order-maintenance (which had been the rule in the South) gave way to a stricter effort to impose middle-class standards on the entire community, the resentment remained. In Wilson's words:

One reason for the increasing complaints of "police harassment" may be that, in the large cities, Negroes are being brought under a single standard of justice; one reason for the complaints of discrimination may be that this process is proceeding unevenly and imperfectly. As the populations of our large cities become, through continued migration, more heavily Negro, more heavily lower-income, and more youthful, we can expect these complaints to increase in number and frequency, especially if, as seems likely, organizations competing for leadership in the central cities continue to seek out such issues in order to attract followers.

Having so accurately foreseen what was coming, Wilson (in collaboration with George Kelling) later developed the well-known "broken-windows" hypothesis, which has served as the basis of the "neighborhood-policing" movement. Wilson and Kelling decided that the watchman style had been correct in one respect—order maintenance does matter. "A broken window that remains broken is a signal that no one cares and an invitation for more broken windows," they wrote. Or, as a resident of Washington Heights put it during the tensions last summer:

I know the police are never going to clean up the drug problem in this neighborhood because they can't even deal with the problem of double-parked cars.

Wilson and Kelling's neighborhood policing is now the basis of a reform movement that is being instituted all over the country—even in places where it does not seem entirely appropriate. Foot patrolmen are now walking the beats of South-Central Los Angeles, trying to win the trust of the community—even though in such neighborhoods they may be the only people around not traveling by car.

BUT whether or not neighborhood policing will do any good, one thing remains clear: to concentrate on police "harassment" and "brutality" is to divert attention from the real problem that faces our society, which is the terrible upsurge of violent crime over the past five years. Worse yet, this focus creates a climate and leads to policies which can only have the effect of making it harder for the police to do their job, and perhaps also of making them less willing to do it.

In Los Angeles last May, the police department hesitated to mount a show of force when the Rodney King verdict was handed down because officials feared they would be blamed for igniting violence. "It would have been seen as provocative," said Willie Williams, who succeeded Daryl Gates as L.A. police chief in June. As it was, there were many reports of police passivity in the face of looting and arson, and order was not restored until three days later when 9,000 National Guardsmen and federal troops hit the streets.

In Minneapolis (which not only has a civilian-review board but also an organization in which members of the major drug gangs work together with the police in trying to establish domestic tranquility), the cops are feeling anxious and inhibited. Says Jerry Larson, a veteran detective and vice president of the city's Police Federation (the policemen's union):

The mayor told us for years that gangs here wouldn't be a problem. We warned him they would and now we've got a problem. You can't handle these gangs without getting pro-active and having all this constant criticism from the political establishment makes us real leery about doing our jobs. It'll be like New York, where the police just drive by things. I know some New York coppers and they say, "The hell with it. If those people aren't killing each other, we're not getting out of our cars."

In New York City itself, as though to confirm Larson's observation, Officer Todd Jamison declared in responding to charges of police brutality after an arrest that left one of his colleagues injured: "There are certain things where we have the power of discretion, we can turn our heads and say, why get involved?" An even more striking comment was made by Officer O'Keefe. When asked why he had not drawn his gun sooner in his mortal struggle with Garcia in Washington Heights, O'Keefe replied: "The truth is, in the current climate, a cop is more worried about getting in trouble than getting killed."

A poignant incident that occurred in Chicago drives the point home. When the Chicago Bulls won the National Basketball Association championship in June 1992, thousands of the city's residents—nearly all of them black—celebrated by rampaging through the downtown stores, breaking windows, looting, and turning over parked cars. (The *New York Times* reported that, of the 100 people injured during the riots, 94 were police officers.) Picking up a pattern which had been established in the Los Angeles riot a month before, the mobs singled out Korean-owned businesses for attack. Park Jung, the 32-year-old owner of a men's clothing store on the West Side, found more than 100 people trying to break through his storefront. When he appealed for help to several police officers who were standing idly by, they refused, advising him to "take care of your life and go home." He left and his store was destroyed.

"What else could I do?" Mr. Park said. "I hate America. I'm going back to Korea."

But those of us who are staying here in America will have greater and greater cause to rue the fact that the police are being morally disarmed and demoralized by a climate of opinion that seems to regard them as a bigger threat to society than the criminals they have to confront—and by whom they are being increasingly outgunned. For many years, criminologists have tried to dismiss swings in the crime rate with the bland assertion that they represent shifts in the crime-prone population of young males. But the current outburst has occurred during a trough in the population cycle. As Dean Fox points out:

What we've seen in the past few years is nothing compared with what we'll see in the next decade and on into the next century. Right now, we have the fewest 18-to-24-year-olds we've had since 1965, but next year they will start to go back up.

In other words, the worst is yet to come, and if the police continue to be incapacitated by a fixation on their occasional misbehavior, we—and most especially the young blacks among us—will have even less protection against violent crime in the future than we do today.

The Future of Diversity in America: The Law Enforcement Paradigm Shift

Charles M. Bozza, Ph.D

Dr. Charles M. Bozza is a police Commander for the City of Irvine, California. He has been a university lecturer and a college instructor for over 20 years. He has published numerous articles in police journals, both nationally and internationally, and is the author of two books on law enforcement. Recently he has published several articles on the future of cultural diversity in America. Dr. Bozza is a futurist and forecaster on law enforcement and leadership trends; he is an officer in the Society of Police Futurists International. His Ph.D. is in Human Behavior and Leadership.

Diversity has become a central issue to most community leaders and law enforcement officers today because of its tremendous impact on the American society. People continue to cry out for help and understanding and at the forefront is the law enforcement officer who provides the ever so needed emergency service. Law enforcement needs to understand how to deal with people from other backgrounds in today's society or be prepared for the results of lack of understanding. The 1990s are a time when the American culture is in a state of flux hurling to the future at warp speed. No longer are the whites of European decent the dominate culture of this country. If one looks out they will see a mosaic of enriched peoples in all shades of color. The first line of defense in dealing with conflicts among people is the police (Trojanowicz and Bucqueroux, 1991).

In the past decade the terms cross-cultural, inter-cultural, multi-cultural, and cultural have become part of popular terminology amongst scholars, politicians, activists, and philanthropists. It appears that being associated with people, groups, or organizations that strive to promote cross-cultural awareness or study people who are ethnically different has become a popular trend and one that must be understood by the law enforcement administrator and officer. Yet, there are few recent empirical studies that address issues concerning many ethnic groups, especially those which have immigrated to the United States in the latter part of the twentieth century. In fact, although there is much confusion about terminologies, there has been little effort in distinguishing the differences between common words like ethnicity, race and culture.

UNDERSTANDING WHAT IS MEANT BY ETHNICITY, CULTURE, AND RACE

The term race was first used in English approximately three hundred years ago and since then it has become one of the most misused and misunderstood words commonly referred to in everyday speech (Rose, 1964). In a universal context, the term race refers to a system by which both plants and animals are classified into subcategories aceording to specific physical and structural characteristics. When it pertains to the human group, Kroginan (1945) defines race as " . . . a subgroup of peoples possessing a definite combination of physical characteristics, of genetic origin, the combination of which to varying degrees distinguishes the subgroup from other subgroups of mankind." Differences which are physical such as skin pigmentation, head form, facial features, stature, and the color distribution and texture of body hair are among the most commonly recognized factors distinguishing races of people. In the past law enforcement has taken the stereotype position the most people fall into the categories of white, black, brown, or other.

Most people, however, not familiar with the term race also use it in contexts which have social implications and this is the cause for the confusion. Mack (1948) submits that race in the biological sense has no biological consequences. However, people believe that race has very profound social consequences. Therefore, individuals as part of their socialization accept myths and stereotypes regarding skin, color, stature, and so forth to be social facts (Atkinson, 1989).

Ethnicity refers to a group classification in which the members share a unique social and cultural heritage passed on from one generation to the next (Rose, 1964). Often times, many individuals use the terms race and ethnicity interchangeably because of the erroneous assumption that ethnicity has a biological or genetic foundation. For example, many groups are identified as racial groups although there is no evidence of biological or genetic foundations to support these claims. Jews, for instance, are frequently associated with being of a distinct race but as Thompson and Hughes (1958) point out, "Jews are not a biological race because the people known as Jews are not enough like each other and too much like

From *Journal of Contemporary Criminal Justice*, Vol. 8, No. 3, August 1992, pp. 208-216. Reprinted with permission from *Journal of Contemporary Criminal Justice*, California State University, Long Beach, Department of Criminal Justice.

other people to be distinguished from them." Jews, therefore, comprise what scholars refer to as an ethnic group.

The most confusing relationship is the one involving culture with race and ethnicity. Moore (1974) illustrates this confusion:

> Sometimes we tend to confuse race and ethnic groups with culture. Great races do have different cultures. Ethnic groups within races differ in cultural content. But, people of the same racial origin and some ethnic groups differ in their cultural matrices. All browns, or blacks, or whites, or yellows, or reds, are not alike in the cultures in which they live and have their being.

Culture, then, at the micro level may exist within ethnic groups and within racial groups. Traditionally, the word culture has been identified with the field of anthropology. To this day scholars credit anthropologists for the creation of the study of culture. Anthropologists define culture as patterns acquired and transmitted by symbols, constituting the distinctive achievement of human groups, including their embodiments in artifacts; the essential core of culture consists of traditional ideas and especially their attached values (Kroeber and Klukhohn, 1952).

Today, the term culture is not only used in many of the social science disciplines, but it is commonly used in the hard sciences and in business as well. For instance, many scholars and business consultants specialize in examining corporate cultures. Lorenz (1991) defines corporate culture as "who we are, what we do, and how things work around here." Needless to say, this definition does not quite parallel the one presented earlier which was synthesized by anthropologists.

Consequentially, culture has developed many new meanings not only to law enforcement but all of society without any significant scholarly work conducted on the formulation of a new universal definition or definitions unique to various disciplines. Thus, the term culture is used in many contexts and individuals define it based on their own professional, sociological, and theoretical orientations.

In order to facilitate the comprehension of goals and/or issues many have developed interesting combinations of the word culture, such as cross-cultural, multi-cultural, inter-cultural, and so on. These terms are sometimes used interchangeably and sometimes to indicate opposite sides of an issue; it all depends on one's theoretical or practical framework. Law enforcement officers of the past have taken it upon themselves to also define culture in the terms of "Blue Humor" without thinking through the implications. An example of this would he referring to people of black origin as "Gorillas of the Mist."

In the 1980s, these combination of terms using the word culture had become so popular in various societal circles that even social scientists began using the terms to grab their audiences. They found these terms useful when writing grant proposals and requesting funds for research projects. Basically, these combination terms became marketing tools. It need not be implied that scholars do not have the right to use marketing terms, however, what happens is that they become so involved with the selling part of their professions that they often forget the purpose of their roles. In their role as scientists, they need to be especially sensitive to the biases and unexamined assumptions that too often wander into scientific concepts. Scholars and law enforcement officers need to devote more time on clarifying the terms that have created so much confusion in lieu of using these new terms to promote their goals.

WHAT IS DIVERSITY

When one thinks about diversity one also thinks about minority groups. Historically, the term minority was formed to represent more Americans, Latinos, East-Asians, Pacific Islanders, and Native-Americans. Today, although the term is still used by all organizations in the private and public sector, it is an obsolete concept because, many cultures, races, and ethnicities are not recognized by the government or corporations as minority groups. They are labeled as immigrant groups. Why? Because minority groups mentioned above are protected by laws and have access to avenues not provided to the so called "immigrant groups." Thus, the word "minority" does not truly represent all minorities but a selected few. Since this word misrepresents many non-minority groups which are racially, culturally, and ethnically different many scholars have started to use terms like "underrepresented" or "ethnic" to refer to many racial and immigrant groups in the United States.

Recently, the term minority has been abandoned by scholars specializing in the traditional "minority groups" because it has negative implications, and plus it is misleading since it is not factual. These groups may be minorities individually, however, collectively they will be the clear majority by the year 2000, it is projected that in California the hispanics will be the majority. Moreover, today women have also joined other groups and they are also referred to as an underrepresented group (Fateri, 1989).

What seems to be the major variable affecting the slow growth in the understanding of the underrepresented groups is the group of people who label themselves or who are labeled as experts on diversity. Haro (1991) complains that many of the supposed "authorities" at conferences seem to be overnight gurus on minority concerns. He cites several examples to support his argument. He states that a former university president who had originally gained recognition for his research on white executives started appearing on panels as an expert on the future of cultural diversity. This ex-president never appointed or groomed any minority administrators, even though he headed an institution where minorities made up more than half of the student body.

Diversity issues have become so important that even bodies which accredit secondary schools, colleges, and universities have recently commenced serious discussions about their own diversity policies. Jaschik (1992) reported that the Middle States adopted a policy stating that its diversity standards would not be used as a condition for accrediting institutions and that colleges could define for themselves how the standards would be applied. This revelation received a prompt response from the Education Secretary, Alexander, who asked this accrediting body to revise its new policy. Recently, the Western Association of Schools and Colleges decided to examine its policies on diversity. Since colleges and universities set the standard for the society on new societal philosophies, all organizations are monitoring the progress of universities for proper direction in their own training programs. More and more schools today are seeking teachers who have received "multi-cultural" training in college (Nicklin, 1991a). Moreover, school systems who have realized their diversity training deficiencies are looking up to universities for new curricula guidance (Nicklin, 1991b).

Berkin (1991) explains that the reason for this immense interest in diversity is not only because of the influx of so many immigrant groups into the United States but also because for more than two decades, scholars interested in creating intellectual space for new perspectives such as feminism and the experiences of underrepresented groups have entered universities in increasing numbers. These new entrants to the scholarly circles have voiced doubts about traditional definitions of proper subject matter and interpretive models. Their attempt to redefine and reinterpret, what should be taught and introduce topic areas such as "women's culture," has been met with a counter attack from supporters of the established thought. Tarnas (1991), for instance, made the attempt to illustrate, in his popular document, why the traditional western culture deserves more attention and why the traditional westerners should not reject their heritage.

Perhaps law enforcement has come upon its own answer to cultural dilemma. By using a community-based policing model that solves this problem by direct interaction and communications with its service population, [they learn] first hand the cultural differences and [work] with them within the framework of the law and community standards.

SOCIETAL THEONES ON DIVERSITY: A PARADIGM SHIFT

Thomas Kuhn (1970), perhaps one of the intellectual gurus of this century, reported the shift in the human kind's pattern of thought. He called it the paradigm shift, a term commonly used today not only in the academic fields but also in the business realms. Unfortunately, Kuhn did not spend adequate time writing and clarifying thoughts on the diverse issues law enforcement is now taking time to clarify. Training in many states is currently

being prepared to give the law enforcement official a better understanding of what is ahead in the communities where we deliver service.

What has happened in the American society in the past few decades is that there has been a shift in its structure. In the past, many immigrant groups in the U.S. were, for the most part, from European countries or East Asian countries and they came to the United States gradually and for economic reasons. Recently, immigrant groups have been coming from all over the world and for varying reasons (Fateri, 1986). Therefore, the degree of adaptation and adjustments are not comparable since the cultures, races, and ethnicities of the peoples are very different and the quantity of immigrants and the differences of identities are far greater. Thus, the melting pot concept which may have been attractive and possible in the past is no longer a logical alternative in a society with numerous races, ethnicities, and cultures.

In its early stages of development, the United States projected an image of the cultural melting pot, a nation in which all nationalities, ethnicities, and races melted into one culture. Inherent in the melting pot concept was the perspective that a new and unique culture would continually emerge as each new immigrant group affected the existing culture (Krug, 1976). The melting pot philosophy was not subscribed to by many because it was believed that the "heart of the United States" was an American culture that was based primarily on the values and races of early immigrants, principally English, Irish, German, and Scandinavian groups. Opponents of this concept believed that instead of melting all cultures into one, an effort needed to be made to culturally assimilate all immigrant groups (Fairchild, 1926). Later, in the 1950s and 1960s there were growing objections to the assimilation theory because it called for relinquishing traditional ethnic values and norms in favor of those of the dominant culture.

Today, the melting pot theory and the assimilation concept are still in contention although the former is favored more than the latter simply because it is better understood. Although both of these philosophies are acceptable and possibly practical in other societies, they are not functional in the American society. What may work is the "salad howl" concept, also referred to as the mosaic: the various ingredients or parts exist together, but rather than melting, the components remain intact and distinguishable while contributing to a whole that is richer than its parts alone.

WHAT DOES THE FUTURE HOLD

The United States today is structured like a salad bowl, where ethnic, racial and cultural groups function independently while contributing to the whole society, but it operates as if it was structured like a melting pot. Alvin Toffler (1990) submits that Los Angeles with its Korea town, its Vietnamese suburbs, its strong and growing Chicano population, its roughly seventy-five ethnically oriented publications, not to mention its Jews, Africans, Japanese, Chinese, and its large Iranian population provides an example of the new and future diversity. The serious question posed is whether we want to operate realistically and effectively as a society in the future? Certainly, all law enforcement organizations want to succeed in implementing their goals and objectives, therefore, we need to accept the reality and organize ourselves in accord with the status quo and not the way society needs to be philosophically or the way the society needs to be structured. Our society is the result of an evolutionary process which is consistently and continually being influenced by rearrangements and introduction of new and different economic, social, political and cultural variables. Few other societies are affected to this degree, therefore, the challenge we face in operating within these boundaries and under these circumstances is rather unique. Toffler (1990) recommends that government will need new legal and social tools they now lack, if they are to referee increasingiy complex, potentially violent disputes.

Since law enforcement organizations possess a structure, a mission, and a system of operation, they can effectively learn about and communicate with the many groups that are, or need to be, of interest to them (Bozza & Fateri, 1990), whereas, the ethnic groups within the society may not have such capabilities or motivations. Law enforcement organizations need to be in the vanguard of this social and legal change that is occurring now and will continue in the future in our nation. The idea is to learn more about these groups so that the society would operate more effectively by being able to improvise and adapt. Most importantly the interaction with these groups through various policing methods and community service would not only increase tolerance among all groups but increase our appreciation of people who are culturally different. The acquisition of knowledge and information is central to proper and efficient management. The successful law enforcement organization of the future will develop systems to learn about all of the underrepresented ethnic and non-ethnic groups that affect their operation. These organizations will take the initiative to acquire the necessary knowledge which would help them to make intelligent decisions.

Marvin Cetron and Owen Davies (1991), respected futurists, projected with optimism that the guiding theme of the 90s will be to restore peace by the joint effort of the entire world community. This is one forecast which many wish to become a self-fulfilling prophecy, and we, as responsible members of the society and law enforcement professionals can contribute and support this new ideology by changing our thinking patterns first and then our national policies on how we see others.

REFERENCES

Atkinson, D. R., Morten, G., Sue, D. W. (1989). *Counseling American Minorities*. Dubuque, Iowa: William C. Brown Publishing.

Berkin, Carol. (1991). "Dangerous Courtesies Assault Women's History." *The Chronicle of Higher Education*. December 11, A-44.

Bozza, C. M., and Fateri, F. (1990). "Methods Dealing With Cross Cultural Concerns: A Case Study of the Iranian New Year." *Journal of California Law Enforcement*. California Peace Officers, Education Research and Training Foundation, Sacramento, Ca. Vol. 24, No. 3.

Centron, M. J., and Davies, O. (1991). *Crystal Globe: The Haves and Haves-Nots of the New World Order*. St. Martin's Press.

Fairchild, H. P. (1926). *The Melting Pot Mistake*. Boston: Little, Brown, & Company.

Fateri, Fardad. (1986). "The Politics of the Iranian Exiles in Southern California: A Case Study of Political Activists." Master's Thesis. California State University, Fullerton.

Fateri, Fardad. (1989). "Sex Role Orientation and Perceived Leadership Behavior of Male and Female Middle Managers Working for Electronic Firms. A Doctoral Dissertation." U.S. International University, San Diego.

Haro, R. P. (1991). "So Called Experts on Cultural Diversity Need to Be Subjected to Careful Scrutiny." *The Chronicle of Higher Education*. November 13, B-2.

Jaschik, Scott. (1992). "Middle States' Decision on Diversity Standards Seen Enhancing Federal Role in Accreditation." *The Chronicle of Highher Education*. January 8, A36.

Kroeber, A. L., and Kluckholm, C. (1952). *Culture: A Critical Review of Concepts and Definitions*. New York: Vintage Books.

Krogman, W. M. (1945). "The Concept of Race." In R. Linton, *The Science of Man in the World Crisis*. (pp. 38–62). New York: Columbia University Press.

Krug, M. (1976). *The Melting Pot of the Ethnics*. Bloomington, Ind.: Phi Delta Kappa Educational Foundation.

Kuhn, Thomas. (1970). *The Structure of Scientific Revolutions*. University of Chicago Press.

Lorenz, John. (1991). "Shifting the Corporate Culture." Orange County *Business Journal*. December 9, C-5.

Mack, R. W. (1968). *Race, Class, and Power*. New York: American Book Company.

Moore, B. M. (1974). "Cultural Differences and Counseling Perspectives." *Texas Personnel and Guidance Association Journal*, 3, 39–44.

Nicklin, J. L. (1991a). "Teacher Education Programs Face Pressure to Provide Multicultural Training." *The Chronicle of Higher Education*. November 27, A-11.

Nicklin, J. L. (1991b). "School Systems Seek Guidance From Universities in Bringing More Diversity to Curricula." *The Chronicle of Higher Education*. November 27, A-16.

Rose, P. I. (1964). *They and We: Racial and Ethnic Relations in the United States*. New York: Random House.

Tarnas, Richard. (1991). *The Passion of the Western Mind*. New York: Harmony Books.

Thompson, E. T., and Hughes, E. C. (1958). *Race: Individual and Collective Behavior*. Glencoe, Ill.: Free Press.

Trojanowicz, Robert, and Bucqueroux, Bonnie. (1991). *Community Policing and The Challenge of Diversity*. Flint, Mich. National Center for Community Policing School of Criminal Justice, Michigan State University.

Toffler, Alvin. (1990). *Power Shift*. New York: Bantam Books.

DRAGONS AND DINOSAURS:
The Plight of Patrol Women

Traveling in the male world is like going to a foreign country. Women have to learn the language, study maps and read guidebooks, and figure out the best way to get from place to place. We aren't surprised that we often feel frustrated, frightened and lonely. We know we women have come from one tradition and that these people come from another. We may continue to think our culture is better than theirs but also that if we keep hanging in there, some day we may enjoy this foreign culture (Hennig and Jardin, 1977: 214-215).

Donna C. Hale
Shippensburg University

Stacey M. Wyland
Pennsylvania State Police

This analogy for prospective women managers is also appropriate for women on patrol who for the past twenty years have been struggling for acceptance and recognition by their male peers and supervisors. Little did women in policing imagine that the videotape of Rodney King's beating by four Los Angeles Police officers would result in the Los Angeles City Council recommending that more women patrol officers be hired. Unfortunately, it is often these serendipitous events that lead to the discovery of what we already knew in this case, that women are effective as patrol officers. The Christopher Commission's role in investigating the Rodney King incident was extremely important to the status of women on patrol because it resulted in illuminating the performance evaluation studies of the late 1970s that overall concluded that women are effective on patrol (Bloch and Anderson, 1974; Bloch, Anderson and Gervais, 1973; Craig, 1976; Milton, Abramowitz, Crites, Gates, Mintz and Sandler, 1974; Sichel, Friedman, Quint and Smith, 1978). These findings, however, did not result in the acceptance of women on patrol. The organizational culture of policing as man's work has been entrenched since the nineteenth century and is very evident today in the attitudes of male peers and supervisors.

What *Time* reporter Jeanne McDowell describes (February 17, 1992) regarding the effective performance of women on patrol is not surprising. This information was reported at the time the performance evaluation studies were conducted fifteen years ago. It is ironic that the police organization has not accommodated the entry of women on patrol. Although the Equal Employment Opportunity Act and Commission have been in existence to ensure women's entry into patrol work, the organization has effectively kept the percentage of women on patrol below ten percent. The time has arrived to acknowledge that women can do patrol, and that they should not have to continually prove that they can do so.

The Christopher Commission "unearthed" these findings that women on patrol communicate effectively without using physical force. This discovery resulted in the city council of Los Angeles recommending that its police department increase female sworn officers to forty-three percent within the next seven years (*Time*, 1992: 72). In order to accomplish this feat, the police department needs to develop strategies to recruit and retain women as patrol officers.

Before discussing strategies to recruit and retain women in policing, it is important to examine the research that supports the fact that women can do patrol work. Consequently, the first section of this article is referred to as "old wine in new bottles" because most of the information presented in the recent *Time* article is based on the performance evaluation studies of the 1970s. It is evident from this reexamination of the performance evaluations that the problem is not that women cannot do patrol work; the problem is the resistance that male police officers either as peers or supervisors hold against women doing what is considered "men's work"

(Balkin, 1988; Bell, 1982; Milton, 1975; Golden, 1981; Charles, 1982; Lord, 1986; Martin, 1990; Price, 1985; Remmington, 1983; Jones, 1986). It is unfortunate that it takes the brutality of the Rodney King videotaped beating to trigger a resurgence of the research substantiating that women can do patrol.

Old Wine in New Bottles: Are Women Better Cops?

Since the early 1970s, patrol women have struggled to be accepted as equals in what has traditionally been a male bastionpatrol. The resistance and hostility towards women is primarily based on stereotypes and myths regarding the ability of women to do what is considered a man's job (Bell, 1982). The literature on women in policing is replete with conclusions that women as patrol officers are not accepted by their male peers and supervisors. If women decide to remain in patrol, they experience and endure sexual harassment and discrimination. If they stay, women must find ways of coping or adjusting to the culture. Susan Martin (1979) has written extensively on the ways women have "adjusted" to the male world of policing. Perhaps her best known work is her description of the POLICEwoman and the policeWOMAN. Women have also resorted to litigation to secure their positions in policing (Hale and Menniti, 1993).

The aftermath of King's assault resulted in the establishment of the Christopher Commission. This is not new. A cursory examination of any introductory text on policing refreshes our memories of earlier studies conducted as a result of police misconduct. For example, the Wickersham and Lenox Commissions reports from the early 1900s; the Knapp Commission investigation of corruption in the New York City Police Department; and, the Kerner Commission that investigated reasons for rioting and destruction in American cities during the summer of 1967 (Inciardi, 1990: 302). Furthermore, it is interesting that although the Commission concluded that "there were numerous causes [of the rioting and destruction], it specified "aggressive preventive patrol, combined with police misconduct in the forms of brutality, unwarranted use of deadly force, harassment, verbal abuse, and discourtesy" as stimuli for the disruptions" (Inciardi, 1990: 302).

During the Christopher Commission's investigation experts testified that women are successful on patrol. Many of these experts' research substantiates the findings of the earlier performance evaluation studies of women on patrol that women could indeed accomplish the requisite duties of patrol.

The most significant contribution of *Time* reporter Jeanne McDowell was that her article reminded us what we already knewwomen are effective at communication and calming volatile and potential violent situations. This information is a given: we have research that supports women are capable of patrol; what we need to do now is to keep these very capable women on the job. As McDowell (1972: 70) reported " . . .

women constitute only 9% of the nation's 523,262 police officers . . . ." After twenty years of meeting resistance by police departments, it is now time to examine the organizational culture of police departments and change the environment so women can be accepted as patrol officers.

Based on McDowell's report and the twenty-year-old research we know that: (1) women are better than men in talking people out of violence; (2) police work is not predominately violent; and, (3) physical size is irrelevant because violence is so little a part of police work. These same conclusions from the Washington, D.C. study are substantiated by those reported in *Time* (May 27, 1974) once again from a study in the nation's capital, there was little difference in the abilities of men and women to deal with violent, or potentially violent situations. Women were similar or equal to men in the percentage of arrests made that resulted in conviction, their attitude toward the public, the number of incidents they were involved in that required back-up support from other officers, the number of injuries they sustained on the job, and even the number of driving accidents they had."

And twenty years ago in 1972, *Time* (May 1: 60) reported that many police departments were assigning women patrol officers to do what was traditionally considered men's work handling domestic disputes. The reason for this change was that women appeared to be more successful at calming disputes. Over the years research by Kennedy and Homant (1983) indicated that victims of domestic violence believed female officers were more patient and took more time to deal with the conflict. These studies reported that female officers were more tactful and subtle, stayed longer, and were concerned about root causes of conflict. Women were described as having "a soothing and calming effect."

Also in 1972, *Newsweek* (October 23: 117) reported that the major objections to the entry of women on patrol in Washington, D.C., Boston, Miami and New York were: (1) women were presumed incapable of dealing with violent situations; (2) the chivalry factor; and (3) physical size. Effectiveness of women patrol officers was reported in handling family disputes, juvenile delinquency, shoplifting and drugs. Therefore, comparing these early articles regarding the effectiveness of women on patrol with McDowell's (1992) report twenty years later, it is clear that the conclusions regarding the effectiveness of women on patrol have not changed. Interestingly, however, in both articles the dissatisfaction with the uniform women were required to wear is similar. McDowell reports "[I]n most places it means wearing an uncomfortable uniform designed for a man, including bulletproof vests that have not been adapted to women's figures." The 1972 article discusses women on patrol wearing skirts and carrying their guns in their purses.

Before we leave this section, it is important to examine a classic article published in 1981 by Van Wormer and to briefly update her advantages and disadvantages of using men on patrol. Her first advantage was superior physical strength combined with stamina to subdue a suspect. Research now substantiates that although women do not have the same upper body strength of their male counterparts they can be trained to compensate for lack of strength (Charles 1981, 1982). Earlier, Talney (1969: 50) pointed out that

> . . . it is not unreasonable . . . to suggest that well-trained women officers could counter many kinds of disturbances and disorders which equally well-trained men could not. . . . male officers are assaulted because . . . they represent a male authority figure which within the value system of many criminals makes them fair game . . . particularly if the encounter takes place in the presence of their peer group where such values are shared.

Talney (1969: 50) continues that female officers could avoid assaults because it is unheroic to assault a female . . . even a female police officer. "Furthermore, the public image of women facing unruly crowds could do much to swing public support to the side of proper police authority."

Van Wormer's second advantage was that men can handle long hours, nights, and rotating shifts. This is one area that women have difficulty with especially if they are single parents. In general, men do not encounter these problems because they have a spouse at home who is the primary caretaker of home and children.

The third advantage focuses on aggressiveness of men. Dranov (1985: 174-175) indicates that some male officers are unsure about the reliability of a woman partner to back them up. Lewis Sherman (1975: 435) found that although females were less aggressive and tend to make fewer arrests than men, they were effective at patrol.

The final advantage is that males have related job experience, primarily military experience. This may have been true in the 1970s, but it would be interesting to examine this in 1993 to see if recruits are coming from the military, college campuses, or other blue-collar occupations? This is important for recruitment practices because it is necessary to learn just what the military experience has in common with police work. It may be that a college education is more beneficial, since officers spend the majority of their time providing services to the community. Finally, individuals may be attracted to police work because it does not require a college degree, but pays a higher salary than many other blue collar occupations.

According to Van Wormer, there are more complaints against men on patrol. The article by McDowell (1992) verifies that when the Christopher Commission investigated the Los Angeles Police Department after the King beating, it found "that the 120 officers with the most use-of-force reports were all men. Civilian complaints against women are also consistently lower. In San Francisco. . . . female officers account for only 5% of complaints although they make up 10% of the 1,839-person force."

Van Wormer points out that male officers provoke violence and are more physically brutal. This has been supported by the performance evaluation research that reported women on patrol as more effective in dealing with conflict because they rely on mediation and intervention techniques. Dranov's (1985: 213) response that "the ability to subdue someone is not as important as the ability to communicate intelligently reflects the overall consensus of the research that women are effective." But, the comment by a deputy sheriff in southern California probably reflects many male's attitudes that physical size is more important than communication styles. The deputy sheriff stated "I don't care if a dame is Calamity Jane and can shoot a button off my vest. My biggest weapons are that I'm tall and pretty intimidating. These gals could only intimidate my little sister" (Newsweek, October 23, 1972: 117). As Katherine Perkins, Detroit police officer, pointed out "Any fool can shoot a gun. What you really need is intelligence and sensitivity—and that's what women bring to the job" (Dreifus, 1981: 58). This is similar to Elizabeth Watson's statement in the McDowell article that "intelligence, communication, compassion and diplomacy" (1992: 70) is required in policing.

Van Wormer stresses that women have a disarming affect and are better at public relations. Male officers often have poor reputations. Furthermore, male officers are not effective at questioning rape victims. Rape is a painful experience for female victims to report rape to male officers; and, male officers may either be insensitive or feel uncomfortable with this type of case, similar to child abuse investigations. Historically, female officers were hired to deal with women as offender and victims because of their gender. It was believed that women would be more sympathetic/empathetic in these situations. It is interesting to note, however, that the English policewomen Lilian Wyles reported in her autobiographical account of her experience at Scotland Yard that male officers tried to shield policewomen from investigations regarding sexual offenses. The reason cited was the belief that middle class women should be protected from these type of situations that may either sully or embarrass them.

Van Wormer's comments that male officers are reluctant to accept women on patrol and may overprotect them. This chivalry is a result of both stereotypes and socialization. Also, Van Wormer points out that historically, women in policing have had more education than men. This is well documented in the early literature of policewomen in America. Men were hired because of their physical size; women were required to have higher education for their positions. In the early 1970s Perlstein (1972: 46) found that 35.3 percent of the women police in his study had higher educational levels. He concluded that more education results in less police authoritarism.

To conclude this section on the effectiveness of women on patrol, it should be noted that in 1980 the Los Angeles Police Department doubled the number of its female officers. Commander Ken Hickman used this opportunity to complete his dissertation research by comparing the records of sixty-eight female cops hired to go out on patrol after 1980 with those of male officers hired at the same time. In an examination of 6,000 daily field activity reports he found that male-female teams were just as productive in initiating potentially hazardous calls as were male-male teams and the individual top initiators of potentially hazardous activities were female. He also found that recruit training officers rated men lower than women in tactics, initiative and self-confidence, writing and communication, and public contacts. Also, the I.Q.s of the female recruits were higher and academically the women surpassed their male classmates in the police academy. Assessing physical fitness and height, Hickman found that these correlated with success in the field for only four percent of all police officers. Women officers got significantly more commendations from the public. He found that both men and women had similar numbers of complaints by the public. Productivity levels were high for the police women in the crime-ridden South Bureau. He also found that the females' communication skills were better and this was an advantage for them for them in domestic violence situations (Elias, 1984:17).

It is evident from this examination of the performance evaluation research on women on patrol that women can handle patrol work. It is no longer necessary to debate or discuss the effectiveness of women on patrol. It is time, however, to address the greater issue of how women can unconditionally be accepted by their peers and supervisors. Twenty years ago, Lewis Sherman (1973: 384, 393) reported the benefits of hiring women patrol officers as:

(1) a reduction in the incidence of violence between police officers and citizens;

(2) increased quality of police service because women accentuate the service role of police work more than men;

(3) improved police community relations because women are more visible than men, make more contacts, and citizens will assist police women upon request;

(4) police men can learn from the police women that an officer can be efficient without using force;

(5) police women more effective than police men in settling problems reported by women from low-income neighborhoods;

(6) a police department becomes more democratic and responsive to the community by hiring personnel who are more representative of the community's population; and,

(7) lawsuits charging sex discrimination could be avoided by the police department that develops and implements job-related selection, recruitment and promotional standards and tests.

Lewis Sherman's (1975: 438) conclusion that "the question of whether women could perform general patrol duties was primarily political rather than scientific [was evident] from the very beginning." He points out that "in many respects, the enormous efforts that have gone into evaluating the performance of women have been a diversion from what has always been the most genuinely important question in police research what kind of person makes a good police officer? As he stated:

> Gender is not a relevant characteristic of that person. It is only a reflection of our prejudiced and conservative views that we should ever have thought it might be. The unassailable fact is that some women are good police officers and some women are not just like men. Our quest still remains to define and measure a good copman or woman.

In the next section, a discussion of recruitment and retention is presented. The major problem for police departments is not recruiting women—the problem is retention because many police departments are locked in a "time-warp" that perpetuates the myth that only men can do patrol. Although research clearly substantiates that patrol is primarily service, and women can handle any physical problems requiring strength by using "karate, twist locks or a baton instead of their fists" (McDowell, 1992), their male counterparts cannot accept reality. Men still perceive police work as a man's domain where women will only get in the way, cannot be depended upon for backup, or may get hurt. The expression "old habits die hard" is evident. The nineteenth century machismo legacy is slow to die in the police organizational culture.

Recommendations for Recruitment and Retention

The major problems facing the recruitment and retention of women as patrol officers are the political, cultural and structural systems of the police organization. Therefore, in order to change the milieu of policing that is vested in traditions of machoism and sexism, it requires a leader who takes the responsibility of slaying the dragons and replacing the dinosaurs who keep the old traditions alive and well. These changes require a "transformational" leader who will work to change both the political and cultural systems of the police department. To begin the change the leader first must develop a vision of women as patrol officers; next, mobilize the department to work toward achieving the new vision and lastly, institutionalizing the changes over time (Tichy and Ulrich, 1984: 344).

Tichy and Ulrich (1984: 345) state that before an organization will change there must be a "trigger" that indicates change is needed. Although for the past twenty years we have known that women are capable of performing patrol, it takes a horrific incident like the Rodney King beating to recognize the effectiveness of women on patrol. As discussed earlier, this incident led to the Los Angeles City Council's recommendation that the percentage of female patrol officers be increased to forty-three percent in the next seven years. The new police chief of the Los Angeles Police Department, Willie Williams, must create an agenda that requires improving police community relations in addition to hiring more female and minority police officers. He will need to rely on effective recruitment and retention strategies to change the organizational culture.

One area that must be addressed in hiring more female officers is how to retain them on the force once they are hired. In general, women are kept out of male-dominated occupations by hostility, sexual harassment and male attitudes (Jacobs, 1989). The presence of women in a traditionally male domain is threatening and they are perceived and treated as outsiders. They are treated paternalistically and prevented from learning tasks that will later help with promotions, or with hostility, or both (Padavic and Reskin, 1990). Furthermore, Cockburn (1985), Dreifus (1980) and Hunt (1990) report the presence of women in traditionally blue-collar male occupations may challenge the men's "culturally-granted gender power" (Cockburn, 1985 in Padavic and Reskin, 1990: 617).

The Christopher Commission did not address how to deal with the resistance by the dinosaurs who believe women have no place on patrol. This resistance is based on three interrelated systems: technical, political and cultural. For example, technical resistance includes the uniforms that women wear. Even twenty years after the performance evaluation studies, improper fit of uniforms and bullet proof vests and size of handguns for women is still a problem. Another example of the technical aspects is the emphasis in the training academies on the physical testing as well as firearms training.

The political resistance in police departments is based on entrenched rules of patrol work established and maintained by the older male officers and supervisors. Especially evident in police departments are policies, or lack of policies regarding pregnancy and disability leaves for patrol women as well as flex shifts for women who have child care responsibilities. These policies also reflect the cultural aspect of the organization that resists changing the culture to accommodate the entry of women on patrol. Anecdotal information reveals that men become upset when women get special consideration because they are pregnant, or have child care responsibilities. Because of these responsibilities, women often move into administrative positions to have the more conventional shift of 8 a.m. to 5 p.m. Unfortunately, this removes the patrol women from the street where their visibility is important. Gender neutral shifts, flex shifts, child care programs and paternity leaves would improve the organizational culture for both male and female officers.

An examination of the litigation regarding sexual harassment and discrimination toward women on patrol reveals the hostility women have encountered. Simply stated, men do not want women on patrol (Hale and Menniti, 1993). In order for women to remain on patrol, the police leader must change the environment emphasizing that harassment and discrimination will not be tolerated. It must be clearly communicated that women will be hired in police departments and that if these policies are violated, recriminations will follow. The leader must make sure that all members of the department are trained regarding sexual harassment and sexual discrimination.

During the recruitment stage it is crucial to explain what the duties of a patrol officer are as well as preparing women for the resistance they will encounter. Timmins and Hainsworth (1989: 204) found that women police officers believed that although admission requirements were usually clear, many of the women were uncertain about why they were hired, what sex roles they should play as women cops; what problems they were likely to encounter; and what the police academy experience was supposed to do for them.

During the recruitment process police departments need to include female police officers as recruiters. Advertisements should depict women officers conducting patrol work as well as describing the department's policy of hiring, paying and deploying women the same as men (Sulton and Townsey, 1981). Once women are recruited, special workshop courses should be included in the police recruit training for both male and female recruits describing the stress of the job as well as explaining to both men and women officers that the evaluation research supports that women can do patrol. Also, in the recruit academy as well as later in-service training, time must be allocated to describing and discussing ethics and police work. Officers need to address issues of police violence and corruption through both presentation and discussion groups. In addition, training should include policies on sexual harassment and discrimination and explaining that these policies will be enforced. All these activities support the commitment that the police organization has to improving the organizational climate for both male and female officers.

Lastly, the changes regarding recruitment and retention of women on patrol must institutionalize the opportunity for promotion of qualified officers. This means that the existing performance evaluations/appraisal must be redesigned to reflect what patrol work is. It is also important that women patrol officers be trained by women patrol officers, or by men who are aware that women can do patrol work effectively.

These changes in the police organization will not take place overnight. They involve a major commitment by both the department's leadership and the local form of government to establish a police department that represents the community. Women as patrol officers should not have to encounter resistance by the peers and supervisors. Although dragons and dinosaurs die slowly; change must begin now. As Betty

Friedan once said "A girl [sic] should not expect special privileges because of her sex but neither should she adjust to prejudice and discrimination" (Warner, 1992: 312). The evaluation research reveals that women did not expect special privileges as patrol officers—they just wanted the opportunity to do the job. The role of the police leader is to change the technical, political and cultural resistance in the police department.

References

Balkin, Joseph. (1988). "Why Policemen Don't Like Policewomen." *Journal of Police Science and Administration,* 16(1): 29-38.

Bell, Daniel J. (1982). "Policewomen: Myths and Reality." *Journal of Police Science and Administration,* 10(1): 112-120.

Bloch, Peter B. and Deborah Anderson. (1974). *Policewomen on Patrol: Final Report.* Washington, DC: Police Foundation.

Bloch, Peter, Deborah Anderson and Pamela Gervais. (1973). *Policewomen on Patrol—Major Findings: Final Report, Volume 1.* Washington, DC: Police Foundation.

Charles, Michael T. (1981). "The Performance and Socialization of Female Recruits in the Michigan State Police Training Academy." *Journal of Police Science and Administration,* 9(2): 209-223.

Charles, Michael T. (1980). "Policewomen and the Physical Aspects of Policing." *Law and Order,* 28(9): 83-89.

Cockburn, Cynthia. (1985). *Machinery of Dominance.* London: Pluto. Craig, G.B. (1976). *Women Traffic Officer Project: Final Report.* Sacramento, California: Department of California Highway Patrol.

Dranov, Paula. (1985). "The Lady is a Cop." *Cosmopolitan,* 199: 174-177, 213.

Dreifus, Claudia. (1981). "Why Two Women Cops Were Convicted of Cowardice." *Ms.,* 9(4): 57-58, 63-64.

Dreifus, Claudia. (1980). "People Are Always Asking Me What I'm Trying to Prove . . ." *Police Magazine* :18-25.

Elias, M.K. (1984). "The Urban Cop: A Job for a Woman." *Ms.,* 12: 17.

None cited. (1972). "Female Fuzz." *Newsweek,* 80: 117.

Golden, Kathryn. (1981). "Women as Patrol Officers: A Study of Attitudes." *Police Studies,* 4: 29-33.

Hale, Donna C. and Daniel J. Menniti. (1993). "Discrimination and Harassment: Litigation by Women in Policing." In *It's A Crime: A Critical Look at Women's Issues in Criminal Justice.* Edited by Roslyn Muraskin and Ted Alleman. Needham Heights, Massachusetts: Regents/Prentice-Hall.

Hennig, Margaret and Anne Jardim. (1977). *The Managerial Woman.* New York, New York: Pocket Books.

Hunt, Jennifer C. (1985). "The Logic of Sexism Among Police." *Women & Criminal Justice,* 1(2): 3-30.

Inciardi, James A. (1990). *Criminal Justice.* Third Edition. New York, New York: Harcourt Brace Jovanovich, Publishers.

Jacobs, Jerry. (1989). *Revolving Doors.* Stanford, California: Stanford University Press.

Jones, Sandra. (1986). "Women Police: Caught In The Act." *Policing,* 2(2): 129-140.

Kennedy, Daniel B. and Robert J. Homant. (1983). "Attitudes of Abused Women Toward Male and Female Police Officers." *Criminal Justice and Behavior,* 10(4): 391-405.

Lord, Lesli Kay. "Policewomen." (1989). In *The Encyclopedia of Police Science.* Edited by William G. Bailey. New York, New York: Garland Publishing, Inc., 491-502.

Lunneborg, Patricia. (1990). *Women Changing Work.* New York, New York: Bergin and Garvey Publishers.

Martin, Susan E. (1979). "Policewomen and Policewomen: Occupational Role Dilemmas and Choices for Female Officers." *Journal of Police Science and Administration,* 7(3): 314-323.

Martin, Susan E. (1989). "Women on the Move?: A Report on the Status of Women in Policing." *Women & Criminal Justice,* 1(1): 21-40.

McDowell, Jeanne. (1992). "Are Women Better Cops?" *Time,* 139(7): 70-72.

Milton, Catherine Higgs, Ava Abramowitz, Laura Crites, Margaret Gates, Ellen Mintz and Georgette Sandler. (1974). *Women in Policing: A Manual.* Washington, DC: Police Foundation.

Padavic, Irene and Barbara F. Reskin. (1990). "Men's Behavior and Women's Interest in Blue-Collar Jobs." *Social Problems,* 37(4): 613-627.

Perlstein, Gary R. (1972). "Policewomen and Policemen: A Comparative Look." *Police Chief,* 39(3): 72-74, 83.

The President's Commission on Law Enforcement and Administration of Justice. (1967). *Task Force Report: The Police.* Washington, DC: The US Government Printing Office.

Remmington, Patricia Weiser. (1983). "Women in the Police: Integration or Separation?" *Qualitative Sociology,* 6(2): 118-135.

Report of the National Advisory Commission on Civil Disorders. (1968). New York, New York: E.P. Dutton.

Reskin, Barbara F. (1988). "Bringing the Men Back In: Sex Differentiation and the Devaluation of Women's Work." *Gender and Society,* 2: 58-81.

Sherman, Lewis J. (1973). "A Psychological View of Women in Policing." *Journal of Police Science and Administration,* 1(4):383-394.

Sherman, Lewis J. (1975). "An Evaluation of Policewomen on Patrol in a Suburban Police Department." *Journal of Police Science and Administration,* 3(4):434-438.

Sichel, Joyce L., Lucy N. Friedman, Janet C. Quint, and Michael E. Smith. (January, 1978). *Women on Patrol: A Pilot Study of Police Performance in New York City.* Washington, DC: National Institute of Law Enforcement and Criminal Justice, Law Enforcement Assistance Administration, US Department of Justice.

Sulton, Cynthia G. and Roi D. Townsey. (1981). *A Progress Report on Women in Policing.* Washington, DC: Police Foundation.

Talney, Ronald G. (1969). "Women in Law Enforcement: An Expanded Role." *Police,* 14: 49-51.

Tichy, Noel M. and David O. Ulrich. (Fall, 1984). "The Leadership Challenge—A Call for the Transformational Leader." *Sloan Management Review,* 59-68. Reprinted in *Classic Readings in Organizational Behavior.* Edited by J. Steven Ott. Belmont, California: Wadsworth, Inc., 1989, 344-355.

Timmins, William M. and Brad E. Hainsworth. (1989). "Attracting and Retaining Females in Law Enforcement: Sex-Based Problems of Women Cops in 1988." *International Journal of Offender Therapy and Comparative Criminology,* 33(3): 197-205.

Van Wormer, Katherine. (1981). "Are Males Suited to Police Patrol Work?" *Police Studies,* 3(4): 41-44.

Warner, Carolyn. (1992). *The Last Word: A Treasury of Women's Quotes.* Englewood Cliffs, New Jersey: Prentice-Hall.

None Cited. (1980). "Women Cops on the Beat." *Time,* 115: 58

None Cited. (1972). "The Women in Blue." *Time,* 99: 60.

Wyles, Lilian. (1952). *A Woman at Scotland Yard.* London: Faber and Faber, Limited.

Police-Killers Offer Insights Into Victims' Fatal Mistakes

Francis X. Clines

Special to The New York Times

WASHINGTON, March 3—The cop killer was deep in an eerie narrative, not bragging, not regretting, just lost in the vivid detail as he recalled casually ambushing a highway patrolman too busy with a clipboard and driver's license to see the end approaching.

"Not watching me at the time, I stuck my wallet back into my pocket and pulled out my pistol and shot him," the killer recollected into the video camera.

"He looked up just in time to see the gun going off," the bald, rather harmless-appearing man, in prison now for a life sentence, continued as he recalled the need he saw for a second shot. "I saw him move, an arm or hand, and I shot him again. I killed him. I shot him in the head and killed him."

Looking for Answers

The television screen boxed in the killer brightly before turning blank, and Edward F. Davis of the Federal Bureau of Investigation clearly felt the passion of that interview all over again. And again, he focused not on the cold-blooded confession, but on the unusual critique he drew from the killer of what the policeman had

done wrong and how he might have lived.

"Before in police literature, the good guys always evaluated the bad guys," Mr. Davis said, describing the turn-about of a new F.B.I. approach to fathoming what may be the ultimate antisocial outrage of gun-encrusted America, the killing of police officers, lately at the rate of six a month.

"What we're doing now is having the *bad* guys make a conscious evaluation of the *good* guys' conduct." Mr. Davis said of the three-year project of delving into cop-killers' tales. With his colleague, Anthony J. Pinizzotto, an F.B.I. agent with a doctorate in psychology, he is seeking advice from the killers on what their victims did wrong.

Interviews with 50 murderers have produced the bureau's first sketch of a typical victim officer: someone with a tendency to use less force than other officers and to rely on an instinctive read of a situation and so drop his guard. By the testimony of the officer's killer as well as mournful colleagues, the victim is likely to be a hard-working, laid-back person who "tends to look for good in others" and not follow all the rules, like waiting for backup help.

"The killers are telling the same things the academy instructors have been saying over and over," Mr. Davis said, emphasizing that carelessness about police procedures can

easily prove fatal. The killers' taped voices are presenting these findings more graphically than the traditional police academy lessons.

A Killer's Perspective

After years of cataloguing the forensic minutiae of each police killing—740 in the past decade—the F.B.I. accepted a proposal in 1989 from Mr. Davis and a colleague, James Baugh, that the bureau focus on the questions of precisely how and why, in the eyes of the killers, the attacks happened. Mr. Davis and Mr. Pinizzotto then traveled to 38 prisons to interview 50 murderers of 54 police officers.

Their work is now being presented at police conferences and academies. Like sketching a criminal, the two men listened to the killers and sketched the profile of a typical victim officer in a 60-page summary of their research called "Killed in the Line of Duty."

No less fascinating for the interrogators were the profiles of the killers, who formed a diverse group of criminal personalities. Fourteen percent, for example, said they might have acted differently had the officer victims been female. Only 1 of the 54 victims was a woman, reflecting the average of such killings for the past decade; two of the killers were women.

"Our bottom line is, 'Don't listen to us; listen to the killers,' " Mr. Davis said as the next taped killer filled the television screen at an F.B.I. office here. The killer, a meek, slender young man, offered a clipped, authoritative critique of why his victim, an officer stopping him after an armed robbery, was too careless for his own good.

Too Little Control

"He did not take control of me," said the young felon, as if that was why he now faces a lifetime in prison.

The killer listened as the question was plainly put to him: What might the officer have done differently to live?

"He never controlled my actions successfully," the convict scolded quietly, noting that the officer had foolishly kept his pistol holstered even as he watched his killer wheel around and fire point-blank.

The police turn to murderers for lifesaving advice.

The interviews, conducted under a painstaking method adapted from the bureau's protocol for serial killers and rapists, averaged more than five hours each. The focus ranged from the killers' recollections of their childhoods to their rationales, feelings and detailed descriptions of killing police officers.

A few officers viewing the tapes have objected to the pragmatic, unaccusing style of Mr. Davis, a 52-year-old veteran officer and F.B.I. agent, and Mr. Pinizzotto, a 42-year-old psychologist. The two members of the F.B.I.'s uniform crime reports section take this as a compliment in their stated assurances to the killers of not raking over guilt and blame but salvaging some life-saving clues for killers as well as victims.

A Crucial Shortcoming

They are already emphasizing the need to deal with a glaring shortcoming they have found: the dearth of training in what to do when a gunman has control of an officer. To draw in turn is folly, the F.B.I. has found, just as to surrender a police pistol can also be fatal.

"It's intriguing," Mr. Pinizzotto said of the talks with the killers. "Their victims stood guard protecting the rights of the citizenry, and these murders have a special symbolism."

Mr. Pinizzotto found that the killers ranged from a nonviolent career thief who suddenly killed when cornered to a passive, dependent young woman who became alarmed as her lover was arrested as an armed robber at a motel. The woman pulled a gun from her miniskirt pocket and killed two surprised policemen.

"How do these things happen? Why? Especially, why?" Mr. Pinizzotto asked. He noted that as complex as the research project had been

the team's next one would be even more so. The two men intend to interview officers who survived life-threatening wounds and ask them what went wrong and how they were almost killed.

'Look What Happened'

"This will be much tougher because they'll have to say, 'Not only did I make [a] mistake, but look what happened,' " Mr. Pinizzotto said.

Of course, there are cases in which an officer made all the recommended moves and yet still died, he said. But the F.B.I. is finding repeated accounts of sloppiness as it gathers killers' accounts of the final actions of many of the victims. This finding leaves the two agents chilled in the face of one murderer's tale, in particular:

"I grabbed the gun in the car and told my two friends I'm going back there and I'm going to shoot this man," one hard-eyed man recalled on the tapes.

The man, who had just committed an armed robbery, was angry at being pulled over by a patrol car for driving erratically. He saw his chance when the policeman became overly busy with his radio: "He wasn't looking at me when I approached the car, which gave me the advantage to get real close to him. He stayed on the radio and when he noticed somebody standing near, all he did was look at me with the corner of his eye. I pointed my gun to his chest and shot him."

The Judicial System

Our system of criminal justice is an adversarial system and the protagonists are the state and the criminal defendant. The courtroom is where the drama is played out, and we look to the courts to preserve our liberties and ensure a fair trial.

"The Judicial Process: Prosecutors and Courts" outlines the roles of prosecutors, defense counsels, and the courts in the criminal justice process. "Abuse of Power in the Prosecutor's Office" is a critical analysis of the office of prosecutor. The article is presented, not as an indictment of all prosecutors, but to stimulate discussion as to the potential for abuse. On the other hand, the role of the public defender is presented in a sympathetic light in "The Trials of the Public Defender."

"Twelve Good Reasons: How Lawyers Judge Potential Jurors" explores the selection process of juries including questions of race, class, gender, or religion.

"Double Exposure: Did the Second Rodney King Trial Violate Double Jeopardy?" explores the philosophical and constitutional issues involved in the retrial of the police officers involved in the arrest of Rodney King.

Looking Ahead: Challenge Questions

What can be done to ensure fairness in the prosecutor's office?

Does the "public defender" concept provide fair representation?

What are the "double jeopardy" issues in the retrial of the L.A. police officers?

Unit 4

The Judicial Process: Prosecutors and Courts

The courts participate in and supervise the judicial process

The courts have several functions in addition to deciding whether laws have been violated

The courts—
• settle disputes between legal entities (persons, corporations, etc.)
• invoke sanctions against law violations
• decide whether acts of the legislative and executive branches are constitutional.

In deciding about violations of the law the courts must apply the law to the facts of each case. The courts affect policy in deciding individual cases by handing down decisions about how the laws should be interpreted and carried out. Decisions of the appellate courts are the ones most likely to have policy impact.

Using an arm of the State to settle disputes is a relatively new concept

Until the Middle Ages disputes between individuals, clans, and families, including those involving criminal acts, were handled privately. Over time, acts such as murder, rape, robbery, larceny, and fraud came to be regarded as crimes against the entire community, and the State intervened on its behalf. Today in the United States the courts handle both civil actions (disputes between individuals or organizations) and criminal actions.

An independent judiciary is a basic concept of the U.S. system of government

To establish its independence and impartiality, the judiciary was created as a separate branch of government co-equal to the executive and the legislative branches. Insulation of the courts from political pressure is attempted through—
• the separation of powers doctrine
• established tenure for judges
• legislative safeguards
• the canons of legal ethics.

Courts are without the power of enforcement. The executive branch must enforce their decisions. Furthermore, the courts must request that the legislature provide them with the resources needed to conduct their business.

Each State has a system of trial and appeals courts

Generally, State court systems are organized according to three basic levels of jurisdiction:

• **Courts of limited and special jurisdiction** are authorized to hear only less serious cases (misdemeanors and/or civil suits that involve small amounts of money) or to hear special types of cases such as divorce or probate suits. Such courts include traffic courts, municipal courts, family courts, small claims courts, magistrate courts, and probate courts.

• **Courts of general jurisdiction**, also called major trial courts, are unlimited in the civil or criminal cases they are authorized to hear. Almost all cases originate in the courts of limited or special jurisdiction or in courts of general jurisdiction. Most serious criminal cases are handled by courts of general jurisdiction.

• **Appellate courts** are divided into two groups, intermediate appeals courts, which hear some or all appeals that are subject to review by the court of last resort, and courts of last resort, which have jurisdiction over final appeals from courts of original jurisdiction, intermediate appeals courts, or administrative agencies. As of 1985, 36 States had intermediate appellate courts, but all States had courts of last resort.

The U.S. Constitution created the U.S. Supreme Court and authorized the Congress to

From *Report to the Nation on Crime and Justice,* Bureau of Justice Statistics, U.S. Department of Justice, March 1988, pp. 81-82, 71-72, 74-75.

establish lower courts as needed

The Federal court system now consists of various special courts, U.S. district courts (general jurisdiction courts), U.S. courts of appeals (intermediate appellate courts that receive appeals from the district courts and Federal administrative agencies), and the U.S. Supreme Court (the court of last resort). Organized on a regional basis are U.S. courts of appeals for each of 11 circuits and the District of Columbia. In Federal trial courts (the 94 U.S. district courts) more than 300,000 cases were filed in 1985; there was one criminal case for every seven civil cases. In 1985 more than half the criminal cases in district courts were for embezzlement, fraud, forgery and counterfeiting, traffic, or drug offenses.

Court organization varies greatly among the States

State courts of general jurisdiction are organized by districts, counties, dual districts, or a combination of counties and districts. In some States the courts established by the State are funded and controlled locally. In others the court of last resort may have some budgetary or administrative oversight over the entire State court system. Even within States there is considerable lack of uniformity in the roles, organization, and procedures of the courts. This has led to significant momentum among States to form "unified" court systems to provide in varying degrees, for uniform administration of the courts, and, in many cases, for the consolidation of diverse courts of limited and special jurisdiction.

Most felony cases are brought in State and local courts

The traditional criminal offenses under the English common law have been adopted, in one form or another, in the criminal laws of each of the States. Most cases involving "common law" crimes are brought to trial in State or local courts. Persons charged with misdemeanors are usually tried in courts of limited jurisdiction. Those charged with felonies (more serious crimes) are tried in courts of general jurisdiction.

In all States criminal defendants may appeal most decisions of criminal courts of limited jurisdiction; the avenue of appeal usually ends with the State supreme court. However, the U.S. Supreme Court may elect to hear the case if the appeal is based on an alleged violation of the Constitutional rights of the defendant.

Courts at various levels of government interact in many ways

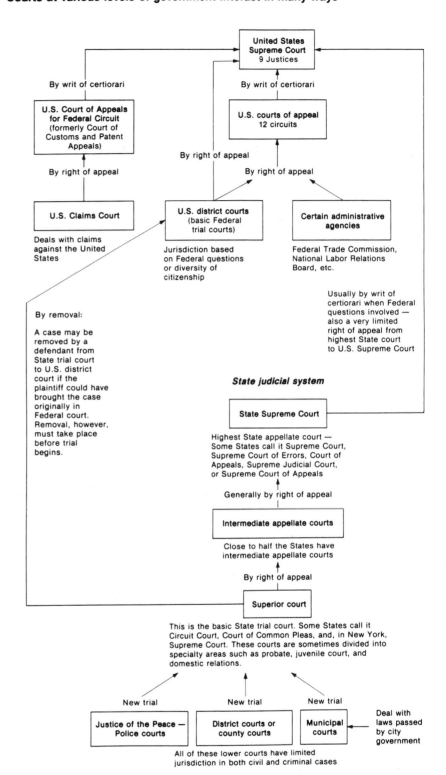

Updated and reprinted by permission from *The American Legal Environment* by William T. Schantz. Copyright © 1976 by West Publishing Company. All rights reserved.

State courts process a large volume of cases, many of them minor

In 1983, 46 States and the District of Columbia reported more than 80 million cases filed in State and local courts. About 70% were traffic-related cases, 16% were civil cases (torts, contracts,

Differences in how prosecutors handle felony cases can be seen in 4 jurisdictions

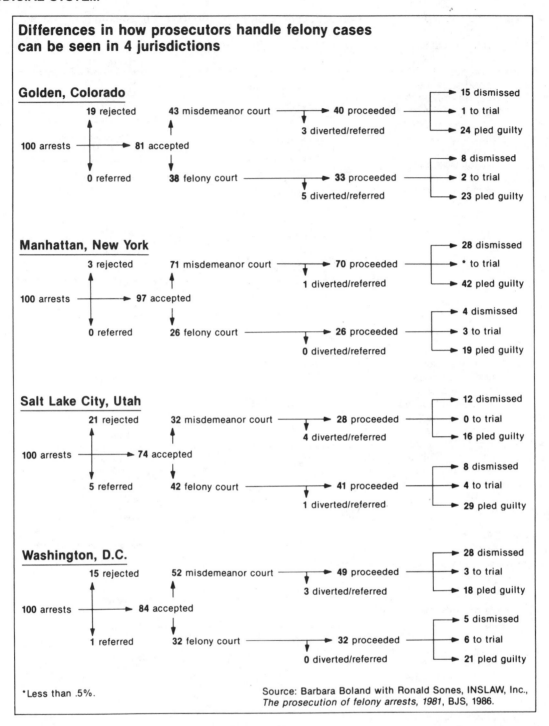

Golden, Colorado

19 rejected	43 misdemeanor court → 40 proceeded	→ 15 dismissed
	↓ 3 diverted/referred	→ 1 to trial
		→ 24 pled guilty
100 arrests → 81 accepted		
0 referred	38 felony court → 33 proceeded	→ 8 dismissed
	↓ 5 diverted/referred	→ 2 to trial
		→ 23 pled guilty

Manhattan, New York

3 rejected	71 misdemeanor court → 70 proceeded	→ 28 dismissed
	↓ 1 diverted/referred	→ * to trial
		→ 42 pled guilty
100 arrests → 97 accepted		
0 referred	26 felony court → 26 proceeded	→ 4 dismissed
	↓ 0 diverted/referred	→ 3 to trial
		→ 19 pled guilty

Salt Lake City, Utah

21 rejected	32 misdemeanor court → 28 proceeded	→ 12 dismissed
	↓ 4 diverted/referred	→ 0 to trial
		→ 16 pled guilty
100 arrests → 74 accepted		
5 referred	42 felony court → 41 proceeded	→ 8 dismissed
	↓ 1 diverted/referred	→ 4 to trial
		→ 29 pled guilty

Washington, D.C.

15 rejected	52 misdemeanor court → 49 proceeded	→ 28 dismissed
	↓ 3 diverted/referred	→ 3 to trial
		→ 18 pled guilty
100 arrests → 84 accepted		
1 referred	32 felony court → 32 proceeded	→ 5 dismissed
	↓ 0 diverted/referred	→ 6 to trial
		→ 21 pled guilty

*Less than .5%.

Source: Barbara Boland with Ronald Sones, INSLAW, Inc., *The prosecution of felony arrests, 1981*, BJS, 1986.

small claims, etc.), 13% were criminal cases, and 1% were juvenile cases. Civil and criminal cases both appear to be increasing. Of 39 States that reported civil filings for 1978 and 1983, 32 had increases. Of the 36 States that reported criminal filings for both years, 33 showed an increase in the volume of criminal filings.

In the 24 States that could report, felony filings comprised from 5% to 32% of total criminal filings with a median of 9%.

Victims and witnesses are taking a more significant part in the prosecution of felons

Recent attention to crime victims has spurred the development of legislation and services that are more responsive to victims.
• Some States have raised witness fees from $5–10 per day in trial to $20–30 per day, established procedures for victim and witness notification of court proceedings, and guaranteed the right to speedy disposition of cases

• 9 States and the Federal Government have comprehensive bills of rights for victims

• 39 States and the Federal Government have laws or guidelines requiring that victims and witnesses be notified of the scheduling and cancellation of criminal proceedings

• 33 States and the Federal Government allow victims to participate in criminal proceedings via oral or written testimony.

The prosecutor provides the link between the law enforcement and adjudicatory processes

The separate system of justice for juveniles often operates within the existing court organization

Jurisdiction over juvenile delinquency, dependent or neglected children, and related matters is vested in various types of courts. In many States the juvenile court is a division of the court of general jurisdiction. A few States have statewide systems of juvenile or family courts. Juvenile jurisdiction is vested in the courts of general jurisdiction in some counties and in separate juvenile courts or courts of limited jurisdiction in others.

The American prosecutor is unique in the world

First, the American prosecutor is a public prosecutor representing the people in matters of criminal law. Historically, European societies viewed crimes as wrongs against an individual whose claims could be pressed through private prosecution. Second, the American prosecutor is usually a local official, reflecting the development of autonomous local governments in the colonies. Finally, as an elected official, the local American prosecutor is responsible to the voters.

Prosecution is the function of representing the people in criminal cases

After the police arrest a suspect, the prosecutor coordinates the government's response to crime—from the initial screening, when the prosecutor decides whether or not to press charges, through trial. In some instances, it continues through sentencing with the presentation of sentencing recommendations.

Prosecutors have been accorded much discretion in carrying out their responsibilities. They make many of the decisions that determine whether a case will proceed through the criminal justice process.

Prosecution is predominantly a State and local function

Prosecuting officials include State, district, county, prosecuting, and commonwealth attorneys; corporation counsels; circuit solicitors; attorneys general; and U.S. attorneys. Prosecution is carried out by more than 8,000 State, county, municipal, and township prosecution agencies.[1] In all but five States, local prosecutors are elected officials. Many small jurisdictions engage a part-time prosecutor who also maintains a private law practice. In some areas police share the charging responsibility of local prosecutors. Prosecutors in urban jurisdictions often have offices staffed by many full-time assistants. Each State has an office of the attorney general, which has jurisdiction over all matters involving State law but generally, unless specifically requested, is not involved in local prosecution. Federal prosecution is the responsibility of 93 U.S. attorneys who are appointed by the President subject to confirmation by the Senate.

The decision to charge is generally a function of the prosecutor

Results of a 1981 survey of police and prosecution agencies in localities of over 100,000 indicate that police file initial charges in half the jurisdictions surveyed. This arrangement, sometimes referred to as the police court, is not commonly found in the larger urban areas that account for most of the UCR Index crime. Usually, once an arrest is made and the case is referred to the prosecutor, most prosecutors screen cases to see if they merit prosecution. The prosecutor can refuse to prosecute, for example, because of insufficient evidence. The decision to charge is not usually reviewable by any other branch of government.

Some prosecutors accept almost all cases for prosecution; others screen out many cases

Some prosecutors have screening units designed to reject cases at the earliest possible point. Others tend to accept most arrests, more of which are dismissed by judges later in the adjudication process. Most prosecutor offices fall somewhere between these two extremes.

Arrest disposition patterns in 16 jurisdictions range from 0 to 47% of arrests rejected for prosecution. Jurisdictions with high rejection rates generally were found to have lower rates of dismissal at later stages of the criminal process. Conversely, jurisdictions that accepted most or all arrests usually had high dismissal rates.

Prosecutorial screening practices are of several distinct types

Several studies conclude that screening decisions consider—
• evidentiary factors
• the views of the prosecutor on key criminal justice issues
• the political and social environment in which the prosecutor functions
• the resource constraints and organization of prosecutorial operations.

Jacoby's study confirmed the presence of at least three policies that affect the screening decision:
• Legal sufficiency—an arrest is accepted for prosecution if, on routine review of the arrest, the minimum legal elements of a case are present.
• System efficiency—arrests are disposed as quickly as possible by the fastest means possible, which are rejections, dismissals, and pleas.
• Trial sufficiency—the prosecutor accepts only those arrests for which, in his or her view, there is sufficient evidence to convict in court.

The official accusation in felony cases is a grand jury indictment or a prosecutor's bill of information

According to Jacoby, the accusatory process usually follows one of four paths:
• arrest to preliminary hearing for bind-over to grand jury for indictment
• arrest to grand jury for indictment
• arrest to preliminary hearing to a bill of information
• a combination of the above at the prosecutor's discretion.

Whatever the method of accusation, the State must demonstrate only that there is probable cause to support the charge.

The preliminary hearing is used in some jurisdictions to determine probable cause

The purpose of the hearing is to see if there is probable cause to believe a crime has been committed and that the defendant committed it. Evidence may be presented by both the prosecution and the defense. On a finding of probable cause the defendant is held to answer in the next stage of a felony proceeding.

The grand jury emerged from the American Revolution as the people's protection against oppressive prosecution by the State

Today, the grand jury is a group of ordi-

4. THE JUDICIAL SYSTEM

nary citizens, usually no more than 23, which has both accusatory and investigative functions. The jury's proceedings are secret and not adversarial so that most rules of evidence for trials do not apply. Usually, evidence is presented by the prosecutor who brings a case to the grand jury's attention. However, in some States the grand jury is used primarily to investigate issues of public corruption and organized crime.

Some States do not require a grand jury indictment to initiate prosecutions

Grand jury indictment required	Grand jury indictment optional
All crimes	Arizona
New Jersey	Arkansas
South Carolina	California
Tennessee	Colorado
Virginia	Idaho
	Illinois
All felonies	Indiana
Alabama	Iowa
Alaska	Kansas
Delaware	Maryland
District of Columbia	Michigan
Georgia	Missouri
Hawaii	Montana
Kentucky	Nebraska
Maine	Nevada
Mississippi	New Mexico
New Hampshire	North Dakota
New York	Oklahoma
North Carolina	Oregon

Ohio	South Dakota
Texas	Utah
West Virginia	Vermont
	Washington
Capital crimes only	Wisconsin
Connecticut	Wyoming
Florida	
Louisiana	**Grand jury lacks authority to indict**
Massachusetts	
Minnesota	
Rhode Island	Pennsylvania

Note: With the exception of capital cases a defendant can always waive the right to an indictment. Thus, the requirement for an indictment to initiate prosecution exists only in the absence of a waiver.
Source: Deborah Day Emerson, *Grand jury reform: A review of key issues*, National Institute of Justice, U.S. Department of Justice, January 1983.

The secrecy of the grand jury is a matter of controversy

Critics of the grand jury process suggest it denies due process and equal protection under the law and exists only to serve the prosecutor. Recent criticisms have fostered a number of reforms requiring due process protections for persons under investigation and for witnesses; requiring improvements in the quality and quantity of evidence presented; and opening the proceeding to outside review. While there is much variation in the nature and implementation of reforms, 15 States have enacted laws affording the right to counsel, and 10 States require evidentiary standards approaching the requirements imposed at trial.

The defense attorney's function is to protect the defendant's legal rights and to be the defendant's advocate in the adversary process

Defendants have the right to defend themselves, but most prefer to be represented by a specialist in the law. Relatively few members of the legal profession specialize in criminal law, but lawyers who normally handle other types of legal matters may take criminal cases.

The right to the assistance of counsel is more than the right to hire a lawyer

Supreme Court decisions in *Gideon* v. *Wainwright* (1963) and *Argersinger* v. *Hamlin* (1972) established that the right to an attorney may not be frustrated by lack of means. For both felonies and misdemeanors for which jail or prison can be the penalty, the State must provide an attorney to any accused person who is indigent.

The institutional response to this Constitutional mandate is still evolving as States experiment with various ways to provide legal counsel for indigent defendants.

ABUSE OF POWER IN THE PROSECUTOR'S OFFICE

Bennett L. Gershman

Bennett L. Gershman is professor of law at Pace University. He is the author of Prosecutorial Misconduct *and several articles on law dealing with such topics as entrapment and police and prosecutorial ethics. For ten years, he was a prosecutor in New York.*

The prosecutor is the most dominant figure in the American criminal justice system. As the Supreme Court recently observed, "Between the private life of the citizen and the public glare of criminal accusation stands the prosecutor. [The prosecutor has] the power to employ the full machinery of the State in scrutinizing any given individual." Thus, the prosecutor decides whether or not to bring criminal charges; whom to charge; what charges to bring; whether a defendant will stand trial, plead guilty, or enter a correctional program in lieu of criminal charges; and whether to confer immunity from prosecution. In jurisdictions that authorize capital punishment, the prosecutor literally decides who shall live and who shall die. Moreover, in carrying out these broad functions, the prosecutor enjoys considerable independence from the courts, administrative superiors, and the public. A prosecutor cannot be forced to bring criminal charges, or be prevented from bringing them. Needless to say, the awesome power that prosecutors exercise is susceptible to

abuse. Such abuses most frequently occur in connection with the prosecutor's power to bring charges; to control the information used to convict those on trial; and to influence juries.

The prosecutor's charging power includes the virtually unfettered discretion to invoke or deny punishment, and therefore the power to control and destroy people's lives. Such prosecutorial discretion has been called "tyrannical," "lawless," and "most dangerous." Prosecutors may not unfairly select which persons to prosecute. But this rule is difficult to enforce, and the courts almost always defer to the prosecutor's discretion. In one recent case, for example, a prosecutor targeted for prosecution a vocal opponent of the Selective Service system who refused to register, rather than any of nearly a million nonvocal persons who did not register. The proof showed that the defendant clearly was selected for prosecution not because he failed to register but because he exercised his First Amendment rights. This was a legally impermissible basis for prosecution. Nevertheless, the courts refused to disturb the prosecutor's decision, because there was no clear proof of prosecutorial bad faith. Many other disturbing examples exist of improper selection based on race, sex, religion, and the exercise of constitutional rights. These cases invariably are decided in the prosecutor's favor. The reasoning is circular. The courts presume that prosecutors act in good faith, and that the prosecutor's expertise, law enforcement plans, and priorities are ill suited to judicial review.

Unfair selectivity is one of the principal areas of discretionary abuse. Another is prosecutorial retaliation in the form of increased charges after defendants raise statutory or constitutional claims. Prosecutors are not allowed to be vindictive in response to a defendant's exercise of rights. Nevertheless, proving vindictiveness, as with selectiveness, is virtually impossible. Courts simply do not probe the prosecutor's state of mind. For example, prosecutors often respond to a defendant's unwillingness to plead guilty to a crime by bringing higher charges. In one recent case, a defendant charged with a petty offense refused to plead guilty despite prosecutorial threats to bring much higher charges. The prosecutor carried out his threat and brought new charges carrying a sentence of life imprisonment. The court found the prosecutor's conduct allowable. Although the prosecutor behaved in a clearly retaliatory fashion, the court nevertheless believed that the prosecutor needed this leverage to make the system work. If the prosecutor could not threaten defendants by "upping the ante," so the court reasoned, there would be fewer guilty pleas and the system would collapse.

Finally, some prosecutions are instituted for illegitimate personal objectives as opposed to ostensibly valid law enforcement objectives. Such prosecutions can be labeled demagogic and usually reveal actual prosecutorial malice or evil intent. Telltale signs of demagoguery often include the appearance of personal vendettas, political crusades, and witch hunts. Examples of this base practice abound. They have involved prosecutions based on racial or political hostility; prosecutions motivated by personal and political gain; and prosecutions to discourage or coerce the exercise of constitutional rights. One notorious example was New Orleans District Attorney James Garrison's prosecution of Clay Shaw for the Kennedy assassination. Other examples have included the prosecutions of labor leader James Hoffa, New York attorney Roy Cohn, and civil rights leader Dr. Martin Luther King.

HIDING EVIDENCE

A prosecutor's misuse of power also occurs in connection with legal proof. In the course of an investigation, in pretrial preparation, or even during a trial, prosecutors often become aware of information that might exonerate a defendant. It is not unusual for the prosecutor to have such proof, in view of the acknowledged superiority of law enforcement's investigative resources and its early access to crucial evidence. The adversary system relies on a fair balance of opposing forces. But one of the greatest threats to rational and fair fact-finding in criminal cases comes from the prosecutor's hiding evidence that might prove a defendant's innocence. Examples of prosecutorial suppression of exculpatory evidence are numerous. Such conduct is pernicious for several reasons: It skews the ability of the adversary system to function properly by denying to the defense crucial proof; it undermines the public's respect for and confidence in the public prosecutor's office; and it has resulted in many defendants being unjustly convicted, with the consequent loss of their liberty or even their lives.

Consider the following recent examples. Murder convictions of Randall Dale Adams in Texas, James Richardson and Joseph Brown in Florida, and Eric Jackson in New York all were vacated because the prosecutors hid crucial evidence that would have proved these defendants' innocence. The Adams case—popularized by the film *The Thin Blue Line*—depicts Texas "justice" at its worst. Adams was convicted in 1977 of murdering a policeman and sentenced to die largely on the testimony of a juvenile with a long criminal record who made a secret deal with the prosecutor to implicate Adams, and the testimony of two eyewitnesses to the killing. The juvenile actually murdered the policeman, as he later acknowledged. At Adams' trial, however, the prosecutor suppressed information about the deal and successfully kept from the jury the juvenile's lengthy record.

The prosecutor also withheld evidence that the two purported eyewitnesses had failed to identify Adams in a line-up, and permitted these witnesses to testify that they had made a positive identification of Adams. A Texas court recently freed Adams, finding that the prosecutor suborned perjury and knowingly suppressed evidence.

Richardson—whose case was memorialized in the book *Arcadia* was condemned to die for poisoning to death his

tor misrepresented to the jury that ballistics evidence proved the defendant's guilt, when in fact the prosecutor knew that the ballistics report showed that the bullet that killed the deceased could not have been fired from the defendant's weapon.

Eric Jackson was convicted of murder in 1980 for starting a fire at Waldbaum's supermarket in Brooklyn in which a roof collapsed and six firefighters died. Years later, the attorney who repre-

---

Abuses most frequently occur in connection with the prosecutor's power to bring charges, to control the information used to convict those on trial, and to influence juries.

---

seven children in 1967. The prosecutor claimed that Richardson, a penniless farm worker, killed his children to collect insurance. A state judge last year overturned the murder conviction, finding that the prosecutor had suppressed evidence that would have shown Richardson's innocence. The undisclosed evidence included a sworn statement from the children's babysitter that she had killed the youngsters; a sworn statement from a cellmate of Richardson's that the cellmate had been beaten by a sheriff's deputy into fabricating his story implicating Richardson; statements from other inmates contradicting their claims that Richardson confessed to them; and proof that Richardson had never purchased any insurance.

Brown's murder conviction recently was reversed by the Eleventh Circuit. Brown was only hours away from being electrocuted when his execution was stayed. That court found that the prosecutor "knowingly allowed material false testimony to be introduced at trial, failed to step forward and make the falsity known, and knowingly exploited the false testimony in its closing argument to the jury." The subornation of perjury related to the testimony of a key prosecution witness who falsely denied that a deal had been made with the prosecutor, and the prosecutor's misrepresentation of that fact to the court. In addition, the prosecu-

sented the families of the deceased firemen in a tort action discovered that one of the prosecutor's expert witnesses at the trial had informed the prosecutor that the fire was not arson related, but was caused by an electrical malfunction. At a hearing in the fall of 1988, the prosecutor consistently maintained that nothing had been suppressed and offered to disclose pertinent documents. The judge rejected the offer and personally inspected the prosecutor's file. The judge found in that file two internal memoranda from two different assistant district attorneys to an executive in the prosecutor's office. Each memorandum stated that the expert witness had concluded that the fire had resulted from an electrical malfunction and had not been deliberately set—and that the expert's conclusion presented a major problem for the prosecution. None of this information was ever revealed to the defense. On the basis of the above, the court vacated the conviction and ordered the defendant's immediate release.

To be sure, disclosure is the one area above all else that relies on the prosecutor's good faith and integrity. If the prosecutor hides evidence, it is likely that nobody will ever know. The information will lay buried forever in the prosecutor's files. Moreover, most prosecutors, if they are candid, will concede that their inclination in this area is not to reveal information that might damage his or her case. Ironically, in this important area in which the prosecutor's fairness, integrity, and good faith are so dramatically put to the test, the courts have defaulted. According to the courts, the prosecutor's good or bad faith in secreting evidence is irrelevant. It is the character of the evidence that counts, not the character of the prosecutor. Thus, even if a violation is deliberate, and with an intent to harm the defendant, the courts will not order relief unless the evidence is so crucial that it would have changed the verdict. Thus, there is no real incentive for prosecutors to disclose such evidence.

Hopefully, in light of the recent disclosures of prosecutorial misconduct, courts, bar associations, and even legislatures will wake up to the quagmire in criminal justice. These bodies should act vigorously and aggressively to deter and punish the kinds of violations that recur all too frequently. Thus, reversals should be required automatically for deliberate suppression of evidence, and the standards for reversal for nondeliberate suppression relaxed; disciplinary action against prosecutors should be the rule rather than the exception; and legislation should be enacted making it a crime for prosecutors to willfully suppress evidence resulting in a defendant's conviction.

MISBEHAVING IN THE COURTROOM TO SWAY THE JURY

Finally, the prosecutor's trial obligations often are violated. The duties of the prosecuting attorney during a trial were well stated in a classic opinion fifty years ago. The interest of the prosecutor, the court wrote, "is not that it shall win a case, but that justice shall be done. As such, he is in a peculiar and very definite sense the servant of the law, the twofold aim of which is that guilt shall not escape or innocence suffer. He may prosecute with earnestness and vigor—indeed, he should do so. But, while he may strike hard blows, he is not at liberty to strike a foul one."

Despite this admonition, prosecutors continually strike "foul blows." In one leading case of outrageous conduct, a prosecutor concealed from the jury in a murder case the fact that a pair of undershorts

with red stains on it, a crucial piece of evidence, was stained not by blood but by paint. In another recent case, a prosecutor, in his summation, characterized the defendant as an "animal," told the jury that "the only guarantee against his future crimes would be to execute him," and that he should have "his face blown away by a shotgun." In another case, the prosecutor argued that the defendant's attorney knew the defendant was guilty; otherwise he would have put the defendant on the witness stand.

The above examples are illustrative of common practices today, and the main reason such misconduct occurs is quite simple: It works. Indeed, several studies have shown the importance of oral advocacy in the courtroom, as well as the effect produced by such conduct. For example, a student of trial advocacy often is told of the importance of the opening statement. Prosecutors would undoubtedly agree that the opening statement is indeed crucial. In a University of Kansas study, the importance of the opening statement was confirmed. From this study, the authors concluded that in the course of any given trial, the jurors were affected most by the first strong presentation that they saw. This finding leads to the conclusion that if a prosecutor were to present a particularly strong opening argument, the jury would favor the prosecution throughout the trial. Alternatively, if the prosecutor were to provide a weak opening statement, followed by a strong opening statement by the defense, then, according to the authors, the jury would favor the defense during the trial. It thus becomes evident that the prosecutor will be best served by making the strongest opening argument possible, thereby assisting the jury in gaining a better insight into what they are about to hear and see. The opportunity for the prosecutor to influence the jury at this point in the trial is considerable, and many prosecutors use this opportunity to their advantage, even if the circumstances do not call for lengthy or dramatic opening remarks.

An additional aspect of the prosecutor's power over the jury is suggested in a University of North Carolina study, which found that the more arguments counsel raises to support the different substantive arguments offered, the more the jury will believe in that party's case. Moreover, this study found that there is not necessarily a correlation between the amount of objective information in the argument and the persuasiveness of the presentation.

For the trial attorney, then, this study clearly points to the advantage of raising as many issues as possible at trial. For the prosecutor, the two studies taken together would dictate an "action-packed" opening statement, containing as many arguments as can be mustered, even those that might be irrelevant or unnecessary to convince the jury of the defendant's guilt. The second study would also dictate the same strategy for the closing argument. Consequently, a prosecutor who through use of these techniques attempts to assure that the jury knows his case may, despite violating ethical standards to seek justice, be "rewarded" with a guilty verdict. Thus, one begins to perceive the incentive that leads the prosecutor to misbehave in the courtroom.

Similar incentives can be seen with respect to the complex problem of controlling evidence to which the jury may have access. It is common knowledge that in the course of any trial, statements fre-

dence on the decisions of jurors. The authors of the test designed a variety of scenarios whereby some jurors heard about an incriminating piece of evidence while other jurors did not. The study found that the effect of the inadmissible evidence was directly correlated to the strength of the prosecutor's case. The authors of the study reported that when the prosecutor presented a weak case, the inadmissible evidence did in fact prejudice the jurors. Furthermore, the judge's admonition to the jurors to disregard certain evidence did not have the same effect as when the evidence had not been mentioned at all. It had a prejudicial impact anyway.

However, the study also indicated that when there was a strong prosecution case, the inadmissible evidence had little, if any, effect. Nonetheless, the most significant conclusion from the study is that inadmissible evidence had its most prejudicial impact when there was little other evidence upon which the jury could base a decision. In this situation, "the controversial evidence becomes quite salient in the jurors' minds."

Finally, with respect to inadmissible evidence and stricken testimony, even if

---

In one leading case of outrageous conduct, a prosecutor concealed from the jury in a murder case the fact that a pair of undershorts with red stains on it, a crucial piece of evidence, was stained not by blood but by paint.

---

quently are made by the attorneys or witnesses despite the fact that these statements may not be admissible as evidence. Following such a statement, the trial judge may, at the request of opposing counsel, instruct the jury to disregard what they have heard. Most trial lawyers, if they are candid, will agree that it is virtually impossible for jurors realistically to disregard these inadmissible statements. Studies here again demonstrate that our intuition is correct and that this evidence often is considered by jurors in reaching a verdict.

For example, an interesting study conducted at the University of Washington tested the effects of inadmissible evi-

one were to reject all of the studies discussed, it is still clear that although "stricken testimony may tend to be rejected in open discussion, it does have an impact, perhaps even an unconscious one, on the individual juror's judgment." As with previously discussed points, this factor—the unconscious effect of stricken testimony or evidence—will generally not be lost on the prosecutor who is in tune with the psychology of the jury.

The applicability of these studies to the issue of prosecutorial misconduct, then, is quite clear. Faced with a difficult case in which there may be a problem of proof, a prosecutor might be tempted to try to sway the jury by adverting to a matter that might be highly prejudicial. In this connection, another study has suggested that the jury will more likely consider inadmissible evidence that favors conviction.

Despite this factor of "defense favoritism," it is again evident that a prosecutor may find it rewarding to misconduct himself or herself in the courtroom. Of course, a prosecutor who adopts the unethical norm and improperly allows jurors to hear inadmissible proof runs the risk of jeopardizing any resulting conviction. In a situation where the prosecutor feels that he has a weak case, however, a subsequent reversal is not a particularly effective sanction when a conviction might have been difficult to achieve in the first place. Consequently, an unethical courtroom "trick" can be a very attractive idea to the prosecutor who feels he must win. Additionally, there is always the possibility of another conviction even after an appellate reversal. Indeed, while a large number of cases are dismissed following remand by an appellate court, nearly one-half of reversals still result in some type of conviction. Therefore, a prosecutor can still succeed in obtaining a conviction even after his misconduct led to a reversal.

An additional problem in the area of prosecutor-jury interaction is the prosecutor's prestige; since the prosecutor represents the "government," jurors are more likely to believe him. Put simply, prosecutors are the "good guys" of the legal system, and because they have such glamor, they often may be tempted to use this advantage in an unethical manner. This presents a problem in that the average citizen may often forgive prosecutors for ethical indiscretions, because conviction of criminals certainly justifies in the public eye any means necessary. Consequently, unless the prosecutor is a person of high integrity and able to uphold the highest moral standards, the problem of courtroom misconduct will inevitably be tolerated by the public.

Moreover, when considering the problems facing the prosecutor, one also must consider the tremendous stress under which the prosecutor labors on a daily basis. Besides the stressful conditions faced by the ordinary courtroom litigator, prosecuting attorneys, particularly those in large metropolitan areas, are faced with huge and very demanding caseloads. As a result of case volume and time demands, prosecutors may not be able to take advantage of opportunities to relax and recover from the constant onslaught their emotions face every day in the courtroom.

Under these highly stressful conditions, it is understandable that a prosecutor occasionally may find it difficult to face these everyday pressures and to resist temptations to behave unethically. It is not unreasonable to suggest that the conditions under which the prosecutor works can have a profound effect on his attempt to maintain high moral and ethical standards. Having established this hy-

---

An unethical courtroom ''trick'' can be a very attractive idea to the prosecutor who feels he must win.

---

pothesis, we see yet another reason why courtroom misconduct may occur.

WHY PROSECUTORIAL MISCONDUCT PERSISTS

Although courtroom misconduct may in many instances be highly effective, why do such practices continue in our judicial system? A number of reasons may account for this phenomenon, perhaps the most significant of which is the harmless error doctrine. Under this doctrine, an appellate court can affirm a conviction despite the presence of serious misconduct during the trial. As one judge stated, the "practical objective of tests of harmless error is to conserve judicial resources by enabling appellate courts to cleanse the judicial process of prejudicial error without becoming mired in harmless error."

Although this definition portrays harmless error as having a most desirable consequence, this desirability is undermined when the prosecutor is able to misconduct himself without fear of sanction. Additionally, since every case is different, what constitutes harmless error in one case may be reversible error in another case. Consequently, harmless error determinations do not offer any significant precedents by which prosecutors can judge the status of their behavior. Moreover, harmless error determinations are essentially absurd. In order to apply the harmless error rule, appellate judges attempt to evaluate how various evidentiary items or instances of prosecutorial misconduct may have affected the jury's verdict. Although it may be relatively simple in some cases to determine whether improper conduct during a trial was harmless, there are many instances when such an analysis cannot be properly made but nevertheless is made. There are numerous instances in which appellate courts are deeply divided over whether or not a given error was harmless. The implications of these contradictory decisions are significant, for they demonstrate the utter failure of appellate courts to provide incentives for the prosecutor to control his behavior. If misconduct can be excused even when reasonable judges differ as to the extent of harm caused by such misbehavior, then very little guidance is given to a prosecutor to assist him in determining the propriety of his actions. Clearly, without such guidance, the potential for misconduct significantly increases.

A final point when analyzing why prosecutorial misconduct persists is the unavailability or inadequacy of penalties visited upon the prosecutor personally in the event of misconduct. Punishment in our legal system comes in varying degrees. An appellate court can punish a prosecutor by simply cautioning him not to act in the same manner again, reversing his case, or, in some cases, identifying by name the prosecutor who misconducted himself. Even these punishments, however, may not be sufficient to dissuade prosecutors from acting improperly. One noteworthy case describes a prosecutor who appeared before the appellate court on a misconduct issue for the third time, each instance in a different case.

Perhaps the ultimate reason for the ineffectiveness of the judicial system in curbing prosecutorial misconduct is that prosecutors are not personally liable for their misconduct. During the course of a trial, the prosecutor is absolutely shielded from any civil liability that might arise due to his or her misconduct, even if that misconduct was performed with malice. To be sure, there is clearly a necessary level of immunity accorded all government officials. Without such immunity, much of what is normally done by officials in authority might not be performed, out of fear that their practices would later be deemed harmful or improper. Granting prosecutors a certain level of immunity is reasonable. Allowing prosecutors to be completely shielded from civil liability in the event of misconduct, however, provides no deterrent to courtroom misconduct.

For the prosecutor, the temptation to cross over the allowable ethical limit must often be tremendous, because of the distinct advantages that such misconduct creates with respect to assisting the prosecutor to win his case by effectively influencing the jury. Most prosecutors must inevitably be subject to this temptation. It takes a constant effort on the part of every prosecutor to maintain the high moral standards necessary to avoid such temptations. Despite the frequent occurrences of courtroom misconduct, appellate courts have not provided significant incentives to deter it. Inroads will not be made in the effort to end prosecutorial misconduct until the courts decide to take a stricter, more consistent approach to this problem.

THE TRIALS OF THE
Public
Defender

**Overworked and underpaid lawyers serve up a brand of
justice that is not always in their clients' best interests**

JILL SMOLOWE

EVERY DAY, AS HE AMBLES through the cobwebbed halls of the New Orleans criminal court building, public defender Richard Teissier feels he violates his clients' constitutional rights. The Sixth Amendment established, and the landmark *Gideon* Supreme Court case affirmed, the right of poor people to legal counsel. At any given moment, when Teissier is representing some 90 accused murderers, rapists and robbers, his office has no money to hire experts or track down witnesses; its law library consists of a set of lawbooks spirited away from a dead judge's chambers.

With so many clients and so few resources, Teissier decided he could not possibly do justice to them all. So he filed suit against himself. He demanded that the court judge his work inadequate, and find more money for more lawyers. A judge agreed and declared the state's indigent-defense system unconstitutional. The ruling is now on appeal before the Louisiana Supreme Court. "This is a test of whether there is justice in the United States," Teissier says. "If you're only going to pay it lip service then get rid of *Gideon*."

Thirty years ago last week, the Supreme Court unanimously voted in favor of Clarence Earl Gideon, an uneducated gambler and petty thief who insisted on his right to legal counsel. "Any person

haled into court who is too poor to hire a lawyer cannot be assured a fair trial unless counsel is provided for him," wrote Justice Hugo Black. "This seems to us to be an obvious truth." Over the next two decades the court expanded the protection to apply to all criminal cases and stressed that the representation must be "effective." But today, as defenders of indigents handle a flood of cases with meager resources, the debate rages on whether the promise of *Gideon* has been fulfilled.

Most public defenders think not. In Memphis, lawyers lament the plead-'em-and-speed-'em-through pace. "It reminds me of the old country song we have here in Tennessee: 'We're not making love, we're just keeping score,' " says chief public defender AC Wharton. Across the country, lawyers watch with frustration as the bulk of criminal-justice funds goes to police protection, prisons and prosecutors, leaving just 2.3% for public defense services. "We aren't being given the same weapons," says Mary Broderick of the National Legal Aid and Defender Association. "It's like trying to deal with smart bombs when all you've got is a couple of cap pistols."

During the war on crime of the '70s and the war on drugs of the '80s, funneling money to defend suspects was a low priority. Meanwhile, the ranks of police and prosecutors were beefed up, leading to

more arrests, more trials and more work for public defenders. "Indigent defense is a cause without a constituency," says Stephen Bright, director of the Southern Center for Human Rights. Over the years, states have unenthusiastically devised three strategies to handle indigent cases: public defender offices, court-appointed lawyers and contract systems. In all cases, the emphasis is on holding costs down. Justice—and sometimes people's lives—can get lost in the mix.

PUBLIC DEFENDERS: NO RESPECT

"Felonies worry you to death, misdemeanors work you to death," says Mel Tennenbaum, a division chief in the Los Angeles public defenders' office. "We're underappreciated and misunderstood." L.A. lawyer David Carleton had his teeth loosened by a client who didn't like his plea arrangement. Manhattan's Judith White needs all seven days of the week to handle her load of drug cases—a task she continues to tackle even since a crack addict murdered her father four years ago. When Lynne Borsuk filed a motion with Georgia's Fulton County Superior Court seeking to reduce her load of 122 open cases, she was demoted to juvenile court. She was lucky; others have been fired for similar actions.

Across the country, the lawyers who staff big-city public defender offices strike a common note: they get no respect. "Clients figure if we were really good, we'd be out there making big money," says Maria Cavalluzzi, a Los Angeles public defender. In courthouse waiting areas—known variously as the Tombs, the Pits, the Tank—defendants cavalierly dismiss their free counselors as "dump trucks," a term that reflects their view that public defenders are more interested in dumping cases than mounting rigorous defenses.

The typical public defender is underpaid and overwhelmed. When Jacquelyn Robins was appointed New Mexico's state public defender in 1985, there were six lawyers in Albuquerque's Metro court to handle the annual load of 13,000 misdemeanor cases. Three years later Robins persuaded state legislators to put up funds for three more lawyers. Even then, lawyers could manage only cursory conferences with clients just 30 minutes before their court appearance. In 1991 Robins again went begging for dollars. When she was accused of having a "management problem," she quit. The move caused such a furor that the Governor promised additional funds. Albuquerque's chief public defender, Kelly Knight, now has 16 lawyers, but the pace is still grueling. "I'm 34, not married, and I have no children," Knight says. "But I'm really, really burned out." She plans to take a sabbatical next year—whether she is granted one or not.

In Los Angeles, which boasts one of the best public defender programs in the country, salaries start at $42,000 and go as high as $97,000. A staff of 570 lawyers juggles roughly 80,000 cases a year. The work is often thankless, but every so often a case upholds the promise of *Gideon*. Earlier this month Frank White, 36, a tall, muscular man covered with tattoos, landed in L.A. County court, accused of murdering a tiny Korean woman with his bare fists. White, diagnosed as a paranoid schizophrenic, refused to take his medication and grew angry when the deputies would not remove his handcuffs. White glared as he stalked into the courtroom and dropped heavily into the seat beside public defender Mark Windham. Without a word, Windham slid his chair closer to his explosive client until they were touching shoulders. And there he stayed throughout the proceeding. "Male bonding," a sheriff's deputy quipped. But to everyone's astonishment, White quieted down. "I did it to make him and everyone else in the room feel better," Windham explained.

Seasoned defense lawyers know the value of the small gesture. And the large. Anticipating the guilty verdict returned by the jury two weeks ago, Windham built a parallel argument that White was not guilty by reason of insanity. If the jury agrees, White will be locked up in a hospital instead of being imprisoned.

ASSIGNED ATTORNEYS: NO EXPERIENCE

In smaller cities, defendants are usually assigned attorneys by the court. Often these lawyers, who tend to be young and inexperienced or old and tired, receive only $20 to $25 an hour. Capital cases go for as little as $400. At Detroit's Recorder's Court, lawyers are paid a flat fee: $1,400 for first-degree murder, $750 for lesser offenses that carry up to a life sentence. "The more time you spend on a case, the less money you make," says attorney David Steingold, a 14-year veteran. Hence lawyers have learned to plead cases quickly and forgo time-consuming motions, a phenomenon known among lawyers as the "plea mill."

Slapdash pleas are sometimes less brutal than the farcical trials that can result when ill-prepared lawyers are thrown in over their heads. In 1983 a man named Victor Roberts and an accomplice stole a car and drove to an Atlanta suburb hunting for a house to burglarize. Posing as insurance salesmen, they entered the home of Mary Jo Jenkins. A skirmish ensued and a gun went off, shooting Jenkins through the heart. H. Geoffrey Slade, a lawyer for 13 years, was assigned to handle the capital case. When he realized he was in over his head and requested co-counsel, the court appointed Jim Hamilton, 75, who had almost no criminal experience.

Their efforts, while well intended, served no one's interests. They conducted no investigation. They interviewed no witnesses in person. They never visited the crime scene. During the trial they introduced no evidence in Roberts' defense. The prosecution, meanwhile, trotted out gory photographs of Jenkins—taken after she had been autopsied. Slade knew enough to object, but he was overruled. The jury deliberated only 45 minutes; Roberts found himself on death row. A federal judge subsequently ordered a new trial, on the ground that the first had been "fundamentally unfair," in part because Roberts' lawyers had failed to "adequately and effectively investigate" the crime. Pretrial proceedings are scheduled to get under way this month—10 years after Roberts' arrest.

CONTRACT LAWYERS: NO SATISFACTION

A variation on court-appointed attorneys, popular in rural areas, is a contract system under which lawyers receive a flat rate. The fee is usually so meager that these attorneys maintain a private practice on the side. Such a system, says Bright, results in "lawyers who view their responsibilities as unwanted burdens, have no inclination to help the client and have no incentive to learn or to develop criminal trial skills." When expenses mount, they economize by refusing the collect calls of their jailed clients. Under a contract system, says L.A.'s Tennenbaum, "you don't investigate, you don't ask for continuances, you plead at the earliest possible moment."

Or worse. In Indiana's Marion County, which includes Indianapolis, reform was sparked after a 1991 study documented abuses in a system where the six superior court judges hired defense lawyers for $20,800 a year to handle the area's indigent work on a part-time basis. Bobby Lee Houston, a truck driver, hired a private counselor whom he couldn't afford when he was arrested in 1989 on charges of child molestation. The lawyer urged him to plead guilty and serve five years; Houston insisted he was innocent. He wrote to a judge complaining of delays and, after 14 months, was assigned David Sexson, one of the contract lawyers. Sexson suggested that Houston plead guilty and get off with time served. Houston was firm: no dice.

One month later, Houston's case was dismissed—but no one bothered to tell him. It would be four more months before Houston learned that he was a free man. After 19 pointless months in a jail cell, Houston has his own bottom line: "Justice is a money thing."

That is precisely what Clarence Earl Gideon complained of in 1962 when he put pencil to lined paper in his Florida cell and and wrote the Supreme Court: "The question is very simple. I requested the court to appoint me attorney and the court refused." Since then, lawyers and judges have stated and restated Gideon's assertion of a fundamental right to adequate representation. Chief Justice Harold Clarke of the Georgia Supreme Court warned state legislators earlier this year, "We need to remember that if the state can deny justice to the poor, it has within its grasp the power to deny justice to anybody." Richard Teissier and his fellow public defenders surely would agree with Judge Clarke: Justice on the cheap is no justice at all. —*Reported by Julie Johnson/ Washington, Michael Riley/New Orleans and James Willwerth/Los Angeles*

Twelve Good Reasons

How lawyers judge potential jurors

SHEILA ANNE FEENEY

(Sheila Anne Feeney is a Daily News staff writer.)

"If a Presbyterian enters the jury box, carefully rolls up his umbrella, and calmly and critically sits down, let him go. He is cold as the grave. ...The Baptists are more hopeless than the Presbyterians. ...You do not want them on the jury, and the sooner they leave, the better."

Fifty-seven years ago, the famed criminal defense attorney Clarence Darrow wrote an Esquire magazine essay on the art of picking a jury. Defense lawyers would be "guilty of malpractice" for not giving the nod to an Irishman — certain to identify with an accused criminal, Darrow wrote. Similarly, he urged colleagues to pack the jury box with Jews and agnostics.

Offensive? Sure. Nonetheless, jury selection and behavior have vexed attorneys, beguiled court buffs and miffed potential jurors since the first court gavel descended, generating not only studies and papers, but also a folklore rife with stereotypes, mythology and superstitions.

Picking a sympathetic jury is so crucial to winning a case that sometimes lawyers hire consultants. Cathy Bennett, one of the best-known jury-selection consultants before her death last year, helped pick the Florida panel that acquitted William Kennedy Smith of rape charges. Bennett believed that asking potential jurors about definitive life experiences, about whom they admire, and then analyzing body language as they replied, was more revealing than generalizations about appearance, ethnicity and occupation. (Bennett's husband, Robert Hirschhorn, continues their Texas consulting business.)

"We spend our lives trying to read their minds and no matter how hard we try, we just can't," sighs Mark A. Longo, a Brooklyn attorney who specializes in civil litigation. When representing a defendant in a personal injury case, Longo concedes to a weakness for middle-aged women with children ("they're skeptical people"), scientific types, engineers and homeowners. Of the last grouping, he says, "They pay insurance premiums. And although you're absolutely not allowed to mention that fact, everyone is sophisticated enough to know" that premiums are linked to payouts.

Generalizations about race, religion, relatives and reading materials continue to be routine during voir dire (jury selection). "If your last name is Slotnick and your husband is a criminal defense attorney, you will never be picked as a juror.

"Ask my wife. It makes her very angry," says Barry Slotnick, who won Bernhard Goetz an acquittal on attempted murder charges.

Slotnick is the first to admit: "I'm not looking for a fair juror, I'm looking for someone who will acquit."

According to conventional wisdom, people with science backgrounds are thought to be good for the prosecution, social workers and artistic types are supposedly sympathetic to the defense.

Slotnick says he is less influenced by race and occupation than by apparel, body language and professed habits: "People who read the National Review are more conservative. In the Goetz case, I would want National Review readers. In most others, I would not."

"I very often look for jurors who run against type," muses David Lewis, who defended Carolyn Warmus against murder charges in her first trial, which ended in a hung jury. (Warmus was later convicted in a second trial.) When Lewis represented a man accused of killing his gay lover, his lead juror was a "devout Baptist who said homosexuality was an abomination unto God." He picked her because he believed she would take her oath not to hold her prejudice against the defendant "more seriously than any other juror." His client was acquitted.

Older homemakers in traditional marriages tend to judge date-rape victims more harshly than younger women or men, and are particularly harsh if the victim has "a non-traditional lifestyle," notes Manhattan sex crimes prosecutor Linda Fairstein. It's dangerous to rely on "over-generalizations" during voir dire, says Fairstein, but schools and seminars teach prosecu-

"People who are discriminated against — be they black, obese or physically disabled — tend to identify with the defendant."

tors to exclude people by occupation. "They tell you to pick Con Ed and phone workers — people in stable jobs for a long time."

Former Brooklyn judge and prosecutor Alan Broomer contends that race is a factor: "People who are discriminated against — be they black, obese or physically disabled — tend to identify with the defendant." People of color in poor neighborhoods often have a "tremendous prejudice" against the police, Broomer adds.

The Supreme Court has repeatedly ruled that potential jurors may not be excluded simply because of their race, but that does not stop some attorneys from making racist assumptions. The Supreme Court has yet to render an opinion on excluding jurors by gender.

Residency is also used to form assumptions about a juror's predisposition, hence the expression "Bronx jury" — describing the borough where, it is believed, record punitive damages are handed down and accused criminals may have a better chance of acquittal. Likewise, you have "Simi Valley" juries, where police are thought to have an advantage.

Even Broomer revises his stereotype that "prejudice by blacks, for blacks" benefits criminal defendants when it comes to stereotyping Staten Island. In Richmond County, says Broomer, who served there for six months, "The blacks and Puerto Ricans are just as conservative as the whites — even more so."

Hard as it may be to believe, some people lie so they

can get on a jury. But they are less likely to fib about their life experiences, however, which is why folks are so often asked about their background.

Cathy Bennett had a remarkable gift for paying attention to "verbal and nonverbal cues lawyers don't hear or see," notes Lewis, who consulted her on his cases.

"Some of us thought she was a witch." He recalls questioning a Bensonhurst woman of Italian descent on a case involving an accused gunrunner for the Irish Republican Army. "I fought like hell to keep her off on the theory that the Italians and the Irish don't get along. Everything about her — based on stereotypic thinking — was bad to me." Yet Bennett demanded he clear the woman for the jury.

Lo and behold, "the woman goes ahead and leads the jury to an acquittal. Her boyfriend gave her the book 'Trinity' to read during the trial and her boyfriend's name turns out to be Sean Cronin," marvels Lewis, laughing at the lesson he learned. His bias-busting schooling was not over yet. Several months after the trial, Sean Cronin visited Lewis because he needed a lawyer. "Sean Cronin," says Lewis, "turned out to be black."

DOUBLE EXPOSURE

DID THE SECOND RODNEY KING TRIAL VIOLATE DOUBLE JEOPARDY?

DARLENE RICKER

Darlene Ricker, an attorney in Laguna Beach, Calif., is a former staff writer and editor for the Boston Globe *and the* Los Angeles Times. *She has written widely on the Rodney King case.*

In this country, a person shall not "be subject for the same offense to be twice put in jeopardy of life or limb."

Or shall he?

After the second Rodney King prosecution, many have questioned whether the double jeopardy clause has become more rhetoric than bedrock. The rule appears to have been swallowed by the "dual sovereignty" exception, which allows separate jurisdictions to prosecute the accused for the same conduct if it violates both a state and a federal law.

What may sound acceptable in theory can have dangerous applications. Has the dual sovereignty exception become a political tool, to be employed whenever society feels the wrong verdict was rendered?

Apparently so, say many defense lawyers. They claim that federal Section 1983 suits in particular, such as the King retrial, present the perfect forum to trigger the legal fiction of dual sovereignty. The strong political interest invoked in cases of alleged police abuse of racial minorities somehow outweighs the accused's right to have to walk the hot coals of the judicial system only one time.

That debate rocked the American Civil Liberties Union in April, at approximately the time the split verdict in the federal King retrial was announced. In the fall of 1992, several months after the acquittals in the first King trial, the organization had temporarily suspended its longstanding policy of opposition to the dual sovereignty exception.

After reconsidering the issue and debating it internally for close to six months, the national board of the ACLU voted to maintain its existing policy against the exception.

That created shock waves in Los Angeles, where an emotional public—and a vocal ACLU affiliate—

opposed that position. So did a significant minority in the national organization, according to Paul Hoffman, legal director of the ACLU of Southern California.

"We believe there should be [a dual sovereignty exception] for civil rights violations because the government has a special responsibility to vindicate federal interests protected by the civil rights statutes," said Hoffman.

His affiliate believed that rationale applied in the King case, calling for the federal government to step in after the first state acquittals. The chapter has continued to maintain that position—and continues to be at odds with the national ACLU.

"We feel the state proceedings were fundamentally flawed because of the change of venue," said Hoffman. "That state procedural mechanism undermined the fairness of the first prosecution."

Hoffman says he is not suggesting there should automatically be a federal prosecution after a state acquittal in civil rights cases. "That power should be exercised with restraint and only when something was seriously wrong with the first prosecution. If the government is convinced that the prior state trial was fair, it may not be appropriate to bring a second prosecution."

William Harris, an attorney in Pasadena, Calif., takes issue with the local ACLU stance. "A criminal defendant who passes through the crucible once and survives is entitled to some peace," he said. "The danger [of the dual sovereignty exception] is that it tends to be invoked only in response to politically unpopular or 'politically incorrect' acquittals."

San Francisco Bay area attorney Alan Ellis agrees. "It has always struck me as a legal fiction that if you rob a bank, you have automatically committed two crimes—one against the state and one against the federal government," said Ellis, a federal criminal appellate lawyer who has taught constitutional law and is a past president of the National Association of Criminal Defense Lawyers.

"It seems to be that if you run the gauntlet once and survive, they get to make you run through it again. That just doesn't pass the smell test," he said. "It is particularly odious when the second prosecution is done for political reasons. The government is walking a very thin line."

Laurie L. Levenson, a professor of criminal law and evidence at Loyola Law School in Los Angeles and a former federal prosecutor, disagrees. She insists that the officers in the King case "were not running the same gauntlet" the second time.

"This was not a duplicate case," said Levenson, who observed the entire federal King trial. Although the two prosecutions involved the same incident, she points to crucial differences in the elements, legal standards and evidence.

First, the burden of proof was higher for federal prosecutors because they had to prove that the officers acted with the specific intent to deprive King of his civil rights, said Levenson. (The state charge of using excessive force was a general intent crime.) Further, the prosecution's evidence was more extensive in the federal trial, including such prosecution witnesses as King himself and a renowned use-of-force expert.

Levenson declined to characterize the second trial as a "political" prosecution. "While there is political interest in cases like this, there are a lot of mechanisms in the [judicial] system that kept this from becoming a 'political case,'" she said. "President Bush didn't indict the four officers; the grand jury did."

Such cases, she said, hinge on two important competing interests —the state's interest in federalism and the government's interest in protecting citizens' civil rights.

The concept of federalism allows the state the opportunity to "clean its own house" before the federal government decides to step in, said Levenson. The dual sovereignty exception serves a valuable purpose in providing each prosecuting authority a separate opportunity to protect its own interests, she said. "Frankly, I believe this doctrine will be around for a long time to come."

". . . you can't be tried twice for the same act . . ."

Los Angeles attorney Harland Braun hopes that is not the case. He defended officer Theodore Briseno in the federal King trial, in which his client was again acquitted. To Braun, the notion of dual sovereignties in modern America is "preposterous."

He points to the historical roots of the double jeopardy bar, which originated in Europe when England agreed to recognize judgments from France. Although the two countries were enemies, the British felt it would be unfair to prosecute a person who had already been tried in another country.

"That was exactly what was meant when the double jeopardy clause was adopted in the Bill of Rights—you can't be tried twice for the same act, period," said Braun. "There is no reason to deviate from history."

In reality, he said, there are no dual sovereigns in the United States. "We don't have kings or competing monarchs. The people delegate their authority to be divided between the federal and state governments."

To ensure that the system works properly, Braun recently made this proposal: An accused who may face federal prosecution could notify the federal authorities that the state is proceeding against him. The federal government would then have 30 to 60 days to decide whether to take over the case. Such a program, said Braun, would eliminate "tag-team prosecutions."

That is what happened in the King case, he said. "Look at what happened to [officer Stacey] Koon. He was tried and acquitted, then he was tried and convicted. Any way you slice it, that's double jeopardy."

Civil rights advocates, however, see the issue differently. Renowned civil rights attorney Morris Dees of the Southern Poverty Law Center in Montgomery, Ala., said the dual sovereignty exception, when correctly applied, "does not offend my sensibilities of fair play."

As a classic example, Dees points to the case of a Montgomery man whose bank account mistakenly showed a $50,000 deposit. The man withdrew the windfall and was charged in state court with embezzlement. After his acquittal on the state charges, federal prosecutors stepped in and indicted him for bank fraud. The man unsuccessfully argued double jeopardy on the grounds that the second prosecution involved the same operative facts.

"Here you had the same bank, the same money, the same actions by the accused," said Dees. "But you have two separate entities, each with its own agenda. The state likened the crime to stealing money; the federal government likened it to using money that is not yours." The elements of the federal charge turned out to be more appropriate, he said.

Dees draws a parallel to the dual prosecutions in the King case. "The state charges of excessive force probably didn't fit nearly as well as did the federal charges. There was clearly a violation of Mr. King's [federal] civil rights," he said.

In such cases, however, Dees feels the federal government should not wait for the outcome of the state case to prosecute. "If it is so egregious a violation of one's civil rights, federal prosecutors should just move ahead," he said.

Traditionally, however, the federal government has rarely chosen to prosecute police officers for civil rights violations—whether or not there has been a prior state trial. Such federal prosecutions have consistently averaged 40 to 60 per year; in 1992, after the outcry over the King case, the national figure was 68.

In the 10 years preceding the King case, there were only three federal prosecutions of police officers in Los Angeles for civil rights violations. Dees points to a Texas civil rights case he handled, in which the federal government declined to step in. Three police officers had allegedly beaten inmate Loyal Garner to death; the state immediately indicted them for Texas civil rights violations.

After an acquittal, the state brought new charges of murder against the police officers. They were convicted.

In rejecting their double jeopardy claim, the Texas Supreme Court upheld the conviction because the elements of murder and a civil rights violation are different. After that ruling, the federal government declined to try the officers on federal civil rights charges.

Constitutional scholars, such as Professor Sheldon Nahmod of Chicago-Kent College of Law, suggest that certain factors should trigger a second prosecution by federal authorities in civil rights cases. A critical consideration, said Nahmod, is whether the first prosecution was "somehow unfair, tainted or flawed."

Many felt that was the case in the state prosecution of the four officers who beat Rodney King. A number of unusual factors, said Nahmod, set the King case apart from other civil rights cases, particularly the videotape of the beating and the change of venue that drew an all-white jury.

He adds to that what he calls the "political" factor—the appearance of unfairness that "impugned the integrity of the entire criminal justice process"—and the resultant political pressure to retry the case.

However, Nahmod believes that the dual sovereignty exception should be applied sparingly. "Ordinarily, even if double jeopardy technically does not apply, we ought not expend government resources on a second trial if the first prosecution was fair," he said.

Another factor is the personal toll a second trial takes on the defendant. To put an accused through a criminal prosecution once is extremely stressful, he said; to do so twice is "devastating." Such could be the situation for Miami police officer William Lozano, who was involved in a shooting that resulted in two black men dead—and three days of rioting in 1989. Lozano was

convicted of state manslaughter charges.

An appellate court ruled that the proceedings had been unfair because jurors feared a not-guilty verdict would lead to more violence, a similar theme voiced in Los Angeles during the King case. Lozano was retried and acquitted this May, shortly after the verdicts were announced in the federal King retrial.

Roberto Martinez, the acting U.S. attorney in Miami, immediately announced that the Justice Department would pursue a federal civil rights investigation into Lozano's actions (the result of which had not been announced at press time).

Miami attorney Roy Black, who represented the officer in both state trials and on appeal, said the Lozano case would not be well-suited to a federal civil rights prosecution.

The state of Florida—under then-State Attorney Janet Reno—already investigated and found no state civil rights violations. (Reno, as U.S. attorney general, has recused herself from considering the federal civil rights issue as to Lozano.)

Should the federal government decide to prosecute Lozano, said Black, the emotional impact would be tremendous. "The case went on for four-and-a-half years, through two full trials. Now, when you think it's over, to start again would be an emotional blow," he said. "That's why we have the double jeopardy clause.

"The men who founded this country put the double jeopardy clause in the Constitution to protect citizens from unwarranted persecution by the government. The founders knew that if you put someone through multiple prosecutions, eventually you can break him. We should give more emphasis to the double jeopardy clause."

Attorney John Barnett, who successfully represented officer Theodore Briseno in the state King prosecution, agrees. He views the dual sovereignty exception as an impermissible basis "for violating the double jeopardy clause." That basis may well have outlived its usefulness.

The reason for the dual sovereignty exception stems from the decades-old belief that local prosecutors in the South were incapable of prosecuting or unwilling to prosecute serious civil rights violations, said Barnett. That made it necessary for the federal government

"to step in as a sort of pater familias and put an end to the killing of the 'freedom riders,'" he said.

Today, said Barnett, that theory has "absolutely no application absent fraud [on the part of prosecutors]." In the King case, he said, the theory would not apply unless it could be shown that "a large metropolitan district attorney's office was

---

The U.S. Supreme Court has traditionally taken a hard-line stance on double jeopardy challenges.

---

incapable of or unwilling to prosecute the officers." Since that was not the case in Los Angeles, Barnett views the federal prosecution of the King case as a "drastic contravention" of the federal Constitution.

"The very people who promoted this violation of the Constitution in the 1970s—civil libertarians—never foresaw this consequence. They should be scandalized now that [the dual sovereignty exception] is being used as a political tool," he said.

Barnett said he tries many cases in which individuals are acquitted of civil rights violations, but are not re-prosecuted "because it is not the politically expedient thing to do."

To suggest that the retrial of the officers in the King case is "just business as usual" is "just wrong," argued Barnett. "What is the next step?"

He suggests this forces the accused to make a frightening election: that he would rather be convicted at the first trial in state court because he will do less time than he would if convicted federally and subjected to the federal sentencing guidelines. "The irony is that you punish people for being acquitted," said Barnett.

What is most troublesome, he said, is that "the momentary satisfaction of the masses should not dictate justice."

Barnett is also disturbed that many people in the legal system (such as criminal defense attorneys and some judges) "ignore the implications of the federal [King] prosecution because, generally, they disagree with the Simi Valley verdict."

Nancy Hollander, president of the National Association of Criminal Defense Attorneys, feels strongly that the King case was double jeopardy. "You can't decide constitutional issues based on how you would like the law to come out," she said.

She draws a parallel to freedom of speech issues. "When a person stands on a street corner and shouts, 'I love America,' he isn't likely to be arrested. When that same person says something offensive, we realize why we have the First Amendment." The same is true for the double jeopardy clause, said Hollander, be-cause the issue tends to arise only in politically motivated prosecutions.

"If one conceives of the government as a unitary entity, it is certainly true that prosecutors were given two chances to secure a conviction against these police officers [in the King case]," said UCLA law professor Peter Arenella. (Note: The two officers convicted in the federal King trial are appealing the verdicts.)

However, he does not feel the double jeopardy issue will prevail on appeal. The U.S. Supreme Court has traditionally taken a hard-line stance on double jeopardy challenges.

In recent years, said Arenella, the High Court has shown no interest in revisiting its traditional interpretation of the double jeopardy clause. Arenella considers it "highly unlikely" that the Court would overturn the two federal convictions in the King case on a double jeopardy challenge.

"The racial unrest and turmoil generated after the first acquittals make the [King] case a politically charged vehicle in which to reconsider the wisdom of the dual sovereignty exception."

Juvenile Justice

A century ago, children found guilty of committing crimes were punished as if they were adults. Since there were few specialized juvenile detention institutions, children were thrown into jails and prisons with murderers, thieves, drunks, tramps, and prostitutes, with no protection and no programs for rehabilitation.

The establishment of a special criminal justice system for the handling of juvenile offenders was hailed in the 1920s by humanitarians, reformers, and social scientists, and accepted, somewhat reluctantly, by the legal profession and the police. Only recently has the cry of dissent been heard.

Judge Ben Lindsay and others who pioneered the juvenile court movement believed that juveniles sinned out of ignorance, because of the growing pains of adolescence, or because they were corrupted by adults. They believed that a juvenile court should concern itself with finding out why a juvenile was in trouble and what society could do to help him or her. They saw the juvenile judge as parental, concerned, and sympathetic, rather than prosecutive and punitive.

The proponents of this system were, of course, thinking of the delinquents of their time—the runaway, the truant, the petty thief, the beggar, the sexual experimenter, and the insubordinate. Today, however, the juvenile in court is more likely to be on trial for murder, gang rape, arson, or mugging. The 1990s also differ from the 1920s in other ways. Juvenile courts are everywhere, as are juvenile police, juvenile probation officers, and juvenile prisons. Literally hundreds of thousands of American juveniles enter this system annually.

It is clear at this time that the winds of change are blowing across the nation's juvenile justice system. Traditional reforms are being replaced by a new and more conservative agenda. This new reform movement emphasizes the welfare of victims, a punitive approach toward serious juvenile offenders, and protection of children from physical and sexual exploitation. Policies that favor diversion and deinstitutionalization are less popular. After many years of attempting to remove status offenders from the juvenile justice system, there are increasing calls for returning truants, runaways, and other troubled youth to juvenile court jurisdiction. In spite of these developments, however, there are many juvenile justice reformers who remain dedicated to advancing due process rights for children and reducing reliance on incarceration.

Clearly, there is conflict and tension between the old and new juvenile justice reform agendas. The articles in this section evaluate problems with the current juvenile justice system and present some possible solutions.

The first essay, "Handling of Juvenile Cases," draws distinctions between juvenile cases and adult cases, explains the circumstances under which juveniles may be tried in criminal courts, and reveals that juveniles receive dispositions rather than sentences.

Transformation in the philosophy and underlying goals of the juvenile justice system has been well documented over the past decade, according to "Punishment, Accountability, and the New Juvenile Justice." Because of the change in the mission of juvenile justice, critical issues need to be addressed.

Are existing delinquency causation theories adequate to the task of explaining female delinquency and official reactions to girls' deviance? The answer is clearly no, according to the author of the next essay, "Girls' Crime and Woman's Place." She maintains that the academic study of delinquent behavior usually focuses on male delinquency alone.

The ultimate authority for the resolution of problems of dysfunctional families is the juvenile court. "The Juvenile Court and the Role of the Juvenile Court Judge" surveys the origin, purposes, and duties of this court and the unique role of the judge.

"Kids, Guns, and Killing Fields," asserts that a plague of youth violence seems to be sweeping the nation. Attorney General Janet Reno discusses what she believes needs to be done to help prevent youth violence in "The Whole Child Approach to Crime."

A Connecticut youth, bored with school and full of fatalism, tells of life in the street and drug dealing in the article "Fernando, 16, Finds a Sanctuary in Crime."

This unit closes with "Street Gang Trends Give Little Cause for Optimism." This essay tells of the current pervasiveness of gangs, extending from prison systems to the suburbs.

Looking Ahead: Challenge Questions

When the juvenile court was first conceived, what convictions did its pioneers hold about juvenile offenders?

Some argue that the failure of the juvenile court to fulfill its rehabilitative and preventive promise stems from a grossly oversimplistic view of the phenomenon of juvenile criminality. Do you agree? Why or why not?

Do you believe the departure of the juvenile justice system from its original purpose is warranted?

Why do some young people become members of gangs?

Handling of Juvenile Cases

Cases involving juveniles are handled much differently than adult cases

The juvenile court and a separate process for handling juveniles resulted from reform movements of the late 19th century

Until that time juveniles who committed crimes were processed through the criminal courts. In 1899 Illinois established the first juvenile court based on the concepts that a juvenile was a salvageable human being who needed treatment rather than punishment and that the juvenile court was to protect the child from the stigma of criminal proceedings. Delinquency and other situations such as neglect and adoption were deemed to warrant the court's intervention on the child's behalf. The juvenile court also handled "status offenses" (such as truancy, running away, and incorrigibility), which are not applicable to adults.

While the juvenile courts and the handling of juveniles remain separated from criminal processing, the concepts on which they are based have changed. Today, juvenile courts usually consider an element of personal responsibility when making decisions about juvenile offenders.

Juvenile courts may retain jurisdiction until a juvenile becomes legally an adult (at age 21 or less in most States). This limit sets a cap on the length of time juveniles may be institutionalized that is often much less than that for adults who commit similar offenses. Some jurisdictions transfer the cases of juveniles accused of serious offenses or with long

criminal histories to criminal court so that the length of the sanction cannot be abridged.

Juvenile courts are very different from criminal courts

The language used in juvenile courts is less harsh. For example, juvenile courts—
• accept "petitions" of "delinquency" rather than criminal complaints
• conduct "hearings," not trials
• "adjudicate" juveniles to be "delinquent" rather than find them guilty of a crime
• order one of a number of available "dispositions" rather than sentences.

Despite the wide discretion and informality associated with juvenile court proceedings, juveniles are protected by most of the due process safeguards associated with adult criminal trials.

Most referrals to juvenile court are for property crimes, but 17% are for status offenses

Reasons for referrals to juvenile courts

11%	**Crimes against persons**	
	Criminal homicide	1%
	Forcible rape	2
	Robbery	17
	Aggravated assault	20
	Simple assault	59
		100%
46%	**Crimes against property**	
	Burglary	25%
	Larceny	47
	Motor vehicle theft	5
	Arson	1

	Vandalism and trespassing	19
	Stolen property offenses	3
		100%
5%	**Drug offenses**	100%
21%	**Offenses against public order**	
	Weapons offenses	6%
	Sex offenses	6
	Drunkenness and disorderly conduct	23
	Contempt, probation, and parole violations	21
	Other	44
		100%
17%	**Status offenses**	
	Running away	28%
	Truancy and curfew violations	21
	Ungovernability	28
	Liquor violations	23
		100%
100%	Total all offenses	

Note: Percents may not add to 100 because of rounding.
Source: *Delinquency in the United States 1983*, National Center for Juvenile Justice, July 1986.

Arrest is not the only means of referring juveniles to the courts

While adults may begin criminal justice processing only through arrest, summons, or citation, juveniles may be referred to court by law enforcement agencies, parents, schools, victims, probation officers, or other sources.

Law enforcement agencies refer three-quarters of the juvenile cases, and they are most likely to be the referral source in cases involving curfew violations, drug offenses, and property crimes. Other referral sources are most likely in cases involving status offenses (truancy, ungovernability, and running away).

 From *Report to the Nation on Crime and Justice*, Bureau of Justice Statistics, U.S. Department of Justice, March 1988, pp. 78-79, 95.

"Intake" is the first step in the processing of juveniles

At intake, decisions are made about whether to begin formal proceedings. Intake is most frequently performed by the juvenile court or an executive branch intake unit, but increasingly prosecutors are becoming involved. In addition to beginning formal court proceedings, officials at intake may refer the juvenile for psychiatric evaluation, informal probation, or counseling, or, if appropriate, they may close the case altogether.

For a case involving a juvenile to proceed to a court adjudication, the intake unit must file a petition with the court

Intake units handle most cases informally without a petition. The National Center for Juvenile Justice estimates that more than half of all juvenile cases disposed of at intake are handled informally without a petition and are dismissed and/or referred to a social service agency.

Initial juvenile detention decisions are usually made by the intake staff

Prior to holding an adjudicatory hearing, juveniles may be released in the custody of their parents, put in protective custody (usually in foster homes or runaway shelters), or admitted to detention facilities. In most States juveniles are not eligible for bail, unlike adults.

Relatively few juveniles are detained prior to court appearance

One juvenile case in five involved secure detention prior to adjudication in 1983. Status offenders were least likely to be detained. The proportion of status offenders detained has declined from 40% in 1975 to 11% in 1983.

All States allow juveniles to be tried as adults in criminal courts

Juveniles are referred to criminal courts in one of three ways—

• **Concurrent jurisdiction**—the prosecutor has the discretion of filing charges for certain offenses in either juvenile or criminal courts

• **Excluded offenses**—the legislature excludes from juvenile court jurisdiction certain offenses usually either very minor, such as traffic or fishing violations, or very serious, such as murder or rape

• **Judicial waiver**—the juvenile court waives its jurisdiction and transfers the case to criminal court (the procedure is also known as "binding over" or "certifying" juvenile cases to criminal courts).

Under certain circumstances, juveniles may be tried in criminal courts

Age at which criminal courts gain jurisdiction of young offenders ranges from 16 to 19

Age of offender when under criminal court jurisdiction	States
16 years	Connecticut, New York, North Carolina
17	Georgia, Illinois, Louisiana, Massachusetts, Missouri, South Carolina, Texas
18	Alabama, Alaska, Arizona, Arkansas, California, Colorado, Delaware, District of Columbia, Florida, Hawaii, Idaho, Indiana, Iowa, Kansas, Kentucky, Maine, Maryland, Michigan, Minnesota, Mississippi, Montana, Nebraska, Nevada, New Hampshire, New Jersey, New Mexico, North Dakota, Ohio, Oklahoma, Oregon, Pennsylvania, Rhode Island, South Dakota, Tennessee, Utah, Vermont, Virginia, Washington, West Virginia, Wisconsin, Federal districts
19	Wyoming

Source: "Upper age of juvenile court jurisdiction statutes analysis," Linda A. Szymanski, National Center for Juvenile Justice, March 1987.

12 States authorize prosecutors to file cases in the juvenile or criminal courts at their discretion

This procedure, known as concurrent jurisdiction, may be limited to certain offenses or to juveniles of a certain age. Four States provide concurrent jurisdiction over juveniles charged with traffic violations. Georgia, Nebraska, and Wyoming have concurrent criminal jurisdiction statutes.

As of 1987, 36 States excluded certain offenses from juvenile court jurisdictions

Eighteen States excluded only traffic, watercraft, fish, or game violations. Another 13 States excluded serious offenses; the other 5 excluded serious

offenses and some minor offenses. The serious offenses most often excluded are capital crimes such as murder, but several States exclude juveniles previously convicted in criminal courts.

48 States, the District of Columbia, and the Federal Government have judicial waiver provisions

Youngest age at which juvenile may be transferred to criminal court by judicial waiver	States
No specific age	Alaska, Arizona, Arkansas, Delaware, Florida, Indiana, Kentucky, Maine, Maryland, New Hampshire, New Jersey, Oklahoma, South Dakota, West Virginia, Wyoming, Federal districts
10 years	Vermont
12	Montana
13	Georgia, Illinois, Mississippi
14	Alabama, Colorado, Connecticut, Idaho, Iowa, Massachusetts, Minnesota, Missouri, North Carolina, North Dakota, Pennsylvania, South Carolina, Tennessee, Utah
15	District of Columbia, Louisiana, Michigan, New Mexico, Ohio, Oregon, Texas, Virginia
16	California, Hawaii, Kansas, Nevada, Rhode Island, Washington, Wisconsin

Note: Many judicial waiver statutes also specify offenses that are waivable. This chart lists the States by the youngest age for which judicial waiver may be sought without regard to offense.

Source: "Waiver/transfer/certification of juveniles to criminal court: Age restrictions: Crime restrictions," Linda A. Szymanski, National Center for Juvenile Justice, February 1987.

A small proportion of juvenile cases are referred to criminal court

Recent studies found that most juveniles referred to criminal court were age 17 and were charged with property offenses. However, juveniles charged with violent offenses or with serious prior offense histories were more likely to be adjudicated in criminal court. Waiver of juveniles to criminal court is less likely where court jurisdiction extends for several years beyond the juvenile's 18th birthday.

Juveniles tried as adults have a very high conviction rate, but most receive sentences of probation or fines

More than 90% of the judicial waiver or concurrent jurisdiction cases in Hamparian's study resulted in guilty verdicts, and more than half the convictions led to fines or probation. Sentences to probation often occur because the criminal courts view juveniles as first offenders regardless of their prior juvenile record. However, serious violent juvenile offenders are more likely to be institutionalized. In a study of 12 jurisdictions with Habitual Serious or Violent Juvenile Offender Programs, 63% of those con-

other agencies were handled informally without the filing of a petition. About 20% of all cases involved some detention prior to disposition.

Of about 600,000 cases in which petitions were filed, 64% resulted in formal adjudication. Of these, 61% resulted in some form of probation, and 29% resulted in an out-of-home placement.

charged by the police with robbery or burglary revealed more similarities in their disposition patterns than the aggregate juvenile court statistics would suggest. For both types of offenses, juvenile petitions were filed and settled formally in court about as often as were complaints filed and convictions obtained in the cases against adults. The juveniles charged with the more serious offenses and those with the more extensive prior records were the most likely to have their cases reach adjudication. At the upper limits of offense and prior record severity, juveniles were committed to secure institutions about as frequently as were young adults with comparable records.

Juveniles receive dispositions rather than sentences

victed were sentenced to prison and 14% to jail. The average prison sentence was 6.8 years.

Correctional activities for juveniles tried as adults in most States occur within the criminal justice system

In 1978, in more than half the States, youths convicted as adults and given an incarcerative sentence could only be placed in adult corrections facilities. In 18 jurisdictions, youths convicted as adults could be placed in either adult or juvenile corrections facilities, but sometimes this discretion was limited by special circumstances. Only 6 jurisdictions restricted placements of juveniles convicted as adults to State juvenile corrections institutions. Generally, youths sentenced in this manner will be transferred to adult facilities to serve the remainder of their sentence on reaching majority.

Juvenile court dispositions tend to be indeterminate

The dispositions of juveniles adjudicated to be delinquent extend until the juvenile legally becomes an adult (21 years of age in most States) or until the offending behavior has been corrected, whichever is sooner.

Of the 45 States and the District of Columbia that authorize indeterminate periods of confinement—
• 32 grant releasing authority to the State juvenile corrections agency
• 6 delegate it to juvenile paroling agencies
• 5 place such authority with the committing judges
• 3 have dual or overlapping jurisdiction.

Most juvenile cases are disposed of informally

In 1982 about 54% of all cases referred to juvenile courts by the police and

The juvenile justice system is also undergoing changes in the degree of discretion permitted in confinement decisions

Determinate dispositions are now used in six States, but they do not apply to all offenses or offenders. In most cases they apply only to specified felony cases or to the juveniles with prior adjudications for serious delinquencies.

California imposes determinate periods of confinement for delinquents committed to State agencies based on the standards and guidelines of its paroling agency. Four States have similar procedures, administered by the State agencies responsible for operating their juvenile corrections facilities.

As of 1981 eight States had serious-delinquent statutes requiring that juveniles who are either serious, violent, repeat, or habitual offenders be adjudicated and committed in a manner that differs from the adjudication of other delinquents. Such laws require minimum lengths of commitment, prescribe a fixed range of time for commitment, or mandate a minimum length of stay in a type of placement, such as a secure institution.

Dispositions for serious juvenile offenders tend to look like those for adults

Aggregate statistics on juvenile court dispositions do not provide an accurate picture of what happens to the more serious offenders because many of the cases coming before juvenile courts involve minor criminal or status offenses. These minor cases are more likely to be handled informally by the juvenile court.

An analysis of California cases involving older juveniles and young adults

Most juveniles committed to juvenile facilities are delinquents

	Percent of juveniles
Total	100%
Delinquents	74
Nondelinquents	
Status offenders	12
Nonoffenders (dependency, neglect, abuse, etc.)	14

Source: BJS Children in Custody, 1985, unpublished data.

The outcomes of juvenile and adult proceedings are similar, but some options are not available in juvenile court

For example, juvenile courts cannot order the death penalty, life terms, or terms that could exceed the maximum jurisdiction of the court itself. In Arizona the State Supreme Court held that, despite statutory jurisdiction of the juvenile courts to age 21, delinquents could not be held in State juvenile corrections facilities beyond age 18.[3]

Yet, juvenile courts may go further than criminal courts in regulating the lifestyles of juvenile offenders placed in the community under probation supervision. For example, the court may order them to—
• live in certain locations
• attend school
• participate in programs intended to improve their behavior.

The National Center for Juvenile Justice estimates that almost 70% of the juveniles whose cases are not waived or dismissed are put on probation; about 10% are committed to an institution.

Punishment, Accountability, and the New Juvenile Justice

by Martin L. Forst, D. Crim. and Martha–Elin Blomquist, Ph.D.

The juvenile justice system has undergone radical change in the past three decades. The procedural revolution that began at the end of the 1960s with the Gault decision has more recently evolved into a substantive revolution. The changes in juvenile justice have been many and in some instances drastic, particularly in the apparent demise of the rehabilitative ideal. New theories or models have emerged, incorporating terminology such as punishment, justice, and accountability into the vocabulary of juvenile justice practitioners and the lexicon of state juvenile codes.

The transformation in the philosophy and underlying goals of the system has been well-documented over the past decade or so.[1] It is now time to ask critical questions about the significance and meaning of this transformation and to bring attention to unresolved issues. This article suggests the issues that need to be addressed in order to make both practical and philosophical sense out of the changes in the mission of "juvenile justice."

The Background

Based on a variety of criticisms,[2] a movement arose within the last decade to make substantive changes in the philosophy of juvenile court and juvenile corrections law, including dispositional decision–making policy. This movement has rejected the rehabilitative ideal as traditionally conceived and has renewed interest in public protection, punishment, justice and accountability. As Gardner summarizes: "...[a] revolution in substantive theory is presently taking place as one jurisdiction after another expresses disenchantment with the rehabilitative ideal and embraces explicitly punitive sanctions as appropriate for youthful offenders."[3]

Notwithstanding their incongruities and unknown consequences, proposals to orient the philosophy and administration of the juvenile justice system around punishment and public protection have been supported by a diverse set of scholars, lawmakers, and practitioners. For example, the prestigious Joint Commission on Juvenile Justice Standards of the Institute of Judicial Administration and the American Bar Association (IJA/ABA) proposed in 1980 that the principles of criminal law and procedure replace the rehabilitative model of juvenile justice.[4] The Joint Commission advocated that juvenile justice sanctions be offense–based rather than based on the needs of the offender and that determinate sentencing should replace the traditional indeterminate sentencing system.

Moreover, these ideas have been supported by a variety of children's rights advocates who believe that a youth has a right to be punished for the offense committed rather than a need to be treated for what others perceive to be wrong with him or her. Other commentators have been concerned with the inequities and injustices resulting from the traditional offender–based system. Offense–based dispositions, by contrast, presumably prevent unjust and disproportionate periods of incarceration often found under a rehabilitation–oriented system. As Fox notes, "punishment clearly implies limits, whereas treatment does not."[5] Under this theory, a youth would not be incarcerated longer than is justified by the nature of the delinquent conduct, and certainly no longer than an adult convicted of the same offense.

Much of the philosophical and structural transformation, despite its lofty theory, is a direct result of public pressure to crack down on juve-

By Martin L. Forst and Martha-Elin Blomquist, "Punishment, Accountability, and the New Juvenile Justice," Volume 43, No. 1. *Juvenile and Family Court Journal, National Council of Family Court Judges* (1992), pp. 1-10. Reprinted by permission.

149

niles -- to get tough with kids. Drs. Norman and Gillespie conclude, "The mood of the nation continues to move toward punishment and incapacitation of offenders."[6] Many statutory revisions are clearly designed to mollify the public's sense of fear and anger over juvenile crime.[7] Cracking down on juveniles has been accomplished in a variety of ways. Revising transfer laws to allow more juveniles to be tried as adults in criminal courts is but one example.[8] Moreover, numerous statutory changes have made sanctions meted out *within* the juvenile justice system more punitive. For example, the new Texas determinate sentencing law for juveniles, passed in 1987, provides that juveniles who have been adjudicated delinquent for one of six serious, violent offenses may receive a determinate sentence of as long as 30 years' confinement.[9]

Law and order groups have continued to propose more restrictive policies for controlling and sanctioning juvenile crime. The goal of these proposals is to make the juvenile justice system more like the criminal justice system. These proposals have resulted in "criminalizing" the juvenile justice system.

Moving To New Models

To institute these substantive reforms, many state legislatures have modified -- sometimes extensively -- the purpose clauses of their juvenile court or juvenile corrections statutes.[10] In some states, policy-makers simply added new phrases to the traditional language of *parens patriae* and "the best interests of the child"; in other states they replaced these time-honored goals all together. The new phraseology more closely approximates the underlying purposes of the criminal justice system -- e.g., public protection, accountability, justice, punishment, deterrence, and incapacitation. Although these theoretical concepts are familiar to the criminal process, they remain confused and ill-defined in the juvenile justice system, particularly to the extent that they are merely grafted onto existing child welfare-based philosophies of traditional juvenile court law.

Examples of the new philosophies in juvenile justice abound. In passing the Juvenile Justice Act of 1977, Washington became the first state drastically to revamp its juvenile justice philosophy and enact a determinate sentencing statute for juvenile offenders. Mary Kay Becker, principal sponsor of the bill, said of the new statute:

"[T]he broad purpose of [the bill] should

be fairly clear. In terms of the philosophical polarities that have characterized the juvenile court debate for more than a century, the new law moves away from the *parens patriae* doctrine of benevolent coercion, and closer to a more classical emphasis on justice. The law requires the court to deal more consistently with youngsters who commit offenses. The responsibility of providing services to youngsters whose behavior, while troublesome, is noncriminal, is assigned to the Department of Social and Health Services and the agencies with whom it may contract. The juvenile court is to view itself primarily as an instrument of justice rather than as a provider of services."[11]

This dramatic philosophical change is also demonstrated in the specific objectives of the legislation: (1) "Make the juvenile offender accountable for his or her criminal behavior," and (2) "Provide punishment commensurate with the age, crime, and criminal history of the juvenile offender."[12] This requirement of commensurate punishment creates the foundation for Washington's determinate sentencing system for juveniles.

Maine's statutes also permit the juvenile court to punish a child. Specifically, juvenile court law authorizes judges to remove a juvenile from parental custody for the minor's welfare or safety, or when "the protection of the public would otherwise be endangered, or where necessary *to punish* a child adjudicated...as having committed a...crime (emphasis added).[13]

The California legislature has made a number of significant changes in the codes pertaining to the philosophy and operation of the juvenile court as well. Statutory revisions enacted in the past ten years have made accountability, victims' rights, and public safety high priorities in the juvenile justice system. The current statement of purpose of the juvenile court law reads, in relevant part:

"The purpose of the [Arnold-Kennick Juvenile Court Law] is to provide for the protection and safety of the public and each minor under the jurisdiction of the juvenile court. . . . Minors under the jurisdiction of the juvenile court as a consequence of delinquent conduct, shall in conformity with the interests of public safety and protection, receive care, treatment and guidance which is consistent with their best interest, which holds them accountable for their behavior, and which is appropriate for their circumstances. *Such guidance may include punishment. . . .*" (emphasis added)[14]

But unlike Maine's statute, California law places a restriction on the punishment to be imposed: "Punishment for the purposes of this chapter does not include retribution."[15]

Minnesota's juvenile law incorporates slightly different terminology, requiring the juvenile court and system "promote public safety and reduce juvenile delinquency by maintaining the integrity of the substantive law by prohibiting certain behavior and by developing individual responsibility for lawful behavior."[16] The use of the phrase "promote the public safety" in the Minnesota statute suggests a social defense or public protection rationale, rather than a "justice" model. But the combined usage of "public safety" and "individual responsibility" is confusing. While these terms have some commonsensical appeal, their meaning or relationship to one another is unclear. Is public safety promoted by enhancing individual responsibility? If protecting the public conflicts with the promotion of individual responsibility, how would Minnesota law resolve the conflict?

Experts have used different terms to describe this shift in juvenile justice philosophy and structure. Scholars speak of new "models" of the juvenile justice system. Among others, these include the "criminal" model,[17] "punitive" model,[18] "penal" model,[19] "justice" model,[20] "accountability" model,[21] and "determinate sentencing" model.[22] Often these new terms or concepts are used interchangeably; insufficient thought has been given to the differences, sometimes subtle, among these models. In addition, the logical corollaries of the models have not been adequately explored. A number of issues need further clarification and analysis.

Addressing Unresolved Issues

Exploring The Nature of Punishment

Punishment is what the founders of the juvenile justice system presumably wanted to avoid. The idea was to extricate juveniles from the punitive adult system and to treat their underlying problems. As Melton explains, "At its deepest roots, [the] paternalistic vision of the juvenile court was based on the moral premise that youth do not deserve punishment for their violations of the law."[23]

But times have changed -- and so have statutes. The juvenile justice statutes in Washington, Maine, and California, as noted above, specifically mention the goal of punishment. And in Judge McGee's opinion, "There should be some form of punishment involved in every delinquency disposition, clearly identified to the perpetrator as being his just deserts."[24]

But what is punishment, particularly within the context of the juvenile justice system? There appear to be two substantially different conceptions. Punishment is viewed as retributive by some and utilitarian by others.

Gardner clearly summarizes the retributivist position. In his view, ". . . punishment entails the purposeful infliction of suffering upon an offender for his offense. . . ."[25] Moreover, ". . . the primary thrust of punishment, rather than seeking to benefit the offender, is to exact from the recipient his debt to society, a payment of which nullifies his guilt."[26] This is a common theme. The retributivist position is thus "backward looking." That is, the key factor in disposition is the offense that took place in the past; the sanctioning system is based on the *offense*. The treatment needs of the offender are of little or no importance to the retributivist.[27]

By contrast, some commentators, particularly practitioners within the system, conceive of punishment in utilitarian, even humanitarian terms. They view punishment as an instrument of change for misbehaving youths. Some contend, for example, that punishment can be useful in helping foster a sense of responsibility in juveniles.[28] For this reason, according to Judge McGee, the juvenile court should punish juvenile offenders. "By doing so, the juvenile court is not repudiating its mission, it is helping to fulfill it."[29] Thus, punishment is miraculously transformed into rehabilitation.

California's statute is unique and raises profound issues. As noted above, the juvenile court in California is authorized to punish a juvenile offender; but the statute also provides that the punishment cannot be *retributive*. What does this mean? What is the difference between "retributive" punishment and "regular" or non-retributive punishment? Are the goals of these two types of punishment the same or different?

Presumably if the juvenile court is allowed to dispense punishment, the child must be protected from disproportionate punishment. As Fox asserts, "punishment implies limits."[30] If the idea is to punish the child and punishment implies limits, then the limits should be based on the seriousness of the offense. How is this reflected in California law? Does non-retributive punishment also imply limits? Or can non-retributive punishment be disproportionate to the seriousness of the offense? Is non-retributive punishment meant to right a wrong that has taken place in the past or is it intended to change a juvenile's personality or attitude?

To the extent that there is a move to punishment in juvenile justice, the logical corollaries must be more fully explored and articulated. Changing to a punishment-based system, particularly with a retributivist basis, has profound implications for sentencing structure, dispositional alternatives, and the internal logic of the entire juvenile justice system.

What Is "Justice" In Juvenile Justice?

The meaning of "justice" in juvenile justice has long been confused and the subject of debate. It might be argued that the concept does not belong in the juvenile system to the extent that the system's focus is on the best interests of the child and his or her rehabilitation. Thus under the rehabilitative model, with its indeterminate sentencing scheme, there is no necessary relationship between the offense committed and the disposition -- that is, between the harm done and, for example, the length of stay in an institution.

Conversely, it could be argued that justice is what has long been missing from the juvenile justice system. But this begs the question: what is, or should be, "justice" within the context of the juvenile justice system? Moreover, what is the relationship between justice and punishment?

Justice and punishment seem somehow to be related. To be just, punishment must be proportionate to the seriousness of the offense committed. Seriousness is generally determined by the harmfulness of the act and the degree of culpability of the offender.[31] This notion is summarized in the simple phrase: "let the punishment fit the crime." This, in turn, implies a gradation of offenses by seriousness. It also implies some corresponding ranking of severity of punishment. Based on this internal logic, Washington state has adopted a determinate sentencing scheme for juvenile offenders.

California has at least partially adopted a just deserts schema. Prompted by the State Supreme Court's ruling in *People v. Olivas* to extend equal protection of the law to the term of confinement served by youthful offenders committed to the California Youth Authority,[32] the legislature modified the indeterminate sentencing law applicable to juveniles. As part of a major reform package adopted in 1976 which affected several aspects of the juvenile justice system, legislators enacted the provision that:

> ". . . in any case in which the minor is removed from the physical custody of his . . . guardian as a result of an order of wardship, the order shall specify that the minor may not be held in physical confinement for a period in excess of the maximum term of confinement which would be imposed upon an adult convicted of the offense . . . which brought the minor under the jurisdiction of the juvenile court."[33]

With a justice or just deserts philosophy, it follows that limits must be placed on dispositional alternatives, and specifically on the degree of punishment meted out to juvenile offenders. These limits can be, and often are, in direct conflict with the traditional goals and structure of the juvenile justice system.

Accountability

Some authorities use the term "accountability" to describe the new models of juvenile justice. Maloney, Romig, and Armstrong, for example, claim that accountability is one of the core values in the recent juvenile court and probation movement. According to them, "Accountability is firmly grounded in the justice theme that the system must respond to illegal behavior in such a way that the offender is made aware of and responsible for the loss, damage, or injury perpetrated upon the victim."[34]

But even this simple assertion raises questions. What is the relationship between accountability and justice or punishment? What is the relationship of accountability to individual responsibility? Does holding a youth accountable mean that the youth will be made to understand and appreciate the wrongfulness of his or her acts? Or does it mean the youth will be held personally responsible for the harm done and punished in direct proportion (no more and no less) to the offense?

Maloney, Romig, and Armstrong seem to use the term in the former way. That is, accountability appears to mean making the juvenile aware of and accept responsibility for his or her wrongful acts. Through the juvenile justice experience, accountability is something to be instilled into the misbehaving youth. For example, Maloney, Romig, and Armstrong suggest that restitution is one of the more promising approaches available to the court "for imposing a tangible and enforceable form of accountability on juvenile offenders."[35] Moreover, "Accountability has taken the form of imparting some sense of individual responsibility and social awareness to the youthful offender."[36] But is accountability something that one *instills* in a juvenile? Or is it something that one inflicts, like punishment, proportionate to the offense?

It is easy to envision the conflicts that could arise with differing notions of accountability -- that is, instilling a sense of responsibility or inflicting punishment for wrongdoing. Take, for example, a 16-year-old armed robber with one prior adjudication for the same offense. Suppose that "justice" (i.e., proportionate punishment as defined by the legislature or a sentencing commission) dictates that a youth spend two years in confinement at a training school. Suppose further that at the end of the two year period the youth does not appreciate or acknowledge the wrongfulness of his or her acts? Should the youth be released at the end of the two year period? If accountability is related to instilling values and fostering responsibility, the answer is no. If accountability is related to just and proportionate punishment, the answer is yes.

Individual Responsibility

Punishment and accountability are related, in some manner, to responsibility. Generally, the infliction of punishment on a person for his or her acts presumes that a person is responsible for those acts. The law does not allow the punishment of the mentally ill or idiots, because they do not possess the requisite mental intent *(mens rea)* to be morally culpable. For the state to punish, the person receiving the punishment must be viewed as a responsible actor. One of the emerging issues in juvenile justice is whether juveniles -- or which juveniles under what circumstances -- are responsible moral actors.

The traditional view is that juveniles are not fully responsible, especially for criminal activity. Even the IJA/ABA Standards provide, "Juveniles may be viewed as incomplete adults, lacking in full moral and experiential development."[37] This leads some authorities, like Zimring, to conclude that juvenile offenders must be protected from the full burden of adult responsibility while being "pushed along by degrees toward moral and legal accountability, that we consider appropriate to adulthood."[38]

But the current trend is to hold juveniles responsible (and accountable) for their actions. Melton observes, "As the rehabilitative underpinnings of the juvenile court have withered away, courts have increasingly been faced with the problem of determining individual juveniles' responsibility, especially in those jurisdictions in which punitive purposes have been expressly recognized in juvenile codes."[39] Gardner, moreover, concludes, "Because punishment is justifiable only if its recipient is a 'person' capable of moral agency, the movement toward a punitive model seriously questions the existing view that juveniles lack capacity for rational decision-making."[40]

Some states have officially adopted the view that juveniles are, at least in some instances, responsible moral actors. For example, in California, the administrative policies instituted by correctional officials in the California Youth Authority (CYA) system have begun to focus on the goals of accountability and public protection. In the comprehensive statement of mission and directions used by the Department of the Youth Authority in 1983, the Director stated that, "the most effective way to protect the public is to ensure that offenders are held accountable for their antisocial behavior."[41] According to this policy document, accountability "refers to the ward accepting *full responsibility* for his or her own behavior, including the commitment offense and behavior while in the institution and on parole" (emphasis added).[42]

As noted, this view of the individual responsibility of juveniles conflicts with traditional conceptions of juvenile responsibility and compelling legal precedent. In *Eddings v. Oklahoma,* the United States Supreme Court mentioned that children have a "special place" in the law, and this is evidenced by the fact that every state in the country has a separate juvenile court system.[43] The Court also expressed in *Eddings* that juveniles possess a lower level of maturity than adults: "Our [American] history is replete with laws and judicial recognitions that minors, especially in their earlier years, generally are less mature and responsible than adults."[44] The Court also stated, ". . . Even the normal 16-year-old customarily lacks the maturity of an adult."[45]

The issue of maturity -- and responsibility -

– of juveniles surfaced again in *Thompson v. Oklahoma*. The Supreme Court stated:

"There is also broad agreement on the proposition that adolescents as a class are less mature and responsible than adults. We stressed this difference in explaining the importance of treating the defendant's youth as a mitigating factor in capital cases. . . . [Moreover] . . . [i]nexperience, less education, and less intelligence make a teenager less able to evaluate the consequences of his or her conduct while at the same time he or she is much more apt to be motivated by mere emotion or peer pressure than is an adult. The reasons why juveniles are not trusted with the privileges and responsibilities of an adult also explain why their irresponsible conduct is not as morally responsible as that of an adult."[46]

This logic led the Court to conclude that ". . . less culpability should attach to a crime committed by a juvenile than to a comparable crime by an adult."[47]

A conflict -- or Catch 22 -- is becoming apparent. On the one hand, juvenile law traditionally holds that juveniles should not be punished because they are *not* responsible actors. On the other hand, some authorities now hold that juveniles should be punished in order to *make* them more responsible. But issues remain unresolved: are juveniles fully responsible for their criminal actions? Under what conditions, if any, are they as responsible as adults? And how is punishment related to levels of responsibility?

The Infancy Defense

To the extent that the juvenile court has historically not been concerned with culpability, responsibility and punishment, the infancy defense was deemed to be irrelevant. Some states have continued to maintain this traditional view. As recently as a 1981, for example, the Rhode Island Supreme Court held,

"Once one accepts the principle that a finding of delinquency or waywardness in a juvenile proceeding is not the equivalent of a finding that the juvenile has committed a crime, there is no necessity of a finding that the juvenile has such maturity that he or she knew what he or she was doing was wrong."[48]

In the trend toward punishment, an opposing position is set forth: "Juvenile proceedings are 'criminal' in nature when punishment is the sanction imposed."[49] If juvenile court proceedings are now deemed criminal in nature, should not the infancy defense be relevant? Some jurisdictions are coming to that conclusion. For example, in *State v. Q.D.*, the Washington Supreme Court held, "The principles of construction of criminal statutes, made necessary by our recognition of the criminal nature of juvenile court proceedings, also compel us to conclude that [the infancy defense] applies to proceedings in juvenile courts."[50]

Thus, to the extent that juvenile codes now authorize punishment for juveniles, it follows that juveniles should be allowed to use the traditional criminal defenses. As Melton contends, "If juveniles are to be subjected to *any* punishment, then they should be provided the protections embedded within criminal procedure, modified as necessary to ensure that such proceedings meet the special demands of fundamental fairness as applied to youth."[51]

Mixed Goals and Continuing Confusion

Some states, as well as some scholars, have tried to blend the new goals of the juvenile justice system with the traditional goals. This mixed bag is evident in the statutory provisions of a few states. For example, the purpose of Florida's revised juvenile code is:

"*to protect society* more effectively by *substituting for retributive punishment*, whenever possible, methods of offender *rehabilitation and rehabilitative restitution*, recognizing that the application of *sanctions* which are consistent with the *seriousness of the offense* is appropriate *in all cases*" (emphasis added).[52]

The language of the Florida law is particularly confusing. On the one hand, the law appears to retain the traditional goal of rehabilitation, which implies variable lengths of confinement based on the ability of each youth to meet his or her treatment goals. On the other hand, the law implies a just deserts orientation, stressing that sanctions be proportionate to the seriousness of the criminal conduct in all cases. These two principles appear to be diametrically opposed. Which one is it going to be?

In a similar vein, Maloney, Romig, and Armstrong advocate a "balanced approach" to juvenile probation -- and presumably to the rest of the juvenile court and correctional process. They claim that there are four "core values" that shape the juvenile court and probation movement: community protection, accountability, competency development, and individualized assessment and treatment.[53]

But these values can -- and often do -- conflict. Accountability, to the extent that it is associated with justice and punishment, may dictate that a youth stay in an institution for a specified period of time, based on the seriousness of the offense. However, community protection may demand that the youth remain incarcerated for a longer period; conversely, a youth's progress in treatment and rehabilitation may suggest a shorter period of confinement. Which core value is to be followed? How are conflicts to be resolved? Who is to resolve these conflicting principles? It may be difficult, but it may be necessary to acknowledge that some principles do not fit well with other principles. It simply will not work to say that the juvenile court should punish a juvenile offender in direct proportion to his or her offense (just deserts) and at the same time individualize the youth's sentence depending on his or her treatment needs.

The new "balanced" approach is probably not much different than in the "good old days" when statutes provided little, if any, guidance to juvenile court judges or officials (parole board or correctional personnel) who were responsible for deciding when juveniles were to be released from institutional placement. In reality, the balanced approach used to mean a lack of standards or guidelines for decision-making. In practice, some judges and correctional officials would emphasize public protection, others rehabilitation, and still others accountability for misdeeds. The same situation appears true today. The modern balanced approach perpetuates a muddled jurisprudence for responding to different types of juvenile offenders under different fact situations. It does not clearly delineate how much weight is to be given to each of the core values under different circumstances. Without such guidance, judges and correctional officials are likely to rely on their own values, and the "balance" may become skewed by personal bias or community pressures.

Conclusion

The juvenile justice system is wrestling with a changing philosophy. Disenchantment with the old system has demanded revision. But because of the lack of clarity of the emerging concepts, there is no consensus about the nature and purpose of the new vision of juvenile justice. Enormous confusion remains over the meaning of the new models and how they should be operationalized.

In responding to demands from the public to "crack down on crime" and give public protection a higher priority in crime control policies, lawmakers have used various terms to describe the juvenile justice system's new mission. Some of the new terms conflict with the traditional juvenile justice language that continues to govern the legal framework of many state juvenile justice systems.

Ambiguity over the new terms or models gives juvenile court judges, as well as correctional officials and staff, confused messages as to the purpose or purposes of the system and the relative priority of the system's various goals. "Accountability," for example, is currently an ill-defined concept that means substantially different things to different people. The accountability model is broad enough to encompass all of the ideas of justice, just deserts, punishment, non-retributive punishment, public safety, preventive detention, responsibility, and culpability. Accountability has also given rebirth to the tarnished concepts of treatment and rehabilitation to the extent that it has been associated with the moral improvement of the youthful offender.

Perhaps all of the philosophical debate is simply a guise or smokescreen, used to gloss over an underlying political and social agenda: crack down on kids and put them away for longer periods of time to satisfy the public's thirst for vengeance and demand for public protection. The new models in juvenile justice may not have grown out of an evolving jurisprudence of juvenile justice, but rather out of a political expediency to give juveniles longer and harsher sentences. Whatever the motivations for moving to new models, policy-makers must begin to clarify the goals and mission of the juvenile justice system, and must specify exactly how the system should respond to different types of offenders and offenses.

Biographical Sketches

Martin L. Forst is Senior Research Associate at the URSA Institute in San Francisco. He received a doctorate in Criminology from the University of California at Berkeley, and is the author or co-author of several books and articles.

Martha–Elin Blomquist is Assistant Professor of Criminal Justice Administration at California State University, Bakersfield. She received her Ph.D in Jurisprudence and Social Policy from Boalt Hall School of Law, University of California at Berkeley. She is the co–author of *Missing Children: Rhetoric and Reality.*

Authors' Addresses:

Martin L. Forst, D. Crim
Senior Research Associate
URSA Institute
185 Berry Street, Suite 6600
San Francisco, California 94107

and

Martha–Elin Blomquist, Ph.D.
Assistant Professor
Criminal Justice Administration
California State University
Bakersfield, California 93302

Notes

[1]For example, see: P. Tamilia, "The Recriminalization of the Juvenile Justice System –– The Demise of the Socialized Court," 31(2) *Juvenile and Family Court Journal,* 15–22 (1980); B. Feld, "Criminalizing Juvenile Justice: Rules of Procedure for the Juvenile Court," 69 *Minnesota Law Review* 141–276 (1984); J. Glen, "Juvenile Court Reform: Procedural Process and Substantive Stasis," 1970 *Wisconsin Law Review* 431–449; B. Feld, "The Juvenile Court Meets the Principle of Offense: Punishment, Treatment and the Difference It Makes," 68 *Boston University Law Review* 821–915 (1988); M. Forst and M. Blomquist, "Cracking Down on Juveniles: The Changing Ideology of Youth Corrections," 5 *Notre Dame Journal of Law, Ethics and Public Policy* 323–375 (1991).

[2]For example, see: F. A. Allen, "The Juvenile Court and the Limits of Juvenile Justice," 11 *Wayne Law Review* 676–687 (1965); M. Wolfgang, "Abolish the Juvenile Court System," 2(10) *California Lawyer* 12–13 (1982); E. van den Haag, *Punishing Criminals.* New York: Basic Books, Inc. (1975); W. Arnold, "Race and Ethnicity Relative to Other Factors in Juvenile Court Dispositions," 77 *American Journal of Sociology* 211–222 (1971); B. Boland and J.Q. Wilson, "Age, Crime and Punishment," 51 *The Public Interest* 22–34 (1978).

[3]M. Gardner, "Punitive Juvenile Justice: Some Observations on a Recent Trend," 10 *International Journal of Law and Psychiatry* 129–151 (1987), at p. 131–132.

[4]Institute of Judicial Administration/American Bar Association (IJA/ABA) Joint Commission on Juvenile Justice Standards, Standards Relating to Disposition (1980). Also see: F. McCarthy, "Delinquency Dispositions Under the Juvenile Justice Standards: The Consequences of a Change of Rationale," 52 *New York University Law Review*

1093–1119 (1977). McCarthy states, ". . . the standards advocate as the principal aim of the juvenile justice system the effective punishment of juveniles whose conduct endangers public safety" at p. 1094.

[5]S. Fox, "The Reform of the Juvenile Court: The Child's Right to Punishment," 25 *Juvenile Justice* 2–9 (1974), at p. 2.

[6]M. Norman and L. Gillespie, "Changing Horses: Utah's Shift in Adjudicating Serious Juvenile Offenders," 12 *Journal of Contemporary Law* 85–98 (1986), at p. 85.

[7]For example, see: R. Dawson, "The Third Justice System: The New Juvenile–Criminal System of Determinate Sentencing for the Youthful Violent Offender in Texas," 19 *St. Mary's Law Journal* 943–1016 (1988); Note, "The Serious Young Offender Under Vermont's Juvenile Law: Beyond the Reach of *Parens Patriae,"* 8 *Vermont Law Review* 173–202 (1983); R. McNally, "Juvenile Court: An Endangered Species," 47 *Federal Probation* 32–37 (1983).

[8]For example, see: B. Feld, "The Juvenile Court Meets the Principle of the Offense: Legislative Changes in Juvenile Waiver Statutes," 78 *Journal of Criminal Law and Criminology* 471–533 (1987); C. Rudman, E. Hartstone, J. Fagan, and M. Moore, "Violent Youth in Adult Court: Process and Punishment," 32 *Crime and Delinquency* 75–96 (1986).

[9]Dawson (1988), *supra,* note 7.

[10]Feld (1988), *supra,* note 1.

[11]M. K. Becker, "Washington State's New Juvenile Code: An Introduction," 14 *Gonzaga Law Review* 289–312 (1979), at p. 308.

[12]Washington Revised Codes, Section 13.40.010(2)(c)-(d).

[13]Maine Revised Statutes Annotated, Title 15, Section 3002.1(c).

[14]California Welfare and Institutions Code, Section 202.

[15]*Id.*

[16]Minnesota Statutes, Section 260.011(2).

[17]For example, see: McCarthy (1977), *supra,* note 4.

[18]For example, see: M. Gardner (1987), *supra,* note 3.

[19]For example, see: S. Wizner and M. Keller, "The Penal Model of Juvenile Justice: Is Juvenile Court Delinquency Jurisdiction Obsolete?" 52 *New York University Law Review* 1120–1135 (1977).

[20]For example, see: C. Springer, *Justice for Juveniles,* U.S. Department of Justice, Office of Juvenile Justice and Delinquency Prevention, Washington, D.C., April 1986.

[21]For example, see: M. Gardner, "The Right of Juvenile Offenders to be Punished: Some Implications of Treating Kids as Persons," 68 *Nebraska Law Review* 182–215 (1989).

[22]For example, see: B. Benda and D. Waite, "A Proposed Determinate Sentencing Model in Virginia: An Empirical Evaluation," 39(1) *Juvenile and Family Court Journal* 55–71 (1988).

[23]G. Melton, "Taking *Gault* Seriously: Toward a New Juvenile Court," 68 *Nebraska Law Review* 146–181 (1989), at p. 151.

[24]C. McGee, "Measured Steps Toward Clarity and Balance in the Juvenile Justice System," 40(3) *Juvenile and Family Court Journal* 1–23 (1989), at p. 16.

[25]Gardner (1989), *supra,* note 21 at p. 185.

[26]*Id.* at p. 184.

[27]For example, see: A. von Hirsch, *Doing Justice.* New York: Hill and Wang, 1976.

[28]R. Barnum, "The Development of Responsibility: Implications for Juvenile Justice," in Francis X. Hartman (ed.), *From Children to Citizens,* 1987, p. 74. Also see: McGee (1989), *supra,* note 24, at p. 16. He states, "Sometimes punishment alone is enough. ... A young petit thief might *learn* lesson enough by a sentence including a few days of incarceration and an additional restitution order."

[29]McGee (1989), *supra,* note 24, at p. 16.

[30]Fox, *supra,* note 5.

[31]von Hirsch (1976), *supra,* note 27.

[32]*People v. Olivas,* 17 Cal.3d 236, 551 P.2d 375 (1976).

[33]California Welfare and Institutions Code, Section 726(c).

[34]D. Maloney, D. Romig, and T. Armstrong, "Juvenile Probation: The Balanced Approach," 39(3) *Juvenile and Family Court Journal* 5–8 (1988), at p. 6.

[35]*Id.*

[36]*Id.*

[37]IJA/ABA Standards (1980), *supra,* note 4, at p. 19 note 5, (quoting Cohen, Position Paper, Juvenile Justice Standards Project, No. 18, 1974).

[38]F. Zimring, *The Changing Legal World of Adolescence.* New York: The Free Press, (1982), at p. 95–96.

[39]Melton (1989), *supra,* note 23 at p. 178.

[40]Gardner (1989), *supra,* note 21, at p. 195.

[41]Department of the Youth Authority. Mission Statement, Premises, Expanded Directional Statements, Sacramento, CA (1983), at p. 5.

[42]*Id.*

[43]*Eddings v. Oklahoma,* 455 U.S. 104 (1982), quoting from *May v. Anderson,* 345 U.S. 528, 536 (1952).

[44]455 U.S. 104, 115–116 (1982).

[45]*Id.* at p. 116.

[46]*Thompson v. Oklahoma,* 487 U.S. 815, 835 (1988).

[47]*Id.*

[48]*In re Michael,* 423 A.2d 1180, 1183 (1981).

[49]Gardner (1987), *supra,* note 3, at p. 147.

[50]*State v. Q.D.,* 685 P.2d 557, 560 (1984).

[51]Melton (1989), *supra,* note 23 at p. 180.

[52]Florida Statutes Annotated, Section 39.001(2)(a).

[53]Maloney et al. (1988), *supra,* note 34.

Girls' Crime and Woman's Place: Toward a Feminist Model of Female Delinquency

This article argues that existing delinquency theories are fundamentally inadequate to the task of explaining female delinquency and official reactions to girls' deviance. To establish this, the article first reviews the degree of the androcentric bias in the major theories of delinquent behavior. Then the need for a feminist model of female delinquency is explored by reviewing the available evidence on girls' offending. This review shows that the extensive focus on disadvantaged males in public settings has meant that girls' victimization and the relationship between that experience and girls' crime has been systematically ignored. Also missed has been the central role played by the juvenile justice system in the sexualization of female delinquency and the criminalization of girls' survival strategies. Finally, it will be suggested that the official actions of the juvenile justice system should be understood as major forces in women's oppression as they have historically served to reinforce the obedience of all young women to the demands of patriarchal authority no matter how abusive and arbitrary.

Meda Chesney-Lind

Meda Chesney-Lind: Associate Professor of Women's Studies and an Associate Researcher with the Center for Youth Research at the University of Hawaii, Manoa.

I ran away so many times. I tried anything man, and they wouldn't believe me. . . . As far as they are concerned they think I'm the problem. You know, runaway, bad label. (Statement of a 16-year-old girl who, after having been physically and sexually assaulted, started running away from home and was arrested as a "runaway" in Hawaii.)

You know, one of these days I'm going to have to kill myself before you guys are gonna listen to me. I can't stay at home. (Statement of a 16-year-old Tucson runaway with a long history of physical abuse [Davidson, 1982, p. 26].)

Who is the typical female delinquent? What causes her to get into trouble? What happens to her if she is caught? These are questions that few members of the general public could answer quickly. By contrast, almost every citizen can talk about "delinquency," by which they generally mean male delinquency, and can even generate some fairly specific complaints about, for ex-

ample, the failure of the juvenile justice system to deal with such problems as "the alarming increase in the rate of serious juvenile crime" and the fact that the juvenile courts are too lenient on juveniles found guilty of these offenses (Opinion Research Corporation, 1982).

This situation should come as no surprise since even the academic study of delinquent behavior has, for all intents and purposes, been the study of male delinquency. "The delinquent is a rogue male" declared Albert Cohen (1955, p. 140) in his influential book on gang delinquency. More than a decade later, Travis Hirschi, in his equally important book entitled *The Causes of Delinquency,* relegated women to a footnote that suggested, somewhat apologetically, that "in the analysis that follows the 'non-Negro' becomes 'white,' and the girls disappear."

This pattern of neglect is not all that unusual. All areas of social inquiry have been notoriously gender blind. What is

perhaps less well understood is that theories developed to describe the misbehavior of working- or lower-class male youth fail to capture the full nature of delinquency in America; and, more to the point, are woefully inadequate when it comes to explaining female misbehavior and official reactions to girls' deviance.

To be specific, delinquent behavior involves a range of activities far broader than those committed by the stereotypical street gang. Moreover, many more young people than the small visible group of "troublemakers" that exist on every intermediate and high school campus commit some sort of juvenile offense and many of these youth have brushes with the law. One study revealed, for example, that 33% of all the boys and 14% of the girls born in 1958 had at least one contact with the police before reaching their eighteenth birthday (Tracy, Wolfgang, and Figlio, 1985, p. 5). Indeed, some forms of serious

From *Crime & Delinquency,* Vol. 35, No. 1, January 1989, pp. 5-29. © 1989 by The National Council on Crime and Delinquency, Sage Publications. Reprinted by permission.

delinquent behavior, such as drug and alcohol abuse, are far more frequent than the stereotypical delinquent behavior of gang fighting and vandalism and appear to cut across class and gender lines.

Studies that solicit from youth themselves the volume of their delinquent behavior consistently confirm that large numbers of adolescents engage in at least some form of misbehavior that could result in their arrest. As a consequence, it is largely trivial misconduct, rather than the commission of serious crime, that shapes the actual nature of juvenile delinquency. One national study of youth aged 15-21, for example, noted that only 5% reported involvement in a serious assault, and only 6% reported having participated in a gang fight. In contrast, 81% admitted to having used alcohol, 44% admitted to having used marijuana, 37% admitted to having been publicly drunk, 42% admitted to having skipped classes (truancy), 44% admitted having had sexual intercourse, and 15% admitted to having stolen from the family (McGarrell and Flanagan, 1985, p. 363). Clearly, not all of these activities are as serious as the others. It is important to remember that young people can be arrested for all of these behaviors.

Indeed, one of the most important points to understand about the nature of delinquency, and particularly female delinquency, is that youth can be taken into custody for both criminal acts and a wide variety of what are often called "status offenses." These offenses, in contrast to criminal violations, permit the arrest of youth for a wide range of behaviors that are violations of parental authority: "running away from home," "being a person in need of supervision," "minor in need of supervision," being "incorrigible," "beyond control," truant, in need of "care and protection," and so on. Juvenile delinquents, then, are youths arrested for either criminal or noncriminal status offenses; and, as this discussion will establish, the role played by uniquely juvenile offenses is by no means insignificant, particularly when considering the character of female delinquency.

Examining the types of offenses for which youth are actually arrested, it is clear that again most are arrested for the less serious criminal acts and status offenses. Of the one and a half million youth arrested in 1983, for example, only 4.5% of these arrests were for such serious violent offenses as murder, rape, robbery, or aggravated assault (McGarrell and Flanagan, 1985, p. 479). In contrast, 21% were arrested for a single offense (larceny, theft) much of

which, particularly for girls, is shoplifting (Sheldon and Horvath, 1986).

Table 1 presents the five most frequent offenses for which male and female youth are arrested and from this it can be seen that while trivial offenses dominate both male and female delinquency, trivial offenses, particularly status offenses, are more significant in the case of girls' arrests; for example the five offenses listed in Table 1 account for nearly three-quarters of female offenses and only slightly more than half of male offenses.

More to the point, it is clear that, though routinely neglected in most delinquency research, status offenses play a significant role in girls' official delinquency. Status offenses accounted for about 25.2% of all girls' arrests in 1986 (as compared to 26.9% in 1977) and only about 8.3% of boys' arrests (compared to 8.8% in 1977). These figures are somewhat surprising since dramatic declines in arrests of youth for these offenses might have been expected as a result of the passage of the Juvenile Justice and Delinquency Prevention Act in 1974, which, among other things, encouraged jurisdictions to divert and deinstitutionalize youth charged with noncriminal offenses. While the figures in Table 1 do show a decline in these arrests, virtually all of this decline occurred in the 1970s. Between 1982 and 1986 girls' curfew arrests increased by 5.1% and runaway arrests increased by a striking 24.5%. And the upward trend continues; arrests of girls for running away increased by 3% between 1985 and 1986 and arrests of girls for curfew violations increased by 12.4% (Federal Bureau of Investigation, 1987, p. 171).

Looking at girls who find their way into juvenile court populations, it is apparent that status offenses continue to play an important role in the character of girls' official delinquency. In total, 34% of the girls, but only 12% of the boys, were referred to court in 1983 for these offenses (Snyder and Finnegan, 1987, pp. 6–20). Stating these figures differently, they mean that while males constituted about 81% of all delinquency referrals, females constituted 46% of all status offenders in courts (Snyder and Finnegan, 1987, p. 20). Similar figures were reported for 1977 by Black and Smith (1981). Fifteen years earlier, about half of the girls and about 20% of the boys were referred to court for these offenses (Children's Bureau, 1965). These data do seem to signal a drop in female status offense referrals, though not as dramatic a decline as might have been expected.

For many years statistics showing

large numbers of girls arrested and referred for status offenses were taken to be representative of the different types of male and female delinquency. However, self-report studies of male and female delinquency do not reflect the dramatic differences in misbehavior found in official statistics. Specifically, it appears that girls charged with these noncriminal status offenses have been and continue to be significantly overrepresented in court populations.

Teilmann and Landry (1981) compared girls' contribution to arrests for runaway and incorrigibility with girls' self-reports of these two activities, and found a 10.4% overrepresentation of females among those arrested for runaway and a 30.9% overrepresentation in arrests for incorrigibility. From these data they concluded that girls are "arrested for status offenses at a higher rate than boys, when contrasted to their self-reported delinquency rates" (Teilmann and Landry, 1981, pp. 74–75). These findings were confirmed in another recent self-report study. Figueira-McDonough (1985, p. 277) analyzed the delinquent conduct of 2,000 youths and found "no evidence of greater involvement of females in status offenses." Similarly, Canter (1982) found in the National Youth Survey that there was no evidence of greater female involvement, compared to males, in any category of delinquent behavior. Indeed, in this sample, males were significantly more likely than females to report status offenses.

Utilizing Canter's national data on the extensiveness of girls self-reported delinquency and comparing these figures to official arrests of girls (see Table 2) reveals that girls are underrepresented in every arrest category with the exception of status offenses and larceny theft. These figures strongly suggest that official practices tend to exaggerate the role played by status offenses in girls' delinquency.

Delinquency theory, because it has virtually ignored female delinquency, failed to pursue anomalies such as these found in the few early studies examining gender differences in delinquent behavior. Indeed, most delinquency theories have ignored status offenses. As a consequence, there is considerable question as to whether existing theories that were admittedly developed to explain male delinquency can adequately explain female delinquency. Clearly, these theories were much influenced by the notion that class and protest masculinity were at the core of delinquency. Will the "add women and stir approach" be sufficient? Are these really theories of delin-

5. JUVENILE JUSTICE

TABLE 1:   Rank Order of Adolescent Male and Female Arrests for Specific Offenses, 1977 and 1986

1977	*% of Total Arrests*	*1986*	*% of Total Arrests*	*1977*	*% of Total Arrests*	*1986*	*% of Total Arrests*
Male				*Female*			
(1) Larceny-Theft	18.4	(1) Larceny-Theft	20.4	(1) Larceny-Theft	27.0	(1) Larceny-Theft	25.7
(2) Other Offenses	14.5	(2) Other Offenses	16.5	(2) Runaway	22.9	(2) Runaway	20.5
(3) Burglary	13.0	(3) Burglary	9.1	(3) Other Offenses	14.2	(3) Other Offenses	14.8
(4) Drug Abuse Violations	6.5	(4) Vandalism	7.0	(4) Liquor Laws	5.5	(4) Liquor Laws	8.4
(5) Vandalism	6.4	(5) Vandalism	6.3	(5) Curfew & Loitering Violations	4.0	(5) Curfew & Loitering Violations	4.7

	1977	*1986*	*% N Change*		*1977*	*1986*	*% N Change*
Arrests for Serious Violent Offenses[a]	4.2%	4.7%	2.3	Arrests for Serious Violent Offenses	1.8%	2.0%	+1.7
Arrests of All Violent Offenses[b]	7.6%	9.6%	+10.3	Arrests of All Violent Offenses	5.1%	7.1%	+26.0
Arrests for Status Offenses[c]	8.8%	8.3%	−17.8	Arrests for Status Offenses	26.9%	25.2%	−14.7

SOURCE: Compiled from Federal Bureau of Investigation (1987, p. 169).
a. Arrests for murder and nonnegligent manslaughter, robbery, forcible rape, and aggravated assault.
b. Also includes arrests for other assaults.
c. Arrests for curfew and loitering law violation and runaway.

quent behavior as some (Simons, Miller, and Aigner, 1980) have argued?

This article will suggest that they are not. The extensive focus on male delinquency and the inattention the role played by patriarchal arrangements in the generation of adolescent delinquency and conformity has rendered the major delinquency theories fundamentally inadequate to the task of explaining female behavior. There is, in short, an urgent need to rethink current models in light of girls' situation in patriarchal society.

To understand why such work must occur, it is first necessary to explore briefly the dimensions of the androcentric bias found in the dominant and influential delinquency theories. Then the need for a feminist model of female delinquency will be explored by reviewing the available evidence on girls' offending. This discussion will also establish that the proposed overhaul of delinquency theory is not, as some might think, solely an academic exercise. Specifically, it is incorrect to assume that because girls are charged with less serious offenses, they actually have few problems and are treated gently when they are drawn into the juvenile justice system. Indeed, the extensive focus on disadvantaged males in public settings has meant that girls' victimization and the relationship between that experience and girls' crime has been systematically ignored. Also missed has been the central role played by the juvenile justice system in the sexualization of girls' delinquency and the criminalization of girls' survival strategies. Finally, it will be suggested that the

official actions of the juvenile justice system should be understood as major forces in girls' oppression as they have historically served to reinforce the obedience of all young women to demands of patriarchal authority no matter how abusive and arbitrary.

THE ROMANCE OF THE GANG OR THE *WEST SIDE STORY* SYNDROME

From the start, the field of delinquency research focused on visible lower-class male delinquency, often justifying the neglect of girls in the most cavalier of terms. Take, for example, the extremely important and influential work of Clifford R. Shaw and Henry D. McKay who beginning in 1929, utilized an ecological approach to the study of juvenile delinquency. Their impressive work, particularly *Juvenile Delinquency in Urban Areas* (1942) and intensive biographical case studies such as Shaw's *Brothers in Crime* (1938) and *The Jackroller* (1930), set the stage for much of the subcultural research on gang delinquency. In their ecological work, however, Shaw and McKay analyzed only the official arrest data on male delinquents in Chicago and repeatedly referred to these rates as "delinquency rates" (though they occasionally made parenthetical reference to data on female delinquency) (see Shaw and McKay, 1942, p. 356). Similarly, their biographical work traced only male experiences with the law; in *Brothers in Crime*, for example, the delinquent and criminal careers of five brothers were followed for fifteen years. In none of these works was any justification given for the equation of male delinquency with delinquency.

Early fieldwork on delinquent gangs in Chicago set the stage for another style of delinquency research. Yet here too researchers were interested only in talking to and following the boys. Thrasher studied over a thousand juvenile gangs in Chicago during roughly the same period as Shaw and McKay's more quantitative work was being done. He spent approximately one page out of 600 on the five of six female gangs he encountered in his field observation of juvenile gangs. Thrasher (1927, p. 228) did mention, in passing, two factors he felt accounted for the lower number of girl gangs: "First, the social patterns for the behavior of girls, powerfully backed by the great weight of tradition and custom, are contrary to the gang and its activities; and secondly, girls, even in urban disorganized areas, are much more closely supervised and guarded than boys and usually well incorporated into the family groups or some other social structure."

Another major theoretical approach to delinquency focuses on the subculture of lower-class communities as a generating milieu for delinquent behavior. Here again, noted delinquency researchers concentrated either exclusively or nearly exclusively on male lower-class culture. For example, Cohen's work on the subculture of delinquent gangs, which was written nearly twenty years after Thrasher's, deliberately considers only boys' delinquency. His justification for the exclusion of the girls is quite illuminating:

My skin has nothing of the quality of down or silk, there is nothing limpid or flute-like about my voice, I am a total

TABLE 2: Comparison of Sex Differences in Self-Reported and Official Delinquency for Selected Offenses

	Self-Report[a] M/F Ratios (1976)	Official Statistics[b] M/F Arrest Ratio	
		1976	1986
Theft	3.5:1 (Felony Theft) 3.4:1 (Minor Theft)	2.5:1	2.7:1
Drug Violation	1:1 (Hard Drug Use)	5.1:1	6.0:1 (Drug Abuse Violations)
Vandalism	5.1:1	12.3:1	10.0:1
Disorderly Conduct	2.8:1	4.5:1	4.4:1
Serious Assault	3.5:1 (Felony Assault)	5.6:1	5.5:1 (Aggravated Assault)
Minor Assault	3.4:1	3.8:1	3.4:1
Status Offenses	1.6:1	1.3:1	1.1:1 (Runaway, Curfew)

a. Extracted from Rachelle Canter (1982, p. 383).
b. Compiled from Federal Bureau of Investigation (1986, p. 173).

loss with needle and thread, my posture and carriage are wholly lacking in grace. These imperfections cause me no distress—if anything, they are gratifying—because I conceive myself to be a man and want people to recognize me as a full-fledged, unequivocal representative of my sex. My wife, on the other hand, is not greatly embarrassed by her inability to tinker with or talk about the internal organs of a car, by her modest attainments in arithmetic or by her inability to lift heavy objects. Indeed, I am reliably informed that many women—I do not suggest that my wife is among them—often affect ignorance, frailty and emotional instability because to do otherwise would be out of keeping with a reputation for indubitable femininity. In short, people do not simply want to excel; they want to excel as a man or as a woman [Cohen, 1955, p. 138.]

From this Cohen (1955, p. 140) concludes that the delinquent response "however it may be condemned by others on moral grounds has least one virtue; it incontestably confirms, in the eyes of all concerned, his essential masculinity." Much the same line of argument appears in Miller's influential paper on the "focal concerns" of lower-class life with its emphasis on importance of trouble, toughness, excitement, and so on. These, the author concludes, predispose poor youth (particularly male youth) to criminal misconduct. However, Cohen's comments are notable in their candor and probably capture both the allure that male delinquency has had for at least some male theorists as well as the fact that sexism has rendered the female delinquent as irrelevant to their work.

Emphasis on blocked opportunities (sometimes the "strain" theories)

emerged out of the work of Robert K. Merton (1938) who stressed the need to consider how some social structures exert a definite pressure upon certain persons in the society to engage in nonconformist rather than conformist conduct. His work influenced research largely through the efforts of Cloward and Ohlin who discussed access to "legitimate" and "illegitimate" opportunities for male youth. No mention of female delinquency can be found in their *Delinquency and Opportunity* except that women are blamed for male delinquency. Here, the familiar notion is that boys, "engulfed by a feminine world and uncertain of their own identification . . . tend to 'protest' against femininity" (Cloward and Ohlin, 1960, p. 49). Early efforts by Ruth Morris to test this hypothesis utilizing different definitions of success based on the gender of respondents met with mixed success. Attempting to assess boys' perceptions about access to economic power status while for girls the variable concerned itself with the ability or inability of girls to maintain effective relationships, Morris was unable to find a clear relationship between "female" goals and delinquency (Morris, 1964).

The work of Edwin Sutherland emphasized the fact that criminal behavior was learned in intimate personal groups. His work, particularly the notion of differential association, which also influenced Cloward and Ohlin's work, was similarly male oriented as much of his work was affected by case studies he conducted of male criminals. Indeed, in describing his notion of how differential association works, he utilized male examples (e.g., "In an area where the delinquency rate is high a boy who is

sociable, gregarious, active, and athletic is very likely to come in contact with the other boys, in the neighborhood, learn delinquent behavior from them, and become a gangster" [Sutherland, 1978, p. 131]). Finally, the work of Travis Hirschi on the social bonds that control delinquency ("social control theory") was, as was stated earlier, derived out of research on male delinquents (though he, at least, studied delinquent behavior as reported by youth themselves rather than studying only those who were arrested).

Such a persistent focus on social class and such an absence of interest in gender in delinquency is ironic for two reasons. As even the work of Hirschi demonstrated, and as later studies would validate, a clear relationship between social class position and delinquency is problematic, while it is clear that gender has a dramatic and consistent effect on delinquency causation (Hagan, Gillis, and Simpson, 1985). The second irony, and one that consistently eludes even contemporary delinquency theorists, is the fact that while the academics had little interest in female delinquents, the same could not be said for the juvenile justice system. Indeed, work on the early history of the separate system for youth, reveals that concerns about girls' immoral conduct were really at the center of what some have called the "childsaving movement" (Platt, 1969) that set up the juvenile justice system.

"THE BEST PLACE TO CONQUER GIRLS"

The movement to establish separate institutions for youthful offenders was part of the larger Progressive movement, which among other things was keenly concerned about prostitution and other "social evils" (white slavery and the like) (Schlossman and Wallach, 1978; Rafter, 1985, p. 54). Childsaving was also a celebration of women's domesticity, though ironically women were influential in the movement (Platt, 1969; Rafter, 1985). In a sense, privileged women found, in the moral purity crusades and the establishment of family courts, a safe outlet for their energies. As the legitimate guardians of the moral sphere, women were seen as uniquely suited to patrol the normative boundaries of the social order. Embracing rather than challenging these stereotypes, women carved out for themselves a role in the policing of women and girls (Feinman, 1980; Freedman, 1981; Messerschmidt, 1987). Ultimately, many of the early childsavers' activities revolved around the monitoring of young girls', particularly immigrant girls', behavior to prevent their straying from the path.

This state of affairs was the direct consequence of a disturbing coalition between some feminists and the more conservative social purity movement. Concerned about female victimization and distrustful of male (and to some degree female) sexuality, notable women leaders, including Susan B. Anthony, found common cause with the social purists around such issues as opposing the regulation of prostitution and raising the age of consent (see Messerschmidt, 1987). The consequences of such a partnership are an important lesson for contemporary feminist movements that are, to some extent, faced with the same possible coalitions.

Girls were the clear losers in this reform effort. Studies of early family court activity reveal that virtually all the girls who appeared in these courts were charged for immorality or waywardness (Chesney-Lind, 1971; Schlossman and Wallach, 1978; Shelden, 1981). More to the point, the sanctions for such misbehavior were extremely severe. For example, in Chicago (where the first family court was founded), one-half of the girl delinquents, but only one-fifth of the boy delinquents, were sent to reformatories between 1899–1909. In Milwaukee, twice as many girls as boys were committed to training schools (Schlossman and Wallach, 1978, p. 72); and in Memphis females were twice as likely as males to be committed to training schools (Shelden, 1981, p. 70).

In Honolulu, during the period 1929–1930, over half of the girls referred to court were charged with "immorality," which meant evidence of sexual intercourse. In addition, another 30% were charged with "waywardness." Evidence of immorality was vigorously pursued by both arresting officers and social workers through lengthy questioning of the girl and, if possible, males with whom she was suspected of having sex. Other evidence of "exposure" was provided by gynecological examinations that were routinely ordered in virtually all girls' cases. Doctors, who understood the purpose of such examinations, would routinely note the condition of the hymen: "admits intercourse hymen rupture," "no laceration," "hymen ruptured" are typical of the notations on the forms. Girls during this period were also twice as likely as males to be detained where they spent five times as long on the average as their male counterparts. They were also nearly three times more likely to be sentenced to the training school (Chesney-Lind, 1971). Indeed, girls were half of those commit-

ted to training schools in Honolulu well into the 1950s (Chesney-Lind, 1973).

Not surprisingly, large numbers of girls' reformatories and training schools were established during this period as well as places of "rescue and reform." For example, Schlossman and Wallach note that 23 facilities for girls were opened during the 1910–1920 decade (in contrast to the 1850–1910 period where the average was 5 reformatories per decade [Schlossman and Wallach, 1985, p. 70]), and these institutions did much to set the tone of official response to female delinquency. Obsessed with precocious female sexuality, the institutions set about to isolate the females from all contact with males while housing them in bucolic settings. The intention was to hold the girls until marriageable age and to occupy them in domestic pursuits during their sometimes lengthy incarceration.

The links between these attitudes and those of juvenile courts some decades later are, of course, arguable; but an examination of the record of the court does not inspire confidence. A few examples of the persistence of what might be called a double standard of juvenile justice will suffice here.

A study conducted in the early 1970s in a Connecticut training school revealed large numbers of girls incarcerated "for their own protection." Explaining this pattern, one judge explained, "Why most of the girls I commit are for status offenses, I figure if a girl is about to get pregnant, we'll keep her until she's sixteen and then ADC (Aid to Dependent Children) will pick her up" (Rogers, 1972). For more evidence of official concern with adolescent sexual misconduct, consider Linda Hancock's (1981) content analysis of police referrals in Australia. She noted that 40% of the referrals of girls to court made specific mention of sexual and moral conduct compared to only 5% of the referrals of boys. These sorts of results suggest that all youthful female misbehavior has traditionally been subject to surveillance for evidence of sexual misconduct.

Gelsthorpe's (1986) field research on an English police station also revealed how everyday police decision making resulted in disregard of complaints about male problem behavior in contrast to active concern about the "problem behavior" of girls. Notable, here, was the concern about the girls' sexual behavior. In one case, she describes police persistence in pursuing a "moral danger" order for a 14-year-old picked up in a truancy run. Over the objections of both the girl's parents and the Social Services Department and in the face of a written confirmation from a surgeon

that the girl was still premenstrual, the officers pursued the application because, in one officer's words, "I know her sort . . . free and easy. I'm still suspicious that she might be pregnant. Anyway, if the doctor can't provide evidence we'll do her for being beyond the care and control of her parents, no one can dispute that. Running away is proof" (Gelsthorpe, 1986, p. 136). This sexualization of female deviance is highly significant and explains why criminal activities by girls (particularly in past years) were overlooked so long as they did not appear to signal defiance of parental control (see Smith, 1978).

In their historic obsession about precocious female sexuality, juvenile justice workers rarely reflected on the broader nature of female misbehavior or on the sources of this misbehavior. It was enough for them that girls' parents reported them out of control. Indeed, court personnel tended to "sexualize" virtually all female defiance that lent itself to that construction and ignore other misbehavior (Chesney-Lind, 1973, 1977; Smith, 1978). For their part, academic students of delinquency were so entranced with the notion of the delinquent as a romantic rogue male challenging a rigid and unequal class structure, that they spent little time on middle-class delinquency, trivial offenders, or status offenders. Yet it is clear that the vast bulk of delinquent behavior is of this type.

Some have argued that such an imbalance in theoretical work is appropriate as minor misconduct, while troublesome, is not a threat to the safety and well-being of the community. This argument might be persuasive if two additional points could be established. One, that some small number of youth "specialize" in serious criminal behavior while the rest commit only minor acts, and, two, that the juvenile court rapidly releases those youth that come into its purview for these minor offenses, thus reserving resources for the most serious youthful offenders.

The evidence is mixed on both of these points. Determined efforts to locate the "serious juvenile offender" have failed to locate a group of offenders who specialize only in serious violent offenses. For example, in a recent analysis of a national self-report data set, Elliott and his associates noted "there is little evidence for specialization in serious violent offending; to the contrary, serious violent offending appears to be embedded in a more general involvement in a wide range of serious and non-serious offenses" (Elliott, Huizinga, and Morse, 1987). Indeed, they went so far as to speculate that arrest histories that tend to highlight particular types of offenders reflect variations in police policy, practices, and processes of uncovering crime as well as underlying offending patterns.

More to the point, police and court personnel are, it turns out, far more interested in youth they charge with trivial or status offenses than anyone imagined. Efforts to deinstitutionalize "status offenders," for example, ran afoul of juvenile justice personnel who had little interest in releasing youth guilty of noncriminal offenses (Chesney-Lind, 1988). As has been established, much of this is a product of the system's history that encouraged court officers to involve themselves in the noncriminal behavior of youth in order to "save" them from a variety of social ills.

Indeed, parallels can be found between the earlier Progressive period and current national efforts to challenge the deinstitutionalization components of the Juvenile Justice and Delinquency Prevention Act of 1974. These come complete with their celebration of family values and concerns about youthful independence. One of the arguments against the act has been that it allegedly gave children the "freedom to run away" (Office of Juvenile Justice and Delinquency Prevention, 1985) and that it has hampered "reunions" of "missing" children with their parents (Office of Juvenile Justice, 1986). Suspicions about teen sexuality are reflected in excessive concern about the control of teen prostitution and child pornography.

Opponents have also attempted to justify continued intervention into the lives of status offenders by suggesting that without such intervention, the youth would "escalate" to criminal behavior. Yet there is little evidence that status offenders escalate to criminal offenses, and the evidence is particularly weak when considering female delinquents (particularly white female delinquents) (Datesman and Aickin, 1984). Finally, if escalation is occurring, it is likely the product of the justice system's insistence on enforcing status offense laws, thereby forcing youth in crisis to live lives of escaped criminals.

The most influential delinquency theories, however, have largely ducked the issue of status and trivial offenses and, as a consequence, neglected the role played by the agencies of official control (police, probation officers, juvenile court judges, detention home workers, and training school personnel) in the shaping of the "delinquency problem." When confronting the less than distinct picture that emerges from the actual distribution of delinquent behavior, however, the conclusion that agents of social control have considerable discretion in labeling or choosing not to label particular behavior as "delinquent" is inescapable. This symbiotic relationship between delinquent behavior and the official response to that behavior is particularly critical when the question of female delinquency is considered.

TOWARD A FEMINIST THEORY OF DELINQUENCY

To sketch out completely a feminist theory of delinquency is a task beyond the scope of this article. It may be sufficient, at this point, simply to identify a few of the most obvious problems with attempts to adapt male-oriented theory to explain female conformity and deviance. Most significant of these is the fact that all existing theories were developed with no concern about gender stratification.

Note that this is not simply an observation about the power of gender roles (though this power is undeniable). It is increasingly clear that gender stratification in patriarchal society is as powerful a system as is class. A feminist approach to delinquency means construction of explanations of female behavior that are sensitive to its patriarchal context. Feminist analysis of delinquency would also examine ways in which agencies of social control—the police, the courts, and the prisons—act in ways to reinforce woman's place in male society (Harris, 1977; Chesney-Lind, 1986). Efforts to construct a feminist model of delinquency must first and foremost be sensitive to the situations of girls. Failure to consider the existing empirical evidence on girls' lives and behavior can quickly lead to stereotypical thinking and theoretical dead ends.

An example of this sort of flawed theory building was the early fascination with the notion that the women's movement was causing an increase in women's crime; a notion that is now more or less discredited (Steffensmeier, 1980; Gora, 1982). A more recent example of the same sort of thinking can be found in recent work on the "power-control" model of delinquency (Hagan, Simpson, and Gillis, 1987). Here, the authors speculate that girls commit less delinquency in part because their behavior is more closely controlled by the patriarchal family. The authors' promising beginning quickly gets bogged down in a very limited definition of patriarchal control (focusing on parental supervision and variations in power within the family). Ultimately, the authors' narrow formulation of patriarchal control results in their arguing that mother's work force participation (particularly in high status occupations) leads to increases in daughters' delinquency since these girls find themselves in more "egalitarian families."

This is essentially a not-too-subtle variation on the earlier "liberation" hypothesis. Now, mother's liberation causes daughter's crime. Aside from the methodological problems with the study (e.g., the authors argue that female-headed households are equivalent to upper-status "egalitarian" families where both parents work, and they measure delinquency using a six-item scale that contains no status offense items), there is a more fundamental problem with the hypothesis. There is no evidence to suggest that as women's labor force participation accelerated and the number of female-headed households soared, aggregate female delinquency measured both by self-report and official statistics either declined or remained stable (Ageton, 1983; Chilton and Datesman, 1987; Federal Bureau of Investigation, 1987).

By contrast, a feminist model of delinquency would focus more extensively on the few pieces of information about girls' actual lives and the role played by girls' problems, including those caused by racism and poverty, in their delinquency behavior. Fortunately, a considerable literature is now developing on girls' lives and much of it bears directly on girls' crime.

CRIMINALIZING GIRLS' SURVIVAL

It has long been understood that a major reason for girls' presence in juvenile courts was the fact that their parents insisted on their arrest. In the early years, conflicts with parents were by far the most significant referral source; in Honolulu 44% of the girls who appeared in court in 1929 through 1930 were referred by parents.

Recent national data, while slightly less explicit, also show that girls are more likely to be referred to court by "sources other than law enforcement agencies" (which would include parents). In 1983, nearly a quarter (23%) of all girls but only 16% of boys charged with delinquent offenses were referred to court by non-law enforcement agencies. The pattern among youth referred for status offenses (for which girls are overrepresented) was even more pronounced. Well over half (56%) of the girls charged with these offenses and 45% of the boys were referred by sources other than law enforcement (Snyder and Finnegan, 1987, p. 21; see also Pope and Feyerherm, 1982).

The fact that parents are often committed to two standards of adolescent behavior is one explanation for such a disparity—and one that should not be discounted as a major source of tension even in modern families. Despite expectations to the contrary, gender-specific socialization patterns have not changed very much and this is especially true for parents' relationships with their daughters (Katz, 1979). It appears that even parents who oppose sexism in general feel"uncomfortable tampering with existing traditions" and "do not want to risk their children becoming misfits" (Katz, 1979, p. 24). Clearly, parental attempts to adhere to and enforce these traditional notions will continue to be a source of conflict between girls and their elders. Another important explanation for girls' problems with their parents, which has received attention only in more recent years, is the problem of physical and sexual abuse. Looking specifically at the problem of childhood sexual abuse, it is increasingly clear that this form of abuse is a particular problem for girls.

Girls are, for example, much more likely to be the victims of child sexual abuse than are boys. Finkelhor and Baron estimate from a review of community studies that roughly 70% of the victims of sexual abuse are female (Finkelhor and Baron, 1986, p. 45). Girls' sexual abuse also tends to start earlier than boys (Finkelhor and Baron, 1986, p. 48); they are more likely than boys to be assaulted by a family member (often a stepfather)(DeJong, Hervada, and Emmett, 1983; Russell, 1986), and as a consequence, their abuse tends to last longer than male sexual abuse (DeJong,Hervada, and Emmett, 1983). All of these factors are associated with more severe trauma—causing dramatic short- and long-term effects in victims (Adams-Tucker, 1982). The effects noted by researchers in this area move from the more well known "fear, anxiety, depression, anger and hostility, and inappropriate sexual behavior" (Browne and Finkelhor, 1986, p. 69) to behaviors of greater familiarity to criminologists, including running away from home, difficulties in school, truancy, and early marriage (Browne and Finkelhor, 1986).

Herman's study of incest survivors in therapy found that they were more likely to have run away from home than a matched sample of women whose fathers were "seductive" (33% compared to 5%). Another study of women patients found that 50% of the victims of child sexual abuse, but only 20% of the nonvictim group, had left home before the age of 19 (Meiselman, 1978).

Not surprisingly, then, studies of girls on the streets or in court populations are showing high rates of both physical and sexual abuse. Silbert and Pines (1981, p. 409) found, for example, that 60% of the street prostitutes they interviewed had been sexually abused as juveniles. Girls at an Arkansas diagnostic unit and school who had been adjudicated for either status or delinquent offenses reported similarly high levels of sexual abuse as well as high levels of physical abuse; 53% indicated they had been sexually abused, 25% recalled scars, 38% recalled bleeding from abuse, and 51% recalled bruises (Mouzakitas, 1981).

A sample survey of girls in the juvenile justice system in Wisconsin (Phelps et al., 1982) revealed that 79% had been subjected to physical abuse that resulted in some form of injury, and 32% had been sexually abused by parents or other persons who were closely connected to their families. Moreover, 50% had been sexually assaulted ("raped" or forced to participate in sexual acts)(Phelps et al., 1982, p. 66). Even higher figures were reported by McCormack and her associates (McCormack, Janus, and Burgess, 1986) in their study of youth in a runaway shelter in Toronto. They found that 73% of the females and 38% of the males had been sexually abused. Finally, a study of youth charged with running away, truancy, or listed as missing persons in Arizona found that 55% were incest victims (Reich and Gutierres, 1979).

Many young women, then, are running away from profound sexual victimization at home, and once on the streets they are forced further into crime in order to survive. Interviews with girls who have run away from home show, very clearly, that they do not have a lot of attachment to their delinquent activities. In fact, they are angry about being labeled as delinquent, yet all engaged in illegal acts (Koroki and Chesney-Lind, 1985). The Wisconsin study found that 54% of the girls who ran away found it necessary to steal money, food, and clothing in order to survive. A few exchanged sexual contact for money, food, and/or shelter (Phelps et al., 1982, p. 67). In their study of runaway youth, McCormack, Janus, and Burgess (1986, pp. 392–393) found that sexually abused female runaways were significantly more likely than their nonabused counterparts to engage in delinquent or criminal activities such as substance abuse, petty theft, and prostitution. No such pattern was found among male runaways.

Research (Chesney-Lind and Rodriguez, 1983) on the backgrounds of adult women in prison underscores the important links between women's childhood victimizations and their later criminal careers. The interviews revealed that virtually all of this sample were the victims of physical and/or sexual abuse as youngsters; over 60% had been sexually abused and about half had been raped as young women. This situation prompted these women to run away from home (three-quarters had been arrested for status offenses) where once on the streets they began engaging in prostitution and other forms of petty property crime. They also begin what becomes a lifetime problem with drugs. As adults, the women continue in these activities since they possess truncated educational backgrounds and virtually no marketable occupational skills (see also Miller, 1986).

Confirmation of the consequences of childhood sexual and physical abuse on adult female criminal behavior has also recently come from a large quantitative study of 908 individuals with substantiated and validated histories of these victimizations. Widom (1988) found that abused or neglected females were twice as likely as a matched group of controls to have an adult record (16% compared to 7.5). The difference was also found among men, but it was not as dramatic (42% compared to 33%). Men with abuse backgrounds were also more likely to contribute to the "cycle of violence" with more arrests for violent offenses as adult offenders than the control group. In contrast, when women with abuse backgrounds did become involved with the criminal justice system, their arrests tended to involve property and order offenses (such as disorderly conduct, curfew, and loitering violations) (Widon, 1988, p. 17).

Given this information, a brief example of how a feminist perspective on the causes of female delinquency might look seems appropriate. First, like young men, girls are frequently the recipients of violence and sexual abuse. But unlike boys, girls' victimization and their response to that victimization is specifically shaped by their status as young women. Perhaps because of the gender and sexual scripts found in patriarchal families, girls are much more likely than boys to be victim of family-related sexual abuse. Men, particularly men with traditional attitudes toward women, are likely to define their daughters or stepdaughters as their sexual property (Finkelhor, 1982). In a society that idealizes inequality in male/female relationships and venerates youth in women, girls are easily defined as sexually attractive by older men (Bell, 1984). In addition, girls' vulnerability to both physical and sexual abuse is heightened by norms that require that they stay at home where their victimizers have access to them.

Moreover, their victimizers (usually males) have the ability to invoke official agencies of social control in their efforts to keep young women at home and vulnerable. That is to say, abusers have traditionally been able to utilize the uncritical commitment of the juvenile justice system toward parental authority to force girls to obey them. Girls' complaints about abuse were, until recently, routinely ignored. For this reason, statutes that were originally placed in law to "protect" young people have, in the case of girls' delinquency, criminalized their survival strategies. As they run away from abusive homes, parents have been able to employ agencies to enforce their return. If they persisted in their refusal to stay in that home, however intolerable, they were incarcerated.

Young women, a large number of whom are on the run from homes characterized by sexual abuse and parental neglect, are forced by the very statutes designed to protect them into the lives of escaped convicts. Unable to enroll in school or take a job to support themselves because they fear detection, young female runaways are forced into the streets. Here they engage in panhandling, petty theft, and occasional prostitution in order to survive. Young women in conflict with their parents (often for very legitimate reasons) may actually be forced by present laws into petty criminal activity, prostitution, and drug use.

In addition, the fact that young girls (but not necessarily young boys) are defined as sexually desirable and, in fact, more desirable than their older sisters due to the double standard of aging means that their lives on the streets (and their survival strategies) take on unique shape—one again shaped by patriarchal values. It is no accident that girls on the run from abusive homes, or on the streets because of profound poverty, get involved in criminal activities that exploit their sexual object status. American society has defined as desirable youthful, physically perfect women. This means that girls on the streets, who have little else of value to trade, are encouraged to utilize this "resource" (Campagna and Poffenberger, 1988). It also means that the criminal subculture views them from this perspective (Miller, 1986).

FEMALE DELINQUENCY, PATRIARCHAL AUTHORITY, AND FAMILY COURTS

The early insights into male delinquency were largely gleaned by inten-

sive field observation of delinquent boys. Very little of this sort of work has been done in the case of girls' delinquency, though it is vital to an understanding of girls' definitions of their own situations, choices, and behavior (for exceptions to this see Campbell, 1984; Peacock, 1981; Miller, 1986; Rosenberg and Zimmerman, 1977). Time must be spent listening to girls. Fuller research on the settings, such as families and schools, that girls find themselves in and the impact of variations in those settings should also be undertaken (see Figueira-McDonough, 1986). A more complete understanding of how poverty and racism shape girls' lives is also vital (see Messerschmidt, 1986; Campbell, 1984). Finally, current qualitative research on the reaction of official agencies to girls' delinquency must be conducted. This latter task, admittedly more difficult, is particularly critical to the development of delinquency theory that is as sensitive to gender as it is to race and class.

It is clear that throughout most of the court's history, virtually all female delinquency has been placed within the larger context of girls' sexual behavior. One explanation for this pattern is that familial control over girls' sexual capital has historically been central to the maintenance of patriarchy (Lerner, 1986). The fact that young women have relatively more of this capital has been one reason for the excessive concern that both families and official agencies of social control have expressed about youthful female defiance (otherwise much of the behavior of criminal justice personnel makes virtually no sense). Only if one considers the role of women's control over their sexuality at the point in their lives that their value to patriarchal society is so pronounced, does the historic pattern of jailing of huge numbers of girls guilty of minor misconduct make sense.

This framework also explains the enormous resistance that the movement to curb the juvenile justice system's authority over status offenders encountered. Supporters of the change were not really prepared for the political significance of giving youth the freedom to run. Horror stories told by the opponents of deinstitutionalization about victimized youth, youthful prostitution, and youthful involvement in pornography (Office of Juvenile Justice and Delinquency Prevention, 1985) all neglect the unpleasant reality that most of these behaviors were often in direct response to earlier victimization, frequently by parents, that officials had, for years, routinely ignored. What may be at stake in efforts to roll back deinstitutionaliza-

tion efforts is not so much "protection" of youth as it is curbing the right of young women to defy patriarchy.

In sum, research in both the dynamics of girls' delinquency and official reactions to that behavior is essential to the development of theories of delinquency that are sensitive to its patriarchal as well as class and racial context.

REFERENCES

Adams-Tucker, Christine. 1982. "Proximate Effects of Sexual Abuse in Childhood." *American Journal of Psychiatry* 193: 1252–1256.

Ageton, Suzanne S. 1983. "The Dynamics of Female Delinquency, 1976–1980.," *Criminology* 21:555–584.

Bell, Inge Powell. 1984. "The Double Standard: Age." in *Women: A Feminist Perspective*, edited by Jo Freeman. Palo Alto, CA: Mayfield.

Black, T. Edwin and Charles P. Smith, 1981. *A Preliminary National Assessment of the Number and Characteristics of Juveniles Processed in the Juvenile Justice System.* Washington, DC: Government Printing Office.

Browne, Angela and David Finkelhor, 1986. "Impact of Child Sexual Abuse: A Review of Research," *Psychological Bulletin* 99:66–77.

Campagna, Daniel S. and Donald I. Poffenberger, 1988. *The Sexual Trafficking in Children*, Dover, DE: Auburn House.

Campbell, Ann. 1984. *The Girls in the Gang.* Oxford: Basil Blackwell.

Canter, Rachelle J. 1982. "Sex Differences in Self-Report Delinquency," *Criminology* 20:373–393.

Chesney-Lind, Meda. 1971, *Female Juvenile Delinquency in Hawaii*, Master's thesis, University of Hawaii.

_____1973. "Judicial Enforcement of the Female Sex Role," *Issues in Criminology* 3:51–71.

_____1978. "Young Women in the Arms of the Law," In *Women, Crime and the Criminal Justice System*, edited by Lee H. Bowker, Boston: Lexington.

_____1986. "Women and Crime: The Female Offender," *Signs* 12:78–96.

_____1988. "Girls and Deinstitutionalization: Is Juvenile Justice Still Sexist?" *Journal of Criminal Justice Abstracts* 20:144–165.

_____and Noelie Rodriguez 1983. "Women Under Lock and Key," *Prison Journal* 63:47–65.

Children's Bureau, Department of Health, Education and Welfare, 1965. *1964 Statistics on Public Institutions for Delinquent Children.* Washington, DC; Government Printing Office.

Chilton, Roland and Susan K. Datesman, 1987, "Gender, Race and Crime: An Analysis of Urban Arrest Trends, 1960–1980," *Gender and Society* 1:152–171.

Cloward, Richard A. and Lloyd E. Ohlin, 1960. *Delinquency and Opportunity*, New York: Free Press.

Cohen, Albert K., 1955. *Delinquent Boys: The Culture of the Gang*, New York: Free Press.

5. JUVENILE JUSTICE

Datesman, Susan and Mikel Aickin, 1984, "Offense Specialization and Escalation Among Status Offenders," *Journal of Criminal Law and Criminology,* 75:1246–1275.

Davidson, Sue, ed. 1982. *Justice for Young Women.* Tucson, AZ; New Directions for Young Women.

DeJong, Allan R., Arturo R. Hervada, and Gary A. Emmett, 1983. "Epidemiologic Variations in Childhood Sexual Abuse," *Child Abuse and Neglect* 7:155–162.

Elliott, Delbert, David Huizinga, and Barbara Morse, 1987, "A Career Analysis of Serious Violent Offenders," In *Violent Juvenile Crime: What Can We Do About It?* edited by Ira Schwartz, Minneapolis, MN: Hubert Humphrey Institute.

Federal Bureau of Investigation, 1987. *Crime in the United States 1986,* Washington, DC; Government Printing Office.

Feinman, Clarice, 1980. *Women in the Criminal Justice System,* New York; Praeger.

Figueira-McDonough, Josefina, 1985. "Are Girls Different? Gender Discrepancies Between Delinquent Behavior and Control," *Child Welfare* 64:273–289.

———1986, "School Context, Gender, and Delinquency," *Journal of Youth and Adolescence* 15:79–98.

Finkelhor, David, 1982. "Sexual Abuse: A Sociological Perspective," *Child Abuse and Neglect* 6:95–102.

———and Larry Baron. 1986. "Risk Factors for Child Sexual Abuse," *Journal of Interpersonal Violence* 1:43–71.

Freedman, Estelle, 1981. *Their Sisters' Keepers,* Ann Arbor; University of Michigan Press.

Geltshorpe, Loraine, 1986. "Towards a Sceptical Look at Sexism," *International Journal of the Sociology of Law* 14:125–152.

Gora, JoAnn, 1982. *The New Female Criminal: Empirical Reality or Social Myth,* New York: Praeger.

Hagan, John, A. R. Gillis, and John Simpson, 1985. "The Class Structure of Gender and Delinquency: Toward a Power-Control Theory of Common Delinquent Behavior," *American Journal of Sociology* 90:1151–1178.

Hagan, John, John Simpson, and A. R. Gillis, 1987. "Class in the Household: A Power-Control Theory of Gender and Delinquency," *American Journal of Sociology* 92:788–816.

Hancock, Linda. 1981. "The Myth that Females are Treated More Leniently than Males in the Juvenile Justice System." *Australian and New Zealand Journal of Criminology* 16:4–14.

Harris, Anthony, 1977. "Sex and Theories of Deviance," *American Sociological Review* 42:3–16.

Herman, Jullia L. 1981. *Father-Daughter Incest.* Cambridge, MA; Harvard University Press.

Katz, Phyllis A. 1979. "The Development of Female Identity," In *Becoming Female: Perspectives on Development,* edited by Claire B. Kopp, New York; Plenum.

Koroki, Jan and Meda Chesney-Lind. 1985, *Everything Just Going Down the Drain.* Hawaii; Youth Development and Research Center.

Lerner, Gerda. 1986. *The Creation of Patriarchy.* New York: Oxford.

McCormack, Arlene, Mark-David Janus, and Ann Wolbert Burgess, 1986. "Runaway Youths and Sexual Victimization: Gender Differences In an Adolescent Runaway Population," *Child Abuse and Neglect* 10:387–395.

McGarrell, Edmund F. and Timothy J. Flanagan, eds. 1985. *Sourcebook of Criminal Justice Statistics—1984.* Washington, DC; Government Printing Office.

Meiselman, Karen. 1978. *Incest.* San Francisco: Jossey-Bass.

Merton, Robert K. 1938. "Social Structure and Anomie," *American Sociological Review* 3(October):672–782.

Messerschmidt, James, 1986. *Capitalism, Patriarchy, and Crime: Toward a Socialist Feminist Criminology,* Totowa, NJ: Rowman & Littlefield.

———1987. "Feminism, Criminology, and the Rise of the Female Sex Delinquent, 1880–1930," *Contemporary Crises* 11: 243–263.

Miller, Eleanor, 1986. *Street Woman,* Philadelphia: Temple University Press.

Miller, Walter B. 1958, "Lower Class Culture as the Generating Milieu of Gang Delinquency," *Journal of Social Issues* 14:5–19.

Morris, Ruth, 1964, "Female Delinquency and Relational Problems," *Social Forces* 43:82–89.

Mouzakitas, C. M. 1981, "An Inquiry into the Problem of Child Abuse and Juvenile Delinquency," In *Exploring the Relationship Between Child Abuse and Delinquency,* edited by R. J. Hunner and Y. E. Walkers, Montclair, NJ: Allanheld, Osmun.

National Female Advocacy Project, 1981. *Young Women and the Justice System: Basic Facts and Issues.* Tucson, AZ; New Directions for Young Women.

Office of Juvenile Justice and Delinquency Prevention, 1985. *Runaway Children and the Juvenile Justice and Delinquency Prevention Act: What is the Impact?* Washington, DC; Government Printing Office.

Opinion Research Corporation, 1982, "Public Attitudes Toward Youth Crime: National Public Opinion Poll." Mimeographed. Minnesota; Hubert Humphrey Institute of Public Affairs, University of Minnesota.

Peacock, Carol, 1981. *Hand Me Down Dreams.* New York: Shocken.

Phelps, R. J. et al. 1982. *Wisconsin Female Juvenile Offender Study Project Summary Report,* Wisconsin: Youth Policy and Law Center, Wisconsin Council of Juvenile Justice.

Platt, Anthony M. 1969. *The Childsavers,* Chicago: University of Chicago Press.

Pope, Carl and William H. Feyerherm. 1982. "Gender Bias in Juvenile Court Dispositions," *Social Service Review* 6:1–17.

Rafter, Nicole Hahn, 1985. *Partial Justice.* Boston: Northeastern University Press.

Reich, J. W. And S. E. Gutierres, 1979, "Escape/Aggression Incidence in Sexually Abused Juvenile Delinquents," *Criminal Justice and Behavior* 6:239–243.

Rogers, Kristine, 1972. "For Her Own Protection. . . . Conditions of Incarceration for Female Juvenile Offenders in the State of Connecticut," *Law and Society Review* (Winter):223–246.

Rosenberg, Debby and Carol Zimmerman, 1977. *Are My Dreams Too Much To Ask For?* Tucson, A. Z: New Directions for Young Women.

Russell, Diana E. 1986. *The Secret Trauma: Incest in the Lives of Girls and Women,* New York: Basic Books.

Schlossman, Steven and Stephanie Wallach, 1978. "The Crime of Precocious Sexuality: Female Juvenile Delinquency in the Progressive Era," *Harvard Educational Review* 48:65–94.

Shaw, Clifford R. 1930. *The Jack-Roller,* Chicago: University of Chicago Press.

———1938. *Brothers in Crime,* Chicago: University of Chicago Press.

———and Henry D. McKay, 1942. *Juvenile Delinquency in Urban Areas,* Chicago: University of Chicago Press.

Shelden, Randall, 1981. "Sex Discrimination in the Juvenile Justice System: Memphis, Tennessee, 1900–1917." In *Comparing Female and Male Offenders,* edited by Marguerite Q. Warren. Beverly Hills, CA: Sage.

———and John Horvath, 1986. "Processing Offenders in a Juvenile Court: A Comparison of Males and Females." Paper presented at the annual meeting of the Western Society of Criminology, Newport Beach, CA, February 27–March 2.

Silbert, Mimi and Ayala M. Pines, 1981. "Sexual Child Abuse as an Antecedent to Prostitution," *Child Abuse and Neglect* 5:407–411.

Simons, Ronald L., Martin G. Miller, and Stephen M. Aigner, 1980. "Contemporary Theories of Deviance and Female Delinquency: An Empirical Test," *Journal of Research in Crime and Delinquency* 17:42–57.

Smith, Lesley Shacklady, 1978. "Sexist Assumptions and Female Delinquency," In *Women, Sexuality and Social Control,* edited by Carol Smart and Barry Smart, London: Routledge & Kegan Paul.

Snyder, Howard N. and Terrence A. Finnegan, 1987. *Delinquency in the United States.* Washington, DC: Department of Justice.

Steffensmeier, Darrell J. 1980 "Sex Differences in Patterns of Adult Crime, 1965–1977," *Social Forces* 58:1080–1109.

Sutherland, Edwin, 1978. "Differential Association." in *Children of Ishmael: Critical Perspectives on Juvenile Justice,* edited by Barry Krisberg and James Austin. Palo Alto, CA: Mayfield.

Teilmann, Katherine S. and Pierre H. Landry, Jr. 1981. "Gender Bias in Juvenile Justice." *Journal of Research in Crime and Delinquency* 18:47–80.

Thrasher, Frederic M. 1927. *The Gang.* Chicago: University of Chicago Press.

Tracy, Paul E., Marvin E. Wolfgang, and Robert M. Figlio. 1985. *Delinquency in Two Birth Cohorts: Executive Summary.* Washington, DC: Department of Justice.

Widom, Cathy Spatz. 1988. "Child Abuse, Neglect, and Violent Criminal Behavior." Unpublished manuscript.

The Juvenile Court and the Role of the Juvenile Court Judge

Judge Leonard P. Edwards

Introduction

One of the principal tasks of a democratic society is to nurture its children to a successful, productive adult life. In the United States we rely primarily upon the family to provide to children most of what they need.

> *It is cardinal with us that the custody, care and nurture of the child reside first in the parents, whose primary function and free-dom include preparation for obligations the state can neither supply nor hinder.[1]*

Other institutions participate in the socialization process, notably schools, churches, and recreational groups, but the fundamental authority for child rearing resides with a child's family.

When the family fails or is unable to rear its child within acceptable norms, society has an interest in intervening to achieve its own goals. Dysfunctional families which are unable to raise their children within societal norms threaten the viability of the social order.[2]

Our legislatures and courts have recognized the importance of responding to family dysfunction. Numerous laws detail society's response to a family which cannot control a child's delinquent behavior, *a family which cannot adequately provide for a child, a family which cannot protect a child from abuse, or a family which cannot or refuses to educate its child.*

The ultimate authority for the resolution of these problems is the juvenile court. The person given the responsibility for carrying out the mandates of the legislature is the juvenile court judge. There are many other persons and institutions the child and family may encounter prior to reaching the court, but if all else fails, the legislatures in the United States have entrusted the authority to address the problems facing dysfunctional families and children to the juvenile court.

Our government's selection of the juvenile court as the institution to fulfill these functions raises a number of important questions:

> *Is the juvenile court a wise choice? Are there better alternatives than turning to the court system for the resolution of these problems? Are the tasks facing the juvenile court judge consistent with the traditional judicial role? Is the judiciary prepared to meet the challenges set by the legislature? What changes are necessary in the judiciary in order to meet these challenges?*

By Judge Leonard P. Edwards, "The Juvenile Court and the Role of the Juvenile Court Judge," Volume 43, No. 2. *Juvenile and Family Court Journal, National Council of Family Court Judges* (1992), pp. 1-2, 25-32. Reprinted by permission.

This paper . . . discusses the role of the juvenile court judge. . . .

[A] conclusion of this paper is that . . . the role of juvenile court judge must be recognized and supported by the judiciary and by the community. . . . Finally, it must be recognized by all that the juvenile court and the agencies serving it cannot alone solve the problems facing children and families in our society today. While the juvenile court must play a key leadership role, the

entire community must join in the efforts to support children and preserve families.

[Editor's Note: This article is part four of a six-part essay. Parts one, two, three, five, and six review the origin of the juvenile court, the status of and alternatives to the juvenile court, expectations fulfillment for the juvenile court judge, and, finally, the conclusion. These parts may be referenced in Volume 43, No. 2, 1992 edition of *Juvenile Family Court Journal.*]

IV. The Role of the Juvenile Court Judge

The most important person in the juvenile court is the juvenile court judge.[172] The descriptions of the different systems reveal the unique role of the juvenile court judge, a role that includes many non-traditional functions. The role of the juvenile court judge combines judicial, administrative, collaborative and advocacy components.

The most traditional role of the juvenile court judge is to decide the legal issues in each of the described categories of cases. The judge must determine issues such as whether certain facts are true, whether a child should be removed from a parent, what types of services should be offered to the family and whether the child should be returned to the family and the community or placed permanently in another setting.

Clearly these are critical decisions, not only for the family before the court, but also for society. Given the importance of the family in the United States, such determinations have profound implications for the manner in which families will

survive. Juvenile court judges are the gatekeepers for systems which incarcerate society's youth and place society's children in foster care. Their decisions provide a measure of our society's confidence in the viability of the family.

Moreover, the attitude of the juvenile court judge will significantly influence the manner in which others view children before the court. An exchange in the Manhattan Family Court reflects one way in which the court can have an impact upon the care of children. The father's attorney commented on the conditions in the home for seventeen adopted children (urine smell, limited food, poor lighting, no bed sheets).

> It may not be the best of care out in Nassau County, but the children are surviving. They're doing okay.

> The judge responded: I don't want the children to survive. I want them to thrive.[173]

Juvenile court judges' decisions also set standards within the community and in the systems connected to the court. The juvenile court judge who removes a child for selling drugs, who refuses to hear a truancy petition because it is not important enough or who returns a child to her family in spite of drug abuse by one of the family members is setting standards which may have a significant impact on how police, probation, social services and other service providers respond to similar cases in the future. Unless an appellate court overturns these decisions, the standards set in the juvenile court will remain as the community's standards for these types of cases.

As an integral part of the decision-making process, the judge must make certain that the parties appearing before the court receive the legal and constitutional rights to which they are entitled. These rights include notice of the legal proceedings, the right to have counsel, and counsel at state expense in many situations,[174] the right to a hearing, to confront and cross examine witnesses, the right to remain silent and the right to a timely hearing on the truth of the allegations. In many cases the court must make certain that families have been provided with services before formal legal action was initiated. With regard to many of these rights, it is the duty of the judge to determine in court whether the party understands the right and wishes to exercise or waive it.

The role of the juvenile court judge includes ensuring that the systems which detect, investigate, resolve and bring cases to court are working efficiently and fairly and that adequate resources exist to respond to the caseloads. For example, the juvenile court judge must ensure that there are enough judicial officers to complete the work of the court.[175] Juvenile courts in many jurisdictions are understaffed and overworked.[176] Within the judiciary it is often difficult to persuade those judicial officers with administrative responsibility that the juvenile court must have sufficient judicial resources to manage the caseloads.[177] Sometimes this lack of judicial resources exists throughout the judiciary,[178] but more frequently the juvenile court receives fewer positions because it is perceived as less important.[179] The problem has been exacerbated with the marked increase in dependency cases over the past five years.[180] In the wake of the higher child abuse and neglect reports, dependency caseloads have risen several-fold. Many juvenile court judges have been struggling with local governments to secure adequate judicial resources to manage the new demands upon the juvenile courts.

Judicial officers cannot function without adequate staff and space. Juvenile courts often find themselves with inadequate staff to meet the legal mandates set by the legislature.[181] The juvenile court judge must work with other branches of government to make certain each is available for the court.

Judges do not work in a vacuum. They learn of the situation facing children and their families from the legal proceedings, the reports from social service agencies, probation departments and from the parties and their attorneys. The quality of a judge's decision about children and their families is directly related to the quality of information the judge receives. Our legal system is built upon a process in which attorneys for the parties are given the duty to present evidence to the court and to test any evidence presented from other sources. From the different perspectives of the parties, the court is able to determine what happened and what should be done.

An important role for the juvenile court judge is to make certain that there are adequate numbers of attorneys of satisfactory quality to complete the work of the court.[182] The juvenile court judge must work with the funding authorities to supply these attorneys and to ensure they are trained. Dependency cases are particularly expensive for the government, as attorneys and guardians ad litem[183] may represent the state or petitioning party, the child and each parent if there is a conflict of interest. Compared to civil cases, in which the government supplies no attorneys, the juvenile court is an expensive operation.

The role of the juvenile court judge as the provider of due process and the role as fiscal manager may be in conflict in one or more of these areas. Providing free attorneys for accused delinquents has never been politically popular, and funders demand to know why every accused delinquent child needs to have an attorney. It is no wonder that some juvenile court judges do not appoint counsel for children in every case[184] or are perceived as favoring waiver of that right.[185]

Similarly, in dependency cases, if the government represents both the petitioner and the child, or if one attorney represents both parents, it would save the cost of an attorney, but it may mean that the remaining attorney has conflicting positions to represent to the court. Juvenile court judges understandably have taken different sides of this debate.[186]

The juvenile court also has the responsibility

of setting the standards by which the juvenile system will be governed. In this way the court provides leadership both to the community and to all participants in the juvenile court system.[187] Cases which do not reach the court but which are resolved by police, probation, social workers or the prosecutor also come under the purview of the juvenile court judge. Only the most serious cases should reach the juvenile court. The majority of cases should be resolved fairly and efficiently by other agencies. It is the role of the juvenile court judge to ensure that this process is implicitly fair to all parties.[188]

> The presiding judge of the juvenile court shall initiate meetings and cooperate with the probation department, welfare department, prosecuting attorney, law enforcement, and other persons and agencies performing an intake function to establish and maintain a fair and efficient intake program designed to promote swift and objective evaluation of the circumstances of any referral and to pursue an appropriate course of action.[189]

The juvenile court judge must know how cases which do not reach the juvenile court are being resolved. What types of alternative dispute resolution techniques are being employed and by whom? What standards do police, probation and prosecution utilize and under what authority? Some may argue that such comprehensive knowledge is unnecessary. Upon reflection, however, it becomes clear that the public holds the juvenile court judge accountable for the failings in a system over which he or she presides.[190]

After the court has made its dispositional orders, it must also monitor the progress of the child, the family and the supervising agency to make certain that each one carries out the terms of its orders.[191] This is no easy task. For the court to monitor services effectively, the judge must become knowledgeable about the services available in the community as well as services which should be available.[192] Review hearings provide one vehicle for the court to assess the situation from month to month. While in all types of juvenile cases reviews are a sound judicial policy, in dependency matters the legislature has mandated judges to review regularly the status of children in placement. This judicial review is the principal mechanism ensuring reunification services are being provided and for preventing unnecessarily long placements and

unnecessary movements of children from home to home, so-called foster care drift.

In some jurisdictions the juvenile court judge is the administrator of the juvenile probation department and court staff who work in the juvenile justice system.[193] This administrative oversight may include responsibility over court personnel including other judges, referees, attorneys, social investigators, clerical workers, support personnel, psychologists, psychiatrists and physicians. The role may also include supervision of the operation of foster homes, detention facilities, the court clinic and aftercare facilities. The juvenile court judge may also have some responsibility for the management of financial services. This administrative role will necessarily take time from the judge's judicial duties. It may also expose the judge to liability for administrative errors such as overcrowding of the juvenile detention facility.[194] On the other hand, the juvenile court judge as administrator is ideally situated to coordinate services between the court and probation departments.[195]

Some critics have argued that this administrative role is inappropriate for the juvenile court judge.[196] Other commentators assert that probation services should be under juvenile court control. They point out that probation is an integral part of the judicial function in the juvenile court and that the juvenile court judge has an interest in maintaining a satisfactory level of service.[197] In some states the juvenile court has no administrative oversight of probation services, while in some states the court has limited control over the selection and administration of probation services.[198] Ironically, as Joseph White points out,

> [w]hichever structure the interested reader may consider . . . certain factors . . . have critical impact. These include the amount of money available for these services, the quality of the personnel with which the system is staffed, and the personal leadership of the judiciary in stimulating community interest and support. Each of these attributes is a *sine qua non* of good services, regardless of the formal administrative structure.[199]

Beyond the confines of the courtroom and the boundaries of the delinquency and dependency systems, the juvenile court judge has an even broader role: providing to the community information about how well the juvenile court is completing the tasks assigned to it.[200] The juvenile court judge both informs and advocates within the community on behalf of children and their families.[201] No other person has the position, perspective or the prestige to speak on behalf of the children and families whose problems are so serious that they must come before the juvenile court. Because of confidentiality laws which restrict the flow of information about most juvenile court cases, it is critical that the juvenile court judge ensure that information about the juvenile court system is made available to the public. Only in this way will the public receive a balanced view of the work of the juvenile court and not rely solely on the spectacular headlines which appear at regular intervals.[202]

> The court must be open to the public and engaged in a continuous dialogue with the public regarding children, parenting, the responsibility of the institutions surrounding children, the responsibilities of the public, and how the court acquits itself of its own responsibilities.[203]

This public role also includes commenting on and, if necessary, drafting legislation which the judge believes is necessary to complete the work of the juvenile court. It is remarkable that juvenile court legislation is often written without significant input from the juvenile court judiciary and that in some jurisdictions juvenile court judges are among the last to learn of legislative changes in their court system. Those states with Juvenile Court Judges Associations have had a much greater impact upon state legislation dealing with juvenile court than those states which have not.[204]

The juvenile court judge has a public role beyond providing information to the community. The judge must also take action to ensure that the necessary community resources are available so that the children and families which come before the court can be well-served.[205] This may be the most untraditional role for the juvenile court judge, but it may be the most important.[206]

What should the judge do when drug counseling is ordered and no drug counseling exists in the community? What should the judge do when a child could be safely returned home if reasonable services were available for the family, but no such services exist? Should the juvenile court judge simply rule on the case before the court and remain indifferent or inactive with regards to the results after the court order has been made?

The clear message from legislators and judges alike is to take action in order to address the deficiencies within the various juvenile court systems.

> Judges should take an active part in the formation of a community-wide, multi-disciplinary "Constituency for Children" to promote and unify private and public sector efforts to focus attention and resources on meeting the needs of deprived children who have no effective voice of their own.[207]

Juvenile court judges have heeded these calls to organize within their own communities. They convene meetings of private and public sector leaders, multi-disciplinary task forces and community-based organizations and provide the information and the leadership to join in concerted efforts to preserve and strengthen families.

Their effectiveness has been noteworthy.[208] In 1978 David Soukoup, a King County, Washington juvenile court judge, asked volunteers within his community to assist abused and neglected children as they went through the dependency court process. His initiative started the Court Appointed Special Advocate Program (CASA), a nationwide endeavor which now has hundreds of programs and over 28,000 volunteers.[209] Other judges have been noteworthy for their leadership in initiating change within their court systems.[210]

In Jefferson Parish, Gretna, Louisiana, Judge Thomas P. McGee used his position as chief judge of the juvenile court to organize within his community on behalf of the children and families who appear in his court. Under his leadership the juvenile court was able to develop a system to detect learning disabilities in children who appeared before the juvenile court and ensure that each was properly educated. He has helped other juvenile court judges and communities organize effective responses for learning disabled children. His successes in his own court and nationally are based upon his belief in judges becoming catalysts for reform.[211]

A Nevada Juvenile Court judge, Judge Charles McGee, was instrumental in creating the Children's Cabinet. A private, non-profit organization, the Children's Cabinet is intended to "fill the gaps" between existing services to children in Nevada and lead in the identification of new programs and resources for families. In its first five years of existence, through the development of new programs this unique public-private venture has served thousands of families.

Among its many programs the cabinet has developed the Truancy Center, the School Early Intervention Program, the Homeless Youth Project and Northern Nevada's first Family preservation program. While volunteers are a critical component in all of its efforts, the Cabinet has sponsored some programs which are managed and staffed exclusively by volunteers. In 1989 the Cabinet published "Nevada's Children: Our Most Precious Resource?", a collection of statistics and information about Nevada's children. Its efforts have added greatly to the lives of children and families in Northern Nevada.[212]

In 1953 in Oakland County, Michigan, Chief Judge Eugene Arthur Moore convened a small group of citizens and community leaders to develop a community-based prevention program. By 1984 there were 26 locally-based youth assistance programs in Oakland County. In 1989 more than 47,000 county residents voluntarily participated in Youth Assistance Primary Prevention programs. The program has been so successful it received the Kendall I. Lingle Community Resources Award from the National Council of Juvenile and Family Court Judges in 1991.[213]

In 1985 in San Bernardino County, California, Juvenile Court Presiding Judge Patrick Morris convened a county-wide meeting of private and public sector persons interested in working on behalf of children. The result was the creation of the Children's Network, now in its seventh year of coordinating agencies, professionals, businesses and citizens and developing resources on behalf of children.[214] Many other examples exist in juvenile courts throughout the country.[215]

Perhaps the best formal expression of the full role of the juvenile court judge was recently adopted by the California Judicial Council. In Rule 24 the Judicial Council wrote that juvenile court judges are encouraged to:

(1) Provide active leadership within the community in determining the needs and obtaining and developing resources and services for at-risk children and families. At-risk children include delinquent, dependent and status offenders.

(2) Investigate and determine the availability of specific prevention, intervention and treatment services in the community for at-risk children and their families.

(3) Exercise their authority by statute or rule to review, order and enforce the delivery of specific services and treatment for children at risk and their families.

(4) Exercise a leadership role in the development and maintenance of permanent programs of interagency cooperation and coordination among the court and the various public agencies that serve at-risk children and their families.

(5) Take an active part in the formation of a community-wide network to promote and unify private and public sector efforts to focus attention and resources for at-risk children and their families.

(6) Maintain close liaison with school authorities and encourage coordination of policies and programs.

(7) Educate the community and its institutions through every available means including the media concerning the role of the juvenile court in meeting the complex needs of at-risk children and their families.

(8) Evaluate the criteria established by child protection agencies for initial removal and reunification decisions and communicate the court's expectations of what constitutes "reasonable efforts" to prevent removal or hasten return of the child.

(9) Encourage the development of community services and resources to assist homeless, truant, runaway and incorrigible children.

(10) Be familiar with all detention facilities, placements and institutions used by the court.

(11) Act in all instances consistently with the public safety and welfare.[216]

Other commentators support this description.[217]

All of these activities may be necessary if the juvenile court judge is going to make it possible for the juvenile court to be an effective institution. Given the nontraditional aspect of many of these tasks, there are numerous challenges facing the judiciary both to educate and socialize juvenile court judges with regard to their distinctive role.

FOOTNOTES

1. " . . . the state's assertion of authority [over the general welfare of children] . . . is no mere corporate concern of official authority. It is the interest of youth itself, and of the whole community, that children be both safeguarded from abuses and given opportunities for growth into free and independent . . . citizens." *Prince v. Massachusetts*, 321 U.S. 158 (1941), citing *Pierce v. Society of Sisters*, 268 U.S. 510.

2. "The costs of such failed socialization is not immediately apparent except in the case of those physically abused and neglected. Further, payment for the failure is deferred and at the same time remote from many people in society, especially those with power. Nonetheless, few would disagree that the price is enormous." "Conclusion" by Francis Hartman, *From Children to Citizen II, The Role of the Juvenile Court*, ed. Francis Hartmann, N.Y.: Springer-Verlag (1987)385. See also "The High Cost of Failure," Chapter One in "Beyond Rhetoric: A New American Agenda for Children and Families," *Final Report of the National Commission on Children*, Washington, D.C. (1991)3-13.

172. "But within the juvenile court itself the judge, regardless of ability, holds the highest status. The judge is the ultimate decision-maker. The coterie of probation, social service, legal and clerical attendants rivet their eyes and ears on his nonverbal language and his utterances." Rubin, H. Ted., *Juvenile Justice: Policy, Practice and Law, op cit.* footnote 45, at p. 351. "From this it should be clear that the judges, and particularly the chief judge, occupy the crucial formal decision-making positions with regard both to individual cases and their disposition, and to procedural, administrative, and program policy." *Judging Delinquents* by Robert Emerson, Aldine Publishing Company, Chicago (1969) 13.

173. Dugger, C. W., "Care Ordered for Children in Abuse Cases," *The New York Times*, 29 May 1991, section B, p. 1.

174. Children in delinquency cases are entitled to counsel at state expense. *In re Gault, op cit* footnote 3. Parents in those proceedings are entitled to have counsel, but normally not at state expense. In addition there is usually a prosecutor who brings the petition before the juvenile court. Most states have the same rules for status offense cases. In dependency matters, the parents usually have the right to counsel at state expense. The child will have a guardian ad litem, who may be an attorney, a volunteer, or both. In addition there will usually be an attorney who brings the legal action on behalf of the state.

175. "Judicial Authority and Responsibility: 18 Recommendations on Issues in Delinquency and Abuse/Neglect Dispositions," National Council of Juvenile and Family Court Judges, Reno (1989) at p. 7: "Juvenile and family courts must have an adequate number of qualified judicial officers and other court personnel available to assure the optimum handling of each individual case."

176. The present system permits overloading of non-jury calendars. Because the family (juvenile) courts are non-jury courts, there is almost no limit to the number of non-jury matters than might be assigned to those courts." Senate Task Force on Family Relations Court, Final Report, Sacramento (1990), pp. 8-10. Also see *In re Ashley K., op. cit.* footnote 145.

177. *Ibid.* at p. 4.

178. Lucas, Malcolm M., "Is Inadequate Funding Threatening Our System of Justice?" *Judicature* 74.6 (April–May 1991) 292.

179. Senate Task Force on Family Relations Court, Final Report, *op. cit.* footnote 176, at p. 4, and see Section V. A. *infra* on the "structure of the Court System."

180. Gomby and Shiono, *The Future of Children, op. cit.* footnote 103.

181. Senate Task Force on Family Relations Court, Final Report, *op. cit.* footnote 176, at p. 2 and *In re Ashley K, op. cit.* footnote 145, in which the Appellate Court noted: "All other considerations aside, and there are many, humaneness and plain common sense make it imperative that there be proper judicial case management in child custody cases in Cook County, and that there be a sufficient number of judges to cope with the number of cases in the system" at p. 17.

182. The court should "establish a training program for attorneys representing parents and children and require attorneys who are appointed by the court to attend this program." *Making Reasonable Efforts, op. cit.* footnote 161, at p. 62. And see McCullough, *op. cit.* footnote 152, at p. 59.

183. Since the passage of the Child Abuse Prevention and Treatment Act of 1974 (P.L. 93-247) as a condition of states receiving federal funds, the juvenile court must appoint a guardian ad litem to represent a child in child abuse or neglect cases that result in a judicial proceeding. 42, U.S.C., Paragraph 5103(b)(2)(G)(1976). For a summary of the ways in which each state has responded to the federal mandate see National Study of Guardian ad Litem Representation, Administration for Children, Youth and Families, Office of Human Development Services, U.S. Department of Health and Human Services, CSR, Inc., Washington, D.C. (1990).

184. See Feld, Barry, "The Right to Counsel In Juvenile Court: An Empirical Study of When Lawyers Appear and the Differences They Make," 79 *J.Crim.L. & Criminology, op. cit.* footnote 114, pp. 1185-1346, and Schwartz, *op. cit.* footnote 66 at pp. 40-51.

185. See Schwartz, *op. cit.* footnote 66, at pp. 152-158; Feld, Barry C., "The Juvenile Court Meets the Principal of the Office: Legislative Changes in Juvenile Waiver Statutes," *Journal of Criminal Law and Criminology* 78.3, *op. cit.* footnote 39, at pp. 471-533.

Rubin agrees with Schwartz in asserting that a child in a delinquency proceeding should have an unwaivable right to an attorney. Rubin, *op. cit.* footnote 45, at p. 403.

The author prefers rigorous questioning of the child to the unwaivable right to counsel suggested by Schwartz and Rubin. In Santa Clara County the juvenile court judges have an elaborate *voir dire* which stresses the importance of the legal proceedings and the need for counsel. Only if the child can give intelligent responses to the court's inquiry will a waiver be accepted. Often it is the parent advising the child that an attorney is unnecessary and in that situation the court must be prepared to engage the parents in the waiver discussion. More than 95% of the children in delinquency proceedings are represented by attorneys in this county.

Of course, if the jurisdiction has no resources to employ counsel, the judge may be less willing to engage in this type of *voir dire*. The judge will first have to devise a strategy on how to secure sufficient attorneys for the juvenile court. See the suggestions in footnote 127 and Resources discussion in Part V, *supra*.

186. Different jurisdictions handle this representation in different ways. In some an attorney is appointed to represent the dependent child in every case (Santa Clara County and San Mateo County in California are examples). In other jurisdictions an attorney is appointed to represent the child on a case-by-case basis. This seems to be the minimal requirement of independent representation as stated by the appellate court in the case of *In re Patricia E.* (1985) 175 Cal.App.3d 1. Also see *Making Reasonable Efforts, op. cit.*, footnote 161, at pp. 31-32.

187. "Toward Juvenile Justice" by mark Harrison Moore, in *From Children to Citizens, op. cit.* footnote 7, at p. 177.

188. "Court-Approved Alternative Dispute Resolution: A Better Way to Resolve Minor Delinquency, Status Offense and Abuse/Neglect Cases, *op. cit.* footnote 76, at pp. 4-7 and 25-28. In some states the juvenile court has the obligation to respond to

the needs of children and order both legal intervention and services. Thus, when a local social services department was unwilling to file dependency proceedings to protect a child living in a harmful environment, the judge ordered the agency to file a petition. See *People in the Interest of R. E.* 729 P.2d 1032 (Colo.App.1986) and *In the Interest of J. H.,* 770 P.2d 1355 (Colo.App.1989). In California, a juvenile court judge dismissed a dependency petition after evidence showed a child had been abused in the family home, but stated he was unsure as to the person responsible for the abuse. The Court of Appeals reversed the trial court and ruled that the juvenile court must take jurisdiction of a child under those circumstances. *In re Christina T.,* 184 Cal.App.3d 650, 229 Cal.Rptr.247 (1986). See "The Court: A Child's Last Hope for Protection" by Sue Pachota, *The Rocky Mountain Child Advocate* 1.2 (June/July 1991) at pp. 4–5.

189. Rule 1404(a) Juvenile Court Rules, West's California Juvenile Laws and Court Rules (1991).

190. See *Deprived Children: A Judicial Response, op. cit.* footnote 144, at p. 10. "The public reasonably expects the judiciary is, or ought to be, ultimately accountable for what happens to abused or neglected children who are reported to or handled by government agencies."

191. Jones, Judge William G., "The Special Responsibilities of Juvenile Court Judges," *The Rocky Mountain Child Advocate* 1.2 (June/July 1991) 3.

192. "Monitoring services" is itself a catch-all describing a number of important responsibilities. These have been summarized as requiring the juvenile judge to:

(1) Know what child welfare and family preservation services are available in the community and the problems that can be addressed by these services;

(2) Know which agencies and individuals are responsible for developing policies and providing services to children in the community;

(3) Understand child development and, in particular, the importance of attachment and bonding and the effects of separation on young children;

(4) Encourage the child welfare agency to prevent unnecessary removal by using services to protect children instead of resorting to removal of the child from the home;

(5) Encourage the development of cooperative agreements between law enforcement bodies and the child welfare agency so that law enforcement officers do not remove children from their homes without prior consultation and coordination with the agency;

(6) Be aware of the child welfare agency's performance in providing preventative and reunification services, as well as its rules and regulations on providing these services, and monitor the agency's compliance with the reasonable efforts requirement;

(7) Ensure that the child welfare agency is aware that the failure to make reasonable efforts will result in a failure to receive federal reimbursement;

(8) Establish a training program for all attorneys representing parents and children and require attorneys who are appointed by the court to attend this program;

(9) Be aware of local experts who can testify on the reasonableness and appropriateness of services provided to keep a child in the home and what harm, if any, a child will experience if removed from the home or continued in an out-of-home placement; and

(10) Monitor the court's own record on compliance with the reasonable efforts requirement by monitoring court of appeals' affirmances or reversals of decisions on reasonable efforts.

Making Reasonable Efforts: Steps for Keeping Families Together, The Edna McConnell Clark Foundation, *op. cit.* footnote 161, pp. 41–59.

193. In 22 states and the District of Columbia probation services are administered either by the local juvenile court or by the state administrative office of the courts. In 14 states probation administration is divided between judicial and executive branches. In other states probation is administered either exclusively from the state, from county government or a split between county and state executive branch departments. See "Organization and Administration of Juvenile Services: Probation, Aftercare, and State Delinquent Institutions," Patricia McFall Torbet, Pittsburgh, National Center for Juvenile Justice (1990) at p. iv.

194. See *Doe v. County of Lake, Indian* (1975) 399 F.Supp.553 and *Santiago v. City of Philadelphia* (1977) 435 F.Supp.136, 146.

195. See Rubin, *op. cit.* footnote 45, at pp. 358–359.

196. "The Constitutionality of Juvenile Court Administration of Court Services" by David Gilman in *Major Issues in Juvenile Justice Information and Training,* Columbus, OH, Academy for Contemporary Problems, (1981) 465–474. "Courts as Social Service Agencies: An Idea Carried to Its Illogical Extension" by Jack D. Foster, pp. 475–490. National Advisory Commission on Criminal Justice Standards and Goals, *Corrections* (Washington, D.C.: Government Printing Office, 1973), Standards 8.2, 10.1, 16.4; Institute of Judicial Administration–American Bar Association, *Court Organization and Administration,* Standard 1.2; National Advisory Committee on Criminal Justice Standards and Goals, *Juvenile Justice and Delinquency Prevention,* Standard 19.2; National Advisory Committee for Juvenile Justice and Delinquency Prevention, *Standards for the Administration of Juvenile Justice,* Standards 3.14, 4.1.

197. "The Juvenile court's Administrative Responsibilities," by Holland M. Gary, pp. 337–342, and Rubin, *op. cit.* footnote 45, at pp. 358–359.

198. Torbet, *op. cit.* footnote 193, at pp. 2–13.

199. White, Joseph L., "Major Issues in Juvenile Justice Information and Training: Services to Children in Juvenile Courts: The Judicial-Executive Controversy," Columbus, Ohio, Academy for Contemporary Problems (1981), cited in Torbet, *op. cit.* footnote 193, at p. i.

200. "To protect the institution, to maintain a proper accountability relationship to the community and to the law, and to strengthen the overall capacity of the community to rear children, the judges of the juvenile court must be prepared to exercise leadership by explaining what the court stands for, why it is making the decisions it is making, and what these decisions imply for the conduct of others. This is how legal values acquire social force and standing." Moore, *op. cit.* footnote 7, at p. 181.

201. "The juvenile court judge of the future will be something special. His skill as a jurist will be secondary to his ability to motivate the community behind juvenile causes." "The Juvenile Justice System: Vision for the Future" by Seymour Gelber, *Juvenile and Family Court Journal* (1990), op.cit. footnote 105, pp. 15–18, at p. 18.

202. "As Mother Killed Her Son, Protectors Observed Privacy" by Celia W. Dugger, *The New York Times* 10 Feb. 1992, at p. A1 and A16; "Child Deaths Reveal Failings of System by Celia W. Dugger, *The New York Times* 23 Jan. 1992.

203. Harmann, *op. cit.* footnote 2 at p. 390.

204. Perhaps the most outstanding example of a juvenile court judges association in the United States is the Juvenile Court Judges' Commission in the Commonwealth of Pennsylvania. Established by the Pennsylvania Legislature in 1959, its members are nominated by the Chief Justice of the Pennsylvania Supreme Court and appointed by the Governor for three-year terms. The Commission is responsible for:

(1) Advising juvenile courts concerning the proper care and maintenance of delinquent children;

(2) Establishing standards governing the administrative practices and judicial procedures used in juvenile courts;

(3) Establishing personnel practices and employment standards used in probation offices;

(4) Collecting, compiling and publishing juvenile court statistics; and

(5) Administering a Grant-In-Aid program to improve country juvenile probation services.

The commission also serves as the liaison between the juvenile courts and the Legislature to ensure passage of legislation that is in the best interest of all children coming within the jurisdiction of the court. It provides a monthly newsletter, an annual report and numerous other publications and offers training for judges and probation staff throughout the state.

All significant legislation relating to children who come before the juvenile court in Pennsylvania is either drafted, suggested or supported by the Commission. For example refer to the testimony of Hon. R. Stanton Wettinck, Jr., and James E. Anderson before the Joint State Government Commission, Task Force of Services to Children, September 11, 1990. The legislative program was recognized by the National Council of Juvenile and Family Court Judges in 1987 as being the nation's most outstanding program.

For further information contact the Juvenile Court Judges' Commission, P.O. Box 3222, Harrisburg, PA 17105-3222.

205. "Juvenile and family court judges should play a leadership role in working with key people from all three branches of government, law enforcement, public health, medical, drug treatment service providers, social service workers, and the private sector to develop a comprehensive continuum of family-focused, multi-disciplinary drug treatment and family strengthening services." *Protocol for Making Reasonable Efforts in Drug-Related Dependency Cases, op. cit.* footnote 86 at p. 4.

206. "He can't go out on the street corner and compete with the Salvation Army. But he can appoint a strong citizens' committee, composed of community leaders interested in youth, as an Advisory Council. He can regularly attend its meetings and invite its members individually to attend court hearings, to visit existing facilities—both state and local—to examine some case histories (both successful and unsuccessful); and he can suggest to them important community goals. Perhaps some static will crackle, perhaps a little unpleasant gas will escape to assault the community's olfactory nerve—and all to the good. What is there to fear? Many of us juvenile court judges have 'resources' that couldn't be worse." "The Juvenile Court Examines Itself" by Judge William S. Fort, *NPPA Journal* 5, 404–413, at p. 411.

207. *Deprived Children, op. cit.* footnote 144, at p. 12. "Juvenile and family court judges should play a leadership role in working with key people from all three branches of government, law enforcement, public health, medical, drug treatment providers, social service workers, and the private sector to develop a comprehensive continuum of family-focused, multi-disciplinary drug treatment and family strengthening services. *Protocol for Making Reasonable Efforts in Drug-Related Dependency Cases, op. cit.* footnote 86, at p. 4.

208. Yet many juvenile judges rise to the challenge and do remarkable jobs. Procedural safeguards and due process rights for juveniles are scrupulously observed in their courts. These judges always are seeking better means of detention and reserve the use of correctional institutions as a last resort. They are very committed, work long hours, and sometimes pass up promotions to more highly paid judgeships with greater prestige. The result is that these judges usually change the quality of juvenile justice in their communities." Clemens Bartollas, *Juvenile Delinquency,* MacMillan, New York (1985) 456.

209. See *Advocating for the Child in Protection Proceedings* by Donald N. Duquette, Lexington Books, Lexington, MA (1990) 1–11. For more information on the National CASA Association, write to: National CASA Association, 2722 Eastlake Avenue East, Suite 220, Seattle, Washington 99102.

210. For example see "Family Court Reform in Six Pennsylvania Counties: Profiles of Judges as Reform Activists," Mastrofski, Jennifer, *Family and Conciliation Courts Review* 29.2 (Apr. 1991) 129–149. "Judge Ernestine Gray throws the book at young offenders—and then expects them to read it" by Sylvia Whitman, *Student Lawyer* (Apr. 1987) 12–13. For different examples of juvenile court judges, their backgrounds and accomplishments see *Behind the Black Robes: Juvenile Court Judges and the Court,* by Rubin, H. Ted, Beverly Hills, Sage Library of Social Research (1985).

211. "Preventing Juvenile Crime: What a Judge Can Do" by Judge Thomas P. McGee, *The Judges' Journal* 24 (1986), at pp. 20–23 and 51–52. Also see *Learning Disabilities and the Juvenile Justice System,* by John B. Sikorsky, M.D. and Judge Thomas P. McGee, National Council of Juvenile and Family Court Judges, Reno (1986).

212. For further information about the Children's Cabinet, contact Judge Charles McGee or Executive Director Sheila Leslie at The Children's Cabinet, 1090 S. Rock Blvd., Reno, Nevada, 89502, (702) 785-4000.

213. For further information contact Chief Judge Eugene Arthur Moore, Probate Court, County of Oakland, 1200 N. Telegraph Road, Pontiac, Michigan 48341-1043.

214. For more information about the Children's Network write: Children's Network, County Government Center, 2nd Floor, 385 North Arrowhead Avenue, San Bernardino, California 92415-0121, (714) 387-8966.

215. For example, Kids in Common, Santa Clara County, California (write c/o Supervisor Dianne McKenna, Board of Supervisors, 70 West Hedding Street, San Jose, California 95110).

216. Standards of Judicial Administration Recommended by the Judicial Council, Rule 24, Juvenile Matters, West (1991). Not all states have identified the role of the juvenile court judge as broadly as California. In some the juvenile court judge may feel constrained by ethical considerations to refrain from some of these activities. Nevertheless, the California Rule is the trend throughout the United States, as the following statements indicate: "I am extremely impressed by the 'Appendix to California Rules of Court Division I: Standards of Judicial Administration' and think they should be given wide dissemination among juvenile and family court judges. . . . If these rules could be adopted everywhere, they would go a long way to resolving the conflicts now experienced, and toward improving the administration of juvenile and family justice." Mark Harrison Moore, Review of "Resolving the Ethical, Moral and Social Mandates of the Juvenile and Family Court," Memo to Hunter Hurst, Pittsburgh, National Center for Juvenile Justice (1990).

217. "Judges must assert community leadership for prevention and treatment of substance abuse among juveniles and their families." *Drugs—The American Family in Crisis,* NCJFCJ, Reno, NV (1989), at p. 25. Judges must provide leadership within the community in determining needs and developing resources and services for deprived children and families. Judges must encourage cooperation and coordination among the courts and various public and private agencies with responsibilities for deprived children. Juvenile and family courts must maintain close liaison and encourage coordination of policies with school authorities. Judges should take an active part in the formation of a community-wide, multi-disciplinary "Constituency for Children" to promote and unify private and public sector efforts to focus attention and resources on meeting the needs of deprived children who have no effective voice of their own. *Recommendations 1, 3, 5, and 7, Deprived Children: A Judicial Response, op. cit.* footnote 144.

Kids, Guns, and Killing Fields

James D. Wright, Joseph F. Sheley, and M. Dwayne Smith

James D. Wright is the Charles and Leo Favrot Professor of Human Relations in the department of sociology at Tulane University. He has written widely on problems of firearms and gun control, including two books. His is currently researching the effect of poverty on the urban underclass, alcohol and drug treatment programs for the homeless, and health and other social problems of street children in Latin America.

Joseph F. Sheley is associate professor of sociology at Tulane University. His most recent book is Criminology: A Contemporary Handbook. *He is currently working on a book about firearms and juveniles.*

M. Dwayne Smith is associate professor of sociology at Tulane University. He has written widely on such topics as understanding differences in rates of violent crime among various sub-population in the United States.

A plague of youth violence seems to be sweeping the nation. The number of juveniles, eighteen and under, who are arrested annually for murder increased by nearly a quarter between 1983 and 1988 and then increased again by nearly half between 1988 and 1990. Indeed, homicide is now the leading cause of death for black males aged fourteen to forty-four and the reduction of violence among youths has become a leading public health goal. Incidents that would have seemed shocking and inexplicable just a few years ago—gang warfare, drive-by slayings, wanton brutality, in-school shootings—have somehow become commonplaces of urban existence.

Among the many questions that might be asked about violence committed by and against youths is where and how do these youths obtain firearms? Federal law (the Gun Control Act of 1968) prohibits direct sale of handguns to persons under the age of twenty-one and sale of shoulder weapons to those under eighteen. These provisions have evidently not prevented large numbers of youths from obtaining sophisticated, high-quality guns. How prevalent has gun-carrying become among youths in the central cities? What are the methods and sources by which guns are obtained? Is there anything to be learned about the details of youthful gun acquisition that would be useful in getting them to stop it?

For the past two years, we have been involved in research designed to provide some preliminary answers to these and related questions. We have undertaken extensive surveys concerning firearms and firearms behaviors among two groups of youth: 835 criminally active youth (all males, mostly from large cities) currently serving time in six maximum-security juvenile corrections facilities in four states, and 1,653 students (males and females) in ten inner-city public high schools in five large cities near the six correctional facilities.

Characteristically, our sample is predominantly non-white, poorly educated, average age in the late teens; most respondents are correctly described as inner-city, non-white poor. The four states where we did the research were California, Louisiana, Illinois, and New Jersey; the specific cities where we surveyed were large cities with well-publicized youth violence problems.

Gun Possession

Eighty-six percent of incarcerated juveniles owned at least one firearm at some time in their lives; 83 percent owned a gun at the time they were incarcerated. Of those who had ever owned a gun, two-thirds acquired their first firearm by the age of fourteen. A large majority (73 percent) had owned three or more types of guns; nearly two-thirds (65 percent) owned at least three firearms just before being jailed. In short, the tendency is for these young inmates to have owned guns in both quantity and variety.

Among the incarcerated youths, the revolver was the most commonly owned weapon; 72 percent had owned a revolver at some time in their lives and 58 percent owned one at the time of their current incarceration. Next in popularity was the automatic or semi-automatic pistol, typically chambered for 9 mm or .45 caliber rounds. Two-thirds of the sample had owned such a gun at some time; 55 percent owned one at the time of their incarceration. For more "serious" work, the shotgun was the weapon of choice, sawed-off or unaltered. More than half the sample (51 percent) possessed a sawed-off shotgun at the time of their incarceration. A bit less than half, 47 percent, reported that they had personally cut down a shotgun or rifle to

From *Society,* Vol. 30, No. 1, November/December 1992, pp. 84-89. © 1992 by Transaction. Reprinted by permission.

make it easier to carry or conceal at some point in their lives. Next in popularity were the military-style rifles that have figured so prominently in recent media accounts. Nearly half our respondents said that they had owned such a weapon at some time; more than a third (35 percent) had owned one at the time they went to prison. Other types of guns—regular hunting rifles, derringers, zip guns, and so on—found little favor, having been owned at the time of incarceration by fewer than a quarter.

Similar patterns of ownership, although on a considerably diminished scale, were found for male high school students. (Results presented here from the high school survey are restricted to males only.) Nearly a third (30 percent) of the male students had owned at least one gun in their lives; 22 percent possessed a gun at the time the survey was completed. The most commonly owned weapon was again the revolver (29 percent over the lifetime), followed by the automatic or semi-automatic pistol (27 percent). Fifteen percent owned (or possessed) a revolver and 18 percent an automatic or semi-automatic handgun at the time of the study; 15 percent of the high school males owned three or more guns when they were surveyed.

High school males were more likely to own handguns than shoulder weapons; still, 14 percent had owned a sawed off shotgun at some time, 14 percent had owned an unmodified shotgun, and 14 percent had owned a military-style rifle (6 percent owned a military-style rifle at the time of the survey). In the general gun-owning population, shoulder weapons are about twice as numerous as handguns, and so it is perhaps noteworthy that the male high school students in this sample were more likely to own handguns than shoulder weapons. Unfortunately, no data are available on ownership patterns for male youths in the aggregate or on ownership patterns in inner-city underclass neighborhoods as a whole.

Carrying a gun was also relatively common among our respondents. Among the inmate sample, 55 percent carried a gun all or most of the time in the year or two before being incarcerated and 84 percent carried a gun at least now and then. Among the male high school sample, carrying a gun at least occasionally was more common than gun ownership. Twenty-two percent of the high school males owned a gun at the time of the survey; 12 percent of them reported currently carrying a gun all or most of the time and another 23 percent did so at least now and then, for a combined percentage of 35 percent carrying firearms regularly or occasionally.

Family members and friends of our respondents were also likely to own and carry firearms. Within the families of the incarcerated juveniles, a third reported

siblings who had committed serious crimes; four in ten inmates had siblings who had been jailed; 47 percent had siblings who owned guns. More generally, 79 percent of the inmates came from families where at least some of the males owned guns. Most significantly, 62 percent had male family members who carried guns as they went about their daily business, at least from time to time. Thus, most of our inmate respondents grew up in families where firearms were routinely present and where gun carrying was the norm. The pattern was even sharper for the peers of the incarcerated juveniles. Ninety percent of the inmates had at least some friends and associates who owned and carried guns. Thus, in the social environment inhabited by these juvenile offenders, owning and carrying guns were virtually universal behaviors—not an aberration characteristic of only a few but a fairly normative and widespread standard.

About half of all households in the nation own a firearm of some kind.

Among our high school males, twelve percent reported siblings who had committed serious crimes; seven out of ten said there were males in their families who owned guns; handguns were present in 37 percent of the homes. In the nation as a whole, about half of all households possess a firearm of some sort and handguns are present in approximately a quarter. Two-fifths of the students said there were males in their families who carried guns, at least now and then. Gun owning and carrying were also common among the friends and peers of the students. More than half (57 percent) had friends who owned guns; 42 percent had friends who carried guns.

Quality of Weapons

Perhaps the most striking feature of our data on juvenile gun ownership is the quality of the firearms they possess. Students and inmates who reported ever owning a handgun were asked to describe the characteristics of the type of handgun they had owned most recently. Among these most recently obtained handguns, automatics and semi-automatics predominated: 57 percent of the inmates' and 49 percent of the students' most recently owned handguns were automatics or semi-automatics. The percentages owning revolvers as their most recent handgun (among those who owned any handgun) were 36 and 42 for inmates and male students respectively, with small proportions (7 and 9 percent) owning other types of handguns. Regardless of type, both inmates and students tended to own large caliber guns. Three-fourths of the inmates and two-thirds of the students who owned a handgun possessed guns of at least a .38 caliber or larger, with the 9 mm showing up as the most popular caliber of all. (In a survey of adult felons conducted in the early 1980s, only 7 percent of the most recently owned handguns were 9 mm weapons, compared to 33 percent among the current sample of juvenile offenders, a striking indication of the availability and street popularity that the 9 mm weapons have come to enjoy over the past decade.) Juvenile criminals and male center-city high school students apparently have little use for or interest in light, small-caliber handguns.

Many of the guns the juveniles obtain from their interpersonal networks have been stolen somewhere along the way.

The preferences inferred from patterns of ownership were confirmed in direct questions about desirable handgun features. We asked respondents (both samples) what features they considered important in a handgun; the profile of desirable features was remarkably similar in both groups. Among inmates, the three highest rated traits were firepower, quality of construction, and traceability, followed by being easy to shoot and accurate.

Among male students, quality of construction was the trait most highly rated, followed by ease of shooting, accuracy, traceability, and firepower. Neither inmates nor students indicated much preference for small, cheap guns, nor were they attracted to ephemeral characteristics of weapons such as "scary looking" or "good looking." The preference was clearly for high-firepower hand weapons that are well-made, are accurate, easy to shoot, and not easily traced—in other words, guns suitable for "serious" work against well-armed adversaries.

Availability of Guns

The number and variety of guns owned by our juveniles suggest that guns are abundant and readily accessible to juveniles in the neighborhoods from which our respondents were drawn. We asked our

respondents how difficult it was to obtain a gun. Seventy percent of the inmates and 41 percent of the male students felt that they could get a gun with "no trouble at all;" an additional 17 percent of the inmates and 24 percent of the male students said it would be "only a little trouble." Only 13 percent of the inmates and 35 per cent of the male students perceived access to guns as a "lot of trouble" or "nearly impossible."

We also asked both groups how they would go about getting the gun. It is obvious from their answers that family, friends, and street contacts were the main sources of guns for the juveniles we surveyed. Drug dealers and junkies seemed to be the major suppliers after family, friends, and other street sources, this for both inmates and students. Purchasing a gun at a gun shop, or asking someone else to do so, was perceived by 28 percent of the students as a reliable method; only 12 percent of the inmates considered it so, or viewed it as necessary. Theft was twice as likely to be mentioned by the inmates as by the students, although relative to other sources, it was not prominent for either group. Perhaps there was little need to seek guns through theft, or to bother with normal retail outlets, when they were readily available through personal contacts or easily obtained through street sources.

Guns are easily stolen and they are apparently stolen in large numbers by both juvenile and adult criminals, not so much because felons look for guns to steal but because guns are commonly owned consumer goods that they routinely encounter in the course of their criminal activities. Since our respondents could trace the lineage of their firearms only to the person from whom they obtained them, our data are inadequate to estimate the percentage of the juvenile firearms supply that originally enters the chain of commerce through theft, but the percentage must certainly be a large one. Guns obtained from junkies, drug dealers and other street sources are almost certainly stolen weapons; otherwise, the street price of guns would presumably be much higher.

Obviously, many of the guns these juveniles obtain from their interpersonal networks have been stolen somewhere along the way. It is therefore highly likely that theft and burglary are the ultimate source of many, perhaps most, guns that fall into the hands of juveniles, but only occasionally the proximate source. Firearms now in circulation—through theft or other means—are sufficiently numerous that a youth seeking a gun need only check his network of family, friends, and street contacts to obtain one. Besides, shopping around in the network will often produce the desired type of weapon; theft leaves the type of weapon to fate. The role of the personal network in obtaining guns is demonstrated by yet another finding. Federal law bars juveniles from purchasing firearms through normal retail outlets. This provision of the law is readily circumvented by persuading someone who is of legal age to make the purchase in one's behalf, and so we asked both groups of respondents whether they had ever done so.

Thirty-two percent of the inmates and 18 percent of the male students had indeed asked someone to purchase a gun for them in a gun shop, pawnshop, or other retail outlet; thus, the strategy was quite common. When queried whom they had asked to purchase these guns, 49 percent of the inmates and 52 percent of the students mentioned a friend; 14 percent of the inmates and 18 percent of the students had turned to family members. Only 7 percent of the inmates and 6 percent of the students had sought help from strangers.

Using an intermediary to purchase a gun illustrates the difficulties society faces in restricting juvenile access to firearms. Direct purchase of handguns by persons under age twenty-one is forbidden but it is not illegal for juveniles to own handguns; they can legally receive handguns as a gift, for example. The line between a legitimate gift and a proxy purchase, however, is obviously obscure. It is also illegal to transfer a weapon to anyone with a felony record, whether through a private or normal retail transaction.

But the center-city underclass neighborhoods are evidently populated by many people who are willing to break the law; clearly, our juvenile felons do not encounter any apparent difficulty in finding someone who will deal them a firearm. Thus, as long as guns are available to anyone, they will also be available to any juvenile with the means and motive to exploit his network of family, friends, and acquaintances.

We also asked several questions about where and how they had obtained their most recent handguns, military-style weapons, and conventional rifles and shotguns. The patterns of actual acquisition closely mirrored the results reported above. Informal purchases, swaps, and trades with family, friends, acquaintances, and street sources were the predominant means of gun acquisition for both inmates and male high school students; conventional cash transactions with legitimate over-the-counter retailers were uncommon—although somewhat more common for students than inmates.

The sources and methods by which juveniles obtain guns are strikingly similar to the sources and methods exploited by adult felons for the same purpose; in both cases, informal, off-the-record transactions predominate. Most of the sources for both juvenile and adult felon firearms can be counted on to ask no questions; most of the transactions are entirely private affairs that

are for all practical purposes impossible to regulate and that leave no discernible trace.

As far as we can tell, there is nothing special about how and where juveniles obtain guns that would make the informal juvenile market different from (or easier to disrupt than) the larger informal market through which firearms circulate to adult felons, juvenile criminals, even center-city high school students, and, one supposes, pretty much anyone else who wants a firearm but have some reason to avoid the normal retail channels. Keeping guns out of the hands of juveniles turns out to involve exactly the same difficulties as keeping them from the hands of adult felons, and while many mechanisms have been suggested to accomplish this worthwhile goal, none has yet proven to be very effective.

Street Prices

Aside from convenience, there is another good reason why juveniles prefer informal and street sources over normal retail outlets. Guns obtained from informal and street sources are considerably less expensive. We asked our respondents (both groups) how much they had paid for their most recent handgun, military-style rifle, and standard rifle or shotgun. (The question was only asked of respondents who indicated that the acquisition had been a cash purchase, as opposed to barter, trade, or theft). The findings indicate that street prices are quite low. A substantial majority of handguns and conventional shoulder weapons obtained in a cash transaction with an informal source were purchased for $100 or less; most of the military-style rifles obtained from such sources were purchased for $300 or less. Considering the general quality of the firearms in question, the cash prices paid on the street were clearly much less than the normal retail cost.

Status or Survival?

It has been claimed with some frequency that juveniles own and carry guns mainly as a means of achieving or maintaining status among their peers. In this view, the gun is principally a symbol for toughness or machismo and its primary function is to make an impression on one's peers. This theory does not appear to describe our respondents. We asked both inmates and students to agree or disagree, "In my crowd, if you don't have a gun people don't respect you." Eighty-six percent of the inmates and 90 percent of the male students rejected this statement, most of them strongly. We also asked them to agree or disagree, "My friends would look down on me if I did not carry a gun."

Eighty-nine percent of the inmates and 91 percent of the students also disagreed with this statement, again most of them strongly.

Inmates who said they carried guns at least occasionally, but not "all of the time," were asked about the circumstances in which they were most likely to carry a gun. The least likely circumstance in which inmates would carry guns was when they were "out raising hell," presumably a peer-linked activity. They were also relatively unlikely to carry guns when they were "hanging out with friends" or when they were with friends who were themselves carrying guns. If it were simply a matter of status or reputation, one would expect these to be the most, not the least, likely circumstances in which they would carry.

Self-protection from enemies was the primary reason given for carrying a gun.

Finally, we asked both samples about the reasons why they had purchased their most recent weapons. "To impress people" and "because my friends had one" were among the least important of all the reasons we asked about, regardless of weapon type and for students and inmates equally. Instead, the responses to these various questions were overwhelmingly dominated by themes of self-protection and self-preservation—that is, survival in the urban street environment. The most frequent circumstances in which inmates carried guns were when they were in a strange area (66 percent), when they were out at night (58 percent), and whenever they thought they needed to protect themselves (69 percent); the most important reason for having obtained one's most recent gun (students and inmates alike) was to protect myself. The desire for protection and the need to arm oneself against enemies were the primary reasons to obtain a gun, easily outpacing all other motivations.

Our respondents had plenty to protect themselves against. Substantial numbers of both groups had been shot, shot at, stabbed, or otherwise wounded in their young lives; even more had been threatened with physical violence at one time or other. Everyday life in the social milieu in which our respondents live is clearly fraught with danger. If one's enemies and even perfect strangers possess the weapons and mentality that allow them to take a life quickly and easily from a distance, then it would be the height of folly not to do likewise.

Even the perpetrators of violence faced significant risks from their victims and rivals. To illustrate, 70 percent of the inmate sample had been "scared off, shot at, wounded or captured" by an armed victim at least once in their lives.

Self-protection was also a factor in the circumstances in which our inmates had actually fired their guns. The behavior was quite common: three-quarters of the inmates had fired a gun at a person at least once. Sixty-nine percent had fired in what they considered self-defense. More than half had also fired shots during crimes and drug deals. Better than six in ten had fired their weapons in fights and to scare someone.

The evidence we have assembled intimates that juveniles who own and carry guns are strongly motivated to do so. The behavior, it appears, is largely if not strictly utilitarian; the odds of surviving are seen to be better if one is armed than if not. Unfortunately, the implications of this result are not encouraging. The decision that one's very survival depends on being armed makes a weapon a bargain at nearly any cost.

Juvenile Crime

Discussion of juvenile crime is dominated by the imagery of guns, drugs, gangs, and wanton violence. As the rate of crime and violence committed by and against juveniles has increased, the imagery has become progressively more horrifying. Media accounts have transformed the troubled teens of a decade ago into roving bands of well-armed marauders indiscriminately spraying bullets. For all the media copy that these themes and images command, there has been little credible research on where, how, and why juveniles acquire, carry, and use guns. Our research was designed to provide some reliable, quantitative information on these and related topics.

Concern about juvenile crime and violence has resurfaced periodically throughout the twentieth century, but still one senses that our situation today is qualitatively different from anything in the past. The juvenile felons we analyzed here were generally better armed, more criminally active, and more violent than were the adult felons of a decade ago. Even at that, one is struck less by the armament than by the evident willingness to pull the trigger.

From the viewpoint of public policy, it matters less, perhaps, where these juveniles get their guns than where they get the idea that it is acceptable to kill. It may be convenient to think that the problems of juvenile violence could be magically solved by cracking down or getting tough, but this is unlikely. The problem before us is not so much one of getting guns out of the hands of juveniles as it is reducing the motivations for juveniles to arm themselves in the first place. Convincing inner-city juveniles, or adults, not to own, carry, and use guns requires convincing them that they can survive in their neighborhoods without being armed, that they can come and go in peace, that their unarmed condition will not cause them to be victimized, intimidated, or slain. In brief, it requires a demonstration that the customary agents of social control can be relied upon to provide for personal security. So long as this is believed not to be the case, gun ownership and carrying in the inner city will remain widespread.

This is much easier said than accomplished. Center-city residents who own and carry guns, whether adult or juvenile, do so mainly for personal security. If the inner cities were made safer, then fewer people would be motivated to own and carry guns, and that would make them safer still. Even at that, one must be concerned that gun-carrying has become sufficiently well-established as a cultural practice, at least among certain groups in the inner city, that the behavior would continue even after conditions themselves dramatically improved. Greater investment in community policing and problem solving would repay itself many times over. Police departments who work closely with the residents of central city neighborhoods to reduce drug traffic, property crime, gang activity, and acts of violence make themselves a critical part of those communities, increase the perceived sense of security, and directly undercut the otherwise widespread impression among many in the inner city that the police themselves are an alien and hostile force.

Not every neighborhood in every large city is a killing field and not all residents of the center city go about their daily business armed. But the violence and fear of violence that pervade inner-city life, especially in minority and underclass neighborhoods, should not be understated. In the past few years, homicide rates in nearly every major city have reached record-setting highs. Arrests for drug offenses have swollen jail and prison populations well beyond capacity; every city of which we are aware finds itself plagued by increasingly violent youth gangs. Surveys of young children in the inner cities report astonishingly high percentages (nearly half in some cases) who say they have seen someone shot or seen a dead body in the streets. In circumstances such as these, possession of a firearm provides a necessary, if otherwise undesirable, edge against the uncertainty of police protection and the daily threat of intimidation or victimization. When the ability of society to protect people from one another becomes problematic, as it evidently has, then we should not be surprised that people take aggressive measures to protect themselves.

Center-city minority and underclass neighborhoods have become remarkably unsafe because decades of indifference to the social and economic problems of the cities has bred an entire class of people, especially young people, who no longer have much stake in their future. Isolation, hopelessness, and fatalism, coupled with the steady deterioration of stabilizing social institutions in the inner city and the inherent difficulties of maintaining security through normal agents of social control, have fostered an environment where "success" implies predation and survival depends on one's ability to defend against it.

Whether predator or prey, the larger urban environment encourages one to be armed. Widespread joblessness and lack of opportunities for upward mobility seem in most accounts to lie at the very heart of the dilemma. In the end, stricter gun control laws, more aggressive enforcement of existing laws, a crack-down on drug traffic, police task forces directed at juvenile gangs, metal detectors at the doors of schools, periodic searches of lockers and shake-downs of students, and other similar measures do not adequately address the true need, the economic, social and moral resurrection of the inner city. Just how this might be accomplished, and at what cost, remains debatable; the evident need to do so is not.

The Whole Child Approach to Crime

The juvenile justice system cannot labor by itself to reverse societal damage done to children, our new U.S. attorney general told the Coalition for Juvenile Justice in April. The following excerpts from her address tell what needs to be done to help prevent youth violence.

Janet Reno

Janet Reno is Attorney General of the United States.

When I first took office as prosecutor in Dade County Fla., I wanted to do everything I could to beef up our juvenile division; make it one of the best possible. I started focusing on 14-, 16- and 17-year-olds but quickly learned that we would never have enough money to change all the delinquent children unless we started much earlier.

Then we looked at dropout programs in the middle schools and that was too late. We tried early intervention programs in the elementary schools and that was too late.

During the crack epidemic advent in Dade County in 1985, doctors took me to the neonatal unit at Jackson Memorial Hospital, but they pointed out to me that it was too late even for small babies.

I began to hear about child welfare and see juvenile justice people and the child welfare people. But too often they don't seem to talk to each other and if they do, they don't talk in a coordinated way.

What we have at stake is not just one component, not just an adult prosecutor or people who focus on juvenile justice or people who focus on child welfare or people who focus on pediatric issues. What we have at stake is children and families throughout America.

I became convinced that unless we as a nation focused on children, all my efforts as prosecutor would be for naught. Everything I saw as a prosecutor—crime and drugs, delinquency and dropouts, youth gangs, teen pregnancy, teen suicide and the great increase in the number of homeless children—was the symptom of a deeper problem in society. For the last 30 or 40 years America has forgotten and neglected its children.

> *Everything I saw as a prosecutor—crime and drugs, delinquency and dropouts, youth gangs, teen pregnancy, teen suicide and the great increase in the number of homeless children—was the symptom of a deeper problem in society. For the last 30 or 40 years America has forgotten and neglected its children.*

I would like to challenge us all—myself and the Department of Justice included—to start to work with others, with the Department of Education, the Department of Health and Human Services and all the federal, state and local agencies that touch children.

We've got to forge a bond between Washington and local government. It can't be Washington saying we know best. It's got to be us asking the people in communities what the problems are and what the best solutions are. The best solutions are out in the communities and the neighborhoods of America.

There are bold, innovative programs being tried at every level, and we've got to come together to take the limited resources of government and provide a national agenda for children.

The first step is to focus on the parents. We've got to support parents, understanding that the best institution for caring for children, for nurturing them, for giving them a strong and healthy environment is the family.

A single mother can do a beautiful job if she's given some support, a helping hand, a little push to get her off to a fresh start and to self-sufficiency. But she can't do it if she struggles to get a minimum wage job and finds herself worse off than if she hadn't gone to work in the first place.

Let's make sure that every child in America has appropriate and preventive health care. There is something terribly wrong with a nation that is interested in dollars and cents but hasn't made sure that all of its children are inoculated.

We've got to make sure that education is available to all our children in a manner that reflects the diversity of America, that appreciates our cultural difference.

We have got to make sure that education is relevant to our children. They want to learn.

But as we focus on education, let us understand why so many of our children aren't going to school. Let's not wait

Reprinted with permission from *Spectrum*, Vol. 66, No. 3, Summer 1993, pp. 31-36. © 1993 by The Council of State Governments.

until they are delinquent at 13, when at eight years old they were out of school 15 days in three months and nobody checked on them.

Nothing frustrates me more than to see the police taking a child to school, the school calls home, nobody comes to get the child and the child is sent home on the bus.

Let's forge an alliance among the social service agencies, the police and schools in every neighborhood of America to make sure that when that mother does not come, the child is taken home by community-friendly police officers and social workers to try to force an action to prevent the problem in the future, rather than waiting until that child at 13 holds somebody up with a gun and gets into real trouble.

Let's save him early but let's do it without labeling. More people tell me that if they transfer a kid from one school to another, he gets rid of the label and starts over again. We shouldn't have to transfer him from one school to another.

We've got to realize that kids develop at different rates, that they've got to be given a chance, that they can make a difference, that they want to be somebody and that if we peel that label off and never put it on we can make such a difference.

Let's understand that children want to socialize with their peers, but they like having adults around, too. If they're drifting around the housing development in the afternoon while their mother is working, or drifting around the middle-class neighborhood while both parents are working and nobody is really focusing on them, we don't know what they're going to get into.

Let's look at the after-school time and the night-time hours. If we make an investment, not just recreation and sports but a variety of programs, after school and in the evening, we can make such a difference. Those programs don't cost that much and they save us millions of dollars in terms of crime prevented.

Let's teach children relevant skills. Has it ever puzzled you to watch somebody graduate from high school without a skill that can enable them to earn a living wage? They go on to college and get a degree in English literature. They can tell you what Blake means in *The Tiger*, but can they get a job? No. They might be able to get a job as a paralegal if they take a special course at the junior college.

Let us suggest to all American high schools that students be required not only to have a certain number of years of algebra or geometry or foreign language, but that they've got to graduate with a skill that can enable them to earn a living wage.

When a person graduates from college with a degree in English literature, he can at least be the radiologist or the X-ray technician at the local hospital dealing with the latest new machines.

Let's give them an opportunity to contribute to their community. I don't think I have ever met a youngster who didn't want to be somebody, who didn't want to contribute, who didn't want to make a difference. Let's let each one of them know that in big and small ways they can make a difference.

Let's give them an opportunity to belong, not to a youth gang that tears the fabric of society around them, but to constructive groups that can build the fabric of society around a neighborhood.

Let's give them an opportunity to feel competent. If a youngster doesn't know how to play a sport but is marvelous on the computer, if he brings to school a polished piece of carving, if he writes a poem or puts two lines together, figure out the way to make him feel competent.

Let's give our youth an opportunity to be involved, to contribute through public service programs such as the Civilian Conservation Corps that helped give youth an opportunity during the depression, or the Peace Corps.

When you raise children, you set guidelines, you punish them when they violate the guidelines, but you also, if you're a good parent, give them love and support and encouragement along the way.

Let's understand that we can do something about violence up front. One of the extraordinary lessons that the 1980s taught us is that drug abuse education, prevention and treatment worked far better than jail.

Let's look at violence in the same way. Let's not wait until a 14-year-old puts a gun to a tourist's head. Let's understand the patterns when that child is in elementary school through conflict resolution programs, which are springing up in elementary schools and middle schools throughout this nation.

Let's understand that violence is one of the greatest public health problems in America today. It is not going to be solved just by adult jails or by juvenile detention facilities or by youth in prisons.

It is going to be solved by working together up front to provide a nurturing environment where a child can learn that we don't solve problems by conflict that leads to violence.

Let's start challenging TV. My mother would never let us have a television because she thought it would contribute to mind rot. I think if she were raising children now, she would also say it contributes to violence.

We put labels on our cigarettes because they cause cancer. I didn't think the Federal Communications Commission should prevent us from putting labels or taking steps to ensure TV programs for children don't promote violence.

A large number of kids who come into the juvenile justice system as delinquents maybe will be there a second time. But after the second time they won't be back, no matter what we do.

Let's try to identify them, get them off on the right foot with the limited resources we have and wish them well. But let us understand that there are children in America today who are coming into the juvenile justice system with the fabric of society literally ripped away because we have forgotten children for the last 30 years. We not only have to wish them well and say let's work on this young man, we have to reknit the fabric of society around them. And we can't do it by diverting them into a program when there are obvious gaps.

We cannot take a 13-year-old child of a crack addict who has helped raise his five siblings and been bounced from his grandmother to his uncle, put him in a diversion program and think he will succeed.

Let's get rid of the categories and labels, such as "delinquent" and "abused." Let's understand that there are children crying out for help, and we have to work together in a comprehensive effort to help these children have a chance.

5. JUVENILE JUSTICE

Youth violence is the greatest single crime problem in America today. Many people suggest it's drugs, but too many of us have seen a kid walk into a courtroom or detention center, not on drugs but totally cynical and mean. If you get to know that child, there is strength and warmth and love. He's just been deprived for too long.

Let us understand that children are thumbing their nose at police officers. We've got to work together with the police to develop reasonable, fair, humane sanctions for our children that send a message. We've got to see that those fair and humane sanctions are carried out when appropriate.

Most of all, we've got to give our children a chance to live in a nurturing, thriving environment and I analogize it to this: When you raise children, you set guidelines, you punish them when they violate the guidelines, but you also, if you're a good parent, give them love and support and encouragement along the way.

Somehow or another we have to devise that environment, particularly in the case of children who don't have the nurturing support around them. We've got to give them the opportunity to grow, but we have got to spell out boundaries and sanctions that can have an impact.

Most of all, we have got to send a message that we will not, we cannot and we won't lose a generation.

We've got to be bold. We've got to give juvenile court judges more authority than they've had. Their hands have been tied because of excesses over the years.

We've got to look at what we are doing with children in America. There is a tendency to think a child's violent, so put him in the detention center and throw the key away; he's committed two violent crimes, so send him to the adult system. I have done that when there was no other way because the juvenile justice system was bankrupt, but we cannot forget that child in detention, we cannot forget that child in the jail.

Let's look at juvenile detention and correctional facilities. Let's look at the overcrowding, the lack of health care and the lack of substance-abuse treatment. Otherwise, we are never going to change those children's lives and some of the situations of confinement we have them in.

Let's understand what we're doing in terms of confining kids. If we confine them and then dump them back into the community with nothing more, it's not going to make any difference. If we send them off to that wonderful school upstate where they learn how to take care of cows and then bring them back to Liberty City without aftercare and a coherent pattern of treatment, that's going to be a big waste of everybody's dollars.

Let's try to develop programs within our community that understand that in most cases, if a child is properly supervised, he will not have to be detained.

There will be rare exceptions. There is always going to be that terrible person who is the exception, but we can do so much if we understand that he is coming back to the community in pretty short order, anyway, and that we can make a difference by providing a coherent pattern.

Let's understand that we've got to forge new ideas. A year ago, we developed a team in a neighborhood plagued by a terrible youth gang, by drugs and crime. A team made up of a highly respected police officer, a social worker, a public health nurse and a community organizer began working in a housing development.

The police officer and social worker would go to court, tell the judge that a kid, with supervision by the police officer and community, could stay out of detention and asked if they could place him in this special program and monitor him.

Crime was so significantly reduced by August 1992 that the police wanted to replicate this program in other jurisdictions with similar problems.

We can do so much if we form youth teams, new ideas, new concepts.

The single most important message we have to send is that somehow or other in America we are going to have to place children first again.

Children of the Shadows

Fernando, 16, Finds a Sanctuary in Crime

John Tierney

Special to The New York Times

BRIDGEPORT, Conn.— Fernando Morales was glad to discuss his life as a 16-year-old drug dealer, but he had one stipulation owing to his status as a fugitive. He explained that he had recently escaped from Long Lane School in Middletown, Conn., a state correctional institution that became his home after he was caught with $1,100 worth of heroin known as P.

"The Five-O caught me right here with the bundles of P," he said, referring to a police officer, as he stood in front of a boarded-up house on Bridgeport's East Side. "They sentenced me to 18 months, but I jetted after four. Three of us got out a bathroom window. We ran through the woods and stole a car. Then we got back here and the Five-O's came to my apartment, and I had to jump out the side window on the second floor."

What Future?

Since his escape in December, Fernando had been on the run for weeks. He still went to the weekly meetings of his gang, but he was afraid to go back to his apartment, afraid even to go to a friend's place to pick up the three guns he had stashed away. "I would love to get my baby, Uzi, but it's too hot now."

He knew the police were still looking for him, which was why he made a special request before agreeing to be interviewed.

"Could you bring a photographer here?" he asked me holding a bundle right there on the front page so the cops can see it. They're going to bug out."

The other dealers on the corner looked on with a certain admiration. They realized that a publicity campaign might not be the smartest long-term career move for a fugitive drug dealer—"man, you be the one bugging out," another dealer told him—but they also recognized the logic in Fernando's attitude. He was living his life according to a common assumption on these streets: There is no future.

When you ask the Hispanic teenagers selling drugs here what they expect to be doing in five years you tend to get a lot of bored shrugs. Occasionally they'll talk about being back in school or being a retired drug dealer in a Porsche. But the most common answer is the one that Fernando gave without hesitation or emotion: "Dead or in jail."

The story of how Fernando got that way is a particularly sad one, but the basic elements are fairly typical in the lives of drug dealers and gang members in any urban ghetto. He has grown up amid tenements, housing projects, torched buildings and abandoned factories. His role models have been adults who used "the city" and "the state" primarily as terms for the different types of welfare checks. His neighborhood is a place where 13-year-olds know by heart the visiting hours at local prisons.

It is also a place where drugs and gangs are always around and parents are often missing. When Fernando and his relatives try to explain what went wrong in his life, they see a cycle over two generations. It began with a father addicted to drugs and alcohol, chronically jobless, prone to battering and abandoning his family. By the time death came, the son was on the street selling the bundles that destroyed the father.

The Family
A Mother Leaves, A Father Drinks

Fernando Morales was born in Bridgeport on Sept. 16, 1986, and his mother moved out a few months later. Since then he has occasionally run into her on the street. Neither he nor his relatives can say exactly why she left—or why she didn't take Fernando and her other son with her—but the general assumption is that she was tired of being hit by their father.

The father, Bernabe Morales, who was 24 years old and had emigrated from Puerto Rico as a teen-ager, moved the two boys in with his mother at the P. T. Barnum public housing project. Fernando lived there until the age of 8, when his grandmother died.

"She was the only one who was really there for him, and it was terri-

From *New York Times*, April 13, 1993, pp. A1, B6. © 1993 by The New York Times Company. Reprinted by permission.

ble for him when she died," said Camilia Mendez, an older cousin who lived there as well. "At the funeral he was going crazy thinking about one night his uncle came in drunk and started hitting her, Nando tried to stop it. He picked up a pool stick and swung it at his uncle, but it hit her by mistake. At the funeral he kept screaming out her name and saying, '"I'm sorry, I didn't mean to hit you."

'Very Bad Life'

After that Fernando and his brother Bernard lived sometimes with their father and his current girlfriend, sometimes with relatives in Bridgeport or Puerto Rico. They eventually settled with their father's cousin, Monserrate Bruno, who already had 10 children living in her two-bedroom apartment.

"Nando's had a very bad life—different parents all the time," said Mrs. Bruno, who is now his legal guardian. "Living with his father was bad for him. The father would get drunk and beat him up. One time Nando came over here crying at 3 in the morning and said his father wanted to cut his penis off with a scissors."

Fernando was reluctant to talk about his father or the traumas of his youth. He said he had fond memories of his grandmother and of his two years in Puerto Rico—"They don't sell there on the streets"—but not much else.

"I used to always bug out," he said. "They had to lock me in my room all the time. One time in school the principal made me bend over and whacked me, so I got mad and picked up a chair and hit him in the head. My father's sister took me in for a little while, but she didn't like me because I used to beat up her kids and make trouble. I used to burn things—if I see a rug, I get some matches."

His relatives say they tried but failed to give him the parental guidance that was missing. He seemed lost and would sometimes refer to himself [as] a hand-me-down Raggedy Ann doll. When the mood struck he would go to video arcades instead of school. He often dismissed his relatives' warnings or help by saying, "I'm going to end up like my father."

"School was corny. I was smart, I learned quick, but I got bored. I was just learning things when I could be out making money." Fernando Morales

---

His father, by all accounts, was a charming, generous man when sober but something else altogether when drinking or doing drugs. He was arrested more than two dozen times, usually for fighting or for drugs, and spent five years in jail while Fernando was growing up. He lived on welfare, odd jobs, and money from selling drugs, a trade that was taken up by both his sons.

At times he tried to be conscientious. Fernando's second-grade teacher, Richard Patton, recalls that Fernando's father was one of the few parents who picked up his child every day after school. But then he started showing up drunk for parent-teacher conferences, and before long he was off to jail.

Fernando's brother Bernard, a year older, also traced their problems to their father. "They be saying you can live anywhere and it don't affect you—that's stupid. It would have made a difference if we would have had somebody taking care of us. My father would always say, 'Stay in school, don't drop out, don't drink or do drugs.' But he never did anything about it himself, so what's the use? It's funny how you can learn to memorize those words."

The 'Industry'
Moving Up in the Drug Trade

Fernando's school days ended two years ago, when he dropped out of ninth grade. "School was corny," he explained. "I was smart, I learned quick, but I got bored. I was just learning things when I could be out making money.'

Fernando might have found other opportunities—he had relatives working in fast-food restaurants and car repair shops, and one cousin tried to interest him in a job distributing bread that might pay $700 a week—but nothing with such quick rewards as the drug business flourishing on the East Side.

He had friends and relatives in the business, and he started as one of the runners on the street corner making sales or directing buyers to another runner holding the marijuana, cocaine, crack, or heroin. The runners on each block buy their drugs—paying, for instance $200, for 50 bags of crack that sell for $250—from the block's lieutenant, who supervises them and takes the money to the absentee dealer called the owner of the block.

By this winter Fernando had moved up slightly on the corporate ladder. "I'm not the block lieutenant yet, but I have some runners selling for me," he explained as he sat in a bar near the block. Another teen-ager came in with money for him, which he proudly added to a thick wad in his pocket. "You see? I make money while they work for me."

Fernando still worked the block himself, too, standing on the corner watching for cars slowing down, shouting out "You want P?" or responding to veteran customers for crack who asked, "Got any slab, man?" Fernando said he usually made between $100 and $300 a day, and that the money usually went as quickly as it came.

He had recently bought a car for $500 and wrecked it making a fast turn into a telephone pole. He spent money on gold chains with crucifixes, rings, Nike sneakers, Timberland boots, an assortment of Russell hooded sweatshirts called hoodies, gang dues, trips to New York City, and his 23-year-old girlfriend.

OTHER VOICES
'You Do What You Have to Do'

The following text was taken from more than 20 hours of discussions with teenagers from the New York City region. [Excerpts appear within each of the article series "The Children of the Shadows," New York Times, April 4–25, 1993.]

Q *Is there strength in numbers? Do you feel compelled to form a group to survive?*

BERNARDO VASQUEZ, *17, Manhattan (A. Philip Randolph High School):* If you want to understand gangs look at rap music. . . . There's a group called the Geto Boys. And one of the guys, Scarface, has a song where he's a little kid. And he explains how that little kid found family and togetherness. . . . How you find togetherness and family and support from a gang. You know, like your mother's probably whoring around or something like that. She ain't giving you that hug and that love. Every human being needs love. . . . So if you get it from your brothers and you form a gang.

ZAIRE GRAHAM, *17, Bronx (High School of Fashion Industries):* I definitely think there's strength in numbers, whether it's negative or positive.

BARBARA FUENTES, *16, Hartford, Hartford Public High School):* The Latin Kings and Los Solidos, and Las Solidas, and the Latin Queens, they think they're a family . . . but they hurt people. . . . If you're going to hang with somebody you should hang with them for positive reasons.

Q *But why do kids do that?*

WUBNESH HYLTON, *19, Brooklyn (Hunter College):* Everybody has a crew though. Everybody has a crew they swing with. . . . It's just natural.

Q *There are people who say that the drug dealers in our communities are looked up to.*

ZAIRE They could say they looked up to the materialistic part, or in the power and respect part. They don't see that his life is in danger.

Q *But at the same time, teen-agers look down on people who work at McDonald's. Why?*

WUBNESH Because it's just cheesy, man. It's just like at the bottom. Flipping greasy burgers. You got to wear those clothes. It's just like the worst. . . . So you do what you have to do to get by. And if that means scamming, that's what you do.

Q *How much are you touched by drugs? How much of a presence do drugs really have?*

ZAIRE I think right now among teen-agers weed is the biggest thing.

Q *Mostly marijuana?*

WUBNESH It's like drinking a soda, you know. Or smoking a cigarette.

ZAIRE . . . You ask people 'why do you smoke weed?' Nobody knows . . . It's like, 'I don't know. I just do it.'

Q *Does it matter that it's against the law?*

JUAN RIVERA, *18, Brooklyn, (Bushwick High School):* Around my way when people smoke weed they just walk down the street, they walk right by the precinct with it. . . . And the cops, they don't do anything about it either, you know.

WUBNESH Everybody sells it . . . You can grow it on your window sill, you know.

His dream was to get out of Bridgeport. "I'd be living fat somewhere. I'd go to somewhere hot, Florida or Puerto Rico or somewhere, buy me a house, get six blazing girls with dope bodies." In the meantime, he tried not to think about what his product was doing to his customers.

"Sometimes it bothers me. But see, I'm a hustler. I got to look out for myself. I got to be making money. Forget them. If you put that in your head, you're going to be caught out. You going to be a sucker. You gong to be like them." He said he had used marijuana, cocaine and angel dust himself, but made a point of never using crack or heroin, the drugs that plagued the last years of his father's life.

At the end, at age 40, the father was living in a rooming house with Donna Strawn, a middle-aged woman who described herself as his fiancée and as a person with her own history of drugs and prison. Ms. Strawn, who had left behind four children in California, said that she had tried to get Fernando's father to intervene as they saw Fernando drop our of school and sell drugs.

"But he'd just throw up his hands and say he didn't know what to do," she said. "Or he might get upset and go take a drink. He felt really guilty because he wasn't the father he should be."

On his final night, last May 23, Fernando's father and Miss Strawn got into an argument about a stereo speaker of hers that he had sold. "He was out of it," she recalled. "His eyes were rotating in his head. He was ramming me in the face with his head. I told him, 'I have no family here and I'm going to let you kill me? I don't think so.' I got a knife and tried to stab him but I stabbed the bed."

The police broke up the fight and arrested Fernando's father, who was taken to police headquarters and charged with third-degree assault and refusing to be fingerprinted. That night he hanged himself in his cell, according to the police and the Medical Examiner. An autopsy found evidence of acute cocaine and ethanol intoxication.

5. JUVENILE JUSTICE

The Gangs
'Like a Family' or Drug Dealers?

"I cried a little, that's it," was all that Fernando would say about his father's death. But he did allow that it had something to do with his subsequent decision to join a Hispanic gang named Ñeta. He went with friends to a meeting, answered questions during an initiation ceremony, and began wearing its colors, a necklace of red, white and blue beads.

"It's like a family, and you need that if you've lost your own family," he said. "At the meetings we talk about having heart, trust, and all that. We don't disrespect nobody. If we need money, we get it. If I need anything, they're right there to help me."

Ñeta is allied with Bridgeport's most notorious gang, the Latin Kings, and both claim to be peaceful Hispanic cultural organizations opposed to drug use. But they are financed at least indirectly by the drug trade, because many members like Fernando work independently in drug operations, and the drug dealers' disputes can turn into gang wars.

Gang meetings are often devoted to adjudicating or avenging acts of disrespect, which is such a central concept on the streets that the language has evolved with a host of synonyms: you can dis someone, play someone, rank someone, try someone, or, when it starts to get violent, beef someone. This can eventually lead to killing someone, which occurred 17 times last year in the 12 blocks of the East Side.

Fernando and the other teen-agers on the street professed to be inured to the violence. They were used to seeing teen-agers in wheelchairs at local night clubs. They casually chatted about gang "missions"—which can range from "beat-downs" of errant members to drive-by shootings—and the proper way to coat a bullet with Teflon so that it can penetrate a bulletproof vest. Fernando lamented that he couldn't yet afford a rocket launcher.

'I Like Guns'

"I like guns, I like stealing cars, I like selling drugs, and I like money," he said. "I got to go to the block. That's where I get my spirit at. When I die, my spirit's going to be at the block, still making money. Booming."

It was hard to tell whether he really believed what he was saying about his life and death. Fernando sounded callous and fatalistic most of the time, but occasionally another side came out. One evening, as he and a friend who was high on angel dust sat in a restaurant laughing about a police car they had stolen, two police officers appeared at the entrance. The two teen-agers turned quiet and stared uneasily at their plates until the officers left.

Then a waitress, Valerie Mendez, who was married to an older cousin of Fernando's and had known him since childhood, came over to the table. She looked in disgust at him and his gold chain and black stocking cap.

"Are you happy now?" she asked. "That's how it going to be the rest of your life. You did it your way because it was easy, and now you're never going to have a life. You'll always be looking over your shoulder. You were smart enough to know better. Why are you going around like a títere?"

He knew that títere meant hoodlum, and he did not have an answer for her. For a moment he looked like nothing more than an embarrassed, baby-faced 16-year-old. After she went away, he said softly, "No, I don't always want to be a bum. I want to be an actor. That's all I wanted to be since I was young. I always loved cameras and performing in front of people. I like to go on TV. Man, I be straight, I be so happy, I leave everything on the street."

For a moment, at least, he could imagine a future. But he was not ready to do anything about it.

"I'm chilling now," he said in late January, during his last interview. (After the interview he lost touch with this reporter, and the two have not talked since.) "I'll be selling till I get my act together. I'm just a little kid. Nothing runs through my head. All I think about is doing crazy things. But when I be big, I know I need education. If I get caught and do a couple of years, I'll come out and go back to school. But I don't have that in my head yet. I'll have my little fun while I'm out."

[This is the fifth of a ten-part series, "The Children of the Shadows," *New York Times*, April 4–25, 1993. *Ed.*]

Street Gang Trends Give Little Cause for Optimism

Robert Dart

Robert Dart is commander of the Gang Crime Section of the Chicago Police Department.

Gangs reportedly existed in America as early as 1760. Accounts have surfaced periodically since then of street gangs menacing our colonial neighborhoods. But it was not until 1927, when Frederic M. Thrasher wrote *The Gang, A Study of 1,313 Gangs in Chicago,* a book that even today serves as a primer for law enforcement and academia, that gangs were recognized as a part of our social fabric. There were the Irish gangs, followed by Germans, Italians, Blacks and Hispanics. Every race and virtually every ethnic group has contributed to the street gang phenomenon and image that Chicago is the gangster capital of the United States, with machine guns firing from open touring cars.

But those gangs were simply delinquent compared to the gangs of the 1990s. Around 1964 modern street gangs first began to appear on the streets of Chicago. Sociologists posit that it was migration from southern states and movements within the city that created unstable neighborhood environments, ripe for gang activity. Individual street gangs began to posture and engage in minor extortion and robbery of "ma-and-pa" grocery stores, along with turf posturing. Law enforcement in the mid-1960s did not track gang homicides or other crimes perpetrated by the gangs.

As one gang grew in strength and power, opposing gangs were forced to respond in kind. Finally, around 1969, the "nation" gangs—the first gang evolution—appeared on the streets of Chicago. Individual groups formalized loose alliances with other street gangs by establishing gang nations, such as the Black P Stone Nation and Black Disciple Nation. At about the same time the Crips and Bloods were forming in south Los Angeles. They appear to have been born out of the same need; gang members must always have an enemy.

The gangs discovered that academics who studied them (and probably inadvertently glorified them) could also attract financing. In the late 1960s through the early 1970s, foundations and philanthropists begin to pump money into the gangs with various goals in mind. Even the federal government directed grants and economic assistance into their criminal coffers. Indeed there were rumors that gangs had been recruited by

some aspiring politicians to ensure the outcome of local elections by turning out voters to vote the "right" way. Even President Nixon joined the crowd by extending a formal invitation to the leadership of a notorious South Side gang to attend his inauguration in 1969. At that same time, the first Chicago Police Department gang officer was ambushed and murdered by the gangs. More were, unfortunately, destined to follow.

It became evident that the gangs were not going to disappear from the scene. Money and power were too easy to come by for them. They had spread from the inner city to establish safe houses, gun stores and narcotic stash pads in suburbia. They were jumping on jumbo jets and travelling to Los Angeles, Las Vegas, New York and Bermuda. Through terror tactics and mystique they were able to move into the labor unions and dominate a number of businesses. National magazines wrote of them as if they were Robin Hood and his merry band instead of the gangsters they were, and authors rushed to the scene as if they were benign modern pirates.

In response, the police rapidly developed anti-gang expertise. The Gang Intelligence unit was formed in Chicago in February 1967. Predecessor units had traditionally attacked the body of

From *CJ the Americas,* Vol. 5, No. 6, December/January 1993, pp. 5-6, 8. Reprinted by permission.

189

the gang but now the hierarchy was being targeted for long range in-depth investigations that would result in substantial prison sentences. Successes became more frequent, and more and more leaders and soldiers were being sent away to state and federal prisons. But law enforcement was unable to foresee two phenomena beginning to manifest themselves to the jails. The police paid no heed as to what gang affiliation or faction they were sending up the river, so rivals found themselves in the same institution and in many cases on the same tier. They carried their gang colors into the penal system with them and found that they had many of the same enemies inside as they did on the outside.

Gang members, by design, were being transferred throughout the system to preclude violence from occurring as they grew stronger in a specific institution. A perceived need arose for them to form some type of gang identification system and alliance inside to protect and project their power as well as their will within their new environment.

Thus in the late 1970s the People and the Folks umbrella organizations—the second gang evolution—began to appear. Not autonomous or individual gangs, but rather an umbrella grouping that would place a member on one side or another in the constant struggle for control and protection from the other side, not unlike NATO and the (former) Soviet bloc alliances. At the same time as the troublesome inmate was transferred his family, in many cases, would follow. Little did the criminal justice system realize at that time that it was spreading the cancer of gangs far and wide, and could unwittingly be providing a national framework for the gangs to develop and exploit years later.

In 15 short years the gangs had developed from small enclaves in the inner city to nations in the communities as well as the prison systems. They had spread their wings from a few city blocks of turf into the suburbs inhabited by people who had fled the high crime cityscape years earlier. Armed with the experience and knowledge of the past it was difficult not to wonder what direction the gangs were travelling tomorrow and how far off was the third evolution.

Gang murders mounted throughout the nation exacerbated by the enhanced killing power of the preferred 9mm cartridge and the proliferation of the easily convertible semi-automatics such as the Intratech 9, Mac 10 and the Uzi. The drive-by shooting was becoming commonplace and more lethal not only in sprawling metropolises but in bedroom communities as well. These were no longer wars over turf, or colors or gang loyalty—these were full-scale narcotic wars.

The third evolution was occurring. The gangs were now doing street corner dope sales tallying thousands and thousands of dollars a day, but the leadership, not the kid on the corner pitching the dope, was raking in the money.

In the early summer of 1992, Chicago saw the first evidence of southern California Crips successfully attempting a foray into narcotics in Chicago. It was initially thought that Chicago gangs would drive the newcomers from their established turf, but it did not happen that way. The reason was simple—this new dope was plentiful and cheaper.

The Crips were formed in south Los Angeles and Compton, California, in the late 1960s and have now spread throughout the western United States. In fact, their constitution maintains that they are not a gang, that there is no leader but rather a board of commissioners whose decisions are final. A national union of gangs was becoming a reality. Prior to 1957 few in law enforcement believed that there was a national organized crime structure until a patrolling New York state trooper discovered the now-famous Appalachia meeting.

But in Chicago it was not simply a marriage between Midwest gangsters and West Coast hoodlums. For the first time, there was a suspension of traditional street gang rivalries to facilitate the sale of narcotics. People and Folk rivalries appeared, in many cases, to be set aside for the sale of narcotics. Profit, rather than colors, was the driving force in this alliance.

In 15 short years the gangs had developed from small enclaves in the inner city to nations in the communities as well as the prison systems. They had spread their wings from a few city blocks of turf into the suburbs inhabited by people who had fled the high crime cityscape years earlier.

Not only were street gangs of national renown uniting, but Jamaicans, Virgin Islanders and Belizeans were also entering the picture. In about 1982 the Jamaicans introduced their own crack cocaine, and accompanying cold-blooded violence, to New York. The notoriously violent Jamaican posses, formed during the bloody 1979–80 Jamaican national election in which some 800 people were killed, spread quickly to New York City, Miami and Los Angeles, and were now emerging in Chicago. The street gang had moved from the inner city to suburbia, nationally across state lines, and was now spanning international borders.

But this was not the first time gangs had done business on an international scale. In the summer of 1986, Libyan operatives from Colonel Moammar Gadhafi met for the first of two clandestine meetings in Panama with Chicago street gang representatives. Speculation as to the purpose of these meetings ranged from negotiating for asylum from prosecution in Chicago to seeking money to carry out terrorist activities. It was then that the gang purchased a LAW missile from FBI agents with the intent to commit terrorist acts by targeting a law enforcement facility or specific gang officers, or both. Later it was reported that this gang sent members halfway around the world to Libya and other Middle East countries.

It is unthinkable that an urban inner city street gang could ever aspire to status as a national narcotic cartel functioning autonomously from any other force, or is it? What we are witnessing today would certainly conform with the definitions employed by the President's Commission on Law Enforcement and Administration of Justice (1968) and the President's Commission on Organized Crime (1986). Law enforcement must begin to think globally of a response to this catastrophe. There are independent writings on gangs, mostly from sociologists and other academicians. Many police departments are quickly forming gang units in response as the gangs move from city jurisdictions to suburban jurisdictions with impunity. Generic street gang conferences are being conducted across the nation to discuss history, organization, profiles and to some degree movements. Now is the time to adopt a new approach—we must address the demise of these transnational organizations, not rehash their history and violence and endeavors.

Law enforcement cannot afford to stay on the same plane as ten years ago and witness the gangs' continued advancement across the United States. Metropolitan police departments are now liaising with each other in the hope of tracking the gangs and recognizing their trends. As these organizations cross political and crime boundaries, local and federal law enforcement agencies are strengthening their partnership in this battle. Jurisdictions with analogous gangs must actively meet for intelligence sharing and for developing harmonious and complementary enforcement strategies and tactics if these problems are going to be vigorously addressed and dismantled. Whether one chooses to call them street gangs or tomorrow's organized crime, one thing is certain—a national strategy must be developed by the leaders of our cities to combat this poisonous phenomenon.

Punishment and Corrections

In the American system of criminal justice, the term "corrections" has a special meaning. It designates programs and agencies that have legal authority over the custody or supervision of persons who have been convicted of a criminal act by the courts.

The correctional process begins with the sentencing of the convicted offender. The predominant sentencing pattern in the United States encourages maximum judicial discretion and offers a range of alternatives from probation (supervised conditional freedom within the community), through imprisonment, to the death penalty. Selections in this unit focus on the current condition of the penal system in the United States and the effects that sentencing, probation, imprisonment, and parole have on the rehabilitation of criminals.

"Sentencing and Corrections" illustrates how society, through sentencing, expresses its objectives for the correctional process. The objectives are deterrence, incapacitation, rehabilitation, retribution, and restitution.

The number of state and federal prisoners grew by 48,384 in 1991 and reached another record high at year's end, according to the Bureau of Justice Statistics. As of December 31, 1991, there were 823,414 men and women being held under state or federal jurisdiction. At the end of 1980 there were 329,821 such inmates.

The increased number of drug-law convictions during the last decade has had a dramatic impact on the nation's prisons. Although about 1 out of every 13 new prisoners had been convicted of a drug offense during 1981, by the end of the decade almost 1 in 3 new admissions was for a drug-law violation.

Some 60 percent of inmates released from state and federal lockups return to prison. Recidivism contributes greatly to the overcrowding that plagues prisons throughout the United States. Crowded, tense conditions make survival the principal goal. Rehabilitation is pushed into the background in the effort to manage incipient chaos. Other issues and aspects of the correctional system—women in prison, alternatives to prison, drug treatment programs, building more prison cells, intensive supervision probation/parole, and the death penalty are other topics in this unit.

"Women in Jail: Unequal Justice" cites the enormous disparity in the treatment of men and women in prison.

The essay "Pennsylvanians Prefer Alternatives to Prison" tells of citizen support for alternatives in order to make punishment fit the crime, change the future behavior of offenders, and save money.

Not unlike other drug addicts, Bill Gidden's life was one of craving and satisfaction. He began drug treatment in prison, and now he is out, clean, and trying to stay that way. His story is told in "The Detoxing of Prisoner 88A0802."

In "Do We Need More Prisons?" two opposing voices are heard. One maintains prisons are an essential ingredient in fighting crime. The other says prisons have not made us safer.

Supporters of intensive probation/parole supervision point out that this form of release into the community emphasizes close monitoring of offenders and rigorous conditions. Research findings are presented in "Evaluating Intensive Supervision Probation/Parole."

Finally, the most controversial punishment of all is under discussion in " 'This Man Has Expired.' "

Looking Ahead: Challenge Questions

If you were to argue the pathology of imprisonment, what points would you make? On the other hand, if you were to justify continued imprisonment of offenders, what would you stress?

If you were a high-level correctional administrator and had the luxury of designing a "humane" prison, what would it be like? What aspects of a traditional prison would you keep? What would you eliminate? What new strategies or programs would you introduce?

What are your feelings about the death penalty? Do you think it is an effective deterrent to murder?

Unit 6

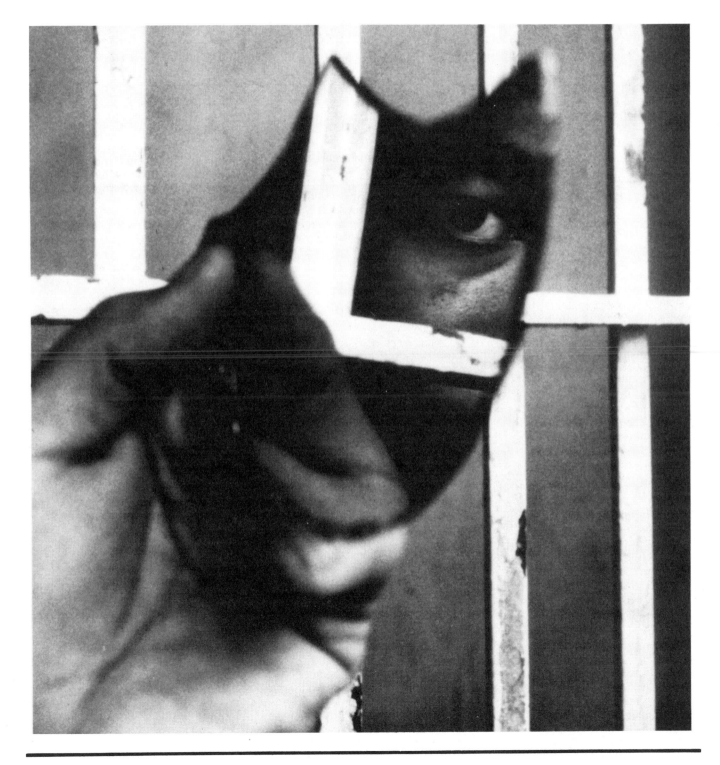

Sentencing and Corrections

Through sentencing, society attempts to express its goals for the correctional process

The sentencing of criminals often reflects conflicting social goals

These objectives are—
• **Retribution**—giving offenders their "just deserts" and expressing society's disapproval of criminal behavior
• **Incapacitation**—separating offenders from the community to reduce the opportunity for further crime while they are incarcerated
• **Deterrence**—demonstrating the certainty and severity of punishment to discourage future crime by the offender (specific deterrence) and by others (general deterrence)
• **Rehabilitation**—providing psychological or educational assistance or job training to offenders to make them less likely to engage in future criminality
• **Restitution**—having the offender repay the victim or the community in money or services.

Attitudes about sentencing reflect multiple goals and other factors

Research on judicial attitudes and practices in sentencing revealed that judges vary greatly in their commitment to various goals when imposing sentences. Public opinion also has shown much diversity about the goals of sentencing, and public attitudes have changed over the years. In fashioning criminal penalties, legislators have tended to reflect this lack of public consensus.

Sentencing laws are further complicated by concerns for—
• **Proportionality**—severity of punishment should be commensurate with the seriousness of the crime
• **Equity**—similar crimes and similar criminals should be treated alike
• **Social debt**—the severity of punishment should take into account the offender's prior criminal behavior.

Judges usually have a great deal of discretion in sentencing offenders

The different sentencing laws give various amounts of discretion to the judge in setting the length of a prison or jail term. In a more fundamental respect, however, the judge often has a high degree of discretion in deciding whether or not to incarcerate the offender at all. Alternatives to imprisonment include—
• probation
• fines
• forfeiture of the proceeds of criminal activity
• restitution to victims
• community service
• split sentences, consisting of a short period of incarceration followed by probation in the community.

Often, before a sentence is imposed a presentence investigation is conducted to provide the judge with information about the offender's characteristics and prior criminal record.

Disparity and uncertainty arose from a lack of consensus over sentencing goals

By the early 1970s researchers and critics of the justice system had begun to note that trying to achieve the mixed goals of the justice system without new limits on the discretionary options given to judges had—
• reduced the *certainty* of sanctions, presumably eroding the deterrent effect of corrections
• resulted in *disparity* in the severity of punishment, with differences in the sentences imposed for similar cases and offenders
• failed to validate the effectiveness of various rehabilitation programs in changing offender behavior or predicting future criminality.

Recent sentencing reforms reflect more severe attitudes and seek to reduce disparity and uncertainty

Reforms in recent years have used statutory and administrative changes to—
• clarify the aims of sentencing
• reduce disparity by limiting judicial and parole discretion
• provide a system of penalties that is more consistent and predictable
• provide sanctions consistent with the concept of "just deserts."

The changes have included—
• making prison mandatory for certain crimes and for recidivists
• specifying presumptive sentence lengths
• requiring sentence enhancements for offenders with prior felony convictions
• introducing sentencing guidelines
• limiting parole discretion through the use of parole guidelines
• total elimination of discretionary parole release (determinate sentencing).

States use a variety of strategies for sentencing

Sentencing is perhaps the most diversified part of the Nation's criminal justice process. Each State has a unique set of sentencing laws, and frequent and substantial changes have been made in recent years. This diversity complicates the classification of sentencing systems. For nearly any criterion that may be considered, there will be some States with hybrid systems that straddle the boundary between categories.

From *Report to the Nation on Crime and Justice,* Bureau of Justice Statistics, U.S. Department of Justice, March 1988, pp. 90-93.

The basic difference in sentencing systems is the apportioning of discretion between the judge and parole authorities

Indeterminate sentencing—the judge specifies minimum and maximum sentence lengths. These set upper and lower bounds on the time to be served. The actual release date (and therefore the time actually served) is determined later by parole authorities within those limits.

Partially indeterminate sentencing—a variation of indeterminate sentencing in which the judge specifies only the maximum sentence length. An associated minimum automatically is implied, but is not within the judge's discretion. The implied minimum may be a fixed time (such as 1 year) for all sentences or a fixed proportion of the maximum. In some States the implied minimum is zero; thus the parole board is empowered to release the prisoner at any time.

Determinate sentencing—the judge specifies a fixed term of incarceration, which must be served in full (less any "goodtime" earned in prison). There is no discretionary parole release.

Since 1975 many States have adopted determinate sentencing, but most still use indeterminate sentencing

In 1976 Maine was the first State to adopt determinate sentencing. The sentencing system is entirely or predominantly determinate in these 10 States:

California	Maine
Connecticut	Minnesota
Florida	New Mexico
Illinois	North Carolina
Indiana	Washington

The other States and the District of Columbia use indeterminate sentencing in its various forms. One State, Colorado, after changing to determinate sentencing in 1979, went back to indeterminate sentencing in 1985. The Federal justice system has adopted determinate sentencing through a system of sentencing guidelines.

States employ other sentencing features in conjunction with their basic strategies

Mandatory sentencing—Law requires the judge to impose a sentence of incarceration, often of specified length, for certain crimes or certain categories of offenders. There is no option of probation or a suspended sentence.

Mandatory sentencing laws are in force in 46 States (all except Maine, Minnesota, Nebraska, and Rhode Island) and the District of Columbia. In 25 States imprisonment is mandatory for certain repeat felony offenders. In 30 States imprisonment is mandatory if a firearm was involved in the commission of a crime. In 45 States conviction for certain offenses or classes of offenses leads to mandatory imprisonment; most such offenses are serious, violent crimes, and drug trafficking is included in 18 of the States. Many States have recently made drunk driving an offense for which incarceration is mandated (usually for relatively short periods in a local jail rather than a State prison).

Presumptive sentencing—The discretion of a judge who imposes a prison sentence is constrained by a specific sentence length set by law for each offense or class of offense. That sentence must be imposed in all unexceptional cases. In response to mitigating or aggravating circumstances, the judge may shorten or lengthen the sentence within specified boundaries, usually with written justification being required.

Presumptive sentencing is used, at least to some degree, in about 12 States.

Sentencing guidelines—Explicit policies and procedures are specified for deciding on individual sentences. The decision is usually based on the nature of the offense and the offender's criminal record. For example, the prescribed sentence for a certain offense might be probation if the offender has no previous felony convictions, a short term of incarceration if the offender has one prior conviction, and progressively longer prison terms if the offender's criminal history is more extensive.

Sentencing guidelines came into use in the late 1970s. They are—
• used in 13 States and the Federal criminal justice system
• written into statute in the Federal system and in Florida, Louisiana, Maryland, Minnesota, New Jersey, Ohio, Pennsylvania, and Tennessee
• used systemwide, but not mandated by law, in Utah
• applied selectively in Massachusetts, Michigan, Rhode Island, and Wisconsin
• being considered for adoption in other States and the District of Columbia.

Sentence enhancements—In nearly all States, the judge may lengthen the prison term for an offender with prior felony convictions. The lengths of such enhancements and the criteria for imposing them vary among the States.

In some States that group felonies according to their seriousness, the repeat offender may be given a sentence ordinarily imposed for a higher seriousness category. Some States prescribe lengthening the sentences of habitual offenders by specified amounts or imposing a mandatory minimum term that must be served before parole can be considered. In other States the guidelines provide for sentences that reflect the offender's criminal history as well as the seriousness of the offense. Many States prescribe conditions under which parole eligibility is limited or eliminated. For example, a person with three or more prior felony convictions, if convicted of a serious violent offense, might be sentenced to life imprisonment without parole.

Sources: Surveys conducted for the Bureau of Justice Statistics by the U.S. Bureau of the Census in 1985 and by the Pennsylvania Commission on Crime and Delinquency in 1986.

Sentencing guidelines usually are developed by a separate sentencing commission

Such a commission may be appointed by the legislative, executive, or judicial branch of State government. This is a departure from traditional practice in that sentences are prescribed through an administrative procedure rather than by explicit legislation.

In some States the guidelines are prescriptive in that they specify whether or not the judge must impose a prison sentence and the presumptive sentence length. In other States the guidelines are advisory in that they provide information to the judge but do not mandate sentencing decisions.

To determine whether a prison sentence should be imposed, the guidelines usually consider offense severity and the offender's prior criminal record. A matrix that relates these two factors may be used.

6. PUNISHMENT AND CORRECTIONS

Sentencing matrix

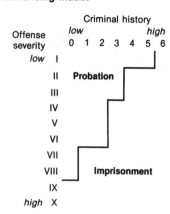

Adapted from *Preliminary report on the development and impact of the Minnesota sentencing guidelines,* Minnesota Sentencing Guidelines Commission, July 1982.

Sentencing guidelines used in the Federal justice system were developed by the United States Sentencing Commission. The guidelines provide for determinate sentencing and the abolition of parole. Ranges of sentence length are specified for various offense classifications and offender characteristics. The judge must provide written justification for any sentence that deviates from the guideline range; sentences that are less severe can be appealed by the prosecution, and sentences that are more severe can be appealed by the defense.

Changes in sentencing have brought changes in correctional practices

Many sentencing reforms have led to changes in the way correctional systems operate:

The proliferation of determinate and mandatory sentences during the past decade, together with dissatisfaction about the uncertainties of indeterminate sentencing (especially the linking of release decisions to rehabilitative progress or predictions of future behavior), have led to modifications in parole decisionmaking. Many States now use parole guidelines, and many have modified their use of "goodtime" and other incentives for controlling inmate behavior and determining release dates.

New administrative requirements, such as collection of victim restitution funds, operation of community service programs, and levying fees for probation supervision, room and board, and other services, have been added to traditional correctional practices.

Changes in sentencing laws and practices may be affecting the size of the correctional clientele. Such changes include—
• using determinate and mandatory sentencing
• limiting or abolishing parole discretion

• lowering the age at which youthful offenders become subject to the adult criminal justice system
• enacting in a few jurisdictions laws providing for life imprisonment without the possibility of parole.

Forfeiture is a relatively new sanction

What is forfeiture?

Forfeiture is government seizure of property derived from or used in criminal activity. Its use as a sanction aims to strip racketeers and drug traffickers of their economic power because the traditional sanctions of imprisonment and fines have been found inadequate to deter or punish enormously profitable crimes. Seizure of assets aims not only to reduce the profitability of illegal activity but to curtail the financial ability of criminal organizations to continue illegal operations.

There are two types of forfeiture: civil and criminal

• **Civil forfeiture**—a proceeding against property used in criminal activity. Property subject to civil forfeiture often includes vehicles used to transport contraband, equipment used to manufacture illegal drugs, cash used in illegal transactions, and property purchased with the proceeds of the crime. No finding of criminal guilt is required in such proceedings. The government is required to post notice of the proceedings so that any party who has an interest in the property may contest the forfeiture.

• **Criminal forfeiture**—a part of the criminal action taken against a defendant accused of racketeering or drug trafficking. The forfeiture is a sanction imposed on conviction that requires the defendant to forfeit various property rights and interests related to the violation. In 1970 Congress revived this sanction that had been dormant in American law since the Revolution.

The use of forfeiture varies greatly among jurisdictions

The Federal Government originally provided for criminal forfeiture in the Racketeer Influenced and Corrupt Organization (RICO) statute and the

Comprehensive Drug Prevention and Control Act, both enacted in 1970. Before that time civil forfeiture had been provided in Federal laws on some narcotics, customs, and revenue infractions. More recently, language on forfeiture has been included in the Comprehensive Crime Control Act of 1984, the Money Laundering Act of 1986, and the Anti-drug Abuse Act of 1986.

Most State forfeiture procedures appear in controlled substances or RICO laws. A few States provide for forfeiture of property connected with the commission of any felony. Most State forfeiture provisions allow for civil rather than criminal forfeiture. A recent survey responded to by 44 States and territories found that under the controlled substances laws most States provide only for civil forfeiture. Eight States (Arizona, Kentucky, Nevada, New Mexico, North Carolina, Utah, Vermont, and West Virginia), however, have criminal forfeiture provisions.[1] Of the 19 States with RICO statutes, all but 8 include the criminal forfeiture sanction.[2]

What is forfeitable?

Originally most forfeiture provisions aimed to cover the seizure of contraband or modes of transporting or facilitating distribution of such materials. The types of property that may be forfeited have been expanded since the 1970s to include assets, cash, securities, negotiable instruments, real property including houses or other real estate, and proceeds traceable directly or indirectly to violations of certain laws. Common provisions permit seizure of conveyances such as airplanes, boats, or cars; raw materials, products, and equipment used in manufacturing, trafficking, or cultivation of illegal drugs; and drug paraphernalia.

How long does it take to determine if property can be forfeited?

In most cases some time is provided before the actual forfeiture to allow persons with an interest in seized property to make a claim. Seized property is normally kept for 6 months to 1 year before being declared forfeit and disposed of. Contraband or materials that are illegal *per se*, such as drugs, are disposed of relatively quickly. Cars, airplanes, boats, and other forms of transportation are usually kept for about 6 months before disposal. Real property is often kept for longer periods. Administrative forfeitures usually take less time than ones that require judicial determination.

Because of the depreciation in value of many assets over time and the cost of storing or caring for such assets, forfeiture may result in a cost rather than revenue to the prosecuting jurisdiction.

What happens to forfeited property?

The disposition of forfeited property is controlled by statute or in some States by their constitutions. In many cases, the seizing agency is permitted to place an asset in official use once it has been declared forfeit by a court. Such assets are usually cars, trucks, boats, or planes used during the crime or proceeds of the crime.

For assets that are sold, the proceeds are usually used first to pay any outstanding liens. The costs of storing, maintaining, and selling the property are reimbursed next. Some States require that, after administrative costs are reimbursed, the costs of law enforcement and prosecution must be paid. More than half the States provide that any outstanding balance go to the State or local treasury, or a part to both.

In eight States law enforcement agencies can keep all property, cash, or sales proceeds. If the State constitution governs distribution, the receiving agency is usually the State or local school system. Some States have specified the recipients to be special programs for drug abuse prevention and rehabilitation.

In 1984 the Federal Government established the Department of Justice Assets Forfeiture Fund to collect proceeds from forfeitures and defray the costs of forfeitures under the Comprehensive Drug Abuse Prevention and Control Act and the Customs Forfeiture Fund for forfeitures under customs laws. These acts also require that the property and proceeds of forfeiture be shared equitably with State and local law enforcement commensurate with their participation in the investigations leading to forfeiture.

Women in Jail: Unequal Justice

An unprecedented influx of female inmates leaves prisons overcrowded and overwhelmed

Californians call it The Campus, and with its low-lying, red-brick buildings set against 120 acres of dairy land, the California Institution for Women at Frontera looks deceptively civilized. The illusion ends inside. Constructed in the early 1950s as a repository for 800 or so wayward ladies, Frontera today holds more than 2,500 women at any given moment. The convicts complain that guards spy on them while they're showering or using the toilet. Inspectors have found rodent droppings and roaches in the food. In a lawsuit against the state, inmates charged that shower drains get so backed up, they have to stand on crates to avoid the slime.

A continent away, New York City's Rose M. Singer jail stands as a testimony to penal enlightenment. Because most inmates are young and sometimes high-spirited, the jail can feel a bit like a boarding school for girls. But the starkly lit hallways and pervasive smell of disinfectant are constant reminders of the true purpose of the place. And even though it was completed only two years ago, it is already seriously overcrowded—a dining room has been turned into a dorm. Above all, the inmates hate the lack of privacy. Says Carmen Gonzalez, who is serving nine months for selling crack, "I wish I was in a cell."

Stiff penalties: For years, the ranks of convicted criminals have been swelling steadily, bringing the nation's prison system perilously close to an overload. The vast majority—94.4 percent—of those inmates are men. But even in jail, women are breaking down the barriers to equal achievement. The Bureau of Justice Statistics reported last week that the female prison population jumped 21.8 percent from 1988 to 1989—the ninth consecutive year that

the rate of increase at women's institutions far outstripped the men's. The number of women doing time has doubled to 40,000 in the last five years (chart). The main reason is drugs. Stiffer penalties are on the books throughout the country and women, who have turned to crack in a way they never embraced other narcotics, have been caught in the sweep. Judges have also shown a greater willingness to incarcerate women than in the past, when chivalry extended even to lawbreakers. "Courts used to look at it as if they were sentencing a mother," says Gary Maynard, Oklahoma's corrections director. "Now they look at it as if they are sentencing a criminal."

Prisons have been largely unprepared to handle the unique problems of their growing female populations. "We assumed that they could benefit from the same programs as men," says Dan Russell, administrator of Montana's division of corrections. "But women have a lot of psychological and medical needs" that men do not. Often, children are at the heart of the matter. Three quarters of the women are mothers, and many of them single parents. In recent years, a number of prisons have created programs to provide greater contact between kids and inmate moms (box). And public officials have begun to acknowledge—sometimes nudged along by lawsuits—that prisons do not provide women with the same rehabilitation or educational programs as men. Inequities in the correctional system, says Washington, D.C., Superior Court Associate Judge Gladys Kessler, "are a mirror of the sex discrimination that occurs in the nonprison population."

Fed by steamy, seamy '50s movies like "Reform School Girl," Americans have had a long fascination with women behind bars. The reality is a good deal more disturb-

ing—and pathetic. The typical offender, according to a 1988 national study conducted for the American Correctional Association, is a young minority mother. In general, she is slightly better educated and less violent than her male counterpart. Many inmates were victims themselves—of poverty, physical violence or sexual abuse. Though most poor people are obviously law abiding, some analysts say more

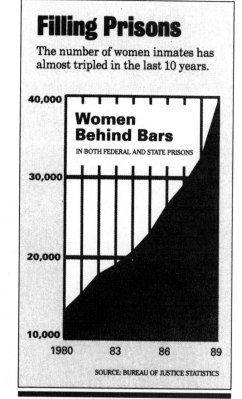

Filling Prisons

The number of women inmates has almost tripled in the last 10 years.

Women Behind Bars
IN BOTH FEDERAL AND STATE PRISONS

SOURCE: BUREAU OF JUSTICE STATISTICS

'Dear Mommy, How Are You Doing?'

It is Mother's Day at the Lorton Correctional Complex outside Washington, D.C., and Michael, 10, is waiting impatiently as the women in camouflage pants file into the gym. Finally, Jennifer Nimmons, who is serving 18 months on a drug charge, arrives and Michael rushes into her arms. He has brought his mother a present: a cutout of a dancing bear with a letter on its stomach, which he reads aloud. "Dear Mommy, How are you doing in the hospital? Have a happy mother's day, this is a poem for you. 'Roses are red, Violets are blue, You are the best mother, I ever wrote to'." Then he asks: "Is this a hospital?"

Confused, enraged, hurt—children like Michael are innocent victims of their mothers' crimes. Until recently, prison officials didn't recognize that a child's emotional dependence doesn't stop just because his mother lands behind bars. Now attitudes are changing: institutions around the country have put programs in place to foster that vital relationship.

Some of the most innovative begin at birth. Federal prisons separate mothers and newborns after 24 hours, and few state pens allow inmates to spend time with infants. The Rose M. Singer Center on Rikers Island is a heartening contrast. The mothers' cells surround the glass-walled nursery on three sides, and an intercom system keeps them in constant touch. If kids cry, moms can rush to their aid—the cells are never locked. Because a female federal prisoner is likely to do time far from home, a program called PACT (Parents and Children Together) is designed to improve long-distance parenting. "We counsel inmates to get as involved as possible by calling teachers on a regular basis," says Jaretta Jones, an instructor at the federal penitentiary in Lexington, Ky.

Psychic costs: Penal authorities have also become more sensitive about the psychic costs to kids. Some children feel guilty about their parents' predicaments—imagining, for example, if they hadn't opened the door for the cops, Mom would be free. The Huron Valley Women's Facility in Ypsilanti, Mich., provides kids with therapy after visits. "If we are going to lock up these mothers, we have to take some responsibility for those children," says Marilyn Marshall, a vocational counselor at the prison. "They will certainly be our next generation of prisoners unless we pay attention now."

---

women have taken to crime to support their families as economic conditions have worsened. In Florida last year, more than two thirds of the men were working at the time of their arrest, while 73.8 percent of the women were jobless.

New Breed: Women prisoners have always been easier to manage than the men—they're more prone to verbal than physical abuse. But that may be changing. Some penologists worry that the lack of space will not only exacerbate existing problems—for example, fights stemming from lesbian jealousies—but provoke the women into new forms of aggression. "The recidivism, as well as the level of violence, seems to be directly linked to the amount of overcrowding," says Rebecca Jurado, an attorney with the ACLU of southern California.

Drugs, in particular, have stimulated violent outbreaks. More than half the women in the federal system were convicted on drug charges. And the problem doesn't stop at the prison gate. Mary Vermeer, a deputy warden in Perryville, Ariz., says new inmates are delighted to discover that, despite efforts to stem the flow, the drug pipeline makes it almost as easy to get a fix inside as out. At Frontera, crack houses and shooting galleries operate in portable toilets in the yard. Old-timers complain about the new breed of "druggie." "They don't care about nothing," says Delores Lee, 37, who is doing 25 years in Florida on a murder conviction. "They steal; they break things."

AIDS also contributes to the crisis atmosphere in American prisons. So far, there are no national figures measuring the disease among the convict population. An official Massachusetts study based on 400 inmates who volunteered to be tested found that 35 percent of the women were HIV-positive, compared with 13 percent of the men. In California, any woman who tested positive was put into a segregated AIDS unit—whether or not she was actually ill. As a result of a discrimination lawsuit, many HIV inmates at Frontera have been mainstreamed during the day—but must return to their separate quarters to sleep.

Though few would argue that male convicts are socially well adjusted, penal experts tend to agree that female inmates require—and desire—more psychological counseling. Many women feel enormous guilt about their kids. "When men get arrested, they ask for a lawyer," says Brenda Smith, an attorney at the National Women's Law Center in Washington, D.C. "When women get arrested, they ask about their children." The children effectively serve as hostages on the outside, ensuring that the women make few demands. "The No. 1 issue for women is getting their kids back," says Sarah Buel, a battered-women's advocate in Massachusetts. "The unwritten rule is, don't make a fuss and we'll help you get [them] back."

Prison officials have begun to acknowledge the enormous disparity in the treatment of men and women. In a number of recent lawsuits, women plaintiffs have accused the system of gender bias. A major problem is "overincarceration." Because of a lack of facilities, many low-security inmates have landed in medium-security penitentiaries. Many of the women have been subjected to greater restrictions, such as strip searches, than their crimes warrant—and which their male counterparts are largely spared.

Some social critics believe the states should help inmates break the cycle of abuse and poverty that led many of them into crime in the first place. They also argue that the system should recognize that women generally pose less of a threat to public safety than men and deserve more lenient sentences. "Assuming that we want to help offenders, the best place to do this is not in prison," says Nicole Hahn Rafter, author of "Partial Justice," a history of women's prisons. That attitude is unlikely to win much support, particularly now that public opinion favors strict penalties. But it is clear that the overcrowded conditions and lack of rehabilitation programs doubly punish women—and do little to advance the society's interests.

ELOISE SALHOLZ *with* LYNDA WRIGHT *in Los Angeles,* CLARA BINGHAM *in Washington,* TONY CLIFTON *in New York,* GINNY CARROLL *in Houston,* SPENCER REISS *in Miami,* FARAI CHIDEYA *in Boston and bureau reports*

Pennsylvanians Prefer Alternatives to Prison

Steven Farkas

The Pennsylvanian public strongly supports the use of alternative sanctions for nonviolent offenders, according to a recent study conducted by the Public Agenda Foundation. Pennsylvanians did not perceive alternative sentences to be a lenient, "slap-on-the-wrist" response to crime. While policymakers like alternative sentences principally for the budgetary savings they promise, citizens saw alternatives as inherently attractive options. Citizens liked alternatives because they allow the criminal justice system to react in a calibrated way to make the punishment fit the crime, because they hope alternatives will change the future behavior of offenders, and because they think alternatives will save money.

DESCRIPTION OF THE STUDY

In October 1992, Public Agenda—a nonprofit, nonpartisan research and public education organization—conducted a sur-

vey for the Edna McConnell Clark Foundation with a demographically and geographically representative sample of about 400 citizens in six areas across Pennsylvania. Participants' attitudes about criminal justice issues were gauged through two questionnaires and through focus group discussions.

Each participant:

☛ filled out a questionnaire (the pretest) that gauged attitudes on criminal justice issues and asked the respondent to sentence 24 hypothetical offenders to prison or probation;

☛ watched a 22-minute video produced by Public Agenda about prison overcrowding and five alternative sentences—strict probation, strict probation plus restitution, strict probation plus community service, house arrest, and boot camp—along with the main arguments for and against using the alternatives;

☛ met in a small group of about 15 people to discuss the issues for about 90 minutes under the guidance of a neutral moderator. The alternatives were summarized on a sheet of paper handed out to each participant during the discussion; and

☛ filled out a second questionnaire (the posttest) sentencing the same 24 offenders, but with the five alternative sentences added to the sentencing options.

INITIAL RESULTS

Initially, Pennsylvanians expressed typical "get-tough" attitudes toward the crime problem. Most wanted longer prison sentences for convicted offenders, most wanted convicted offenders to serve at least some time in prison, and most thought judges were "too soft." Although the vast majority (85 percent) knew their state's prisons were overcrowded, strong majorities rejected build-

From *Overcrowded Times*, Vol. 4, No. 2, April 1993, pp. 1, 13-15. Reprinted by permission.

Pennsylvanians Prefer Alternatives

ing more prisons if this meant increasing taxes or cutting public services. By a two to one margin, Pennsylvanians were not concerned whether prison overcrowding amounted to cruel and unusual punishment. In the focus group discussions, many respondents said overcrowding added to the deterrent value of prisons and expressed little sympathy for incarcerated offenders. A woman from the Wilkes-Barre area expressed this sentiment when she said, "It's [prison] not supposed to be nice for you. They're in there to be punished."

PREDISPOSITION FOR ALTERNATIVES

These pretest attitudes seemingly illustrate the dynamic that created the present budgetary and overcrowding pressures. But the public's approach to the crime problem is actually more complex and flexible than these initial "lock-'em-up" attitudes indicate. Even in the pretest—before viewing the video and participating in discussion—an overwhelming 85 percent of Pennsylvanians favored finding "new ways to punish offenders that are less expensive than prison but harsher than probation." In the pretest, three-fourths (76 percent) favored the use of alternative sentences such as restitution and community service. Pennsylvanians support alternative sentencing not only in the abstract. When asked to sentence a variety of 24 hypothetical offenders, majorities preferred applying alternatives over prison and probation to most cases.

SENTENCING OF 24 HYPOTHETICAL OFFENDERS

Table 1 on page 14 briefly describes the 24 hypothetical cases and Pennsylvanians' sentencing preferences for those offenders in the pretest and posttest. The cases

Table 1: Comparison of Sentencing Twenty-four Hypothetical Cases

Description of Offense	Pretest Prison	Posttest Prison	Posttest Alternatives
	%	%	%
BURGLARY/EMBEZZLEMENT:			
Burglary, first offense, 15-year-old, unarmed	9	2	69
Burglary, first offense, unarmed, $5,000 stereo from a store	37	5	83
Embezzlement, first offense, $250,000 in forged checks	64	24	71
Burglary, second offense, armed, $5,000 stereo	87	47	51
FORCE OR THREAT OF FORCE:			
Armed robbery, first offense, pointed a loaded gun at a victim	76	39	56
Rape, first offense, forced rape in a park	96	77	22
PETTY THEFT:			
Shoplifting, first offense, male, $150 radio from a store	13	3	60
Purse snatching, second offense, 15-year-old male	37	4	91
Shoplifting, fifth offense, female, $150 dress from a store	71	22	73
Same offense as above, but head of household	45	13	81
Shoplifting, third offense, male, $150 radio from a store	82	20	78
Shoplifting, fifth offense, male, $150 radio from a store	92	47	51
Same offense as above, but head of household	56	27	69
DRUNK DRIVING/JOYRIDING:			
Joyriding, first offense	13	2	61
Drunk driving, first offense	18	4	64
Drunk driving, second offense, crashed into fire hydrant	62	18	80
BAR BRAWLS:			
Bar brawl, second offense, no injury	17	2	78
Bar brawl, second offense, injured victim	62	18	79
DRUG CRIMES:			
Drug possession, first offense, two grams of cocaine—a probable user	23	9	71
Drug possession, first offense, ten grams of cocaine—a probable drug dealer	48	17	76
Drug dealer, first offense	52	18	67
Drug dealer/addict, third offense, sought treatment	63	28	69
Drug dealer/addict, fifth offense, sought treatment	75	53	41
OTHERS:			
Statutory rape, first offense, 21-year-old male with a 15-year-old female, no force involved	24	15	57

Source: *Punishing Criminals: The People of Pennsylvania Speak Out.* 1993. Prepared by the Public Agenda Foundation for the Edna McConnell Clark Foundation.

range in severity from joyriding to rape, but the bulk of the offenses were of moderate severity (e.g., property or drug crimes)—the types of crimes criminal justice experts often cite as most appropriate for alternative sentences. The cases also present scenarios that introduce gender, juvenile offenders, and mitigating circumstances such as being the household provider.

In the pretest—before the educational intervention and given only the options of prison and probation—majorities sentenced 15 offenders to prison and nine to probation. In the posttest—after the intervention and with five alternative sentences added to their sentencing options—majorities sentenced 22 of the 24 offenders to alternative sentences. Only two offenders were sentenced to prison in the posttest, and no offender was sentenced to probation. These results are very similar to comparable studies that Public Agenda conducted in Alabama in 1989 and in Delaware in 1991. A woman from Exton explained her support for alternative sentences by saying, "I like the idea of progressive punishment. In every school discipline code you don't go from one suspension to expulsion—there are steps all the way up. If they do it properly, you're going to stop them somewhere down the line."

A brief review of the public's sentencing patterns illustrates their preference for alternative sentences, especially in cases involving nonviolent offenses. Majorities sentenced four of the five drug offenders to prison in the pretest but in the posttest four of the five were instead sentenced to alternatives. For example, while a 48 percent plurality of pretest respondents favored prison for a first-time offender convicted of selling 10 grams of cocaine, three-fourths (76 percent) in the posttest sentenced him to alternatives. Policymakers heartened by the potential savings engendered by

moving an offender from prison "down" to alternatives should note that the public also moved offenders from probation "up" to alternatives. For example, while two-thirds (66 percent) of pretest respondents had opted to sentence to probation an offender convicted of possession of two grams of cocaine, 71 percent sentenced him to alternatives in the posttest. A Philadelphia man said of probation, "It's a joke! They feel 'Okay, I commit a crime, you put me on probation. Probation is a joke so I'll go do something else.' They should put them in there, maybe boot camp, on the first offense. Maybe it'll make them think twice."

The public drew the line, however, when it came to violent criminals or the most persistent offenders. More than three-fourths (77 percent) in the posttest opted to imprison an offender convicted of mugging and raping a woman (96 percent had wanted to imprison him in the pretest). A 53 percent posttest majority wanted to imprison a drug dealer convicted of his fifth offense (75 percent had wanted to imprison him in the pretest).

PERCEPTIONS OF ALTERNATIVES

Respondents were generally hopeful about the impact of alternative sentences and did not perceive them to be lenient. An overwhelming 86 percent agreed that, "alternatives give judges the flexibility to make the punishment fit the crime." A man from the Wilkes-Barre area said, "I like these alternatives for a judge because he has a little more right to treat a person as an individual." Respondents also expect alternatives to save taxpayers money: fully 79 percent agree that "alternative sentences are a less expensive way to punish offenders." Another two-thirds (66 percent) thought that, "alternatives improve the chances that an offender will be rehabilitated." Only 24 percent agreed with the state-

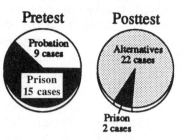

Figure 1: Comparison of Sentencing Twenty-four Hypothetical Cases

Pretest

Probation 9 cases
Prison 15 cases

Posttest

Alternatives 22 cases
Prison 2 cases

Source: *Punishing Criminals: The People of Pennsylvania Speak Out.* 1993. Prepared by the Public Agenda Foundation for the Edna McConnell Clark Foundation.

ment that, "alternatives are not harsh enough;" 61 percent disagreed.

PREFERRED ALTERNATIVES

When asked which of the five alternatives should be used most often, respondents preferred three alternatives: boot camp, strict probation plus restitution, and strict probation plus community service. When posttest respondents sentenced the 24 hypothetical offenders, they most often relied on those same three alternatives. Strict probation alone and house arrest were the least preferred alternatives.

The Pennsylvanians clearly voiced their preference for sanctions that force convicted offenders to work or pay back the victim or the community for crimes committed. There was a sense that work offered a chance for rehabilitation. One woman said of boot camp, "This teaches self-discipline to some kids that have never had it at home." Restitution was perceived as especially appropriate for property crimes. A woman from the Pittsburgh area said, "Generally the people who embezzle have homes, take vacations. Why should they be able to do that and not pay restitution to the person they embezzled?" However, the public disliked house arrest because the option lacked a work component. A Wilkes-Barre man said, "It's not getting at the cause of the crime. With a white-collar criminal their home is an entertainment capital itself. So they are stuck in their own home with their VCR, three color TVs. Where's the punishment there?"

PERCEPTIONS OF PRISON

It is interesting to note parallels between the public's views of prisons and their least preferred alternatives. A majority (60 percent) thought Pennsylvania's inmates "spend most of their time watching television, playing cards or basketball and not having to work." Almost half (49 percent) thought that "Pennsylvania's prisons turn most offenders into hardened criminals who are more likely to commit crime when they leave prison."

RESPONSE TO VIOLATIONS OF ALTERNATIVE SENTENCES

Respondents' reactions to an offender who violated the terms of his alternative sentence (strict probation) is enlightening in that they reflect a desire for enforcement of sanctions and an overall

strategy toward crime—tough but calibrated. Sixty percent wanted more severe alternatives for a man convicted of shoplifting who oversleeps and therefore misses a meeting with his probation officer, with only 5 percent opting for prison. When the offender is described as failing a drug test, 62 percent moved him to more severe alternatives and another 26 percent to prison. When the offender repeats his shoplifting offense, 55 percent moved him to tougher alternatives and 39 percent to prison.

MANDATORY SENTENCES

The issue of mandatory sentences is a vexing one for criminal justice experts. On the one hand, there is public support and even insistence on the adoption of mandatory sentences. On the other hand, such sentencing aggravates fiscal burdens and overcrowded prison conditions. Not surprisingly, our survey found large and stable majorities supporting mandatory sentences. About three-fourths of the public favored mandatory sentences, even after reading two arguments for and three against the policy. The public's attraction to manda-

tory sentences may be explained by their overwhelming agreement with the statement that "mandatory sentencing laws stop some judges from being too lenient on offenders." For the public, mandatory sentences may represent a kind of insurance policy guaranteeing offenders will receive some level of punishment. It is interesting to speculate on what the public's response would be to mandatory punishments, such as alternative sentences, that do not involve prison.

CONCLUSION

In Pennsylvania, as in Delaware and Alabama, the public displays a strong willingness to support alternatives to incarceration for nonviolent offenders. This study shows that the public's approach to criminal justice issues is pragmatic and nuanced, not ideological or "knee-jerk." Support for alternatives was steady across racial, political, gender, education, and geographic groupings. The boundaries of political permission—the leeway and support to undertake change that citizens will give their governmental leadership—seem to extend to the substantial but delimited use of alternatives.

THE DETOXING OF PRISONER 88A0802

*Like many junkies and crackheads who haunt American cities,
Bill Giddens was a one-man crime wave. Fourteen months ago, he entered
an in-prison 'therapeutic community.' Now he's out, clean and
trying to stay that way.*

Peter Kerr

Peter Kerr is a reporter for The Times

THE 200 INMATES AT THE PHOENIX HOUSE DRUG TREAT-
ment unit at the State Medium Security Facility in
Marcy, N.Y., are cordoned off from the 1,300 other
prisoners by a high chain-link fence topped with
barbed wire. When they march out of the treatment
zone for meals, stepping smartly in double file, other
prisoners glare and mutter "crackheads" and "snitches"
at them. They are hated because their life, inside a
protected world each day, violates the unwritten laws
of prison.

"You *must* have hospital corners," says Bill Giddens,
a slender prisoner of 6 foot 2 and 180 pounds. Giddens
is touring rows of cubicles separated by chest-high
partitions. Men stand attentively next to beds made
tight enough to bounce coins off. He walks the shiny
waxed floors with heavy socks pulled over his shoes so
he will not leave a mark. An assistant with a clipboard
trails behind.

"This is the place where you get your pride and
quality," Giddens says as he runs his long bony fingers
down walls, behind chairs and over hidden flat sur-
faces. "Dust on a partition divider." The assistant
makes a note.

Bill Giddens is an unlikely drill sergeant. One
day six years ago the shoe of a police officer
pressed down so hard on his face he thought his
skull would crack. Cold grains of concrete dug into his
cheek. Yet as he lay surrounded by a circle of armed
officers, he struggled to reach for one of their revolvers.
By the frenzied calculus of a heroin addict, he imag-

ined that he could outgun them all. As happens so
often in the Williamsburg section of Brooklyn where
Giddens grew up, a crowd gathered to see detectives
arrest the young man—one more terrifying figure from
the neighborhood who deserved to go prison.

Bill Giddens, like the legions of junkies and crackheads who haunt many communities, had been a one-
man crime wave: in two years he had robbed more than
200 people. His was a life of craving and satiation. He
knew little of guilt or responsibility. He was the type
who long ago led criminal-justice experts to abandon
the idea that predatory street criminals could be
rehabilitated.

But at drug-treatment programs, like the one at the
Marcy prison, in more than a dozen states from California to Connecticut, criminal-justice officials now report
enough success to begin to transform their thinking.
Two decades ago, they concluded that such programs
were just about worthless. Now they are finding that,
with the help of new research and revised techniques,
prison and post-prison "therapeutic communities," as
the programs are called, have significant potential if
operated correctly. Inmates can readily obtain drugs
somewhere in most prisons, and freeing them of addiction is a momentous event. This is true not only for the
individual inmate, but also for society.

A relatively small number of severe addicts commit
a high percentage of street crime. By targeting them,
these programs may thus have impact. This realization
comes just at a time when a rebellion is building
against the 1980's approach of lock 'em up and throw
away the key—if only because states find they soon
have to make room for other prisoners. In April, two
well-known Federal judges in New York, Whitman
Knapp and Jack B. Weinstein, declared they would no

longer preside over drug cases because the Government's emphasis on long imprisonment without treatment, rehabilitation or prevention was a failure. And last month, the new Attorney General, Janet Reno, called for revision of the national strategy for coping with drugs and crime. Treatment programs in prisons are to be a principal part of that new approach.

So the question reverberates: This time around, have prison authorities hit on a form of rehabilitation that works?

Prisoners inside the beige walls of Marcy's barracks J-2 rise at 5 A.M.

They march half a mile to breakfast and back. Then they stand in a circle, arms around each other's shoulders and chant the Phoenix House philosophy – a kind of prayer for redemption and strength:

> Rise from the ashes of our defeat to take our rightful place in society.
> Society will accept us, for once we have regained our dignity, we will be society.

At a nearby barracks, an encounter session among another circle of green-clad men is reaching full boil. Inmates are challenging R. B., a former drug dealer in his 20's. R. B. has said he is a good father because he bought his family a respectable home in Queens and pampered his little girl with expensive toys and clothes.

"I indict your butt," shouts one prisoner.

"If I need your help, I'll ask for it," snaps R. B., a thickset black slouched in his chair, his arms folded defiantly. "My kid doesn't know what I do on the street."

"It doesn't take much for her to figure out what's going on," says Dana Macklin, a 28-year-old former dealer with a daughter of his own. "Are you aware of this criminal history, what effect it is going to have on your kid?"

"Yeah," barks another inmate, "your best thinking is what got you into jail."

R. B. shakes his head. "My little girl doesn't know what I do."

A deputy director of the program, Manny Rivera, a 52-year-old former prisoner with a rhythmic voice, swept-back hair and dark, lively eyes has been watching.

"Look at this from another point of view." He paces with coffee cup in his hand. "What does a young girl, wherever she lives, what does she need from a father? Who is going to tuck her in tonight? Who is going to fluff up the pillow?"

The men's faces are tough. Some are marred by knife wounds. One has the tattoo of a tear under his eye, a sign that he has killed someone.

All are silent.

"Who is going to tell her everything is going to be all right?," Manny says. "What man is going to be there for her? You are not that man now."

R. B.'s eyes are downcast.

"I went to jail the last time when I was 40," Manny says. "I don't want that for you, man. We just want what is best for you."

The theory of the therapeutic community is this: to treat addiction, one must change a person's values, thinking, moods, behavior and spirituality. The therapeutic community aims to resocialize people and force them to embrace responsibility, honesty and caring for others. It attempts to teach them to recognize their own feelings and think and speak clearly and honestly.

Some prisoners call what is going on brainwashing, or mind control. For many, however, the therapeutic community is the first family they have ever really had. In fact the prisoners call themselves a family. Other versions of the therapeutic community exist outside of prison, not only for treating drug addiction but also for helping alcoholics and the mentally ill.

As Giddens tells it, it was an excruciating breakthrough to learn to step back, look at himself objectively, and express feelings in full sentences.

"Talking with me before I came here, it was always yes-no, I mean you would of thought you were talking to a mute, I mean, I always thought I would always say the wrong thing." He pauses, looks at my notebook and begins to articulate each word slowly. "I am deeply gratified that I have gotten my communication skills up to par. I guess what I have learned here in treatment is that to feel and know yourself is to be strong. I am not ashamed of who is inside Bill."

Giddens takes me back to his "cube" and, from the back of a cabinet, pulls out six shrunken gray objects, with a year written on each in black magic marker. When he arrived in prison, he got six oranges and on each birthday marked off another year. Today they are private symbols of his wasted years.

"They are dried up, no color, no smell, no juice left in them," Giddens says quietly.

Bill Giddens was born in Brooklyn in 1957 to a single mother who went on and off welfare. By 13, he was drinking wine and smoking marijuana in a local park and, with friends in the ninth grade, he learned to jump out from hidden spots in subway stations, grab people from behind and rob them.

He won a basketball scholarship to North Carolina A.&T., but dropped out of college after three months and returned to the neighborhood. In the years that followed, he drifted from job to job, fathered two children and eventually slipped into heavy drug use. A yearlong stint at a state minimum-security prison for car theft, Giddens recalls, had about as much effect as a drop of water on a chunk of wax.

"Nice countryside," he says. "You get pretty much everything you want. I guess I just took to it pretty well."

By 1985 Giddens was shooting up heroin three or four times a day. To support the $90-a-day habit, he says he sometimes robbed as many as two people a day. He often confronted them in elevators or building entryways. They were usually compliant, so he says he did not have to hurt them. It all seemed easy. But one morning when he went out to buy a bottle of orange juice, he was jumped by six policemen and arrested for robbery.

He spent the next five and a half years in some of New York State's toughest prisons. Everyone owned a weapon, be it a knife sharpened from a steel bedpost part or a razor blade tucked between gum and cheek. Drugs were easy to obtain. Giddens learned to trust no one and show no weakness. In Sing Sing, he said, prison society tested a new arrival by having one longtime inmate offer a cigarette. Saying "thank you" with a tone of relief or appreciation betrayed fear and weakness. Within days, the new prisoner was told he was in debt and had to do what the gang commanded. Unless he refused and fought, he would be marked forever as a victim.

Giddens refused to take anything from anyone.

The current national turn back to rehabilitation arises in part from desperation.

With the end of the Reagan-Bush years when the Federal Government frowned on rehabilitating prisoners, courts have ordered more than 40 states to relieve overcrowding. Staggering numbers of young minority men are under the supervision of the criminal-justice system (by one study, about one in four black men ages 20 to 29 is in prison, on probation or on parole). Incarceration costs $25,000 a year per prisoner in New York. The present number of prisoners is expected to rise from more than 1.3 million to more than 2 million people by the year 2000; small wonder that many criminal-justice experts say the Government must take a new approach.

"The great drug triumph of the Reagan-Bush years—the decline in the number of marijuana and cocaine users—produced few visible social benefits," says a leading authority on drug enforcement, Mark A. R. Kleiman, an associate professor of public policy at the John F. Kennedy School of Government at Harvard. "Hard-core problem users were not the ones who stopped using drugs. But they are where the crime, violence and disorder come from."

The program at Marcy, which has been run by Phoenix House along with the Department of Corrections since 1990, is one of seven in New York State. It chooses prisoners who have no convictions for violent or heinous crimes and are available for release within two years. If they join and succeed at 6 to 12 months of therapy, they can be released for up to one year more of treatment in a residential therapeutic community in Queens. Or the most promising are released to live at home, work and attend therapy sessions at night. In either case, they are required to stay in the program, attending intensive encounter sessions until they have been in treatment for two years. If their behavior turns erratic or they fail a weekly urine test for drugs, they are returned to prison.

The attraction is that if they agree to treatment, they may get out of prison early. But once they enter treatment they cannot choose to leave until it's over.

Arriving at the treatment unit, Bill Giddens recalls, was like passing through the looking glass. When he got off the bus, several inmates grabbed his bags and ran ahead with them into the dormitory. Giddens thought this was a test and was heading for a fight. But inside he found his bags on his bed and the perpetrators smiling, welcoming him aboard.

"I was most worried by the fact that the inmates were in charge," Giddens says. "I thought I would be subject to someone disrespecting me and abusing me and no one there to do anything about it. The next day I saw a circle of men were cursing, screaming."

He says they began to insult one member viciously. "I see it in his face that this guy wants to jump someone. I say to myself, Bill, stay clear, someone's gonna get hurt. But afterwards, they get up and they hug each other. I say, this is weird stuff. I gotta learn how the game goes so I do not stand out."

Giddens practiced for hours in advance what he would say in meetings. He grew angry when others, particularly younger men or those with worse criminal records, tried to correct him. Slowly he became aware of his rage at a world that treated him as worthless. Even worse, he loathed himself because he believed the world was right.

The idea is that even when prisoners are not attending their intensive therapy sessions, which may be twice a day, they are working together, recording each others missteps and attempting to rise in a hierarchy by demonstrating empathy, honesty and dedication to work.

A new arrival usually starts at the bottom, sweeping, mopping, cleaning toilets. A first promotion allows him to work as a barber, or a maintenance worker, and beyond that, in more attractive jobs like supply clerk, or the organizer of group meetings. At the top is a ladder of leadership positions, with individuals often rising and falling, depending on how their peers and counselors judge their progress. It all amounts to a 24-hour-a-day floating psychotherapy session, in which men experience a level of scrutiny and intimacy they have never known before.

Over eight months, Giddens began to believe he could change, stay free of drugs and crime and begin to organize a life outside. But he learned that that life outside was more complicated than when he left it. The mother of his children had become a crack addict, and last July, his 11-year-old son and his 7-year-old daughter were separated and sent to live with what he believed were insensitive foster families.

He became desperate to retrieve his children: "I felt that they were doing time, for what I have done."

To prepare for life outside, he used his first three-day furlough to wander through department stores and in the legal district of downtown Brooklyn and strike up conversations with sales people, legal secretaries and lawyers. He wanted to practice talking to articulate people. He got in touch with relatives to see if they knew of any kind of menial job. And he met with his children at a city social service center. He promised they would be together sometime soon.

One day after he returned from that furlough, I walked with him to the prison dining hall. Looking up at him as he towers over me, I found my own mind spinning off a bit: I thought both that I liked him and that he scared me.

Soft-spoken, self-effacing, Giddens had the manner of an earnest student. Yet I could also imagine him in a dark subway entrance or in an alleyway, pointing a gun at my head. In my imagination he was demanding my wallet, my watch and my wedding ring. Was this "Raising Arizona," the film in which prison therapy turns ordinary bank robbers into "emotionally integrated" bank robbers, who terrorize the countryside while getting in touch with their feelings.

Can six months, a year, two years of treatment undo decades of antisocial behavior?

How will the best of the inmates in this program fare, once they are alone, in poor neighborhoods, where unemployment is above 20 percent, where old friends are addicts, and crime and drugs still seem, to so many, to be the only way out?

Those same thoughts come to mind as I interview David Jordan, a 25-year-old, short, rotund former crack dealer from Harlem who never finished the ninth grade. Jordan, or Jelly, as they call him, left school to pursue a career as a break dancer on Manhattan sidewalks. He hit it big, appearing in television commercials and touring in concerts. But when work suddenly disappeared, he figured only the drug trade offered him same quick status and money.

"The program says if you stick to it you can do it," Jelly says. "I know I am being trained. The way I speak. The way I present myself. I am starting to feel good about myself. But my people, we don't have much. I am poor. I am poorly educated. When I get outside, I need an income and I feel like if I believe in this too much, am I setting myself up for a fall.

"Sometimes I am faking changes and it's like a war inside me." he adds: "I don't know which side is real . . . I don't know which side I'm on."

Doubts about rehabilitation took hold in the early 1970's, and were expressed in a seminal article in The Public Interest in 1974. It concluded that "with few and isolated exceptions, the rehabilitative efforts that have been reported so far have no appreciable effect on recidivism." From that article, and a book called "The Effectiveness of Correctional Treatment," by Douglas S. Lipton, Robert Martinson and Judith Wilks, published the following year, the belief that "Nothing works," entered the corrections vocabulary. Much of the financing for rehab efforts disappeared.

But drug-related crime has continued to increase in the last decade, despite increased prison sentences for criminals. Between 1978 and 1992, the number of people behind bars grew from 466,000 to 1,326,000. Of people arrested in the 22 largest cities, the Federal Government has found that 55 to 80 percent test positive for drug use. Meanwhile, studies show that a few heavy users commit a disproportionate share of street crimes. Heavy heroin addicts, known among criminal-justice experts as "predators," for example, commit 10 times as many thefts, 15 times as many robberies, 20 times as many burglaries as offenders who don't use drugs. If such offenders can stay off of drugs, research indicates, their criminal activity drops precipitously.

Yet Federal policy during the Reagan-Bush years gave much higher priority to seizing drugs at the borders, fighting drug production overseas and making arrests, than to drug treatment. Justice Department officials who tried to expand treatment programs in prison were rebuffed.

Lipton, one of the authors who once helped promote the "nothing works" theory, now says that the earlier research did not fully explore the potential of therapeutic communities. He says he has found what he regards as surprisingly positive results in a therapeutic community in a state prison on Staten Island with prisoners who on average had been arrested four times. The study of 450 prisoners who started the program between 1977 and 1984 found that 27 percent were rearrested in the three years after they left prison. That compared with a 41 percent rate for those who had no treatment at all. Lipton, a researcher at National Development and Research Institutes, a nonprofit corporation for drug and AIDS research in New York, argues that if prisons target the worst predators, good programs could have a striking impact on street crime. A program in the Oregon State Hospital in Salem showed that 71 percent of the program's graduates were not reincarcerated within three years after release, compared with only 26 percent of inmates who dropped out in less than one month. In addition, studies of graduates of therapeutic communities outside of prisons, where most therapeutic communities operate, show significant reduction in long-term drug use.

Harry K. Wexler, a researcher in the field, says programs often failed in the past because staff workers were poorly trained and treatment did not continue after a prisoner was released.

Critics say some of the current research may be misleading, that, for instance, it may be measuring the behavior of the prisoners who are most likely to succeed. A survey of drug treatment research published by the Federal Institute of Medicine, showed that if one combined the graduates of the Oregon program and those that dropped out in less than one month, the percentage reincarcerated was 36 percent. By comparison, of Oregon parolees who got no treatment 37 percent were reincarcerated.

Others like Mark Kleiman of Harvard agree that therapeutic communities undoubtedly reduce criminal behavior. But how much, they say, is still unclear.

Giddens made a list of all the women he knew and wrote to the only one who never used drugs and always held a steady job. Now they're dating.

Dr. Mitchell S. Rosenthal, president of Phoenix House, the largest residential drug treatment organization in the country, also cautions against rushing overoptimistically to build therapeutic communities. It takes years, Rosenthal says, to cultivate good programs, which rely on experienced counselors who are often graduates of the programs themselves. And aftercare programs are essential. Other experts, like Bruce Carnes, who served in the Bush anti-drug program, ask whether it is fair to give treatment to criminals when other people not in prison—teen-agers in housing projects, for example—are turned away because of limited public funds.

But even if success rates turn out to be low, the arithmetic of treatment is compelling. Therapeutic communities cost about $2,500 to $5,000 per inmate per year. In a state where keeping a prisoner behind bars costs $25,000 a year, treatment pays for itself if just one in five participants serves just one year less. Operators of the Staten Island program, for example, say they far surpass that success rate. Besides, there are immense added savings if any of those prisoners stay off drugs permanently: Innocent people are not mugged, children and spouses do not suffer abuse, AIDS transmission by drug users is reduced and drug-related violence is lessened.

If such thinking seems theoretical, one has only to look at Texas and Alabama. Last year, Texas, which has more than a half-million people in prison or under supervision of probation and parole authorities, established a program to allow judges to sentence convicts to new therapeutic communities instead of prisons. Financed by a $1 billion bond issue, the state intends to create a virtually separate prison system of treatment, with 14,000 new beds. In Alabama, where the number of prisoners has risen to 18,000 from 5,000 in 1980, the state has committed 1,000 beds to drug treatment programs and is also designing separate facilities. Other programs are under way in California, Connecticut, Colorado, Delaware, Florida, Georgia, Hawaii, Minnesota, New Jersey, North Carolina, North Dakota, Ohio, Oregon, Pennsylvania, Virginia, Washington, D.C., Wisconsin, as well as in city and county jails in Illinois and Arizona.

"Our failures on work release have been cut nearly in half," says Dr. Merle Friesen, director of treatment for the Alabama Department of Corrections, referring to temporary release of prisoners for job programs. "People down here are conservative but they aren't dumb. They know that addicts are either stealing or they are about to start."

One day last fall, Bill Giddens awoke at 4 A.M. and moved quietly through the dark, still barracks. He placed a pair of loafers on the chair in one prisoner's cubicle, a sweater in another, a baseball hat in another. When the men in unit J-2 awoke, those with the least to wear found gifts from the man who was going home.

Freedom struck Giddens harshly as he stepped off the bus at the Port Authority Terminal in New York. On a subway platform, he saw two large police officers threatening to arrest a small young man. He walked away.

The weeks that followed were hard. He moved in with his mother and brother in a crowded apartment in the projects of Williamsburg. In contrast to prison, where he had worked his way to the top of society, he found himself at the bottom again, begging for work of any kind.

Day after day he walked into stores and offices in Manhattan, hair neatly combed, in a freshly ironed shirt, saying he was looking for a job. Everyone said no. Officials of the foster care system were reluctant to let his children come to live with his mother, because she had already taken in two other children who belonged to another relative who had become a drug addict.

In his old neighborhood he felt isolated. "I saw one guy I used to do stickups with," he says. "He's out there looking bad. No shoes. Hair's nappy. In my whole neighborhood the guys who are alive haven't moved anywhere. But as soon as they talk to me, see my expressions, they know not to say, 'Hey, Bill, let's hang out.' "

One night I took him to dinner in Greenwich Village. Giddens clearly tensed as we ordered from the menu. When a waitress asked him to repeat himself, he seemed crestfallen, as if he had failed a test. Later we walked the streets crowded with shoppers. At a corner, he stared at the passers-by. I asked, "What is it?"

"Sometimes I look around and I say, Bill, are you the only one around here who doesn't have a real job?," he said. "You are 35 years old and you don't have anything and it is your own fault."

After about a month, Giddens had one of his first successes. He made a list of all the women he knew and sent a letter to the only one he could think of who never used drugs and always had a steady job. He had not seen her in 18 years.

She called. Giddens explained that he had been in prison and that he was starting a new life. "Well, why did you call *me?*" she says. He replied: "Well, to be honest, I went down the list of all the women I knew and you were the pick of the litter." She laughed, and agreed to a date. They have been seeing each other ever since.

After six weeks he found a part-time job as an usher at Broadway theaters run by the Nederlander organization, which paid him between $85 and $185 a week.

But then the job disappeared and he was unemployed for more than a month. Later with the help of Phoenix House, he got work at a stapler factory. He got up every day at 5:30 A.M. and rode the subway an hour and a half to work. Three evenings a week he attended therapy sessions and twice a week met with probation officers. Typically he got home at 11 P.M. On a salary of less than $200 a week, he was able to put $10 each Friday into savings. But after seven weeks, that job disappeared as well.

Then he seemed to wobble. His counselors found him a gritty, low-paying job in a recycling plant but he quit without promptly telling them. Not a good sign. They told me I should stop seeing him without a counselor present. They worried that my interviews might be making him think he was a celebrity and that his struggles in half-finished treatment were over.

But at the end of May, after weeks of searching, he found himself a job as an assistant in a recreation program run by a nonprofit agency in Brooklyn, earning $300 a week. No one can guarantee that Bill Giddens will succeed. Some of the men who left Marcy at about the same time have already been sent back. But his counselors, so far, are encouraged. So is he.

"All I want is a good place for my kids to come to after school that they can call home," he said. "When I see my kids they ask, 'Dad, when will we be together?' I just tell them soon, soon. It will be soon."

Do we need more prisons?

Point ▶▶▶▶▶▶▶▶▶▶▶

Ann W. Richards

Ann W. Richards is governor of Texas.

I f government's most sacred and fundamental obligation is to protect its citizens, government is failing to meet its obligation. Throughout this nation, crime and the fear of crime have fundamentally altered the way we live. People all over America, Texans included, lack the assurance that the criminal justice system is making their cities safer, their homes more secure, their streets free from violent crime. We read too many newspaper stories, see too many horror stories on the evening news, talk with too many friends and acquaintances who have been crime's victims, to believe that we have made our communities safe places for our families.

Making America a safer, more secure place to live is not an easy task. It requires a comprehensive approach, a battle on numerous fronts. Building more prisons is an absolutely crucial component of this multifront strategy.

If our criminal justice system is to be effective, the perpetrator of a crime must know that punishment will be swift and sure. Violent criminals must know that many years will pass before they walk free again. They must serve the bulk of the sentence assessed. And we must be assured that the criminal comes out of prison a changed human being.

To meet those objectives, we have to build enough prison cells to end the revolving-door system that turns criminals loose after they have served only a fraction of their sentences. Last year in Texas, our prisons admitted more than 46,000 new prisoners, enough to fill almost all the space we have. Obviously, something has to give. Either you let some out, or you don't let new ones in — or you build more space. Other states confront the same dilemma.

We need more prison space. Here in Texas, we have no choice. Our prisons are so crowded that we have had to resort to releasing violent prisoners after they have served a mere fraction of their sentences. Some 17,000 felons are clogging up our county jails, because our prison cells are occupied. Thousands of warrants go unserved because of a lack of space.

Even though we have added thousands of prison beds in the past two years and have nine prisons under construction, the backlog is so great that jail overcrowding will continue. With a backlog larger than the total prison population of 36 states, Texas has to build more prisons.

Building more prisons is not a panacea; we understand that fact. If prisons are mere holding spaces,

◀◀◀◀◀◀◀ Counterpoint

Anne M. Larrivee

Maine Rep. Anne M. Larrivee serves on the Joint Select Committee on Corrections, the Maine Criminal Justice Commission and is a member of the Campaign for an Effective Crime Policy.

W e only need more prisons if they're working. So, let's take a critical look at what has happened in the last 10 years. As statistics from the American Correctional Association clearly show, per 100,000 of population we have doubled the number of people behind bars from 1980 to 1990. And in 1992 according to *Americans Behind Bars: One Year Later*, the U.S. rate of incarceration rose 6.8 percent to 455 per 100,000 population, number one in the world. In second place was South Africa, with 311 per 100,000 incarcerated. Their rate declined in 1991 by 6.6 percent. Our incarceration rate has risen more than 100 percent in the last decade and is still going up. If incarceration works to deter crime, ask yourself if you feel 100 percent safer from crime than you did in 1980. Our streets do not feel safer to me. There has been little impact on crime rates in relationship to the tremendous increase in numbers incarcerated. A recent FBI report shows that 1991 was the bloodiest on record with murders up 5.4 percent from the previous year.

There is no disagreement that perpetrators of violent crimes (rape, robbery, assault) must be incapacitated by prison sentences. However, a study by the National Council on Crime and Delinquency found that 80 percent of those going to prison are not serious or violent criminals but are guilty of low-level offenses; minor parole violations; and property, drug and public disorder crimes. Alternatives such as intensive probation, electronic monitoring, restitution and fines for appropriate offenders have shown to be more effective and less costly than incarceration. Warehousing these prisoners at a cost of about $50,000 per bed for construction and $20,000 per year must be rationally analyzed. We must be sure we are not reacting to cries for a popular "get tough" philosophy by simply increasing the number of prisons and the length of the sentences when we can show no better than a negligible effect on crime. If the goals of incarceration are incapacitation, deterrence, punishment and rehabilitation we must scrutinize the effectiveness of our current sentencing structures and building plans. And we must avoid being lured into decisions to satisfy the need for a politically correct voting record.

Most people understand the need to fund prisons, but want to know their investment is working. They want to be assured that they will be safer, criminals will be punished, and that imprisonment will work.

Point

nothing but criminal warehouses, we will never be able to build all that we need.

We must make sure that the right people are occupying prison cells. We must use the prisons to keep violent criminals off the street. We must lock away the people who have no regard for the life or safety of other human beings.

Of course, we cannot look the other way when nonviolent crime occurs. But too often, the hot-check writer or the young first-time burglar ends up occupying prison space that ought to be reserved for murderers and rapists. That's not smart. We need what the professionals call "alternative sentencing" — electronic monitoring, restitution centers, boot camp, intensive supervision probation. We have to make sure that tax money does not become a scholarship to crime school, otherwise known as prison.

Finally, we need to make sure that the prison experience cuts into the cycle of crime, especially into the escalating cycle created by drugs in our society. We know that eight out of 10 people serving time in our state prisons committed crimes that were directly related to their abuse of alcohol and drugs. Six out of 10 prison inmates are rearrested within three years of their release, and drug offenders have a recidivism rate 25 percent higher than other offenders.

Here in Texas, we have set aside 12,000 prison cells for inmates who were put in prison because drugs or alcohol took insidious control of their lives. We are telling them in no uncertain terms that if they want to get out and stay out, they must undergo rigorous treatment and stop alcohol and drug use.

When inmates are forced to confront their addiction and the harm it has done to their lives and the lives of others, three out of four serve their time and never come back. We know we are cutting costs and crime when an inmate leaves prison clean and sober and determined to stay that way. That is what prisons are supposed to do; they are supposed to change people's lives for the better.

We know that building more prisons will not, in and of itself, eliminate crime. But refusing to build them does not work either. Prisons have their place in a carefully designed, comprehensive system of criminal justice. Our job is not only to build them, but to make sure they function effectively.

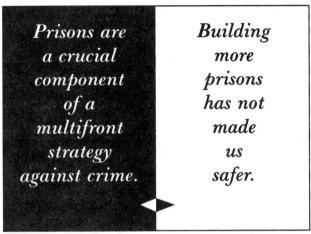

Prisons are a crucial component of a multifront strategy against crime.

Building more prisons has not made us safer.

Counterpoint

I doubt that you could find a handful of voters who think we have crises licked because we now put 100 percent more people behind bars. When informed that from 1982 to 1989 the cost for corrections for the nation per $100 of personal income rose 54 percent while education costs increased only 6 percent, they would wonder how much more good money should be thrown after bad to the detriment of education, health care, early intervention and other methods of building a healthier society.

When we rely on putting people behind bars to decrease crime rates what we fail to recognize is that 98 percent of inmates *will* be out on our streets again. With the trend moving toward incarcerating more and more, funding that could be used for treatment within the prison walls is going to bricks and mortar. The effect is that many inmates are walking out the door with their proverbial new suit and $3 in their pocket with the same problems they brought in, with the same behaviors intact and most likely, new ones learned behind bars. If certain of those inmates had escaped two weeks prior to release, we would have put out APB's, started the manhunts and advised citizens to lock their doors. Ask your corrections officials who's due to be released in the next year from your prisons and if they would feel safe having those inmates in their neighborhoods. Simply building more capacity has not worked.

The answer to the question "Do we need more prisons?" must be no. No, because prison terms are not working; and no, because we are not safer. When the only tool you have is a hammer, every problem looks like a nail. Justice does not mean prisons and only prisons. In an era of scarce resources, we must use more tools, cheaper tools and more effective tools than simply "locking them up," which is costing taxpayers dearly while doing precious little to insure their safety.

Let's look deeper.

Evaluating Intensive Supervision Probation/ Parole: Results of a Nationwide Experiment

Joan Petersilia and Susan Turner

Joan Petersilia is Director, Criminal Justice Program, RAND Corporation, and Associate Professor with the School of Social Ecology at the University of California, Irvine. Susan Turner is a Researcher, Criminal Justice Program, with RAND Corporation. This document is based on the research performed under NIJ Grant No. 90–DD–CX–0062. A fuller discussion of the research can be found in Petersilia, Joan, and Susan Turner. "Intensive Probation and Parole." In *Crime and Justice: An Annual Review of Research*, vol. 17. ed. Michael Tonry. Chicago: University of Chicago Press, forthcoming 1993.

Sentencing practices in this country suggest that offenses can be divided into two categories. When the crime is relatively serious, offenders are put behind bars; when it is less so, they are put on probation, often with only perfunctory supervision. This two-fold division disregards the range of severity in crime, and as a result, sentencing can err in one direction or another: either it is too harsh, incarcerating people whose crimes are not serious enough to warrant a sanction this severe, or too lenient, putting on probation people whose crimes call for more severe punishment. This need for more flexible alternatives— punishments that in harshness fall between prison and probation—led many States to experiment with intermediate sanctions, such as intensive supervision probation/ parole (ISP).[1]

Intensive supervision probation/parole is a form of release into the community that emphasizes close monitoring of convicted offenders and imposes rigorous conditions on that release. Most ISP's call for:

● Some combination of multiple weekly contacts with a supervising officer.

● Random and unannounced drug testing.

● Stringent enforcement of probation/ parole conditions.

● A requirement to participate in relevant treatment, hold a job, and perhaps perform community service.

Interest in ISP's has been generated in part by the increased proportion of serious offenders among the probation population, a group whose needs and problems may not be effectively addressed by routine probation. Another reason for interest in ISP's is the greater flexibility in sentencing options that they permit. They are better able than the traditional alternatives—prison or probation—to fit the punishment to the crime.

The problem

The population on probation is a particular focus of ISP's. This population has been growing, increasing 5 to 7 percent each year from 1985 to 1990. At the end of 1990, two-thirds of all people who were under correctional supervision were on probation.[2] More importantly, the type of offender on probation has also changed. More of the current probation population consists of people convicted of felonies than misdemeanors.[3]

As a sentencing option, routine probation was neither intended nor structured to handle this type of offender. One reason is that felons are not good risks for routine probation. A recent report by the Bureau of Justice Statistics revealed that 43 percent of felons on State probation were rearrested for another felony within 3 years.[4] This threat to public safety underscores the need for sentencing alternatives. Moreover, the need is even greater in view of budget cuts at probation agencies.

At the other extreme, reliance on imprisonment has limitations. Prison populations have tripled since 1975. States have responded to the increased need with enormous investments in prison construction. Yet the level of violent crime is now substantially higher than it was a decade ago, indicating that the prospect of imprisonment has not had the deterrent effect that investment in prisons hoped to buy.[5] It has also meant that 36 States are currently operating all or part of their correctional systems under court orders or consent decrees to reduce crowding.[6]

The rationale for ISP's

Since neither prison nor routine probation can fully respond to the current situation,

From *National Institute of Justice (NIJ)/Research in Brief*, May 1993, pp. 1-11. Reprinted by permission.

ISP's have increasingly been viewed as an alternative. Indeed, these programs have been hailed by many as the most promising criminal justice innovation in decades. Between 1980 and 1990 every State adopted some form of ISP for adult offenders.[7] The Federal system has not been as aggressive as the States in ISP experiments, although there are a few programs in selected districts.

A growing number of jurisdictions have come to believe that by providing increased supervision of serious offenders in the community, ISP's can both relieve prison crowding and lessen the risks to public safety that such offenders pose— and all at a cost savings. In addition to these practical considerations, many believe ISP's should be adopted as a matter of principle, to meet the need for greater latitude in sentencing and to achieve the sentencing objective of just deserts.

The practical argument is the one advanced most often. ISP's are believed to be cost-effective, either in the short run or the long run. Prison-diversion programs (see "Types of ISP's") are thought to be able to reduce corrections costs because they presumably cost less than prison. Probation-enhancement programs are believed to prevent crime because the close surveillance they provide should deter recidivism.

Types of ISP's

ISP's are usually classified as prison diversion, enhanced probation, and enhanced parole. Each has a different goal.

Diversion is commonly referred to as a "front door" program because its goal is to limit the number of offenders entering prison. Prison diversion programs generally identify lower risk, incoming inmates to participate in an ISP in the community as a substitute for a prison term.

Enhancement programs generally select already sentenced probationers and parolees and subject them to closer supervision in the community than regular probation or parole. People placed in ISP enhanced probation or enhanced parole programs show evidence of failure under routine supervision or have committed offenses generally deemed to be too serious for supervision on routine caseloads.

With lower recidivism, the need for imprisonment is also reduced, since fewer offenders will be reprocessed by the system.

Assumptions about the effect of ISP's on crime control involve comparisons of various types of sanctions. Prison is assumed to provide the strongest, and routine supervision the weakest, crime control. ISP's are a middle ground, with more control than routine supervision but less control than prison. Theoretically, offenders in ISP programs are deterred from committing crimes because they are under surveillance, and they are constrained from committing crimes because the conditions of the program limit their opportunities.

Initial reactions to ISP's

Some of the enthusiasm for ISP's was generated by early reports from programs like that of the Georgia Department of Corrections, which seemed to bear out many of the assumptions and to produce a number of benefits.[8] Many ISP programs claimed to have saved at least $10,000 a year for each offender who otherwise would have been sentenced to prison.[9] Participants in the Georgia program, which served as the model for programs adopted elsewhere, had low recidivism, maintained employment, made restitution, and paid a monthly supervision fee.

In other places where ISP's were adopted, evaluations produced mixed results, with some sites reporting cost savings (Illinois and New Jersey, for example), while others did not (such as Massachusetts and Wisconsin); and some reporting reduced recidivism (Iowa, for example), while others did not (such as Ohio and Wisconsin).

The ambiguous results of these programs indicate that assumptions about the ability of ISP's to produce practical results— relieve prison crowding, lower costs, and control crime—may not have been well-founded. Reservations have been raised by independent agencies (such as the U.S. General Accounting Office), as well as by a number of scholars, including proponents of the ISP concept.[10] It appears not that the ISP's themselves have failed, but that the objectives set for them may have been overly ambitious, raising expectations they have been unable to meet.

The evidence seems better able to support the argument based on principle. That is, because ISP's are more punitive than routine probation and parole and because they provide for greater surveillance, they may be able to achieve the goal of permitting needed flexibility in sentencing.

The demonstration project

To test the relative effectiveness of ISP's and traditional sanctions, NIJ evaluated a demonstration project sponsored by the Bureau of Justice Assistance (BJA). The demonstration, which involved 14 programs in 9 States, ran from 1986 to 1991 and involved about 2,000 offenders. NIJ commissioned the RAND Corporation to evaluate the programs in a project supported by the Institute as well as BJA.

The participating jurisdictions (see exhibit 1) were asked to design an ISP program and were given wide latitude in doing so. Only two sites (Marion County, Oregon, and Milwaukee, Wisconsin) selected prison diversion programs, in which lower risk offenders who would have entered prison were diverted into the community. All others chose either probation enhancement or parole enhancement programs for the more serious offenders who were then under community supervision.

The offenders whom the jurisdictions chose to target had to meet only two criteria: they had to be adults and they could not be currently convicted of a violent crime. Once these criteria were met, the jurisdictions were free to focus on whatever type of offender population they wished: probationers and/or parolees, people currently in jail, or people who were prison bound.

They were also free to tailor their programs to meet local needs. For example, several sites designed their programs specifically for drug offenders. However, for a variety of reasons, the agencies were unable to place many offenders in drug, alcohol, or other such treatment programs. Thus, the ISP's evaluated were not primarily service and treatment programs, but rather were oriented more toward surveillance and supervision. (See "Study Methods.")

Effectiveness of ISP's

The demonstration was intended to answer the question of how participation in an ISP affected offenders' subsequent criminal behavior (that is, its effect on recidivism). The evaluation was intended to bring to light information about cost-effectiveness and extent of offender participation in counseling, work, and training programs. The effect of ISP's on prison crowding was not a study aim, but it has been a major policy interest in all ISP programs. The participating sites had their own objectives and interests. Most wanted to learn whether ISP's are an effective intermediate sanction, in which probation and parole conditions are monitored and enforced more credibly.

Overall, the results revealed what *cannot* be expected of ISP's as much as what *can* be. Most notably, they suggest that the assumptions about the ability of ISP's to meet certain practical goals—reduce prison crowding, save money, and decrease recidivism—may not have been well-founded and that jurisdictions interested in adopting ISP's should define their goals carefully. Other study findings indicate that ISP's were most successful as an intermediate punishment, in providing closer supervision of offenders and in offering a range of sentencing options between prison and routine probation and parole.

The programs were effective as surveillance. The ISP programs were designed to be much more stringent than routine supervision, and in every site they delivered more contacts and monitoring than did the routine supervision provided in the control groups. Most of the ISP's were significantly higher than the control programs

Study Methods[11]

Program design

All jurisdictions selected by the Bureau of Justice Assistance for participation in the demonstration and evaluation were asked to design and implement an ISP program that was to be funded for 18 to 24 months. The jurisdictions also were required to receive training and technical assistance, both provided by outside consultants.[12] In addition, they took part in the independent evaluation, which required their gathering data about the program.

The population studied consisted of approximately 2,000 adult offenders who were not currently convicted of a violent crime (homicide, rape, robbery, and assault). The vast majority of the offenders were men in their late 20's and early 30's, and most had long criminal records. In other respects, sites varied. Some, for example, chose offenders with more serious prison records than others. The nature of their offenses varied, as did their racial composition. The proportion of offenders who had prison records varied by site. For example, 86 percent of the offenders in Dallas had served a prison term, while for Contra Costa the figure was only 5 percent.

Because each site was allowed to design its own ISP, no two programs were identical. They adopted whatever components of the general ISP model they wished (such as random urine testing, curfews, electronic monitoring, and treatment referrals).

Close supervision of offenders was one of the few required program components. It consisted of weekly contacts with the officers, unscheduled drug testing, and stricter enforcement of probation/parole conditions.

Random assignment

The study was conducted as a randomized experiment. Indeed, the study may well be the largest randomized experiment in corrections ever undertaken in the United States. At each site, along with the experimental group, a control group of offenders was set up to serve as a comparison. The offenders in the control group were not part of the program but instead were given a different sanction (either prison or routine probation or parole, for example).[13] After the jurisdictions selected the pool of offenders they deemed eligible for ISP programs, the researchers assigned them randomly to one or the other of the two groups.

Having a control group with which to compare findings ensured that the results were the product of the manipulated variables of the ISP program rather than of differences among the offenders in the two groups. Previous ISP evaluations lacked matching comparison groups.

Data collection

For each offender, in both the experimental and the control groups, data collection forms were completed by the participating agency in the respective jurisdictions. A *background assessment* recorded demographic information, prior criminal record, drug dependence status, and similar information. The other forms—*6- and 12-month reviews*—recorded probation and parole services received, participation in treatment and work programs, and recidivism during the 1-year followup. Also recorded on this form were the number of drug tests ordered and taken, the types of drugs for which the offender tested positive, and the sanction imposed.

Measuring program effects

Separate calculations were devised for estimating costs and for measuring program implementation, the effect of the ISP's on recidivism, and the effect on social adjustment (percentage of offenders who attended counseling, participated in training, were employed, and the like).

in number of face-to-face contacts with supervisors, telephone and collateral contacts, law enforcement checks, employment monitoring, and drug and alcohol testing. (See exhibit 2 for findings on contacts and drug tests.)

The data reveal no straightforward relationship between contact levels and recidivism; that is, it is not clear whether the surveillance aspect of the ISP had a positive effect on offenders' subsequent behavior. For example, although the average number of face-to-face contacts in Seattle was 3.4 per month and the average in Macon was much higher at 16.1, the percentage of ISP offenders arrested at both sites was about the same—46 percent in Seattle and 42 percent in Macon.

This finding must, however, be qualified by the nature of the data. The ISP programs were "packages" of contacts and services, and for this reason it is difficult to distinguish the specific effect of individual components of a package (such as contact level, drug testing, and electronic monitoring) on recidivism.

The programs were effective as intermediate sanctions. In a sense, this issue is the same as the preceding one if more frequent contacts and drug testing are viewed as punishment. Most of the ISP's had significantly higher levels of the features that curtail freedom.[14] Both coercion and enforced diminution of freedom were higher for most ISP's than for the control group when measured by the criminal justice system response to offenders' technical violations.[15] In fact, the response to this type of violation gives ISP's their greatest punitive value. The rate of technical violations was high, making the resultant coercion and diminution of freedom experienced by the offenders an added punitive sanction as well as creating a public safety benefit.

The General Accounting Office, in its report on intermediate punishments, noted that if judged by a standard of zero risk, all ISP programs fail to protect public safety.[16] However, what most of these programs try to achieve is a more stringent punishment for at least some of the serious offenders who now receive only nominal supervision. Judged by that criterion, virtually all of the sites succeeded. It is also possible that the closer surveillance imposed on ISP participants may increase the probability that they are caught for a larger percentage of the crimes they commit.

Exhibit 2. Number of Monthly Face-to-Face Contacts and Drug Tests During 1-Year Followup

| | Face-to Face Contacts | | Drug Tests | |
	ISP	Controls	ISP	Controls
Contra Costa County, California	2.7	0.5*	1.7	0.2*
Los Angeles County, California	4.1	0.6*	0.5	0.2*
Seattle, Washington	3.4	0.8*	0.4	0.1*
Ventura County, California	7.4	3.0*	2.7	1.3*
Atlanta, Georgia	12.5	14.9	4.8	4.9
Macon, Georgia	16.1	17.7	5.8	3.7*
Waycross, Georgia	22.8	22.4	14.2	1.6*
Santa Fe, New Mexico	10.6	2.8*	2.9	1.1*
Des Moines, Iowa	5.8	3.8*	2.8	1.0*
Winchester, Virginia	8.1	1.9*	1.5	0.4*
Dallas, Texas	3.3	1.5*	0.1	0.0*
Houston, Texas	4.0	1.9*	0.7	0.0*
Marion County, Oregon**	12.2	n/a	2.2	n/a
Milwaukee, Wisconsin	8.8	n/a	0.7	n/a
AVERAGE	5.8 [a]	1.6 [b]	1.4 [a]	0.2 [b]

* Indicates that ISP and control are significantly different, p <.05.

** Based on 6-month followup only.

[a] Weighted average of ISP in all sites.
[b] Weighted average of routine probation in Contra Costa, Los Angeles, Seattle; routine probation/parole in Santa Fe, Des Moines, Winchester; routine parole in Dallas and Houston.

To test this effect, researchers conducted interviews with ISP participants in the Contra Costa site to discuss their perceptions of the harshness of the program. The interview findings confirmed that these offenders viewed the likelihood of their being caught for probation violations to be higher than for offenders who were on routine probation. They felt this to be particularly true when the violations involved drugs. In addition, the ISP offenders believed they would be treated more harshly for most types of violations than would their counterparts who were on routine supervision.

Evidence also suggests that some offenders may view ISP's as even more punitive and restrictive of freedom than prison. Among offenders at the Oregon site, 25 percent who were eligible for prison diversion chose not to participate. The reason may be that Oregon's crowded prisons made it unlikely that anyone sentenced to a year would serve the full term, while offenders assigned to ISP's could be certain of a full year of surveillance in the program. As prisons become more crowded and length of sentence served decreases, ISP's may come to seem increasingly punitive to offenders.

The effect on recidivism

The major recidivism outcome measures were officially recorded arrests and technical violations. On these measures, the ISP programs were not as successful as on others.

ISP participants were not subsequently arrested less often, did not have a longer time to failure, and were not arrested for less serious offenses than control group members. The findings reveal that in 11 of the 14 sites, arrest rates during the 1-year followup were in fact higher for ISP participants than for the control group (although not significantly so). At the end of the 1-year period, about 37 percent of the ISP participants and 33 percent of control offenders had been arrested. (See exhibit 3.)

These findings should be interpreted with caution, because officially recorded recidivism may not be as accurate an indicator of an individual's criminality as it is a measure of the impact of the ISP program on the criminal justice system. That is, officially recorded recidivism measures enforcement—the system's ability to detect crime and act on it (through arrests).

As noted earlier, with an ISP program, surveillance may be so stringent as to increase the probability that crimes (and technical violations) will be detected and an arrest made. In this way ISP's may increase officially recorded recidivism. Thus, it may be that an ISP offender is committing the same number or fewer crimes than someone on routine supervision, who has a lower probability of being arrested for them. The ISP offender, whose behavior is more closely monitored, may be caught in the enforcement net, while the offender on routine probation or parole may escape it.

Effect of technical violations. If technical violations are interpreted as another measure of recidivism, the findings are also less positive for the ISP's than the controls. An average of 65 percent of the ISP clients had a technical violation compared with 38 percent for the controls. (See exhibit 3.) However, technical violations can be interpreted as effects of the program itself rather than as evidence of criminal activity or recidivism. For one thing, the view of technical violations as a proxy for crime commission is only an assumption. Noncompliant behavior such as disregarding curfews, using alcohol and drugs, and missing treatment sessions may not necessarily signal that the ISP participant is going to commit "new" or "real" crimes.

To test the hypothesis that revoking offenders for technical violations prevents arrests for new crimes, the researchers examined the ISP programs in California and Texas. They computed correlations between number of arrests and number of technical violations and found few statistically significant relationships. In other words, offenders who committed technical violations were no more likely to be arrested for new crimes than those who did not commit them. Moreover, when convictions for arrests during the 1-year followup were examined for all sites, the researchers found no difference in the rates of the ISP offenders and the control group.

ISP's were consistently associated with higher rates of technical violations because of the closer supervision given to those in the programs. If stringent conditions are imposed and people's behavior is monitored, they have more opportunities for violations and for being found out than if there are few conditions and few contacts. For example, the requirement of frequent drug testing alone is virtually guaranteed to generate a large number of technical viola-

tions. Few of the sites had many low-risk[17] offenders. The higher the risk, the more likely that offenders are involved with drugs. At most of the sites, drug-related technical violations accounted for a large proportion of all technical violations. Offenders under routine supervision were not subjected to such close scrutiny and would not therefore have had as many opportunities to commit technical violations of the conditions of their probation or parole.

Effect of type of ISP program. Because only 2 of the 14 sites implemented prison diversion programs and their programs experienced difficulties, the research remains inconclusive regarding the ability of this type of ISP to relieve prison crowding. (See "The Experience of the Prison Diversion Programs.")

The findings for parole and probation enhancement ISP's suggest that commitments to prison and jail may actually increase under the program. The reason is the large number of technical violations, which lead to a higher percentage of ISP offenders than controls being recommitted to jail and prison. At a minimum, ISP programs attempt to increase the credibility of community-based sanctions by making certain that the conditions ordered by the court, including those considered "technical" in nature, are monitored, enforced, and if violated, punished by imprisonment. Depending on how severely ISP staff and their respective courts choose to treat ISP infractions, commitments to prison and jails may rise precipitously.

Data from the Houston site illustrate this point. The Houston ISP was a parole-enhancement program that targeted people under supervision who had a high probability of returning to prison. ISP participants were not arrested for new crimes more often than the controls (who were on routine parole), but were returned to prison more frequently for more technical violations. Fully 81 percent of the ISP offenders had technical violations, compared with 33 percent of offenders in the control group. As a result, five times as many ISP offenders were returned to prison for technical violations as those on routine supervision (21 percent versus 4 percent), and at the end of the 1-year followup, about 30 percent of ISP participants were in prison, compared with only 18 percent of the control group.[18]

Thus, in Houston, putting people on ISP added more offenders to the prison population than did routine parole. This is interpreted as an effect of the ISP program itself—which tends to generate more technical violations—rather than the result of differences between the ISP experimental and control groups. Any other differences were eliminated through random assignment of offenders to both groups.

Cost benefits

Are ISP's a cost-saving alternative? Like other questions about ISP's, this too has an ambiguous answer—one that depends on what is being compared to what. Compared with routine probation, ISP's are more costly because they are highly labor intensive. Because supervision is intensive, ISP's require lower caseloads—typically 25 offenders per supervisor or team of supervisors. An increase of only 100 offenders in an ISP would call for hiring and training 4 to 8 new employees.

If the cost of ISP's is compared to that of imprisonment, the opposite is true. Virtually no one would question the claim that it is more expensive to keep an offender in prison than on probation. The costs per day for imprisonment are much higher per offender than the costs per day for an ISP. Obviously, ISP's cost less than building new prisons.

Length of time under each sanction also has to be taken into consideration when comparing costs of prison and ISP's. The average cost per year per imprisoned offender is $12,000 and per ISP offender only $4,000. However, if the ISP offender would have otherwise served time in prison (had he or she not been placed in an ISP) for a period of only 3 months, the cost would be $3,000—less than the $4,000 it costs for 1 year of an ISP program. In addition, some of the ISP participants spent part of the followup year incarcerated rather than in the ISP program, thus eliminating part of the cost savings of diversion from prison.

Again, it should be kept in mind in interpreting these findings that the ISP programs resulted in more incarcerations and consequently higher costs than routine probation/parole because of the higher number of technical violations. Across the 12 probation/parole enhancement programs, high violation and incarceration rates for ISP offenders drove up the estimated costs, which averaged $7,200 per offender for the year, compared with about $4,700 for the control group on routine supervision.

Exhibit 3. **Offender Recidivism During 1-Year Followup**

	Percentage of Offenders With Any Arrest		Percentage of Offender With Technical Violations		Percentage of Offenders Returned to Prison	
	ISP	Controls	ISP	Controls	ISP	Controls
Contra Costa County, California	29	27	64	41*	2	4
Los Angeles County, California	32	30	61	57	26	22
Seattle, Washington	46	36	73	48*	6	5
Ventura County, California	32	53*	70	73	23	28
Atlanta, Georgia	12	04	65	46	23	4
Macon, Georgia	42	38	100	96	8	21
Waycross, Georgia	12	15	38	31	4	0
Santa Fe, New Mexico	48	28	69	62	14	17
Des Moines, Iowa	24	29	59	55	39	23
Winchester, Virginia	25	12	64	36*	14	8
Dallas, Texas	39	30	20	13	28	17
Houston, Texas	44	40	81	33*	35	20*
Marion County, Oregon	33	50	92	58	50	25
Milwaukee, Wisconsin	58	03*	92	17*	35	3*
AVERAGE	37 [a]	33 [b]	65 [a]	38 [b]	24	15

* Indicates that ISP and control are significantly different, p <.05.

[a] Weighted average of ISP in all sites.

[b] Weighted average of routine probation in Contra Costa, Los Angeles, Seattle; routine probation/parole in Santa Fe, Des Moines, Winchester; routine parole in Dallas and Houston.

Results for treatment

Treatment and service components in the ISP's included drug and alcohol counseling, employment, community service, and payment of restitution. On many of these measures, ISP offenders participated more than did control group members (see exhibit 4); and participation in such programs was found to be correlated with a reduction in recidivism in at least some sites.

When figures from all sites are examined, they reveal that participation in counseling was not high in either the experimental or control groups, but it was higher for ISP offenders. Forty-five percent of ISP offenders received some counseling during the followup period, compared with 22 percent of the controls.

Overall figures indicate that more than half of the ISP participants were employed compared with 43 percent of the offenders who were on routine supervision. In 4 of the 14 sites (Contra Costa, Los Angeles, Seattle, and Winchester), ISP offenders were significantly more likely than controls to be employed.

Participation in community service varied considerably by site. The highest rate (more than two-thirds of offenders) was reported in the three Georgia sites, where community service has historically played a major role in the ISP design. In seven of the ISP programs, 10 percent or fewer offenders participated in community service, and at no site did ISP offenders participate significantly more often than routine supervision offenders.

Although restitution was paid by only a small minority of offenders, the rate was higher among ISP offenders than those on routine supervision (12 percent and 3 percent, respectively, paid some restitution).

Analysis of the programs in California and Texas revealed a relationship between treatment participation and recidivism. A summary score was created for each offender, with one point assigned for participation in any of four treatment or service programs. Analysis revealed that higher levels of program participation were associated with a 10- to 20-percent reduction in recidivism. However, because offenders were not randomly assigned to participate in these activities within the experimental and control groups, it is not possible to determine whether the lower recidivism was the effect of the treatment or of selec-

tion bias. In other words, the positive outcomes may be a function not of the treatment but of the type of offender who entered the treatment program. Nevertheless, the results are consistent with literature showing positive outcomes of treatment.

The ISP programs in the demonstration project were by design oriented more toward surveillance than treatment, with funds used largely for staff salaries rather than for treatment service. Sites had to rely on existing treatment programs, which in some communities were quite minimal. This raises the issue of whether participation in treatment would have been higher had more resources been allocated to it.

Policy implications

Jurisdictions that wish to adopt ISP's might want to revise the model represented in the demonstration to create a better "fit" with their particular needs.

Making controls more stringent. ISP contact levels were greater than with routine supervision, but it might be argued that the programs were not "intensive" enough. It appears that more stringent conditions could be required of ISP's. In the demonstration, ISP contacts of any type amounted, on average, to a total of less than 2 hours per month per offender (assuming that 20 minutes, on average, was spent per face-to-face contact). The same is true of drug testing—the average

---

The Experience of the Prison Diversion Programs

Prison diversion programs in this study did not provide data on the effect of ISP's on prison crowding. Of the two participating sites that implemented prison diversion programs in the demonstration, one had too few eligible offenders to yield usable results. In the other, the use of randomization was overridden by the jurisdiction, thereby foiling its purpose. The selection process at these two sites therefore makes it impossible to state with certainty the effect of ISP's in reducing prison crowding.

The experience of the two sites (Marion County, Oregon, and Milwaukee, Wisconsin) does reveal a number of insights into the issues jurisdictions face when making decisions about selecting convicted offenders for diversion into the community.

Marion County, Oregon

Marion County set eligibility requirements so stringent that few offenders could qualify for the prison diversion ISP. The study's mandated criterion of excluding offenders currently convicted of violent crimes was extended to exclude offenders with any prior record of violence. Examination of the Marion County data revealed that, in addition, a large percent of potential participants who had current burglary convictions were rejected. Although this offense is considered nonviolent, evidently Marion County did not wish to place burglars into ISP programs.

The three criteria—exclusion of violent offenders, people with any history of violence, and convicted burglars—shrank the pool of eligibles considerably. Furthermore, the local Marion County judge imposed the requirement of informed consent from the offender, producing a sample too small to yield statistically reliable results.

Milwaukee, Wisconsin

In Milwaukee, judges and probation/parole officers overrode the researchers' random assignment of offenders into the experimental and control groups. Milwaukee initially had two pools of eligibles: "front-end" cases consisting of high-risk offenders newly convicted of nonviolent felonies, and "back-end" cases consisting of probation or parole violators who were facing revocation. Regardless of the random designation made by the researchers, most front-end cases were sentenced to prison rather than diversion to an ISP. Of the back-end cases, more than half were sent to routine probation or parole.

That only two sites chose prison diversion suggests the level of concern on the part of the criminal justice system about the risks involved in sending convicted offenders into the community. Further evidence of this concern is the response of these two sites in placing additional restrictions on program implementation.[19]

for all sites was just over two tests per month. If the amount of time spent in contacts were greater (that is, if conditions were tougher), the result might be less recidivism. Jurisdictions would have to decide how much more restrictive the conditions should be and would have to weigh possible benefits against the probable higher cost.

Increasing treatment. Jurisdictions might want to strengthen the treatment component of ISP's in hopes of a positive behavioral effect that would lower recidivism. As stated earlier, at the California and Texas sites the recidivism of offenders who received any counseling (for drugs or alcohol), held jobs, paid restitution, and did community service was 10 to 20 percent lower than those who did not.

Overall outcomes might have been even more positive had a greater proportion of the offenders participated in treatment.[20] Participation in drug treatment, in particular, might have had a high payoff. In all the sites, about half the offenders were judged drug dependent by their probation or parole officers. Yet ISP staff often reported difficulties obtaining drug treatment for these people, and at some sites a large percentage of all offenders in need of drug treatment went untreated.[21] It comes as no surprise, therefore, that about one-third of all new arrests were drug-related. A high priority for future research would be evaluation of ISP programs in which treatment plays a major role.[22]

Deemphasizing technical violations. Jurisdictions might want to reexamine the assumption of technical violations as a proxy for criminal behavior. Offenders who commit this type of violation constitute a considerable proportion of the prison population. On any given day, about 20 percent of new admissions nationwide consist of parole or probation violators,[23] and the resultant crowding means early release for other offenders.

The experience of the State of Washington in rethinking parole and probation revocations is instructive. There, the State legislature, responding to the heavy flow of technical violations attendant on stringent parole and probation conditions, set new rules. The rules require conditions be set according to the specific offense and the particular offender's past criminal behavior; they effectively bar the imposition of conditions affecting all offenders. In addition, the new rules state that prison

Exhibit 4. **Representative Program Participation**

| | Percentage of Offenders in Any Counseling During 1-Year Followup | | Percentage of Offenders With Any Paid Employment During 1-Year Followup | |
	ISP	Controls	ISP	Controls
Contra Costa County, California	39	14*	41	26*
Los Angeles County, California	16*	02	45	18*
Seattle, Washington	42	14*	31	08*
Ventura County, California	78	76	80	79
Atlanta, Georgia	48	48	54	65
Macon, Georgia	65	50	85	71
Waycross, Georgia	100	88	92	96
Santa Fe, New Mexico	100	59*	86	79
Des Moines, Iowa	59	41*	76	70
Winchester, Virginia	32	12	89	56*
Dallas, Texas	04	02	37	33
Houston, Texas	55	32*	61	61
Marion County, Oregon	50	n/a	33	n/a
Milwaukee, Wisconsin	54	n/a	54	n/a
AVERAGE	45 [a]	22 [b]	56 [a]	43 [b]

* Indicates that ISP and control are significantly different, p <.05.

[a] Weighted average of all sites.
[b] Weighted average of routine probation in Contra Costa, Los Angeles, Seattle; routine probation/parole in Santa Fe, Des Moines, Winchester; routine parole in Dallas and Houston.

cannot be used as a sanction for technical violations; the maximum sentence is 60 days in jail.[24]

No empirical studies have been performed yet, but Washington officials believe that as a result of the new rules, revocations for technical violations have decreased while arrest rates for new crimes have remained roughly the same.[25] If Washington is successful, it may mean that jurisdictions will have more prison space for really serious offenders and therefore increase public safety by decreasing the number of people sent to prison for technical violations of parole and probation.

Handling costs. When considering the issue of affordability, jurisdictions need to keep in mind its relation to program goals. The more constraints a program imposes and/or the more it is service- and treatment-oriented, the higher will be the cost. In Ventura and Houston, for example, stringent conditions and rigorous response to technical violations drove up costs. On the other hand, future evaluations might reveal that the return on investment in programs with these types of emphasis may be lower recidivism.

Judging outcomes. In assessing the success of ISP's (and deciding whether to invest further in them), jurisdictions need to use the same criterion for deciding whether a program is affordable; that is, does it achieve the goals set? One of the study's strongest implications is that jurisdictions need to establish very clearly their intentions for the ISP's they develop and structure the programs accordingly. If jurisdictions are interested primarily in imposing intermediate sanctions, even if the result is not lower recidivism, that goal should be made clear. Otherwise, the public may interpret the recidivism rates as an indication of program failure.

If jurisdictions are primarily interested in reducing recidivism, prison crowding, and system costs, ISP programs as currently structured may not meet all their expectations. These more "practical" objectives were set on the basis of overly ambitious assumptions and on the early results of a few programs that received a great deal of attention and perhaps unwarranted enthusiasm. The findings of this evaluation provide further evidence that surveillance-oriented ISP's will have difficulty in fully achieving these objectives.

If jurisdictions target objectives based more on intermediate sanctions principles, ISP's hold promise. By setting this type

of objective, they may be able to impose more stringent controls on offenders than are possible with routine probation and parole, and they may achieve greater flexibility in sentencing decisions by punishments that more closely fit the crimes committed. Developing an array of sentencing options is an important and necessary first step to creating a more comprehensive and graduated sentencing structure. This goal alone can provide the justification for continued development of ISP and other intermediate sanctions.

Is prison diversion viable? The evaluation findings indicate that prison diversion and, by extension, reduction of prison crowding, is particularly difficult to implement. This difficulty is reflected in the decision by only 2 of the 14 sites to adopt this type of program. The criteria these two jurisdictions used to assign offenders to the programs also suggest a measure of reluctance. (See "The Experience of the Prison Diversion Programs.") The experience with prison diversion in this study indicates that the criminal justice system and the general public do not at present seem receptive to this type of ISP. A targeted public and judicial education campaign would be required to overcome that reluctance.

Future research

The major issue for further research is determining whether ISP, a concept that may be sound in theory, might be structured and implemented differently to produce better results. The experience of the California sites suggest, for example, that certain program components could be manipulated. At these sites, a higher level of offender participation in treatment and service programs was associated with lower recidivism. In Ventura, which had the highest levels of surveillance, arrest rates were lower than among the controls. A revised ISP model could answer these and other questions:

● Would ISP's reduce recidivism if resources were sufficient to obtain treatment drug offenders need?

● Would more intensive surveillance lower recidivism?

● Would more selective conditions of parole and probation lower revocation rates?

● What combination of surveillance and treatment would produce the best results?

The study findings indicate a number of additional areas for research:

The potential of ISP as prison diversion. The limited number of study sites selecting this option and their restrictions on the programs indicate major concerns about ISP for prison diversion. Researchers may want to examine the nature of the potential pool of eligibles, document the most commonly utilized criteria for ISP eligibility, and depending on the criteria, simulate the prison population that would qualify.

Testing of different offender populations. The ISP model in this study was tested primarily on drug-involved offenders who had committed serious crimes. Studies have shown that the more experienced the offenders, the lower they rate the risk of being caught and confined.[26] For this reason, models using a population of less serious offenders might result in greater deterrence.

The effects of different ISP components. The random assignment in this study permitted testing the effect of the entire ISP "package," but made it impossible to test the effect of a particular program component. By extension, it was not possible to determine how changing a component might change the effects. Future research could be designed specifically to test the incremental impact of various ISP conditions (such as drug testing and drug and alcohol treatment) on offender behavior.

Effectiveness over time. Recent research indicates that a 1-year followup, the time period on which the evaluation of outcomes was based, may not be long enough.[27] Future research might focus on whether longer followup might ultimately result in behavioral differences between ISP offenders and controls.

Technical violations and criminal behavior. The study revealed that technical violations resulted in many recommitments to prison and jail. As noted earlier, the view that such recommitments prevent crime may be only an assumption. The policy significance of technical violations suggests that research is needed in a number of areas:

● Empirical evidence of the relationship of technical violations to criminal behavior.

● The types of technical conditions currently imposed at sentencing.

● How technical conditions are used by community corrections to manage offenders, encourage rehabilitation, and protect the community.

● Trends in the growth of the technical violator population and the effect on jails and prisons.

● Innovative programs, policies, and statutes that have emerged to deal with technical violators.

Appropriate outcome measures. Recidivism is a key outcome used in evaluating all types of interventions, and because success in rehabilitation has been far from complete, it is almost the only measure used in corrections.

In reaffirming its commitment to ISP and to its focus on rehabilitation, the American Probation and Parole Association issued a position paper that identifies behavioral change, not recidivism, as the appropriate outcome measure. Such change includes negotiation skills, managing emotions, and enhanced values and attitude shifts.

Given the centrality of recidivism to research and practice, it is essential to examine its appropriateness as a measure for certain interventions. For some programs, recidivism may be one of many measures, but perhaps not the primary one.

These are not the only issues for a future criminal justice research agenda, but they are currently the most pressing for research on the future of intensive supervision probation and parole.

Notes

1. The results of NIJ-sponsored research into four major types of intermediate sanctions are summarized in Gowdy, Voncile B., *Intermediate Sanctions.* Research in Brief. Washington, D.C.: U.S. Department of Justice, National Institute of Justice, forthcoming, 1993.

2. Bureau of Justice Statistics, *Probation and Parole 1990.* Bulletin. Washington, D.C.: U.S. Department of Justice, Bureau of Justice Statistics, November 1991.

3. The figure for felonies is 48 percent, and for misdemeanors, it is 31 percent, according to Bureau of Justice Statistics. *Correctional Populations in the United States, 1990.* Washington D.C.: U.S. Department of Justice, Bureau of Justice Statistics, July 1992.

4. Langan, Patrick A., and Mark A. Cuniff. *Recidivism of Felons on Probation, 1986–89.* Special Report. Washington, D.C.:U.S. Department of Justice, Bureau of Justice Statistics, February 1992.

5. A discussion of recent findings about the rise in the rate of violent crime despite the increase in the number of people incarcerated is presented in the National Research Council's *Understanding and Preventing Violence*, ed. Albert J. Reiss, Jr., and Jeffrey A. Roth, Washington, D.C.: National Academy Press, 1993: 292–294.

6. Macguire, Kathleen, and Timothy J. Flanagan, eds. *Sourcebook of Criminal Justice Statistics—1991.* Washington, D.C.: U.S. Department of Justice, Bureau of Justice Statistics, 1992.

7. General Accounting Office. *Intermediate Sanctions: Their Impacts on Prison Crowding, Costs, and Recidivism Are Still Unclear.* Gaithersburg, Maryland: General Accounting Office, 1990.

8. For descriptions of the Georgia program, see Erwin, Billie S. "Turning Up the Heat on Probationers in Georgia." *Federal Probation*, vol. 50 (1986):2.

See also:
Petersilia, Joan. *Expanding Options for Criminal Sentencing.* Santa Monica, California: RAND Corporation, 1987.

Byrne, James M., Arthur J. Lurigio, and Christopher Baird. "The Effectiveness of the New Intensive Supervision Programs." *Research in Corrections*, vol. 2 (1989).

The results of a National Institute of Justice evaluation of the program are presented in Erwin, Billie S., and Lawrence A. Bennett. *New Dimensions in Probation: Georgia's Experience With Intensive Probation Supervision (IPS).* Research in Brief. Washington, D.C.: U.S. Department of Justice, National Institute of Justice, January 1987.

9. Byrne, Lurigio, and Baird, "The Effectiveness of the New Intensive Supervision Programs."

10. General Accounting Office, *Intermediate Sanctions.* See also Morris, Norval, and Michael Tonry. *Between Prison and Probation: Intermediate Punishments in a Rational Sentencing System.* New York: Oxford University Press, 1990.

11. For more information on the experiences of the sites in implementing the experiments, see Petersilia, Joan. "Implementing Randomized Experiments: Lessons for BJA's Intensive Supervision Project." *Evaluation Review*, vol. 13, 5.

12. The training component was directed by Rutgers University, the technical assistance by the National Council on Crime and Delinquency.

13. In the Georgia and Ventura sites, the control programs were another form of intensive supervision. References to all ISP's mean all 14 experimental programs. References to ISP enhancement programs mean all experimental ISP's except Milwaukee and Marion, which adopted prison diversion programs. References to routine supervision probation and parole mean the control programs in eight sites: Contra Costa, Los Angeles, Seattle, Santa Fe, Des Moines, Winchester, Dallas, and Houston.

14. This meets the definition of effective sentencing proposed by Morris and Tonry. It involves "the curtailment of freedom either behind walls or in the community, large measures of coercion, and enforced diminutions of freedom." (*Between Prison and Probation*)

15. A violation that does not consist of committing a crime or is not prosecuted as such is usually called a technical violation. It is behavior forbidden by the court order granting probation or parole but not forbidden by legal statute. Examples are failure to observe curfew, abstain from alcohol, or attend treatment sessions.

16. General Accounting Office, *Intermediate Sanctions.*

17. The risk score was constructed from the following variables: drug treatment needs, age at first or current conviction, previous probation terms, previous probation and parole revocations, previous felony convictions, and type of current offense.

18. Turner, Susan, and Joan Petersilia. "Focusing on High-Risk Parolees: An Experiment to Reduce Commitments to the Texas Department of Corrections." *Journal of Research in Criminology and Delinquency*, vol. 29, 1 (1992): 34–61

19. NIJ has provided support to RAND to evaluate a prison diversion program in Minnesota that promises to furnish more reliable evidence on the impact of this type of sanction.

20. Some recent literature gives credibility to this notion. See Anglin, M. Douglas, and Yih-Ing Hser. "Treatment of Drug Abuse." In *Crime and Justice: An Annual Review of Research, Volume 13: Drugs and Crime.* ed. Michael Tonry and James Q. Wilson. Chicago: University of Chicago Press, 1990; and Paul Gendreau and D.A. Andrews. "Tertiary Prevention: What the Meta-Analyses of the Offender Treatment Literature Tell Us About 'What Works.'" *Canadian Journal of Criminology*, vol. 32 (1990):173–184.

21. For a more complete presentation of this finding, see Petersilia, Joan, Susan Turner, and Elizabeth Piper Deschenes. "Intensive Supervision Programs for Drug Offenders." In J. Byrne, A. Lurigio, and J. Petersilia. *Smart Sentencing: The Emergence of Intermediate Sanctions.* Newbury Park, California: Sage Publications, 1992.

22. NIJ is providing RAND with support for a randomized field experiment, currently being conducted in Maricopa County, Arizona, that will test the impact on probationers of different levels of treatment.

23. Petersilia, Joan, and Susan Turner. "Reducing Prison Admissions: The Potential of Intermediate Sanctions." *The Journal of State Government*, vol. 62 (1989):2.

6. PUNISHMENT AND CORRECTIONS

24. Washington State Sentencing Guidelines Commission. *Preliminary Evaluation of Washington State's Sentencing Reform Act.* Olympia, Washington: Washington State Sentencing Guidelines Commission, 1983.

25. Greene, Richard. "Who's Punishing Whom?" *Forbes*, vol. 121, 6 (1988): 132–133.

26. Paternoster, R. "The Deterrent Effect of the Perceived Certainty and Severity of Punishment: A Review of the Evidence and Issues." *Justice Quarterly*, 4 (1987).

27. Anglin, M.D., and W.H. McGlothlin. "Outcomes of Narcotic Addict Treatment in California." In *Drug Abuse Treatment Evaluation: Strategies, Progress, and Prospect*, ed. F.M. Tims and J.P. Ludford. National Institute on Drug Abuse Research Monograph No. 51. Rockville, Maryland: U.S. Department of Health and Human Services, National Institute on Drug Abuse, 1984.

Findings and conclusions of the research reported here are those of the authors and do not necessarily reflect the official position or policies of the U.S. Department of Justice

'THIS MAN HAS EXPIRED'

WITNESS TO AN EXECUTION

ROBERT JOHNSON

ROBERT JOHNSON *is professor of justice, law, and society at The American University, Washington, D.C. This article is drawn from a Distinguished Faculty Lecture, given under the auspices of the university's senate last spring.*

The death penalty has made a comeback in recent years. In the late sixties and through most of the seventies, such a thing seemed impossible. There was a moratorium on executions in the U.S., backed by the authority of the Supreme Court. The hiatus lasted roughly a decade. Coming on the heels of a gradual but persistent decline in the use of the death penalty in the Western world, it appeared to some that executions would pass from the American scene [cf. *Commonweal*, January 15, 1988]. Nothing could have been further from the truth.

Beginning with the execution of Gary Gilmore in 1977, over 100 people have been put to death, most of them in the last few years. Some 2,200 prisoners are presently confined on death rows across the nation. The majority of these prisoners have lived under sentence of death for years, in some cases a decade or more, and are running out of legal appeals. It is fair to say that the death penalty is alive and well in America, and that executions will be with us for the foreseeable future.

Gilmore's execution marked the resurrection of the modern death penalty and was big news. It was commemorated in a best-selling tome by Norman Mailer, *The Executioner's Song*. The title was deceptive. Like others who have examined the death penalty, Mailer told us a great deal about the condemned but very little about the executioners. Indeed, if we dwell on Mailer's account, the executioner's story is not only unsung; it is distorted.

Gilmore's execution was quite atypical. His was an instance of state-assisted suicide accompanied by an element of romance and played out against a backdrop of media fanfare. Unrepentant and unafraid, Gilmore refused to appeal his conviction. He dared the state of Utah to take his life, and the media repeated the challenge until it became a taunt that may well have goaded officials to action. A failed suicide pact with

his lover staged only days before the execution, using drugs she delivered to him in a visit marked by unusual intimacy, added a hint of melodrama to the proceedings. Gilmore's final words, "Let's do it," seemed to invite the lethal hail of bullets from the firing squad. The nonchalant phrase, at once fatalistic and brazenly rebellious, became Gilmore's epitaph. It clinched his outlaw-hero image, and found its way onto tee shirts that confirmed his celebrity status.

Befitting a celebrity, Gilmore was treated with unusual leniency by prison officials during his confinement on death row. He was, for example, allowed to hold a party the night before his execution, during which he was free to eat, drink, and make merry with his guests until the early morning hours. This is not entirely unprecedented. Notorious English convicts of centuries past would throw farewell balls in prison on the eve of their executions. News accounts of such affairs sometimes included a commentary on the richness of the table and the quality of the dancing. For the record, Gilmore served Tang, Kool-Aid, cookies, and coffee, later supplemented by contraband pizza and an unidentified liquor. Periodically, he gobbled drugs obligingly provided by the prison pharmacy. He played a modest arrangement of rock music albums but refrained from dancing.

Gilmore's execution generally, like his parting fete, was decidedly out of step with the tenor of the modern death penalty. Most condemned prisoners fight to save their lives, not to have them taken. They do not see their fate in romantic terms; there are no farewell parties. Nor are they given medication to ease their anxiety or win their compliance. The subjects of typical executions remain anonymous to the public and even to their keepers. They are very much alone at the end.

In contrast to Mailer's account, the focus of the research I have conducted is on the executioners themselves as they carry out typical executions. In my experience executioners—not unlike Mailer himself—can be quite voluble, and sometimes quite moving, in expressing themselves. I shall draw upon their words to describe the death work they carry out in our name.

DEATH WORK AND DEATH WORKERS

Executioners are not a popular subject of social research, let alone conversation at the dinner table or cocktail party. We simply don't give the subject much thought. When we think of executioners at all, the imagery runs to individual men of disreputable, or at least questionable, character who work stealthily behind the scenes to carry out their grim labors. We picture hooded men hiding in the shadow of the gallows, or anonymous figures lurking out of sight behind electric chairs, gas chambers, firing blinds, or, more recently, hospital gurneys. We wonder who would do such grisly work and how they sleep at night.

This image of the executioner as a sinister and often solitary character is today misleading. To be sure, a few states hire free-lance executioners and traffic in macabre theatrics. Executioners may be picked up under cover of darkness and some may still wear black hoods. But today, executions are generally the work of a highly disciplined and efficient team of correctional officers.

Broadly speaking, the execution process as it is now practiced starts with the prisoner's confinement on death row, an oppressive prison-within-a-prison where the condemned are housed, sometimes for years, awaiting execution. Death work gains momentum when an execution date draws near and the prisoner is moved to the death house, a short walk from the death chamber. Finally, the process culminates in the death watch, a twenty-four-hour period that ends when the prisoner has been executed.

This final period, the death watch, is generally undertaken by correctional officers who work as a team and report directly to the prison warden. The warden or his representative, in turn, must by law preside over the execution. In many states, it is a member of the death watch or execution team, acting under the warden's authority, who in fact plays the formal role of executioner. Though this officer may technically work alone, his teammates view the execution as a shared responsibility. As one officer on the death watch told me in no uncertain terms: "We all take part in it; we all play 100 percent in it, too. That takes the load off this one individual [who pulls the switch]." The formal executioner concurred. "Everyone on the team can do it, and nobody will tell you I did it. I know my team." I found nothing in my research to dispute these claims.

The officers of these death watch teams are our modern executioners. As part of a larger study of the death work process, I studied one such group. This team, comprised of nine seasoned officers of varying ranks, had carried out five electrocutions at the time I began my research. I interviewed each officer on the team after the fifth execution, then served as an official witness at a sixth electrocution. Later, I served as a behind-the-scenes observer during their seventh execution.

The results of this phase of my research form the substance of this essay.

THE DEATH WATCH TEAM

The death watch or execution team members refer to themselves, with evident pride, as simply "the team." This pride is shared by other correctional officials. The warden at the institution I was observing praised members of the team as solid citizens—in his words, country boys. These country boys, he assured me, could be counted on to do the job and do it well. As a fellow administrator put it, "an execution is something [that] needs to be done and good people, dedicated people who believe in the American system, should do it. And there's a certain amount of feeling, probably one to another, that they're part of that—that when they have to hang tough, they can do it, and they can do it right. And that it's just the right thing to do."

The official view is that an execution is a job that has to be done, and done right. The death penalty is, after all, the law of the land. In this context, the phrase "done right" means that an execution should be a proper, professional, dignified undertaking. In the words of a prison administrator, "We had to be sure that we did it properly, professionally, and [that] we gave as much dignity to the person as we possibly could in the process....If you've gotta do it, it might just as well be done the way it's supposed to be done—without any sensation."

In the language of the prison officials, "proper" refers to procedures that go off smoothly; "professional" means without personal feelings that intrude on the procedures in any way. The desire for executions that take place "without any sensation" no doubt refers to the absence of media sensationalism, particularly if there should be an embarrassing and undignified hitch in the procedures, for example, a prisoner who breaks down or becomes violent and must be forcibly placed in the electric chair as witnesses, some from the media, look on in horror. Still, I can't help but note that this may be a revealing slip of the tongue. For executions are indeed meant to go off without any human feeling, without any sensation. A profound absence of feeling would seem to capture the bureaucratic ideal embodied in the modern execution.

The view of executions held by the execution team members parallels that of correctional administrators but is somewhat more restrained. The officers of the team are closer to the killing and dying, and are less apt to wax abstract or eloquent in describing the process. Listen to one man's observations:

It's a job. I don't take it personally. You know, I don't take it like I'm having a grudge against this person and this person has done something to me. I'm just carrying out a job, doing what I was asked to do....This man has been sentenced to death in the courts. This is the law and he broke this law, and he has to suffer the consequences. And one of the consequences is to put him to death.

I found that few members of the execution team support the death penalty outright or without reservation. Having seen executions close up, many of them have lingering doubts about the justice or wisdom of this sanction. As one officer put it:

I'm not sure the death penalty is the right way. I don't know if there is a right answer. So I look at it like this: if it's gotta be done, at least it can be done in a humane way, if there is such a word for it. . . . The only way it should be done, I feel, is the way we do it. It's done professionally; it's not no horseplaying. Everything is done by documentation. On time. By the book.

Arranging executions that occur "without any sensation" and that go "by the book" is no mean task, but it is a task that is undertaken in earnest by the execution team. The tone of the enterprise is set by the team leader, a man who takes a hard-boiled, no-nonsense approach to correctional work in general and death work in particular. "My style," he says, "is this: if it's a job to do, get it done. Do it and that's it." He seeks out kindred spirits, men who see killing condemned prisoners as a job—a dirty job one does reluctantly, perhaps, but above all a job one carries out dispassionately and in the line of duty.

To make sure that line of duty is a straight and accurate one, the death watch team has been carefully drilled by the team leader in the mechanics of execution. The process has been broken down into simple, discrete tasks and practiced repeatedly. The team leader describes the division of labor in the following exchange:

the execution team is a nine-officer team and each one has certain things to do. When I would train you, maybe you'd buckle a belt, that might be all you'd have to do. . . . And you'd be expected to do one thing and that's all you'd be expected to do. And if everybody does what they were taught, or what they were trained to do, at the end the man would be put in the chair and everything would be complete. It's all come together now.

So it's broken down into very small steps. . . .

Very small, yes. Each person has *one* thing to do.

I see. What's the purpose of breaking it down into such small steps?

So people won't get confused. I've learned it's kind of a tense time. When you're executin' a person, killing a person—you call it killin', executin', whatever you want—the man dies anyway. I find the less you got on your mind, why, the better you'll carry it out. So it's just very simple things. And so far, you know, it's all come together, we haven't had any problems.

This division of labor allows each man on the execution team to become a specialist, a technician with a sense of pride in his work. Said one man,

My assignment is the leg piece. Right leg. I roll his pants leg up, place a piece [electrode] on his leg, strap his leg in. . . . I've got all the moves down pat. We train from different posts; I can do any of them. But that's my main post.

The implication is not that the officers are incapable of performing multiple or complex tasks, but simply that it is more efficient to focus each officer's efforts on one easy task.

An essential part of the training is practice. Practice is meant to produce a confident group, capable of fast and accurate performance under pressure. The rewards of practice are reaped in improved performance. Executions take place with increasing efficiency, and eventually occur with precision. "The first one was grisly," a team member confided to me. He explained that there was a certain amount of fumbling, which made the execution seem interminable. There were technical problems as well: The generator was set too high so the body was badly burned. But that is the past, the officer assured me. "The ones now, we know what we're doing. It's just like clockwork."

THE DEATH WATCH

The death-watch team is deployed during the last twenty-four hours before an execution. In the state under study, the death watch starts at 11 o'clock the night before the execution and ends at 11 o'clock the next night when the execution takes place. At least two officers would be with the prisoner at any given time during that period. Their objective is to keep the prisoner alive and "on schedule." That is, to move him through a series of critical and cumulatively demoralizing junctures that begin with his last meal and end with his last walk. When the time comes, they must deliver the prisoner up for execution as quickly and unobtrusively as possible.

Broadly speaking, the job of the death watch officer, as one man put it, "is to sit and keep the inmate calm for the last twenty-four hours—and get the man ready to go." Keeping a condemned prisoner calm means, in part, serving his immediate needs. It seems paradoxical to think of the death watch officers as providing services to the condemned, but the logistics of the job make service a central obligation of the officers. Here's how one officer made this point:

Well, you can't help but be involved with many of the things that he's involved with. Because if he wants to make a call to his family, well, you'll have to dial the number. And you keep records of whatever calls he makes. If he wants a cigarette, well he's not allowed to keep matches so you light it for him. You've got to pour his coffee, too. So you're aware what he's doing. It's not like you can just ignore him. You've gotta just be with him whether he wants it or not, and cater to his needs.

Officers cater to the condemned because contented inmates are easier to keep under control. To a man, the officers say this is so. But one can never trust even a contented, condemned prisoner.

The death-watch officers see condemned prisoners as men with explosive personalities. "You don't know what, what a man's gonna do," noted one officer. "He's liable to snap, he's liable to pass out. We watch him all the time to prevent him from committing suicide. You've got to be ready—he's liable to do anything." The prisoner is never out of at least one officer's sight. Thus surveillance is constant, and control, for all intents and purposes, is total.

Relations between the officers and their charges during the death watch can be quite intense. Watching and being watched are central to this enterprise, and these are always engaging activities, particularly when the stakes are life and death. These relations are, nevertheless, utterly impersonal; there are no grudges but neither is there compassion or fellow-feeling. Officers are civil but cool; they keep an emotional distance from the men they are about to kill. To do otherwise, they maintain, would make it harder to execute condemned prisoners. The attitude of the officers is that the prisoners arrive as strangers and are easier to kill if they stay that way.

During the last five or six hours, two specific team officers are assigned to guard the prisoner. Unlike their more taciturn and aloof colleagues on earlier shifts, these officers make a conscious effort to talk with the prisoner. In one officer's words, "We keep them right there and keep talking to them— about anything except the chair." The point of these conversations is not merely to pass time; it is to keep tabs on the prisoner's state of mind, and to steer him away from subjects that might depress, anger, or otherwise upset him. Sociability, in other words, quite explicitly serves as a source of social control. Relationships, such as they are, serve purely manipulative ends. This is impersonality at its worst, masquerading as concern for the strangers one hopes to execute with as little trouble as possible.

Generally speaking, as the execution moves closer, the mood becomes more somber and subdued. There is a last meal. Prisoners can order pretty much what they want, but most eat little or nothing at all. At this point, the prisoners may steadfastly maintain that their executions will be stayed. Such bravado is belied by their loss of appetite. "You can see them going down," said one officer. "Food is the last thing they got on their minds."

Next the prisoners must box their meager worldly goods. These are inventoried by the staff, recorded on a one-page checklist form, and marked for disposition to family or friends. Prisoners are visibly saddened, even moved to tears, by this procedure, which at once summarizes their lives and highlights the imminence of death. At this point, said one of the officers, "I really get into him; I watch him real close." The execution schedule, the officer pointed out, is "picking up momentum, and we don't want to lose control of the situation."

This momentum is not lost on the condemned prisoner. Critical milestones have been passed. The prisoner moves in a limbo existence devoid of food or possessions; he has seen the last of such things, unless he receives a stay of execution and rejoins the living. His identity is expropriated as well. The critical juncture in this regard is the shaving of the man's head (including facial hair) and right leg. Hair is shaved to facilitate the electrocution; it reduces physical resistance to electricity and minimizes singeing and burning. But the process has obvious psychological significance as well, adding greatly to the momentum of the execution.

The shaving procedure is quite public and intimidating. The condemned man is taken from his cell and seated in the middle of the tier. His hands and feet are cuffed, and he is dressed only in undershorts. The entire death watch team is assembled around him. They stay at a discrete distance, but it is obvious that they are there to maintain control should he resist in any way or make any untoward move. As a rule, the man is overwhelmed. As one officer told me in blunt terms, "Come eight o'clock, we've got a dead man. Eight o'clock is when we shave the man. We take his identity; it goes with the hair." This taking of identity is indeed a collective process— the team makes a forceful "we," the prisoner their helpless object. The staff is confident that the prisoner's capacity to resist is now compromised. What is left of the man erodes gradually and, according the officers, perceptibly over the remaining three hours before the execution.

After the prisoner has been shaved, he is then made to shower and don a fresh set of clothes for the execution. The clothes are unremarkable in appearance, except that velcro replaces buttons and zippers, to reduce the chance of burning the body. The main significance of the clothes is symbolic: they mark the prisoner as a man who is ready for execution. Now physically "prepped," to quote one team member, the prisoner is placed in an empty tomblike cell, the death cell. All that is left is the wait. During this fateful period, the prisoner is more like an object "without any sensation" than like a flesh-and-blood person on the threshold of death.

For condemned prisoners, like Gilmore, who come to accept and even to relish their impending deaths, a genuine calm seems to prevail. It is as if they can transcend the dehumanizing forces at work around them and go to their deaths in peace. For most condemned prisoners, however, numb resignation rather than peaceful acceptance is the norm. By the account of the death-watch officers, these more typical prisoners are beaten men. Listen to the officers' accounts:

A lot of 'em die in their minds before they go to that chair. I've never known of one or heard of one putting up a fight. . . . By the time they walk to the chair, they've completely faced it. Such a reality most people can't understand. Cause they don't fight it. They don't seem to have anything to say. It's just something like "Get it over with." They may be numb, sort of in a trance.

They go through stages. And, at this stage, they're real humble. Humblest bunch of people I ever seen. Most all of 'em is real, real weak. Most of the time you'd only need one or two people to carry out an execution, as weak and as humble as they are.

These men seem barely human and alive to their keepers. They wait meekly to be escorted to their deaths. The people who come for them are the warden and the remainder of the death watch team, flanked by high-ranking correctional officials. The warden reads the court order, known popularly as a death warrant. This is, as one officer said, "the real deal," and nobody misses its significance. The condemned prisoners then go to their deaths compliantly, captives of the inexorable, irresistible momentum of the situation. As one officer put it, "There's no struggle. . . . They just walk right on in there." So too, do the staff "just walk right on in there," following a routine they have come to know well. Both the condemned and the executioners, it would seem, find a relief of sorts in mindless mechanical conformity to the modern execution drill.

WITNESS TO AN EXECUTION

As the team and administrators prepare to commence the good fight, as they might say, another group, the official witnesses, are also preparing themselves for their role in the execution. Numbering between six and twelve for any given execution, the official witnesses are disinterested citizens in good standing drawn from a cross-section of the state's population. If you will, they are every good or decent person, called upon to represent the community and use their good offices to testify to the propriety of the execution. I served as an official witness at the execution of an inmate.

At eight in the evening, about the time the prisoner is shaved in preparation for the execution, the witnesses are assembled. Eleven in all, we included three newspaper and two television reporters, a state trooper, two police officers, a magistrate, a businessman, and myself. We were picked up in the parking lot behind the main office of the corrections department. There was nothing unusual or even memorable about any of this. Gothic touches were notable by their absence. It wasn't a dark and stormy night; no one emerged from the shadows to lead us to the prison gates.

Mundane considerations prevailed. The van sent for us was missing a few rows of seats so there wasn't enough room for all of us. Obliging prison officials volunteered their cars. Our rather ordinary cavalcade reached the prison but only after getting lost. Once within the prison's walls, we were sequestered for some two hours in a bare and almost shabby administrative conference room. A public information officer was assigned to accompany us and answer our questions. We grilled this official about the prisoner and the execution procedure he would undergo shortly, but little information was to be had. The man confessed ignorance on the most basic points. Disgruntled at this and increasingly anxious, we made small talk and drank coffee.

At 10:40 P.M., roughly two-and-a-half hours after we were assembled and only twenty minutes before the execution was scheduled to occur, the witnesses were taken to the basement of the prison's administrative building, frisked, then led down an alleyway that ran along the exterior of the building. We entered a neighboring cell block and were admitted to a vestibule adjoining the death chamber. Each of us signed a log, and was then led off to the witness area. To our left, around a corner some thirty feet away, the prisoner sat in the condemned cell. He couldn't see us, but I'm quite certain he could hear us. It occurred to me that our arrival was a fateful reminder for the prisoner. The next group would be led by the warden, and it would be coming for him.

We entered the witness area, a room within the death chamber, and took our seats. A picture window covering the front wall of the witness room offered a clear view of the electric chair, which was about twelve feet away from us and well illuminated. The chair, a large, high-back solid oak structure with imposing black straps, dominated the death chamber. Behind it, on the back wall, was an open panel full of coils and lights. Peeling paint hung from the ceiling and walls; water stains from persistent leaks were everywhere in evidence.

Two officers, one a hulking figure weighing some 400 pounds, stood alongside the electric chair. Each had his hands crossed at the lap and wore a forbidding, blank expression on his face. The witnesses gazed at them and the chair, most of us scribbling notes furiously. We did this, I suppose, as much to record the experience as to have a distraction from the growing tension. A correctional officer entered the witness room and announced that a trial run of the machinery would be undertaken. Seconds later, lights flashed on the control panel behind the chair indicating that the chair was in working order. A white curtain, opened for the test, separated the chair and the witness area. After the test, the curtain was drawn. More tests were performed behind the curtain. Afterwards, the curtain was reopened, and would be left open until the execution was over. Then it would be closed to allow the officers to remove the body.

A handful of high-level correctional officials were present in the death chamber, standing just outside the witness area. There were two regional administrators, the director of the Department of Corrections, and the prison warden. The prisoner's chaplain and lawyer were also present. Other than the chaplain's black religious garb, subdued grey pinstripes and bland correctional uniforms prevailed. All parties were quite solemn.

At 10:58 the prisoner entered the death chamber. He was, I knew from my research, a man with a checkered, tragic past. He had been grossly abused as a child, and went on to become grossly abusive of others. I was told he could not describe his life, from childhood on, without talking about confrontations in defense of a precarious sense of self—at home, in school, on the streets, in the prison yard. Belittled by life and choking with rage, he was hungry to be noticed. Paradoxically, he had found his moment in the spotlight, but it was a dim and unflattering light cast before a small and unappreciative audience. "He'd pose for cameras in the chair—for the attention," his counselor had told me earlier in the day. But the truth was that the prisoner wasn't smiling, and there were no cameras.

The prisoner walked quickly and silently toward the chair, an escort of officers in tow. His eyes were turned downward, his expression a bit glazed. Like many before him, the prisoner had threatened to stage a last stand. But that was lifetimes ago, on death row. In the death house, he joined the humble bunch and kept to the executioner's schedule. He appeared to have given up on life before he died in the chair.

En route to the chair, the prisoner stumbled slightly, as if the momentum of the event had overtaken him. Were he not held securely by two officers, one at each elbow, he might have fallen. Were the routine to be broken in this or indeed any other way, the officers believe, the prisoner might faint or panic or become violent, and have to be forcibly placed in the chair. Perhaps as a precaution, when the prisoner reached the chair he did not turn on his own but rather was turned, firmly but without malice, by the officers in his escort. These included the two men at his elbows, and four others who followed behind him. Once the prisoner was seated, again with help, the officers strapped him into the chair.

The execution team worked with machine precision. Like a disciplined swarm, they enveloped him. Arms, legs, stomach, chest, and head were secured in a matter of seconds. Electrodes were attached to the cap holding his head and to the strap holding his exposed right leg. A leather mask was placed over his face. The last officer mopped the prisoner's brow, then touched his hand in a gesture of farewell.

During the brief procession to the electric chair, the prisoner was attended by a chaplain. As the execution team worked feverishly to secure the condemned man's body, the chaplain, who appeared to be upset, leaned over him and placed his forehead in contact with the prisoner's, whispering urgently. The priest might have been praying, but I had the impression he was consoling the man, perhaps assuring him that a forgiving God awaited him in the next life. If he heard the chaplain, I doubt the man comprehended his message. He didn't seem comforted. Rather, he looked stricken and appeared to be in shock. Perhaps the priest's urgent ministrations betrayed his doubts that the prisoner could hold himself together. The chaplain then withdrew at the warden's request, allowing the officers to affix the death mask.

The strapped and masked figure sat before us, utterly alone, waiting to be killed. The cap and mask dominated his face. The cap was nothing more than a sponge encased in a leather shell with a metal piece at the top to accept an electrode. It looked decrepit and resembled a cheap, ill-fitting toupee. The mask, made entirely of leather, appeared soiled and worn. It had two parts. The bottom part covered the chin and mouth, the top the eyes and lower forehead. Only the nose was exposed. The effect of a rigidly restrained body, together with the bizarre cap and the protruding nose, was nothing short of grotesque. A faceless man breathed before us in a tragicomic trance, waiting for a blast of electricity that would extinguish his life. Endless seconds passed. His last act was to swallow, nervously, pathetically, with his Adam's apple bobbing. I was struck by that simple movement then, and can't forget it even now. It told me, as nothing else did, that in the prisoner's restrained body, behind that mask, lurked a fellow human being who, at some level, however primitive, knew or sensed himself to be moments from death.

The condemned man sat perfectly still for what seemed an eternity but was in fact no more than thirty seconds. Finally the electricity hit him. His body stiffened spasmodically, though only briefly. A thin swirl of smoke trailed away from his head and then dissipated quickly. The body remained taut, with the right foot raised slightly at the heel, seemingly frozen

there. A brief pause, then another minute of shock. When it was over, the body was flaccid and inert.

Three minutes passed while the officials let the body cool. (Immediately after the execution, I'm told, the body would be too hot to touch and would blister anyone who did.) All eyes were riveted to the chair; I felt trapped in my witness seat, at once transfixed and yet eager for release. I can't recall any clear thoughts from that moment. One of the death watch officers later volunteered that he shared this experience of staring blankly at the execution scene. Had the prisoner's mind been mercifully blank before the end? I hoped so.

An officer walked up to the body, opened the shirt at chest level, then continued on to get the physician from an adjoining room. The physician listened for a heartbeat. Hearing none, he turned to the warden and said, "This man has expired." The warden, speaking to the director, solemnly intoned: "Mr. Director, the court order has been fulfilled." The curtain was then drawn and the witnesses filed out.

THE MORNING AFTER

As the team prepared the body for the morgue, the witnesses were led to the front door of the prison. On the way, we passed a number of cell blocks. We could hear the normal sounds of prison life, including the occasional catcall and lewd comment hurled at uninvited guests like ourselves. But no trouble came in the wake of the execution. Small protests were going on outside the walls, we were told, but we could not hear them. Soon the media would be gone; the protestors would disperse and head for their homes. The prisoners, already home, had been indifferent to the proceedings, as they always are unless the condemned prisoner had been a figure of some consequence in the convict community. Then there might be tension and maybe even a modest disturbance on a prison tier or two. But few convict luminaries are executed, and the dead man had not been one of them. Our escort officer offered a sad tribute to the prisoner: "The inmates, they didn't care about this guy."

I couldn't help but think they weren't alone in this. The executioners went home and set about their lives. Having taken life, they would savor a bit of life themselves. They showered, ate, made love, slept, then took a day or two off. For some, the prisoner's image would linger for that night. The men who strapped him in remembered what it was like to touch him; they showered as soon as they got home to wash off the feel and smell of death. One official sat up picturing how the prisoner looked at the end. (I had a few drinks myself that night with that same image for company.) There was some talk about delayed reactions to the stress of carrying out executions. Though such concerns seemed remote that evening, I learned later that problems would surface for some of the officers. But no one on the team, then or later, was haunted by the executed man's memory, nor would anyone grieve for him. "When I go home after one of these things," said one man, "I sleep like a rock." His may or may not be the sleep of the just, but one can only marvel at such a thing, and perhaps envy such a man.

CRIME CLOCK
1992

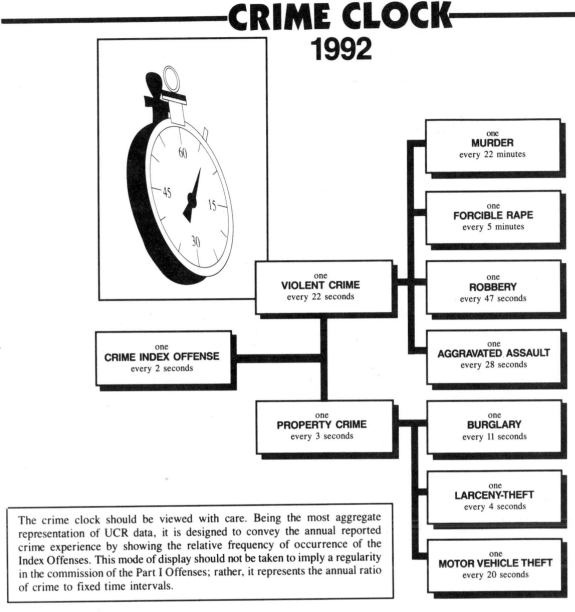

one
MURDER
every 22 minutes

one
FORCIBLE RAPE
every 5 minutes

one
VIOLENT CRIME
every 22 seconds

one
ROBBERY
every 47 seconds

one
CRIME INDEX OFFENSE
every 2 seconds

one
AGGRAVATED ASSAULT
every 28 seconds

one
PROPERTY CRIME
every 3 seconds

one
BURGLARY
every 11 seconds

one
LARCENY-THEFT
every 4 seconds

one
MOTOR VEHICLE THEFT
every 20 seconds

The crime clock should be viewed with care. Being the most aggregate representation of UCR data, it is designed to convey the annual reported crime experience by showing the relative frequency of occurrence of the Index Offenses. This mode of display should not be taken to imply a regularity in the commission of the Part I Offenses; rather, it represents the annual ratio of crime to fixed time intervals.

Crime in the United States 1992

Crime Index Total

The Crime Index total dropped 3 percent to nearly 14.5 million offenses in 1992, the first decline recorded since 1984. In the cities collectively and the suburban counties, the Index was also down 3 percent from 1991, while the rural counties registered a 1-percent decrease. This downward trend was evident in all city population groups with those having a million or more inhabitants showing the largest decrease, 8 percent. Five- and 10-year percent changes showed the 1992 national experience was 4 percent above the 1988 level and 19 percent higher than in 1983.

Geographically, the largest volume of Crime Index offenses was reported in the most populous Southern States, which accounted for 38 percent of the total.

Following were the Western States with 24 percent, the Midwestern States with 21 percent, and the Northeastern States with 17 percent. All regions except the West showed Crime Index decreases from 1991 to 1992.

Seasonality figures show Crime Index offenses occurred most frequently in the month of August and least often in February.

Rate

Crime rates relate the incidence of crime to population. Nationwide in 1992, there were an estimated 5,660 Crime Index offenses for each 100,000 in population. The Crime Index rate was highest in metropolitan areas and lowest in rural counties. While the national 1992 Crime Index rate fell 4 percent from 1991, it showed virtually no change from the 1988 level and was 9 percent above the 1983 total.

Table 1.—Index of Crime, United States, 1973-1992

Population[1]	Crime Index total[2]	Modified Crime Index total[3]	Violent crime[4]	Property crime[4]	Murder and non-negligent man-slaughter	Forcible rape	Robbery	Aggra-vated assault	Burglary	Larceny-theft	Motor vehicle theft	Arson[3]
					Number of Offenses							
Population by year:												
1983-233,981,000	12,108,600		1,258,090	10,850,500	19,310	78,920	506,570	653,290	3,129,900	6,712,800	1,007,900	
1984-236,158,000	11,881,800		1,273,280	10,608,500	18,690	84,230	485,010	685,350	2,984,400	6,591,900	1,032,200	
1985-238,740,000	12,431,400		1,328,800	11,102,600	18,980	88,670	497,870	723,250	3,073,300	6,926,400	1,102,900	
1986-241,077,000	13,211,900		1,489,170	11,722,700	20,610	91,460	542,780	834,320	3,241,400	7,257,200	1,224,100	
1987-243,400,000	13,508,700		1,484,000	12,024,700	20,100	91,110	517,700	855,090	3,236,200	7,499,900	1,288,700	
1988-245,807,000	13,923,100		1,566,220	12,356,900	20,680	92,490	542,970	910,090	3,218,100	7,705,900	1,432,900	
1989-248,239,000	14,251,400		1,646,040	12,605,400	21,500	94,500	578,330	951,710	3,168,200	7,872,400	1,564,800	
1990-248,709,873	14,475,600		1,820,130	12,655,500	23,440	102,560	639,270	1,054,860	3,073,900	7,945,700	1,635,900	
1991-252,177,000	14,872,900		1,911,770	12,961,100	24,700	106,590	687,730	1,092,740	3,157,200	8,142,200	1,661,700	
1992-255,082,000	14,438,200		1,932,270	12,505,900	23,760	109,060	672,480	1,126,970	2,979,900	7,915,200	1,610,800	
Percent change: number of offenses:												
1992/1991	−2.9		+1.1	−3.5	−3.8	+2.3	−2.2	+3.1	−5.6	−2.8	−3.1	
1992/1988	+3.7		+23.4	+1.2	+14.9	+17.9	+23.9	+23.8	−7.4	+2.7	+12.4	
1992/1983	+19.2		+53.6	+15.3	+23.0	+38.2	+32.8	+72.5	−4.8	+17.9	+59.8	
					Rate per 100,000 Inhabitants							
Year:												
1983	5,175.0		537.7	4,637.4	8.3	33.7	216.5	279.2	1,337.7	2,868.9	430.8	
1984	5,031.3		539.2	4,492.1	7.9	35.7	205.4	290.2	1,263.7	2,791.3	437.1	
1985	5,207.1		556.6	4,650.5	7.9	37.1	208.5	302.9	1,287.3	2,901.2	462.0	
1986	5,480.4		617.7	4,862.6	8.6	37.9	225.1	346.1	1,344.6	3,010.3	507.8	
1987	5,550.0		609.7	4,940.3	8.3	37.4	212.7	351.3	1,329.6	3,081.3	529.4	
1988	5,664.2		637.2	5,027.1	8.4	37.6	220.9	370.2	1,309.2	3,134.9	582.9	
1989	5,741.0		663.1	5,077.9	8.7	38.1	233.0	383.4	1,276.3	3,171.3	630.4	
1990	5,820.3		731.8	5,088.5	9.4	41.2	257.0	424.1	1,235.9	3,194.8	657.8	
1991	5,897.8		758.1	5,139.7	9.8	42.3	272.7	433.3	1,252.0	3,228.8	659.0	
1992	5,660.2		757.5	4,902.7	9.3	42.8	263.6	441.8	1,168.2	3,103.0	631.5	
Percent change: rate per 100,000 inhabitants:												
1992/1991	−4.0		−.1	−4.6	−5.1	+1.2	−3.3	+2.0	−6.7	−3.9	−4.2	
1992/1988	−.1		+18.9	−2.5	+10.7	+13.8	+19.3	+19.3	−10.8	−1.0	+8.3	
1992/1983	+9.4		+40.9	+5.7	+12.0	+27.0	+21.8	+58.2	−12.7	+8.2	+46.6	

[1]Populations are Bureau of the Census provisional estimates as of July 1, except 1980 and 1990 which are the decennial census counts.
[2]Because of rounding, the offenses may not add to totals.
[3]Although arson data are included in the trend and clearance tables, sufficient data are not available to estimate totals for this offense.
[4]Violent crimes are offenses of murder, forcible rape, robbery, and aggravated assault. Property crimes are offenses of burglary, larceny–theft, and motor vehicle theft. Data are not included for the property crime of arson.
All rates were calculated on the offenses before rounding.

Regionally, the Crime Index rates ranged from 6,388 in the West to 4,837 in the Northeast. The 2-year percent changes (1992 versus 1991) showed declines in all regions.

Nature

The Crime Index is composed of violent and property crime categories, and in 1992, 13 percent of the Index offenses reported to law enforcement were violent crimes and 87 percent, property crimes. Larceny-theft was the offense with the highest volume, while murder accounted for the fewest offenses.

Property estimated in value at $15.8 billion was stolen in connection with all Crime Index offenses, with the largest losses due to thefts of motor vehicles; jewelry and precious metals; and televisions, radios, stereos, etc. Law enforcement agencies nationwide recorded a 36-percent recovery rate for dollar losses in connection with stolen property. The highest recovery percentages were for stolen motor vehicles, consumable goods, livestock, clothing and furs, and firearms.

Law Enforcement Response

Law enforcement agencies nationwide recorded a 21-percent clearance rate for the collective Crime Index offenses in 1992 and made an estimated 2.9 million arrests for Index crimes. Crimes can be cleared by arrest or by exceptional means when some element beyond law enforcement control precludes the placing of formal charges against the offender. The arrest of one person may clear several crimes, or several persons may be arrested in connection with the clearance of one offense.

The Index clearance rate has remained relatively stable throughout the past 10-year period. As in 1992, the clearance rates in both 1988 and 1983 were 21 percent.

Total Crime Index arrests, as well as those of adults, dropped 2 percent in 1992 when compared to 1991. During the same time period, juvenile (persons under 18) arrests for the Index were up 1 percent, and those of persons under age 15 increased 2 percent. In fact, juvenile arrests increased over 1991 for all offenses except burglary and motor vehicle theft, for which arrest volumes were down 1 and 4 percent, respectively. Adult arrests declined for all offenses with the exception of aggravated assault which showed a 4-percent increase, 1992 versus 1991.

Considering the individual offenses composing the Index, only aggravated assault and arson showed increases in arrest totals from 1991 to 1992. Decreases for the remain-

CRIME INDEX OFFENSES REPORTED

ing Index offenses ranged from 1 percent for forcible rape to 5 percent for murder.

As in past years, larceny-theft arrests accounted for the highest volume of Crime Index arrests at 1.5 million.

MURDER AND NONNEGLIGENT MANSLAUGHTER

DEFINITION

Murder and nonnegligent manslaughter, as defined in the Uniform Crime Reporting Program, is the willful (non-negligent) killing of one human being by another.

TREND

Year	Number of offenses	Rate per 100,000 inhabitants
1991	24,703	9.8
1992	23,760	9.3
Percent change	−3.8	−5.1

Volume

The total number of murders in the United States during 1992 was estimated at 23,760. Monthly figures show that more persons were murdered in August in 1992, while the fewest were killed during February.

Murder by Month, 1988-1992

[Percent distribution]

Months	1988	1989	1990	1991	1992
January	8.2	8.1	7.9	8.0	8.1
February	7.2	7.1	7.0	7.0	7.5
March	7.7	7.8	8.0	7.7	8.2
April	7.7	7.9	7.4	7.8	8.0
May	7.8	7.8	8.1	8.1	8.5
June	7.7	8.2	8.4	8.6	7.9
July	8.9	9.1	9.6	9.1	9.1
August	9.5	9.0	9.3	9.4	9.1
September	8.9	8.8	9.2	8.8	8.7
October	8.9	8.9	8.8	8.6	8.0
November	8.2	8.5	7.6	7.8	8.1
December	9.2	8.7	8.8	9.0	8.8

When viewing the four regions of the Nation, the Southern States, the most populous region, accounted for 41 percent of the murders. The Western States reported 23 percent; the Midwestern States, 20 percent; and the Northeastern States, 17 percent. Among the regions, only the Western States registered an increase from 1991 to 1992, 3 percent.

The murder volume was down 4 percent nationwide in 1992 from 1991. In the Nation's cities overall, murder decreased 5 percent, with the greatest decline—12 percent—registered in cities with populations of 50,000 to 99,999. The suburban counties recorded a 3-percent drop in their murder volumes and the rural counties, an 8-percent decrease for the 2-year period.

[There has been] a 15-percent rise nationally in the murder

counts from 1988 to 1992. The 10-year trend showed the 1992 total 23 percent above the 1983 level.

Rate

Down 5 percent from the 1991 rate, the national murder rate in 1992 was 9 per 100,000 inhabitants. Five- and 10-year trends showed the 1992 rate was 11 percent higher than in 1988 and 12 percent above the 1983 rate.

On a regional basis, the South averaged 11 murders per 100,000 people; the West, 10 per 100,000; and the Northeast and Midwest, 8 per 100,000. Compared to 1991, murder rates in 1992 declined in three of the four geographic regions with the only increase in the West, 1 percent.

The Nation's metropolitan areas reported a 1992 murder rate of 10 victims per 100,000 inhabitants. In the rural counties and in cities outside metropolitan areas, the rate was 5 per 100,000.

Nature

Supplemental data provided by contributing agencies recorded information for 22,540 of the estimated 23,760 murders in 1992. Submitted monthly, the data consist of the age, sex, and race of both victims and offenders; the types of weapons used; the relationships of victims to the offenders; and the circumstances surrounding the murders.

Based on this information, 78 percent of the murder victims in 1992 were male; and 88 percent were persons 18 years of age or older. Forty-seven percent were aged 20 through 34 years. Considering victims for whom race was known, an average of 50 of every 100 were black, 48 were white, and the remainder were persons of other races.

FORCIBLE RAPE

DEFINITION

Forcible rape, as defined in the Program, is the carnal knowledge of a female forcibly and against her will. Assaults or attempts to commit rape by force or threat of force are also included; however, statutory rape (without force) and other sex offenses are excluded.

TREND

Year	Number of offenses	Rate per 100,000 inhabitants
1991	106,593	42.3
1992	109,062	42.8
Percent change	+2.3	+1.2

Volume

An estimated 109,062 forcible rapes were reported to law enforcement agencies across the Nation during 1992. The 1992 total was 2 percent higher than the 1991 level.

Geographically, 37 percent of the forcible rape total in 1992 was accounted for by the most populous Southern States, 25 percent by the Midwestern States, 24 percent by the Western States, and 14 percent by the Northeastern States. Two-year trends showed that all regions experienced volume increases over 1991 figures, ranging from 1 percent in the Midwest to 3 percent in the South.

Forcible Rape by Month, 1988-1992

[Percent distribution]

Months	1988	1989	1990	1991	1992
January	7.4	7.4	7.6	7.1	7.0
February	7.3	6.3	6.7	7.0	7.6
March	8.0	7.7	7.9	7.9	8.6
April	8.0	8.3	8.1	8.3	8.5
May	9.0	8.6	9.1	9.2	8.9
June	8.7	8.9	9.0	9.2	8.7
July	9.9	10.0	9.6	9.5	9.4
August	9.8	9.5	9.4	9.7	9.6
September	9.0	8.8	9.1	8.8	8.7
October	8.4	8.9	8.4	8.6	8.4
November	7.6	8.3	7.7	7.8	7.6
December	6.8	7.3	7.4	6.8	7.0

The greatest numbers of forcible rapes were reported during the summer months.

Rate

By Uniform Crime Reporting definition, the victims of forcible rape are always female. In 1992, an estimated 84 of every 100,000 females in the country were reported rape victims, an increase of 1 percent over the 1991 rate. Since 1988, the female forcible rape rate has risen 15 percent.

Female forcible rape rates for 1992 showed there were 90 victims per 100,000 females in MSAs, 73 per 100,000 females in cities outside metropolitan areas, and 49 per 100,000 females in rural counties. Although MSAs record the highest rape rates, they have shown the smallest change over the past 10 years. During this time, the greatest rate increase was shown in cities outside metropolitan areas, 78 percent. MSAs and rural areas showed lesser increases, 18 percent and 69 percent, respectively.

Regionally, in 1992, the highest female rape rate was in the Western States, which recorded 91 victims per 100,000 females. Following were the Southern States with a rate of 90, the Midwestern States with 89, and the Northeastern States with 58. Over the last 10 years, regional increases in the forcible rape rate were 48 percent in the Midwest, 34 percent in the South, 14 percent in the Northeast, and 6 percent in the West.

Nature

Rapes by force constitute the greatest percentage of total forcible rapes, 86 percent of the 1992 experience. The remainder were attempts or assaults to commit forcible rape. The number of rapes by force increased 3 percent in 1992 over the 1991 volume, while attempts to rape decreased 3 percent. Ten years of data show the percentage of rapes by force increasing.

As for all other Crime Index offenses, complaints of forcible rape made to law enforcement agencies are sometimes found to be false or baseless. In such cases, law enforcement agencies "unfound" the offenses and exclude them from crime counts. The "unfounded" rate, or percentage of complaints determined through investigation to be false, is higher for forcible rape than for any other Index crime. In 1992, 8 percent of forcible rape complaints were "unfounded," while the average for all Index crimes was 2 percent.

Law Enforcement Response

Nationwide, as well as in the cities, over half of the forcible rapes reported to law enforcement were cleared by arrest or exceptional means in 1992. Rural and suburban county law enforcement agencies cleared a slightly higher percentage of the offenses brought to their attention than did city law enforcement agencies.

Geographically, clearance rates for the regions were lowest in the Midwestern States and highest in the Southern States.

Of the total clearances for forcible rape in the country as a whole, 14 percent involved only persons under 18 years of age. The percentage of juvenile involvement varied by community type, ranging from 12 percent in the Nation's cities to 21 percent in suburban counties.

Law enforcement agencies nationwide made an estimated 39,100 arrests for forcible rape in 1992. Of the forcible rape arrestees, about 3 of every 10 were in the 18- to 24-year age group. Over half of those arrested were white.

The number of arrests for forcible rape fell 1 percent nationwide. Decreases of 2 percent were experienced in the Nation's cities and 4 percent in suburban counties from 1991 to 1992, while forcible rape arrests were up 7 percent in the rural counties.

ROBBERY

DEFINITION

Robbery is the taking or attempting to take anything of value from the care, custody, or control of a person or persons by force or threat of force or violence and/or by putting the victim in fear.

TREND

Year	Number of offenses	Rate per 100,000 inhabitants
1991	687,732	272.7
1992	672,478	263.6
Percent change	-2.2	-3.3

Volume

Reported robberies in 1992 were estimated at 672,478 offenses, accounting for 5 percent of all Index crimes and 35 percent of the violent crimes. Robberies occurred most frequently in December and least often in April during 1992.

Robbery by Month, 1988-1992

[Percent distribution]

Months	1988	1989	1990	1991	1992
January	8.6	8.8	8.7	8.7	9.0
February	7.9	7.4	7.3	7.5	8.0
March	8.0	8.0	8.1	8.0	8.1
April	7.3	7.3	7.2	7.4	7.8
May	7.6	7.6	7.7	7.8	7.9
June	7.6	7.6	7.8	7.8	7.9
July	8.4	8.4	8.5	8.4	8.4
August	8.7	8.6	8.8	8.8	8.6
September	8.7	8.6	8.6	8.5	8.3
October	9.1	9.2	8.9	9.2	8.7
November	9.0	9.0	8.7	8.7	8.3
December	9.2	9.3	9.6	9.2	9.0

Nationally, the 1992 robbery volume was 2 percent lower than the 1991 level. This downward trend was also evident in the suburban counties and in cities overall, with 3-percent declines in each. Robberies were up 2 percent in the rural counties.

Distribution figures for the regions showed that the most populous Southern States registered 32 percent of all reported robberies. Two-year trends show the number of robberies in 1992 was down in three of the four regions as compared to 1991. The declines were 6 percent in the Midwest, 4 percent in the Northeast, and 3 percent in the South. The West showed a 5-percent increase during the same time period.

In 1992, the number of robbery offenses was 24 percent higher than in 1988 and 33 percent above the 1983 total.

Rate

The national robbery rate in 1992 was 264 per 100,000 people, 3 percent lower than in 1991. In metropolitan areas, the 1992 rate was 323; in cities outside metropolitan areas, it was 70; and in the rural areas, it was 16. With 1,076 robberies per 100,000 inhabitants, the highest rate was recorded in cities with a million or more inhabitants.

A comparison of 1991 and 1992 regional robbery rates per 100,000 inhabitants showed the Midwest's rate of 207 down 7 percent; the rates of 241 in the South and 336 in the Northeast each down 4 percent; and the West's rate of 295 up 3 percent.

Nature

In 1992, a total estimated national loss of $565 million was due to robberies. The value of property stolen during robberies averaged $840 per incident, up from $817 in 1991. Average dollar losses in 1992 ranged from $402 taken during robberies of convenience stores to $3,325 per bank robbery. The impact of this violent crime on its victims cannot be measured in terms of monetary loss alone. While the object of a robbery is to obtain money or property, the crime always involves force or threat of force, and many victims suffer serious personal injury.

As in previous years, robberies on streets or highways accounted for more than half (56 percent) of the offenses in this category. Robberies of commercial and financial establishments accounted for an additional 21 percent, and those occurring at residences, 10 percent. The remainder were miscellaneous types. From 1991 to 1992, bank robbery and miscellaneous robbery volumes each increased 1 percent. Decreases were experienced for all other robbery categories.

Robbery, Percent Distribution, 1992

[By region]

	United States Total	North-eastern States	Mid-western States	Southern States	Western States
Total[1]	100.0	100.0	100.0	100.0	100.0
Street/highway	55.6	62.7	60.0	50.4	51.8
Commercial house	11.9	10.3	10.1	12.0	14.5
Gas or service station	2.5	2.1	3.1	2.5	2.6
Convenience store	5.3	2.4	3.2	8.6	5.6
Residence	10.1	10.3	9.4	12.0	7.9
Bank	1.7	1.0	1.1	1.3	3.2
Miscellaneous	13.1	11.4	13.2	13.3	14.4

[1]Because of rounding, percentages may not add to totals.

AGGRAVATED ASSAULT

DEFINITION

Aggravated assault is an unlawful attack by one person upon another for the purpose of inflicting severe or aggravated bodily injury. This type of assault is usually accompanied by the use of a weapon or by means likely to produce death or great bodily harm.

TREND

Year	Number of offenses	Rate per 100,000 inhabitants
1991	1,092,739	433.3
1992	1,126,974	441.8
Percent change	+3.1	+2.0

Volume

Totaling an estimated 1,126,974 offenses nationally, aggravated assaults in 1992 accounted for 58 percent of the violent crimes. Geographic distribution figures show that 40 percent of the aggravated assault volume was accounted for by the most populous Southern Region, 25 percent by the Western Region, 19 percent by the Midwestern Region, and 16 percent by the Northeastern Region. Among the regions, the Northeast and Midwest registered declines in aggravated assaults.

The 1992 monthly figures show that the greatest number of aggravated assaults was recorded during July, while the lowest volumes occurred during February.

In 1992, aggravated assaults were up 3 percent nationwide as compared to 1991. For the same time period, cities collectively experienced a 2-percent increase in the aggravated assault volume, with cities from 25,000 to 49,999 in population recording the greatest rise, 7 percent. Cities with a million or more inhabitants experienced the only

Aggravated Assault by Month, 1988-1992

[Percent distribution]

Months	1988	1989	1990	1991	1992
January	7.2	7.5	7.4	6.9	7.3
February	7.0	6.6	6.7	6.6	7.3
March	7.9	7.9	7.8	7.7	8.0
April	8.1	8.1	8.2	8.1	8.7
May	8.9	8.9	9.0	9.1	9.2
June	9.0	8.9	9.4	9.3	8.9
July	9.8	9.6	10.1	9.7	9.4
August	9.8	9.2	9.3	9.9	9.1
September	9.0	8.8	8.9	9.0	8.6
October	8.4	9.1	8.3	8.6	8.5
November	7.5	7.9	7.4	7.6	7.6
December	7.5	7.5	7.5	7.6	7.4

decline, 2 percent. The suburban counties registered a 4-percent increase and the rural counties, a 6-percent rise for the 2-year period.

Five- and 10-year trends for the country as a whole showed aggravated assaults up 24 percent above the 1988 level and 73 percent over the 1983 experience.

Rate

Up 2 percent above the 1991 rate, there were 442 reported victims of aggravated assault for every 100,000 people nationwide in 1992. The rate was 19 percent higher than in 1988 and 58 percent above the 1983 rate.

Higher than the national average, the rate in metropolitan areas was 492 per 100,000 in 1992. Cities outside metropolitan areas experienced a rate of 373, and rural counties, a rate of 174.

Regionally, the aggravated assault rates ranged from 513 per 100,000 people in the West to 347 per 100,000 in the Midwest. Compared to 1991, 1992 aggravated assault rates were up in two of the four regions; the South and West registered increases of 5 and 3 percent, respectively. The Northeast and Midwest showed declines, 1 and 2 percent, respectively.

Nature

In 1992, 31 percent of the aggravated assaults were committed with blunt objects or other dangerous weapons.

Aggravated Assault, Type of Weapons Used, 1992

[Percent distribution by region]

Region	Total all weapons[1]	Fire- arms	Knives or cutting instru- ments	Other weapons (clubs, blunt objects, etc.)	Personal weapons
Total	100.0	24.7	18.2	31.3	25.7
Northeastern States	100.0	16.9	21.5	31.2	30.4
Midwestern States	100.0	29.8	18.6	33.9	17.6
Southern States	100.0	26.8	19.8	31.8	21.7
Western States	100.0	23.1	13.8	28.8	34.2

[1]Because of rounding, percentages may not add to totals.

Of the remaining weapon categories, personal weapons such as hands, fists, and feet were used in 26 percent of the offenses; firearms in 25 percent; and knives or cutting instruments in the remainder.

From 1991 to 1992, assaults with firearms rose by 5 percent, those involving personal weapons increased 4 percent, and those involving blunt objects or other dangerous weapons were up 2 percent. Aggravated assaults by knives or cutting instruments showed the only decline, 1 percent.

BURGLARY

DEFINITION

The Uniform Crime Reporting Program defines burglary as the unlawful entry of a structure to commit a felony or theft. The use of force to gain entry is not required to classify an offense as burglary.

TREND

Year	Number of offenses	Rate per 100,000 inhabitants
1991	3,157,150	1,252.0
1992	2,979,884	1,168.2
Percent change	−5.6	−6.7

Volume

An estimated 2,979,884 burglaries occurred in the United States during 1992. These offenses accounted for 21 percent of the Crime Index total and 24 percent of the property crimes.

Distribution figures for the regions showed that the highest burglary volume occurred in the most populous Southern States, accounting for 41 percent of the total. The Western States followed with 24 percent, the Midwestern States with 20 percent, and the Northeastern States with 16 percent.

In 1992, the highest burglary totals were recorded during August, while the lowest count was reported in February.

Burglary by Month, 1988-1992

[Percent distribution]

Months	1988	1989	1990	1991	1992
January	8.4	8.8	8.8	8.1	8.6
February	7.8	7.3	7.5	7.3	7.7
March	8.1	8.2	8.1	8.1	8.2
April	7.5	7.7	7.8	7.9	7.8
May	8.1	8.4	8.1	8.3	8.2
June	8.0	8.3	7.9	8.2	8.1
July	8.8	9.2	8.9	9.2	9.0
August	9.3	9.3	9.0	9.2	9.0
September	8.6	8.6	8.3	8.6	8.4
October	8.5	8.5	8.5	8.6	8.3
November	8.4	8.1	8.3	8.0	8.2
December	8.5	7.8	8.7	8.6	8.3

Nationwide, the burglary volume dropped 6 percent in 1992 from the 1991 total. By population group, decreases were registered in all city groupings; the largest decrease was in cities with populations of 1 million or more, which showed a 9-percent decline.

Geographically, all four regions of the United States reported decreases in burglary volumes during 1992 as compared to 1991. Both the Northeastern States and the Southern States experienced 7-percent declines. The Midwestern States showed a 6-percent decrease; and the Western States reported the smallest change, a 2-percent decline.

Longer term national trends show burglary down 7 percent from the 1988 volume and 5 percent below the 1983 level.

Rate

A burglary rate of 1,168 per 100,000 inhabitants was registered nationwide in 1992. The rate was 7 percent lower than in 1991 and 13 percent below the 1983 rate. In 1992, for every 100,000 in population, the rate was 1,265 in the metropolitan areas, 1,012 in the cities outside metropolitan areas, and 661 in the rural counties.

Regionally, the burglary rate was 1,379 in the Southern States, 1,273 in the Western States, 964 in the Midwestern States, and 935 in the Northeastern States. A comparison of 1991 and 1992 rates showed decreases of 8 percent in the South, 7 percent in the Midwest and Northeast, and 4 percent in the West.

Nature

Two of every 3 burglaries in 1992 were residential in nature. Sixty-nine percent of all burglaries involved forcible entry, 23 percent were unlawful entries (without force), and the remainder were forcible entry attempts. Offenses for which time of occurrence was reported were evenly divided between day and night.

Burglary victims suffered losses estimated at $3.8 billion in 1992, and the average dollar loss per burglary was $1,278. The average loss for residential offenses was $1,215, while for nonresidential property, it was $1,400. Compared to 1991, the 1992 average loss for residential property declined, while for nonresidential property the average was up. Both residential and nonresidential burglary volumes showed declines from 1991 to 1992, 5 and 6 percent, respectively.

Law Enforcement Response

Geographically in 1992, a 13-percent clearance rate was recorded for burglaries brought to the attention of law enforcement agencies across the country. In the South, the clearance rate was 15 percent; in the Northeast and West, 13 percent; and in the Midwest, 12 percent.

Rural county law enforcement cleared 16 percent of the burglaries in their jurisdictions. Agencies in suburban counties cleared 14 percent, and those in cities, 13 percent.

LARCENY-THEFT

DEFINITION

Larceny-theft is the unlawful taking, carrying, leading, or riding away of property from the possession or constructive possession of another. It includes crimes such as shoplifting, pocket-picking, purse-snatching, thefts from motor vehicles, thefts of motor vehicle parts and accessories, bicycle thefts, etc., in which no use of force, violence, or fraud occurs.

TREND

Year	Number of offenses	Rate per 100,000 inhabitants
1991	8,142,228	3,228.8
1992	7,915,199	3,103.0
Percent change	−2.8	−3.9

Volume

Larceny-theft, estimated at 7.9 million offenses during 1992, comprised 55 percent of the Crime Index total and 63 percent of the property crimes. Similar to the experience in previous years, larceny-thefts were recorded most often during the month of August and least frequently in February.

When viewed geographically, the Southern States, the most populous region, recorded 38 percent of the larceny-theft total. The Western States recorded 24 percent; the Midwestern States, 22 percent; and the Northeastern States, 16 percent.

Larceny-Theft by Month, 1988-1992

[Percent distribution]

Months	1988	1989	1990	1991	1992
January	7.6	8.0	8.2	7.8	8.2
February	7.5	7.2	7.4	7.5	7.8
March	8.2	8.2	8.2	8.2	8.3
April	7.8	8.0	7.9	8.1	8.1
May	8.3	8.6	8.3	8.4	8.2
June	8.5	8.7	8.3	8.5	8.5
July	9.0	9.2	8.9	9.2	9.1
August	9.5	9.5	9.1	9.3	9.1
September	8.5	8.3	8.2	8.3	8.4
October	8.7	8.6	8.7	8.7	8.6
November	8.2	8.0	8.1	7.9	7.9
December	8.3	7.7	8.4	8.2	8.0

Compared to 1991, the 1992 volume of larceny-thefts showed a decline of 3 percent in the Nation, in all cities collectively, and in suburban counties. The rural counties showed a decline of less than 1 percent.

Regionally, larceny declines were recorded in the Northeast, 6 percent; in the Midwest, 4 percent; and in the South, 2 percent. The number of larceny-thefts in the West showed no change.

The 5- and 10-year national trends indicated larceny was up 3 percent over the 1988 total and 18 percent above the 1983 level.

Rate

The 1992 larceny-theft rate was 3,103 per 100,000 United States inhabitants. The rate was 4 percent lower than in 1991 and 1 percent under the 1988 level. When compared to 1983, the rate showed an increase of 8 percent. The 1992 rate was 3,378 per 100,000 inhabitants of metropolitan areas; 3,601 per 100,000 population in cities outside metropolitan areas; and 1,036 per 100,000 people in the rural counties.

For all regions, the larceny-theft rate per 100,000 inhabitants declined from 1991 levels. The rate in the Northeast was 2,443, a decline of 6 percent; the Midwest's 1992 rate of 2,928 was down 5 percent; and rates of 3,388 in the South and 3,452 in the West were down 4 and 2 percent, respectively.

Nature

During 1992, the average value of property stolen due to larceny-theft was $483, a slight increase from $478 in 1991. When the average value was applied to the estimated number of larceny-thefts, the loss to victims nationally was $3.8 billion for the year. This estimated dollar loss is considered conservative since many offenses in the larceny category, particularly if the value of the stolen goods is small, never come to law enforcement attention. Losses in 24 percent of the thefts reported to law enforcement in 1992 ranged from $50 to $200, while in 36 percent, they were over $200.

Losses of goods and property reported stolen as a result of pocket-picking averaged $430; purse-snatching, $292; and shoplifting, $106. Thefts from buildings resulted in an average loss of $802; from motor vehicles, $555; and from coin-operated machines, $141. The average value loss due to thefts of motor vehicle accessories was $297 and for thefts of bicycles, $231.

Thefts of motor vehicle parts, accessories, and contents made up the largest portion of reported larcenies—37 percent. Also contributing to the high volume of thefts were shoplifting, accounting for 16 percent; thefts from buildings, 14 percent; and bicycle thefts, 6 percent. The remainder were distributed among pocket-picking, purse-snatching, thefts from coin-operated machines, and all other types of larceny-thefts.

Larceny Analysis by Region, 1992

[Percent distribution]

	United States Total	North-eastern States	Mid-western States	Southern States	Western States
Total[1]	100.0	100.0	100.0	100.0	100.0
Pocket-picking	1.0	3.4	.7	.5	.5
Purse-snatching	.9	1.8	1.0	.7	.7
Shoplifting	15.8	14.2	14.0	15.9	18.3
From motor vehicles (except accessories)	22.6	21.7	18.4	20.8	29.4
Motor vehicle accessories	14.0	13.9	14.0	15.5	11.8
Bicycles	5.9	6.2	5.0	5.1	7.8
From buildings	14.0	18.0	19.5	10.5	12.2
From coin-operated machines	.9	1.6	.6	.9	.8
All others	24.8	19.1	26.7	30.2	18.7

[1]Because of rounding, percentages may not add to totals.

MOTOR VEHICLE THEFT

DEFINITION

Defined as the theft or attempted theft of a motor vehicle, this offense category includes the stealing of automobiles, trucks, buses, motorcycles, motorscooters, snowmobiles, etc.

TREND

Year	Number of offenses	Rate per 100,000 inhabitants
1991	1,661,738	659.0
1992	1,610,834	631.5
Percent change	−3.1	−4.2

Volume

An estimated total of 1,610,834 thefts of motor vehicles occurred in the United States during 1992. These offenses comprised 13 percent of all property crimes. The regional distribution of motor vehicle thefts showed 32 percent of the volume was in the Southern States, 27 percent in the Western States, 23 percent in the Northeastern States, and 18 percent in the Midwestern States.

The 1992 monthly figures showed that the greatest number of motor vehicle thefts was recorded during the month of August, while the lowest count was in February.

Motor Vehicle Theft by Month, 1988-1992

[Percent distribution]

Months	1988	1989	1990	1991	1992
January	8.0	8.3	8.5	8.3	8.8
February	7.6	7.3	7.6	7.5	7.9
March	7.9	8.1	8.4	8.2	8.2
April	7.4	7.5	7.9	7.8	7.8
May	7.8	8.0	8.1	8.1	8.1
June	8.0	8.2	8.1	8.2	8.2
July	8.8	8.8	8.8	8.7	8.8
August	9.4	9.0	8.8	8.9	8.9
September	8.7	8.5	8.4	8.3	8.2
October	9.0	9.0	8.8	8.7	8.6
November	8.7	8.7	8.3	8.5	8.3
December	8.7	8.5	8.4	8.8	8.2

The number of motor vehicle thefts fell 3 percent nationally and in the cities overall from 1991 to 1992. During the same period, the suburban counties experienced a 2-percent drop and the rural counties, a 6-percent decline.

Geographically, three regions experienced motor vehicle theft decreases, while the Western Region showed a 3-percent increase.

[T]he volume of motor vehicle thefts in 1992 increased 12 percent over the 1988 volume.

Rate

The 1992 national motor vehicle theft rate—631 per 100,000 people—decreased 4 percent from the rate in

1991. The rate was 8 percent higher than in 1988 and 47 percent above the 1983 rate.

For every 100,000 inhabitants living in MSAs, there were 758 motor vehicle thefts reported in 1992. The rate in cities outside metropolitan areas was 217 and in rural counties, 109. As in previous years, the highest rates were in the Nation's most heavily populated municipalities, indicating that this offense is primarily a large-city problem. For every 100,000 inhabitants in cities with populations over 250,000, the 1992 motor vehicle theft rate was 1,591. The Nation's smallest cities, those with fewer than 10,000 inhabitants, recorded a rate of 246 per 100,000 and the rural counties, a rate of 117 per 100,000.

Among the regions, the motor vehicle theft rates ranged from 799 per 100,000 people in the Western States to 477 in the Midwestern States. The Northeastern States' rate was 727 and the Southern States' rate, 578. All regions except the Western States registered rate decreases from 1991 to 1992.

An estimated average of 1 of every 120 registered motor vehicles was stolen nationwide during 1992. Regionally, this rate was greatest in the Northeast where 1 of every 89 motor vehicles registered was stolen. The other three regions reported lesser rates—1 per 98 in the West, 1 per 135 in the South, and 1 per 168 in the Midwest.

Nature

During 1992, the estimated value of motor vehicles stolen nationwide was nearly $7.6 billion. At the time of theft, the average value per vehicle stolen was $4,713. The recovery percentage for the value of vehicles stolen was higher than for any other property type. Relating the value of vehicles stolen to the value of those recovered resulted in a 64-percent recovery rate for 1992.

Eighty percent of all motor vehicles reported stolen during the year were automobiles, 15 percent were trucks or buses, and the remainder were other types.

Motor Vehicle Theft, 1992

[Percent distribution by region]

Region	Total[1]	Autos	Trucks and buses	Other vehicles
Total	100.0	79.6	15.1	5.4
Northeastern States	100.0	92.4	4.8	2.9
Midwestern States	100.0	83.7	11.1	5.2
Southern States	100.0	74.2	18.7	7.1
Western States	100.0	72.8	21.6	5.6

[1]Because of rounding, percentages may not add to totals.

Glossary

Abet To encourage another to commit a crime. This encouragement may be by advice, inducement, command, etc. The abettor of a crime is equally guilty with the one who actually commits the crime.

Accessory after the Fact One who harbors, assists, or protects another person, although he knows that person has committed a crime.

Accessory before the Fact One who helps another to commit a crime, even though he is absent when the crime is committed.

Accomplice One who is involved in the commission of a crime with others, whether he actually commits the crime or abets others. The term *principal* means the same thing, except that one may be a principal if he commits a crime without the aid of others.

Acquit To free a person from an accusation of criminal guilt; to find "not guilty."

Affidavit A written declaration or statement sworn to and affirmed by an officer having authority to administer an oath.

Affirmation To swear on one's conscience that what he says is true. An *oath* means that one calls upon God to witness the truth of what he says.

Alias Any name by which one is known other than his true name. *Alias dictus* is the more technically correct term but it is rarely used.

Alibi A claim that one was in a place different from that charged. If the person proves his alibi, he proves that he could not have committed the crime charged.

Allegation The declaration of a party to a lawsuit made in a pleading, that states what he expects to prove.

Amnesty A class or group pardon (e.g., all political prisoners).

Appeal A case carried to a higher court to ask that the decision of the lower court, in which the case originated, be altered or overruled completely.

Appellate Court A court that has jurisdiction to hear cases on appeal; not a trial court.

Arraignment The appearance before the court of a person charged with a crime. He or she is advised of the charges, bail is set, and a plea of "guilty" or "not guilty" is entered.

Arrest To take a person into custody so that he may be held to answer for a crime.

Autopsy A post-mortem examination of a human body to determine the cause of death.

Bail Property (usually money) deposited with a court in exchange for the release of a person in custody to assure later appearance.

Bail Bond An obligation signed by the accused and his sureties, that insures his presence in court.

Bailiff A court attendant whose duties are to keep order in the courtroom and to have custody of the jury.

Bench Warrant An order by the court for the apprehension and arrest of a defendant or other person who has failed to appear when so ordered.

Bill of Rights The first ten amendments to the Constitution of the United States which define such rights as: due process of law, immunity from illegal search and seizure, the ban on cruel and unusual punishment, unreasonably high bail, indictment by a grand jury, and speedy trial.

Bind Over To hold for trial.

"Blue" Laws Laws in some jurisdictions prohibiting sales of merchandise, athletic contests, and the sale of alcoholic beverages on Sundays.

Booking The procedure at a police station of entering the name and identifying particulars relating to an arrested person, the charges filed against him, and the name of the arresting officer.

Burden of Proof The duty of affirmatively proving the guilt of the defendant "beyond a reasonable doubt."

Calendar A list of cases to be heard in a trial court, on a specific day, and containing the title of the case, the lawyers involved, and the index number.

Capital Crime Any crime that may be punishable by death or imprisonment for life.

Caseload The number of cases actively being investigated by a police detective or being supervised by a probation or parole officer.

Change of Venue The removal of a trial from one jurisdiction to another in order to avoid local prejudice.

Charge In criminal law, the accusation made against a person. It also refers to the judge's instruction to the jury on legal points.

Circumstantial Evidence Indirect evidence; evidence from which the principal fact can be proved or disproved by inference. Example: a finger-print found at the crime scene.

Citizen's Arrest A taking into custody of an alleged offender by a person not a law enforcement officer. Such an arrest is lawful if the crime was attempted or committed in his presence.

Code A compilation, compendium, or revision of laws, arranged into chapters, having a table of contents and index, and promulgated by legislative authority. Criminal code; penal code.

Coercion The compelling of a person to do that which he is not obliged to do, or to omit doing what he may legally do, by some illegal threat, force, or intimidation. For example: a forced confession.

Commit To place a person in custody in a prison or other institution by lawful order.

Common Law Law that derives its authority from usage and custom or court decisions.

Commutation To change the punishment meted out to a criminal to one less severe. Executive clemency.

Complainant The victim of a crime who brings the facts to the attention of the authorities.

Complaint A sworn written allegation stating that a specified person committed a crime. Sometimes called an *information*. When issued from a *Grand Jury*, it is called an *indictment*.

Compulsion An irresistible impulse to commit some act, such as stealing, setting a fire, or an illegal sexual act.

Confession An admission by the accused of his guilt; a partial admission (e.g., that he was at the crime scene; that he had a motive) is referred to as "an admission against interest."

Confinement Deprivation of liberty in a jail or prison either as punishment for a crime or as detention while guilt or innocence is being determined.

Consensual Crime A crime without a victim; one in which both parties voluntarily participate (e.g., adultery, sodomy, etc.).

Conspiracy A secret combination of two or more persons who plan for the purpose of committing a crime or any unlawful act or a lawful act by unlawful or criminal means.

Contempt of Court Behavior that impugns the authority of a court or obstructs the execution of court orders.

Continuance A delay in trial granted by the judge on request of either the prosecutor or defense counsel; an adjournment.

Conviction A finding by the jury (or by the trial judge in cases tried without a jury) that the accused is guilty of a crime.

Corporal Corporal punishment is pain inflicted on the body of another. Flogging.

Corpus Delicti The objective proof that a crime has been committed as distinguished from an accidental death, injury or loss.

Corrections Area of criminal justice dealing with convicted offenders in jails, prisons; on probation or parole.

Corroborating Evidence Supplementary evidence that tends to strengthen or confirm other evidence given previously.

Crime An act or omission prohibited and punishable by law. Crimes are divided into *felonies* and *misdemeanors;* and recorded as "crimes against the person" (murder, rape, assault, robbery) and "crimes against property" (burglary, larceny, auto theft). There are also crimes against public morality and against public order.

Criminal Insanity Lack of mental capacity to do or refrain from doing a criminal act; inability to distinguish right from wrong.

Criminalistics Crime laboratory procedures (e.g., ballistics, analysis of stains, etc.).

Criminology The scientific study of crime and criminals.

Cross-Examination The questioning of a witness by the party who did not produce the witness.

Culpability Guilt; *see also mens rea.*

Defendant The person who is being prosecuted.

Delinquency Criminality by a boy or girl who has not as yet reached the age set by the state for trial as an adult (the age varies from jurisdiction to jurisdiction and from crime to crime).

Demurrer In court procedure, a statement that the charge that a crime has been committed has no sufficient basis in law, despite the truth of the facts alleged.

Deposition The testimony of a witness not taken in open court but taken in pursuance of authority to take such testimony elsewhere.

Detention To hold a person in confinement while awaiting trial or sentence, or as a material witness.

Deterrence To prevent criminality by fear of the consequences; one of the rationalizations for punishing offenders.

Direct Evidence Proof of facts by witnesses who actually saw acts or heard words, as distinguished from *Circumstantial Evidence.*

Direct Examination The first questioning of a witness by the party who produced him.

Directed Verdict An instruction by the judge to the jury to return a specific verdict. A judge may not direct a guilty verdict.

Discretion The decision-making powers of officers of the criminal justice system (e.g., to arrest or not, to prosecute or not, to plea-bargain, to grant probation, or to sentence to a penal institution).

District Attorney Prosecutor; sometimes County Attorney, (U.S. Attorney in Federal practice).

Docket The formal record maintained by the court clerk, listing all cases heard. It contains the defendant's name, index number, date of arrest, and the outcome of the case.

Double Jeopardy To be prosecuted twice for the same offense.

Due Process Law in its regular course of administration through the courts of justice. Guaranteed by the 5th and 14th Amendments.

Embracery An attempt to influence a jury, or a member thereof, in their verdict by any improper means.

Entrapment The instigation of a crime by officers or agents of a government who induce a person to commit a crime that he did not originally contemplate in order to institute a criminal prosecution against him.

Evidence All the means used to prove or disprove the fact at issue.

Ex Post Facto After the fact. An ex post facto law is a criminal law that makes an act unlawful although it was committed prior to the passage of that law.

Examination An investigation of a witness by counsel in the form of questions for the purpose of bringing before the court knowledge possessed by the witness.

Exception A formal objection to the action of the court during a trial. The indication is that the excepting party will seek to reverse the court's action at some future proceeding. *Objection.*

Exclusionary Rule Rule of evidence which makes illegally acquired evidence inadmissible; *see* Mapp vs. Ohio.

Expert Evidence Testimony by one qualified to speak authoritatively on technical matters because of his special training or skill.

Extradition The surrender by one state to another of an individual accused of a crime.

False Arrest Any unlawful physical restraint of another's freedom of movement. Unlawful arrest.

Felonious Evil, malicious, or criminal. A felonious act is not necessarily a felony, but is criminal in some degree.

Felony Generally, an offense punishable by death or imprisonment in a penitentiary.

Forensic Relating to the court. Thus, forensic medicine would refer to medicine in relation to court proceedings and the law in general.

Grand Jury A group of 16 to 23 citizens of a county who examine evidence against the person suspected of a crime, and hand down an indictment if there is sufficient evidence to warrant one.

Habeas Corpus (Writ of) An order that requires a jailer, warden, police chief, or other public official to produce a person being held in custody before a court in order to show that they have a legal right to hold him in custody.

Hearsay Evidence not originating from the witness' personal knowledge.

Homicide The killing of a human being; may be murder, negligent or non-negligent manslaughter, or excusable or justifiable homicide.

Impeach To discredit. To question the truthfulness of a witness. Also: to charge a president or governor with criminal misconduct.

Imprisonment The act of confining a convicted felon in a federal or state prison.

In Camera In the judge's private chambers; in secrecy; the general public and press are excluded.

Indictment The document prepared by a prosecutor and approved by the grand jury which charges a certain person with a specific crime or crimes for which that person is later to be tried in court. Truebill.

Inference A conclusion one draws about something based on proof of certain other facts.

Injunction An order by a court prohibiting a defendant from committing an act.

Intent A design or determination of the mind to do or not do a certain thing. Intent may be determined from the nature of one's acts. Mens Rea.

Interpol International Criminal Police Commission.

Jail A short-term confinement institution for the detention of persons awaiting trial and the serving of sentences by those convicted of misdemeanors and offenses.

Jeopardy The danger of conviction and punishment that a defendant faces in a criminal trial. *Double Jeopardy.*

Judicial Notice The rule that a court will accept certain things as common knowledge without proof.

Jurisdiction The power of a court to hear and determine a criminal case.

Jury A certain number of persons who are sworn to examine the evidence and determine the truth on the basis of that evidence. Grand jury; trial jury.

Juvenile Delinquent A boy or girl who has not reached the age of criminal liability (varies from state to state) and who commits an act which would be a misdemeanor or felony if he were an adult. Delinquents are tried in *Juvenile Court* and confined to separate facilities.

L.E.A.A. Law Enforcement Assistance Administration, U.S. Dept. of Justice.

Leniency An unusually mild sentence imposed on a convicted offender; clemency granted by the President or a state governor; early release by a parole board.

Lie Detector An instrument which measures certain physiological reactions of the human body from which a trained operator may determine whether the subject is telling the truth or lies; polygraph; psychological stress evaluator.

Mala In Se Evil in itself. Acts that are made crimes because they are, by their nature, evil and morally wrong.

Mala Prohibita Evil because they are prohibited. Acts that are not wrong in themselves but which, to protect the general welfare, are made crimes by statute.

Malfeasance The act of a public officer in committing a crime relating to his official duties or powers. Accepting or demanding a bribe.

Malice An evil intent to vex, annoy, or injure another; intentional evil.

Malicious Prosecution An action instituted in bad faith with the intention of injuring the defendant.

Mandamus A writ that issues from a superior court, directed to any person, corporation, or inferior court, requiring it to do some particular thing.

Mens Rea A guilty intent.

Miranda Warning A police officer when taking a suspect into custody must warn him of his right to remain silent and of his right to an attorney.

Misdemeanor Any crime not a *Felony*. Usually, a crime punishable by a fine or imprisonment in the county or other local jail.

Misprision Failing to reveal a crime.

Mistrial A trial discontinued before reaching a verdict because of some procedural defect or impediment.

Modus Operandi Method of operation by criminals.

Motions Procedural moves made by either defense attorney or prosecutor and submitted to the court, helping to define and set the ground rules for the proceedings of a particular case. For example: to suppress illegally seized evidence or to seek a change of venue.

Motive The reason for committing a crime.

N.C.C.D. National Council on Crime and Delinquency.

No Bill A phrase used by a *Grand Jury* when they fail to indict.

Nolle Prosequi A declaration to a court, by the prosecutor that he does not wish to further prosecute the case.

Nolo Contendre A pleading, usually used by a defendant in a criminal case, that literally means "I will not contest."

Objection The act of taking exception to some statement or procedure in a trial. Used to call the court's attention to some improper evidence or procedure.

Opinion Evidence A witness' belief or opinion about a fact in dispute, as distinguished from personal knowledge of the fact. Expert testimony.

Ordinance A statute enacted by the city or municipal government.

Organized Crime The crime syndicate; cosa nostra; Mafia; an organized, continuing criminal conspiracy which engages in crime as a business (e.g., loan sharking, illegal gambling, prostitution, extortion, etc.).

Original Jurisdiction Trial jurisdiction.

Over Act An open or physical act, as opposed to a thought or mere intention.

Pardon Executive clemency setting aside a conviction and penalty.

Parole A conditional release from prison, under supervision.

Penal Code The criminal law of a jurisdiction, (sometimes the criminal procedure law is included but in other states it is codified separately).

Penology The study of punishment and corrections.

Peremptory Challenge The act of objecting to a certain number of jurors without assigning a cause for their dismissal. Used during the *voir dire* examination.

Perjury The legal offense of deliberately testifying falsely under oath about a material fact.

Petit Jury The ordinary jury composed of 12 persons who hear criminal cases. Determines guilt or innocence of the accused.

Plea-Bargaining A negotiation between the defense attorney and the prosecutor in which defendant receives a reduced penalty in return for a plea of "guilty."

Police Power The authority of the legislation to make laws in the interest of the general public, even at the risk of placing some hardship on individuals.

Post Mortem After death. Commonly applied to examination of a dead body. An autopsy is a post mortem examination to determine the cause of death.

Preliminary Hearing A proceeding in front of a lower court to determine if there is sufficient evidence for submitting a felony case to the grand jury.

Presumption of Fact An inference as to the truth or falsity of any proposition or fact, made in the absence of actual certainty of its truth or falsity or until such certainty can be attained.

Presumption of Law A rule of law that courts and judges must draw a particular inference from a particular fact or evidence, unless the inference can be disproved.

Prima Facie So far as can be judged from the first appearance or at first sight.

Prison Federal or state penal institution for the confinement of convicted felons. Penitentiary.

Probation A penalty placing a convicted person under the supervision of a probation officer for a stated time, instead of being confined.

Prosecutor One who initiates a criminal prosecution against an accused. One who acts as a trial attorney for the government as the representative of the people.

Provost Marshal Military police officer in charge of discipline, crime control and traffic law enforcement at a military post.

Public Defender An appointed or elected public official charged with providing legal representation for indigent persons accused of crimes.

Reasonable Doubt That state of mind of jurors when they do not feel a moral certainty about the truth of the charge and when the evidence does not exclude every other reasonable hypothesis except that the defendant is guilty as charged.

Rebuttal The introduction of contradicting testimony; the showing that statements made by a witness are not true; the point in the trial at which such evidence may be introduced.

Recidivist A repeater in crime; a habitual offender.

Recognizance When a person binds himself to do a certain act or else suffer a penalty, as, for example, with a recognizance bond. Release on recognizance is release without posting bail or bond.

Relevant Applying to the issue in question; related to the issue; useful in determining the truth or falsity of an alleged fact.

Remand To send back. To remand a case for new trial or sentencing.

Reprieve A stay of execution or sentence.

Search Warrant A written order, issued by judicial authority in the name of the state, directing a law enforcement officer to search for personal property and, if found, to bring it before the court.

Sentence The punishment (harsh or lenient) imposed by the trial judge on a convicted offender; major options include: fines, probation, indeterminate sentencing (e.g., three to ten years), indefinite sentencing (e.g., not more than three years), and capital punishment (death).

Stare Decisis To abide by decided cases. The doctrine that once a court has laid down a principle of law as applicable to certain facts, it will apply it to all future cases when the facts are substantially the same.

State's Evidence Testimony given by an accomplice or participant in a crime, tending to convict others.

Status Offense An act which is punishable only because the offender has not as yet reached a statutorily prescribed age (e.g., truancy, running away, drinking alcoholic beverages by a minor, etc.).

Statute A law.

Stay A stopping of a judicial proceeding by a court order.

Subpoena A court order requiring a witness to attend and testify in a court proceeding.

Subpoena Duces Tecum A court order requiring a witness to testify and to bring all books, documents, and papers that might affect the outcome of the proceedings.

Summons An order to appear in court on a particular date, which is issued by a police officer after or instead of arrest. It may also be a notification to a witness or a juror to appear in court.

Suspect One whom the police have determined as very likely to be the guilty perpetrator of an offense. Once the police identify a person as a suspect, they must warn him of his rights (Miranda warning) to remain silent and to have legal advice.

Testimony Evidence given by a competent witness, under oath, as distinguished from evidence from writings and other sources.

Tort A legal wrong committed against a person or property for which compensation may be obtained by a civil action.

Uniform Crime Reports (U.C.R.) Annual statistical tabulation of "crimes known to the police" and "crimes cleared by arrest" published by the Federal Bureau of Investigation.

Venue The geographical area in which a court with jurisdiction sits. The power of a court to compel the presence of the parties to a litigation. See also *Change of Venue*.

Verdict The decision of a court.

Victimology Sub-discipline of criminology which emphasizes the study of victims; includes *victim compensation*.

Voir Dire The examination or questioning of prospective jurors.

Waive To give up a personal right. For example: to testify before the grand jury.

Warrant A court order directing a police officer to arrest a named person or search a specific premise.

Witness One who has seen, heard, acquired knowledge about some element in a crime. An *expert witness* is one who, though he has no direct knowledge of the crime for which the defendant is being tried, may testify as to the defendant's sanity, the amount of alcohol in the deceased's blood, whether a signature is genuine, that a fingerprint is or is not that of the accused, etc.

Index

Credits/ Acknowledgments

Cover design by Charles Vitelli

1. Crime and Justice In America
Facing overview—The Dushkin Publishing Group, Inc. photo by Pamela Carley. 100—*FBI Law Enforcement Bulletin,* September 1993.

2. Victimology
Facing overview—United Nations photo by John Isaac.

3. Police
Facing overview—Insurance Institute for Highway Safety.

4. The Judicial System
Facing overview—EPA Documerica.

5. Juvenile Justice
Facing overview—United Nations photo by John Robaton.

6. Punishment and Corrections
Facing overview—Criminal Justice Publications, New York.

ANNUAL EDITIONS ARTICLE REVIEW FORM

■ NAME: _____ DATE: _____

■ TITLE AND NUMBER OF ARTICLE: _____

■ BRIEFLY STATE THE MAIN IDEA OF THIS ARTICLE: _____

_____

_____

_____

_____

■ LIST THREE IMPORTANT FACTS THAT THE AUTHOR USES TO SUPPORT THE MAIN IDEA:

_____

_____

_____

_____

_____

_____

■ WHAT INFORMATION OR IDEAS DISCUSSED IN THIS ARTICLE ARE ALSO DISCUSSED IN YOUR TEXTBOOK OR OTHER READING YOU HAVE DONE? LIST THE TEXTBOOK CHAPTERS AND PAGE NUMBERS:

_____

_____

_____

_____

_____

_____

■ LIST ANY EXAMPLES OF BIAS OR FAULTY REASONING THAT YOU FOUND IN THE ARTICLE:

_____

_____

_____

_____

■ LIST ANY NEW TERMS/CONCEPTS THAT WERE DISCUSSED IN THE ARTICLE AND WRITE A SHORT DEFINITION:

_____

_____

_____

_____

_____

_____

We Want Your Advice

ANNUAL EDITIONS: CRIMINAL JUSTICE 94/95
Article Rating Form

Here is an opportunity for you to have direct input into the next revision of this volume. We would like you to rate each of the 42 articles listed below, using the following scale:

1. Excellent: should definitely be retained
2. Above average: should probably be retained
3. Below average: should probably be deleted
4. Poor: should definitely be deleted

Your ratings will play a vital part in the next revision. So please mail this prepaid form to us just as soon as you complete it.
Thanks for your help!

Annual Editions revisions depend on two major opinion sources: one is our Advisory Board, listed in the front of this volume, which works with us in scanning the thousands of articles published in the public press each year; the other is you—the person actually using the book. Please help us and the users of the next edition by completing the prepaid article rating form on this page and returning it to us. Thank you.

Rating	Article	Rating	Article
	1. An Overview of the Criminal Justice System		24. Abuse of Power in the Prosecutor's Office
	2. The Campus Crime Wave		25. The Trials of the Public Defender
	3. Breeding Hate		26. Twelve Good Reasons: How Lawyers Judge Potential Jurors
	4. Seeking the Roots of Violence		27. Double Exposure: Did the Second Rodney King Trial Violate Double Jeopardy?
	5. Tunnel Vision: The War on Drugs, 12 Years Later		
	6. Street Guns: A Consumer Guide		28. Handling of Juvenile Cases
	7. The Untold Story of the L.A. Riot		29. Punishment, Accountability, and the New Juvenile Justice
	8. The Fear of Crime		
	9. Hunted: The Last Year of April LaSalata		30. Girls' Crime and Woman's Place: Toward a Feminist Model of Female Delinquency
	10. 'Til Death Do Us Part		
	11. When Men Hit Women		31. The Juvenile Court and the Role of the Juvenile Court Judge
	12. The Reasonable Woman		
	13. Incest: A Chilling Report		32. Kids, Guns, and Killing Fields
	14. Repeating a Study, If Not Its Results: Five Projects Rethink Domestic-Violence Response		33. The Whole Child Approach to Crime
			34. Fernando, 16, Finds a Sanctuary in Crime
	15. Where to Now on Domestic Violence? Studies Offer Mixed Policy Guidance		35. Street Gang Trends Give Little Cause for Optimism
	16. The Most Stressful Job in America: Police Work in the 1990s		36. Sentencing and Corrections
			37. Women in Jail: Unequal Justice
	17. Public Solidly Favors Mixed Police/Civilian Review Boards		38. Pennsylvanians Prefer Alternatives to Prison
	18. Beyond 'Just the Facts, Ma'am'		39. The Detoxing of Prisoner 88A0802
	19. Is Police Brutality the Problem?		40. Do We Need More Prisons?
	20. The Future of Diversity in America: The Law Enforcement Paradigm Shift		41. Evaluating Intensive Supervision Probation/Parole: Results of a Nationwide Experiment
	21. Dragons and Dinosaurs: The Plight of Patrol Women		
	22. Police-Killers Offer Insights Into Victims' Fatal Mistakes		42. 'This Man Has Expired'
	23. The Judicial Process: Prosecutors and Courts		

(Continued on next page)

ABOUT YOU

Name_____ Date_____

Are you a teacher? ☐ Or student? ☐

Your School Name _____

Department _____

Address _____

City _____ State _____ Zip _____

School Telephone # _____

YOUR COMMENTS ARE IMPORTANT TO US!

Please fill in the following information:

For which course did you use this book? _____

Did you use a text with this Annual Edition? ☐ yes ☐ no

The title of the text? _____

What are your general reactions to the Annual Editions concept?

Have you read any particular articles recently that you think should be included in the next edition?

Are there any articles you feel should be replaced in the next edition? Why?

Are there other areas that you feel would utilize an Annual Edition?

May we contact you for editorial input?

May we quote you from above?